How Sweet the Sound

The Spirit of African American History

How Sweet the Sound

The Spirit of African American History

Edited by

Nancy-Elizabeth Fitch

College of New Rochelle

HARCOURT BRACE COLLEGE PUBLISHERS

Fort Worth   Philadelphia   San Diego   New York   Orlando   Austin   San Antonio
Toronto   Montreal   London   Sydney   Tokyo

Publisher:	Earl McPeek
Acquisitions Editor:	David C. Tatom
Developmental Editor:	Margaret McAndrew Beasley
Market Strategist:	Steve Drummond
Project Editor:	Travis Tyre
Art Director:	Burl Sloan
Production Manager:	Diane Gray
Cover:	Gary Logan

ISBN: 0-15-501302-5
Library of Congress Catalog Card Number: 98-89630

Address for orders:
Harcourt Brace & Company
6277 Sea Harbor Drive
Orlando, FL 32887-6777
1-800-782-4479

Address for editorial correspondence:
Harcourt Brace College Publishers
301 Commerce Street, Suite 3700
Fort Worth, TX 76102

Web site address:
http://www.hbcollege.com

Printed in the United States of America

9 0 1 2 3 4 5 6 7 8   016   9 8 7 6 5 4 3 2

To my mother, Nancy-Elizabeth Mariah Harvey Fitch
For my nephew, Saliym Surya; our cousins, Michael,
Morgan, and Charlie
And goddaughter Gillian
It is due to the encouragement of colleague friends Philip,
Floyd, and Joseph that this book has happened.
God bless the work and all of you.

Preface

How Sweet the Sound: The Spirit of African American History is an anthology of readings and historical texts that reveals the African American experience. What is significant about the materials selected for this volume is that they are based on the oral rather than the alphabetically-written tradition. They are discussions about the folk traditions of the African American community in the United States, not only in the verbal arts but also in concepts such as movement and dance. The oral tradition, in this volume, is the implicit language of architecture and of space and place, within the parameters where a people define themselves and their individual and community values; in rituals, ceremonies, and music; the visual arts; and in the rhythms of life from worldview or cosmology; and human language and speechmaking.

How Sweet the Sound is addressed to the student who is beginning the study of African American cultural history and who has acquired some basic knowledge of U.S. history. This text is also intended to accompany more traditional textbooks on American history, African American history, American studies, African American studies, historiography, and culture studies. It can stand alone for the more advanced student who is interested in reading and understanding the American experience from a different textual-reading perspective— from texts meant to be heard and seen rather than merely read silently from a book. It is for the student and instructor interested in locating oral texts and documentation within the discipline of western historiography, which is founded on the written document and often misses oral folk traditions for a variety of reasons, including cultural (as in class), social, and political.

How Sweet the Sound is a collection of essays, articles, and oratory by eminent scholars, thinkers, and regular people who study and/or live within the universe of African American history, literature, and culture. The essays are based on life in the community and on the daily living of black folk whose very act of surviving, under adversities— located in what culture scholar Paul Gilroy has called the "memory of slavery,"— are powerful testimonies to the strength of the human spirit. Building upon Melville Herskovits, W.E.B. Du Bois, and Katherine Dunham's seminal works on African cultural survivalisms in the Americas, this collection finds *nummo* to be central to the understanding of the meaning of African American history in the United States. *Nommo* or *nummo* means "the spoken word," and it is important to both the continental and diasporic African existence.

How Sweet the Sound is also a history text grounded in the Little (rather than the Great) tradition of African American folk and their community life and development. To the extent possible, this text has sought the work of historians, folklorists, and students of culture whose writings not only are *read* but invite the reader to *hear* the voices of the people themselves and to visualize their community life and activities.

The themes that are identified and discussed include *cosmology;* the concept of *movement* (in this context, dance); the establishment of *places and spaces* that provide a language of expression for an entity called "African America"; *rituals, ceremonies,* and *music;* plastic and other of the *visual arts;* dynamics of *language,* and the art of *speech-making*. The text ends on the threshold of the written text where most western historiography begins.

This anthology attempts to introduce new material and new ways of thinking and reading about familiar historical information. In addition to the oral method of reading African American history, the introduction explains the paradigm used in the anthology. Each of the seven chapters that follow begins with an introductory statement that presents the main issues raised in the subsequent essays and ends with a suggested reading list that leads readers to additional sources for further reading. An appendix is included, as well as a subject index, because the thematic foundations may occur in more than one chapter.

Acknowledgments

The evolution of a paradigm for reading African American history in a different way— with other texts— and the subsequent locating and compiling of materials to support the discussion of oral traditions in the study of U.S. history, has taken a number of years. Many colleagues, friends, and family members have offered me support, encouragement, information, direction, and have also opened their homes to me. I am ultimately responsible for the final work, but I would be remiss if I did not thank the following persons who accompanied me on this extended journey.

First, I owe an incredible debt to Drake Bush, the initial acquisitions editor who signed my project and shepherded it through early drafts. I have worked with two subsequent developmental editors to whom I am also grateful: Pam Hatley and Margaret McAndrew Beasley. I also wish to thank the rest of the team at Harcourt College Publishers: David C. Tatom, acquisitions editor; Travis Tyre, project editor; Diane Gray, production manager; and Burl Sloan, art director.

My appreciation also goes to the Jesse Ball duPont Foundation, along with the Virginia Foundation for Independent Colleges, who awarded me an Eminent Scholars Fellowship in History, which was used during the academic year at Randolph-Macon Woman's College. With that fellowship, I began work on the first manifestation of this work. I would like to thank Drs. Robert Spivey; Peter Marcy; and most especially, Margaret Pertzoff, former chair of the department of history and Theodore H. Jack, professor of history, for making that year possible; as well as former president Linda Lorimer; Drs. Floyd W. Hayes III; Philip Stump; Carla Heath; Sonja Peterson-Lewis; Joseph H. Autry III; Marie H. Martin; and Bonnie Eilen; also Farah Naim; Thelma Williams, C. Martin; Marion Stump; Christine Marcroullier; Marilyn Johnson Hayes; Robert F. Fitch III; Carole W. Robinson; Nicola James, and my late grandmother Alsia Penola Zeigler; the staffs of Richmond, Virginia's Valentine Museum; the Hampton University Archives; the Bard Graduate Center Library in Manhattan and Robert Meier and Paul Palmiere of Bronxville,New York's, Concordia College Computer Services. Also, I wish to thank the late Dr. John Henrik Clarke, who was Hunter College's

Professor Emeritus of Africana and Puerto Rican Studies, for his early and continuing faith in me.

I acknowledge the contributions of the reviewers who commented on various drafts of the manuscript: Judith Kerr, Towson State University; Rick G. Moniz, Chabot College; William D. Piersen, Fisk University; Gerald L. Smith, Memphis State University; Marshall F. Stevenson, Dillard University; Sterling Stuckey, University of California, Riverside; Henry L. Suggs, Clemson University; Carol Wilson, Washington College.

Finally, I thank my mother to whom *How Sweet the Sound* is dedicated. From her, I learned my first poem "The Lord's Prayer" and developed an interest in my southern heritage and family. It was she who insisted I study American history in graduate school, in order to find out who I was. And as I grew up, she gave me my first lessons in the history of black people. She is, I realize, also the only teacher of African descent I have had in my entire educational career from kindergarten to doctorate.

Nancy-Elizabeth Fitch

Contents

Preface   *vii*

Introduction The Spirit of African American History   1

Chapter 1 African and African American Cosmology   25

From the Shores of Africa   *Vincent Harding*   40

Slavery and the Circle of Culture   *Sterling Stuckey*   59

Gullah Attitudes Toward Life and Death   *Margaret Washington Creel*   138

A Wild African Tribe   *William S. McFeely*   164

Chapter 2 Movement or Dance   174

The Limbo Dance and History, Fable, and Myth in the Caribbean and Guianas
   Wilson Harris   181

The Association of Movement and Music as a Manifestation of a Black Conceptual
   Approach to Music Making   *Olly W. Wilson*   189

An Aesthetic of the Cool: West African Dance   *Robert Farris Thompson*   200

Primitive African Dance and Its Influence on the Churches of the South
   Pearl Primus   212

Total Transcription of a Sermon-Poem   *Reverend W. T. Goodwin*   215

Chapter 3 Space and Place   231

Shotgun Houses   *John Michael Vlach*   239

"Poor People Done It Like That"   *John Michael Vlach*   243

Gracia Real de Santa Teresa de Mose: A Free Black Town in Spanish Colonial Florida
   Jane Landers   252

From Plantation to Campus: Progress, Community, and the Lay of the Land in
   Shaping the Early Tuskegee Campus   *Kendrick Ian Grandison*   276

Tradition and Innovation in African-American Yards   *Grey Gundaker*   305

Chapter 4 Plastic and Other Visual Arts   332

Another Face of the Diamond   *Judy McWillie*   336

African Symbolism in Afro-American Quilts   *Maude Southwell Wahlman*   345

Vision in Afro-American Folk Art   *William Ferris*   357

James Hampton: The Throne of the Third Heaven of the Nations. Millennium
   General Assembly   *Lynda Roscoe Hartigan*   373

Chapter 5   Rituals, Ceremony, and Music   383
      Negro Baptizings   *Ruby Terrill Lomax*   386
      Festivity and Celebration in a Black Methodist Tradition, 1813–1981
            Lewis V. Baldwin   391
      Women and Ritual Authority in Afro-American Baptist Churches of Rural Florida
            Audrey L. Brown   399
      We Got Our Way of Cooking Things: Women, Food, and Preservation of Cultural
            Identity among the Gullah   *Josephine A. Beoku-Betts*   414
      I Got the Blues   *Alan Lomax*   432

Chapter 6   Dynamics of Language   459
      Gullah: A Creole Language   *Charles Joyner*   461
      Ezekiel and the Vision of Dry Bones   *Reverend Carl J. Anderson*   487

Chapter 7   African American Speechmaking   496
      Oration in Memory of Abraham Lincoln   *Frederick Douglass*   503
      The Negro in Retrospect and Prospect   *Mary McLeod Bethune*   511
      For the Best and the Brightest   *Vincent Harding*   518

Selected Bibliography   533
Photo and Literary Credits   539
Index   541

We are the people of the spoken word, we are a people of the danced word, we are a people of the sung word, We are a people of the musical word.

Vincent Harding

How Sweet the Sound

The Spirit of African American History

Introduction

THE SPIRIT OF AFRICAN AMERICAN HISTORY

How Sweet the Sound: The Spirit of African American History is an anthology of readings relating to African American culture. It also extends the parameters of the meaning of "text" in revealing the history of African Americans in the United States, specifically discussing "texts" beyond those alphabetically written or printed as in a book.[1] The anthology is predicated on the idea that history is an evolutionary process involving movement and motion, change and transformation, and not a rigidly horizontal progression with a defined beginning, middle, and end. African American history is perceived in an active mode where ordinary people live and daily make history as they work, play, sing, dance, and pray. The underlying idea is that history is not passive. It is not a book, sitting on the library shelf, that simply records events from the distant past with no living or informing legacy. In fact, however, history is connected to the present and beyond. This is certainly true of the African American experience in the United States.

How Sweet the Sound is also based on the belief that the history of these African Americans is especially informed by what cultural sociologist and literary historian Paul Gilroy, in *The Black Atlantic. Modernity and Double Consciousness,*[2] has called the "memory of slavery." It is indeed a memory of past "terrors" and horror. In the present and beyond, Gilroy believes, this may lead, may already have led, to what he calls a "redemptive critique" of that legacy. This concept of redemptive critique implies an offsetting of the moral costs and losses due to the Atlantic slave trade and the subsequent enslavement of African peoples, a critique that seeks to ransom those three centuries of

---

[1] There are "texts," for example textiles, that tell a story or through pictographs (pictures) or symbols convey parables and truisms. They are in effect also "written" texts but not alphabetically written ones. In fact, the word *text* means "to weave." See Geoffrey Parrinder's *African Mythology* (London: Paul Hamlyn, 1967, p. 46) about the connection between the word and weaving, and also Marcel Griaule's *Conversations with Ogotemmeli. An Introduction to Dogon Religious Ideas,* especially the chapter entitled, "Third Day. The Second Word and Weaving," pp. 24–29 (London: Oxford University Press. Published for the International African Institute, 1970 [1965]). (Translation of *Dieu d'Eau: Entretiens avec Ogotemmeli* by Ralph Butler and then by Audrey I. Richards and Beatrice Hooke), and "Tenth Day. The Word and the Craft of Weaving," pp. 69–74.

[2] Harvard University Press, 1993.

An Ivory Coast weaver at Washington D.C.'s Textile Museum "writing" at the loom. Though the weaver is preliterate, neither reads nor writes, he speaks French and weaves textiles that are written in parables and folktales.

European captors from the sins incurred as a result of slavery. The redemptive process is meant to take apart (or deconstruct) and analyze that legacy and find its meaning. Slavery's "redeeming" nature may serve to direct *modern* society, which has been born out of the "memory of slavery," into transforming racial subordination, inequality, and their languages into a language of struggle and protest, liberation, and ultimately of racial harmony. So it is that the capture and enslavement of West African peoples defined the world in which *they* lived, worked, played, suffered, and persevered for almost three centuries. The legacy that has been left, however, is not only for African Americans but has been left on American, in fact on Western society itself, specifically the color line and the various responses to it. But it is the spirit in which these "memor(ies) of slavery" and their legacy are presented and then interpreted, along with the lessons of a people's courage and survival, that might yet transform not only black lives in 1999 and beyond, but the lives of all Americans as we enter an even more culturally and ethnically diverse United States of the twenty-first century.

We begin in West Africa. The readings recall some of the experiences of African peoples during the Atlantic slave trade and the Middle Passage, that involuntary journey of African captives between the coasts of West Africa and the Americas. They recall as well some of the cultural influences from the Caribbean where, for varying lengths of time, some captive persons were "seasoned" or broken: those attempts by European captors to break their spirit, the better to ensure their forced labor. Some of the travail of a people is also noted, not only in servitude but after it legally ended, still living with racism and discrimination and the insidious dynamics of the color line, which would continue to restrict their lives in many ways.

   How Sweet the Sound illustrates how African Americans as captives, enslaved persons, and citizens of the United States struggled to transcend those adversities and forge a community of persons— together finding their way in a hostile space/place. Therefore, in order to better show historical process and action, this anthology is not divided into the traditional divisions of historical or temporal time consisting of past, present, and future. It does not follow a chronological order: it follows a thematic one. And it is cyclical and circular in nature, not only in terms of time but in terms of movement and space as well as worldview. *How Sweet the Sound* is also a discussion about the continuity of *ethos,* meaning the values, character, and spirit of this particular American community, descended from West African captives who were forcibly brought to the Americas. A people whose ancestral home is (informed by) the American South and by the symbol *Sankofa,* which is the backward-looking bird illustrating the Ashanti and Gyaman peoples of Ghana and Côte d'Ivoire, respectively, and meaning "Go back, look everywhere, and take" or, as Kwaku Ofori-Ansa translated it, "it is not a taboo to go back and retrieve if you forget."[3]

   In fact, *How Sweet the Sound* follows a developmental organization illustrating the evolving of this African and also American circle of persons. It is visually developmental in the same sense as a palimpset—a parchment on which only traces and fragments rather than a complete written text of previous writing and information—is visible. New information, and new developments, continue to be written atop these traces of older data, renewing and refining what was there previously—in other words, not moving horizontally beyond the old data but building on and transforming what is already there. This volume, then, discusses a series of building blocks on which the U.S. African American community was established. Like the objects in the residential "junk" or "spirit" yards, discussed in Chapter 3, "Spaces and Places,"—sites where old and lost or discarded things have been recycled and new uses found for them—values, traditions, memories of Africa, times of travail and struggle, and the will to survive have been retrieved and transformed into instruments of the spirit. They would carry the community even through the challenges of the present and beyond, having been brought back from the dust heap of time and having been resurrected to sustain the community and praise its communal life. This is one meaning of circularity for the black community here in the United States.

   How Sweet the Sound consists of seven areas of readings. It begins with African (-derived) American perceptions of the physical and spiritual realms in African and African American cosmology, and with the resulting uses of space/place. It ends with the

---

[3] See Clementine M. Kaik-Nzuji's *Tracing Memory. A Glossary of Graphic Signs and Symbols in African Art and Culture* (Hull, Quebec: Canadian Museum of Civilization, 1996, p. 75 [nos. 2 and 3]), and Dr. Ofori-Ansa's chart, "Meaning of Symbols in Adinkra Cloth" (Hyattsville, Md.: Sankofa Publications, 1993 [1978]).

dynamics of language, closing with examples from African American speechmaking. These vernacular or folk oral traditions have evolved from some fundamental understandings and beliefs about African American physical space, spiritual and mental landscapes, and conceptualizations about both even in such tangible representations as quilt and basket making. Furthermore, ideas and thought are visualized in dance and sacred and secular rituals and ceremonies. We might call those physical spaces and spiritual and mental landscapes—even the philosophical beliefs, traditions, and thought determined in part by geography, climate, and topography—part of the *cosmology,* or worldview of the African American, a cosmology African-descended persons in the United States created from both the experience and the "memory of slavery."

As a distinct "Africanist" American culture in the United States evolves,[4] there are building blocks of African American experience to discuss including movement (or dance); ritual, ceremony, and music; and plastic and other visual (tangible) arts. But the six theme areas, after the discussion of cosmology, are not meant to be all-inclusive of this experience. They are considered critical, however, to an understanding of the cultural backdrop that signifies this particular branch of the American family, which is a syncretic group of persons who are Old World (West African) and new Western men and women (for example, Caribbean but in this volume predominantly North American). A people who had to forge a new identity and ethos as a result of the devastations brought by the Atlantic slave trade that would not only fetter their bodies but make serious assaults against their sense of self and worth. A people who, in order to survive and even transcend the effects of oppressive life conditions, had to make adaptations to hostile physical, intellectual, and spiritual environments.

Discussion of these themes begins with Chapter 1 on cosmology—African and African American understanding and use of the spiritual and physical dimensions and spaces of human existence. This discussion continues in subsequent chapters as follows:

- Movement or Dance (Chapter 2)
- Space and Place (Chapter 3)
- Plastic and Other Visual Arts (Chapter 4)
- Rituals, Ceremony, and Music (Chapter 5)
- Dynamics of Language (Chapter 6)
- African American Speechmaking (Chapter 7)

The seven thematic chapters (see discussion later in this introduction) contribute to the concept of African American unity symbolized by the circle. They constitute a circular view of history rather than a horizontal or linear perspective divided into three discrete segments of time that typifies Western historical tradition. The circular movement,

---

[4] This "Africanist" American culture alludes to the syncretic nature of being African American in the United States and is consistent with W. E. B. Du Bois's concept of the "double consciousness" of a people who are reconciling two seemingly opposing sides of themselves, one "American" and the other "Negro," or, in 1990s terminology, "African American." Thus syncretism, in this case, involves not only those two elements but the combination of them which creates the third. See footnote 6 in Chapter 1, "African and African American Cosmology."

with all time flowing through and upon what has already preceded it, forming an unbroken circle and symbolizing continuity of culture, heritage, and history (which is a discipline about time), is what fundamentally, I believe, has made it possible for African Americans to persevere and survive.

Chapter themes of black struggle, perseverance, community, and the centrality of movement, particularly dance, and of the spoken word and other forms of oral tradition, also flow into one another, reappearing again and again from one chapter to the next and reenforcing what has been discussed previously. The manner in which individuals and groups of persons physically establish space and build on, and within, it—organize it—are nonverbal forms of vernacular language. They are, later in the volume, further articulated with verbal or spoken language and the rhetorical and oratorical forms that it takes. The selections within these chapters illuminate some of the compelling forces and ideas leading African and African-descended peoples through the historical process in the United States: from "slavery to freedom," from "plantation to factory" to cyberspace, from civil (human) rights movements to elective politics: forces that have led not only to physical liberation from bondage but to freedom of thought and expression.

I conclude this anthology with chapters on "Dynamics of Language" and "African American Speechmaking" that place you on the threshold of *written* historical texts with which we, as students of Western history, are most familiar. Ending *How Sweet the Sound: The Spirit of African American History* there does not suggest the writing and printing of books is unimportant or secondary. That would be absurd. It does suggest, however, that that particular written format (specifically the alphabetic versus the symbolic or that which illustrates cultural and historical stories that are created, for example, in the weaving of textiles) is already accessible to the student of history. It suggests that other "texts" should be as accessible, if not acceptable, within the discipline of history.

CHAPTER THEMES

African and African American Cosmology

The physical environment and topography, the spiritual and philosophical beliefs and traditions coming from them, the sense and definition of time,[5] even climatic conditions, tell us much about why an ethnic group's history is what it is. They tell us why people act and do the things they do and avoid what they do not. These elements constitute an

---

[5] An important, in this case, if not much debated discussion of time in African thought (specifically in southern Zaire) has been led by John Mbiti. His definition of the past, or *tene,* lends itself to the symbolism of the circle as used in this anthology. Newell S. Booth in "Time and Change in African Traditional Thought," in the *Journal of Religion in Africa* 7, fasc. 2 (1975): 81–91, elaborates on Mbiti's thesis discussing the connection of "time" in African terms, meaning not numbers (i.e., dates and hours) but cycles in the natural world, to human activity and community events. Booth also explains that the concept of future means the "completion of events that have already begun to take place." This ties the future to the past, to tradition, and finally to the ancestors and then, necessarily, to the ringshout, rites of homecoming (burials), and to the concepts of rebirth, recycling, and renewal (or other ways of looking at the cyclical and the circular, i.e., history).

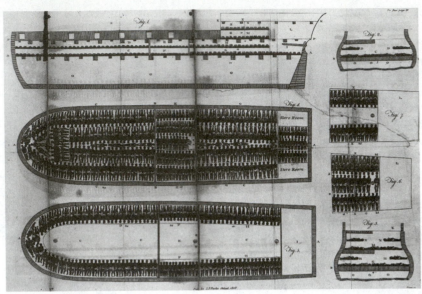

Cutaways of a slaving ship transporting "black gold" or African captives across the Atlantic during the Middle Passage. It illustrates how human "cargo" was placed in the lower decks.

African people's worldview or philosophy (or way) of life, in other words, a people's cosmology.

Movement or Dance

Movement in this chapter means the physicality in music, namely dance, as well as the physicality often accompanying verbal expression. The late anthropologist and choreographer/dancer Pearl Primus was a trained cultural observer who found significance in the motion of the hand gestures, body swaying, and facial expressions of the black preacher and his congregation in the United States as they were singing, praying, or testifying together. She connected these movements, an aspect of dance, with Africa and the Caribbean. Of course, in any discussion of the movement of African Americans we must again consider their migratory history: movements of West African peoples to the Western Hemisphere and often from the Caribbean to the North American mainland. In interpreting African American movement, for example dance and other body motions, we see the influences of these migrations. Wilson Harris's essay, "The Limbo Dance and History, Fable, and Myth in the Caribbean and Guianas,"[6] connects the artistry of the "limbo" dance with the necessary bending and cramping movements of African captives as they tried to exercise their "limbs" on slaver (or cargo) ships. These African captives, Harris contends, created an art form born of the "dislocations" of the Middle Passage as

[6] Wilson Harris, "History, Fable, and Myth in the Caribbean and Guianas," *Caribbean Quarterly,* 16(2) (1970): 1–32 [excerpts, pp. 6–17, 25].

well as of the physical necessity to make bodily adaptations, if not contortions, in order to negotiate restricted spaces and places. Katherine Dunham would probably add, that in the movements created by these awkward physical exertions, these soon-to-be en-slaved persons, many who would then be "bent over" in southern cotton fields, were going through a process of purification from the wash of their sweat, from physical exertion, was generating. In an interview, Dunham addressed this issue:

> Dance [for which we could substitute the word "movement"] can free people from some of their oppressions. Just by using the body in its rhythmic patterns, it heightens circulation. Then if you work hard enough, so that water is running off you, there is a purifying process . . .[7]

The chapter "Movement or Dance" shows that music is an important aspect of the African American historical process, and another medium with which to understand and interpret the history of black people in the Western Hemisphere. It is an integral part of the discursive oral tradition that extends beyond the verbal arts to include movement as in dance. In "Space and Place," the connective for African American building and housing traditions might be the shotgun house, adapted from the courtyard structure of traditional African housing and brought to the American South from Haiti. Likewise, a primary connective between continental Africa and diasporic Africa was and is dance. Both shotgun house and dance illustrate the communal nature of black people.

African American dance has roots in "the shout,"[8] in the voodoo dances of Congo Square in Louisiana where many Haitians migrated, and in the modern dance choreography of such artists and cultural scholars as Katherine Dunham and Pearl Primus. Dunham has written seminally on the connections between African dance/motion and the history of African culture, anthropology, and the moral sense that yet survives in the Western Hemisphere. She argues convincingly that it is *motion* which connects the diaspora with the continent. Through dance, we can see that Alfred N. Hunt's theory that the American South is "the northern extremity of Caribbean culture," expounded in *Haiti's Influence on Antebellum America,*[9] opens the door to that "extremity" (Africa *via* the Caribbean experience) being at least Harlem, New York. But that "extremity" is probably even further north, among those places in the industrial Midwest impacted by the Great Migration (1915–1919) of black persons from the South as well as the music (vocal, instrumental, and dance) they brought with them and the worldviews that came with the music. That music, those ballads, those stories expressed in song and movement, transformed the American eastern seaboard and the industrial Midwest with its style and elegance and the memories and history of other times.

---

[7] Brian Lanker, *I Dream a World: Portraits of Black Women Who Changed America* (New York: Stewart, Tabori & Chang, 1989), p. 28.

[8] See Jacqui Malone, *Steppin' on the Blues. The Visible Rhythms of African American Dance* (Urbana: University of Illinois Press, 1996) especially Chapters 1 and 2: "'Gimme de Kneebone Bent': Music and Dance in Africa" and "'Keep to the Rhythm and You'll Keep to Life': Meaning and Style in African American Vernacular Dance," respectively (pp. 9–36).

[9] Albert N. Hunt, *Haiti's Influence on Antebellum America: Slumbering Volcano in the Caribbean* (Baton Rouge: Louisiana State University Press, 1988).

Through music and motion, we see an Africanist perspective on the world distinct from that of the West in terms of timing, sound (rhythm and discordance vs. melody and harmony), listener involvement (call and response vs. "audience" passivity), story content, and as a vehicle of historical transmission and information. The nexus between sound and movement is evident as well in the chapter "Ritual, Ceremony, and Music." Sound and movement illustrate the important role music has played in African American survival and on that community's thought, beliefs, and oral traditions. Sound and movement bring an integration of material and spiritual worlds and provide clues not only to the community's survival but to its transcendence over the negative influences brought about by the founding economic and social principles of the United States. Those principles, which justified the institution of slavery, led not only to centuries of enslavement but also bolstered accompanying cultural and intellectual ideologies in the Western world that adversely impacted—and to varying degrees continue to do so—persons of African descent, for example the alleged mental inferiority of African-descended persons reenforced by nineteenth-century pseudoscience and social Darwinism.

Historian Sterling Stuckey, in *Slave Culture: Nationalist Theory and the Foundations of Black America*,[10] suggests the first pan-African nationalist element in enslaved societies in the American colonies was found in music. He claims persuasively that it was in the ringshout. The ringshout is a spiritual circle dance that many blacks would bring with them into their adopted Christian denominations most notably the Pentecostal and Holiness churches. The sacred "shout" was the one cultural commonality shared and claimed by all West Africans who found themselves away from home and in the Americas. Captive Africans, in their national and cultural diversity, did not share either common language or common religion. In *The Souls of Black Folk*,[11] Du Bois, however, names one of the "gifts" the African brought to America as being that of the spirit and things spiritual. The dance was the vehicle through which spirit forces could be unleashed, to manipulate and (re)arrange space and place, even in servitude, through freedom of expression in movement and in joined voices as in the shout— openly to aspire toward freedom. Done any other way, for example in writing or oratory, such expression would be potentially deadly, for it would have suggested insurrection—which the American slavocracy feared the most and punished most severely—as well as suggesting, if not in fact proving, the equality and humanity of the enslaved person. The ritualistic ringshout, however, served all those political and ideological purposes in addition to those that were spiritual.

It was also important that this early African American "sacred" dance, as was the spiritual (Du Bois's "sorrow songs"), was double textual. It had at least two levels of meaning. The dominant American society attempted to rout out Africanisms or African cultural heritage by prohibiting the speaking of African languages, the giving of African names, the practice of African religions—even instruction in the reading and writing of English. These restrictions on cultural expression were to control the budding community building

---

10 Sterling Stuckey, *Slave Culture: Nationalist Theory and the Foundation of Black America* (New York: Oxford University Press, 1987).

11 W. E. B. Du Bois, *The Souls of Black Folk* [1903], (Reprint, New York: Signet Classic, 1986).

among African Americans. However, singing and dancing were allowed, if not encouraged. Those who exercised political and social control over African Americans failed to recognize this was no mere music making or even necessarily a form of entertainment. It was a manifestation of Africanisms and a means of unifying disparate West African societies, under siege in the Americas, into a community or nation.

In more contemporary times, dance would provide the opportunity for white young people to be influenced by that other seminal element in U.S. culture, the African and African-descended. Rock and roll, rhythm and blues, and currently hip hop or rap *culture* would have them mimic certain segments (and thus certain values) of the black community. Music and dance would be connectives in the midst of color lines and would make African American cultural influence significant in American society and to an extent that would be the inverse of the community's political influence. So powerful was that influence that major black music figures were mimicked by whites, the latter being more acceptable to the cultural principles of some white parents. Pat Boone and Elvis Presley, themselves on opposite sides of the spectrum, both tempered the oftentimes frenzied following of seemingly less controllable originators of that music and of American popular culture like Chuck Berry and Little Richard.

Music and especially dance, as discussed in these essays, have also been used when necessary as a way of "masking"—or a form of masquerade—of keeping the community's secrets and protecting and moving it toward its aspirations of liberation and self-direction. It was a masquerade often misread as an acceptance of servitude, misread even as contentment. Music and dance have been, in fact, a means of expressing aspirations of freedom through the exhibition of aspects of it through motion. And it was in full view, not hidden. Thus movement, or dance, as with post-Reconstruction era migration also known as "voting with one's feet," has been not only cultural but political statement and a critique of life in the United States.

Space and Place

In discussions of African American cultural history, space and place (1) in the sense of physical environment, (2) what is situated and placed in that environment, (3) place as location, that is, cities, educational and cultural sites, or (4) place in the sense of social position (during the slavocracy this would include the location of slave living quarters in relationship to the plantation manor house) all help define status and locate the people who live, work, pray, survive, and, as they transcend adversity, even struggle to thrive within these spaces and places. For most cultural groups, land—as in a country, the place where groups of people live with cultural commonality, autonomy, self-determination, and self-governance—is where their history begins and is acted out.[12]

---

[12] Because African captives coming to the Western Hemisphere were of different cultural groups and societies, the concept of cultural continuity refers to the syncretic group they created—in what becomes the United States—the African American. Such artifacts as the sacred ringshout and basket making and wood carving and virtuosity in the verbal arts are a few of the evidences of cultural connections between Africa and the African diaspora—those other places where Africans live whether brought by force or personal choice.

Plantation workers, men and women including the elderly, picking cotton.

African Americans, the descendants of those captives torn involuntarily from their homelands, for the most part lack knowledge of their particular ancestral country or society of origin. This can, as a result, skew their sense of who they are as it relates to (1) where their forebears originally came from (a specific place rather than a continental region), (2) how they lived, and (3) what their beliefs and values were. For African Americans, this situation is critical, for that point of origin is where the African-descended person, now in the Western Hemisphere, had ancestors who were free persons able to exercise personal autonomy in a world in which they predominated. This is a reality often lost in the discussion in which many African Americans, and their fellow citizens, debate the history and legacy of the contemporary black person. And this is why Gilroy's concept of the "memory of slavery" is so pivotal. The history of black people in the Americas all too often begins with the subject of "slavery" rather than with "captivity" or enslavement. The latter presupposes prior freedom and other spatial and societal existences and legacies as well as distinctive cultural views about life and the place of African peoples in the universe that are not imposed or informed by servitude.

This sense of self-identity and group identity, informed also by African continental and diasporic spaces and places (those locations where African persons dispersed, either by force or will, throughout the world, e.g., the Caribbean), was purposefully obscured, and knowledge, especially of self, was then denied them. This was a direct result of the Atlantic slave trade and the very dynamics of enslavement itself, which controlled physical movement and the ability to determine one's own destiny and even one's freedom of thought. The African American's sense, then, of the origins of their

Enslaved persons being marched in a coffle, as part of the domestic slave trade.

syncretic African American culture, as described by W. E. B. Du Bois, as twoness and double consciousness—at the same time "Negro" and also "American"—must come through their various migratory experiences in and outside the Americas.

These migratory experiences begin with being "stolen away" from Africa and thus from family, community, and traditions. They continue with the Middle Passage from the coasts of West Africa across the Atlantic Ocean to the Americas—in the holds of over-packed slaver ships. Then from auction blocks and slave markets, in the Caribbean, and from port-of-entry cities in New England and the South—to the southern plantation it-self. This process of human transporting was also a socialization process to distance the captive and future American slaves from their homeland not only geographically but psy-chologically. It was to create a fracture or breakage in the continuity of their culture and

Faces of the African Slave Trade: Enslaved persons who were taken from a dhow that was captured by the HMS Undine.

history. This breakage could distort the enslaved people's worldview and certainly was meant to break their spirit in ways that would make control over these forced plantation laborers easier. And there would be further movement or threats of this level of control on land[13] as they were led in internal marches by slave traders and drivers. They would be moved from Upper to Lower South, following the fortunes of the cash crop that would unilaterially entrench African slavery in North America—"King Cotton."

After the Civil War, movement from "plantation to factory" would involve migration from rural farms and towns to urban industrial centers especially in the North but also within the South. But it would be in the American South, where slavery especially took root, that a "way of life," even a "racial" way of life for both black and white people living there, would be forged and become distinctively "southern" in terms of cuisine, language, and architecture. It would be a place, too, that would leave indelible markings on the African American, culturally and aesthetically. Those markings would also travel, along with the African American, out of the South to the North and West.

---

13 Enslaved persons who were perceived "difficult" or liable to attempt escape, as well as previous escapees, were threatened with being sent further south where the work and climate were deemed uniformly harsh(er) and the inhumanity of slave owners and overseers legend. Threat of this internal "deeper south" migration also meant the breakup of families and communities. Thus it was a deterrent to certain behaviors inimical to the interests of slave owners and the plantation system. This was part of the domestic slave trade, which became very important after the legal cessation of the international slave trade in 1808 as enunciated in the American Constitution.

Booker T. Washington, founder and builder of Tuskegee Institute (now University), in front of a Louisiana crowd on his last summer tour of the South.

During the post-Reconstruction period, which was also the era of Booker T. Washington, blacks in the South witnessed one man's plan or strategy for a *reconstructed* black existence, in fact, a reconstructed southland. For Washington, its author, and his followers, it would mean that southern blacks would remain in the South and that region would be the firmament, the land, the earth, the home place on which they would build an economically autonomous community, but one that would also benefit the entire region including whites. The end of enslavement was a time, however, when black expectations for full integration into American society, including political and social, were at their highest. Some of the newly freed African Americans, who had never known Africa personally or through the stories of elderly relatives, would take this opportunity— freedom of movement—to migrate from their ancestral southern American homeland and become pioneers by establishing residential African American spaces in places like the Oklahoma Territory. They would establish towns like Langston, Taft, and Boley, in addition to southern black places like Mound Bayou, Mississippi, and Eatonville, Florida. Places where white Americans would have minimal and even no influence over their daily lives.[14]

---

[14] See Toni Morrison's (negative) twist on the concept of separate black and white spaces in her novel *Paradise* (New York: Knopf, 1998).

African Americans' sense of history and of space and place would prove to be portable, but there would still be cultural continuity whether they went to the urban South, the industrial North, or the frontiers of the western territories. The homeland of these descendants of original African captives would be the American South, with distant remembrances or consciousness of Africa. But there would be even more recent consciousness of the southland, which now informed their African American ethos. That consciousness was carried along wherever else they went. They would carry their evolving American Africanness, their double-consciousness and syncreticism, into other aspects of their lives. There would be surviving ideas, beliefs, and traditions—African "survivalisms" so named by anthropologists such as Melville Herskovits, discussed by W. E. B. Du Bois in *The Negro*,[15] and visualized in dance by anthropologist and choreographers/ dancers Katherine Dunham and Pearl Primus—visible in African American aesthetic and oral traditions. These survivalisms would surface in movement (dance) and the plastic arts, in establishment of black spaces and places and in language.

"Space and Place" considers African American building and housing traditions, the vernacular or "folk" architecture, those artifacts that went into living spaces and distinguished black community life, other black institutional sites, and consideration of space itself—as a place to be autonomous, free, and oneself. You will see connections between the African continent, other countries of the African diaspora, especially in the Caribbean, and the United States. These "connections" support Herskovits's theory of the continuity of the black experience that is purposefully maintained despite the disruptive influences of captivity, Middle Passage, servitude, and racism resulting from the Atlantic slave trade and the planting of the European in the Americas.

"Space and Place" comments on the traditional cosmological and spiritual aspects of black people synthesizing traditions from Africa, the Caribbean, and the United States. Some of those traditions are sites like the residential yards discussed in this chapter that become "praise" and "sacred" places masquerading as "junk" yards to the outside world. Mundane or everyday material objects, most discarded and now having a second life, are used to make spiritual statements about life, death, the afterlife, and relationships between the living and those who have passed on and become the ancestors. In this chapter, we see some of the foundations of an African*ist,* not "African" but "African-descended," worldview that reflects the cyclical nature of African-derived existence: the rebirth of persons and of community, the recycling of "things," the adapting and improvising on the environment to make something new or better. This recycling in traditional African society, according to Newell S. Booth, is called "the tradition of renewal."[16] All this takes place within a political, social, and economic environment that, for over two hundred years, denied the African American was even human.

This ability to change the physical environment, to retain discarded things and give them new life, to hold on to surviving elements of Africanness, would occur in a

---

15 W. E. B. Du Bois's *The Negro* [1915], (Reprint, New York: Oxford University Press, 1982).

16 Newell S. Booth, "Time and Change in African Traditional Thought," *Journal of Religion in Africa 7,* fasc. 2 (1975): 89–90.

country determined to rout out that heritage with its cyclical thought and beliefs and substitute in its stead a perpetual slave "state" of mind. The ability to change one's environment, to adapt even to a hostile one and survive in it, provides glimpses of how black people used ancient "knowledge" of spiritual things to create for themselves sources of power—at a time when they were "unschooled"—when there was passage of laws denying them the right to possess a cultivated mind developed through the vehicle of literacy, ownership of their own persons, and unrestricted thought and actions. These spaces and places, whether on earth or in the afterlife, from educational institutions, to dance squares, to sacred land like the burial ground, were sources for the cultivation of black spiritual/mental power. They would make African American communities truly free, even though those who created these institutions were socially, politically, and economically without power.[17] When enslavement ended, those power sources would be maintained and multiplied to curtail the effects of racism and discrimination which, although no longer legal, were (are) still part of the American social pattern.

Finally, African American community building, and political/economic aspirations and potential, concludes "Space and Place." Community building illustrates the desire and need of this circle of people to come together in self-governing, political black spaces/places. It also shows an ongoing African American interest in controlling and guiding the destinies of their own communities and of owning land. One such black space/place is recalled almost in a visual way: Booker T. Washington combined geographic and physical space and landscape along with a mental landscape that forged visions of the economic development of the "black belt."[18] Here he would establish one of the pillars of black higher education—and a critical black space/place—Tuskegee Institute, now Tuskegee University.

Plastic and Other Visual Arts

"Plastic and Other Visual Arts" looks at traditional art forms born in the American South and influencing African American art throughout the United States. And they too are firmly based on Herskovits's survivalisms from the African continent and the Caribbean. Like movement and dance, plastic and other visual arts are concrete representations of African American spirit and life. Once again, through the utilitarian uses of these art forms, the material and spiritual meet. Unlike art placed under glass, these works of art are a vital part of daily life. What we see is representative black Atlantic art, that black convergence of Africa and the African diaspora of the Americas and Europe. Included in this repertoire are examples of what can be called "nonalphabetic" writing. These are the pictographs of storytelling quilts, the ideographs in other quilt designs, the "writing in the spirit," and the "signing" works of other artists. There is also the spiritual throne of folk artist James Hampton, constructed in his garage, a spiritual conceptualization made

---

[17] They may not have had social, political, or economic power to use in their own interests, but they were not powerless *culturally* in transforming even aspects of the larger society.

[18] "Black belt" is (1) that geographic environment of fertile black soil which had supported the slavocracy (especially in Alabama) as well, arguably, as the larger federal economy but (2) also a geographic area with a predominant black population.

A front view of James Hampton's "Throne of the Third Heaven of the Nation's Millennium" General Assembly. It was made of recycled, discarded materials that Hampton collected from the streets, offices, and junkyards of Washington, D.C. where he lived and worked as a federal government employee.

from the discards of life, covered in colored foil and recycled into a praise song.

This is art, also, that exemplifies everyday life in the black community, art created by talented geniuses who are, more importantly, ordinary if not also unrecognized *artistic* members of their communities. These are the works of folk artists whose primary aesthetic purpose is spiritual and only secondarily, if at all, commercial. Author Gregory Day explains it eloquently in an essay[19] about Carolinian traditional arts: these traditional arts are intertwined, he writes, in the "collective labor activities" of the community, that is, hunting and gathering, fishing, gardening, harvesting, house building, and crafts making. This is art meant to be *used,* not only for the mundane but for the sacred: in worship and spiritual rituals. The vehicles may be pottery, sculpture, or even basketry. The latter, which was an integral part of the plantation economy used in winnowing, harvesting, and transporting of the products of slave labor, was and is a foundation of black rural and urban community life when used, for example, as a collection plate during Sunday

---

[19] Gregory Day, "Afro-Carolinian Art. Towards the History of a Southern Expressive Tradition," *Contemporary Art/Southwest* 1 (January-February 1978): 10–21.

[20] Ibid.

A Gullah man and boy engaged by the traditional Sea Island craft of netweaving.

church services.[20]

Textile arts show an association between music and the oral tradition. Within the context of the improvisatory in blues-jazz, this is especially true in quilt making. And in quilting, although an art historically practiced in Africa and the Americas by both men and women, we see women's *power* too. Early American quilts were considered to be protective "medicines of God" by those who used them and those who created them. They were able to counteract negative influences of the unseen spirit world. This associates women, especially, with traditional healing capabilities whether in terms of medicinal treatments for the body or spiritual curatives for the mind and spirit.

The musical tradition, and the more obvious of oral traditions, are also seen in the sculpture of folk artists. The created pieces are often representations from "dreams" and are "signs." Folklorist William Ferris has written about the power and spiritual qualities of this work: "To create a man's image is to have power and control over him. . . . The folk artist thus becomes a powerful and at times frightening force within the black community, somewhat similar to the Griot of West Africa."[21] Or, as with the healing woman mentioned earlier, with the shaman, the medicine woman (or man), the priestess can read signs in the natural world to warn and protect the community.

Rituals, Ceremony, and Music

African American rituals mark a convergence between individual and personal rites of life passages and the communal and public rites of the entire community. Water, music, physical movement—approaching and including dance—play important roles in both sacred and secular ceremonies. Passing over (dying) and life in the hereafter were particularly important life passages for the African American. And especially to those who had themselves known enslavement because these were the first opportunities, in many cases, to contemplate liberation, freedom, and a life free from bondage. They were a captive, Old Testament people, as we see from the texts of their spirituals about Moses leading his people to freedom, God delivering Daniel from the lion's den, and Joshua tearing down the walls of Jericho. These early African Americans closely identified with the biblical Israelites, seeing Jesus as a latter-day Moses who would lead them out of bondage, if not in this life in the next. And the idea of rebirth expressed in baptism, or in the Easter sunrise service, is integral to their belief systems. A proper burial, in the circle of loved ones, was also important for passing over not only into the spiritual world but for the early African captive's belief in the body returning "home" across the water to Africa.

"Rituals, Ceremony, and Music" also contributes to the idea of an African circular view of history: of individual life that does not start and then progress toward an end but that flows back into the life (re)cycle of the community. Rather than thinking of time in terms of beginning, middle, and end, African American history can be seen as a continuum. The immediate goals of freedom, education, human and political rights were to enhance the individual and communal lives of African Americans and contribute to their excelling as a community of persons. These goals were not the "end" of the continuum. Looking at time in this way, it is easier to see how the living and those who have passed over and "gone home" could continue an ongoing relationship with one another and have responsibilities toward one another and for the life of the community as a cultural unit.

Important nineteenth-century secular rituals prior to the Civil War often had to do with enslaved people's thoughts about freedom and the political controls of a system of slavery which encouraged them to express themselves "freely" during certain times of the year. These holiday celebrations around harvest time and Christian holidays did not

---

21 William Ferris, "Vision in Afro-American Folk Art: The Sculpture of James Thomas," *Journal of American Folklore* 88: (348), April–June 1975: 127.

occur for altruistic reasons necessarily, but to curb the possibility of slave insurrections. This was especially so after the black Revolution of St. Dominique, now Haiti, under Toussaint Louverture (1743–1803), which made that island nation the first black republic anywhere in the world attempting to establish and live by democratic institutions. Some of these celebrations, like Negro elections and Pinkster festivals,[22] again inverted the power relationship between blacks and whites, allowing African Americans to dress like their "betters"; control their own time, movement, and actions; and assemble and congregate together. But it was also the hope of some masters that these holidays would provide opportunities for those who were enslaved to dull their senses and longing for freedom, so they liberally distributed alcoholic beverages during those times. These occasions for the master class were surely palliatives. But more importantly, they were also occasions for African American community building, the acting out of governance and political situations for the time when they would exercise them in reality.

"Rituals, Ceremony, and Music" is interesting for another reason. It discusses an important and often overlooked aspect of African American cultural history: the pivotal role of black women. Their role in the community's oral traditions is central because these traditions pervaded all aspects of traditional African, and by extension, early African American life. Because black women under enslavement were the first in their communities to make inroads into white society, returning to the circle with knowledge of the dominant society's customs and beliefs, they also influenced that *other* community because of their contact in the early and formative years with the young in the southern European American community. They introduced them to and acquainted them with African American community traditions and lore that became a significant part of what is southern culture. The influence of the southern black woman and the proximity to daily evidences of black life, for the white child, was so pervasive that southern parents of the ruling classes would send their young men, who were being groomed to govern and control, even to the hated North to break that Afro-southern influence and bond which often was evidenced in the way they spoke.

The blues, a secular often profane offshoot of the spirituals (vs. the sacred gospel music), are another aspect of African American oral tradition, thought, and double textuality. Ostensibly discussing life's hardships and disappointments and consequently how it feels to be "down and out," the blues are not really about being sad but are rather a pragmatic, heroic discourse on life at its most absurd.[23] They discuss, for example, racism that has contributed to unemployment, poverty, family breakups, alcoholism, and other social ills adversely impacting on black people in particular and the poor in general. The blues are ritual in the sense of storytelling, performance, and drama (tragedy combined with humor or absurdity). They also represent the masquerade and catharsis. The call-and-response interaction between the leader-artist/performer with follower-audience/

---

[22] See Sterling Stuckey's essay "Slavery and the Circle of Culture" in Chapter 1 especially relating to Negro elections and Pinkster festivals, pp. 104–113.

[23] See Albert Murray's *Stomping the Blues* [1976] (Reprint, De Capo Press, 1989), and *The Blue Devils of Nada. A Contemporary American Approach to Aesthetic Statement* (New York: Vintage International, 1997).

listener/respondent or priest and priestess with church and congregation was communal and acted out by equals, each knowing the respective roles they were to play. The blues are both theater and worship, as is the African American dramatic heritage.[24]

The blues, live, constituted a community of people sharing common experiences of life and offering empathy that was active rather than passive. It is another expression of unity—of the circle. And it is ritualistic. Ma Rainey and Bessie Smith were not only secular blues divas, although that would have been enough. They were also "priestesses." The function of live blues singing was less strident protest than the expression of wry humor signifying the absurdity of and transcendence over the oppression that racism brings in its wake. The blues are about reality and its disappointments, bad luck, failed love, and attempted escapes through life via the bottle or drugs; about lack of meaningful work and affirmative life chances. This is the drama of one aspect of black life: a chronicling of hard times whether of individual or group. And the blues also serve a *griot*-like or chronicler role, for in them is much about the affect of the historical legacy of black people's travail in the United States.

To an extent, the ritual aspects of blues-jazz have been muted. At the turn of the century, white record companies, seeing the music's economic potential within the white community, began taking the storytellers out of the juke joints and clubs and into recording studios, making them more accessible to the larger community. The priests and priestesses of these first rural and then urban venues were in effect taken away from their congregants and the live energy of call and response. The music, in the wider social context, took on the moniker of "race" music, and the vinyl product that was produced became known as the "race" record. If Pinkster festivals and dances were safety valves put in place by whites, the blues were safety valves put in place by blacks[25]—generally those still struggling to survive economically—the working poor rather than the middle class. The absurdities of human existence, and black acknowledgment of them, are among some of the origins of African American humor that is also found in the music. The ability to laugh at one's situation and at oneself is a weapon of survival in an oppressed community's arsenal against forces it can not control either politically or economically. It was also a commentary on the behavior of whites but in a form that would not encourage lethal reprisals toward those making the critique.

Dynamics of Language

"Dynamics of Language" precedes the last chapter, "African American Speechmaking," which brings us full circle. Here again is a representation of the continuum of black peoples in the United States from the time of captivity to the present, most clearly seen in

---

24 See Albert Murray's *Stomping the Blues*.

25 Of course, commercialism of the blues and of other African American cultural artifacts has often muted the self-direction and control of the artist and his or her art form. This is another absurdity surely. For a most visual acting out of this phenomenon, August Wilson's play *Ma Rainey's Black Bottom* (New York: A Plume Book, New American Library, 1985) is an important "text." It should be noted that all of Wilson's plays are written as historical artifacts commenting on and illuminating each decade of the twentieth century in (black) America.

the Sea Islands off the coasts of the Carolinas, Georgia, and Florida—black spaces and places we encounter in Chapter 1 on cosmology and that reappear in subsequent chapters. Because language is the mother of culture, invention, and subsequently of history, we glimpse African-derived American society in the Gullah tongue. This Africanism, Gullah, is the object of much controversy. Even some younger members of contemporary Gullah communities have viewed the language of their forebears, including that of their own parents, as a form of "substandard" English, and the traditional arts of basketry and wood carving, forms of Gullah culture, as unsophisticated and unworthy of passing on.[26]

In fact, Gullah language and culture are the last vestiges of authentic African traditions brought to the United States by some of the first and some of the last African captives. The language is derived from a Caribbean Afro-Pudgin, a created language resulting from a merger of African speech rhythms with African and English words. Gullah, also called Geechee (both words also naming the people themselves), is an *oral* language created in, and for, the present in time. At the moment of its coming forth, Gullah is a living language with its own accompanying gestures and intonations. The gestures and intonations add to an African American oral tradition based on indirection, or circuitous speaking, and double textuality that reveals but also conceals. Gullah is a language that protects and allows its users to "mask" and isolate themselves from the influences of the dominant society. It does this in much the same way as being islanders geographically and physically isolates the inhabitants from the mainland. The language is noted for its uniqueness of verb and pronoun usage, nominal systems of pluralization, nongender distinctions, and present tense active voice. Thus in a sense, it is a *place* located in black consciousness and cosmology.

The importance the Gullah speakers attach to naming traditions and the secrecy of one's real name again show the power *nommo* (the spoken word) has for African-descended peoples. The association of day, weather, and season, which also *place* or locate a person, the circumstances of one's birth, attach a cosmological environment around the individual being named.

African American Speechmaking

With "Dynamics of Language" and "African American Speechmaking," we are developmentally on the threshold of the written tradition in history. But first we have the dynamics of African American communication grounded in the black church and black spirituality: in call and response, the shouts and the ringshout, the speaking in tongues—in the

---

[26] And there has been accompanying migration with implications for the entire community as young people abandon the security of island life that allows them to retain aspects of authentic African culture in the United States for life on the mainland—for work. And as they leave for a more assimilative and seemingly better life, elements of the mainland acquire the firmament on which African American history is established—the land. In doing so, corporate America will also remove the evidences of African continuity in the United States, building on even its sacred grounds (cemeteries). Young people of the twentieth century may not appreciate having a black space/place because they may not understand how priceless was its cost. For one interpretation of this experience, see Julia Dash's womanist film, *Daughters of the Dust* (King on Video, 1992).

rhythms of daily life as well as the rhythms of music, even the rhythms of the universe. In closing this anthology, it is appropriate then to listen to and hear the voices and messages of such ancestors as Frederick Douglass, Dr. Mary McLeod Bethune, and historian-theologian Vincent Harding.

How Sweet the Sound: The Spirit of African American History is panoramic in scope, looking at events, ideas, thought, and worldviews of the evolving African American from the time of enslavement to the twentieth century. The thread running through the volume that informs the African American historical process in the United States is the ongoing struggle for freedom, equality, and the complete liberation of the African American community still attaining its full human rights and the role of culture in that process: culture informed by Africa and the syncretic elements of Caribbean, but most especially by African American society in the United States.

These oral folk expressions are not seen in a limited context of the discipline of "oral history," of a *verbal* recording of history. Like that discipline, however, they are other narrative forms, grounded in vernacular or folk traditions: that is, they are located among ordinary people whose daily living has been informed by established beliefs and traditions from family and community which endured and grew root under extreme forms of racism. The passing down through the generations, in myriad oral forms, of these beliefs, values, and traditions rather than the mere writing down of them is the central interest and purpose for discussion in this anthology. It is especially so because so much of African American historical primary source material has been recorded and documented in formats other than that alphabetically written or printed. This too is a direct result of the restrictive life informed by slavery.

How Sweet the Sound will, it is hoped, add to the American as well as the African American historical discursive tradition by focusing on "texts" that are "spoken," "heard," or "seen." These "spoken," "sung," "shouted," "danced," "performed," "shaped," and "crafted" texts, seen and heard and interpreted in the anthology's selected essays, are documentary, rhetorical artifacts and statements relating the narrative or (his)story of the descendents of West Africans in the United States.

Finally, it should be clear that while touting the oral traditions and expressions of Africanist culture in the United States, *How Sweet the Sound: The Spirit of African American History* produces yet another "written" text. This may appear, at first, to be an oxymoron. It is not. What the reader will discern is a serious attempt to maintain the "sound," tempo, and look of aspects of African American history that are not often considered in the context of scholarly texts and documentary artifacts. It is, in fact, these very sounds, tempos, and visualizations that form the foundation of traditional black folkloric values and systems of thought. They reveal black peoples to themselves and to others. These are, in fact, intellectually vibrant creative forces and engagements that contribute significantly to what the world understands as *American* civilization.

Suggested Reading

Baker, Houston A., Jr. *Blues, Ideology, and Afro-American Literature. A Vernacular Theory.*

Chicago: University of Chicago, 1984.

Booth, Newell S., Jr. "Time and Change in African Traditional Thought." *Journal of Religion in Africa* 7, fasc. 2 (1975): 81–91.

Davis, Charles T., and Henry Louis Gates, Jr., eds. *The Slave's Narrative*. New York: Oxford University Press, 1985.

Davis, David Brion. *The Problem of Slavery in Western Culture*. New York: Cornell University Press, 1969.

Du Bois, W. E. B. *The Negro* [1915]. Reprint, New York: Oxford University Press, 1972.

———. *The Souls of Black Folk* [1903]. Reprint, New York: Signet Classic, 1986.

Ellison, Ralph W. "Twentieth-Century Fiction and the Black Mask of Humanity." In *Shadow and Act,* pp. 24–44. New York: Vintage Books, 1972.

Ferguson, Robert. "'We Hold These Truths': Strategies of Control in the Literature of the Founders." In *Reconstructing American Literary History,* edited by Sacran Bercovitch, pp. 1–28. Cambridge: Harvard University Press, 1986.

Gates, Henry Louis, Jr., ed. *Black Literature and Theory*. New York: Methuen, 1984.

———. *"Race," Writing, and Difference*. Chicago: University of Chicago Press, 1985.

Gilroy, Paul. *The Black Atlantic. Modernity and Double Consciousness*. Cambridge: Harvard University Press, 1993.

Herskovits, Melville. *The Myth of the Negro Past*. Boston: Beacon Press, 1958.

Hogue, W. Lawrence. *Discourse and the Other. The Production of the Afro-American Text*. Durham: Duke University Press, 1986.

Jahn, Janheinz. *Muntu. African Culture and the Western World* [1961]. Reprint, New York: Grove Weidenfeld, 1989.

Jefferson, Thomas. *Notes on the State of Virginia* [1785]. Edited by William Peden. Reprint, Cutchogue, N.Y.: Buccaneer Books, 1994.

Jones, Gayl. *Liberating Voices. Oral Tradition in African American Literature*. New York: Penguin Books, 1991.

Lovejoy, Arthur O. *The Great Chain of Being. A Study of the History of an Idea*. The William James Lectures Delivered at Harvard University, 1933. Cambridge: Harvard University Press, 1936.

Sobel, Mechal. "The West African Sacred Cosmos." In *Trabelin' on the Slave Journey to an Afro-Baptist Faith,* pp. 3–21. Westport, Conn.: Greenwood Press, 1979.

Turner, Elizabeth Hutton, ed. *Jacob Lawrence. The Migration Series*. Washington, D.C.: The Rappahannock Press, in association with The Phillips Collection, 1993.

Selected Videos, Films, CD-ROMS, and Slides

Films for the Humanities & Sciences

We Shall Overcome. Jim Brown, Ginger Brown, Harold Leventhal, George Storey, producers. California Newsreel. Video. Color. 1989.

In Search of the Dream. An Exploration of the Social, Political, Cultural, and Economic Life of African Americans from 1619 to the Present. Hosted by Arthur Ashe, producer. ABC News in association with Bolthead Communications Group. Six-part series. Films for The Humanities & Sciences. Video and Videodisc Program.

Unearthing the Slave Trade. Films for The Humanities & Sciences. 28 minutes. Video. Color.

PBS (Public Broadcasting Service) Videos

Amazing Grace with Bill Moyers. Produced by Public Affairs Television. AMAG-000C-CR94. 90 minutes. 1990.

Eyes on the Prize, Part I. America's Civil Rights Years 1954–1965. [Six-part series: *Awakenings* (1954–1956), 60 minutes; *Fighting Back* (1957–1962), 60 minutes; *Ain't Scared of Your Jails* (1960–1961), 60 minutes; *No Easy Walk* (1961–1963), 60 minutes; *Mississippi: Is This America* (1962–1964), 60 minutes; *Bridge to Freedom* (1965), 60 minutes]. Produced by Blackside, Inc. 1987. EYPZ-000H-CR94. 1987.

The Freedom Station [about Harriet Tubman]. Produced by Maryland Instructional Technology. 30 minutes. 1988.

Juba. JUBA-000-CR94 [Four-part series: *The Legend of Harriet Tubman,* 15 minutes; *Why Stories,* 15 minutes; *Brer Rabbit Stories,* 15 minutes; *How Stories Came to Be,* 15 minutes]. Produced by WETA. 1978.

That Rhythm, Those Blues. From *The American Experience.* George T. Nierenberg, producer. AMEX-110-CR94. 60 minutes. 1988.

Roots of Resistance—A Story of the Underground Railroad. Orlando Bagwell, producer. AMEX-216-CR94. 60 minutes. 1989.

The Second American Revolution, Part I and II [Regarding the twentieth-century civil rights movement]. From *A Walk Through the 20th Century with Bill Moyers.* AWTB-107-CR94 and AWTB-108-CR94. 60 minutes each.

Syracuse University Classroom Film/Video Rental Center

Black American Odyssey [Three parts: *Road to Freedom,* 20 minutes; *Attacking the Color Barrier,* 19 minutes; and *Crusade for Civil Rights,* 21 minutes]. Handel, 1987.

Updata

African American History. CD 1938 DOS MAC.

Other Sources

The Road to Brown [1954 Supreme Court decision]. William A. Elwood, producer/director. Sponsor, The University of Virginia. 47 minutes. Video. 1990.

Shackles of Memory: The Atlantic Slave Trade. Michel Morcan and Jean-Marc Masseaut. Filmmaker's Library. 52 minutes. Video. 1977.

Trouble Behind. Robbie Henson, producer/director. 56 minutes. Video and 16mm. 1990.

Chapter 1

AFRICAN AND AFRICAN
AMERICAN COSMOLOGY

Central to a discussion of African and African American cosmology or worldview is the circle. It is a symbol that represents the joining of the four corners of the earth and the four moments of the sun or the life cycle from birth to rebirth, from sunrise to midnight.[1] It links living people with those who went before them and now reside in the world of the spirits, which is joined to the living world at the boundary line of earth and water. The circle is a symbol that links African and African American history, heritage, traditions, values, and belief systems. And it creates an idea of time and space and being/becoming[2] that has no divisions but instead represents continuity. Like the waves of the ocean or the waters of a river, the circle knows no obvious or discernible beginning or end.

In this opening chapter, four historians, Vincent Harding, Sterling Stuckey, Margaret Washington Creel, and William S. McFeely, discuss fundamental building concepts necessary for the creation of an architectual structure for a new "home/land" for African peoples displaced by the Middle Passage. Those building concepts include the circle as the primary entity that acknowledges the ancestors and the influence they exert on present time, and their connection to those living persons who keep them in their memory—and thus alive—as a part of daily life. This is done by honoring and maintaining their resting places and following their example. The symbol of the circle also represents the African community in the diaspora being *renewed* and *recreated* into something basic to human survival, especially in the context of captivity and enslavement; it is the centrality of

---

[1] For discussion of the Bakongo cross that represents the four corners of the earth and four moments of the sun, see Robert Farris Thompson's *Flash of the Spirit: African and Afro-American Art and Philosophy* (New York: Random House, 1983), and also his *The Four Moments of the Sun* (Washington, D.C.: National Gallery of Art, 1981).

[2] See Mechel Sobel's *Trabelin' On. The Slave Journey to an Afro-Baptist Faith* [1979] (Reprint, Princeton: Princeton University Press, 1988) about the concept of "becoming" (p. 14) and on the "life force"—"being"— whose symbol is water or "the word" *(nommo)* (p. 7) in the chapter "West African Sacred Cosmos" (pp. 1–21). In this chapter, Sobel adds "being" to the usual four categories for the discussion of cosmology: time, space, causality, and purpose.

Sea Island dancers in a ring dance that represents community.

nommo,[3] the spoken word, and the oral and vernacular traditions necessary for the revealing of African American history and heritage, and the centrality of movement (as in dance). Dance as an oral tradition not only represents the rhythms of human life and existence and a ritual acknowledgment of the ancestors but represents also the human capacity to fill space (or a void) and interpret it and oneself in a way that will eventually make it, if Stuckey is correct, the first pan-African nationalist agency. Dance would guide the African American community-in-formation toward freedom through ongoing protest and struggle. Another building concept is a cosmology that with the onset of the Atlantic slave trade must work within a reality that, as Creel suggests, with the architectural structure slavery built, will include arbitrary death and systematic daily attempts to kill the spirit that fuels humanity. Finally, for the purposes of this anthology, there are the building concepts of continuity (the linkages between persons, ideas, and objects from continent to diaspora) and of perpetuity (that which is continuous and infinite).[4] This cosmology, (re)built and improvised on when African captive peoples reach the other side

---

[3] See Geoffrey Parrinder's *African Mythology* in which he discusses, inter alia *nommo* or *nummo* and relates the Dogan creation (of the world) story (pp. 23–24, 27, 46, 48, 62, 76).

[4] Creel adds to African cosmology, which includes the concepts of circularity and continuity, the concept of "perpetuity." See p. 81 of her essay.

of the Atlantic Ocean, is brought by them to riversides on African coasts as journeys to an unknown world begin. It is then carried on shipboard during the Middle Passage and throughout Paul Gilroy's "memory of slavery"[5] and then by that memory's legacy in the era of racism and discrimination. African cosmology is sustained in such community rituals and celebrations as the circle dance known as the ringshout.

Vincent Harding, historian/theologian and social scientist and spiritual leader, opens this chapter on cosmology by placing us, twentieth-century students of history, at the beginning of the process that creates the African American in the United States. His work puts us at the river's edge somewhere in West Africa as the history of the African in America, and particularly the United States, is unfolding. We are waiting with African ancestors who are losing their freedom and with it everything they hold dear and that has meaning. Harding's introduction to his book *There Is a River. The Black Struggle for Freedom in America,* "From the Shores of Africa," reproduced here, is another circle that represents a community-in-formation. It portrays a circle of captive Africans waiting to begin an involuntary journey toward servitude and the establishment of a syncretic group of persons called at various times in what becomes the United States: "African," "Afro-Saxon," "black," "colored," "Negro," "black American," and "Afro-American" and who become in the latter part of the twentieth century "African American." The latter term actually best reflecting the idea of syncreticism and the dual nature and double consciousness of the evolved African people, who began their transformation into "African Americans" on those West African coasts, that W. E. B. Du Bois discussed in "Of Our Spiritual Strivings"[6].

Harding takes professional but instructive risks as a writer of history in placing the reader cum participant among the persons of the ancestors. In effect, he makes us part of the circle and extends the parameters of historical writing and the idea of history as something only in the distant past to something that is immediate. His doing so is consistent with African/African American cosmology—the link is there especially for those of us who

---

[5] See Paul Gilroy's *The Black Atlantic: Modernity & Double-Consciousness* (Cambridge: Harvard University Press, 1995).

[6] W. E. B. Du Bois, "Of Our Spiritual Strivings," *The Souls of Black Folk* [1903] (Reprint, New York: The New American Library, 1969: 43–53). In an interesting discussion by writer Scott Sherman, "Fighting Words: Adolph Reed's Crusade Against the New Black Intellectuals" in *Lingua Franca* (March 1997): 38–48, Sherman mentions Reed's book, *W. E. B. Du Bois and American Political Thought: Fabianism and the Color Line,* subsequently published by Oxford University Press, 1997, where Reed, according to Sherman's interpretation puts a spin on Du Bois's concept of "double consciousness" that most historians and social scientists have accepted as a common condition of the "Negro" ("African American"): the sense of "twoness" that Du Bois writes about in *The Souls of Black Folk.* Reed, a noted political scientist, finds the origins of this philosophical/historical concept to be based on an "elite-driven organizational model" (or class model) suggesting, in Sherman's reading of Reed's manuscript, that Du Bois, therefore, is less a "radical" than a "conservative" thinker. Reed, according to Sherman, believes that after 1903, the year *Souls* was published, Du Bois does not again use "twoness" as the basis for the black condition (although the idea is to be found in the writings of Carter G. Woodson in *Miseducation of the Negro,* in Richard Wright's *The Outsider,* and Margaret Walker's discussion of African American humanism in Charles H. Rowell's "Poetry, History and Humanism. An Interview with Margaret Walker" in *Black World* [December 1975]: 4–17, and in her historical novel *Jubilee*). According to Sherman, Reed also contends that "the implication that millions of people experience a bifurcated identity simply by virtue of their racial status is a plainly essentialist [sic] notion that covers up complexity and diversity within the black community . . . he [Reed] suggests that the ideology of double consciousness is solidly anchored in the upper echelons of the black social hierarchy [The Talented Tenth]. After all, it's the black elite that lives in close proximity to whites and has the most occasion to brood over its 'two souls.'" (p. 47, "Fighting Words")

are African American. We are now what, at those moments, they were becoming—African Americans in the Americas. Being there among the ancestors makes the story palpable: less remote, less distant. Thus the story of the history of loss, strife, struggle, protest, liberation, and celebration in the U.S. African American community begins with *us* not as passive readers but as participants in the cultural beginnings of that experience. It is an experience which, we can clearly see and painfully feel, begins not just with the Middle Passage, not just with enslavement, but with *captive* persons who, like African Americans more than three centuries later, had been free in their movements, in their capacity to grow as human beings, free to think, and to contribute their work, sport, prayers, and spirit to the welfare of their families, ancestors, and respective societies. The present story of African Americans in the United States in 1999 starts in places like Harding's riverside, in the seventeenth, eighteenth, and nineteenth centuries,[7] and with persons like these who are not "African" or "West African" but Igbo, Fon, Yoruba, Dogan, Dahomean, Akan, Angolan, Bambara, Fulani, Mandingo, Kongo, Hausa, and Tiv. Diverse peoples whose contributions to what will become the "*African* American" are reflected in "A Wild African Tribe," in which McFeely describes the countenance of Sea Island boatman Argene Grovner, whose face he perceives as a "defiant banner of Africa," an authentic African face seen in the Gullah peoples on Sapelo Island in the Georgia of the 1990s.

At the river, we can hear the sounds of a cacophony of diverse tongues with a shared painful plea: to be returned to the life they know and to those persons, objects, and rituals that have meaning for them. This embarking on a terrible journey through the unknown allowed them to carry only their memories and the culture that comes with their mother tongue. No longer did they even own or control their own lives and bodies, labor or thoughts. This embarkment, as others before and after it, during the Atlantic slave trade, was marked by loss as well as violence. Harding places us in a circle not only of persons who are ancestors but on a circular journey beginning with *loss* of freedom, then movements toward the regaining of it, and, along the way, to an understanding of what freedom means, the forms it takes, and what aspects of the human spirit lead to it again and sustain it.

We begin with Vincent Harding's work: the process of African American liberation begins with freedom's loss. The circle that includes the "memory of slavery" also includes the almost simultaneous efforts at creating unity, or a new circle, out of (African) diversity, finding a liberatory voice from many tongues, marching as a community to freedom songs starting with the shouts and spirituals, and identifying the drum majors who will lead the march to create another "home/land." This circle of persons, this circle of memories and rituals that links the present with history and legacy, is an architectural foundation for a new home/land and community. This new circle of persons appropriates another sign, giving an African context to "e pluribus unum"—and out of many one.

Images and the ability to visualize them are important in understanding African American history as presented here. Harding's images and those of the other readings discussing cosmology here are palpable:

---

[7] This (his)story begins in Jamestown, Virginia, in 1619 with the twenty African persons who became indentured servants upon arriving at what later becomes the United States.

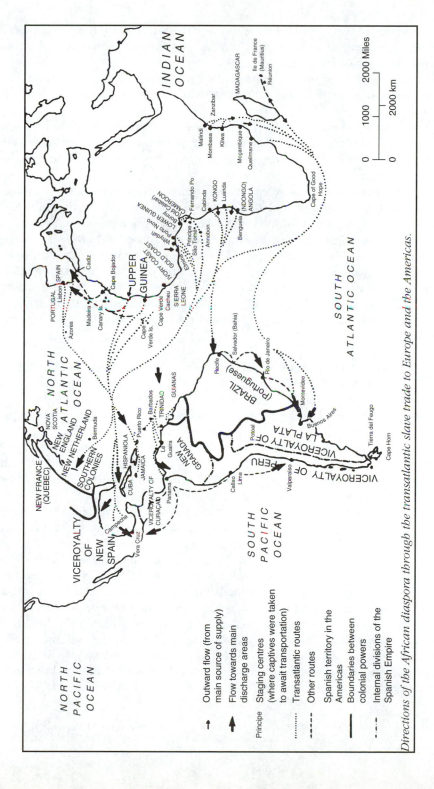

Directions of the African diaspora through the transatlantic slave trade to Europe and the Americas.

- The waters of rivers leading from the various coasts along the western seaboard of the African continent and then flowing into the vast ocean void and moving toward the unknown other side;
- The strange ships with an architecture of little living or breathing space, a floating house of death and dying, and with even stranger-looking men manning them;[8]
- The chains and fetters and foreign non-African languages based almost solely on the impatient if not angry imperative voice of commands and instructions;
- The cacophony of African tongues and voices mostly unintelligible even to the captives themselves;
- And the people—who included spiritual leaders of traditional African religions and Islam; the musicians and singers who would keep the spirit and, without the actual ancestral drums, internalize the drum's marking of the rhythms of life and universe while maintaining ancestral rituals and observances that would become the foundation of (re)new(ed) community; and the master agriculturalists and artisans, children and young people, who would, while being the architects of this American homeland, also new to their European captors, become out of necessity the nationalists and ideologues guiding their people through travail to freedom and the creation of renewed spirit, cooperation, and communalism.

In his essay, McFeely writes of American slavery being more than just a system and an abomination. On the island he studied, the enslaved persons still had names and personal identities remembered by their descendants. This makes this period of slavery not only inhumane but also what he terms a "populated time." So too are Harding's African peoples, whose names may be lost, portrayed as people and not objects of that "peculiar" era and institution. In his depiction of slavery we see African humanity, not just systematic attempts at total dehumanization. As his Africans do, we the readers/participants transcend the mundane and banal and look deeply in the souls of these persons even as they remain unknown to most of us.

The responsibilities of community for the preservation of that which is African in the "African-American," and for an African and then African American cosmology or worldview, (re)occur in McFeely's Sapelo; in Creel's eloquent metaphysical discussion of distinctly spiritual and physical spheres of human existence with the door between them—death—leading to their interconnectiveness; and in Stuckey's seminal discussion of the centrality of the circle in revealing African American cultural history, specifically in ring or circle dances including the ringshout. Here, in Stuckey's work, is found a significant place in African American intellectual history on which to build the idea that African and later African American dance and music became the soil, or the firmament, on which the African American has stood and still stands and on which he or she has built. As some of the ancestors in "From the Shores of Africa" ingested the soil of their homeland upon departing it, the ground of the Americas that African feet touched in the

---

[8] For an interesting account of an African's impression of the European (man and ship) upon first encountering them, see *The Interesting Narrative of the Life of Olaudah Equiano* [1789], edited by Robert J. Allison (New York: St. Martin's Press, 1995).

sacred circle dances they brought with them became the "African in America's" home soil and McFeely's boatman's face a banner or flag of that homeland, defying the conscious effort by the European system of captivity and enslavement to obliterate all that evoked Africa: personal names, African languages and thought processes, religious and spiritual beliefs, sense of history and contribution to human development, and feelings of community—aspects of life that now had to be maintained in memory, oral tradition, and in secret—and were.

In the excerpt by Vincent Harding, it is clear that striking for freedom is costly. But these African captives believed freedom to be priceless even if it meant throwing themselves into shark-infested waters as they were leaving the African continent. Not, as initially interpreted by their captors, in an attempt to "commit suicide" but to rejoin the ancestors and be one again with the soil of Africa. Creel, in her discussion of the spiritual and physical worlds of the enslaved person in the United States, illustrates that this action was a means of continuing human existence, not of ending life. Those persons who were able to achieve a reconciliation with all they were losing might have been the fortunate ones. But reunion with Africa and the ancestors was to be a common dream, especially of those born in Africa or of African parents in America. Reunion would form an important aspect of African American ritual as their new communities in the Western Hemisphere took responsibility, in the burial rites for those passing over, for placing their bodies with heads facing west and near water—so the souls could cross over the ocean for the final homecoming that would bring them back to their beginnings. The return of African descendants to the circle that begins in Africa, the vehicle of water as the connection making the return possible, and the service of living persons in effecting this return through correct burial, not to mention the ringshout itself, again illustrate the significance of circularity and also of water in African-defined and influenced cosmology and culture.

Harding lays the groundwork for Stuckey, Creel, and McFeely to discuss the common threads in African American cultural history that create community and freedom and are themes in this anthology. A proactive community of walkers toward freedom were the ancestors—African and later African American. Even more, they constituted a circle of persons whom adversity brought together and a community that struggle created, nurtured, and harvested. His depiction of coastal-leave taking provides, in the form of traditions, spirit/s, values, and memories, an architecture that provides shelter, nourishment, and raiment to these diverse West Africans. On the other side of the Atlantic, in the places where the Stuckey, Creel, and McFeely histories unfold, the reader sees these same persons, and their descendants, in their compulsion to create a home in the spaces and places that were most hostile to their persons, and, through assaults against their spirit, hostile also to their personhood.[9] Sterling Stuckey's essay "Slavery and the Circle of

---

[9] In this instructive quotation from an 1832 debate in the Virginia House of Delegates, it is clear that the captivity and servitude of African peoples was not just physical and spiritual but also intellectual: "We have, as far as possible, closed every avenue by which light might enter their [the slave's] minds. If we could extinguish the capacity to see the light, our work would be completed; they would then be on a level with the beasts of the field, and we should be safe! I am not certain that we would not do it, if we could find out the process, and that on the plea of necessity." From the American and Foreign Anti-Slavery Society publication, *The American Slave Code in Theory and Practice: Its Distinctive Features Shown by Its Statutes, Judicial Decisions and Illustrative Fact* (1853), p. 323.

Culture,"[10] which opens his influential study of nationalist (nation-forming) tendencies in the preformative moments of community building among African captive peoples, also builds on the cultural elements and histories of these same persons. Here, Stuckey's circle represents the new community-in-formation: Africa's orphaned children in the diasporic wilderness creating their "invisible institution" to be known as "the Black Church," but while that institution is still "invisible," praising the Creator, reflecting the spirit, and remembering the spirits of the ancestors in the act of dancing in a circle counterclockwise and together. This dancing circle is also a form of prayer that Robert Farris Thompson in "From Ancient Loango to Twentieth-Century North America: Roots of the Yard Show," from his *Face of the Gods: Art and Altars and the African Americas,*[11] describes as "space for moving and shouting with the spirit."[12]

The architecture of movement, gesturing, clapping, chanting, shouting, of spiritual, and of call and response, built that new home even before it had roof and walls and became praise/prayer house or church. It also created a new language based on dance, circle dance, and especially ringshout that became a shared *text* of West African peoples of differing tongues and cultural heritages—a text that not only would allow them to reclaim their heritage by honoring the ancestors but also by creating a common goal and language for and of liberation. The ringshout, as a combination of music, dance, and song was part of West African burial and spiritual traditions and the foundation of the language of nationalism and community that in the myriad forms of now African American oral heritage would tell of the power of the spirit, of the ancestor's connection to human life, and of aspirations toward freedom. Through the circle and ring dances, Stuckey reenforces the holistic aspect of African-defined life. Dance is not entertainment or ritual or just *of* the spirit. It is not defined by a particular segment of time or tied to a particular activity. Dance is part of everyday living and, being an integral part of the oral tradition, it is storytelling, history, worship, play. It is also integral to memory and legacy. It is part of the rhythm and drama of human existence. In the context of the ringshout, the counterclockwise movement going against the Western clock and the (ideological) grain, the shuffling, chants, and clapping constitute the new land that is being formed even as the slaving ships are crossing the ocean. This provided a common language, as this diverse group of people had temporarily lost the ability to communicate with others of their number from different cultural and language groups and had not yet, in the case of Africans coming to North America, acquired a common speech in English.

Stuckey is also convincing when he finds in the circle dance, and especially the ringshout, an oppositional *force* to enslavement and servitude. Its nature is part of the masking or masquerading that is an element of the cultural attributes of Africa. That the ringshout can take place at all, in the open, is due in part to its being perceived by the Europeans as a form of aberrant Christianity when, in reality, it was a proactive and

---

10 See Stuckey's *The Ideological Origins of Black Nationalism* (Boston: Beacon Press, 1972).

11 Robert Farris Thompson, *Face of the Gods: Art and Altars and the African Americas.* Published in conjunction with the exhibition of the same title organized and presented by The Museum of African Art (New York: 1993), pp. 74–95.

12 Ibid., p. 81.

creative protest against Middle Passage, auction block, plantation life, and the idea that these captives were chattel. That masking occurs also in the singing of the spirituals and in secular dancing, in mock election and coronation celebrations, and at carnivals where African Americans may be critiquing American society by mimicking and poking fun at those persons who created their oppressive living conditions.

Dance was especially important to persons whose movements, and even thoughts and facial expressions, were restricted or at least disguised. It represented freedom of movement and freedom of expression. It was the only possession enslaved Africans brought with them, besides the air in their lungs to give them breath and energy and their memories of rituals: their ability to cut through air and space with their bodies, their foot and hand movements, and their soaring in dance and shouts. Together the place for the dance became places and spaces to build a new interior home. It formed a new architecture in space that was invisible except when there was dance and performance—a place that while not totally unrestricted still could not have "decorum" imposed on it—a "decorum" that would contain the percussive sounds and noises coming from slapping the skin of the human body, using the body like the drum, as text. It became the architectural structure for a new homeland, a foundation their feet touched and that grounded African peoples. As well, it provided an interior space for freedom in their heads.[13] For those moments, when they at best were observed with amusement by those who did not know what they were seeing (an "invisible institution"), a community was being formed on what was becoming or being transformed into sacred ground. And even more. For a people who were able to bring with them no possessions, the ringshout as it was in its original birthplace was about *being* possessed themselves. The participants were possessed by the spirit and informed by the spirits of their ancestors, which, in those moments, joined them in the earthly realm and gave them possibilities—represented by an ability to transcend the banality of their present condition of earthly servitude—through movement.

The ringshout then was about transcendence and the transporting from the physical to the spiritual back to the physical realm again. And, in fact, for a spiritual people, those realms become indivisible. The masquerading, the presence of spirits unseen in the world, the evolution of the "invisible institution" becoming "the Black Church," and the misperceptions of Europeans about the meaning and significance of the ringshout, even about the cosmology of African life, in some ways will parallel McFeely's discussion of Sapelo. Stuckey does important things in "Slavery and the Circle of Culture": he links dance to music—sees them as *one* system of human expression—links the sacred to the secular and to daily activities of life, and both to the ideological. He associates movement (dance) with nonverbal language and other oral traditions, and he portrays aesthetics as a *place* for societal critique for persons who initially can not openly express their protest and struggle without placing themselves in great danger.

---

13 Following is an eloquent description of the ringshout from Paule Marshall's novel *Praisesong for the Widow* [1983] (New York: E.P. Dutton, 1984, p. 34): "They were propelling themselves forward at a curious gliding shuffle which did not permit the soles of the heavy work shoes they had on to ever once lift from the floor. Only their heels rose and then fell with each step, striking the worn pineboard with a beat that was as precise and intricate as a drum's, and which as the night wore on and the Shout became more animated could be heard all over Tatem."

Margaret Washington Creel's "Gullah Attitudes Toward Life and Death" focuses on the chain of Sea Islands off the coast of South Carolina. The Sea Islands, which extend from South Carolina to Florida, were some of the first places and also last ones to intimately know the settlement of African captives coming directly from the continent, or after a short period of "seasoning" (also known as "breaking-in") from the Caribbean prior to arriving on the North American mainland. The isolation of these offshore islands, ironically, has assisted in the preservation of linkages between African and African American thought and belief systems that are the basis of Sea Island, or Gullah, cosmology even today. Her discussion on the interacting aspects of human existence in life and death (afterlife) further elaborates on the ritualistic life of black persons in the United States, as gleaned in the text of the ringshout, and informs her architecture of "moral order" for the community that is based on cooperative and communal sensibilities as well as on a Creator who demands both cooperation and community from the people.

Creel does something else in this article: she places these life-affirming qualities of African-descended culture within a house of death and destruction, which the system of slavery built, thus explaining the easy and necessary negotiations between the world of the living and that of the spirits. Their interdependency (life and afterlife) make the African American "home" one that is based on "moral order" as a result of the links between ancestors and living persons, between Africa and African diaspora, between individual and community, and between the spiritual and the secular. McFeely illustrates these connections in his discussion of one Sea Island, Sapelo, self-contained, removed, remote from mainland influences and corruptions[14] and with a culture of its own, making it a distinctive community forged out of a slave labor village and transformed into "home"—even with the painful memories and stories that glued the building materials together.

The importance of Gullah society on all the Sea Islands is partly a result of its being a space/place that links Africa with the Americas in a similar, but more affirming way, that the Middle Passage links black people on both sides of the Atlantic Ocean. It is a space/place for the adaptive and the innovative, in the sense of the new, improvisational, and ameliorative, that create the architecture for a new home, one that will make it possible not only to survive enslavement but to live in freedom. For example, Creel writes about Christianity being adapted to Gullah necessity, rather than the reverse, showing how Gullahs focused on the biblical stories of the Israelites being led out of bondage, how they transformed the Bible, which was most often used to justify the servitude of black people, into a Book of Liberation. Along the way, the people she writes about also

---

14 Twentieth-century land and commercial developers, accompanied with lawyers and tax liens to appropriate black land, including even sacred ground where Gullahs are buried, have created what some have called "cultures in conflict." Several articles about this situation, which is jeopardizing Gullah culture and heritage, include Ron Nikon, "Cultures in Conflict. Sea Island Communities Are Fighting for Their Survival, Stirring New Hopes Along the Coast of South Carolina," *Southern Exposure* 21(3) (1993): 53–56; June M. Thomas, "No Place in the Sun for the Hired Help," *Southern Exposure* 10(3) (1982): 35–37; Vernie Singleton, "We Are an Endangered Species. An Interview with Emory Campbell" [executive director of the historic Penn Center on St. Helena Island (SC)], *Southern Exposure* 10(3) (1982):37–38; Maria Mallory, "Is the 'Mecca of Africanism' Not Long for This World?" *Business Week (Industrial/Technology Edition)* (August 15, 1994, No. 3385): 22B–22F; and Nancy L. Mohr, "Treasures on an Island," *American Visions* 4(5) (1989), 29–31.

The Christian river baptism especially practiced by Afro-Baptists as it is reminiscent of African religious water rites.

transformed the Christian god into their own god and, in the form of Jesus, created a mosaic (Moses prototype) model of liberation that was Old Testament and text for spirituals and shouts and other spiritual expression. Creel portrays Gullah existence, on earth and in the hereafter, and the construction of thought about that existence as part of a journey where the moment of passing over is actually a gateway or door leading to an afterlife that is part of human existence and African-derived cosmology. And the ones who have passed over, beings existing in this other realm, are being nourished by those still on earth with food and water and burial articles from their previous existence and representations of rebirth (i.e., Mother's Day cards, pinwheels, clocks with the time stopped, shells, food, water, and holders of water like pitchers left on the burial mound[15]) which allow them to leave behind completely their physical bodies and the world of the living.

Creel's essay can lead us into discussion, as well, of how the two spheres of human existence inform one another, for example in the decorative arts of pottery and wood carving where wood and water spirits can be contained and reside; in burial ornaments and spirit yards with protective qualities that mimic the guardian posts outside African homes where the spirits of the ancestors and the spirits of the natural world (i.e., wood and water spirits) are believed to have energy and the power to ward off evil and mayhem (or create it). She also discusses the symbolism of total immersion in water, an important African rite, which prompted many African Americans to embrace the Baptist

---

[15] See Robert Farris Thompson's work cited earlier, and that of John Michael Vlach and Judy McWillie including their contributions in Chapters 3 and 4 of this anthology. Also refer to Janheinz Jahn's *Muntu. African Culture and the Western World* (rev. ed. New York: Grove Weidenfeld Evergreen, 1990) and the discussion about life and human existence or the worlds of the living and of those who have passed over.

denomination rather than, for example, the more staid Episcopal Church or even the African Methodist Episcopal Church. As the ringshout is about possession of living persons by the ancestors, the total immersion of Baptist baptism allowed the African descendants to merge with the ancestors in the rivers and creeks below which they reside and also be in proximity with powerful water spirits. Sometimes prayer meetings were located around trees where the tree spirits resided to create a spirit world in *physical* time and space. Trees were used as altars in worship, their function unknown often to outside observers. Again we see the influences of water, circularity and continuity, and masking (tree altars). These are constants in African American history and an inheritance from Africa.

Creel, in discussing life and death (afterlife) and how they are related on a daily basis and create unity, again is talking about time and space. Spirituality is indivisible from the physical/secular world and it informs the thoughts, actions, and activities of the African American community. While honoring the ancestors, the African American community also found its "moral order" in the life-affirming qualities of the Creator that support and guide community existence. As Creel paints a picture of the early Gullahs living in the deadly world of slavery, after an equally dangerous captivity and Middle Passage, the connection of the worlds of the quick and the dead and the belief that death actually opens the door to the afterlife were important beliefs that allowed the Gullahs, through the singing of spirituals and the dancing of the ringshout and the near-water burials, not to dwell on death but to embrace it, if necessary, for a "life" of freedom. It also allowed them to live with its constant threat. The text of African American spirituals attest to this.

The texts of dance and song allow for the transcendence over earthly servitude and support the spirit of the community as it overcomes or at least transcends adversity. Part of the transcendence process, heard in the spirituals, is the idea that freedom and life are also part of the next world or the hereafter. The double textuality of ringshout and spiritual and freedom celebrations, sanctioned by the slave system, allows those outside the community the (mis)perception of the aspiration for liberation *after* physical life—as the reward of afterlife—at a later time. In reality, it also meant the hope and possibility of freedom on earth, masked in the cloak of Christian cosmology, which according to Creel, the Gullahs were transforming for their own purposes. The spirits and ancestors, with whom the ringshout dancers immersed themselves, were the guardians of life possessing healing propensities and providing guidance to those left behind.

Furthermore, although this is a discussion of the continuities in African American cultural heritage, Creel also illustrates that it is also about the perpetuity of life as represented in the four moments of the sun, in the circle, and in the Bakongo (the African cross from the Kongo) and Christian crosses—the cycles of life: "rising (birth, beginning, or regrowth), ascendancy (maturity and responsibility), setting (death and transformation), and midnight (existence in the other world and eventual rebirth)."[16] This idea of rebirth not only includes the newborn, possibly being the return of the spirit of an ancestor, into the community of living souls, but the idea of renewal, as seen for example,

---

[16] Creel, p. 81. Also see Robert Farris Thompson's *The Four Moments of the Sun* (Washington, D.C.: National Gallery of Art, 1981).

An enactment of a Yoruba burial ceremony where a priest and priestess pass a newborn back and forth over the grave of a deceased person to establish continuity of human existence between the living and those who have passed on. This enactment was part of a ceremony performed at the African Burial Ground in lower Manhattan.

in the spirit yards filled with retrieved and recycled objects that have been discarded and labeled "junk."[17]

Song and dance were possessions the system of slavery allowed and even encouraged. Not understanding the importance of either and the uses to which they could be put in maintaining the human spirit: to mask true feelings about enslaved person's situations of adversity, in order for them to experience emotions that had freedom at its core and as its inspiration, to affirm humanity, and to experience catharsis that allowed transcendence of reality and over death—both physical and of the spirit—song and dance were also the misbegotten gifts of the captor to the captive.

---

[17] See especially Robert Farris Thompson's chapter "From Ancient Loango to Twentieth-Century North America: Roots of the Yard Show," in his book *Face of the Gods: Art and Altars and the African Americas,* and in Chapter 3 of this anthology, Grey Gundaker's, "Tradition and Innovation in African-American Yards," *African Arts* (April 1993):58–71, 94–96.

To an extent, McFeely's "A Wild African Tribe" is a (re)turning of the circle, that cycle, perhaps, which represents the sun's moment of rebirth and renewal that comes at the midnight hour. Sapelo is a Georgia Sea Island where descendants of enslaved persons, who had worked on the plantation of Thomas Spaulding, now live in their own hammocks, or villages, born out of Spaulding's slave labor village model of "human management." McFeely is visiting the island on the occasion of the 125th anniversary of the First African Baptist Church founded by the grandsons of a Muslim whose name was Bilali and his wife Phoebe, the great-great-great grandfather and grandmother of current residents Allen Green, master basketmaker, and Katie Brown and patriarch of a family composed of many other descendants on the island. McFeely visited that part of the island called "Hog Hammock." It was named for and founded by a black family whose last name was "Hogg." On Sapelo, in Hog Hammock, the people practice traditional Gullah arts of fishing, boating, basketmaking, storytelling, and also serve as a living museum for American and international scholars and researchers who ask questions of them about Gullah language and culture, which is founded on traditional African-derived aesthetics, cosmology, religious beliefs, and culture. McFeely is among Gullah people who remember the stories of the past as told by great-great-great grandparents, who had been captured by slave traders and shared with their children and their children's children what they were doing when they were kidnapped, what it was like on slaver ships, and what life was like on the plantation that evolved into a community their descendants are holding on to tenaciously, land developers notwithstanding. To lose that land would mean to lose their Gullah culture and a *living* African-derived society.

"A Wild African Tribe" is a chapter in *Sapelo's People. A Long Walk into Freedom* about how a Gullah community made a forced "new home," however "bitter[ly]" built, into their own space/place. As we move from Harding's description of captivity, we hear in the oral tradition of the Greens and Grovners, the Carters, the Allens and the Baileys, bits and pieces of the beginnings of enslavement, the stopover in the Caribbean, the slave marts of such cities as Charleston and Savannah, the plantation on what is now, for the most part, the Gullahs' island. These persons also represent Du Bois's hyphenated Americans, which in "Of Our Spiritual Strivings" he called "Negro Americans." They are Gullahs and thus, as with Creel's Gullah people in South Carolina, retained a great deal that was African, passed down generation to generation. But they are living with the past and not dwelling on it, which as McFeely writes, would cause them, in remembering and focusing on it, to experience possibly unnecessary pain by contemplating all the past suffering that locates them on Sapelo today. Slavery is not forgotten, for it contains the story of how common languages and words among the diverse cultural groups who came to the island identified them to one another and how the creation of creole language and culture developed into a community known as Gullah. Africa is not the focus of their lives. What is, rather, is that on this island newly enslaved great-great-great grandparents made someone else's space and place habitable for themselves and finally a possession of their descendants—a place the Gullahs would call their own. What they accomplished, in two hundred years, was the transformation of these "hammocks," or family-based settlements, created by the plantation system for its own benefit, into their "home" and their hammocks. Africa is a place to visit, but reality for the Gullahs is Hog Hammock and the other hammocks on Sapelo.

Along with those Gullah hammocks are their churches, one of which is the First African Baptist Church. But McFeely, in discussing that institution created by the descendants of Muslim ancestors, who maintained Islamic practices and rituals and read the Holy Quran in the Arabic, builds on the idea of cooperation and community when he writes that although descendants of Muslims founded this church "That faith [Islam] was not lost, but rather transferred to another still firmly held."[18] The adaptive, innovative, and the circular still inform. McFeely makes clear that these Sapelo residents are descendants of *survivors* of slavery and the church is an enduring symbol of that and of the bonds of community. After slavery ended, St. Luke's, another Baptist church, was established on Sapelo. Today, the two churches, with different congregations, alternate services weekly, and on the anniversary of First African Baptist both sets of parishioners came to celebrate its survival and its importance to the entire community.

During the era of enslavement, those who came first to the island, and had to train and acclimate newcomers, comforted them by identifying *themselves* as fellow peoples from Africa, if not also from common cultural groups, and as people in similar circumstances (members of an enslaved community) to the newcomers. The Spaulding family that populated Sapelo with forced labor from Africa conceived of "slaves" as having neither history nor heritage prior to what they called "the school of slavery," which theoretically would bring enslaved persons to a level of "civilization" that would make it possible to consider their achieving freedom in the distant future. In the remembered stories from their forebears, Gullah people created a picture of a space and place that was imposed on a frightened people and on the attempts made to create among them a "serf peasantry" with families that settled into island villages like that at Hog Hammock. "The management" of enslaved persons employed by the Spauldings led to, if not encouraged, community and made the descendants of enslaved persons "African Americans," who know the stories but do not dwell on slavery or on Africa, finally owners of the land. And after importation of Africans to the United States legally ended in 1808, natural increase, the consequence of surviving and wanting to have families and loved ones that only the hope of future freedom and faith could create and sustain, made this time of travail McFeely's "populated time."

The Gullahs of the 1990s have a long past, extending back to a place mostly unseen, over the horizon, and across, for many reasons, what is an inhospitable ocean that the islanders, as they do the Georgia mainland, do not give much consideration to. What does inform their lives represents two hundred years of the more immediate past in the United States and the legacy made here on this side of the Atlantic. They have been transformed into Gullahs, a creole people: into African Americans. Their home, a place they made, and the Gullah people who were forged out of people born on the island, who created enduring families in spite of enslavement, are living testament to that. The land of the Gullahs is one of the last African survivalisms in the United States, making them what Caribbean writer Wilson Harris called a gateway people, a third people from the admixture of African, European, and Native American cultures. McFeely talks about the people's gait and walk and how they hold their heads high. He sees all these things as signs. Why dwell on the past when you signify it? He writes that in the color of a boatman's face

---

[18] McFeely, p. 43.

is the flag of African memory and legacy. The memory and legacy are part of the Gullah people, physical locations both external and, being also in their souls, internal: factors that tie them to their origins and the fact of their survival as a unique American people. They do not have to see Africa because Africa is in them, just as the captives we met in Harding ingested into their bodies African soil as they boarded slaver ships. Africa is in the people, on their persons, in their souls, and in the (re)name of their oldest church. It also describes these forced Americans ("African Americans"). Sapelo and other of the Sea Islands, as well as other creole places and spaces and cultural survivals throughout the United States, attest to the continuity of African experience in the Western Hemisphere.

From the Shores of Africa
Vincent Harding
Historian/Theologian

Vincent Harding was director of the Martin Luther King Memorial Center's Institute of the Black World from 1965–1969. The Institute was an influential force in the evolution of the Black Studies movement on campuses throughout the U.S. He is also the author of Martin Luther King: The Inconvenient Hero *(1996) and* Hope *and* History: Why We Must Share the Story of the Movement *(1990) and co-author of Volume 9 of "The Young Oxford History of African Americans" series* We Changed The World: African Americans, 1945–1970 *(1997). A civil rights activist, he was a senior adviser on the award-winning PBS documentary* Eyes on the Prize: America's Civil Rights Years. *Harding currently teaches at the University of Denver's Iliff School of Theology.*

. . . we stood in arms, firing on the revolted slaves, of whom we kill'd some and wounded many . . . and many of the most mutinous leapt over board, and drowned themselves in the ocean with much resolution . . .

John Barbot
Slave Ship Captain, 1701

It began at the edge of our homeland, where the verdant forests and tropical bush gave way gradually to the sandy stretches of the Guinea coast. It began at the mouths of the rivers, from that northern point where the Senegal and the Gambia pour their

Vincent Harding, "From the Shores of Africa," in There Is a River. The Black Struggle for Freedom in America, *pp. 3–23, 339–341 (New York: Harcourt Brace Jovanovich, 1981).*

troubled streams into the waters around Cape Verde, down the thousands of miles of coastline to the place where the mighty river Congo breaks out into the ocean. On these shores near the mouths of these rivers, we first saw the ships.

There was no way to know it then, but their crews of men and boys came from many ports and many pasts to find the shores of Africa. They sailed from Amsterdam and Lisbon, from Nantes and La Rochelle, from Bristol and London, from Newport and Boston on ships with strange names. They came to us on *Brotherhood* and *John the Baptist,* on *Justice* and *Integrity,* on *Gift of God* and *Liberty;* they came on the good ship *Jesus.* But by the time our weary lines of chained and mourning travelers saw the vessels riding on the coastal waves, there could be but one name, one meaning: captivity. Thus it was on the edges of our continent—where some of us gulped down handfuls of sand in a last effort to hold the reality of the land—that the long struggle for black freedom began.[1]

Struggle was inevitable for the captives, and preparations began early. There were many times when the forced marches from the interior or the long rides in the river canoes brought our people to their terrible rendezvous with slavery long before the *Morning Star* and *Mary* had arrived to receive them. Often, even when the ships were anchored in the bay, the involuntary black pilgrims were kept waiting weeks at a time until a slaver's full human cargo had been collected. Then, guarded by other Africans who had made a tragic choice, huddled together in rows of wooden shacks known as "baracoons" and "factories," forced into dungeonlike castles and forts which the Europeans had built on the coasts, or simply settled in open clearings by the riversides, a troubled and bewildered people had time to consider the past and the future, time to ponder this new captivity which dominated the present, time to grapple with the need to break free.[2]

As is so often the case with human struggles for liberation, the first stages of the baracoon-based movements toward black freedom required internal action, exertions of the will. In many places it was probably necessary to break through all the real and fancied barriers of each particular geographic, tribal, and national history represented in these first confused and unlikely pan-African assemblies. For within the flexible matrix of our continental oneness, over the long millennia of the ages, Africa has produced great diversity. Even in the relatively limited setting of the western portions of the continent, which supplied most of the men, women, and children who filled these prison spaces, there was a fascinating, compelling variety of human experience. Wherever they were gathered, in the slave castles at York, or at Cape Coast on Bena Island, or at Atim, or in scores of other places, the African captives were themselves a testimony to this multiformity. They had come from the ocean-tempered coastal area as well as inland forests, from the villages in the mountain shadows and from riverside towns. Some were the products of peoples and nations with long traditions of strong kings, elaborate courts, and well-defined civil services. Most of the others had heard of such things only through the stories of their traders; the sole kingdom they knew was that which encompassed their family, clan, and small tribe. As they identified themselves to one another and spoke their names in those dark prison places, the sounds of their tribes and nations must have tumbled like a waterfall out of the river of the past: Bambara, Malinka, Fon, Dinka, Ewe, Bakongo, Ibo, Yoruba, and hundreds more.

In the same way, the African people who waited against their will for the coming of the European ships were also living testimonies to the breadth and variety of the work and skills of their continent. Imprisoned now in the heart of the earth they had known so well were miners familiar with the long African traditions of iron, gold, and diamond mining. Blacksmiths, their companion artisans, were also captives. Weavers and potters; workers in bronze, copper, and gold; traders whose wide-ranging movements had long ago put Africa in touch with Asia, Asia Minor, and Europe—all of them were now among the prisoners in these cramped and fetid waiting rooms of history. Here were herders, perhaps captured while pursuing their lonely, roaming occupation, and fishermen and fisherwomen. But surely no group was more fully represented in the baracoons than the vast body of farmers. And none was more essential to the life of the people than the priests and musicians who illuminated, intensified, and celebrated the ritual integument and vital religious center of African life. They too were in these terrible temporary settlements by the waters, and their prayers and songs for freedom must have filled the air like a bittersweet dust. Often they were among the natural leaders in planning the struggle to break free.[3]

For struggle was inevitable. Reflection on the great and varied African past was not sufficient. Now all these histories were jammed into one frightening present, and it was evident that we were being rushed forward into a new history, one which had no real precedent in the countless centuries of our past (except for the Moslems among us who told their stories of the captive people who had followed a certain Moses). So by the time the ships arrived, there could no longer be any doubt that we had been captured in our homeland to prepare us for a greater, uncharted, wholly terrifying captivity across the endless waters "far from [our] native clime/Under the white man's menace, out of time."[4]

From the European side, the way to this place of struggle had been ploughed by powerful movements of peoples and institutions. That relatively small continent was bursting with new cultural, political, and economic forces. Religious, civil, and commercial revolutions were creating new men and women, new institutions, new hungers for the riches of other people's lands which could only lead to harsh conflicts. In the fifteenth and sixteenth centuries the recently established monarchies and national states, burgeoning commercial classes, trading companies, and adventurers were all drawn together. The common magnet was the search for gold and other precious goods, for the wealth and power these created, and the new trading routes to the Orient which led to them. At the same time, while their newly redefined religion and philosophy taught these men that human freedom had few limits for the strong, their advances in weaponry convinced them that there was no strength to match their own. Other technological developments, often borrowed by the way of North Africa and Asia Minor, gave them greater confidence on the ocean, new capacities to navigate its reckless wastes, stronger ships to carry them into the sun. Most often the kings, queens, and trading companies, as well as the new public treasuries, provided the capital for the bold explorations. Popes, bishops, and professors provided the blessing and the rationale for their incursions into the lives and histories of other civilizations. Their developing nation states and national consciousness promised glory and recognition to the most successful conquerors and exploiters. Men and boys newly uprooted from the countryside and towns provided the crews and cannon fodder for fierce mutual warfare and for the larger European assault on the peoples of Africa and the Western Hemisphere.

With the merchant marine of Portugal and Spain taking the lead, the men and the ships who carried the banner of this new Europe blundered into the Americas while seeking the way to China. At the same time, still looking for alternative routes to the Orient, searching out trading posts on the way around "the Dark Continent," they discovered Africa's gold and its people. So Christopher Columbus and Vasco de Gama, Bartholomeu Diaz and John Cabot went out in search of wealth, adventure, and a place in history, and they barged into the future on a rising tide of blood. As a result, by the end of the sixteenth century many Europeans realized that across the Atlantic they had found a sparsely populated hemisphere to conquer, exploit, and settle. South of their so often cold and crowded lives, they had also come upon a great, warm black continent to provide the slave workers who would create much of the wealth of the New World. That brutal connection between the vast, potentially profitable lands of the Western Hemisphere, and the apparently inexhaustible sources of captive labor in Africa, became the critical nexus in the mind of Europe's ruling and commercial classes, as they anticipated the wealth and power these human and physical resources would bring to them. Out of that combination of vision, enterprise, and avarice, the African slave trade was born.[5]

Of course long before the ships of Europe arrived, there was a form of human bondage in Africa, just as there was on most of the world's continents. But there is no evidence that the kind of chattel slavery which Europe was to perfect in the New World had taken root in West Africa. The slavery in existence was—as slavery goes— far more humane, since often it was only for prescribed periods of time, and involved no laws aimed at dehumanization. This slavery was not established by the Africans primarily for profit; it did not impose on the victims a mark of essential, intrinsic inferiority; and it was not necessarily passed on to the children of the bondsmen. When the ships came, they brought with them the European passion for profits, the European disease of racism, and the European fondness for power of arms. When these forces encountered all the weaknesses—all the tendencies to fear, deception, and greed—that Africans share with the rest of humankind, the earlier, more flexible patterns of African bondage degenerated into the African slave trade—financed, fueled, and directed by the peoples of Europe, and all too often aided and abetted by African allies.[6]

Attempts had already been made in various places to use the indigenous peoples of the Western Hemisphere, as well as poor white prisoners and indentured servants from England and the continent, as slave workers in the Americas, but none of these experiments had proven successful. In the case of the Indians, escape was too easy on their own native ground. Besides, their numbers were limited, and few had any preparation for the heavy agricultural work and metal mining which European exploitation demanded. In many cases, when they resisted European demands for such slave workers, the native peoples were simply destroyed. On the North American continent— where the need for such work was focused—two other considerations emerged as well. The enslaving of Indians was a direct invitation to their armed retaliation against some of the isolated frontier settlements, which the Europeans did not readily invite.

In addition, one important early source of income for the Europeans in North America was the fur trade with the Indians, which enslavement of the latter would endanger. For these and other reasons, the practice never developed beyond relatively isolated instances.[7]

On the other hand, even those whites brought out of the prisons of England and elsewhere to work as slaves or indentured servants often still had some link to the home countries. Consequently, knowledge of their permanent servitude could produce serious political problems at home for the colonizers of the royal territories, as well as stop the flow of other white servants to the colonies. Besides, the common color and culture that these white servant-slaves shared with other whites in the colonies created thorny social, religious, and psychological problems, and also rendered re-capture more difficult when they escaped. Perhaps even more important was the fact that, as in the case of the Indians, there were simply not enough of them, and they had not developed the natural immunities necessary to become the massive, intensive, often semi-tropical labor force required to satisfy the desire of the companies and monarchs for the largest profits in the shortest time.[8]

As a result, by the end of the seventeenth century, as England and other white-settler countries shifted their attention north from the Caribbean, established claims along the North American coast, and explored the wilderness, Africans became the chosen people for American slavery. Here they were far from home with no natural allies around them, and with no regular means for word of their fate to get back to any political centers which would affect the sources of supply. In most cases they had the needed agricultural experience and natural tropical immunities, and the supply seemed inexhaustible. Then, too—surely of the greatest importance—they were an alien, non-Christian, nonwhite people, easily providing a negative source of identity and a negative rallying point for the New World's white society. And so they were chosen. We were chosen.

By this time England had established its hegemony over "the Trade," as its participants and others euphemistically referred to this commerce in human bondage. With the Royal African Company and scores of independent "adventurers" leading the way, the vessels called *Morning Star* and *Charity, Young Saint Paul* and *Good Intent* were making their laden way from the Guinea coast to Barbados and Jamaica, to Charleston and Norfolk, carrying the peoples of Africa into captivity. There were often impressive profits to be made now in the Trade itself, and especially in that great flowering of agriculture, shipping, and commerce which accompanied the colonizing of the New World, a world that the captive Africans built. Individual owners, trading companies, churches, monarchs—all shared in the wealth. Of course these financial gains were based on working hundreds of thousands and eventually millions of men, women, and children for their lifetime without pay. And so, beginning with their first experimental presence on the tobacco plantations of the Caribbean, Africans gave their involuntary labor to the creation of the new settlement. They blazed the trails, cleared the forests, built the dwellings, tilled the land, planted the seed, harvested the crops, dug the ore, kept the livestock, nursed the children, created and maintained the wealth of the New World—without pay. As a result, there were great profits in Barbados and Hispaniola, in Carolina and Virginia. Indeed, before the American War for Independence, one contemporary English economist would say, "The daily bread of the most-considerable part of our British manufacturers, are owing primarily to the labor of Negroes." That, essentially, is what Eric Williams, C. L. R. James, and Walter Rodney have told us since: Europe's Industrial Revolution, that engine of revolutionary change which released the social, economic, and political energies of the modern world, was built on the black and bloody foundations of our African forebears. That is why the ships continued to come to the coast of Guinea and to wait at the mouths of the rivers.[9]

As the "Black Gold" began pouring into the English colonies of the New World, new patterns of captivity, betrayal, and confusion were established on the continent. African nations like the Fulas, the Mande, the Susu, and the peoples of Dahomey devoted themselves to capturing and keeping other Africans for the slave trade. Ancient political balances and structures of power and alliances were shattered through the introduction of Europe's firearms into the hands of one side or another. Often the arms were used as bribes to encourage leaders to capture men, women, and children from adjoining nations and tribes. Wars were declared for no other reason than to obtain prisoners. Villages were razed; hunting parties never returned home. Families and tribes, and centuries of traditions, were broken. And eventually the trails of the West African lands were beaten smooth by the bare feet of millions of our ancestors, as they made their way down to the rivers and the sea. For a long time the Europeans, sustained by their guns and Bible, and by arrogance and cruelty, were convinced that all things white and Christian were possible. For a long time, partly because of internal weaknesses among the nonwhite peoples, it seemed the Europeans were right—as if, for instance, all the lives and skills and names in those coastal African baracoons were to be annealed into a single hopeless being called Nigger and Slave.[10]

But this was only a part of reality, for in those early precincts of despair, beginning in baracoons and in oceanside forts, under multilayered surfaces of European domination and African betrayal, the struggle for black freedom was breaking out. This, of course, was to be expected. Men, women, and children who for generations had helped create families, tribes, nations, and empires—who had known no other land but the land of their fathers, no other rule but the rule of their African peoples—must have developed within themselves a powerful will to break free from this captivity. Even the Africans who had been prisoners, the disgraced, the twice-captured, must have recognized the desperation of their plight. Too much human life, too much human creativity, too much human hope was compressed in those castles and dungeons for the struggle to be denied.

And so, by the time the ships arrived out of the glaring mirror of sunswept waters, or moved like a visitation of giant fireflies against the darkness of the sea—by the time *Integrity* and *Liberty* and *Black Boy* arrived at Whydah and Malemba—the issues and nature of those early stages of black struggle were starkly defined. At that moment in our history, as the ominous shadows hovered near the coasts, we fought to remain in our homeland, to continue in the experience and tradition our peoples had created, to build and protect the societies we had fashioned under the guidance of the spirits. Our struggle was to resist the breaking of our nations, our families, and the chain of our existence. Our struggle was to free ourselves from the already obviously brutal captivity which was spreading over the people like some cloud of foreboding and death, to free ourselves for the life that our forebears had willed to us and our children. Our struggle was to resist both the European captors and their African helpers, to challenge and seek to break their power to take us away from our homeland. In doing this, we denied the European right to hold us, to rule our lives, to control our destiny. We affirmed our own freedom, our own being.

Struggle was inevitable, and captains of the slave ships knew that they must be prepared for our attempts to break free, especially while their vessels were still near the African coasts. On board an English ship in 1693 (was it *Brotherhood* or *Constant Mary?*—we no longer know) the captain wrote: "When our slaves are aboard we shackle the men two and two, while we lie in port, and in sight of their own country, for 'tis then they attempt to make their escape and mutiny; to prevent which we always keep centinels upon the hatchways, and have a chest full of small arms, ready loaden and primed, constantly lying at hand upon the quarter-deck, together with some granada shells; and two of our quarter-deck guns, pointing on the deck thence, and two more out of the steerage."[11]

If chains and guns were necessary when Africans were stuffed down in the brutal darkness between the decks, then even greater force and threat of force were often deemed necessary when we came up on deck to eat. The captain continues: "They are fed twice a day, at 10 in the morning, and 4 in the evening, which is the time they are aptest to mutiny, being all upon deck; therefore all that time, what of our men are not employ'd in distributing their victuals to them, and settling them, stand to their arms; and some with lighted matches at the great guns that yaun upon them, loaden with partridge, 'til they have done and gone down to their kennels between decks." Such testimony from the men who manned the ships of black captivity was repeated hundreds of times throughout the centuries of the Trade. In spite of their names, many of the vessels were indeed meant to be "kennels" where human beings were forced to exist for weeks and months in conditions not fit for animals. That is why so many hundreds of thousands of our ancestors were ravaged by disease, lying for days in their own excrement, dying in these cattle ships.[12]

Yet the ships were also prisons for humans. That was the meaning of the chains, the guns, and the fearful white men standing with lighted matches at the cannon. For ultimately they knew that we were more than animals, that the secret conversations of the baracoons and lower decks could turn into rebellion at any moment. So as in all prisons, an inordinate amount of the captors' time was spent in simply watching and guarding against any black movement toward freedom. And the life of the sailor guards, locked in a captivity parallel with our own, was often filled with sheer wretchedness.[13]

In the course of the struggles, it developed that the ships were even more than prisons. Ultimately they provided black people with an introduction to the Euro-American state, for they were mini-states with their own polity, their own laws and government; the common sailors were the ships' own indigenous oppressed class. When the Africans were brought on board, much of the machinery of these floating miniatures of England and France, of Virginia and Massachusetts, could be geared toward our captivity, but the internal contradictions did not disappear. At the core of the mini-states, prisons, and kennels it was always possible to discover the social, economic, and political scourges rising out of Europe: racism, capitalism, and the deep human fears they engender. The tie of the ships to European capitalism was evident in the decision to call them "slavers," and in their relationship to the slave "factories," and to the industrial factories at home which made the goods that they brought to trade for humans. To maximize profits, the ships had to herd as many Africans aboard as possible, and to exploit their own white crews.

The racism was just as clearly there, as for instance in the shipboard public executions which usually followed the unending black attempts at resistance and rebellion. Certainly it was unmistakable in the words and intent of William Snelgrave, one of the more famous (because more literary) slaving captains, when in 1727 he reported on the execution of an African who had killed a white man in the struggle for freedom. Snelgrave had the black man hoisted as high as possible above the deck and shot to death in the presence of his fellow Africans. Then, he said, "I ordered the Linguist to acquaint the men-Negroes, 'That now they might judge, no one that killed a white Man should be spared.' " Snelgrave probably did not know it then, but even if he had hoisted the insurrectionary up into the clouds, the struggle would not have ended. Though few of their words survive, the actions of our fathers and mothers in those ships along the coasts declared that many of them were determined to carry on a relentless struggle for freedom. They wanted freedom from the status of animals, the role of prisoners, the domination of white Europeans. They wanted to continue in their people's long stream of history.[14]

In the early struggles on the ships in the coastal waters, the African captives used every available tool to strike for freedom. Sometimes they even broke their chains and transformed them into weapons. Near the end of the seventeenth century, off the shores of the Gulf of Guinea where the castle of Elmina stood, a Dutch captain underestimated the power of the will of his black captives. He fished up an anchor left behind by another ship, and put it down in the hold where the male Africans were being held. The anchor became a signal and a forge. A Dutch writer and a participant in the slave trade, William Bosman, wrote:

> [the men,] unknown to any of the ship's crew, possessed themselves of a hammer; with which, in a short time, they broke all their fetters in pieces upon the anchor; after this they came above deck and fell upon our men; some of whom they grievously wounded, and would certainly have mastered the ship if a French and English ship had not fortunately happened to ly by us and immediately came to our assistance with chalops and men, and drove the slaves under deck: Notwithstanding which before all was appeased about twenty of them were killed.

The lessons then being written in the reddened coastal waters soon entered into the long history of the struggle: blacks have never lacked ingenuity, wisdom, courage, and a deep longing for freedom. But in captivity these were not sufficient: it was not enough to break the chains; it was necessary to master the ship.[15]

Along the African coasts, it was possible to hope for such mastery. So in spite of constant and costly defeats, the struggles for freedom went on. Often women took a crucial part, making full use of the special status and greater freedom of movement accorded them. While the men, except for prescribed times, were kept chained in the communal hole between the decks, the women were allowed to move around the up-per decks by day, and not infrequently after the day had ended. Why? Partly because they were judged less dangerous than the men. Partly too because the captains, who considered themselves humane and Christian, often thought it necessary for the chil-dren to be on deck, and wanted the women to be able to care for them. But also, on many vessels, so that white men from the captain to the cook's helper could unleash their lust against them.[16]

Fortunately for the black struggle, many black women refused to submit to or be corrupted by this most personal of white invasions; instead, they turned the situation to the purposes of their people's fight for freedom. Samuel Waldo, the owner of the slaving ship *Africa,* which operated out of Boston, wrote to his captain in 1734: "For your own safety as well as mine, You'll have the needfull Guard over your Slaves, and putt not too much confidence in the Women nor Children lest they happen to be Instrumental to your being surprised which might be fatall."[17]

By the time of his letter there was much evidence to support such a warning, for black women were regular participants in the struggle for freedom. Their role was ex-emplified in the events on board the English ship *Robert* as it stood off the coast of Sierra Leone in 1721. Among the thirty captives on board was a man who called him-self Captain Tomba, one of the earliest identifiable leaders of the struggle. He and sev-eral other African men and an unnamed woman had developed a plan to attack the crew, overcome them, and make their way back to the shore. The woman, because she had greater freedom of movement, was chosen to inform the men of the best time for the attack.[18]

One night as she roamed the deck, she noted that the number of sailors in the night watch was small enough to make a surprise move feasible. After she managed to inform Tomba, he prepared to act immediately; but only one of the African men who had promised earlier to assist him was now ready to join Tomba and the woman. Nevertheless, these three moved to strike for their freedom. The smallness of their force and an accidental sounding of an alarm worked against them, so that after killing two of the crew they were overwhelmed by others, beaten to the deck, and placed in chains. The ship's doctor who preserved this story of black struggle also recorded its cost: "The Reader may be curious to know their punishment: Why, Captain Harding weighing the Stoutness and Worth of the two Slaves, did as in other Countries they do by Rogues of Dignity, whip and scarify them only; while three others, Abettors, but not Actors, nor of Strength for it, he sentenced to cruel Deaths; making them first eat the Heart and Liver of one of [the whites who was] killed." Such atavistic tendencies, such remembrances of their own tribal pasts, were constantly in evidence among the white exploiters.[19]

And what of the woman who chose the struggle for black freedom over her priv-ileged bondage among white men? We are told that "the woman he hoisted up by the Thumbs, whipp'd and slashed her with Knives, before the other Slaves till she died." And so, not far from the shores of the homeland, the swaying, bleeding body of a sister in struggle bore terrifying witness to the cost of the decision for freedom. Yet perhaps she would have considered this lonely vigil above the sea a better use of her body than any that the crew members had had in mind.[20]

It is only by accident that we learn a name such as that of Captain Tomba, or even catch the disturbingly grand outlines of the woman from Sierra Leone. Most of those Africans who carried on the earliest phases of the movement toward justice are now nameless. This is unfortunate, yet not wholly so, for their very anonymity is a reminder of the broad basis of the struggle, an encouragement to see the relentless surge toward freedom as a movement from the outset belonging to the people.

Even without the faces or the names, what begins to be clear is the stunning, perhaps frightening power resident in those early struggles. For instance, we know only that in 1730 the captive Africans of the Massachusetts schooner *William* conspired together and killed almost all the crew, then made their way back to the nearby shores. On another Massachusetts ship of the same period, "the Negroes got to the powder and Arms, and about 3 o'clock in the morning, rose upon the whites; and after wounding all of them very much, except two who hid themselves; [the blacks] ran the Vessel ashore a little to the Southward of Cape Lopez and made their escape." So too, near the end of 1732, a contemporary account reported that a group of captives from Guinea on board a Bristol slaving ship "rose up and destroyed the whole crew, cutting off the Captain's Head, Legs and Arms."[21]

The sheer ferocity of such confrontations makes it clear that some of the men and women who battled in the coastal waters anticipated the violent future ominously as when, in 1735, the captives on the English ship *Dolphin* "overpowered the crew, broke into the powder room, and finally in the course of their effort for freedom blew up both themselves and the crew." In February 1759, in the Gambia River, a battle on board a New England ship produced a similar outcome. When the vessel had taken on its captives, it was attacked by other Africans from the shore. According to a contemporary white account, the crew "made a good defence; but the Captain finding himself desperately wounded, and likely to be overcome, rather than fall into the Hands of such merciless Wretches, when about 80 Negroes had boarded his Vessel, discharged a Pistol into his magazine, and blew her up; himself and every living soul on Board perished."[22]

In spite of the constant danger of such suicidal white defense, black men and women continued to resist. Still, there were always captains and other white men who claimed to be surprised at such persistent struggle. On another occasion a group of Africans fresh from the Gold Coast attempted an uprising while the ship of the familiar Captain Snelgrave was still near the shore. The fifty white men in the slaver's crew were healthy and well armed; black resistance had not been expected. When the revolt had been crushed, Snelgrave had his translators ask what had induced them to mutiny. According to his own account, the Africans told him that he was "a great Rogue to buy them, in order to carry them away from their own Country, and that they were resolved to regain their Liberty if possible."[23]

It is likely that the version of either the translators or the captain was much milder than the original sentiment; nevertheless, both the words and the deeds of the rebellious Africans were significant, and their meaning was not lost. The captives were challenging the justice, authority, and legitimacy of their captors. Their words, which surely represented the speeches—and the screams—of many other men and women on those voyages, were among the earliest forms of what we shall call the Great Tradition of Black Protest. As such, the speakers and others like them were the first bold face-to-face petitioners against slavery. But they were more besides, for if those European ships indeed represented the rising white racist nation-state and its developing systems of economic and cultural exploitation, then the black voices of the Gold Coast were also part of a beginning tradition of radical challenge to such a state. Albeit unwittingly, they called into question the very roots of the mechanisms of white power and control. Essentially, they declared that for them this system had absolutely no legitimacy; they persistently acted accordingly and often took the consequences. This was black radicalism at the outset.[24]

Everywhere, though, the joint tradition of protest and radicalism raised problems which needed to be solved—harsh questions involving both the goals of the struggle and the nature of the men and forces which opposed black freedom. How could black struggle best break the power of men who were at once driven and imprisoned by the glittering promises of commercial wealth, and blinded by the racism and fear which burrowed deeply within their lives? When such white men were in possession of the ships and weapons, when they had access to the self-destruction levers, what was the proper path of a struggle, what was the goal of the radical movement toward freedom?

While the battles were still being waged in sight of the homeland, at least some issues and answers seemed clear. Africans had shared no significant history with those masters of the slave ships, which were meant to be our prisons and our kennels, providing a brief and horrible introduction to the civilization of the European world, its laws, its impulses, and its conception of our place. Near the coast our challenge was clear, fundamental, and radical in its essential nature: our total struggle on each ship was a total challenge to the control of the white captors, a movement to smash their power, to repossess our history and our future. We wanted their little ships only long enough to return us to our vast continent. Indeed, sometimes we spared their crews if they did not hinder our homeward flight. So for the most part, black struggle and black radicalism were at the beginning a single stream encompassing both words and action.

But what happened on those ships, those thousands of ships which took us out into the ocean, away from the sights and smells of our land, beyond even the far-ranging flight of our birds? What did black struggle for freedom mean out in the vast and seemingly endless arena of that ocean? Was any struggle possible? In such situations African men and women must surely have asked, why challenge the captains and crews, why risk the certainty of death for the uncertainty of the land beyond the ocean, why fly in the face of the eternal east wind?

Already it was evident that from place to place, time to time, and setting to setting, the nature of our struggle was to be transformed and the questions reshaped. So it was on the ocean, as we moved further from the black shores into the agonies of the middle passage. Under those new, unprecedented circumstances the only possible struggle for most captives was to stay alive—an arduous task on many ships, usually demanding all our energies. On too many vessels the focus of this struggle for survival was the food, stingily apportioned by the captains or the owners, while Africans and their children slowly starved. Sometimes our attention was focused on filth and on the disease it engendered, as well as on the strange new diseases brought from the wharfs of Bristol or London—and from the captains' bedrooms—and insinuated into our bodies just as arrogantly as the boats moved into the rivers of our land. Often the focus was on the extended suffering of countless hours in chains, lying on our backs and sides in spaces made for narrow, rigid corpses. But it is likely that for most of us the heart of the new darkness was imprisonment itself. Most of us had not experienced it before—neither the physical imprisonment of kennels, chains, and guns, nor those mental dungeons that white fear and disdain now created around us. In many instances, the shock they induced proved fatal.[25]

It was a long journey to the Western Hemisphere—usually from one to three months, depending on tides and storms, and on the points of departure and landing. Under these circumstances, when even the birds of the homeland could no longer be seen, survival was an understandable obsession, and it was not always possible to perceive the meaning or purpose of any other struggle. In the midst of the journey, on many ships they made us sing and dance. But like so much of our singing and dancing at white command ever since, the activity was not primarily for our benefit or entertainment, but for white profits, ordered because dancing was considered therapeutic, was supposed to ensure us against the "melancholy" that drove countless thousands of Africans to suicide in the course of the middle passage. It was also supposed to help prevent scurvy, though as some observers noted, dancing "was a useless torture for men with swollen limbs." Nevertheless, "while sailors paraded the deck, each with a cat-o'-nine-tails in his right hand, the men slaves "jumped in their irons' until their ankles were bleeding flesh." The men and women often danced separately, their music supplied by a fellow captive who beat on a broken drum or played on the upturned kettle which was, and would continue to be, so ubiquitous in our cultures.[26]

And what were the songs that we sang? One doctor who served on the English ship *Young Hero* probably spoke with great accuracy when he said, "They sing, but not for their amusement. The captain ordered them to sing, and they sang songs of sorrow. Their sickness, fear of being beaten, their hunger, and the memory of their country . . . are the usual subjects." Then late at night, after the songs were over, from the darkness of the lower decks of the *Young Hero* and a thousand other ships, the sailors often could hear "an howling melancholy noise, expressive of extreme anguish." On one such occasion, the ship's doctor said that he asked his black female interpreter to go inquire the cause of the wailing noise. According to the doctor, "she discovered it to be owing to their having dreamt that they were in their own country, and finding themselves when awake, in the hold of a slave ship." At every period of our history, in every place of our captivity, men and women have dreamed that long collective dream of home and then awakened to the brutal reality of the endless night.[27]

On many ships in the Atlantic, out of sight of the shores, there were other awakenings as well. Even in such desolate places, where all cause for hope seemed destroyed, many Africans awoke and insisted on the continuing reality and necessity of struggle. Again, some of the oppressors knew of the black commitment to carry on the fight for freedom, even when the distant homeland was only a dream in the darkness. Thus one white participant in the slave trade wrote: "When we are slaved and out at Sea, it is commonly imagined, the Negroes ignorance of Navigation, will always be a Safeguard; yet, as many of them think themselves bought to eat, and more, that Death will send them into their own Country, there has not been wanting Examples of rising and killing a Ship's Company, distant from Land." They knew the captives would fight, but these Europeans did not think we would struggle against them simply because we knew that we did not belong to them, simply because many African men and women considered any fate better than the continued subjugation they had already experienced briefly among Europeans. Therefore the whites said they could not understand those apparently reckless last stands which often ended with death in the ocean.[28]

One of many such desperate battles took place near the beginning of the eighteenth century on the English ship *Don Carlos,* which had sailed up the Congo River and down again, and was now out to sea. Several crew members had died on the river and others were sick. Nevertheless, in an act of careless overconfidence, the crew had given knives to many of the black men. In addition, the captain later wrote:

> others had pieces of iron they had torn off our forecastle door, as having premeditated a revolt, and seeing all the ship's company, at best but weak and many quite sick, they had also broken off the shackles from several of their companions feet, which served them, as well as . . . all other things they could lay their hands on, which they imagined might be of use for their enterprize. Thus armed, they fell in crouds and parcels on our men, upon the deck unawares, and stabb'd one of the stoutest of us all, who received fourteen or fifteen wounds of their knives, and so expir'd. Next they assaulted our boatswain, and cut one of his legs so round the bone, that he could not move . . . others cut our cook's throat to the pipe, and others wounded three of the sailors, and threw one of them overboard in that condition.[29]

Before long, however, the ship's company rallied behind the ever-present firearms. As the captain later reported, "We stood in arms, firing on the revolted slaves of whom we kill'd some, and wounded many: which so terrified the rest, that they gave way, dispersing themselves . . . between decks, and under forecastle; and many of the most mutinous, leapt over board, and drowned themselves in the ocean *with much resolution, showing no manner of concern for life.*"[30]

What was the basic goal of such desperate struggle, and what manner of men and women were these who threw themselves into the ocean "with much resolution," rather than submit to slavery a long way from home? Obviously, the captain's answer is not that of the black people. The captors and the captives never have the same answers to the basic questions of struggle; most often, not even the same questions. Those who threw themselves resolutely into the ocean in fact had great "concern for life." That was why they fought so relentlessly in a seemingly hopeless situation, driven by a vivid urgency that only those who face bondage can know. They were incited by a wild and terrible hope which winds its way through all the history of our struggle against white domination. They lost the battle to live and be rid of their captors, but they won the struggle to die and be free.[31]

The question then arises: after the struggle to break the oppressors' hold upon our lives is stymied, is suicide another form of battle against that domination? Thousands upon thousands of Africans—we cannot know the number—took that path. For many, of course, it was the traditional pathway back to the homeland, for they believed that death would deliver them to the unseen but well-remembered shores. Sometimes, after the firearms had overwhelmed them, black men and women moved resolutely back into the hold and methodically, unwaveringly—in spite of knives ripping them and hot coals placed at their mouths—starved themselves to death. Others, countless others, took some new occasion to leap over the side of the vessels. This response was so common that the watch was constantly on guard, and special nettings were rigged up to baffle such attempts. Still, this black action was so often successful that schools of sharks followed the vessels.[32]

Consistently, even the reluctant white witnesses spoke of the active resoluteness of the suicides, and at times perceived suggestions of ecstasy in their daring acts. On the French ship *Le Rodeur,* which had left Bonny Town on the Guinea Coast and was several days at sea, there was a sudden commotion. The Africans began charging across the decks in every direction. Eluding the flailing arms of the crew, avoiding the nettings, they hurled themselves into the ocean. An eyewitness later wrote: "The Negroes . . . who had got off, continued dancing about the waves, yelling with all their might, what seemed to me a song of triumph and they were soon joined by several of their companions still on deck. Our ship speedily left the ignorant creatures behind; their voices came fainter and fainter upon the wind; the black head, first of one, then another, disappeared, and then the sea was without a spot; and the air without a sound." On another ship the captain declared—typically—that he would fight the epidemic of suicides among the Ibos on board by public beheadings of all who attempted it. At one of these white rituals several Africans tried again to break loose and leap overboard, and one succeeded. A crew member was lowered to catch him, but the man swam and floated away, and as he went he "made signs which words cannot express [testifying to] his happiness in escaping. He went down and was seen no more."[33]

Once again, the history of the slavers was inadequate to capture the meaning of black struggle. It could not bear the terrible significance of such "songs of triumph," sung in magnificent unity by those Africans on the deck and those moving into the depths of the water. In European eyes these singers could only be "ignorant creatures" whose lives were to be forever blotted from the pages of the world's real history. Even in our own time more recent versions of conventional wisdom would relegate such black action to the category of unfortunate, ineffectual escapism, or of limited passive resistance at best. Contrary to such opinions, both the songs and the singers remain embedded in the black freedom movement in America. No struggle against oppression is ignorant, and to label it escapist is in itself an evasion, an escape from the meanings of the long battle. These forerunners who fought and sang, who starved themselves to death in the darkness of the ships' holds, have forced their way into the ever-flowing river of black struggle. To call such acts "passive resistance" is to deny the existence of vast realms of the spirit, to count resistance only by its outward physical modes. Anyone who has seriously contemplated suicide or attempted fasting surely understands what tremendous action of the will was performed by those men and women who leaped voluntarily into the waters, or who refused food until they died. There was nothing "passive" in such decisions and deeds.

Their form of resistance again challenged and denied the ultimate authority of the white traders over their lives and their spirits. Their actions were unmistakable attacks on the system of slavery and the slave trade, for they refused the system some of its profits, some of its parts—perhaps even threatened some of its self-righteousness of spirit. Whatever else they did, these men and women made a radical break with the situation of their captivity, denying that their lives could belong to any man, especially to the representatives of Europe. Doing so, they took charge of their future, joining it with their own past. Out on the Atlantic, such an action was often the highest form available to many persons who found themselves far from the sands of Africa's shores, far from the birds of the mainland, under the white man's menace, but determined to be free.

Suicide was a last resort. Before its final word was spoken, all the other possible avenues of struggle were often attempted; just as they had been attempted near the shores. The movement never abated, and we are told by a major authority on the subject that from the third decade of the eighteenth century to the end of the slave trade, "tales of mutinies abound in the literature of the slave trade. . . . There is little question but that they became more common as the trade fell into the hands of independent traders, who probably were more careless in their supervision of the negroes, and who carried smaller crews in comparison with the size of their cargoes than had the company vessels." This was a strange but telling testimony, not only to the determined resistance of the forefathers, but to the way in which the very racism and greed for profits which fueled the trade created openings for new struggle and revolt. For this carelessness was a form of disdain for the Africans' love of freedom, a disbelief in their willingness to strike when the opportunity arose. And the smallness of the crews was a way of saving on the initial investments, so that the profit might be even higher. Out on the ocean the captives took advantage of both of these circumstances wherever possible.[34]

In 1727 the English ship *Ferrers* was ten days out from the Guinea Coast. Its captain, surely considering himself liberal and humane, regularly sat among the African captives while they ate their main meal on deck. One day, we are told, the Africans "laid on him, and beat out his Brains with the little Tubs, out of which they eat their boiled Rice." Nor was this an unplanned, impetuous act.

> This mutiny having been plotted amongst all the grown Negroes on board, they run to the forepart of the Ship in a body, and endeavored to force the Barricadeo on the Quarter-Deck, not regarding the Musquets of Half Pikes, that were presented to their Breasts by the white Men, through the Loop-Holes. So that at last the chief Mate was obliged to order one of the Quarter-deck Guns laden with Partridge-Shot, to be fired amongst them; which occasioned a terrible destruction: For there were near eighty Negroes killed and drowned, many jumping overboard when the Gun was fired. This indeed put an end to the Mutiny, but most of the Slaves that remained alive grew so sullen, that several of them were starved to death, obstinately refusing to take any Sustenance.[35]

Eventually, after another attempted uprising, the *Ferrers* was lost in a hurricane off the coast of Jamaica.

Meanwhile the struggles of the forerunners continued on the Atlantic, out beyond the birds of the coasts. In the spring of 1730 the Rhode Island vessel *Little George,* with ninety-six Africans on board, had left the Guinea Coast almost a week behind. Somehow the African men slipped out of their chains and overpowered the crew. Throwing some crew members overboard, the captives gained control of the ship. The remaining crew took refuge in a cabin, holing themselves up there with as much of the firearms and gunpowder as they were able to gather. If the white men expected that the Africans would eventually become frustrated with running the ship, they were sorely disappointed. For although it took them nine days to make a six-day voyage, they returned the ship to the shores of their homeland and left it there—captain, crew, gunpowder, and all.[36]

As the eighteenth century wore on, an increasing number of ships from the North American colonies were taking part in the Trade. Owned and commanded by the rising patriots of New England, they bore down on the continent from ports like Boston, Portsmouth, and Newport, entering the rivers, befouling the shores, to carry black people as slaves for the rising patriots of Virginia, the Carolinas, and Maryland. Our fathers and mothers made no distinctions between those slave ships whose owners were fighting for "freedom," "liberty," and "independence" at home, and the ones who were not; there was no cessation in their struggles when they were herded aboard the North American vessels in the time of freedom's ferment. In 1765 a ship from Providence, Rhode Island, had filled its lower decks with captives and was on its way to the high seas. According to one account, soon after they left the coastal area extensive sickness among the crew forced the captain "to permit some of the Slaves to come upon the Deck and assist the People." An invidious distinction between "Slaves" and "People" had obviously been impressed upon the minds of the Americans, but not the Africans. Indeed, we are told that "these slaves contrived to release the others, and the whole rose upon the People, and endeavored to get Possession of the Vessel; but was happily prevented by the Captain and his Men, who killed, wounded and forced overboard Eighty of them, which obliged the rest to submit."[37]

Meanwhile, the ironies and contradictions built up. So, in the spring of 1776 Thomas Jefferson, representing the cause of American freedom, wrote into his draft of the Declaration of Independence a sharp attack on the English crown for supposedly forcing the colonists to participate in the African slave trade in order to fill the mother country's coffers. At the same time, these Americans seemed to be unreluctant slave traders and slave owners and were actively engaged in suppressing shipboard rebellions carried out in the cause of black freedom. For instance, that fall of Independence, there was word of another African uprising, this time on the Rhode Island–based vessel *Hope*. The ship's doctor told the story:

> We had the misfortune to lose 36 of the best slaves we had by an Insurrection; this unlucky affair happened . . . when there was only the Boatswaine, Carpenter, 3 White people and myself on board. . . . We had 160 Slaves on board and were that day let out of the Deck Chains in order to wash, about 2 O'Clock. . . . They began by seizing upon the Boatswain . . . but he soon got disengaged . . . after receiving a wound on his breast and one under his Chin. . . . They continued to threw [sic] Staves, billets of wood, etc., and in endeavoring to get down the Baricado, or over it for upwards of 40 minutes, when finding they could not effect it all the Fantee and most of the Accra Men Slaves jumped over board.[38]

At the end of his narrative, this doctor found it difficult to account for the struggle: "The only reason we can give for their attempting any thing of the kind, is, their being wearied at staying so long on board the ship." But these captives knew why they struggled, and it had nothing to do with the boredom of the ship. Like the independence struggles of the American colonists—indeed, *more than* the white battles in America—the issue was simply freedom.[39]

Sometimes, of course, other related matters were involved. On June 6, 1796, the captain of the *Mary* out of Providence, Rhode Island, wrote in his log: "This morning found our women slave apartments had been attempted to have been opened by some of the Ship's crew, the locks being Spoiled and Sundered." Four days later the African men attempted an uprising. They failed, but they knew why they rose.[40]

Struggle was inevitable.

We do not know how many battles were actually won in those days of the forerunners, or how often the Africans were able to take over the ships and return to the homeland. Similarly, we do not know how many repossessed their own lives by means of suicide. But we do know that the struggle continued relentlessly, from the river Gambia to Charleston's bay, filling the waters and lining the ocean floor with the bones of those first many thousands gone. Of course we also know that the large majority of uprisings failed, because of the overwhelming fire power of the captors. Nevertheless, even in their failure these battles often led the most honest among the white men to marvel at the unyielding determination of the Africans. In 1790, such testimony emerged from the simple reportage of the English sailor, William Richardson, whose crew had gone to the aid of a French vessel where the Africans were rebelling: "I could not but admire the courage of a fine young black who, though his partner in irons lay dead at his feet, would not surrender but fought with his billet of wood until a pistol ball finished his existence. The others fought as well as they could but what could they do against fire-arms?"[41]

What the learned medical doctor had not been able to see, an ordinary sailor saw clearly. And the question and the issue remain with us through all our history. As the sailor rightly sensed, the issue was never—nor is it now—a matter of superior white cultures, more satisfying ways of life, democracy, free worlds, or higher civilizations. Always, beneath these shibboleths of oppression lurked the demonic forces of white racism and Euro-American capitalism, and deep human fears, fueled and protected by the engines of destruction and warfare ("what could they do against fire-arms?"). It is against that backdrop that we assess the struggles of our fathers and our mothers in the slave ships of Europe. It is in such a setting that we recognize the amazing image of our brother, chained to a dead comrade, facing the bullets of Europe with a piece of wood in his hand. That vision from the past becomes a symbol and a source of the truths we seek for the future. It reminds us that only in the light of the historical realities of our captors, and in the presence of our people's amazing endurance, can we properly understand the river of our struggle and help to guide its continuing movement toward freedom.

Notes

1. Such names of ships are found throughout Elizabeth Donnan's *Documents Illustrative of the Slave Trade to America,* 4 vols. (1935; rpt. New York: Octagon Books, 1965).
2. Among a number of helpful sources for an understanding of the slave trade and particularly the process of collecting captives are Roger Anstey, *The Atlantic Slave Trade and British Abolition, 1760–1810* (Atlantic Highlands, N.J.: Humanities Press, 1975), especially pp. 20–66; K. G. Davies, *The Royal African Company* (London: Longmans, 1957), pp. 240ff; C. Duncan Rice, *The Rise and Fall of Black Slavery* (New York: Harper and Row, 1975), pp. 111–16; Basil Davidson, *The African Slave Trade* (Boston: Atlantic Little-Brown, 1961), especially Chapter 3; Daniel P. Mannix and Malcolm Cowley, *Black Cargoes: A History of the Atlantic Slave Trade* (New York: Penguin, 1962), Chapters 1 and 4. An older and still important work is George E. Dow, *Slave Ships and Slaving* (1927; rpt. New York: Marine Research Society, 1970). In a

more personal and often moving vein, Nathan Huggins, *Black Odyssey* (New York: Pantheon, 1977), pp. 1–56, has provided an important humanized version of the story.

3. Several illuminating general introductions to African life and history have become available during the last decade. Included among these are two works by Basil Davidson, *Africa: History of a Continent* (New York: Macmillan, 1972), and *The African Genius: An Introduction to Social and Cultural History* (Boston: Atlantic Monthly Press, 1970); also [Alvin M. Josephy, Jr, ed.], *The Horizon History of Africa* (New York: American Heritage, 1971). Although not a general history, Walter Rodney's incisive Marxist analysis in *How Europe Underdeveloped Africa* (Washington, D.C.: Howard University Press, 1974) is invaluable, especially Chapter 2.

4. The quotation is from Claude McKay's poem, "Outcast," in Wayne Cooper, ed., *The Passion of Claude McKay: Selected Prose and Poetry, 1912–1948* (New York: Schocken Books, 1973), p. 121.

5. There are several informative discussions of these early contacts and connections. Among the most valuable are A. Ade Boahen, "The Coming of the Europeans," in Josephy, *Horizon History,* pp. 305–27; Carlo M. Cipolla, *Guns, Sails and Empires* (New York: Funk & Wagnalls, 1965), pp. 21–89, 132–48; William H. McNeill, *The Rise of the West* (Chicago: University of Chicago Press, 1963), pp. 569–78 (McNeill's focus on European "pugnacity" is intriguing); Rodney, *How Europe,* Chapters 3 and 4; Eric Williams, *Capitalism and Slavery* (New York: Russell and Russell, 1961), pp. 30–50.

6. Some of the most incisive discussions of this overworked issue are found in Davidson, *African Genius,* Part 4; Davidson, "Slaves or Captives? Some Notes on Fantasy and Fact," in *Key Issues in the Afro-American Experience,* Nathan J. Huggins, Martin Kilson, and Daniel M. Fox, eds., 2 vols. (New York: Harcourt Brace Jovanovich, 1971), I, pp. 54–73; Rodney, "African Slavery and Other Forms of Social Oppression on the Upper Guinea Coast," *Journal of African History,* 7 (1966), 431–43.

7. One of the most recent discussions of the ways in which Native Americans, Europeans, and Africans were approached as a labor force is in Peter H. Wood, *Black Majority* (New York: Knopf, 1974), pp. 37–62. Wood focuses on South Carolina. The Virginia experience has been explored by Edmund S. Morgan, *American Slavery, American Freedom* (New York: W. W. Norton, 1975).

8. The standard monograph on white servitude in the colonies is Abbot E. Smith, *Colonists in Bondage* (1947; rpt. Gloucester, Massachusetts: Peter Smith, 1965). For important treatments since then, see Lerone Bennett, *The Shaping of Black America* (Chicago: Johnson Publishing, 1975), pp. 18–57; Morgan, *American Slavery,* pp. 108–79, 216–18; and Winthrop D. Jordan, *White over Black* (Chapel Hill: University of North Carolina Press, 1968), pp. 52–95. Much insight on this subject was presented even earlier by E. Williams in the first chapter of *Capitalism.*

9. On the development of the slave trade, see Davies, *Royal African,* pp. 213–90; Davidson, *African Slave Trade,* pp. 53–68; Mannix and Cowley, Chapters 2 and 3; E. Williams, *Capitalism,* pp. 30–50. Malachi Postlewayt, the eighteenth-century economist, is quoted in Harold Baron, "The Demand for Black Labor," *Radical America,* 2 (Mar./Apr., 1971), pp. 2–6. The profitability of slavery and its relationship to European economic, political, and social development is still under debate. For a sample of some positions see C. L. R. James, *The Black Jacobins* (1938; rpt. New York: Vintage Books, 1963), pp. 45–61; Rodney, *How Europe,* Chapter 3; E. Williams, *Capitalism,* passim; Robert P. Thomas and Richard N. Bean, "The Fishers of Men: Profits of the Slave Trade," *Journal of Economic History,* 34 (Dec. 1974), pp. 885–914.

10. The destructive effect of the slave trade on African life and culture is noted in Davies, *Royal African,* pp. 278–84; Josephy, *Horizon History,* pp. 305–27; Anstey, *Atlantic,* pp. 69–88, 404;

Rice, *Rise and Fall,* pp. 17–21. See also Rodney, "African Slavery," pp. 431–33, and his "Upper Guinea and the Significance of the Origins of Africans Enslaved in the New World," *Journal of Negro History* (hereafter cited as *JNH*), 54 (Oct. 1969), pp. 327–45; also Davidson, "Slaves or Captives?"

11. Quoted in Mannix and Cowley, p. 108. No extensive work has yet been done on the struggles for black freedom during the middle passage. Two helpful essays are Lorenzo Greene, "Mutiny on the Slave Ships," *Phylon,* 5 (Jan. 1944), pp. 346–54, and Darold D. Wax, "Negro Resistance to the Early American Slave Trade," *JNH,* 51 (Jan. 1966), pp. 1–15. The starting point for any new major study would still be Elizabeth Donnan's monumental *Documents.*

12. Mannix and Cowley, p. 108.

13. Readily accessible works which focus on the middle passage include Davidson, *African Slave Trade;* James Pope-Hennessy, *Sins of the Fathers* (New York: Knopf, 1968); Thomas Howard, ed., *Black Voyage: Eyewitness Accounts of the Atlantic Slave Trade* (Boston: Little, Brown, 1971); Mannix and Cowley. For suggestions on the deadly costs of the trade to the largely white crew members, see Philip D. Curtin, *The Atlantic Slave Trade: A Census* (Madison: University of Wisconsin Press, 1969), pp. 282–86; contemporary testimonies on the same point are in Howard, Chapter 3

14. (Quoted in Donnan II, 350.)

15. *Ibid.,* I, 438, 443.

16. See Mannix and Cowley, p. 104.

17. Donnan, III, 45.

18. *Ibid.,* 226. One can only speculate about this Captain Tomba's possible relation to a leader with the same name among the Baga people of West Africa at about the same period. He is briefly mentioned in Rodney, *How Europe,* p. 80.

19. Donnan, III, 226. This cannibalism did not die out among white oppressors. In many American lynchings, blacks experienced it well into the twentieth century in various tormented forms. For one example, see Ralph Ginzburg, ed., *100 Years of Lynchings* (New York: Lancer Books, 1962), p. 223.

20. Donnan, III, 226.

21. Greene, "Mutiny," p. 349; Donnan, II, 486; Wood, *Black Majority,* pp. 221–22.

22. Benjamin Brawley, *A Social History of the American Negro* (1921; rpt. New York: Macmillan, 1970), p. 43; Donnan, IV, 374.

23. Donnan, II, pp. 354–55.

24. For instance, see Harvey Wish, "American Slave Insurrections before 1861," *JNH,* 22 (July 1937), pp. 299–320.

25. Davidson, *African Slave Trade.* Mannix and Cowley and Pope-Hennessy offer summary accounts of the voyages. Note also McNeill's brief statement on the role of diseases in the European conquests: *Rise of the West,* pp. 571–73. See as well Curtin's cautious statement, *Atlantic Slave Trade,* p. 270.

26. Mannix and Cowley, p. 114.

27. The *Young Hero* event is reported in Mannix and Cowley, pp. 114–16. A similar story of the mournful nighttime songs appears in Robert Dale Owen, *The Wrong of Slavery* (Philadelphia, 1864), p. 52. The hymn in question was composed by one of the most famous of the Christian slaving captains, John Newton: Mannix and Cowley, pp. 133–37.

28. Donnan, II, pp. 281–82.

29. *Ibid.,* I, pp. 456–57.

30. *Ibid.* my emphasis.

31. For example, Mannix and Cowley, pp. 117–22. In addition to other suicides cited below, pp. 18–20, note also the account of the African, Olaudah Equiano (Gustavas Vassa), in Philip D.

Curtin, ed., *Africa Remembered: Narratives by West Africans from the Era of the Slave Trade* (Madison: University of Wisconsin Press, 1967), p. 96.

32. Howard, *Black Voyage,* p. 94.
33. Mannix and Cowley, p. 118.
34. Donnan, II, 361 n. Also Mannix and Cowley, p. 110.
35. Donnan, II, pp. 360–61.
36. *Ibid.*
37. *Ibid.,* III, 213. The same incident is recorded in a slightly different form by Greene, "Mutiny," p. 352.
38. Donnan, II, pp. 323–24.
39. *Ibid.*
40. *Ibid.,* III, pp. 374–75.
41. Mannix and Cowley, pp. 110–11.

Slavery and the Circle of Culture

Sterling Stuckey
Historian

Sterling Stuckey is the author of Going Through the Storm: The Influence of African American Art in History *(1994) and of* The Ideological Origins of Black Nationalism *(1972). His much anthologized article, "Through the Prism of Folklore: The Black Ethos in Slavery" is the basis for* Slave Culture: Nationalist Theory and the Foundation of Black America *(1987) from which this essay is taken. Another article by Stuckey that is of special note is "The Death of Benito Cereno: A Reading of Herman Melville on Slavery (1982)," which he co-authored with Joshua Leslie. Stuckey is currently professor of history at the University of California at Riverside.*

• • •

II

The majority of Africans brought to North America to be enslaved were from the central and western areas of Africa—from Congo-Angola, Nigeria, Dahomey, Togo, the Gold Coast, and Sierra Leone.[1] In these areas, an integral part of religion and culture was movement in a ring during ceremonies honoring the ancestors. There is, in fact, substantial evidence for the importance of the ancestral function of the circle in West

Sterling Stuckey, "Slavery and the Circle of Culture," in Slave Culture. Nationalist Theory and the Foundations of Black America, *pp. 10–43, 53–64 (New York: Oxford University Press, 1987).*

Africa, but the circle ritual imported by Africans from the Congo region was so power-ful in its elaboration of a religious vision that it contributed disproportionately to the centrality of the circle in slavery. The use of the circle for religious purposes in slavery was so consistent and profound that one could argue that it was what gave form and meaning to black religion and art. It is understandable that the circle became the chief symbol of heathenism for missionaries, black and white, leading them to seek either to alter it or to eradicate it altogether. That they failed to do so owes a great deal to Bakongo influence in particular, but values similar to those in Congo-Angola are found among Africans a thousand or more miles away, in lands in which the circle also is of great importance. Thus scholarship is likely to reveal more than we now know about the circle in Africa, drawing West and Central Africa closer together culturally than they were previously thought to be.

The circle is linked to the most important of all African ceremonies, the burial ceremony. As Talbot shows, in discussing dance in Southern Nigeria, "The Ekoi also in some of their dances imitate the actions of birds, but the most solemn of them all is perhaps the Ejame, given at the funeral of great chiefs, when seven men dance in the centre of an immense circle made by the other performers." In that ceremony, the men keep their eyes to the ground and the songs they sing are said to be "so old that their meaning has long since been forgotten," which suggests the ancient quality of dance within the circle, the immemorial regard for the ancestral spirits in a country in which dance exists mainly as a form of worship and appears to have developed as a means of achieving union with God, of "exerting an influence *with his help* on the fertility of men and of crops,"[2] Talbot notes the prime importance of rhythm to dance, and his description of "one variety" of dance parallels descriptions of dance in the ancestral circle in the Congo and in America since "the main object appears to be never to lift the feet off the ground and to leave a clear, even, continuous track." The ordinary method of dancing among the people of Southern Nigeria—among them Ibos, Yorubas, Ibibios, and Efiks—appears monotonous and unattractive

> since it consists of slowly moving round in a circle—always in the opposite direction to the hands of a clock, widdershins—with apparently little variation in the few steps em-ployed. It takes time to appreciate the variety and detail in the different movements and the unceasing, wave-like ripple which runs down the muscles of the back and along the arms to the finger-tips. Every part of the body dances, not only the limbs.[3]

In Bakongo burial ceremonies, according to art historian Robert F. Thompson, bodies were sometimes laid out in state in an open yard "on a textile-decorated bier," as bare-chested mourners danced to the rhythms of drums "in a broken counter-clockwise circle," their feet imprinting a circle on the earth, cloth attached to and trail-ing on the ground from their waists deepening the circle. Following the direction of the sun in the Southern Hemisphere, the mourners moved around the body of the de-ceased in a counterclockwise direction. If the deceased lived a good life, death, a mere crossing over the threshold into another world, was a precondition for being "carried back into the mainstream of the living, in the name and body of grandchildren of suc-ceeding generations." From the movement of the sun, Kongo people derive the circle and its counterclockwise direction in a variety of ways. "Coded as a cross, a quartered circle or diamond, a seashell's spiral, or a special cross with solar emblems at each ending—the sign of the four moments of the sun is the Kongo emblem of spiritual continuity and renaissance. . . . In certain rites it is written on the earth, and a person stands upon it to take an oath, or to signify that he or she understands the meaning of life as a process shared with the dead below the river or the sea—the real sources of earthly power and prestige."[4]

Wherever in Africa the counterclockwise dance ceremony was performed—it is called the ringshout in North America—the dancing and singing were directed to the ancestors and gods, the tempo and revolution of the circle quickening during the course of movement. The ring in which Africans danced and sang is the key to understanding the means by which they achieved oneness in America. Knowledge of the ancestral dance in Dahomey contributes to that understanding and helps explain aspects of the shout in North America that are otherwise difficult to account for. For instance, the solo ringshouts noted by Lydia Parrish in Virginia and North Carolina are in the ring dances of Dahomey done in group *and* solo forms, the two being combined at times. Thus, as the drums sounded, a woman held a sacrifice under her left arm, slowly dancing in a "cleared space three times in a counter-clockwise direction, ending with a series of shuffling steps in front of the drums, while the young women who followed her cried out a shrill greeting to the spirits." Solo dance combined with other patterns of dance:

> With the drums sounding they formed a line of twos, and one couple behind the other they danced in the customary counter-clockwise direction about the edges of the cleared space, finally forming a single line in front of the drums, which they faced as they danced vigorously. Retreating in line to their place on the South side, before the ancestral temple they remained standing there, while one after another of their number danced singly, moving toward the drums and then retreating before circling the dance-space.[5]

An impressive degree of interethnic contact, representing large areas of black Africa, at times took place at such ceremonies in Dahomey. F. E. Forbes, who spent two years in Dahomey and kept a journal of his observations, reports that one such instance of ethnic cross-play involved "groups of females from various parts of Africa, each performing the peculiar dance of her country." When not dancing a dance with elements unique to a given country, they performed dances common to many different countries of Africa: "the ladies would now seize their shields and dance a shield-dance; then a musket, a sword, a bow and arrow dance, in turns." Finally, "they called upon the king to come out and dance with them, and they did not call in vain." The king's response had its own unifying influence and was understood by the women from the various countries of Africa, just as the response of Daha, the chief observed by Herskovits almost a century later, would have been understood by them as he "twice circled the space enclosed by the 'bamboos' in a counterclockwise direction before he retired to the portico, where several of his wives solicitously wiped the perspiration from his face and otherwise attended him."[6]

A Kongo ancestral ritual that is profoundly related to counterclockwise dance among the Kongo people occurs, according to Thompson, when they place a cross in a circle to derive the four moments of the sun. While counterclockwise dance in itself achieved as much, the graphic representation does so in more explicit terms, marking off in precise ways the important stages or moments along the way: "In each rendering the right hand sphere or corner stands for dawn which, in turn, is the sign of life beginning. Noon, the uppermost disk or corner, indicates the flourishing of life, the point of most ascendant power. Next, by the inevitable organic process as we know it, come change and flux, the setting of the sun, and death, marked by the left-hand median point or disk."[7]

The horizontal line of the cross, referred to as the Kalunga line, deserves attention, for we shall later encounter it in American slavery—associated, as in the Congo, with those who lived long and were generous, wise and strong "on a heroic scale." Such people, in the imagination of the Kongo people, "die twice . . . once 'here' and once 'there,' beneath the watery barrier, the line Bakongo call *Kalunga*." According to Thompson, "This is a line marked by the river, the sea, or even dense forestation, a line which divides this world from the next."[8] When that line, which extends from dawn to sunset, is evoked by the Kongo staff-cross, it symbolizes the surface of a body of water beneath which the world of the ancestors is found, and this casts additional light on why water immersion has had such a hold on blacks in America and why counterclockwise dance is often associated with such water rites.

The art historian Suzzane Blier has written that the circle is the most frequently employed linear mode of movement in Togo: "In the funeral, circular lines are formed as clockwise movements when linked to women, but are counter-clockwise motion sequences when employed for men." In the funeral, circular movement is used to represent themes of togetherness and containment. For example, when the deceased is carried around the house before being taken to the cemetery, the act "is said to call together the house ancestors so that they will come to the cemetery for the ceremonies to be performed there." The clockwise movement of women in Togo is a significant departure from the counterclockwise movement indigenous to much of Central and West Africa and does not appear to have an analogue in North America. The most likely explanation for its failure to survive in North America is that Africans from Togo who might have continued the clockwise movement in slavery yielded to the overwhelming preference of other Africans for counterclockwise movement.[9]

An indication of the complex rites to which people other than the Bakongo put the circle is found in ethnic groups from Sierra Leone. The connection of the circle to the ancestors and to the young is so various in that country, from which Africans were imported to American markets, that one better understands the strength and varying patterns of the circle in North America by understanding its antecedents in Sierra Leone. The Sierra Leonean Earl Conteh-Morgan's scholarship illuminates the relationship of the circle to the storyteller as dancing in a counterclockwise direction occurs: "Instances of dancing in a circle occur during storytelling time in the villages as the storyteller sits in the middle while the listeners sit around him and listen attentively." Since storytellers, or griots, focus mainly on the history of their people, ancestors are usually the principal subject of a particular chronicle of the past—the ceremony framed, as it were, by the listeners gathered around the storyteller. Depending on the demands of the narration, they either listen or, on signal from the storyteller, become active participants.

Clapping and dancing usually occur in stories with a song that takes the form of a refrain. The refrain is repeated by the listeners at a signal from the storyteller. Although it may not involve physical touching of the storyteller, it nonetheless gives the whole exercise an air of celebration. It also adds an air of vivid drama in the whole process of storytelling.[10]

Such singing of refrains and clapping of hands as dance occurs in a counter-clockwise direction are similar to those of the dance described by Thompson in the Kongo funeral scene. Conteh-Morgan observed counterclockwise dance among the Bundu in Sierra Leone during a burial ceremony, and such dancing around the deceased, given the prominence of sacred dance in traditional societies, would seem to be widespread in Sierra Leone.[11]

The Sierra Leoneans reveal much about the circle in relation to the life process; indeed, the circle may well be the principal African metaphor for it. Among Mende and Temne secret societies, dancing in a circle with people in the center is a common practice on sacred occasions, for example, during rites of passage for young girls. When they are eligible to be selected for marriage by young men, they go through rites in "the secret house, usually in the bush, or in huts specifically built for that. A couple of days are set aside, or one big day, when they are brought out into the open for all to see as they participate in final ceremonies." At this time, the women stand around the girls, who are generally teenagers, clapping and singing as the girls sit in the middle of the circle. "From time to time, dancing in a circle takes place either by the girls themselves or by the women surrounding them. Touching of the heads or shoulders of those in the center and many types and styles of dancing take place as the music varies in rhythm and tempo."[12]

The circle, among Mende and Temne, is the chief symbol of a ceremony that leads to marriage and the renewal of the life process with the birth of children. Although counterclockwise dance of the Mende and Temne continued in North America as a function primarily of religious activity, it is highly unlikely, considering the mockery that was made of slave marriage in America, that the associated institution of preparation for marriage in the secret house survived even in secrecy in slavery.

Nevertheless, other African institutions and African priests were brought to America in large numbers and, unrecognized by whites, found their places in the circle and elsewhere. Some were among the first and last slave preachers. Herskovits tells us that a variety of them came to the New World, which greatly encouraged the preservation of African values in slavery:

> . . . the river spirits are among the most powerful of those inhabiting the supernatural world, and . . . priests of this cult are among the most powerful members of tribal priestly groups. It will be . . . recalled how, in the process of conquest which accompanied the spread of the Dahomean kingdom, at least (there being no data on this particular point from any other folk of West Africa), the intransigeance of the priests of the river cult was so marked that, more than any other group of holy men, they were sold into slavery to rid the conquerors of troublesome leaders. In all those parts of the New World where African religious beliefs have persisted, moreover, the river cult or, in broader terms, the cult of water spirits, holds an important place. All this testifies to the vitality of this element in African religion, and supports the conclusion, to be drawn from the hint in the Dahomean data, as to the possible influence such priests wielded even as slaves.[13]

Priests were present on the plantations of the South, but whether they were, in specific instances, African-born or products of African influence in America is usually difficult to determine. This distinction is mainly theoretical, since at times one finds their practices, irrespective of the period of slavery, to be of nearly pristine purity and highly esoteric, as when they surface in the folktale. There, as in life, they gathered on the principal occasions of worship, above all at ancestral ceremonies, the most important of which in North America was the ringshout, which often was but one aspect, however important, of multifaceted African religious observance. The ringshout was the main context in which Africans recognized values common to them. Those values were remarkable because, while of ancient African provenance, they were fertile seed for the bloom of new forms. Moreover, understanding the function of ancestral ring ceremonies elsewhere in the Americas makes it possible to determine the function of the ring ceremony in its most arcane form in North America.

The argument that *shout* is used as one of the two words in the phrase *ringshout* because dancing was regarded as "so sinful that it was wise to avoid even the name" is less interesting than the contribution of Lorenzo Turner, whose work on Afro-American culture is of primary importance: "Dr. L. D. Turner has discovered that the Arabic word *saut* (pronounced like our word 'shout'), in use among Mohammedans of West Africa meant to run and walk around the Kaaba." Turner's remark concerning the term is particularly interesting owing to his association of the ringshout with the ritual in which hundreds, tightly assembled, move around the Kaaba in a counterclockwise direction. There is, however, reason to question the view that *saut* refers to "shout." One authority on the Arabic language argues that the word is not pronounced like *shout,* which calls into question Turner's tantalizing view. What is certain is that Moslems move about the Kaaba in a counterclockwise fashion. But it is just as certain that their movement is more of a trot than a dance and that spirit possession apparently has no place in the ceremony around the Kaaba.[14]

Melville and Frances Herskovits, the distinguished anthropological team, note the persistence of the circle ceremony among the descendants of Africans in Suriname who are centuries removed from their ancestral home in the Gold Coast. Indeed, the Suriname bush Negro retained some features of his heritage, including priestly functions, in almost pristine form.[15] With drums speaking to and interpreting the messages of the dead, they dramatized spiritual attitudes through the language of dance, at times moving in a counterclockwise direction. Ashanti dance style was common to the bush Negro and to black Africans generally. R. S. Rattray writes of dance in the Gold Coast at 4 A.M. in a yard "packed with people sitting all around the circle of singers and in the open Verandah Rooms." The head priestess rushed into the yard before disappearing. She returned and "jumped into the ring," clapping her hands, and "began to dance that curious shuffling, stooping, mincing dance alternated with wild gyrations, so peculiar to West Africa." It was that dance, essentially, that was encountered in Suriname. But the Herskovitses found African dance in that country precisely related to elements of ancestral ring dance in North America: the feet executed "figures in place without leaving the ground, the arms hanging loosely at the side." And in generic African style—"the arms flexed and held rigid at the elbow and knees bent but rigid"—as the feet continued to execute intricate steps, "the movement of the feet, angular and precise, was reiterated by the outstretched palms, while all the muscles of the hips took up the rhythm."[16]

Associated with the ancestral ceremonies in Suriname is the Anansi trickster tale told to amuse the deceased during burial ceremonies. The Herskovitses report that in honoring the dead, the bush Negroes of Suriname appreciated the role of humor, not uncommonly turning to the dead to share amusing stories of tricksters. "Some Trickster proverbs were spoken to bear upon the shortcomings of the white man." One or two of the bush Negroes then turned "to repeat to the dead what had been said, and there was great laughter." The father of the dead man assured the anthropologists that "the dead man liked it very much. For the dead, it appears, were especially susceptible to humor and to exceptional occasions." This explains the prominence of trickster tales of Anansi, the spider, being used "to amuse the spirit" of the dead in Suriname.[17] But since tricksters, most notably the hare, pervade much of black Africa, as does the ring ceremony honoring the ancestors, and since the trickster and the circle are associated not only in South America where Africans were enslaved but in North American slavery as well, the evidence implies a wide association of the two in black Africa and, consequently, among numerous African ethnic groups in North America. That may have been the case, for what is more ironic than the continuing interplay of the living and the dead, and where a more appropriate setting for the trickster than in that Spiritual context? Besides, the trickster's character, certainly that of Anansi and Brer Rabbit, is not known to differ significantly from one region to another.

Marshall Stearns offers a description of ring shouts in South Carolina in the 1950s, some years after John and Alan Lomax saw shouts in various parts of the South. Stearns's description is, in most respects, a characteristic one but also helps us understand an abstruse problem, to be considered later, relating to a particular manifestation of the shout:

> The dancers form a circle in the center of the floor, one in back of another. Then they begin to shuffle in a counter-clockwise direction around and around, arms out and shoulders hunched. A fantastic rhythm is built up by the rest of the group standing back to the walls, who clap their hands and stomp on the floor. . . . Suddenly sisters and brothers scream and spin, possessed by religious hysteria, like corn starting to pop over a hot fire. . . . .This is actually a West African circle dance . . . a complicated and sacred ritual.[18]

III

The most stunning illustration of the trickster's involvement in ancestral ceremonies is contained in the tale "Bur Rabbit in Red Hill Churchyard," collected in South Carolina by E.C.L. Adams. In this tale, Rabbit is trickster in ways never before associated with him (except in the work of the great collector and storyteller William John Faulkner): he is keeper of the faith of the ancestors, mediator of their claims on the living, and supreme master of the forms of creativity. As presented in "Red Hill Churchyard," Brer Rabbit is shown as a man of God, and new possibilities are opened for understanding him as a figure in Afro-American folklore heretofore unappreciated for religious functions. In the Adams tale, ancient qualities of African culture, some of the most obscure kind, appear to yield new and original artistic forms within the circle of culture and are directly related to Anansi and Akan priests in the Suriname bush. More precisely, the tale reveals African tradition and the future flowing from it, the ground of spiritual being and the product of its flowering.

But the Red Hill ceremony seems, on its face, just one of the many in which Brer Rabbit uses his fiddle as a kind of magic wand—for example, to realize his will against predators or in competition for the hand of a maiden. What seems equally obvious, though inexplicable, is the strong convergence of the world of the living and that of the dead as a function, it seems, of nothing more than Brer Rabbit's genius with his instrument. That a deeper meaning lies beneath the surface of the tale is suggested, even to one without a command of the African background, by slave folklore, which holds that all sorts of things, under the right conditions, are possible in the graveyard. Headless horsemen race about, a rabbit is seen walking "on he hind legs wid a fiddle in he hands," and the sacred and the secular are one in moments of masterly iconography as the "buck and wing" is danced "on a tombstone." "It look lik in de Christmas ef de moon is shinin' an' dere's snow on de ground, dat is de time when you sees all kind er sights." At such times, day appears to light up the night, but the glow is from the moon and "every star in de element . . . geeing light." The "diff'ence been it ain' look as natu'al."[19] The real seems unreal, the unreal real as the story unfolds in the depths of winter in the South.

> De ground was kiver all over wid snow, an' de palin's on de graveyard fence was cracklin; it been so cold. . . . An' I look an' listen . . . an' I seen a rabbit settin' on top of a grave playin' a fiddle, for God's sake.[20]

The dance of the community of animals occurred:

> All kind 'er little beasts been runnin' round, dancin'. . . . An' dere was wood rats an' squirels cuttin' capers wid dey fancy self, and diff'ent kind er birds an' owl. Even dem ole Owl was sachayin' 'round look like dey was enjoying' dey self.[21]

Brer Rabbit got up from his seat on the tombstone, stopped playing and "put he fiddle under he arm an' step off de grave." Then he gave "some sort er sign to de little birds and beasts, an' dey form dey self into a circle 'round de grave." Within that setting, several forms of music were heard:

> Well, I watch an' I see Br'er Rabbit take he fiddle from under he arm an' start to fiddlin' some more, and he were doin' some fiddlin' out dere in dat snow. An' Br'er Mockin' Bird jine him an' whistle a chune dat would er made de angels weep. . . .[22]

Probably a spiritual, the song whistled by Brer Mockingbird is made sadder as Brer Rabbit accompanies him on the violin, the ultimate instrument for the conveying of pathos. But sadness gives way to a certain joy as Brer Rabbit, with all the subtlety of his imagination, leads Brer Mockingbird as they prefigure a new form of music:

> Dat mockin' bird an' dat rabbit—Lord, dey had chunes floatin' all 'round on de night air. Dey could stand a chune on end, grab it up an' throw it away an' ketch it an' bring it

back an' hold it; an' make dem chunes sound like dey was strugglin' to get away one minute, an' de next dey sound like sump'n gittin' up close an' whisperin'.[23]

The music of Brer Rabbit and Brer Mockingbird resembles the improvisational and ironic flights of sound that characterize jazz, especially on Fifty-second Street in New York in the mid-twentieth century. The close relationship between the music in Red Hill Churchyard and jazz finds further support in the behavior of Brer Rabbit, whose style calls to mind Louis Armstrong's:

> An' as I watch, I see Bur Rabbit lower he fiddle, wipe he face an' stick he han'k'ch'ef in he pocket, an' tak off he hat an' bow mighty nigh to de ground.[24]

That scene and the others recall the broader context of Louis Armstrong's musical environment in New Orleans, where jazz was sacred in funeral ceremonies and where African secret societies were important to its sustenance and definition. A further consideration of the tale reveals its irreducible foundation in Africa.

The Herskovitses' discussion in *Suriname Folklore* of the drum harks back to the Akans of the Gold Coast and enables us, by transferring the power of the drum to the fiddle, to understand the central mystery of the ritual, which at first glance seems inexplicable. The drums have a three-fold power in the mythology of the bush Negro. Of the first power, the Herskovitses write, "Tradition assigns to them the . . . power of summoning the gods and the spirits of the ancestors to appear." After Brer Rabbit stopped fiddling, wiped his face, and with the other animals bowed in a circle before the grave, the storyteller tells us,

> de snow on de grave crack an' rise up, an' de grave open an' I see Simon rise up out er dat grave. I see him an' he look jest as natu'al as he don 'fore dey bury him.[25]

The second power of the drums of the Akans is that of "articulating the message of these supernatural beings when they arrive." A flesh-and-blood character capable of speech, rather than a disembodied spirit, appears as the ancestor in the tale. Consequently, the other characters are able to communicate directly with him, and he is greatly interested in them:

> An' he [Simon] look satisfy, an' he look like he taken a great interest in Bur Rabbit an' de little beasts an' birds. An' he set down on de top of he own grave and carry on a long compersation wid all dem animals.[26]

The third power of the drum is to send the spirits of the gods or ancestors "back to their habitats at the end of each ceremony."

> But dat ain't all. After dey wored dey self out wid compersation, I see Bur Rabbit take he fiddle an' put it under he chin an' start to playin'. An' while I watch, I see Bur Rabbit step back on de grave an' Simon were gone.[27]

The intensity of the dancing in the circle, to the music of Brer Rabbit and Brer Mockingbird, was great, as indicated by the pace of the music and the perspiration of the performers, though snow covered the ground. From internal evidence alone—and a large body of external data also suggests as much—we know the dancers fairly whirled in counterclockwise movement. To them dance was sacred, as in Suriname, where "one of the most important expressions of worship is dancing." There the dancers "face the drums and dance toward them, in recognition of the voice of the god within the instruments."[28] The Gold Coast myth, it appears, was elegantly applied in Red Hill Churchyard, but descriptions of the ceremony there and elsewhere in North America make no mention of dancers facing percussionists as a necessary aspect of ritual. This is not surprising, for drums were rarely available to slaves.

Since the functions of the drum in Suriname and of the violin in South Carolina slavery are the same, on the evidence of the tale and the work of the Herskovitses, it is very tempting to conclude that South Carolina slaves, not having access to the drum, simply switched to the violin to express the threefold power. But a case can be made for another explanation of why slaves in South Carolina, and almost certainly elsewhere, used the violin on so sacred an occasion. In this context, David Dalby's assertion that some understanding of "the history and culture of the great medieval empire of Mali" is crucial to an understanding of slave culture is particularly relevant.

> The civilization of Mali included a rich musical culture, based on an elaborate range of string, wind and percussion instruments and on a long professional training for its musicians. This musical culture has survived in West Africa for at least a thousand years and, by its influence on American music, has enabled the United States to achieve an independence from European musical traditions and to pioneer new forms. A bitter aspect of the American slave trade is the fact that highly trained musicians and poets from West Africa must frequently have found themselves in the power of slaveowners less cultured and well educated than themselves.[29]

Dalby's thesis takes on added significance when one looks at slave culture and discovers the extraordinary degree to which slaves, at gathering after gathering, relied on the fiddle. When one takes into account that the one-string violin was used in the Mali Empire, and is used today among the Songhai of Upper Volta, which is within the boundaries of the old empire, to summon the ancestral spirits, new light is cast on "Bur Rabbit in Red Hill Churchyard," revealing a vital Songhai component in the tale and among South Carolina slaves.[30] The presence of the old Mali Empire, then, is felt in a way that could scarcely be more important—in the ancestral ceremony directed by Brer Rabbit with his fiddle.

Among the ethnic groups of the empire, the violin was widespread, in contrast to the banjo, which was used to accompany the griot's declamation or recitation of stories. Where one had to be apprenticed to griots to learn to master the banjo—in Upper Volta and, possibly, elsewhere in West Africa—a nonprofessional could pick up and, after long practice, achieve mastery of the violin without being apprenticed. The violin was a democratic rather than an aristocratic instrument for the Songhai; this helps explain, together with its use elsewhere in West Africa before and through the centuries of the slave trade, its widespread use by American slaves. In fact, the violin was the most important instrument of slave musicians and important among Northern slaves as well. It is small wonder that in "Bur Jonah's Goat" the storyteller says, "Ef you was to take dat fiddle 'way from him [Brer Rabbit], he would perish 'way and die."[31]

Missionaries in Georgia attempted to eradicate the widespread use of the fiddle on the Hopeton plantation, where five hundred slaves, very large numbers of whom were children and some "old and superannuated," formed a slave community. Sir Charles Lyell, who visited the plantation in the 1840s, wrote about efforts of Methodists to rid slave culture of that instrument even though nothing raucous was associated with ceremonies in which it was played. So pervasive was the use of the fiddle at Hopeton that the Malian tradition of string instruments to which Dalby makes reference is the background against which Lyell's remarks should be placed.

> Of dancing and music negroes are passionately fond. On the Hopeton plantation above twenty violins have been silenced by the Methodist missionaries, yet it is notorious that the slaves were not given to drink or intemperance in their merry-makings.[32]

Even when we include the large numbers of children and the very old, we find the astonishing average, on Hopeton, of approximately one fiddler for every twenty slaves in a population of five hundred. When we exclude the young and old, our calculations show that about one in every ten slaves played the fiddle, which makes it difficult to conceive of any ceremony, especially burial rites, in which not even one fiddle was present. And since slaves from Upper Volta were represented on so large a plantation, there was probably a Songhai presence, with ancestral spirits and gods being called forth with the fiddle, as in Red Hill Churchyard, at least until the campaign against its use was launched. It is a study in contrasting cultures that missionaries thought the fiddle profane in religious ceremonies and the African thought it divine in that context.[33]

The ceremony Brer Rabbit directed in Red Hill Churchyard was one with which great numbers of Africans in North America could identify because it involved a burial rite common in enough particulars to West African ethnic groups as a whole. Whatever their differences in language, slaves from many different ethnic groups might easily, at such a ceremony, assume their places in the circle, dancing and singing around the deceased, whether in Virginia, South Carolina, North Carolina, Georgia, Louisiana, Pennsylvania, Maryland, the District of Columbia, or elsewhere. What is certain is that African customs in a more openly expressed form in the North were more likely to occur secretly and in the inscrutable language of the tale in the South. Since the fear of slave insurrections was much less there than in the South, slaves in Philadelphia, for example, were permitted to come together in large numbers for ceremonies.

> Many [in 1850] can still remember when the slaves were allowed the last days of the fairs for their jubilee, which they employed ("light hearted wretch!") in dancing the whole afternoon in the present Washington Square, then a general burying ground—the blacks joyful above, while the sleeping dead reposed below![34]

The burial ground provided an ideal setting, under the conditions of enslavement, for Africans from different ethnic groups to relate to one another, to find shared religious values that must have been an enormous source of satisfaction as they struggled to prevent their numbers from being smaller still as a result of ethnic allegiances. When customs vital to West Africa as a cultural complex were indulged, such as the relationship and obligations of the living to the ancestors, bonds among Africans of different ethnic groups, if before unknown to them, were recognized and strengthened in America despite differences in language and despite certain differences in burial ceremonies. Occasions for such discoveries were not infrequent, since slaves, permitted to participate in the last days of the fairs, decided that a collective ancestral rite would become an annual event. That meant scores of first-generation members of a particular ethnic group chose to participate in a ceremony practiced in Central Africa and all over West Africa as well. The choice of the graveyard for the setting did not prevent white onlookers from concluding that the slaves were carefree, because they did not understand that African dance was a form of worship essential to sacred ceremony or how painful it was for Africans to practice such a ceremony in an alien land, and as slaves.

> In that field could be seen at once more than one thousand of both sexes, divided into numerous little squads, dancing, and singing, "each in their own tongue," after the customs of their several nations in Africa.[35]

If they had been preserved, the lyrics of what was sung would tell us much about the impact of slavery on the consciousness of first-generation Africans and much about African religious ceremonies generally. But given the context of the songs, the overall meaning is clear enough: they were songs concerning the ancestors, songs some notes of which, like those of Brer Mockingbird in Red Hill Churchyard, conveyed the pain of being on the ground of the dead in an alien land far from the ancestral home. Under those conditions, the degree of musical improvisation must have been exceptional, even for a people noted for improvisational brilliance. Their annual movement to the burial ground in Philadelphia meant a continuing affirmation of their values, so they sang and danced in a circle "the whole afternoon," the ground beneath them being common ground.[36]

But when African languages were sung, the requirements of ethnicity at times made random scatterings of singers unrealistic, which guaranteed the ethnic patterns of behavior in the Philadelphia graveyard. As the English language became more their property, it was easier for the mixture of ethnic peoples to occur in myriad circles in that graveyard and in others. There was, inevitably, some unevenness of movement toward cultural oneness because of the language factor alone; some years in the New World were required before those from different ethnic backgrounds achieved cultural oneness by being able to use the same language. Ironically, it was a degree of harmony that could not be reached through African languages. But from the start of the ceremonies in the graveyard, complementary characteristics of religion, expressed through song, dance, and priestly communication with the ancestors, were organic to Africans in America and their movement in a counterclockwise direction in ancestral ceremonies was a recognizable and vital point of cultural convergence.

Though the number of Africans brought into Pennsylvania in the eighteenth century was small—they accounted for just 2 percent of the state's 333,000 people in 1790—their influence on their descendants for generations determined the nature of most of black religion in the state, and with it sacred song and dance style. This raises a question regarding the relationship of slave culture to demography that deserves an answer different from the one offered until now.[37] From what we know of black religion in Pennsylvania, small numbers of Africans were sufficient to constitute the "critical mass" for the retention of essentials of African religion in slavery. Moreover, what is true of black African culture is true of any culture rich in artistic and spiritual content:

initiation into it in youth guarantees its presence in consciousness, and to a considerable extent in behavior, for a lifetime.

Fortunately for the slave, the retention of important features of the African cultural heritage provided a means by which the new reality could be interpreted and
spiritual needs at least partially met, needs often regarded as secular by whites but as
often considered sacred to blacks. The division between the sacred and the secular, so
prominent a feature of modern Western culture, did not exist in black Africa in the
years of the slave trade, before Christianity made real inroads on the continent.
Consequently, religion was more encompassing to the African in slavery than before,
the ring shout being a principal means by which physical and spiritual, emotional and
rational, needs were fulfilled. This quality of African religion, its uniting of seeming opposites, was perhaps the principal reason it was considered savage by whites. It was
the source of creative genius in the slave community and a main reason that whites
and free blacks thought the slaves lacked a meaningful spiritual life.[38] Opposition to
African religion, therefore, was limited in effectiveness because the African was
thought to have a religion unworthy of the name, when, in fact, his religious vision
was subtle and complex, responsible for the creation of major—and sacred—artistic
forms.

For decades before and generations following the American Revolution, Africans
engaged in religious ceremonies in their quarters and in the woods unobserved by
whites. From the time of the earliest importations of slaves to the outbreak of the Civil
War, millions of slaves did the ring shout, unobserved, with no concern for white approval. But the possibility that whites might discover the guiding principles of African
culture kept blacks on guard and led them, to an astonishing degree, to keep the essentials of their culture from view, thereby making it possible for them to continue to
practice values proper to them. Such secretiveness was dictated by the realities of oppression and worked against whites acquiring knowledge of slave culture that might
have been used to attempt to eradicate that culture. While Lydia Parrish fails to appreciate that political consideration, she effectively draws on African tradition to explain
her difficulty in securing certain types of cooperation:

> It took me three winters on St. Simon's to hear a single slave song, three times as many
> winters to see the religious dance called the ring-shout, still more winters to unearth the
> Buzzard Lope and similar solo dances, and the game songs known as ring-play. . . . The
> secretiveness of the Negro is, I believe, the fundamental reason for our ignorance of the
> race and its background, and this trait is in itself probably an African survival. Melville J.
> Herskovits . . . quotes a Dutch Guiana Bush Negro as saying: "Long ago our ancestors
> taught us that it is unwise for a man to tell anyone more than half of what he knows
> about anything." It is amusing to question Southerners as to the number of times they re-
> member hearing Negroes volunteer information. Not one so far has recalled an instance
> in which something has been told that was not common knowledge.[39]

For the African, dance was primarily devotional, like a prayer, "the chief method of
portraying and giving vent to the emotions, the dramatic instinct and religious fervour of
the race."[40] That whites considered dance sinful resulted in cultural polarization of the
sharpest kind since dance was to the African a means of establishing contact with the

ancestors and with the gods. Because the emotions of slaves were so much a part of dance expression, the whole body moving to complex rhythms, what was often linked to the continuing cycle of life, to the divine, was thought to be debased. But a proper burial, not what whites thought, was what mattered, unless they were present on so sacred an occasion. A proper burial, for the great majority of slaves throughout slavery, was one in accordance with African tradition. "Wen one uh doze Africans die, it wuz bery sad," an old man recalled of slave days in Georgia. "Wen a man's countryman die, he sit right wid um all night. . . . You know . . . doze Africans ain got no Christianity. Dey, ain hab no regluh religion." After praying, before leaving the "settin' up," the countrymen "put deah han on duh frien and say good-bye."[41] The placing of hands on the dead was an African custom practiced in West Africa and elsewhere in the Americas, including Dutch Guiana, just as drumming was practiced in Africa and, when permitted, in slave America. But the drummer's tempo apparently varied from place to place in Africa, ranging from the rapidity of some tribes in the Congo area to the slow beat of the Africans who influenced some of the drumming in Georgia graveyards: "We beat duh drum agen at duh fewnal. We call it duh dead mahch. Jis a long slow beat. Boom-boom-boom. Beat duh drum. Den stop. Den beat it agen."[42] On such occasions, there was at times the singing of African lyrics but more often the new lyrics of the spirituals.

Spirituals were born as the religious vision of the larger society was caught, as by centripetal force, drawn to the innermost regions of black spiritual consciousness and applied to what blacks were experiencing in slavery. In an African ritual setting on one such occasion, a black man got on his knees, his head against the floor, and pivoted as members of the group around him moved in a circle, holding his head "down to the mire," singing "Jesus been down to de mire." The arms of those circling "reached out to give a push" and from overhead looked somewhat like spokes in a wheel—a continuation of a tradition centuries old in Sierra Leone and one maintained well over a century in America, which argues a significant Mende and Temne presence in slavery in Georgia. As descendants of Temnes and Mendes in America sang in this century, inspiration was drawn from awareness that Jesus knew despair. This confronting of tragedy was somehow strangely comforting, the throwing of one's whole being into the performance a possible source of the blues in the song sang—the sacred side of the blues, what they owe to the spirituals:

> You must bow low
> Jesus been down
>   to de mire
> Jesus been down
>   to de mire
> Jesus been down
>   to de mire
> You must bow low
>   to de mire
> Honor Jesus
>   to de mire
> Lowrah lowrah
>   to de mire

Lowrah lowrah
  to de mire
Lowrah lowrah
  to de mire
Jesus been down
  to de mire
You must bow low
  to de mire
low
  to de mire

"The refrain—repeated relentlessly—corresponds in its character and rhythmic beat to that of drums," the words so filled with emotion that, after a while, they dissolve into moans and cries.[43]

For all her merits as a student of folklore, Parrish, who observed that particular shout, never understood the depths of its spirituality. She considered the shout "a kind of religious dance," and this has been the going thesis for well over a century. Nevertheless, she concluded that "Sperrichels were most often sung at night on the plantations when the 'shout'" was held, a context that should have deepened the meaning of the shout for her, as the relationship between the shout and the spirituals deepens the meaning of the latter for us: "The people, young and old would gather in the praise house, or, if there was none, in one of the larger cabins, where the ceremonies were usually prolonged till after midnight, sometimes till 'day clean'." Thus, slave youths were introduced to the circle and to the singing of spirituals within it—all the while dancing in ways scholars acknowledge to be little different from black "secular" dance of today.[44]

IV

Too often the spirituals are studied apart from their natural, ceremonial context. The tendency has been to treat them as a musical form unrelated to dance and certainly unrelated to particular configurations of dance and dance rhythm. Abstracted from slave ritual performance, including burial ceremonies, they appear to be under Christian influence to a disproportionate extent. Though the impact of Christianity on them is obvious and considerable, the spirituals take on an altogether new coloration when one looks at slave religion on the plantations where most slaves were found and where African religion, contrary to the accepted scholarly wisdom, was practiced. Because that was true, principles guiding African culture were found there, none in greater force than the practice of one determination or form leading to and containing vital elements of another. This is seen when one adds to the words of the spirituals the African rhythms that regulate all movement as the worshippers circle counterclockwise in the shout.

The relative simplicity of spirituals sung in the circle was noted by Higginson and others, among them James Weldon Johnson. But the possibility that those who sang them in a circle also sang them outside the circle appears not to have been considered.

Given the complexity and irony of Negro-African culture and the reciprocity of forms that characterize black music in this country, it would follow that, as the contexts in which Higginson observed and discusses the spirituals changed, many of the slaves who sang them in the circle sang them in other contexts as well. Certainly Higginson gives us no reason to doubt it. It is not sufficient then, to ascribe the simplicity of the spirituals when sung in the circle merely to their stage of development. Rather, it is more likely that the songs in the circle are simple because dance is so pronounced and indispensable a component of the ceremony. As a result, the lyrics are driven by complex percussive rhythms, and often give way to chants, whose repetition can have a hypnotic effect and contribute to the high religious purpose of possession.

That the spirituals were sung in the circle guaranteed the continuing focus on the ancestors and elders as the Christian faith answered to African religious imperatives. In that context and in that way, they were sung by the majority of the slaves who sang them as Higginson, a colonel in the Union Army, observed the shout on South Carolina plantations:

> Often in the starlit evening, I have returned from some lonely ride by the swift river . . . and, entering the camp, have silently approached some glimmering fire, round which the dusky figures moved in the rhythmical barbaric dance the negroes call a "shout," chanting, often harshly, but always in the most perfect time some monstrous refrain. Writing down in the darkness, as I best could,—perhaps with my hand in the safe covert of my pocket,—the words of the song, I have afterwards carried it to my tent, like some captured bird or insect, and then, after examination, put it by.[45]

Unlike most students of the spirituals, who treat them as a musical form unrelated to dance, Higginson understood that the rhythms of dance regulated all movement and affected the singing of the lyrics. As the names of those participating in the ceremony were called out, the line between the living and the dead was blurred when the celebrants focused on the ancestors, all to "the measured clapping of hands" and "the clatter of many feet." "Hold Your Light," a favorite of the children as well, was sung:

> *Hold your light, Brudder, Robert,—*
> *Hold your light,*
> *Hold your light on Canaan's shore.*
> *What make ole Satan, for follow me so?*
> *Satan ain't got notin' for do wid me.*
> *Hold your light*
> *Hold your light*
> *Hold your light on Canaan's shore.*[46]

A more resounding but plaintive spiritual was sung, and the participants added names, in turn, as the dust rose about them, the tempo quickening. The song conveyed a sense of the inevitability of death but no longing for it:

> *Jordan River, I'm bound to go,*
> *Bound to go, bound to go,—*
> *Jordan River, I'm bound to go,*
> *And bid 'em fare ye well.*

My Brudder Rober, I'm bound to go,
   Bound to go . . .
My Sister Lucy, I'm bound to go,
   Bound to go . . .[47]

At times hand clapping and foot stomping took on a more sorrowful meaning, underscoring pain, urgency, and a longing not even the ring shout could satisfy:

O, my mudder is gone! my mudder is gone!
My mudder is gone into Heaven, my Lord!
   I can't stay behind!
Dere's room in dar, room in dar,
Room in dar, in de heaven, my Lord!
   I can't stay behind!
Can't stay behind, my dear,
   I can't stay behind!

O, my fader is gone! my fader is gone
My fader is gone into Heaven, my Lord!
   I can't stay behind!
Dere's room in dar, room in dar,
Room in dar, in de heaven, my Lord!
   I can't stay behind!
   Can't stay behind, my dear,
   I can't stay behind![48]

The repetition of stanzas as the dancers circled around and around with ever greater acceleration reinforced and deepened the spirit of familial attachment, drawing within the ancestral orbit slaves who may not have known either a father or a mother, their involvement being an extension of that of others, the circle symbolizing the unbroken unity of the community. Familial feeling in the broad sense of clan and in the personal sense of one's own parents was a dominant, irresistible theme of slave consciousness when "Room in There" was sung. When it was, "every man within hearing, from oldest to youngest, would be wriggling and shuffling as if through some magic piper's bewitchment; for even those who at first affected contemptuous indifference would be drawn into the vortex." Such a response, from the oldest to the youngest, could not easily have been evoked by an appropriation from another culture; rather, the magical pull was àn expression of traditional values of a people, those that moved the oldest to engage in sacred dance and the young to join them in the circle. All within hearing of the shout joined in the last chorus of the song:

I'se been on de road into heaven, my Lord!
   I can't stay behind!
O, room in dar, room in dar,
Room in dar, in de heaven, my Lord!
   I can't stay behind![49]

While the clapping of hands and dance were clear manifestations of the ancestral context of the songs, the monotonous refrains, characteristic of ring shout spirituals, had the effect of reinforcing in the consciousness of the participants the concerns of the song and the ceremony generally, thereby building emotional and physical tension. The wider African context, not the words alone, should be kept in mind when interpreting, as slaves moved in a circle, their meaning when singing:

> *Nobody knows de trubble I sees,*
> *Nobody knows de trubble I sees,*
> *Nobody knows de trubble I sees,*
> *Nobody knows but Jesus.*[50]

And

> *I know moon-rise, I know star-rise,*
> *Lay dis body down.*
> *I walk in de moonlight, I walk in de starlight,*
> *To lay dis body down,*
> *I'll walk in de graveyard, I'll walk through de graveyard,*
> *To lay dis body down.*
> *I'll lie in de grave and stretch out my arms;*
> *Lay dis body down.*
> *I go to de judgement in de evenin' of de day,*
> *When I lay dis body down;*
> *And my soul and your soul will meet in de day*
> *When I lay dis body down.*

Though Higginson read the song brilliantly in noting that in "I'll lie in de grave and stretch out my arms" man's desire for peace had never been "uttered more plaintively," death and reunion with the ancestors—"And my soul and your soul will meet in de day"—a process endlessly renewed, was an aspect of that peace for most Africans in American slavery.[51] The achieving of spiritual peace involved a complex ritual essential for harmony between the living and the dead, command of a symbolic world in which the circle steadily appears.

Although spirituals with poetry of a superior cast, such as "I Know Moonrise," were in fact better suited for being sung outside the ring, to the swaying of bodies, slaves who sang spirituals in the ring shout apparently were the ones who, in the main, sang them outside the ring, for Higginson makes no distinction between them and other blacks. Marshall Stearns writes, "If we start with a more-or-less African example such as the ring-shout, we can see that as the rhythm dwindled, the melody lengthened and harmony developed." In other words, the ring shout itself may well have provided the creative breakthrough that led to spirituals being sung outside the ring:

> This process is enormously complicated by the West African tradition of improvisation, augmented by the free style of the folk hymn—no one melody is sacred; it can always be changed by spontaneous embellishments. Thus, although many Spirituals are written down and ring-shouts generally are not, it is conceivable that the former's sustained melody could have emerged momentarily from a ring-shout. The evolution is fluid, proceeding at different speeds in different mixtures, with much depending upon the performer.[52]

While one differs with Eugene Genovese regarding the extent to which slaves were influenced by Christianity, his discussion of slave religion contains a profound insight: "The black variant of Christianity laid the foundations of protonationalist consciousness and at the same time stretched a universalist offer of forgiveness and ultimate reconciliation to white America."[53] In arguing that protonationalist consciousness was achieved, Genovese sensed a greater degree of autonomy in the slave community than scholars before him had found. Still, he underestimated the degree of nationalist consciousness, for slave consciousness was grounded in a continuing awareness of the fundamentals of African faith. But there is no question of the force of his argument that Christianity enabled the slave to stretch "a universalist offer of forgiveness and ultimate reconciliation" to whites—an achievement that began, if Stearns is right, in the ring shout during moments of sustained melody. Considering their rich experiences with multiple ethnic groups, it is fitting that Africans attempted to make Christianity real in the lives of others—in effect, to give it universal appeal.

Like South Carolina, Virginia offers a rich field for the study of the spiritual in relation to African values. Though the slave trade came to an end in Virginia by 1808, the impact of African culture on slaves there was not that much greater in 1800 than in the 1850s, a consideration, as we shall see, vital to understanding the context in which the spiritual evolved in the South. In this regard, it is essential to study the spiritual within the context of the folktale, especially since African religious culture is expressed more faithfully and with greater power in the tale than in other sources. Nowhere was that culture richer than in Virginia.

By 1800, Virginia contained large numbers of African-born slaves. Between 1727 and 1769, nearly 40,000 slaves were brought into the state, and "Africa overwhelmingly was the source, more than four-fifths of the slaves coming from that continent." With the slave population of Virginia at 187,000 in 1770, slaves formed 40 percent of the inhabitants; by 1790, nearly 60 percent of slaves in the United States resided there and in Maryland.[54] Since the overwhelming majority of the slaves brought into Virginia until the end of the trade were African born, they provided the foundation of values from which slave culture was erected, New World experience being interpreted largely from the African point of view. "At the beginning of the nineteenth century," an authority writes, "Virginia had something over 300,000 Negroes, of whom 285,369 were slaves and 20,124 free Negroes. By 1860, the slaves had increased to 490,865 and the free Negroes to 58,042."[55] One of the blacks born in Virginia near the close of slavery was Simon Brown.

Born into slavery in 1843, Simon participated in the most sacred of rituals in the 1850s by the age of thirteen—a common practice in slave communities in both the North and the South, as children, within a year or two after they were able to walk, joined in some ceremonies, especially in the ring shout. In fact, slave culture was, despite its centeredness upon the elders and ancestors, a culture in which the very young played a more vital role than scholars have assigned them. The preference of slaveholders for African males aged sixteen or under helped determine that role, as did the importance of family to Africans. Consequently, slave culture was preeminently a youth culture in which there was great respect for the aged and for the ancestors. Indeed, in 1750 over half the slave population over much of the Virginia was under sixteen.[56]

Simon Brown's relationship to that tradition was unusual, since he helped to extend slave customs as a practioner in youth and as a storyteller later on. Much of what he recounted had shaped his life in lasting ways and helps explain his precise revelations of slave experiences. His keen intellect and his extraordinary artistic sense enabled Brown to assimilate much of what he witnessed in slavery, to shape it into the folktale, and to do so with a faithfulness as exacting as that of the most gifted historian, working in conventional sources, in recording the past. More than that, his gifts as an artist gave him a dimension of talent rare among historians, the ability to give expression to human feeling as a factor in shaping past and present, the ability to link the subjective to the communal. Those qualities made him a great teacher, able to convey values of slave culture to children at the turn of the century, as other storytellers conveyed them on plantations more than three decades earlier.

One finds in Brown's tales references to the means by which slaves prevented their true feelings from being detected in the presence of the master, and references to what is distinctive about slave culture and why. But many of the tales, certainly the greatest, have a dimension that is so esoteric, so African in meaning, that the master class missed their meaning altogether. On that level, that of Africanity, as we see repeatedly in the tales of Tad, the tale was the greatest device, next to the actual ceremony it recounts, for imparting the values of the culture to the young and for reinforcing them in adults, for preparing slaves to cope with the world of slavery and for revealing the process by which that world unfolded. Like the ring shout that helped give it birth, the spiritual was, for slaves, integral to that process.

How slave experience, including ceremonies in which the spiritual was sung, was communicated to succeeding generations and cultural continuity maintained is demonstrated through the contact between Simon and William John Faulkner, his prize student, who met the ex-slave in Society Hill, South Carolina, in 1900 at the age of nine. Brown became the model storyteller for the young Faulkner, and the latter attempted to tell the tales like Brown, whom he so greatly admired that even now, at the age of ninety-five, he remains inspired by Brown. That inspiration helps explain why Faulkner has held the most precise details of the tales in mind for more than three-quarters of a century. His intelligence, his powers of retention, and an artistry reminiscent of that of Simon Brown are factors in the remarkable correspondence of the tales, like those of Tad, to the *processes* of African culture revealed by art historians, anthropologists, and students in related fields like linguistics and musicology. Transcribed over thirty years after Faulkner first heard them from Brown, but recounted on hundreds of occasions, Faulkner's tales enlarge our knowledge of African religion in America on its own terms and in relation to Christianity in new and striking ways. This is even more remarkable because Brown, no doubt following a practice learned in slavery, refused to respond to inquiries from Faulkner regarding African culture except to say, "We used to have great times." But in "How the Slaves Worshipped" Brown put his finger on important differences between slave religion and that of the master class, suggesting that slaves brought intuitive, aesthetic, and other values to black Christianity, distinguishing it from white Christianity:

> I use' to drive my Massa's family in town to church, in the "two-horse surey," on a Sunday. I had to sit upstairs with the other slaves. We act like we enjoy' the services, but we didn't. . . . But the slave' had they Christian religion too, an' it wasn't cole and "Proper," like in the white folk' church. The fact is, the black folk in my day didn't even

have a church. They meet in a cabin in the cole weather an' outdoors, under a tree or a "brush arbor" in the summer time. Sometimes the Massa's preacher would "talk" at the meetins 'bout bein' obedient to our massas an' good servants, an' 'bout goin' to heaven when we die.' . . . But, oh, my, when my people got together to "Wishop" (Worship) God, the Spirit would "move in the meetin!"[57]

Religion was for many slaves, by the mid-nineteenth century in Virginia, an African version of Christianity marked by an awareness of the limits of the religion of whites.

The folk' would sing an' pray an' "testify," an' clap they han's, jus' as if God was right there in the midst with them. He wasn't way off, up in the sky: He was a-seein' every-body an' a -listen' to ever' word an' a-promisin' to "let His love come down." My people would be so burden' down with they trials an' tribulations, an' broken hearts, that I seen them break down an' cry like babies. . . .Yes sir, there was no pretendin' in those prayer-meetin's. There was a livin' faith in a jus' God who would one day answer the cries of his poor black chillen an' deliver them from they enemies. But they never say a word to they white folks 'bout this kine of faith.[58]

At laying-by time on some plantations, revival meetings were held over several nights in the heat of summer. With "sisters and brothers" clapping their hands and singing and mourners coming to their bench, the slaves sang songs created within the ancestral circle of dancers:

Sister (or brother), you better get ready;
You got to die, you got to die.
It may not be today or t'morrow
You never know the minute or the hour
But you better get ready, you got to die.

It was important to be at peace with oneself. For those sinners who had trouble "comin' through," the slaves sang another spiritual:

Go down to the River of Jordan, go down,
Singing Hallelujah
Singing Hallelujah
Sing Halle-, Sing Halle-,
Sing Hallelujah.[59]

A deacon assisted the preacher with his flock of white-gowned men and women in a ceremony common to West African religions and to Christianity—water immersion, or baptism. As a rule "the converts was made ready to be baptize' the next-comin' Firs' Sunday, soon in the mornin', down by the Mill Pond." The new converts and friends as well as members of their families would make a pilgrimage, Simon Brown tells us, down to the Mill Pond. Herskovits writes, "In ceremony after ceremony witnessed among the Yoruba, the Ashanti, and in Dahomey, one invariable element was a visit to the river or some other body of 'living' water . . . for the purpose of obtaining the liq-uid indispensable for the rites." Thus, Yorubas, Ashantis, and Dahomeans would easily have identified with the pilgrimage to the Mill Pond for a ceremony that was heavily influenced by Bakongo religious ritual.

Simon Brown relates that slaves would secure passes and "come from all 'roun'—in buggies an' carts an' on mule-back"—to attend revival meetings. "But mos' of them walk' on foot. The candidates for baptism would gather 'roun' an' march down the Big Road all dress' in white to the edge of the pond." As they waited for the ceremony to begin and as the congregation began singing a "baptism' song," "one of the Deacons would hole in his han' a long staff built like a cross . . . would wade out into the water, usin' his staff as a soundin' stick in fron' of him. When the staff reach' the proper depth, he would drive it down hard into the bottom." With the cross visible above the water, the preacher was "fetched" by the deacon and stood near it as the congregation sang:

> Wade in the water, Chillen
> Oh wade in the water, chillen,
> Wade in the water, chillen,
> Wade in the water to be baptize'.[60]

The staff made like a cross was, for the Bakongo, "a tree across the water's path, a bridge that mystically put the dead and the living in perpetual communication."[61] In America, therefore, its retention was an illustration, as described by Simon Brown, of how a particular feature of the African religious vision, whatever the fate of its other features, might radiate the fullness of that vision without outsiders having the slightest awareness of its significance. So it was that the deacon in the ceremony was not simply a "deacon" but "the good leader" or priest who was capable of introducing the living to their ancestors through the ritual of water immersion. Moreover, to the Kongo people the staff-cross represented authority that was also legislative, judicial, and executive.[62] On the slave plantation, therefore, the authority of the religious leader might have been enhanced because Africans recalled the enormous authority their religious leaders once held. But given the restraints of slavery, the radically different context in which the staff was revealed, legislative and judicial authority ceased to exist, and political authority, to the extent that it persisted, was so greatly reduced as to be all but unidentifiable in the African sense of leadership. But the remaining substance, the African religious role of the deacon, had political overtones because its meaning was vital to the slave's sense of autonomy, was kept from slaveowners. The white gowns of the slaves as well as the staff-cross recall Bakongo religious mythology:

> In the world below, called *mpemba,* land of kaolin, land of all things white, the lordly dead, through powers commensurate with the relative goodness of their life once lived on earth above, lose the impurities acquired in life, acquire a new freshness of existence, and reenter the world.[63]

The cross portion of the staff symbolizes the four moments of the sun and represents, to the Bakongo, the four corners of the earth and the four winds of heaven. The horizontal axis of the cross signifies the sea or river that divides the world of the living and dead, the heavens above and the earth below, this world and the next. The staff-cross enabled the deacon, as it did the Bakongo king, to traverse the watery barrier—the horizontal portion of the cross—and, like Brer Rabbit in Red Hill Churchyard, to mediate between the world of the living and that of the dead. When the deacon brandished his staff, it was as if the sun in its orbit was suddenly mirrored, revealing the fullness of Bakongo religion. And since those who lived a good life might experience rebirth in generations of grandchildren, the cycle of death and rebirth could hardly have been more suggestive than through the staff-cross—a symbol of communal renewal.[64]

What appears in "How the Slaves Worshipped," despite the African context of the creation of the spirituals, as primarily a Christian ceremony is actually a conversion within the circle of the cross, a movement from one state of being in the Kongo religious system to a higher one. Substantial numbers of Bakongo, Angolans, and west coast Africans were enslaved in Virginia, and even if first-generation Africans were not much in evidence at the ceremony witnessed by Simon Brown, their descendants across a number of ethnic lines were doubtless among those who had come from all around, in buggies and on foot, to participate.

In the ceremony before and at the pond, as in most "Christian" ceremonies on slave plantations, Christianity provided a protective exterior beneath which more complex, less familiar (to outsiders) religious principles and practices were operative. The very features of Christianity peculiar to slaves were often outward manifestations of deeper African religious concerns, products of a religious outlook toward which the master class might otherwise be hostile. By operating under cover of Christianity, vital aspects of Africanity, which some considered eccentric in movement, sound, and symbolism, could more easily be practiced openly. Slaves therefore had readily available the prospect of practicing, without being scorned, essential features of African faith together with those of the new faith.

When the convert in "How the Slaves Worshipped" is held underwater—under the Kalunga line—he "dies a small death, and then is reborn, emerging from a short commune with the ancestors." It is small wonder that Simon Brown tells us that a candidate, after immersion, would "come up from the water so happy he would begin to shout right out in the pond, an' it would take both deacons to bring him safe to shore." More than one song, sung at the Mill Pond, takes on a new meaning now: "Sister, you better get ready/You got to die/You got to die." One can hardly doubt that the meaning was double, as it certainly was for Bakongo in the baptismal ceremony. The convert was wiped with a towel, and then his family or friends would cover him with a quilt as the singing of the congregation evoked the Kalunga line—since it was also imagined as a dense forest or, in Gullah Joe's language, feenda:

> Oh, my soul got happy when I come out the wilderness,
> Come out the wilderness,
> Oh my soul got happy
> When I come out the wilderness,
> I'm leanin' on the Lawd—
>> CHORUS
> I'm a-leaning' on the Lawd,
> I'm a-leaning' on the Lawd,
> I'm a-leaning' on the Lawd,
> Who die' on Cal-va-ree.[65]

That last image was also enriched by the staff-cross, by the African concern for the relationship between the world of the living and that of the dead, because reciprocity was crucial in ceremonies of the Bakongo and of Africans generally. Thompson believes, because of the "wheel" effect, the Kongo cross "should make clear the rhetorical point of its existence, as forever distinguished from the standing emblem of Jesus Christ." The complex uses to which the Kongo peoples put the symbolism of the cross and circle as a cosmogram help explain the power of the two as means of extending the basis of commonality among Virginia slaves and of linking them in cultural unity with Africans practicing the ring shout in the South and the North. Something of the complexity of the circle in the Congo is discussed by Thompson:

> Fu-Kiall's diagrams illustrate the fundamental circularity of the Kongo sign of cosmos, a circularity which bursts into full view where a small shell spirals at the center of one cruciform or, in another instance, where a circle spins around the endings of the cross. . . . Dots or small circles added to the intersecting arms of the Kongo cross indicate man or woman as second suns, moving through time and space, following the circle of the sun.[66]

The cross represented an intricate field of circularity to the Bakongo and Angolan in Virginia, and against that radiating field they placed Christ when converting others to Christianity.[67] Thus, priests through the symbolism of the "long staff built like a cross" maintained an African defining power in the slave community that lent a peculiar irony to the crucifixion, deepening the pain of spirit of those who sang the song under Kongo influence, calling to mind a whole complex ancestral heritage as Christ is imagined on the cross: "I'm a-leanin' on the Lord (3)/Who die' on Cal-va-ree."[68]

In all of the ceremonies we have described, black artists occupied a place beside black religious leaders at the center of slave communities. Both artist and preacher—the two were often the same—thrived among the masses. The preacher was as much a part of the masses as the artist and related to followers in much the same way, the one reaching out to the other as in Africa. At times African art and religion in slavery were sustained by supporters who rivaled the priests and priestesses who stood before them at the ceremonial sites. That process won ultimate sanction in the folk art of the tale and bears a profound relationship to the melding of various African ethnic groups in slavery. In this regard, the evidence drawn on to see the process unfold may at first glance appear to be primarily Christian, as in "How the Slaves Worshipped," but it seldom is. In fact, the great bulk of the slaves were scarcely touched by Christianity, their religious practices being vastly more African than Christian. The slave preacher on the plantation was able to relate to slave communities touched by Christianity and to those with little or no Christian characteristics, the latter because otherwise he could have had no credence whatsoever among the majority of his people.[69]

No less an authority on slave conversion to Christianity than the Reverend Charles C. Jones, writing in 1834, had this to say regarding slaves and Christianity: "It is true they have access to the house of God on the Sabbath; but it is also true that even where the privilege is within their reach, a minority, (and frequently a very small one) embraces it." Moreover, Jones noted the inability of churches in the South and the Southwest to accommodate "one-tenth of the Negro population; besides others (areas of the South) in which there are no churches at all." To compound the problem, Jones concluded, "great numbers of masters have very few or no religious privileges at all." That being the case, William W. Freehling's finding that, as the year 1833 ended, "only twelve white men in the whole South devoted themselves exclusively to ministering to the slaves" underscores the inability of Christianity to Christianize the slaves. "Only one slave in twenty," according to Freehling, "was a communicant in white churches," and those who were in attendance were unprepared to comprehend the erudite sermons addressed to educated citizens. Freehling notes, "As evangelical Christianity swept over the Old South, another burden was added to the uneasy consciences of many slaveholders." The attempt to Christianize slaves was at best "an abortive affair. . . . Protestant sects believed that the Savior had enjoined all Christians to read His words, and planters kept slaves from reading the Scripture."[70]

Not surprisingly, the old Negro preacher and other religious leaders in the slave community were the ones who spoke for their people whatever their ethnic origins. The authority of major religious leaders on the plantations owed much to the divine-kingship systems of West Africa and for that reason was the least likely to be questioned. Whereas the warrior-king was typical of Europe, much of black Africa was characterized by the priest-king, which gave the religious leader a high status in slave communities. In Africa the priest was at times king, reaching his highest rung of authority, performing religious roles that determined the vital functions—presiding over harvests and mediating with ancestral spirits. The life forces were regulated by and passed through the king-priest, whose importance was paramount; this helps explain the authority of the black preacher through slavery and later. Except for that authority the "scattered and often clandestine" praise houses may not have surfaced, without which the Negro spirituals may well not have come into being. It is small wonder that Johnson observed, "The Negro today [1927] is the most priest-governed group in the country."[71] Thus, the powers of priests, and those of artists, especially storytellers and musicians, on the plantations of the South caused African-born slaves to recognize central features of life in the various ethnic homelands as they moved toward a single ethnicity in their new environment, which was precisely the nature of the process Brer Rabbit did so much to further in Red Hill Churchyard.

One errs in assuming that the slave preacher was primarily Christian and did not play a variety of religious roles, especially that of African priest. Indeed, the categories of religious leadership on plantations were so fluid that the functions of class leader, deacon, and "preacher" were often indistinguishable, as they were in cities. The preacher's priestly or African function, and that of deacon and class leader, was guarded from whites, who thought anything African of a religious nature was pagan or heathen, an insult to Christianity. Therefore, if the African religious leader was to operate in the open, the safest cloak to hide behind was that of Christianity. African religious leaders predominated in slavery and in that oppressive environment orchestrated their people's transformation into a single people culturally. James Weldon Johnson makes the penetrating observation that it was through the old Negro preacher that "people of diverse languages and customs who were brought here from diverse parts of Africa and thrown into slavery were given their first sense of unity and solidarity."[72]

Simon Brown was a supreme articulator of that process. His grounding as a storyteller, as we have seen, was lived experience, which must be taken into account in the attempt to understand his tales' remarkable faithfulness to the past. A mulatto house slave, he found the only culture he knew and respected in the quarters. It was there that he witnessed and participated in an African burial ceremony at thirteen. Other youths joined him in becoming inheritors of the culture of their ancestors, directly responsible for the sacred act of digging and filling up the grave, apparently as soon as they were strong enough. In the 1850s, these youths participated in burial customs common to Central and West Africa, customs known to vast numbers of slaves, although by then second- and third-generation Africans [in America] greatly outnumbered those born in Africa. Even slaves to whom aspects of a particular African custom, such as the constructing of the burial mound, were unknown, and therefore not at first understood, got a sense of solidarity with those who knew the custom through the genius of the preacher and that of singers responding to him. Rapport was established through song style, which powerfully affected preaching style, both peculiarly African and widespread, both regulated by the rhythm of dance at the burial site.

Brown tells us that slaves helped each other in illness as in death. If a woman fell ill, "other women came over to help her with the chillen, or to cook the meals, wash the clothes or to do other necessary chores." He recalled medical and other practices that were African:

> It wasn't like it is today, when ever'body seem like they tryin' only to git the dollar. Women would come over jus' to sit a spell an' sing an' pray 'roun' the sickbed. Nobody was lef' to suffer alone. Sometimes a man or woman with a healin' touch would brew a herb tea, mix a poultice, or apply peach tree leaves to the fevered brow, to help the sick git well. All of this lovin' care cheer' up the trouble' soul, whether he got well or died.[73]

When Sister Dicey died, the women washed and dressed her and laid her out in a homemade coffin, resting it on chairs. Slaves from all over came to sit, sing, and pray. "The singin' was mostly sad songs with happy endin's, 'cause the folks felt that now Aunt Dicey was freed from all the trials an' tribulations of slavery an' was safe in Heaben, at res' an' in peace forever more. She wouldn't be a bare-foot slave dress' in rags anymore." And so they sang,

> *I got shoes*
> *You got shoes*
> *All God's chillen got shoes*
> *When I git to Heaben*
> *I'm a-goin' to put on my shoes an'*
> *Walk all over God's heaben*
> *I got a robe*
> *You got a robe*
> *All God's chillen got a robe.*
> *When I git to Heaben*
> *I'm a-goin' to put my robe an'*
> *Shout all over God' Heaben.*[74]

Some of the people "git so happy with this picture of Heaben that they burs' out cryin' an' shoutin' for joy. An' so the 'sittin' up' went on all night—some folks comin' an' goin' all the time." The African custom of "sittin' up" was accompanied by the singing of spirituals, the sadness-joy of the songs in Virginia resembling the feelings at the burial ceremony conducted by Brer Rabbit in Red Hill Churchyard in South Carolina, and by New Orleans blacks in the nineteenth and twentieth centuries.[75]

The next morning, at the grave, the preacher offered Christian words of comfort in an African style that finally led, as the tension mounted, to dance growing out of rejoicing, and to resolution. According to Simon Brown, the preacher's voice carried softly, then with rising emphasis as he sang the sermon:

> "Sister Dicey, since God in His mercy has taken your soul from earth to Heaben, an' out of your misery, I commit your body to the groun', earth to earth, ashes to ashes, dus' to dus', where it will res' in peace. But on that Great Gettin' Up Mornin', when the trumpet of God shall soun' to wake up all the dead, we will meet you in the sky an' join the host' of saints who will go marchin' in. Yes, we'll be in that number, Sister Dicey, when the saints go marchin' in." Before the preacher could finish his benediction, some of the women git so happy that they jus' drown' him out with they singin' an' han' clappin' an' shoutin'.[76]

The variety and depth of African customs in the Virginia slave community of Simon Brown form the background against which "they singin' an' han' clappin' an' shoutin'" should be viewed: the "sittin' up," the African medical practices, the Kongo cross at the baptismal ceremony, the rhythms of song, sermon, and dance—all these elements marked the Virginia slave community as African in important ways. The shouting and hand clapping, in context, then, was the ring shout, the circular movement around the old lady's grave being a key symbol while a sermon was delivered that was as Christian in message as its mode of delivery and the response it evoked were African, its call and response pattern common to blacks the world over. The counterclockwise movement of those at the graveside opposed the movement of the sun. For first-generation Africans from Congo-Angola and for those in their tradition, each rising and setting of the sun was a painful reminder that they were indeed in a new world, but their counterclockwise movement was a form of spiritual and physical resistance to this reality, as it was for some that day at Sister Dicey's grave. What followed, however, was a ceremony practiced by millions in Africa above and below the equator:

> Then the men an' boys begin to fill up the grave. When it was full they roun' it up real purty-like, an' put a wood shingle at the head an' another at the foot of the grave. The women-folk lay some flowers an' "ribbon-grass" on the top, an' put different color' bottles, broken glass an' sea-shells all 'roun' the grave of Aunt Dicey. In that way they show they love for her. It was the bes' that slaves could do in them days, when ever'body was poor an' own' by they massas. But no man could own they souls or keep them from lovin' one another. Them gifts come only from God.[77]

The "sittin' up" and the burial mound are bridges to the hereafter, making communication with God and the ancestors less abstract, because being in proper relation to Sister Dicey eased one's own passage in turn. While the preacher spoke of meeting her on that great getting-up morning, the preparation of the burial mound by relatives meant an awareness that continuing contact with Sister Dicey's spirit was unavoidable. Hence, by being certain that her spirit was at rest, contact with her thereafter was more likely to be of a harmonious kind. The two visions of religion in the tale, the traditional African and the Christian, were complementary and explainable in relation to the African view of religious experience, which does not function from a single set of principles but deals with life at different levels of being. The African spiritual vision of the universe is synthetic, does not claim everything can be deduced from a single principle—that is to say, the center of the African's morality is the life process and the sacredness of those who brought him into existence. The African's relationship to the future is determined by his relationship to the young, his relationship to the past determined by his relationship to his parents. The maintenance of this continuity from generation to generation is justification for his being and the basis on which he determines proper behavior. The needs, physical and spiritual, of the actual, concrete human being are recognized as important, and an attempt is made to satisfy them in African societies; those needs were multiple before Christianity became a part of the African's faith. The absorption of aspects of Christianity—such as a belief in Christ—did not mean they ceased being multiple, as can be seen in burial and other ceremonies in slavery.

Just as slave music reflects the unity of West African culture through syncopation, antiphony, group singing, improvisation, and instruments used, and through its organic tie to dance, the essential unity of large sections of Central and West African religion was reflected in the burial mound of slaves in antebellum America and later. The African character of slave burial ceremony was unmistakable: "Them dishes and bottles what put on the grave is for the spirit and ain't for nobody to touch them. That's for the spirit to feel at home." "You put dishes and bottles and all the pretty pieces what they like on the grave. You always break these things before you put 'em down. You break them so that the chain will be broken. You see, the one person is dead and if you don't break the things, then the others in the family will die, too."[78] Robert Farris Thompson observes,

> Two early twentieth-century graves in Mississippi . . . glitter with surface china, suggesting the rumpled vitality of a vanished life. The use of the fragments seems deliberate: pieces are aligned to show the length of the grave in a simple axial statement. . . . An intimate act characteristic of the deceased is [sometimes] recalled forever on the surface of the grave by means of a particular object selected. What appears to be a random accumulation is in fact the distillation of a life. . . . The deposit of chinaware and other objects on the Afro-American grave is in contrast with the stark plots of grass which cover the graves of Americans of European descent.[79]

The preacher presiding over the deceased, overseeing the ritual, assumes major responsibility for the fate of the deceased's spirit. The obligation of the occasion suggests a power beyond the grave for him, leads him to assume the role of the African priest over the burial mound. Thus, the divine-kingship function of mediating with the ancestors was reborn on the plantations of the South, as Africa was recalled on a level of precise symbolism. Slaves found objects in North America similar to the shells and close enough to the earthenware of West Africa to decorate the grave in an African manner—and in the African manner to celebrate the lives of those who, like Sister Dicey, lived long and won the admiration of their fellows. Africans from different points of the continent shared this vision, which could have *strengthened* an African trait under the conditions of North American slavery: "The fusion of slaves from the Gold Coast, the Congo-Angola area, and other parts of the Guinea Coast in Southern slavery could mean the reinforcement of the African notion that the funeral is the climax of life and that the dead should be honored by having their possessions placed upon the top of their graves."[80]

In *Black Thunder*, a superb treatment of a conspiracy led by Gabriel Prosser in Virginia in 1800, Arna Bontemps portrays a ceremony like the one described by Faulkner, capturing an aspect of the ethos of contempories of Gabriel:

> They were burying old Bundy in the low field by the swamp. They were throwing themselves on the ground and wailing savagely. (The Negroes remembered Africa in 1800.) . . . Down, down, down: old Bundy's long gone now. Put a jug of rum at his feet. Old Bundy with his legs like notty canes. Roast a hog and put it on his grave. Down, down. How them victuals suit you, Bundy? How you like what we brung you?

Faith in the continuing influence of the dead on the living was as great as faith that the living influenced the dead:

> Anybody knows that dying ain't nothing. You got one eye open and one eye shut old man. We going to miss you just the same, though, we going to miss you bad, but we'll meet you on t'other side, Bundy. We'll do that sure's you born.

There was African song—a moaning cry—and dance:

> They had raised a song without words. They were kneeling with their faces to the sun. Their hands were in the air, the fingers apart, and they bowed and rose together as they sang. Up came the song like a wave, and down went their faces in the dirt . . . at the place where the two worlds met.[81]

$$\bullet \quad \bullet \quad \acute{\bullet}$$

VI

[The writer] Fredrika Bremer witnessed, in a "separate place of worship," an expression of Africanity that in some ways seems almost as obscure as the most inaccessible aspect of the ceremony in South Carolina's Red Hill Churchyard or the one in Virginia in which the staff-cross was used as the slaves worshiped. But unlike most African ceremonies in America under review here, the one described by Bremer, which occurred in the 1850s in New Orleans, appears not to have a precise analogue in Africa. Indeed, an incontestably African outlook, such as reverence for the ancestors, is not apparent from Bremer's description despite her belief that what she witnessed, for all the genuineness of its Christianity, was African. Her account of what took place is particularly useful because it is one of the few on record in which the religious ceremonies of slaves in separate churches are described in detail. What Bremer saw occurred under circumstances that the South Carolina jurist thought most likely to encourage the continuation of "African barbarism." She visited what was, despite the passage of thirty years, in some respects—not the least of which was that the New Orleans slaves were "Methodists" with class leaders—the New Orleans counterpart to the Charleston African Church attended by the Vesey conspirators.

[Editor's note: The Denmark Vesey conspiracy took place in Charleston in 1822. Vesey was a free man at the time of his unsuccessful artisan insurrection. Stuckey discusses Vesey's rebellion in detail in the first chapter of *Slave Culture* titled, "Introduction: Slavery and the Circle of Culture (pp. 43–53).]

The Christian and African aspects of the ceremony witnessed in New Orleans so complemented each other, were in such reciprocal relation, that the two faiths appear altogether harmonious though each stands out vividly, the one a catalyst for the other. Yet, as Bremer notes, the defining faith is ultimately African, an "African Tornado," though the setting was one in which "Sunday schools for Negro children" provided "instruction about the Savior." Though she had seen black Methodists in Washington, D.C., where the ring shout was a powerful influence in the lives of blacks, her expectations "were quite exceeded" in New Orleans: "Here we were nearer the tropical sun than at Washington."[82]

Christian elements in the ceremony were unmistakable, as African religious leaders calmly preached the Christian Gospel in an atmosphere otherwise hardly Christian. The tempo of activity at the start of the ceremony was relaxed and slow but quickened as exhorters moved along the benches and stopped to talk to individual worshippers during the "so-called class meeting." "These exhorters," Bremer observes, "go around at the class-meeting to such of the members of their class as they deem to stand in need of consolation or encouragement, talk to them, aloud or in an under voice, receive their confession, impart advice to them, and so on." The exhorters' words quickly served to establish an antiphonal relationship, the action accelerating, the exhorters' calls answered by the consoled, who experienced exaltation and began "to speak and to perorate more loudly and more vehemently than the exhorter himself, and so to overpower him"—a scene not unlike the ceremony around Sister Dicey's grave when the preacher's voice was drowned out by responsive singing and shouting and hand clapping.

> There was one exhorter in particular, whose black, good-natured countenance was illumined by so great a degree of inward light, by so much good-humor and joy, that it was a pleasure to see him and to hear him, too; for although his phrases were pretty much the same, and the same over again, yet they were words full of Christian pith and marrow, and they were uttered with so much cordiality, that they could not do other than go straight to the heart with enlivening power. . . . And it was only as the messenger of the joy in Christ that he preached.[83]

That the preaching of the exhorter—the regular sermon had ended before Bremer and her associates arrived at the church—was Christian underscored the defining power of African religious faith as registered in the response it evoked. Messages such as

> Hold fast by Christ! He is the mighty One! He will help! He will do everything well! Trust in him my sister, my brother. Call upon Him. Yes. Yes. Hold fast by Christ! He is the Lord!

before long evoked a leaping response from the worshipers like "corn starting to pop over a hot fire." It represented the Africanization of Christianity not only in emotive and intuitive force but in a larger religious sense:

By degrees the noise increased in the church and became a storm of voices and cries. The words were heard, "Yes, come, Lord, Jesus! come oh come, oh glory!" and they who thus cried aloud began to leap—leaped aloft with a motion as of a cork flying out of a bottle, while in the air, as if they were endeavoring to bring something down, and all the while crying aloud, "Come, oh come!" And as they leaped, they twisted their bodies round in a sort of corkscrew fashion, and were evidently in a state of convulsion; sometimes they fell down and rolled in the aisle, amid loud, lamenting cries and groans. . . . Whichever way we looked in the church, we saw somebody leaping up and fanning the air; the whole church seemed transformed into a regular bedlam, and the noise and tumult was horrible.[84]

In that atmosphere, the "tropical exhorter, the man with the sunbright countenance," together with the other exhorters, made his rounds, perfectly at home, "as if everything were going on as if it ought to do." Just a few words from an exhorter to a tall, handsome mulatto woman drew words from her that took the shape of art. Like musical instruments at play, the woman and the exhorter preached to each other, conveying a Christian message through an African form. They preached with pleasure until "she sprang aloft with such vehemence that three other women took hold of her by the skirts, as if to hold her on the earth." Still she leaped and twisted and threw her arms about before falling and rolling about "amid convulsive groans." Her rising and walking from one part of the church to another exclaiming "Hallelujah!" meant that Christianity was being used to affirm and spur on the African faith and the African religion Christianity as the ceremony built to a climax:

Amid all the wild tumult of crying and leaping, on the right hand and the left, she continued to walk up and down the church in all directions, with outspread arms, eyes cast upward, exclaiming in a low voice, "Hallelujah! Hallelujah!" At length she sank down upon her knees on the platform by the altar, and there she became still. . . . What has happened to her? we inquired from a young negro girl whom she knew. "Converted!" said she laconically, and joined those who were softly rubbing the palms of the converted.[85]

This scene calls to mind the relationship of the preacher to his congregation in the sanctified churches of Chicago and Harlem, where the congregation is on its feet responding to the preacher, dancing and shouting. Moreover, Melville and Frances Herskovits, in *Rebel Destiny,* note similarities between Suriname blacks, those of the Gold Coast of West Africa, and blacks in sanctified churches in the United States, where the "saints" dance and shout. A marvelous description of the process that occurs when blacks in America in our time are most African when worshiping is found in James Baldwin's *The Fire Next Time.* What is described is of the twentieth century and of the nineteenth, and in a number of respects is remarkably similar to what Bremer found in the New Orleans ceremony. Baldwin writes,

There is no music like that music, no drama like the drama of the saints rejoicing, the sinners moaning, the tambourines racing, and all those voices coming together and crying holy unto the Lord. There is still, for me, no pathos quite like the pathos of those multi-colored, worn, somehow triumphant and transfigured faces, speaking from the depths of a visible, tangible, continuing despair of the goodness of the Lord. I have never seen anything to equal the fire and excitement that sometimes, without warning, fill a church, causing the church, as Leadbelly and so many others have testified, to "rock." Nothing that has happened to me since equals the power and the glory that I sometimes felt when, in the middle of a sermon, I knew that I was somehow, by some miracle, really carrying, as they said, "the Word"—when the church and I were one. Their pain and their joy were mine, and mine were theirs—they surrendered their pain and their joy to me, I surrendered mine to them—and their cries of "Amen!" and "Hallelujah!" and "Yes, Lord!" and "Praise His Name!" and "Preach it, brother!" sustained and whipped on my solos until we all became equal, wringing wet, singing and dancing in anguish and rejoicing, at the foot of the altar.[86]

As W. E. B. Du Bois recognized, possession during religious ceremonies is not new to the world, not the exclusive experience of a particular people, but is ancient and transcultural.[87] The context and content of its occurrence, however, may differ markedly, as we see, in contrast to European tradition, in ring ceremonies designed for ancestors to take possession of the celebrant at the highest point of exaltation. And even when black Christians experienced possession, it was mainly in that same circular context where the degree of emotional fervor and the intensity of convulsions—and the particulars of dance that finally give way to them—were also African. Especially in the tradition of Africans in America, passions are unleashed that are to some extent called forth and polarized by oppression.

The ultimate expression of the passion witnessed by Bremer and Baldwin indicates that the community in which the celebrant attains such a state basically rejects the authority of those who exercise control over it. Since outbursts of general fervor, followed by the incapacitation of some worshipers through possession and convulsions, challenged the master's sense of discipline (unlike drunkenness, in that its sources were not understood and its particular flowering remained, therefore, a mystery). The anthropologist Mary Douglas comments, "I don't ask why people are doing it [having convulsions], but why they are not doing it."[88] That perception enables us to grasp what was powerfully felt by the slave master—that what was not understood and seemed not to lend itself to discipline was threatening and consequently should be discouraged—and this was a principal reason for Africans continuing to practice their religion. But there was a more important reason for the persistence of certain features of the Africans' faith. In slavery, African religion, while losing its character in some respects, was intensified in others because of the need to gain relief, however temporary, from oppression by throwing one's whole being into the ceremony and giving oneself up totally to a more transcendent state, in which the ancestors—and possibly the gods—enter approvingly upon the communal ground of being.[89] In the process, indescribable suffering and grief are given ritualistic expression and briefly overcome, and slaves were aware of how such an experience differed in content and form from white worship, as Simon Brown notes in "How the Slaves Worshipped."

Where slaves had Christianity largely under their control, what usually occurred was what occurred in New Orleans—conversion within the circle of culture. But that conversion in New Orleans, in the case of the slaves observed by Bremer, was under conditions as calculated to protect them from censure as those in the Virginia conversion ceremony described by Simon Brown. In New Orleans and Virginia the exhorter, while consciously Christian, was as African in faith as Brer Rabbit in Red Hill Churchyard. Bremer tells us, "The tornado gradually subsided in the church, shrieking and leaping, admonishing and preaching, all became hushed." The key to the precise nature of African religion in the ceremony is in that sentence. It unlocks mysteries of the relationship of the exhorter and worshiper in the New Orleans church, for in *Elements of Weather* we read, "Tornadoes are revolving storms, turning counterclockwise in the Northern hemisphere."[90]

The ring shout comes vividly to mind, the force of the ceremony witnessed by Bremer suggesting tremendous African religiosity a few years before the end of slavery. Within the circle new life was breathed into Christianity, as the African felt the need for a salvation from slavery that, it must have seemed, only a miracle could effect. Hence the appeal of Christianity: "He is the mighty One! He will help!" But Christ did not replace the God of the Africans, for the African God was more an Absentee Landlord than a personal God on intimate terms with His followers; this helps explain, together with the brutality to which the slaves were subjected, the prominent strain of fatalism in the fabric of so much of black folk life and lore. The circle of culture had plenty of room for Jesus, and there he was received as he could not have been through racist pastoring. In the African Church, there was no segregation, and no one was told he was born to serve. What Bremer witnessed was Christianity shot through with African values, and she said as much. In that church, the Africans did not end their conversion ceremony because whites were present, as they were known to do at camp meeting conversions, for their leaping movement in the church had no apparent connection with the ring shout. It is possible, moreover, that the constricted architecture of the church ruled out the conventional shout except in front of the altar unless the benches were movable (in the New Orleans ceremony in question, there is no indication that they were). What is crucial here is that leaping was at times a variant of the ring ceremony in Africa, which made such a maneuver useful as a force for affirming the African religious vision in America, without being easily associated with the outlawed ring shout. Though not devised to conceal the ring shout, leaping served, like the staff-cross, to give powerful expression to its meaning.

The long and narrow aisles became the place for many to gather and leap as others leaped from where they sat. In this regard, it should be noted that leaping or jumping was associated with the shout by Bishop Payne, who saw the shout performed in and out of churches before all-black groups. Unlike others, he had no illusions about the relationship between the shout and jumping, having seen both in churches in which he was defied, and on one occasion, in Maryland, physically attacked, by his people. Perhaps herein lies part of the answer we are seeking concerning the dance movement employed in New Orleans: since blacks in churches pastored by Payne did not hesitate to do the ring shout collectively, there was no reason for them to jump about to disguise anything, which indicates that the leaping movement referred to by Payne and Bremer—and later by Stearns—may be associated with some versions of the ring ceremony in Africa as in America.[91]

The constricted quarters of the church, the proselytizing manner of the exhorters, and the confessional aspects of Christianity all encouraged a subjective experience of great intensity, which was heightened by the accelerating rhythms of the "preachers" as they faced each other. There was much to confess about oppression, so it is small wonder that slaves in the New Orleans church, like those observed by Simon Brown in "How the Slaves Worshipped," broke down and cried in a tumult of lamentation. The possibility should be seriously entertained that the spirit possession of the ring shout, and as slaves leaped in the air, is a principal source of "shouting" in most black churches today. In that and other respects, the ring ceremony and the art associated with it, such as the spirituals, often underwent change when introduced into the church. But since it was common practice for the ring shout to be seen in front of altars of black churches, the ceremony reaching its high point when spirit possession ensued, the shouting in the ring and that of the leapers probably constitute the antecedents of shouting as we know it in black churches today.

As African dance movement underwent change in the church—except for dance in the area of the altar, in which only so many could participate—the singing of the spirituals was altered, especially when not accompanied by the counterclockwise movements of groups of dancing worshipers. Though the swaying of the body and the clapping of hands could be done from the benches and elsewhere, on the whole it was not nearly as easy to engage the many parts of the body in the performance; this affected the rendering of the spirituals, especially as efforts to rid black churches of the shout and the singing of spirituals while not dancing were mounted before and after emancipation. The deemphasis on dance meant more stress on the words, a development associated with the introduction of choirs and "audiences." Even so, those audiences of slaves and ex-slaves were not like white audiences, which did not sway with the music and erupt, individually and collectively, in responsive song. Meanwhile, the line between the spirituals and Gospel music in the church, as on the plantation, was frequently obliterated in response to the propulsive clapping of hands, stomping of feet, and swaying of bodies. And we should remember that urban slaves were not divorced from the larger black community, in which the shout touched the lives of almost everyone. This could hardly have been otherwise, especially since slaves from the countryside were at times in attendance at slave churches in cities.[92]

Following the lead of whites, some black ministers inveighed against dance in religious ceremonies. But in and out of church blacks found ways of getting around Christian strictures when not ignoring them altogether, as they often did. "I have since heard it said," writes Bremer, "that the Methodist missionaries, who are the most effective teachers of and preachers among the Negroes, are very angry with them for their love of dancing and music, and declare them to be sinful." Though she is correct in noting such hatred of African music and dance—the missionaries would hardly have opposed one without the other, since music and dance were to the African all but inseparable—she is in error when she goes on to state, "And whenever the Negroes become Christian, they give up dancing, having preaching meetings instead, and employ their musical talents merely on psalms and hymns." In fairness to her, it must be said that she made that observation before she attended the camp meetings in which slaves were converted and before she visited the all-black New Orleans church in which slaves worshiped. Still, she would "let them have sacred dances, and let them sing to them joyful songs of praise in the beautiful air beneath the flowering trees," a position opposed by white practitioners of Christianity and by free Negro Christians.[93]

Rather "thoroughly amused by the frolic," Bremer revealed a limited understanding of the precise nature of what she experienced in the African Church. Yet she perceived that it was indeed a religious ceremony and not, because of the vigor of bodily movement or the joy and pain, "semi-religious." In a passage that recalls a Thomas Wentworth Higginson description of a ring shout, Bremer writes, "Of the whole raging, exciting scene there remained merely a feeling of satisfaction and pleasure, as if they had been together at some joyful feast."[94] In her account, we find Africans at home with Christianity because they did not permit the essence of their faith to be violated by their adoption of tenets of the new religion. Indeed, hers is perhaps the best portrayal in print of "Christian" exhorters, amid the most extraordinary African religious passion, serenely going about their work. Despite her belief that blacks were not generally equal to whites, she sensed the potential importance of African religion to America and to the West:

> In spite of all the irrationality and want of good taste which may be felt in such scenes, I am certain that there is in them, although as yet in a chaotic state, the element of true African worship. Give only intelligence, order, system to this outbreak of the warm emotions, longings, and presentiments of life, and then that which now appears hideous will become beautiful, that which is discordant will become harmonious. The children of Africa may yet give us a form of divine worship in which invocation, supplication, and songs of praise may respond to the inner life of the fervent soul!
>
> How many there are, even in our cold North, who in their youthful years have felt an Africa of religious life, and who might have produced glorious flowers and fruits if it only could have existed—if it had not been smothered by the snow and the gray coldness of conventionality—had not been imprisoned in the stone church of custom.[95]

That was slave religion in New Orleans in the fifties, a city noted for Congo Square and public expressions of Africanity, the very name of the square an indication of the place of origin and style of ceremony of many of the slaves in the Louisiana area. More precisely, Congo-Angola blacks, and certainly descendants of Africans from those areas, were found there in abundance during slavery, as were numerous signs of their presence in dance and musical expression, and in the sign of the cross with the circle touching its four points, forming the four corners of the earth. In addition to Congo-Angola blacks, there were many from other African civilizations in Louisiana who interacted musically with each other and, through the relative freedom city life provided, with Europeans.

> The tremendous creative energies released, when Kongo-derived traditions combined in New Orleans with those from the equally sophisticated Malian, Nigerian, and Cameroonian traditional civilizations, must have been amazing. This does not even take into account the final fillip, the blending of all that with the equally complex mix of musics—French, Spanish, and English—in that culturally strategic city.[96]

Frederick Law Olmsted observed that three-fourths of the slaves on Louisiana plantations in the 1850s were "thorough-bred Africans," and he found the same proportion of Africans on Mississippi plantations.[97] He meant thorough-bred in culture, which suggests the continuing power of African culture when passed from one generation to another. His attribution of Africanity to the great bulk of slaves in those states is supported by his observations regarding their religious practices. While walking in "a rather mean neighborhood" in New Orleans one morning, he was drawn to an open door of a church, entered, and was given "the uppermost seat facing the pulpit where there were three other white persons," one of whom "was probably a member of the police force in undress—what we call spy when we detect it in Europe." Scenes of tumult followed that recall those in the African Church visited by Bremer. While many in the congregation had "light hair and hardly any perceptible indications of having African blood," their behavior was generally indistinguishable from that of the darkest of blacks.[98] There was something infectious about the ritual, an "indescribable" ecstasy of "stamping, jumping and clapping of hands":

> The tumult often resembled that of an excited political meeting; and I was once surprised to find my own muscles all stretched, as if ready for a struggle—my face glowing, and my feet stamping—having been affected unconsciously, as men often are, with instinctive bodily sympathy with the excitement of the crowd . . . and I have no doubt that it was [the preacher's] "action" rather than his sentiments, that had given rise to the excitement of the congregation.[99]

With that, Olmsted demonstrated his understanding of a feature of Negro-African culture that is as important to the preacher as to the singer of sacred or secular song. Though the preacher's message was ostensibly Christian, his performance style, as at the church attended by Bremer, was African, the rhythms of his delivery stirring some to jump and clap their hands and others to shriek in a voice "impossible to be expressed in letters." As the first preacher drew his sermon to an end,

> a small old woman, perfectly black, among those in the gallery, suddenly rose, and began dancing and clapping her hands; at first, with a slow and measured movement, and then with increasing rapidity, at the same time beginning to shout "ha! Ha!" The women about her arose also, and tried to hold her as there appeared great danger that she might fall out of the gallery, and those below left their pews that she might not fall on them.[100]

Then "a tall, full-blooded negro" with "a disgusting expression of sensuality, cunning and vanity in his countenance" rose to preach. At times "breaking out into a yell with all the strength of extraordinarily powerful lungs," his striking attitude and extraordinary gestures created an excitement in the congregation that led to "the loudest and most terrific shouts," which could be compared to "nothing else human" one might hear. In language generally unintelligible, the preacher engaged irreligious forces in combat, shadowboxing, countering imaginary blows with "knock-down" replies. As he strode before the congregation and engaged evil, four people went into hysterics, but none so violently as the woman in the gallery.[101] In time, the seeming chaos of ecstasy was ordered by song. The preacher had picked up the sole hymnal in the church and repeated "the number and page and the first two lines" of a song. "These were sung, and he repeated the next, and so on, as in the South Presbyterian Service." As the congregation sang, its movements were those of sacred and secular singing groups in the mid-twentieth century:

> I think every one joined, even the children, and the collective sound was wonderful. The voices of one or two women rose above the rest, and one of these soon began to

introduce variations, which consisted mainly of shouts of oh! oh! at a piercing height. Many of the singers kept time with their feet, balancing themselves on each alternately, and swinging their bodies accordingly.

It is evident, from Olmsted's description of the ceremony, that, while a hymn was being sung, rhythms of the ring shout, which were the rhythms of the spirituals, were being applied as the Africans took possession of the hymn. And there was little apparent concern that whites were present as the preacher raised his voice above all others, clapped his hands, laughed aloud, then danced "first with his back, and then with his face to the audience."[102]

Indeed, Olmsted refers to him as "the dancer," and there is no doubt that he, the other preachers, and the congregation brought dance into the church, as Africans in another part of the city had done when Bremer attended their church. Here, as in the earlier case, the dance was distinctly African, involving a leaping about and a flailing of arms. As the singing ended, the preacher "continued his movements, leaping with increasing agility, from one side of the pulpit to the other," his movements threatening the security of the preachers "shut into the pulpit" as he threw himself back and jammed one, "who was trying to restrain him, against the wall."[103] The architecture of the church not only limited the freedom of the shouters but also, under the circumstances, threatened the physical well-being of those near the shouters. What would otherwise have been a concerted shout involving up to fifteen people was in that setting fragmented by the fear of injury in such constricting surroundings.

The thought that those who danced in the gallery might lose their footing and fall to the main floor caused those below to leave their pews so that the dancer or dancers would not fall upon them. As the tall preacher demonstrated, those in the pulpit were in great enough danger, especially since, as with individual dancers elsewhere, the order of group performance, with its rhythms regulating the movements of all, was in this case absent, the violent jerks of arms and legs "like a supple-jack, in every direction," increasing the danger of injury. It is little wonder that the preacher who leaped about like those who formed the tornado ended up with another preacher "sitting on the stair holding his head on his shoulder, and grasping one of his hands, while his feet were extended up into the pulpit." The prostrate man rose and released the young preacher, who pronounced, ironically enough, "the Apostle's blessing."[104] The poor spy, who had more than enough to report concerning "dance," must have left more than a little confused.

William Wells Brown observed ceremonies in which Negro spirituals were sung and the shout was done with great vigor. His description of African religion in a Nashville church recalls both Bremer and Olmsted, which deepens our understanding of the ring shout and the contexts of its expression after slavery. It was in 1880 that he encountered the shout and thought that it contributed to "moral and social degradation," failing to note the irony of his observation that its practitioners were "generous to a fault." At St. Paul's in Nashville—he does not give its denomination—the minister used a Christian theme to excite those in his congregation to dance. Women first moved their heads, then began "a shout," with five or six "fairly at it, which threw the house into a buzz. Seats were soon vacated near the shouters, to give them more room, because the women did not wish to have their hats smashed by the frenzied sisters."[105] Here was an instance of shouting in coordinated form with little or no leaping, the area of or near the pulpit being the place of ceremony. In that Nashville church, the small ring was enlarged as others joined in, the tempo at intervals challenging some to enter with vigor.

> The shouting now became general; a dozen or more entering into it most heartily. These demonstrations increased or abated, according to movements of the leaders, who were in and about the pulpit; for the minister had closed his discourse and first one, and then another would engage in prayer. The meeting was kept up till a late hour, during which, four or five sisters becoming exhausted, had fallen upon the floor and lay there or had been removed by their friends.[106]

The constraining church architecture, with its benches and chairs, was the setting, undoubtedly, of individual, as opposed to collective, shouting in the black church; indeed, it was the setting in which the shout was practically divorced from dance for those who could not get to an aisle or to the area of the pulpit; overcome nonetheless, one had little choice but to get to one's feet and cry out, struggling for room in which to move.

In the 1880s in Tennessee, there were no signs that the ring and associated forms of religious expression were disappearing. There was "the wildest excitement" at "one of the most refined congregations" in Nashville. Brown concluded that it would not be easy "to erase from the mind of the Negro of the South the prevailing idea that outward demonstrations, such as shouting, the loud 'amen,' and the most boisterous noise in prayer are not necessary of piety."[107] The scene was not dissimilar to what Bremer witnessed—"not less than ten or fifteen were shouting in various parts of the house," and "four or five were going from seat to seat shaking hands with the occupants of the pews"—as call and response punctuated dance and song. Shouting was the ultimate test of religiosity in that Nashville church. One young lady of "good education and refinement" said that "not until she had one shouting spell did most of her Sisters believe she had the witness.'" She was told by one of her sisters, "Sister Smith, I hope to live to see you show that you've got the witness for where the grace of God is, there will be shouting, and the sooner you comes to that point the better it will be for you in the world to come."[108]

Institutions other than the church existed to help blacks prepare for "the world to come." Indeed, as William Wells Brown understood it, a powerful current of African faith swept the black South: "To get religion, join a benevolent society that will pay them 'sick dues' when they are ill, and to bury them when they die, appears to be the beginning, the aim, and the end of the desires of the colored people of the South." In Petersburg, Virginia, he was told that there were "thirty-two different secret societies," and he "met persons who held membership in four at the same time."[109] Brown correctly reasoned that much of the stimulus for the securing of homes and the providing for other expenses is taken away by multiple attachments to secret societies for protection during illness and for burial at death. What he did not know was that without a proper burial it was thought the spirit would be restless and the relatives of the deceased might fall on hard times.

VII

Coming from cultures in which work and art were united so completely that any notion of art for art's sake lacked meaning, Africans in North America created while working, as they had done before. For all the comparative leisure available to whites, the African used his imagination to reflect on life in the new land with an originality sufficient to bring indigenous artistic forms into being. The objective reality that Africans combined, under the humiliating circumstances of slavery, the hardest and most prolonged work with a creativity the Helots never knew, illustrates that their influence on the development of the country, culturally and economically, was greatly disproportionate to their numbers. And slave creativity helped ease the pain of labor that might otherwise have been intolerable. Above all, strength was drawn from the ancestral spirits, and from the Creator of the fruits of labor.

At harvest time in Virginia and elsewhere, dances were held outdoors to climax the planting season, an expression of the slaves' gratefulness to forces bigger than man, to the ancestral spirits for the fertility of the soil and the renewal of the life process. Such celebrations were frequent on the plantations of the South. One survivor of slavery recalled, "Everybody bring some uh duh fus crops. We all gib tanks fuh duh crop an we dance and sing." An elderly Georgia woman, a youth when emancipated from slavery, recalled in the 1930s, "We pray and gib tanks fuh duh crop and pray fuh duh nex yeah. We all eat and sing an dance. One uh duh dances call duh Buzzard Lope. We still dance dat today." Henry Williams, when almost ninety years of age, recalled slave festivals in Georgia in the late 1840s and during the 1850s with an accuracy and vividness that support the sources on the subject. Again there is the same dominating, organizing symbol:

> Remembuh the big times we use tuh have wen I wuz young. We does plenty uh dances in those days. Dance roun in a ring. We has a big time long bout wen crops come in an evrybody bring sumpin tuh eat wut they makes an we all give praise fuh the good crop and then we shouts an sings all night. An wen the sun rise, we stahts tuh dance.[110]

"Hahves time wuz time fuh drums," the ex-slave Katie Brown remembered. It was also time for rattling "dry goad wid seed in um" and for beating flat tin plates. "Dey shout an moob roun in succle an look lak mahch goin tuh heabm."[111]

Harvest festivals were excellent occasions for passing on African cultural traits from one generation to the next. Some of the best dancing and music took place then, because of the high purpose of the occasion. Aware that few if any whites understood the deeper purpose of the festival, blacks found it an ideal situation, within the context of oppression, for them to give full expression to their Africanity:

> We use tuh hab big times duh fus hahves, and duh fus ting wut growed we take tuh duh chuch so as ebrybody could hab a piece ub it. We pray obuh it and shout. Wen we hab a dance, we use tuh shout in a ring. We ain't have wut yuh call a propuh dance tuhday. . . . One uh duh dances wuz called duh Buzzard Lope.[112]

Slave celebrations were regarded by whites, who allowed them to take place, as "innocent pleasures," though harvest festivals had existed for centuries in Africa before blacks had arrived in North America. "The festival dance was commonly a 'cake-walk,'" writes Roscoe Lewis in *The Negro in Virginia*. The slaves assembled in large numbers in "their Sunday best and with glowing tallow dips or pine knots forming a ring of light. . . . The cake-walk has been ascribed to African tribal celebrations." And like dance in African celebrations, the cake-walk and other dances at festival time on Virginia plantations usually represented vital aspects of religious expression. In that context, festivities and work were combined at corn-shucking time, with specific kinds of work an inspiration to slave creativity. While some slaves formed their glowing circle with pine knots, others, in the center, danced "the motions of labor,—swinging a scythe, tossing a pitchfork of hay into a wagon, hoisting a cotton-bale, rolling a hogshead of tobacco, sawing wood, hoeing corn—without the restriction and effort imposed by the load."[113] In that dance the slave reviewed much of the labor performed on the plantation that made it possible for the master to exist and to prosper. In the New World, that kind of festival dance was a means of distancing slaves from the purely exploitative reality of work, of extracting from the experience spiritual and artistic rewards, which helped slaves affirm their dignity through labor.

Important here are the specific forms of work and the uses to which work is put in a ceremony analogous to the martial dances of the various African women in Dahomey. In both cases we have responses to the environment that transcend ethnic considerations but reflect an unmistakable African response to problems common to all. Dances like "pitchin' hay," "corn-shuckin'," "cuttin' wheat," and "spottin'" (dancing with the hands and other parts of the body without moving the feet) are as African as the buzzard lope. So are the "pony's prance," "the Swan's bend," the "kangaroo," and "shooting the chute"—all of which could be a part of dance competitions during festivals and helped establish the precedent for later "cutting" sessions in which jazz artists exchange ideas. Those watching the festival dances usually acclaimed the winners, demanding that the couple continue to dance: "When the judges had made their decisions (it was a brave judge who went against the decision of the crowd), the other couples were called to the sidelines."[114]

In general, Saturday nights were spent as slaves pleased, as long as they remained in the quarters. But when they had the opportunity, they left the quarters for greater privacy in the woods. At times, dances conceived for religious purposes were performed in a setting that to Westerners might appear to serve mainly for entertainment but that to the African was suffused with religious spirit. The use of sacred dance for entertainment was natural to the ancestors of those whose dances today derive mainly from slave sacred dance. Moreover, there is no convincing evidence that the rhythms of sacred dance or music required much change when used outside the circle in which they were most often felt and heard. The scene on one such occasion in Virginia in the late 1840s or 1850s was clearly African; what at first appears secular was from the African vantage point sacred, the influence of Christianity coloring the retrospective view:

> But Sadday nights we'd slip out de quarters an' go to de woods. Was a ole cabin 'bout five miles 'way from de house, an' us would raise all de ruckus dere we wanted. . . . Ev'y gal wid her beau, an' sech music! Had two fiddles, two tangerines, two banjos, an' two sets of bones. Was a boy named Joe dat used to whistle too. Dem devilish boys would git out in de middle of de flo' an' me, Jenny, and de devil right wid 'em.[115]

The African presence was evident in musical instruments, in the formal dance expression, and in the placing of an object on the woman's head as she danced:

> Set a glass of water on my haid, an' de boys would bet on it. I had a great big wreaf roun' my haid an' a big ribbon bow on each side, an' didn't waste a drop of water on none of 'em. Dem was de days when me, Jenny, and de devil was runnin' in de depths of hell.

Apparently that last sentiment was not so firmly held when she was young: "Wouldn't do it now fo' nothin'. Lord Christ in heaven, God knows I didn't know no better."[116] And she was young, considering her testimony in the 1930s, in the last years of slavery, perhaps only in her teens. From the references to her youth, this ex-slave found nothing "sinful" about dancing while in slavery, nor did her peers or most of the older people around them. Sometime following slavery, perhaps much later in life, judging from the strength of African religious values for most ex-slaves decades following slavery, she came to regard such practices of her youth with some regret. Still, there is no reason to believe she lacked the ability or, for that matter, the inclination to do the dances in old age.

Slaves preferred to be as far away from the big house as possible: "We used to git back in de end cabin an' sing an' dance by de fiddle till day break. Sho' had one time, swingin' dem one piece dresses back an' fourth, an' de boys crackin' dey coattails in de wind." In that description by the eighty-two-year-old Charles Hancock, one can imagine the movements of the jitterbug, prominent in the North in the 1940s, but the sacred sources of which predated the arrival of the first African in North America: the left hand of the man clasping the woman's right hand, his right arm around her waist guiding her as they release each other's hand, their attire swinging in the wind. Again, from Hancock's description, emblems of Africanity: "Den dey would set a glass of water on dey haid an' see how many kinds of steps dey could make widout spillin' de water."[117] Improvisational dance under difficult circumstances was a successful test of continuing Africanity, when the water was balanced and a variety of dance figures were executed.

In North Carolina towns, especially on Christmas Day, slaves in groups of ten to twenty played instruments and sang songs "not remarkable for their melody but of pronounced rhythm":

SOLO: Young gal go ROUND de corner!

CHORUS IN HARMONY: My true love gone Down de lane!

SOLO: Wet on de grass where de djew been poured.

CHORUS: Hey, me lady, go Down de road;
    Go DOWN de road; go Down de road!
    My true love gone Down de lane.

As whites and a few blacks crowded before them, one of their number danced up to the crowd for a few coins as others rattled bones, danced, and shouted

> *Hab! Low! Here we go!*
> *Hab! Low! Here we go!*
> *Hab! Low! Kuners comin'*[118]

before disappearing to collect more contributions. This ceremony, which outlasted slavery, was African. Initial performances, dating from the eighteenth century, were very likely conducted for slaves, the singing in African languages. By the nineteenth century, the words of the songs heard by whites were English, but the overall effect of the ceremony could scarcely have been more African to the slaves, nor could the means of achieving it in musical instruments, dance and mode of singing, and attire. Whether in North Carolina cities or in the countryside, the general effect and purpose were African:

> They were dressed in "tatters," strips of cloth of gay colors sewn to their usual garments and producing an effect of exotic grotesquerie. All were men, but a few wore the clothes and acted the parts of women actors . . . frequently wore masks known as kuner-faces. . . . The leader carried a raw-hide whip with which he prevented interference from urchins in the streets.[119]

Thought by Europeans to be mainly for children, the ceremony, called John Kunering, had a deeper significance. The literature of West African secret societies seems to indicate that it was only because the original Kuners and their descendants in America were slaves that children and women were able to congregate before them to be entertained. Of a Nigerian ritual that closely resembles John Kunering, Talbot writes, "In many cases the headdress consists of human masks which appear to have originally represented the ancestors who had returned to life for the occasion; while the dances are expressions of prayer to the forefathers for the granting of fertility in crops and children." Talbot adds, concerning the people of Southern Nigeria, that the mysteries of the ceremony "are kept from women." The principal festival takes place

> in June, when the crops are ripening in the farms, the first fruits begin to come in and the help of the dead is most needed. The eve of the festival is called Ikunle, kneeling, since the principal members spend the whole night in the sacred grove on their knees while they hold communion with, and pray to, the ancestors. . . . The Images, dressed in their long robes with a net or wooden mask over the face, parade the streets, jumping about [dancing] . . . accompanied by friends who keep the bystanders at a distance with their long wands.[120]

The critical point here is that the ceremony was performed to honor the ancestors, especially those who founded towns: "The next morning, following the night in the sacred grove, they form a procession to visit the ruler of the town, who salutes them and receives their blessing, after which a dance is held and the tunes peculiar to them are played." As in Kunering, women were not permitted to participate in the ceremony, and, again as in Kunering, an instrument similar to the whip was used to prevent interference with the ceremony.[121]

Over a period of eight years, during the 1950s and 1960s, Joshua Leslie observed the Egun masquerade on numerous occasions among the Yorubas, for whom the circle was an important, recurring symbol. His description of the Egun secret society recalls Talbot's findings and reinforces the view that Egun rites are an analogue to, perhaps one of the sources of, the Kuners dance in North Carolina, a state in which Yorubas and other Nigerian peoples, including Ibos, were represented:

In traditional Yoruba Society there are masquerades in which the founding fathers of the village or town are worshipped and the wearing of the mask is meant to embody the ancestral figure. Sometimes you get men wearing masks representing all the ancestors of the town. The Egun masquerade is also a way of establishing certain rights and authorities of age and sex. The whip is carried so that certain people can't see the masqueraders—the embodiment of the spirit—carrying the God. Certain families have the right to carry the gods and certain people can't witness them doing so—women and children.[122]

Owing to the impact of Nigerian culture on Dahomey, Africans from Dahomey were familiar with Egun ceremonies, and the presence of Dahomeans in North Carolina, together with Nigerians, could well account for the visibility and strength of Kunering there. Because of that presence, Kunering took at least two forms, with or without the suggestion of female involvement. When some men masqueraded as women, it was apparently because Dahomeans made up the bulk of their ranks—first-generation Yorubas or Ibos would hardly have participated—and Dahomean women were not present to play female roles.

It is obvious . . . that the Egu cult in Abomey has been strikingly assimilated to the Dahomean patterns of ritual observance. . . . One of the outstanding characteristics of the Egungun in Nigeria is the fact that women are strictly prohibited from having any contact with the masked figure; indeed, since for a woman to see any part of the body of a masked dancer meant death for her as well as for the dancer, the contrast of the Abomey Egu ceremony with the Nigerian Egungun customs is apparent at once.[123]

Africans were so given to secret societies, and their purposes and characteristics were generally so similar, that a great many ceremonies across Central and West Africa involving the use of masks and costumes—signs that ancestral figures are being represented—might resemble and be related to John Kunering, and might have enabled Africans from various parts of Africa to identify with and join in Kunering in North Carolina, since masks are used universally to represent ancestral figures. Moreover, a number of African secret societies excluded women and children, keeping them at a distance during their ceremonies, as in the case of the Egun. Yet one Egun ceremony bears, it appears, directly on Kunering. Referring to that ceremony, Talbot remarks, "In several ways it resembles the European Christmas, as it is an occasion for the reunion of the family and of friends, and is treated as a general holiday. . . . Presents are given and the 'play' is repeated in the various 'quarters' of the town."[124] Such practices are not that dissimilar from Kunering in North Carolina, where Africans found reinforcement for Egun-type practices in the Christmas season. Knowing that in North America Christmas was the main religious period for the dominant group when families gathered, exchanged gifts, worshiped, and enjoyed the festivities of the occasion, the slaves took advantage of that time to revive African cultural expression along somewhat similar lines, since in Africa exchanges of gifts at reunions of family and friends on holidays were not uncommon, especially on important religious occasions. Exchanges of gifts, such as they were, among slaves were often accompanied by the receipt of gifts from the master and, in the context of John Kunering, "presents" in the form of donations after performances.

At the elaborate Collins estate, Somerset Place, on Lake Scuppernong, in Washington County, North Carolina, influential whites frequently gathered and witnessed

African rituals, especially John Kunering, which were in full flower in the 1840s and 1850s. The approximately three hundred slaves working "several thousand acres of arable land," which yielded "a princely income" annually, could scarcely have been more African; this was understood by Dr. Edward Warren, who visited the plantation over many years and was an intimate associate of its rich ruler. There he saw Africans and their descendants "John Kunering," decided that the ceremony had some tie to religion as other white observers found the ring shout "semi-religious," and shrewdly but not altogether accurately offered as evidence of the "connection" that the slaves only participated in it on the most sacred Christian holiday.[125]

As African as the Kunering performances in North Carolina town were, they were more rarefied in the countryside at the Collins estate, where the majority of blacks, "never having been brought into relations with other representatives of their race . . . had retained many of the ideas and traditions of their native land." Warren heard some speak a language that probably was typical of that spoken by Africans in places where they outnumbered or had little contact with whites: that is, like Gullah-speaking blacks who lived on the Sea Islands, off the coast of South Carolina and Georgia, they could shift from intelligible English to an incomprehensible mixture, except to the trained ear, of African and English words regulated by African grammar and syntax, the African words increasing in proportion to the desired degree of unintelligibility. Warren thought the mysterious language confined to "'Guinea negroes . . . remnants of the cargoes of African slaves . . . brought into those waters and sold at handsome prices to the neighboring planters."

> These antiquated darkeys spoke a sort of gibberish, which was a medley of their original dialect and the English language, and to me was perfectly unintelligible. They retained all of their original fetich superstitions and were as uncivilized, even in their old age, as when they roamed in youthful freedom among the jungles of the dark continent.[126]

The influence of Africa was present in most if not all aspects of "kunering," especially in the "ragman," the "leading character"

> whose "get-up" consists in a costume of rags, so arranged that one end of each hangs loose and dangles; two great ox horns, attached to the skin of a raccoon, which is drawn over the head and face, leaving apertures only for the eyes and mouth; sandals of the skin of some wild "varmint"; several cow or sheep bells or strings of dried goats' horns hanging around their shoulders, and so arranged as to jingle at every movement; and a short stick of seasoned wood, carried in his hands.[127]

Another "character" in the ceremony, Number Two, was played by "the best looking darkey of the place, who wears no disguise." He wore his "Sunday-go-to-the-meeting suit" and carried a small cup or bowl to collect the "presents." His attire appears to have been perfectly acceptable to the other slaves, even welcome, perhaps an acceptable aspect of improvisation, in that context. In any case, another half a dozen important performers were active, "each arrayed fantastically in ribbons, rags, and feathers, and bearing between them several so-called musical instruments or 'gumba boxes,' which consist of wooden frames covered over with tanned sheep-skins," African-made instruments in North America. These performers were as a rule "followed by a motley crowd of all ages, dressed in their ordinary working clothes, which seemingly comes as a guard of honor to the performers."[128]

Their movement as a group amounted to a procession or parade, first to the great house, where, as they reached the front door, the musicians "beat their gumba-boxes violently" and the "ragman" and character Number Two "entered upon a dance of the most extraordinary character," structured yet allowing for freedom of invention, "a combination of bodily contortions, flings, kicks, gyrations, and antics of every imaginable description, seemingly acting as partners, and yet each trying to excel the other in the variety and grotesqueness of his movements."[129] However assimilated Number Two may have appeared, his performance in the dance was wholly African, the forms of dance and their substance sacred. It thus seems that, despite the Sunday-go-to-meeting attire he wore, he was an African religious figure of some stature on the Collins estate.

In Kunering there was not only the usual improvisation in dance paralleling the endless variations on themes in music but also the extemporaneous creation of song, or so it seemed to Warren, with character Number Two leading with lines full of irony:

My massa am a white man juba!
Old missus am a lady, juba!
De children am de honey-pods, juba! juba!
Krismas come but once a year, juba!
Juba! juba! O, ye juba!
De darkeys lubs de hoe-cake, juba!
Take de "quarter" for to buy it, juba!
Fetch him long, you white folks, juba! juba!
Krismas come but once a year, juba.
Juba! juba! O, ye juba!

Building on the irony of the performance, "the whole crowd joined in the chorus, shouting and clapping their hands in the wildest glee." After singing his song, Number Two danced toward the master "with his hat in one hand and a tin cup in the other, to receive the expected 'quarter,' and while making the lowest obeisance," with great irony shouted, "May de good Lord bless old massa and missus and all de young massas, juba!" All the while the "ragman" was singing "at the top of his voice,"

My massa am a white man juba!
Old missus am a lady, juba!
De children am de honey-pods, juba! juba!
Krismas come but once a year, juba!
Juba! juba! O, ye juba![130]

In that context, the opinion of a great authority on slavery is relevant: "The real feelings and opinions of the slaves were not much known or respected by their masters. The distance between the two was too great to admit of such knowledge." So it was when slaves sang,

I am going away to the Great House farm,
O, yea! O, yea! O, yea!
My old master is a good old master,
O, yea! O, yea! O, yea![131]

Warren was convinced that Kunering "was based on some festive ceremony which the Negroes had inherited from their African ancestors." While in Egypt, he met "the exact counterpart of the old 'Guinea negroes' of the Lake," who evoked memories of his days among slaves in North Carolina. Except for the lyrics of the Kuner song heard at the Collins estate, he had witnessed a ceremony by blacks "absolutely identical" with the one he had seen in Carolina. In Egypt they "amused themselves," he thought, with Kunering "at Byram—the principal feast of the Koran."[132] The finding by Warren is intriguing and deserves investigation because it raises the important question of whether Kunering originated in Egypt and because it strongly suggests that the phenomenon, thought to be widespread in West Africa, was indeed even more pervasive. A critical point is that Warren's reference to the religiosity of Kunering at the Byram feast is further evidence of its religious nature in North American slavery.

The importance of the African religious component was recognized by him more generally. This was a key consideration because the Collins family had a resident pastor to impart Christianity to the hundreds of slaves on the plantation. Consequently, the slaves on the Collins estate received more than the usual amount of attention from whites interested in Africans becoming Christians. Though they were "rampant Christians, with 'the service' on the tips of their tongues," slaves at Somerset Place retained "faith in evil genii, charms, philters, metempsychosis, etc., and they habitually indulged in an infinitude of cabalistic rites and ceremonies." It is small wonder, therefore, that Warren found it "a constant source of interest to see the negroes flocking to church on Sundays, participating in the services—for they knew every word of the 'prayer book'—and partaking of holy communion at the same table with their master and members of his family."[133]

The composition of the crowd of Kuners in the North Carolina countryside, with slaves of all ages represented, guaranteed the persistence of the tradition, the old Africans forming the principal links to the past and being succeeded in that role, in graduated stages, by younger Africans—the whole process sustained by all of the participants, for they came from cultures in which immemorial custom was valued. If, then, the old in slave communities commanded respect on most matters, on those of greatest import to their people cultural transmission was all but guaranteed, especially in religion, with its attendant dances and songs to the ancestors. The scores of young blacks participating in the Kunering ceremony were, therefore, as vital to its perpetuation as the children who participated in the ring shout were to its transmission to succeeding generations.

VIII

The earliest memories of many slave children were of the ceremonies of their parents, relatives, and other blacks in the slave community. It was not, in fact, uncommon for special arrangements to be made for the attendance of infants on such occasions. When one considers that the most important ceremonies occurred in the slave quarters, where the children lived, and in the secrecy of the forests, where the children were found as well, the transmission of culture from the old to the young seems inevitable, a development that could not be prevented, short of the destruction of black people. The preservation of their culture in the North is a measure of the extent to which, year after year, they successfully congregated, then dispersed, retaining values fundamental to their culture though greatly outnumbered.

No doubt the scattering of slaves in tiny numbers in the households of Northern slaveholders contributed to the view, widely entertained by historians, that African culture never took hold in the Northern colonies, let alone lasted throughout and beyond the slave era—not an astonishing view, since African culture is not thought to have taken hold substantially in the South. What was once noted in the nineteenth century but has since been ignored by almost all scholars is that African cultural influence in the North was widespread and continuous during the slave era.[134] The power of that influence was due in part to slaves and free blacks seeking out each other for cultural reinforcement, their relative scarcity contributing to their determination to be in each other's company and to the vitality with which they expressed themselves culturally, dominating the festivals in which they participated.

What the African offered in music and dance to most whites appeared so peculiar in expression and so light of heart, some whites must have thought, as to constitute the soul of holiday cheer. Besides, there were practical reasons for allowing blacks to "amuse" themselves. The calculus of control often required their overindulgence in drink, particularly in the South, where revolt was most feared and measures taken to prevent it exceeded all reasonable lengths. Though the matter of control, for obvious reasons, was not of equal weight in the North, it nonetheless was one reason that whites permitted such ceremonies as New England's election day or parade of governors. The New Englander's disinclination to suppress the African to anything like the degree to which he was suppressed in the South was illustrated by the size of the election day ceremonies in several New England colonies, the masters permitting slaves to travel considerable distances to participate.

New England slaves gathered on holidays in large numbers for public recreation and amusement and, though whites usually did not know it, for religious observance. Hubert H. S. Aimes, an early student of African culture in America, notes that "one of these days was election day when the whole community took a holiday and gathered in towns to vote." It was "the occasion for a pompous and ceremonious parade by the Negroes," a practice apparently begun around 1750 and continued for a century.[135] Though the parades of blacks were African in inspiration and style, their elections were modeled after those of whites. In fact, blacks staged mock elections of their own as a result of encouragement from whites, elections that replicated the form of those of whites.

Between 1730 and 1750, African imports to New England increased substantially, and "at the latter date, numbered as slaves . . . about 3,500." Before that time, blacks were not sufficiently numerous to have introduced and sustained a parade, at least not one impressive in size. By 1780, in Connecticut, however, they numbered 6,000, and the parade was enthusiastically supported in several towns, as it was in Rhode Island towns, where they numbered 4,000 in 1780. Africans seasoned in the West Indies and those directly from Africa constituted the bulk of the slaves brought into New England, that is, most of them were African in sensibility and outlook. Advertisements indicate

Gold Coast Negroes, considered "of highest quality," were most sought after, as "in South Carolina and the West Indies." In 1762, for example, a New England merchant offered "a few prime men and boy slaves from the Gold Coast," which meant that there, as in other sections of New England to which Gold Coast blacks were brought, a ring dance in some form was practiced as in the South and in sections of the North other than New England. According to Lorenzo Greene, Africans were "conspicuously 'played up' in advertising columns of the newspapers, including very likely, agreeable and healthy Negro boys and girls lately imported from Guinea."[136]

Thousands of young Africans, with the permission of their masters, joined older ones in parades in Massachusetts, Rhode Island, and Connecticut:

> They decked themselves out in striking or fantastic costumes, and on horseback or on foot accompanied their "governor" through the streets. The parade included an accompaniment of hideous music, and was followed by a dinner and dance in some commodious hall hired for the purpose. Sometimes, however, the dinner and dance were not preceded by the parade.[137]

Since first-generation Africans constituted the bulk of adult blacks in New England in 1780, whatever the significance of the parade in the minds of the most acculturated among them, the majority paraded, danced, and made music as Africans. This should not surprise us, considering what we know of the functions of dance and music in Africa and their strength in the American South. Moreover, the literature reveals no attempts on the part of white New Englanders to place severe restrictions on the manner in which the slaves carried out either the festivities of the parade or the dinner, which took place in several New England towns, and the dance that followed. The accretions of Africans that made possible New England parades by 1750 guaranteed, since music and dance were at the heart of the parades, a sacred dimension to the ceremonies that allowed ample room for joyous expression and entertainment—as on ceremonial occasions in Africa.

In Rhode Island, election day gave "great delight to the young and animated sons of Africa," who found the time to entertain and instruct by telling tales in their native languages. In fact, the announcement of the election of a new governor of the blacks was known to occasion "a general shout . . . every voice upon its highest key, in all the various languages of Africa," which meant a sense of community, of underlying cultural unity, was felt despite linguistic and other differences among them.[138] Within the language groups represented, on the occasion of the parades and at other times, there were Africans who found it safer and more resonant spiritually to express their deepest concerns and fondest hopes in their native tongues, an aspect of slavery no less real for being largely and forever lost to history. But we do know that Africans were speaking in various languages in New England, as they were in Philadelphia in 1800, and found their native languages an important means of communicating all sorts of sentiments they would not have dared utter in English. The clearest indictments of slavery and the deepest expressions of sorrow must have been spoken in the native tongues and sung as well, but they are unrecorded. We are left, at best, with expressions of joy shouted in many languages upon the announcement of the Negro governor, their essential oneness affirmed through the consensus reached.

A wide range of activity excited Africans on election days. They played games, played on the instruments of their native countries and fiddled, danced and drank. They were the center of attraction for all: when they cudgeled, jumped, and wrestled, whites stood observing, as they did when they paraded before the election ball, which was a favorite. Jane De Forest Shelton notes that it was common for entire families of blacks to participate in the events of the day in Connecticut—"a babe in arms being no drawback, as the tavern keeper set apart a room and provided a caretaker for them" during the dinner and dance. The dancing characteristically lasted into the next day.

> Sometimes more than a dozen little wooly-heads would be under surveillance, while the light-hearted mothers shuffled and tripped to the sound of the fiddle. New Haven and Hartford, as well as intervening towns, were represented. Supper was served for fifty cents each, and they danced and feasted with a delight the more sedate white man can hardly appreciate, spinning out the night and often into the next day.[139]

Platt writes that "the old negroes aided in the plan" of the Negro governor, a plan that, according to Isaac W. Stuart, included "ceremonies." Given the role of elders in Africa in helping to determine the spiritual direction of their people, it follows that old Africans in New England played a similar role, helping to determine what would take place, and how, on election day, the most important public ceremony for New England blacks.

Historians who argue that African dance was "subdued" among slaves in America are contradicted by the vigorous rhythmic motion, and the words of New England Negroes. "A newspaper notice of more than fifty years ago," Shelton wrote in 1894, "strikes the key note of the great day":

ATTENTION . . .

There will be a general election of the colored gentlemen of Connecticut, October first, twelve o'clock noon. The day will be celebrated in the evening by a dance at Warner's tavern, when it will be shown that there is some power left in muscle, catgut, and rosin.

By order of the Governor
From Headquarters.[140]

Slave dance in New England was not substantially different from black dance in the South, on the continent of Africa, or wherever black men and women gathered, for New England slaves had come from many different sections of black Africa, as had slaves in the South and elsewhere in the Americas. The same is largely true of the music made by New England and Southern slaves in the eighteenth century and later. Since African music was described as "hideous" by some whites, the fact that Africans did not regard it that way suggests the presence in New England and the South of an African aesthetic or standard of beauty radically different from that of whites. The rhythms and the means by which they were conveyed formed, across ethnic lines, cultural bonds for slaves on ceremonial occasions generally, helping to determine performance style in dance and song and group interplay, including walking and talking. Such was the case in New England, where the drum was among the instruments "played on." The pronounced rhythms, pervasive both in black Africa and in black

America, despite differences in language, were especially unifying when blacks danced, sang, played instruments, or paraded.

Blacks selected "their best and ablest men" as governors. Though the Negro governor had no legal power, he exercised, together with the lieutenant governor, justices of the peace, and sheriffs he sometimes appointed, "considerable control over the Negroes throughout the state" of Connecticut. The parade, led by a prominent black leader, and the election were used by slaveowners as a means of indirectly ruling blacks. The irony was sharp as the Puritan gentry promoted a certain democracy among blacks the more effectively to enslave them. Respect for Connecticut's Negro governor was substantial enough to reinforce values drawn on for the parade, and other aspects of ceremonies of the blacks, and more:

> The person they selected for the office in question was usually one of much note among themselves, of imposing presence, strength, firmness and volubility, who was quick to decide, ready to command, and able to flog. . . . He settled all grave disputes in the last resort, questioned conduct, and imposed penalties and punishments sometimes for vice. . . . He was respected as "Gubernor" . . . by the Negroes throughout the state, and obeyed almost implicitly.[141]

Platt refers to elderly Negroes aiding the governor in his effort to assure the morality and honesty of their people, a process carried out less obviously to outsiders but apparently with some degree of rigor in slavery and later. Whatever the ultimate intent of New England slaveowners in fostering limited Negro rule, a great deal that was African in morality, especially respect for elders and ancestors and the immemorial uses of art to those ends, was conveyed to younger blacks, extending Africanity over time. We can establish the existence of storytelling in New England by elders, and art there, like the telling of tales in the South, was a primary means of pointing to a terribly complex reality, and the lessons arrived at from dealing with it. A special freedom was afforded slave storytellers in the last half of the eighteenth century, when the number of first-generation Africans was considerable, in the North and the South, because whites did not understand their native tongues (or even acknowledge them as legitimate languages). The stories told in New England, like those collected later by Adams and Faulkner in the South, must have been based mainly on actual experiences at a time when large numbers of New England slaves had experienced the Atlantic voyage. There is little question that, considering the rich variety of African languages heard in New England, tales at least as ethnic as those later rendered in English and collected in the South were routinely told, especially since African cultural resources were then accessible to storytellers who were themselves born in Africa.

If Africans chose their election day leader out of concern for ethnic background, the available documents do not record it. For two, possibly three, generations, those engaged in the selection process were from various ethnic groups, as were those selected to represent them. Yet a common perception of their predicament led first-generation Africans in the North as well as the South to subordinate ethnic prejudices to the demands of the New World, to their interest in rising above their status as an enslaved people, and there is no indication that their masters played off one ethnic group against another. Nevertheless, the influence of the master class was a factor to be reckoned with in the election process and ceremonies. There is some evidence that the prospective governor's financial backing was important to his chances for election, just as the support of their masters made it possible for blacks generally to participate in the events of the day and the night. Nevertheless, the background of oppression led slaves, when the votes were counted and announced, to become more united than before as the "defeated candidate was . . . introduced by the chief marshal and drank the first toast after the inauguration, and all animosities were forgotten." The governor, at dinner, "was seated at the head of the long table, under trees or an arbor, with the unsuccessful candidate at his right and his lady at his left."[142]

Ethnic allegiances were greater in Brazil and in islands like Cuba, where parades paralleling those of the Negro governor occurred. While the concentration of Africans of specific ethnic groups in Cuba and elsewhere in the Americas was greater, African cultural features were not that much greater there than in North America. For instance, Africanity in the parade of kings in Cuba was certainly not in every particular more pronounced than in the parade of governors in New England. Perhaps an important factor regulating perceptions of culture in the West Indies and Brazil is that the white observer, because of the larger numbers of Africans in proportion to whites and the consequent impact of African culture generally, more readily conceded what was African in the cultures of the blacks. In America, by contrast, much of African culture was hidden from whites, and when not hidden, as in the parade of governors, was less likely to be considered influential. But understanding what is African in cultural expression outside America is, as we have seen, an important means of more easily identifying African culture in America. In a passage that bears directly on New England governors, Aimes notes regarding Brazil and Cuba:

> There is an abundance of contemporary evidence showing the condition of the Negroes in these colonies, and the government, in Cuba at least, legally recognized and made use of their African customs as a part of the local police as a means of controlling the Negro population.[143]

A critical passage, from *Letters from Havana, during the Year 1820,* is quoted by Aimes:

> Each tribe or people has a king elected out of their number, whom they rag out with much savage grandeur on the holidays on which they are permitted to meet. . . . Almost unlimited liberty was given to the Negroes. Each tribe, having elected its king and queen, paraded the streets with a flag, having its name and the words *Viva Isabella,* with the arms of Spain, painted on it. Their majesties were dressed in the extreme of the fashion, and were ceremoniously waited on by the ladies and gentlemen of the court. . . . They bore their honors with that dignity which the Negroes love so much to assume.[144]

The behavior of blacks in New England on election day was not dissimilar. Caulkins, an authority on election day, describes Governor Samuel Huntington following an election:

> Riding through the town on one of his master's horses, adorned with painted gear, his aides on each side, *a la militaire,* himself sitting bolt upright and moving with a slow majestic pace, as if the universe was looking on. When he mounted or dismounted, his aides

flew to his assistance, holding his bridle, putting his feet into the stirrup, and bowing to the ground before him. The Great Mogul in a triumphant procession never assumed an air of more perfect self-importance than the Negro Governor.[145]

In each case, the governor or king carried himself as ruler and treated his followers like subjects; in each, African cultural forms were similar enough for the followers to act in concert; in each, the black "ruler" controlled on behalf of others; in each, there was also more latitude for African autonomy than slaveowners imagined, thanks to the impenetrability of numerous African cultural forms, including linguistic ones, to almost all whites. The parallels are strong enough to suggest the existence of elements of a Pan-African culture in New World slavery in the parades of governors and kings and more, especially since substantial numbers of slaves in Cuba and North America came from essentially the same areas of Africa, from the undulating stretch of land along the Guinea Coast that, curving through Angola, helped give the world the ring shout. Related to the question of origins is the fact that, in the New World, Africans evolved along parallel lines in their cultural forms—in Cuba "screeching out the songs of their nations to the music and rattles, tin pans, and tambourines,"[146] in New England shouting approval of election results in "all the various languages of Africa," in Philadelphia singing the various languages of Africa while dancing the ring shout in squads.

The evidence suggests that the parades of kings and governors were parts of a larger cultural configuration, and this reinforces our claim that a Pan-African culture existed in the Americas. For example, in Albany, New York, on Pinkster Hill, there was "this great festival of the negroes," whose similarity to the New England parade of governors and to the Cuban parade of kings is striking. Pinkster festivals occurred at a time "when every family of wealth or distinction possessed one or more slaves." Usually beginning in May and lasting for a whole week, the ceremony was also known as "the carnival of the African race," and it was thought the Africans "indulged in unrestrained merriment and revelry," a judgment made of African rituals generally. The surroundings were at times not unlovely, nature being generous with her beauty despite human oppression. Spring lilacs "were everywhere," and azaleas "saturated the bright morning air with their ever-delicious fragrance," so there were grounds for merriment, especially for the young, white and black, who wore their best clothes for the festival on Albany's Pinkster Hill.[147]

While whites participated in the celebration in a variety of capacities and attended the events of the week in large numbers, apparently mingling freely with the blacks, the center of attention was the black Pinkster king and his throng of followers. And though it is not certain how the idea of a Pinkster king was born or whether he exercised an authority among his own comparable to that of the New England governor or the African king in Cuba, he was treated like a sovereign by his people. It is likely that regard for the Pinkster king extended beyond the days of celebration since, in addition to being a man of impressive manner and carriage, he was nearly seventy, a distinguished elder to the slave population by the time of the last Pinkster celebration, in 1811, and presumably the king of all New York blacks. On that occasion, the crowd wound its way up avenues toward Pinkster Hill over the seven days of the festival. On the second day—the day when the king made his appearance—important whites, carefully guided by trusted slaves through the densely populated streets, could hear before them "sounds of many voices, harmoniously intermingled with the occasional shouts of boisterous mirth," and, on arrival, found the field "darkened" by the gathering crowd,

> consisting chiefly of individuals of almost every description of feature, form and color, from the sable sons of Africa, neatly attired and scrupulously clean in all their holiday habiliments, to the half clad and blanketed children of the forest, accompanied by their squaws, these latter being heavily burdened with all their different wares, such as baskets, moccasins . . . and many other things . . . and boys and girls of every age and condition were everywhere seen gliding to and fro amid this motley group.[148]

Everyone was out to witness the performance of black "royalty," which had stayed in seclusion on the first day, as if to heighten the interest it inevitably provoked among whites and blacks and Indians. A portent of what was to come was the body servant to one of the wealthiest of New Yorkers—a servant acting as master of ceremonies whose "grace and elegance of manner . . . characterized his progress through life until his dying day" and to whom "was unanimously entrusted the arduous duty of reducing to some kind of order this vast mass of incongruent material, which his superior ability soon enabled him to accomplish with complete success."[149] This sense of Negro aristocracy was not uncommon among blacks in the colonial and early national periods or, for that matter, in antebellum America and later, and owes a great deal to African tradition. One need only recall that thousands of members of royal families were removed from Africa and taken to North America, where they often became the slaves of far less cultivated men and women. But some recognition of those traits was accorded at Pinkster ceremonies, as in New England at the governor's parade, and the parallels were also noticeable in other respects:

> The hour of ten having now arrived, and the assembled multitude being considered most complete, a deputation was then selected to wait upon their venerable sovereign king, "Charley of the Pinkster Hill," with the intelligence that his respectful subjects were congregated, and were anxiously desirous to pay all proper homage to his majesty their king. Charles originally came from Africa, having . . . been brought from Angola. . . . He was tall, thin and athletic; and although the frost of nearly seventy winters had settled on his brow, its chilling influence had not yet extended to his bosom, and he still retained all the vigor and agility of his younger years. Such were his manly attributes at this present time. . . . Never, if our memory serve us, shall we forget the mingled sensations of awe and grandeur that were impressed on our youthful minds, when first we beheld his stately form and dignified aspect, slowly moving before us and approaching the centre of the ring.[150]

Arrangements were completed for the dancing to commence, the king having already been greeted by many in the crowd. Assisted by his aides, the master of ceremonies had "partially restored" peace and tranquility as the audience awaited the next, decidedly African stage of the ceremony. The dancers on the green were prepared to dance until exhaustion and joined in the dance at various times with "utmost energy until extreme fatigue or weariness compelled them to retire and give space to a less exhausted set." The intensity of the performance matched that of dancers in Virginia,

South Carolina, North Carolina, and other areas in the South, the rhythms danced to being no less complex since the drum was the principal instrument, and so "the dance went on with all its accustomed energy and might . . . until the shades of night began to fall slowly over the land, and at length deepen into the silent gloom of midnight." Still the performance continued, and the keen observer's eye, "weary in gazing on this wild and intricate maze," sought in the general throng the king, "and there, enclosed within their midst, was his stately form beheld, moving along with all the simple grace and elastic action of his youthful days, and sometimes displaying some of his many amusing antics, to the delight and wonderment of the surrounding crowd. . . . And thus the scene continued until the shades of night and morning almost mingled."[151]

The physical exertion evident here matched the energy expanded in dance on the continent. The infrequent opportunity to congregate contributed to the explosions of energy before the flame of movement died in the dusk of morning. Such opportunity to celebrate—the Pinkster festival began "on the Monday following the Whitsunday or Pentecost of the Catholic and Episcopal churches"—assured a focusing on religious thought and feeling. Despite white participation, the festival was acknowledged to be African. What Dr. James Eights said of Pinkster also applies to John Kunering and to the parade of governors: "The dance had its peculiarities as well as everything else connected with this . . . celebration."[152]

Apart from sharing religious values with them, the Pinkster ceremonies were similar to the parade of governors and kings in dance movement and rhythm, in honor guard and character of the processional. It is clear that Pinkster celebrations and the parade of governors were similar phenomena, variations or replications of roughly equivalent processional and political traditions of certain African regions, as were the counterclockwise dance of Central and West Africa. Moreover, both Pinkster and the parade of governors featured athletic events and "leaders" of similar demeanor inspiring similar respect from blacks and support and attention from whites. The parade of governors and the parade of kings were remarkably similar phenomena, and the Pinkster celebration was sufficiently like each, with the king and his attendants as pivotal figures, to suggest the possibility of similar or related sources. More knowledge of processions in Africa, especially since New York and New England were populated by blacks from essentially the same areas of Africa, will cast more light on patterns of Africanity in both regions and on their relation to those elsewhere in the Americas.

What we know of slave culture in the South, and of that of blacks in the North during and following slavery, indicates that black culture was national in scope, the principal forms of cultural expression being essentially the same. This is attributable mainly to the similarity of the African regions from which blacks were taken and enslaved in North America, and to the patterns of culture shared more generally in Central and West Africa. It should also be taken into account, in examining the national dimensions of black culture, that the scores of thousands of slaves who escaped to the North in the antebellum period served to assist in the sharing of cultural values, which was enhanced also by the relative absence of opportunities for blacks to secure an education in the North.

Evidence of the oneness of black culture in the twentieth century abounds. For example, the spread of Southern black music to the North with the creation of each new form, together with the migration of black musicians and blacks generally, placed Southern values within reach of all strata of Northern black communities. But because much that was Southern was African, Northern and Southern blacks from the start shared an essentially common culture.

In blinding whites to the value of African culture, racism helped the slave, as segregation helped his descendants, preserve essentials of African culture. But the preservation of that culture during slavery owed more to its affirmation by blacks than to the negative thrust of American life. Slave trading to America from 1750 to the end of 1807, a phenomenon largely neglected in its cultural dimension, greatly strengthened African values in America. Still, the preservation of those values in various forms was not an automatic process. On the contrary, slave ingenuity was indispensable to the survival of African culture in America.

IX

Thomas Wentworth Higginson and other Northerners who entered the Sea Islands during the Civil War agreed that the Christianity of blacks was different from that of whites. They knew that Christianity, as practiced by many whites, had no deep roots in slave communities, the ring shout appearing to be as ineradicable as it was pervasive. Moreover, few were the blacks who participated in Christian services who did not infuse them with their own spirituality, thereby transforming Christianity. Some notion of the place of Christianity in the ring shout, a phenomenon that fascinated Higginson, is found in his description of that ritual.

> All over the camp the lights glimmer in the tents, and as I sit at my desk in the open doorway, there come mingled sounds of stir and glee. Boys laugh and shout,—a feeble flute stirs somewhere in some tent, not an officer's,—drums throb far away in another . . . and from a neighboring cook-fire comes the monotonous sound of that strange festival, half pow-wow, half prayer-meeting, which they know only as "shout." These huts are usually enclosed in a little booth, made neatly of palm-leaves and covered in at top, a regular native African hut. . . . This hut is now crammed with men, singing at the top of their voices, in one of their quaint, monotonous, endless, negro-Methodist chants, with obscure syllables recurring constantly, and slight variations interwoven, all accompanied with a regular drumming of the feet and clapping of the hands, like castanets.[153]

The language is Gullah, the rhythms of feet and hands African, the chant African in performance style, the excitement building inside and outside the hut. Men begin to "quiver and dance," a circle forms and winds monotonously "round someone in the center," and excitement grows:

> Some "heel and toe" tumultuously, others merely tremble and stagger on, others stoop and rise, others whirl, others caper sideways, all keep steadily circling like dervishes; spectators applaud special strokes of skill; my approach only enlivens the scene; the circle enlarges, louder grows the singing, rousing shouts of encouragement come in; half bacchanalian, half devout . . . and still the ceaseless drumming and clapping in perfect cadence, goes steadily on. Suddenly there comes a sort of *snap,* and the spell breaks,

amid general sighing and laughter. . . . And this not rarely and occasionally, but night after night.[154]

It should not surprise us that the same people constructed African huts in which they shouted and, as Higginson demonstrates in a passage that recalls Herman Melville's *Redburn,* brought African sensibility to bear on Christianity: "Elsewhere, it is some solitary old cook, some aged Uncle Tiff, with enormous spectacles, who is perusing a hymn-book by the light of a pine splinter, in his deserted cooking booth of Palmetto leaves."[155]

The scenes could scarcely have been very different at the introduction of Christianity into African communities earlier in the century. There was a mixture of Western and African cultural qualities, but the African ones dominated. If there were dances of "red-legged soldiers doing right, and left and 'now-lead-delady-ober," and if psalms were "deaconed out" from memory, the "everlasting shout" was "always within hearing" and elsewhere there were "*conversazioni* around fires, with a woman for queen of the circle,—her Nubian face, gay headdress, gilt necklace, and white teeth, all resplendent in the glowing light." And at times, subtle mocking of Christian prayer:

> And yonder is a stump-orator, perched on his barrel, pouring out his exhortations to fidelity in war and in religion. To-night for the first time I have heard in a different strain, quite saucy, sceptical, and defiant, appealing to them in a sort of French materialistic style, and claiming some personal experience of warfare . . . he hit hard at the religionists: When a man's got de sperrit ob de Lord in him, it weakens him all out, can't hoe de corn . . . I mean to fight de war through, an' die a good sojer wid de last kick,—dat's *my* prayer![156]

The Christmas season was "the great festival of the year for this people." There were "prayer-meetings as late as they desired; and all night, as I waked at intervals, I could hear them praying and 'shouting' and clattering with hands and heels." The shout "seemed to make them very happy, and appeared to be at least an innocent Christmas dissipation, as compared with some of the convivialities of the 'superior race' hereabouts." Praying was endemic to gatherings around camp fires, and that was natural enough since the ring shout, the most sacred slave rite, was itself a form of prayer often engaged in around a fire. So strong was the devotional side of the slave personality that "the greatest scamps kneel and groan in their prayer-meetings with such entire zest."[157]

Incantations were heard everywhere, together with chanting. Especially at dusk the air was full of song and clapping of hands. A song encountered before, one "full of plaintive cadences," a chant of beauty, was recorded as sung by soldiers recruited for service in the Union army:

> *I can't stay behind, my Lord, I can't stay behind!*
> *O, my father is gone, my father is gone,*
> *My father is gone into heaven, my Lord!*
> *I can't stay behind!*
> *Dare's room enough, room enough,*
> *Room enough in de heaven for de sojer:*
> *Can't stay behind!*

It was sung at all seasons, and Higginson heard it one night "and, tracing it into the recesses of a cookhouse . . . found an old fellow coiled away among the pots and provisions," again like some character from a Melville novel, "chanting away with this 'Can't stay behind, sinner,' till I made him leave his song behind."[158]

Edward Channing Gannett's writing on the ring shout echoes Higginson:

> The "shout" is a peculiar service in which a dozen or twenty jog slowly round a circle behind each other with a peculiar shuffle of the feet and shake of arms, keeping time to a droning chant and hand-clapping maintained by bystanders. As the exercise continues, the excitement increases, occasionally becomes hysterical. Some religious meaning is attributed to it. . . .[159]

The hand clappers standing aside serve the role of drummers in Africa or in Suriname, of the violinist in Red Hill Churchyard, but Gannett had no way of seeing such connections. Without a grasp of the African background, there was simply no way for him or any other outsider to understand such phenomena. Yet it is to his credit that he reveals key aspects of slave culture, enabling us to see the confluence of cultural forces from new angles. He tells us, for example, that at least one group of black Baptists in the Sea Islands had "nearly the whole church management" in their hands, and the evidence he presents makes it clear that they grafted African institutions onto the church they attended:

> Subsidiary to the church are local "societies," to which "raw souls" are admitted after they have proved the reality of their "striving." This "striving" is a long process of self-examination and solitary prayer "in the bush," and so unremitting must be the devotion during this stage that even attendance at school is thought to interfere with the action of the Spirit.[160]

The level of self-discipline and meditation here calls to mind Eastern rather than Western religions; the references are to rites of passage through institutionalized societies the practices of which were secret, societies existing prior to the flight of slave masters as the Union forces entered the islands. The intensely religious atmosphere was encouraged by "the plantation leader," a figure whose precise religious role was not defined, but who called slaves to praise meetings three evenings a week and "thrice again on Sundays." Those among them who moved furthest into Christianity— or led whites to think they had—the ones who seemed "to distrust the institution [of the ring shout] a little," found license for it in the Bible, "which records, they say, that 'the angels *shout* in heaven.'" The immediacy of their faith was nearly palpable: "With religious ideas decidedly material, their religious feeling seems to be a real laying hold of spiritual truths." Religion encompassed more for them than for whites, rendering irrelevant the distinction between the sacred and the secular—a false dichotomy to a people for whom emotional fervor and dance were integral to religious expression.

> Religion contributes a large part of life's interest to the inhabitants of Port Royal; perhaps because, as the plant grows toward the light that is natural to it, they moved in the direction where alone they had free action. Not only their souls but their mind finds here its principal exercise, and in great measure it takes the place of social entertainment and amusements.[161]

Black youngsters were eager to "shout," forming themselves into a circle, singing and dancing on the slightest suggestion, assuring the perpetuation of important religious and artistic values of their people. Of all the literature on the shout, Charlotte Forten's writings are the most instructive on the mode of perpetuation. Again and again, she describes the young's unconscious contribution to cultural continuity in black South Carolina. "After school the children went into a little cabin near, where they kindled a fire, and had a grand 'shout.'" In a word, they expressed their regard for the Lord in African form and feeling, putting their stamp on the faith in their time as their parents had before them. "All the children had the shouting spirit. . . . They had several grand shouts in the entry. 'Look Upon the Lord,' which they sang to-night seems to me the most beautiful of all their shouting tunes. There is something within it that goes to the depths of one's soul." On another occasion, children traveled considerable distances to shout together: "This eve our boys and girls with others from across the creek came in and sang . . . several shouting tunes that we had not heard before; they are very wild and strange." One little child exclaimed, "All I want to do is sing and shout."[162] The shout was vigorously pursued in the last few years of slavery, the young regarding the practice as essential to their lives.

> In the evenings, the children frequently came in to sing and shout for us. These "shouts" are very strange,—in truth, almost indescribable. It is necessary to hear and see in order to have any clear idea of them. The children form a ring, and move around in a kind of shuffling dance, singing all the time. Four or five stand apart, and sing very energetically, clapping their hands, stomping their feet, and rocking their bodies to and fro. These are the musicians, to whose performance the shouters keep perfect time.[163]

For all her recognition of the paramount importance of the ring shout to the slave, Forten never suspected a connection between it and their value system—never realized, indeed, that the ceremony was, above all, devoted to the ancestral spirits, to reciprocity between the living and the dead. Had she understood that, she might have seen the relationship between the ring shout and the place of the elders in the life of the slave, for certainly there was no absence of respect among the slaves for old people. Still, her references to the shout convey a sense of abiding commitment to the ceremony on the part of the children. Not only did they emulate their elders by kindling a fire and dancing around it at night, but they rocked to and fro in usual ring shout form. A child named Prince, a large boy from one of the plantations, "was the principal shouter among the children," and he found it impossible "to keep still. . . . His performances were amusing specimens of Ethiopian gymnastics." A child of six named Amaretta was no less dedicated, at times singing a shouting song, also referred to earlier, that was a favorite of the adults. "Hold Your Light on Canaan's Shore," singing the parts to herself as she walked along:

> *What make ole Satan follow me so?*
> *Satan got nuttin' 't all for to do wid me.*
> CHORUS
> *Tiddy [Sister] Rosa, hold your light!*
> *Brudder Tony, hold your light!*
> *All de member, hold bright your light*
>   *On Canaan's shore!*[164]

A partial explanation of why the young ones threw themselves into the shout with such energy and so often, at the urging of others or on their own initiative, is contained in one of Forten's observations: "The children, too, are taught to be very polite to their elders, and it is the rarest thing to hear a disrespectful word from a child to his parent, or to any grown person." Forten's findings regarding the elders are supported by Gannett. A passage from his "The Freedmen of Port Royal" reveals much of African culture in addition to the respect the young have for the elders:

> Orphans are at once adopted by connections, and the sick are well nursed by their friends. The old are treated with great reverence, and often exercise a kind of patriarchal authority. Children are carefully taught "manners," and the common address to each other, as well as to the "buckra people," is marked by extreme courtesy.[165]

It followed that the children would emulate adults in matters of importance, children of "not more than three and four years old" entering the ring "with all their might." Since respect for the ancestors gave birth to the shout, it was natural that there would be respect for the elders, who were "closest to being ancestors."[166] Entering the ring was a means of renewing the most hallowed values of their people, of expressing them through song and dance that would later figure powerfully in the black American's "secular" repertoire.

It was no accident that students of the shout, lacking knowledge of its meaning in the African context, failed to grasp more than a fragment of its significance in the slave community and among free blacks. This was so mainly because blacks, determined to protect their culture, sent forth conflicting, confusing signals to those asking about the shout:

> But the shouting of the grown people is rather solemn and impressive. . . . We cannot determine whether it has a religious character or not. Some of the people tell us that it has, others that it has not. But as the shouts of the grown people are always in connection with their religious meetings, it is probable that they are the barbarous expression of religion, handed down to them from their African ancestors, and destined to pass away under the influence of Christian teachings.[167]

Much of the religious behavior of the elders, from whom children learned the shout, was in slavery concealed from whites in the way blacks generations later concealed African religious values from whites. Though whatever children do seems less threatening to their oppressors, those shouting with all their being found models for that as for other activity in their elders, the line of transmission extending in descending chronological order with the young learning much from each other. Culturally, one can almost see slave society whole by studying the role of slave youth in relation to themselves, their elders, and members of the larger society. In the culture of slave youths, a greatly neglected area, one finds the means by which values of immemorial vintage are preserved and extended into the future, passed on to youth by their elders.

The skill with which slave children mastered an African practice in one area reflects the degree of their command of others and tells us much about how culture is transmitted and received almost as an unconscious ornament of the child's inheritance. It was natural to find in their environment the gift of improvisation in dance, oratory, song, marching step, and the balancing of objects on their heads when marching. In their parades, "the 'route step'" was a challenge to military strictness as "the depths of theological gloom" were contrasted with jubilant chorus—a mixture of joy-pain that characteristically informs black music. The blacks were more at home culturally with themselves: "For all the songs, but especially for their own wild hymns, they constantly improvised" as they marched along. "The little drum corps kept in advance, a jolly crew, their drums slung over their backs, and the drum-sticks perhaps balanced on their heads," like emblems of Africanity. The leader of the parade—the supreme majorette—found in that occasion an opportunity to express qualities of Africanity:

> At the head of the whole force there walked, by some self-imposed preeminence, a respectable elderly female, one of the company laundresses, whose vigorous stride we never could quite overtake, and who had an enormous bundle balanced on her head, while she waved in her hand, like a sword, a long-handled tin dipper.[168]

That the ring shout flourished subterraneously at camp meetings in the state of Georgia and elsewhere—with children present at the ceremony and usually participating—is the surest evidence of its presence among slaves over wide areas of the South when they worshiped alone. If the shout was in fact a prominent, if mostly undetected, aspect of slave worship at camp meetings, then the extent to which Christianity penetrated the slave community without being Africanized must again be considered. The subterranean form taken by the shout at camp meetings was described by Fredrika Bremer, who visited a meeting in Macon, Georgia, in 1850, in which blacks were in the majority, numbering more than three thousand in a setting favorable to African values. The worshipers were separated before a platform on which stood preachers of both races, whites preaching to whites and blacks to blacks.

> The night was dark with thunder-clouds as well as natural darkness; but the rain had ceased, except for a few heavy drops, and the whole wood stood in flames. Upon eight fire-altars, or fire hills as they are called—a sort of lofty table raised on posts around the tabernacle—burned, with a flickering brilliance of flame, large billets of firewood containing a large amount of resin, while on every side in the woods, far away in its most remote recesses, large or smaller fires burned before tents or other places, illuminating the fir-tree stems, which appeared like columns of an immense temple consecrated to fire.[169]

Given the far-flung tents and fires, it is not surprising that Bremer found in each tent of the blacks some new phase of religious exaltation. In one she found "a whole crowd of blacks on their knees, all dressed in white, striking themselves on the breast, and crying out and talking with the greatest pathos." This could easily have been a scene in Dahomey, for there Africans were observed in similar ceremonies beating their breasts, a form of keeping time during musical performances on sacred occasions:

> Their songs are accompanied by gongs and rattles, and by a sound made by beating the chest with the open hand or clinched fist. . . . As the singing of and striking of gongs and chests and the playing of rattles continued, two of the men in the orchestra appeared to be possessed; it seemed that one of these might begin at any instant to dance. After a time, an old woman took up the sacrificial goat. . . . As she did this, the drums began to sound, and holding the sacrifice under her left arm, she slowly danced about the cleared

space three times in a counter-clockwise direction, ending with a series of shuffling steps in front of the drums.[170]

The beating of breasts that was a common phenomenon of ritualistic expression and associated with counterclockwise dance in Dahomey was not the only African practice witnessed. On entering another tent, Bremer saw women

dancing the "holy dance" for one of the newly converted. This dancing, however, being forbidden by the preachers, ceased immediately on our entering the tent. I saw merely a rocking movement of women who held each other by the hand in a circle, singing the while.[171]

Sir Charles Lyell in the 1840s witnessed a similar phenomenon, a modified version of the ring shout resulting from white objections to dance on religious occasions. On the Hopeton plantation, there was a rocking movement in the ring:

At Methodist prayer-meetings, they are permitted to move round rapidly in a ring, joining hands in token of brotherly love, presenting first the right hand and then the left, in which maneuver, I am told, they sometimes contrive to take enough exercise to serve as substitute for the dance. . . .[172]

Yet Lyell seemed unaware of the resentment felt by Africans at having to alter religious preferences because of whites. Bremer understood, as Lyell did not, that once whites were gone, Africans were likely to return to the ring ceremony without restraining themselves. Both observed the ceremony in Georgia conversion activity, so there is little reason to expect different responses to similar religious stimuli from people of essentially the same cultural background, especially considering interaction that had been occurring among them up to that time, transforming them into a single people. As a part of that process, thousands of Africans drawn from scores of plantations had occasion to meet at camp meetings in Georgia and to share religious practices and attitudes both formally and informally.

Whatever Lyell's naîveté regarding the effectiveness of Christian strictures against African religion, he thought Christianity had by no means been absorbed by blacks, which should have led him to suspect that, when they were alone, a different religion might appear. A rather low-level, though commendable, encounter between African and Christian values, he thought, was taking place, and not a creative melding largely under African control, as the presence of the circle indicates:

However much we may feel inclined to smile at some of these outward tokens of conversion, and however crude may be the notions of the Deity which the poor African at first exchanges for his belief in the evil eye and other superstitious fears, it is nevertheless an immense step in his progress toward civilization that he should join some Christian sect.[173]

Missionaries failed to halt African religion in Georgia because it took forms they did not understand or even recognize. Dahomean influence was even greater there than one would have suspected by combining the insights of Bremer and Herskovits; it also appeared in a form and a place in which whites would least expect African religious expression of any kind—in the quilts of slave women. Fashioned from throwaway cloth, slave quilts were used to clothe mysteries, to enfold those baptized with reinforcing symbols of their faith. Such quilts in Georgia bore a remarkable resemblance to Dahomean appliqué cloth. Harriet Powers's Bible quilt is a brilliant example both of that tradition and of Bakongo tradition, combining the two so naturally as to reflect the coming together of Dahomean and Bakongo people in American slavery.[174]

Born in Georgia in 1837, Harriet Powers may have been of Dahomean descent, but her command of Bakongo religious symbols was so profound, their intricacies in her hands so complete, that it is possible she was of Bakongo parentage. Of course, she might have been of both Bakongo and Dahomean heritage. But given the prevalence of ethnic forms in slave communities of the South, she perhaps absorbed the values of an ethnic group she was not born into as easily as she might have taken in those native to one or more parents.[175] The values of both peoples were represented in the Georgia of her youth, and she must have known them in a general religious sense before thinking of them in relation to quilts. We should not forget that Simon Brown, one of the greatest of storytellers and a keeper of Bakongo tradition of the most obscure kind, was born in the big house yet when bearly [sic] in his teens had command of symbols of African religious faith though he was neither a Christian nor, apparently, a devotee of African religion. If he was able to do so at so early an age from the big house, it is not unlikely that Powers in youth could also have absorbed African values either from there or from the quarters.

Her date of birth was approximately that of Brown, which means she was in her teens, as he was, in the 1850s and in her twenties at emancipation. Almost certainly she learned to do quilts before emancipation, since it was not uncommon for adolescent slave girls, or their adolescent descendants in our time, to take to making quilts. Through that process, she transmitted materially what Brown transmitted orally. So faithful is her rendering of the core of Bakongo religious thought that, were it not for the Dahomean features of her work, one might conclude her quilt was done in Congo-Angola. And yet the squared patterns of the fabric and depictions of characters are so close to those of Dahomey that one might, except for the four moments and other Bakongo symbols incorporated into the quilt, conclude it was fashioned there. Thus, her quilt is a symbol of the fusion of African ethnic traditions in slavery and later.

The depiction of crosses in the upper left corner of the quilt, in which four suns are represented, calls to mind the four moments of the sun, especially since the suns are patterned exactly as they are by Bakongo, which suggests that the same religious vision informed the crosses and suns—a vision of circularity.[176] It is also possible, though unlikely, that the particular cross depicted is Dahomean with a meaning different from that of the Bakongo cross. Even if that is so, it seems inconceivable that Bakongo slaves did not, when viewing a cross in such a context, derive four moments and the circle by moving in the accustomed way from one point of the cross to another. Given the Bakongo presence in North America and the influence of that group in the ring shout, in baptismal ceremonies, and in the construction of burial mounds, such an association was almost certainly made by slaves under their influence. That association was logical for slaves who affirmed the circularity of the cross, as in Virginia at baptismal ceremonies in which they sang of Christ dying on Calvary. But the crucifixion or superimposition of Christ is explicitly realized in the lower right-hand corner of the Bible quilt and helps to form an arc around a tiny manger in an extremely sub-tle melding of Christian and African values.[177]

Since Dahomeans were in Virginia in the time of Simon Brown, as they had been before his birth, and since specific reference was made in "How the Slaves Worshipped" to the use of quilts in baptismal ceremonies, one could hardly imagine a more subtle affirmation of African values than that which occurred when a quilt with crosses and suns was used to warm the shivering convert. And though the Ashanti cross, like the Dahomean, may not represent circularity and four moments, such representations might have been associated with it on a plantation on which the staff-cross was brandished and Gold Coast burial mounds constructed. The presence of customs grounded in ancestral concerns, such as the decoration of the burial mound, made it easier to invest another African cross, whether Ashanti or Dahomean, with the values of the Bakongo when the staff-cross was a focal point of ritual. Although these possibilities were real enough, there is no doubt that the Powers quilt, in its exacting reproduction of African symbols and processes, illustrates the persistence of African values in her consciousness at least as late as the 1890s, the decade in which the quilt was made. When asked about the meaning of her quilt, Harriet Powers responded at considerable length and in much detail, asserting that the quilt in every particular is Christian.[178]

Perhaps no one was better qualified to judge the impact of Christianity on free blacks and slaves than Bishop Daniel Alexander Payne, of the African Methodist Episcopal Church (A.M.E.). In 1878, in Philadelphia, Payne attended a "bush meeting" of black Christians and was so disturbed at seeing them do the ring shout that he "requested the pastor to go and stop their dancing." At the pastor's request, "They stopped their dancing and clapping of hands, but remained singing and rocking their bodies to and fro." The momentum of the performance continued through singing and rocking until Payne approached the leader of the shouters and "requested him to desist and to sit down and sing in a rational manner." Payne told him that such worship was "heathenish . . . disgraceful to themselves, the race, and the Christian name," at which point they broke up the ring and "walked sullenly away." But that was not enough for Payne, who had encountered the ring shout over a period of decades and still looked upon it as a powerful, dominating presence among the black masses, in the North and the South.

> After the sermon in the afternoon, having another opportunity of speaking alone to this young leader of the singing and clapping ring, he said: "Sinners won't get converted unless there is a ring." Said I: "You might sing till you fell down dead, and you would fail to convert a single sinner, because nothing but the Spirit of God and the word of God can convert sinners." He replied: "The Spirit of God works upon people in different ways. At camp meeting there must be a ring here, a ring there, a ring over yonder, or sinners will not get converted."[179]

The resistance to the jettisoning of African spiritual values in the conversion to Christianity was widespread among blacks, and no one was more aware of that than Payne, who had a dreadful time and dismal results in the effort, never understanding that the shout was a primary means of contact with and respect for the ancestral spirits

and the source of artistic expression to that end. It is small wonder that Payne, in believing there could be no Christian conversion for his people without abandonment of
the shout, encountered severe and wide opposition, for they believed there could be
no conversion except through the ring. In a word, he was asking them to give up the
products of ancestral genius as well as the means by which spiritual autonomy was
preserved, and with it a certain unity of being. And because the shout, prevalent in the
folktale, associated with the burial mound, and the primary means of encouraging that
unity, was the single most important cause of the formation of a common consciousness and ethos, Payne drew almost uniformly hostile reactions in attempting to extir-
pate it from black Christianity.

Nowhere was that hostility more actively expressed than in Baltimore, Maryland,
though Payne also had problems in Washington, D.C. Having opposed the singing of
spirituals in Bethel Church in Baltimore, he was rejected by a congregation led by two
women who, rising from a front row and approaching the pulpit with clubs, attacked
him and an assistant pastor. "The trouble grew out of my endeavor to modify the ex-
travagances in worship," including "their spiritual songs," he admitted. His assistant
was left in a puddle of blood, but Payne was not seriously injured, the blow directed
at him glancing off his shoulder. Though he contended he was able "to correct some
bad customs of worship, and especially to moderate the singing and praying bands,
which then [1850] existed in the most extravagant form" one wonders whether his successes, if they occurred, lasted, considering a later assertion:

> As to the "songs," as already stated, I had attempted to modify some of the extravagances
> in worship in Bethel Church. These songs were known as "Corn-field Ditties." I left them,
> considering myself unjustly rejected; nor would I return upon being urged by Bishop
> Quinn to go to take possession of the charge, supported by civil and ecclesiastical law. I
> declined on the ground that the people had deliberately rejected me, and as I had always
> exhibited a disinterested friendship for them, and had voluntarily rendered them signal
> service, if they did not want me, I did not want them.[180]

In fact, that is his tone in summing up the movement to end the ring shout of
black Christians. If anything, it is despairing, and Payne favored expulsion of the vast
majority of black Christians from the church as late as the 1870s, if the ring shout
could not be curbed. He admitted success only among the "intelligent," presumably
the tiny minority of "educated" blacks, among whom he succeeded in making the ring
shout appear "disgusting"; the ignorant masses regarded "the ceremony as the essence
of religion," and that applied to the masses in the District of Columbia, Pennsylvania,
Maryland, and other places to which he had traveled. "So much so was this the case
that," like the young man with whom he debated in Philadelphia, "they believed no
conversion could occur without their agency, nor outside of their own ring could any
be a genuine one." Though he remonstrated with numerous pastors for allowing such
practices, he met with the invariable response "that they could not succeed in restraining them, and an attempt to compel them to cease would simply drive them away
from our church."[181]

Payne thought a critical juncture was at hand, that the time had come when the
A.M.E. Church "must drive out this heathenish mode of worship or drive out all the

intelligence, refinement, and practical Christians who may be in her bosom."[182] One can almost sympathize with Payne, despite his ignorance of African religion and its impact on the spiritual, political, and artistic life of blacks and the nation. As slavery ended and the membership of black Baptists and Methodists increased and black churches proliferated, there was simply no easy way for the regular black Christian ministry— those ministers not grounded in the religion of the plantation slave—to affirm the religious vision of the new converts, which was alien to their sense of what was proper. Payne's predicament in 1878 and later was that the majority of black Christians in Pennsylvania and elsewhere seemed actually to be more African in religious practice than European.

> These "Bands" I have had to encounter in many places, and, as I have stated with regard to my early labors in Baltimore, I have been strongly censured because of my efforts to change the mode of worship or modify the extravagances indulged in by the people.[183]

The A.M.E. Church, headquartered in Philadelphia, the home of its founder, Richard Allen, with branches in many states, found its masses infected as by an "incurable religious disease," so much so that it was with Payne "a question whether it would not be better to let such people go out of the Church than remain in it to perpetuate their evil practice and thus do two things: disgrace the Christian name and corrupt others." What was all too frequently observed, that Christianity made little impact on the slave spiritually, was so revolting to Payne that it led him to oppose any semblance of African influence in the black religion of his era. He found the force of African spirituality almost superhuman, calling for a "cure" proportionate to the affliction, one that ruled out any compromise of visions, any synthesis of faiths. A powerful counterforce was needed because some of the most influential and popular preachers labored "systematically to perpetuate this fanaticism."

> How needful it is to have an intelligent ministry to teach these people who hold to this ignorant mode of worship the true method of serving God. . . . My observations lead me to the conclusion that we need more than an intelligent ministry to cure this religious fanaticism. We need a host of Christian reformers like St. Paul.[184]

But it was too late for African religion—and therefore for African culture—to be contained or reversed, because its advocates were practically the whole black population in America: the essential features of the ring shout were present in one form or another, and hardly a state in the Union was without its practitioners during and following slavery. Moreover, the shout continued to form the principal context in which black creativity occurred. Marshall Stearns had this in mind when writing that the "continued existence of the ring-shout is of critical importance to jazz, because it means that an assortment of West African musical characteristics are preserved, more or less intact, in the United States—from rhythms and blue tonality, through the falsetto break and the call-and-response pattern, to the songs of allusion and even the motions of African dance."[185]

The ring shout, prominent in Louisiana well before Bremer and Olmsted observed it in the 1850s, helped form the context in which jazz music was created. With scores of secret societies flourishing in New Orleans, financial as well as spiritual support was available to jazzmen performing on behalf of the societies, including performances at funerals, in which circularity was noted: In church, before reaching the cemetery, those who belonged to the various benevolent societies "circled the casket. Some . . . would shout and scream hysterically." After marching solemnly to the grave, they returned in a different mood, dancing "individual and various dances" as the band "burst into 'Just Stay A Little While,' " with relatives of the deceased "soon trucking with the rest of them."[186]

Of the shout and the life that accompanies it, Stearns offers the important insight that a large number of jazzmen "even among the ultra-moderns are familiar with all or part of it because they lived near one of the sanctified churches during childhood."[187] So it was with Milt Jackson, and so it was with perhaps the most original of jazz composers, Thelonious Monk, who frequently rose from his piano, cigarette in mouth, and proceeded to dance in a counterclockwise direction, his feet beating out intricate figures before he returned to the piano and joined his combo in playing music as advanced as any of his era.[188]

But jazz musicians merely formed the apex of the pyramid. Farther below, down among the masses that produced the jazzman and responded to his art, the ring shout continued to be expressed in even its most complex forms, at times in ways that recalled the Bakongo religious vision with almost startling clarity. Even among a people who practiced the shout vigorously and ubiquitously in the closing decades of the nineteenth century, the discovery of the ritual in the fullness of its Bakongo expression in the 1920s is but additional evidence of their ability to respond to oppression in ways that affirm values proper to them—in the teeth of that oppression. The classic case of such values melded with and transforming Christian values is that of Maum Hester of South Carolina.

> She was possessed with the idea that every day that passed carried with it a record of the deeds and thoughts which had been performed by each person. The sun carried the record somewhere to the center of the earth, where the moon and stars, the signs and seasons, all rested until their appointed time to appear. The "Lawd Jedus" presided over the entrance to this region, and observed the record which each day bore of the doings of mortal men which were to be stored up against the Judgment Day. Maum Hester's chief concern was that the record which the sun bore to her Lawd Jedus each night might prove acceptable to him.[189]

"Only the figure of Jesus Christ identifies Maum Hester's beliefs as Christian; the rest is saturated with Bakongo imagery," writes Anne Spurgeon in a brilliant paper on African spiritual influences in black American culture. Spurgeon's analysis is persuasive, for we have seen that "concepts of heaven and judgment" were not foreign to large numbers of Africans, especially Ibos and Bakongo, entering America.[190] The place of the cosmogram in the shout, however, was inspired in North America by the Bakongo, its presence within a ritual being the source of definitive power to all familiar with the four moments:

> She first opened her shutter wide toward the west, and then told how, as soon as the sun looked in at the window and told her he [the sun] was going to see the "Lawd Jedus," she stood there, "jus' lak-a-dat" . . . and repeated three times this formula: "Do, Lawd Jedus, is I please you dis day?" Each time that she repeated this form of invocation, after

walking around the room in a circle with the peculiar posture, step, and rapt expression which is characteristic of the Negro "shout." . . . After the third question, her emotional state bordered on hysteria. . . . "But de t'ird time, de sun he 'gin move, I see he shoutin'. Den I happy, by I know den I done please de Lawd Jedus dat day!"[191]

The anthropologist and folklorist Zora Neale Hurston makes the pioneering comment that

the Negro has not been christianized as extensively as is generally believed. The great masses are still standing before their pagan altars and calling old gods by a new name . . . so the congregation is restored to its primitive altars under the new name of Christ. Then there is the expression known as "shouting" which is nothing more than a continuation of the African "Possession" by the gods. The gods possess the body of a worshipper and he or she is supposed to know nothing of their actions until the god decamps. This is still prevalent in most Negro protestant churches and is universal in Sanctified churches.[192]

The basis for the shout's flourishing in the North was laid by the great migrations of blacks from the South from the close of the nineteenth century to the 1940s and later. The implications of this movement were enormous not only for black religion but for American culture—a subject of great importance that awaits full exploration. But already we know that the ring shout exists in America today with all the power of its expression more than a century ago. Stearn's and Hurston's suggestion regarding the sanctified church as a harborer of the shout is borne out by Baldwin's *Go Tell It on the Mountain* when, during Sunday morning services in the slums of Harlem in the 1940s—"the sisters in white, the brothers in blue, heads back; the white caps of the women seeming to glow in the charged air like crowns"—the piano player "hit the keys, beginning at once to sing, and everybody joined him, clapping their hands, and rising, and beating the tambourines."

While John watched, the Power struck someone, a man or woman; they cried out, a long wordless crying, and, arms outstretched like wings, they began the Shout. Someone moved a chair a little to give them room, the rhythm paused, the singing stopped, only the pounding feet and the clapping hands were heard; then another cry, another dancer; then the tambourines began again, and the cries rose again, and the music swept on again, like fire, or flood, or judgment. Then . . . like a planet rocking in space, the temple rocked with the Power of God. John watched, watched the faces, and the weightless bodies, and listened to the timeless cries.[193]

Notes

• • •

1. Robert F. Thompson estimates that 30 percent of the Africans brought to North America during the slave trade were brought from the Congo-Angola region of Africa. Phillip Curtin, on whom Thompson relied for the estimate, notes in some detail the complexities involved in determining Congo-Angolan influences in the New World. For example, regarding the nineteenth century, Curtin writes, "The 'Angola' of earlier tables can now be divided into two—'Congo North' taking in coastal points from Cape Lopez southward to and including the mouth of the Congo River, and 'Angola' now taken as Angola proper, the region from

Ambriz southward to Benguela." Thompson argues that what apparently happened in the New World was that "a mixture of Kongo and Kongo-related cultures were brought together" to strengthen the more important and salient "shared general Bakongo cultural traits, a fusion in which the memory and the grandeur and the name of Kongo itself was maintained." The estimate by Thompson of the percentage of Bakongo brought to North America is based on a lecture by Phillip Curtin. Conversation with Robert F. Thompson, July 24, 1986. James Rawley writes that 25 percent of the Africans brought into slavery in North America were from Congo-Angola and almost as many from Nigeria-Dahomey-Togo-Ghana: "Scrutiny of the African origins of American slaves in general reveals that about one-quarter of the whole came from Angola [Congo-Angola] and a lesser portion from the Bight of Biafra. Of the remainder, in descending order, the Gold Coast, Senegambia, the Windward Coast, and Sierra Leone, the Bight of Benin, and Mozambique-Madagascar supplied the rest." See Curtin, *Atlantic Slave Trade,* 241; Robert F. Thompson, *The Four Moments of the Sun* (Washington, D.C.: National Gallery of Art, 1981), 148; and James H. Rawley, *The Transatlantic Slave Trade* (New York: Norton, 1981), 335. A minimum of 50 percent of the Africans brought to North America—to the colonies and states discussed in this volume—were from Congo-Angola and from Nigeria, Dahomey, Togo, the Gold Coast, and Sierra Leone.

2. Talbot, *Southern Nigeria,* 804. Talbot writes, "The vast majority of dances in Southern Nigeria may be said to have to do with fertility in one or other of its aspects. It is interesting to think that it was out of similar dances, from the dithyrambs at the spring festival of Dionysus, of which the main object was the magical promotion of the food supply, that the drama of ancient Greece arose." Ibid.

3. Ibid., 803.

4. Thompson, *Four Moments,* 54, 28.

5. Parrish's observation that "the solo ring performance is apparently the only form in use" in North Carolina and Virginia and that "the ring shout seems to be unknown" is probably wide of the mark, as we shall see. Lydia Parrish, *Slave Songs of the Georgia Sea Islands* (New York: Creative Age Press, 1942), 54; Melville J. Herskovits, *Dahomey,* (New York: Augustin, 1938), 1:216.

6. Herksovits, *Dahomey,* 67–68.

7. Thompson, *Four Moments,* 28.

8. Ibid.

9. Suzzane Blier, "The Dance of Death," *Res* 2 (Autumn 1981):117.

10. Interview with Earl Conteh-Morgan, Spring 1984. Conteh-Morgan's description of the story-teller encircled by his listeners closely resembles Higginson's description of a storytelling scene in the Sea Islands, one that he rightly regarded as a major source of the means by which education occurred in the slave community:

    > Strolling in the cool moonlight, I was attracted by a brilliant light beneath the trees, and cautiously approached it. A circle of thirty or forty soldiers sat around a roaring fire, while the old uncle, Cato by name, was narrating an interminable tale, to the insatiable delight of his audience. . . . It was a narrative, dramatized to the last degree . . . and even I . . . never witnessed such a piece of acting. . . . And all this . . . with the brilliant fire lighting up their red trousers and gleaming from their shining black faces,—eyes and teeth all white . . . This is their university; every young Sambo before me, as he turned over the sweet potatoes and peanuts which were roasting in the ashes, listened with reverence to the wiles of the ancient Ulysses, and meditated the same.

    Thomas Wentworth Higginson, *Army Life in a Black Regiment* (New York: W. W. Norton, 1984), 36–38 (originally published in 1869).

11. Interview with Conteh-Morgan, Spring 1984.

12. Ibid.

13. Melville J. Herskovits, *The Myth of the Negro Past* (Boston: Beacon Press, 1941), 106–7.

14. The Arabic scholar and professor of African history John Hunwick disputes Turner's rendering of the pronunciation of the word *saut. Saut,* according to Hunwick, simply means "voice" or "sound." Interview with Hunwick, Spring 1984.

15. Melville J. Herskovits, *Rebel Destiny* (New York and London: Whittlesey House, McGraw-Hill, 1934), x, and chap. 1.

16. Ibid., 8, 9; R. S. Rattray, *Ashanti* (London: Oxford U. Press, 1923), 209–10.

17. Herskovits, *Rebel Destiny,* 8.

18. Marshall Stearns, *The Story of Jazz* (New York: Oxford U. Press, 1956), 12–13. The Lomaxes saw "shouts" in Texas, Louisiana, and Georgia as well as in the Bahamas, and they saw "voudou rites in Haiti":

    All share basic similarities: (1) the song is "danced" with the whole body, with hands, feet, belly, and hips; (2) the worship is, basically, a dancing-singing phenomenon; (3) the dancers always move counter-clockwise around the ring; (4) the song has the leader-chorus form, with much repetition, with a focus on rhythm rather than on melody, that is, with a form that invites and ultimately enforces cooperative group activity; (5) the song . . . steadily increasing in intensity and gradually accelerating, until a sort of mass hypnosis ensues. . . .

    The Lomaxes added, "This shout pattern is demonstrably West African." See John A. Lomax and Alan Lomax, *Folk Song U.S.A.* (New York: Duell, Sloan and Pearce, 1947), 335. Courlander notes that as the tempo of the shout builds, singing is interspersed with exclamations peculiar to some Negro church ceremonies, until the tempo reaches "a tense peak close to an ecstatic breaking point of excitement," at which time "such exclamations as 'Oh, Lord!' and 'Yes, Lord!' turn into nonsense syllables and cries. . . ." See Harold Courlander, *Negro Folk Music, U.S.A.* (New York: Columbia U. Press, 1963), 194.

19. For Brer Rabbit and headless horseman, see "The Dance of the Little Animals," in Adams, *Nigger to Nigger,* 178; also see "Bur Rabbit in Red Hill Churchyard," Ibid., 171.

20. Adams, "Churchyard," 171.

21. Ibid.

22. Ibid., 172.

23. Ibid.

24. Ibid.

25. Melville and Frances Herskovits, *Suriname Folklore* (New York: Columbia U. Press, 1936), 520.

26. Adams, "Churchyard," 172–73.

27. Ibid., 173.

28. Herskovits, *Suriname Folklore,* 521. As "Churchyard" demonstrates, the absence of explicit references to an African God or to African gods in slave folklore, especially in the tale, should not be taken to mean that slaves, in embracing Christianity, did so without a continuing consciousness of the African Godhead. Moreover, the African God, in conception is close to the Judaic God as presented in Christianity, that is, the conception of God as Spirit. It should also be noted that the exposure to Islam of sizable numbers of blacks in Africa made it easier, because of the Judaic influence in Islam, for some enslaved Africans to accept Christianity. A note of caution must be sounded with respect to slave references to God: for slaves to refer openly to an African God would have invited brutal repression from slave overlords. Mbiti writes of the African God, "It is commonly believed that God is Spirit, even if in thinking and talking about Him African peoples may often use

anthropomorphic images. As far as is known, there are no images or physical representations of God by African peoples . . . one clear indication that they consider Him to be a Spiritual Being." African concepts of God are strongly influenced by the geographical, historical, social, and cultural environment and background of each people, which

> explains the similarities and differences which we find when we consider the beliefs about God from all over the continent. It is this which partly accounts also for the beliefs parallel to those held by peoples of other continents and lands, where the background may be similar to that of African peoples. This does not rule out the fact that through contact with the outside world, some influence of ideas and culture has reached our continent. But such influence is minimal and must have operated in both directions. There are cardinal teachings, doctrines, and beliefs of Christianity, Judaism and Islam which cannot be traced in traditional religions. These major religious traditions, therefore, cannot have been responsible for disseminating those concepts of God in traditional religions which resemble some biblical and semite ideas about God. . . .

John S. Mbiti, *African Religions and Philosophy* (New York: Doubleday, 1969), 38, 44.

29. David Dalby, "Jazz, Jitter and Jam," *New York Times,* Nov. 10, 1970, op-ed page.

30. I wish to thank the anthropologist Paul Riesman for bringing Songhai burial ceremonies, and the place of the violin in them, to my attention. Interview with Riesman, Spring 1982.

31. Adams, "Bur Jonah's Goat," *Nigger to Nigger,* 174. Dalby's thesis regarding Malian influences on slaves in America is supported by linguistic studies of Lorenzo Turner, who notes the prominence of Malian linguistic influences among Gullah-speaking blacks in the Sea Islands of South Carolina and Georgia, where Wolof, Malinke, Mandinka, and Bambara ethnic groups were represented in antebellum America.

32. Sir Charles Lyell, *A Second Visit to the United States of America* (New York: Harper, 1849), 262–69.

33. On the Hopeton plantation, moreover, there was a distinct preference among slaves, during Christian baptism, for "total immersion," a widespread practice in Central and West Africa. On such occasions, the "principal charm" for slave women was "decking themselves out in white robes." Since in Georgia the Episcopal bishop, one Dr. Elliott, "found that the negroes in general had no faith in the efficacy of baptism except by complete immersion, he performed the ceremony as they desired." Lyell, *Second Visit,* 269.

34. John Fanning Watson, *Annals of Philadelphia* (Philadelphia, 1850), 2:265. It is almost certain that slaves in the Philadelphia graveyard were doing the ring shout, for as late as the 1870s the shout was pervasive and powerful among blacks in that city. Blassingame makes mention of the ring shout in treating slave culture, and Raboteau gives more than passing attention to that ritual. Genovese perceptively notes that the dance of the shout is the foundation of jazz dance, and Levine presents the shout over several pages in his work. While these scholars, all important contributors to scholarship on slave culture, were by no means unmindful of the importance of the shout, they did not probe its significance in African ancestral terms. See John W. Blassingame, *The Slave Community* (New York: Oxford U. Press, 1972), 65–66; Albert J. Raboteau, *Slave Religion* (New York: Oxford U. Press, 1978), 66–73, 339–40; Eugene D. Genovese, *Roll, Jordan, Roll* (New York: Pantheon Books, 1974), 233–34; Lawrence W. Levine, *Black Culture and Black Consciousness* (New York: Oxford U. Press, 1977), 37–38; 165–66. Some attention is given to the ring shout in an unpublished essay by Robert L. Hall, "Africanisms in Florida: Some Aspects of Afro-American Religion." Also see Charles Joyner, *Down by the Riverside* (Urbana: U. of Illinois Press, 1984). 160–61.

35. Watson, *Philadelphia,* 265. Although the ring shout was vigorously employed by countless thousands of slaves, some African religious practices either did not survive the slave experience in any significant degree—which is suggested by their relative absence from slave

oral literature—or survived in greatly reduced form: African superstitions, such as the belief that death or sickness resulted from "medicine" used against one and could be prevented by the right "medicine," could not compete with the power of the master class, which was great enough to hold the African in slavery. The overwhelming majority of slaves, consequently, refused to rely on obviously ineffective African means in opposing their white overlord. The classic case of a slave recognizing the limitations of superstition in opposing slavery involved Frederick Douglass and Sandy, "a genuine African" who "had inherited some of the so-called magical powers said to be possessed by the eastern nations." "He told me," Douglass said, "that if I would take that root and wear it on my right side it would be impossible for Covey an overseer to strike me a blow." But when wearing the root and attacked by Covey, "I forgot all about my root, and remembered my pledge to stand up in my own defense. The brute was skillfully endeavoring to get a slipknot on my legs. . . ." See Douglass, *The Life and Times of Frederick Douglass* (New York: Collier Books, 1962), 137, 139, quoted from the rev. ed., 1882. W. E. B. Du Bois captured the essence of the problem for the slave: "Slavery . . . was to him the dark triumph of Evil over him." Since the master was the avatar of that evil, slaves were far too clever to think magic would solve the problem of their oppression. See Du Bois, *The Souls of Black Folk* (Greenwich, Conn.: Fawcett Books, 1953), 146 (originally published in 1903).

36. Watson, *Philadelphia,* 265.
37. Until recently, the existence of African ritual forms in slavery was denied, and areas of heavy concentrations of slaves were not even thought to provide a source of African values. That a handful of persons were able to maintain African explanatory values—values that illumine vital aspects of the culture of their people—was not seriously considered, the focus being on African values in relation to more dominant, it was assumed, Christian values. Now we know that African values not only existed in significant degree but were, as in the case of Pennsylvania slaves, thought of and discussed in African languages on American soil. That this occurred in the North strongly argues that it often occurred when Africans of similar linguistic backgrounds were together—and alone—in Southern slavery.
38. No matter how "contemplative" the African may have appeared, it is doubtful that his religion would have been respected by Christians, who were in a dominating, superior frame of mind. But vigorous movement from the pelvic region while dancing to handclapping and song—dancing until overcome by almost complete exhaustion as the perspiration dampened one's clothing and the ground—was too foreign to white religious sensibility to merit much of a response, short of pity and a certain revulsion.
39. Parrish, *Slaves Songs,* 20.
40. Talbot, *Southern Nigeria,* 802. Dancing affords the African

> the one means of representing, as perfectly as possible, their otherwise inarticulate sense of the mystery of existence, the power of the supernatural influences which enfold them, the ecstasy of joy in life—of youth and strength and love—all the deeper and more poignant feelings so far beyond expression by mere words . . . and, whether the occasion be one of rejoicing or grief, of victory in war or funeral obsequies, of thanksgiving to the gods for their blessings of crops and children or of mere social amusement, it is by far the chief, and almost the only way of picturing and depicting their affections and sensibilities.

Ibid. Of course, dance as a means of expressing victory in warfare ceased to exist in North America. So, too, did dance to urge on those engaged in war at home or away—a practice especially common among Ashanti women, who were found in sizable numbers in the North and the South. For a discussion of the uses of dance and song in urging African men to acts of valor in battle, see Joshua Leslie and Sterling Stuckey, "The Death of Benito Cereno: A Reading of Herman Melville on Slavery, *Journal of Negro History* 67 (Winter 1982): 290; also see Frederick Angustus Ramsayer and Johannes Kuhne, *Four Years in Ashantee,* English trans. (Chicago: U. of Chicago photoduplication, 1967), 52, 209-10.

41. "In the Euro-Christian tradition," writes Courlander, "dancing in church is generally regarded as a profane act." He argues mistakenly, however, that the ring shout reconciled this objection, in that shouters avoided crossing their legs and thereby stopped short of dance—and hence the compromise. For one thing, neither Courlander nor anyone else has demonstrated that the crossing of legs was ever a part, essential or otherwise, of the shout. See Courlander, *Negro Folk Music,* 195.

42. Georgia Writers' Project, *Drums and Shadows* (Westport, Conn.: Greenwood Press, 1973), 107 (originally published in 1940).

43. Parrish, *Slave Songs,* 71. At Possum Point in the Sea Islands, blacks "alluz [always] does [one] dance. We calls it 'Come Down tuh duh Myuh.' We dance roun and shake duh han an fiddle duh foot. One ub us kneel down in duh middle uh duh succle. Den we all call out an rise an shout roun, and we all fling duh foot agen." Georgia Writers' Project, *Drums and Shadows,* 141.

44. Jean and Marshall Stearns, *Jazz Dance* (New York: Shirmer Books, 1964), 31, 32.

45. Higginson, *Black Regiment,* 188.

46. Ibid., 187–88.

47. Ibid., 188.

48. Ibid., 189–90.

49. Ibid., 190.

50. Dena Epstein, *Sinful Tunes and Spirituals* (Urbana: U. of Illinois Press, 1977), 281.

51. Higginson, *Black Regiment,* 199.

52. Stearns, *Story of Jazz,* 130.

53. Genovese, *Roll, Jordan, Roll,* 278.

54. Rawley, *Slave Trade,* 402. As will be evident in the discussion of slave culture that immediately follows, too much attention can be given to whether slaves were African born in considering the continuing African spiritual and artistic influences in American slavery. In Virginia, as in North Carolina, generations passed without large importations of slaves directly from Africa. By 1778, in fact, the trade was effectively outlawed in Virginia, the large slave population even then growing by natural process. Yet almost three-quarters of a century later, extremely esoteric African cultural forms were in evidence there. Thus, the heavy involvement of Virginia slaves in the domestic slave trade as the glutted market was reduced was a development fraught with cultural significance, for by the late-eighteenth-century Virginia slaves, with their largely African spiritual values, were being sold to the lower South and the Southwest, where they had cultural contact with other slaves. For additional data on the Atlantic trade to Virginia, see ibid., 401–4.

55. Ibid., 407. The cultural impact of the trade in Africans to North Carolina from Virginia was considerable. Slaves entering from Virginia were likely, at the least, to want to continue the cultural practices to which they were accustomed. When they were not permitted to do so, the desire to do so must certainly have been there, influencing their thought and, in some degree, regulating their behavior, making it more tentative until new ways became accustomed ways, easing the process of setting aside old ones.

56. William John Faulkner, *The Days When the Animals Talked* (Chicago: Follette Publishers, 1977), 38; Rawley, *Slave Trade,* 407.

57. Faulkner, *The Animals Talked,* 52–59.

58. Ibid., 54.
59. Ibid., 56–57.
60. Ibid., 57.
61. Thompson, *Four Moments*, 35.
62. Ibid., 34, 46.
63. Ibid., 43.
64. Ibid., 43.
65. Faulkner, *The Animals Talked*, 58. See Laurie Abraham, "The Dead Live" (Research paper for History CO1-2, Fall 1985, on Bakongo influences in Virginia during slavery, Reserve Room, Northwestern U. Library). Abraham's analysis of slave song during the conversion ceremony is pathfinding.
66. Thompson, *Four Moments*, 43.
67. Ibid., 43–44. The Kalunga line was represented horizontally on the cross-staff carried by the deacon.
68. Faulkner, *The Animals Talked*, 58.
69. This thesis is borne out by the fact that, as demonstrated here, conversion to Christianity characteristically occurred within the ancestral circle. Moreover, the evidence is overwhelming that slave converts to Christianity preferred to worship alone, often in forests or in praise houses, with no whites in view. It follows that the more African the ceremony, the more likely its occurrence when outsiders were not present.
70. Charles Colcock Jones. *The Religious Instructions of the Negroes in the United States* (Savannah, Ga., 1842), 176; William W. Freehling, *Prelude to Civil War* (New York: Harper & Row, 1965), 73, 337. Raboteau provides insight into the degree of Christian influence in the slave community near the end of slavery, quoting Du Bois's figure of "468,000 black church members in the South in 1859." Raboteau adds a statement that deserves attention: "Within forty years after emancipation, however, a black population of 8.3 million contained 2.7 million church members. This astounding figure sheds some light on the extent to which slaves had adopted Christianity in the antebellum South." Though Raboteau, in his valuable study of slave religion, has carefully set forth the extent to which white Christians converted slaves, one might differ with the conclusion he draws, namely, that much progress was made in this regard during and following slavery. Rather, what is surprising is that so few blacks were members of the Christian faith. Raboteau, *Slave Religion*, 209.
71. James Weldon Johnson, *God's Trombones* (New York: Penguin Books, 1976), 3.
72. Ibid., 2.
73. Faulkner, *The Animals Talked*, 35.
74. Ibid., 37.
75. Ibid., 36; Stearns, *Story of Jazz*, 57–63.
76. Faulkner, *The Animals Talked*, 39.
77. Ibid.
78. Quoted from Georgia Writers' Project, *Drums and Shadows*, by Robert Farris Thompson, "African Influences on the Art of the United States," in Armstead Robinson, ed., *Black Studies in the University* (New Haven: Yale U. Press, 1969), 151. For a fine treatment of slave burial rites, see David Roediger, "And Die in Dixie," *The Massachusetts Review* 22 (Spring 1981), no. 1.
79. Thompson, "African Influences," 150-51.
80. Ibid., 150. A superb student of African and Afro-American cultures, Thompson argues in this essay that "the main outlines" of the West African burial "tradition appear in parts of

Mississippi, Georgia, and South Carolina as an almost classic demonstration of the nature of a generic survival." Ibid. Actually, those outlines are also found in Virginia, as we have seen, and in North Carolina and Arkansas. In West Memphis, Arkansas, the burial mounds of two ex-slaves support their essence. Saucers and cups rest on each mound, as do spoons with handles in the mounds and a pipe the stem of which extends into one of the mounds. The husband had been a mulatto who married a dark-skinned slave—a mulatto who shared the values of the slave community, as did mulattoes generally on plantations. Hazel Todd, the daughter, visited the grave with family members from Detroit, Chicago, and Memphis in the 1950s and observed those objects and broken glass on the mounds. Interview with Todd, Spring 1984.

81. Arna Bontemps, *Black Thunder* (Boston: Beacon Press, 1968), 52 (originally published in 1936). In a close reading of the scene, Anne Spurgeon noted Bontemps's reference to "the place where the two worlds meet," which indicates an uncommon grasp of Bakongo religion on the part of Bontemps and, like his treatment of the burial mound, an unusual understanding of the Bakongo faith. See Anne Spurgeon, "The African Religious Culture of the Afro-Americans" (Seminar paper for History C92, Spring 1985, Reserve Room, Northwestern U. Library).

• • •

82. Fredrika Bremer, *America of the Fifties: Letters of Fredrika Bremer,* ed. Adolph B. Benson (New York: Oxford U. Press, 1924), 275.

83. Ibid., 275–76.

84. Ibid., 276–77; Stearns, *Story of Jazz,* 13.

85. Bremer, *America,* 277–78.

86. James Baldwin, *The Fire Next Time* (New York: Dell, 1962), 49–50.

87. W. E. B. Du Bois, *The Souls of Black Folk,* in John Hope Franklin, ed., *Three Negro Classics* (New York: Avon Books, 1965), 339 (originally published in 1903).

88. Drawing on Douglas, Burns writes, "It is in the interests of authority to control people, and frenzied convulsions are a threat to any attempt at control. . . . Once a people do not subscribe to the authority which aims to control them, convulsions are likely to occur. . . . Mary Douglas added that convulsions can be a form of protest by the 'inferior' members of society. Women are thus more inclined to engage in convulsions." Greg Burns, "Comparisons of Spirit Possession in African and African-American Cultures" (Seminar paper for History C92, Spring 1985, Reserve Room, Northwestern U. Library).

89. Ibid.

90. Thomas A. Blair, *Weather Elements* (New York: Prentice-Hall, 1931), 210.

91. The ring ceremony in Ashanti appears to be one source of the jumping of shouters in North America, the Ashanti priests, dancing in a great circle, leaping and "pirouetting like Russian dancers." Rattray, *Ashanti,* 158. See Daniel Alexander Payne, *Recollections of Seventy Years* (New York: Arno Press, 1968), 92–94 (originally published in 1888).

92. In churches in which the benches were not nailed down, much of the latitude taken under the sky at night or the sun at dawn could be taken. Still, the architecture of the church worked its own, subtle influence even in such circumstances. One should not, however, overemphasize the effects of that architecture, whether benches were nailed down or not, for a great deal of the naturalness—of emotional release and joyous affirmation of the faith—occurred despite the surroundings, an authentic African ceremonial atmosphere being created to remarkable degree. One can make this argument with confidence, because the quality of being able to achieve an authentic emotional experience in an environment far

removed from what the celebrants are accustomed to is an impressive feature of black culture today in America. At the Smithsonian Institution, Southern Negroes repeatedly demonstrated the principle, as was noted by one participant, Jamila, who remarked of those present, "They turned the whole thing into a church. You knew when you saw people walking up there that that's what they were doing. I do believe I was among them in doing that." Quoted in Sterling Stuckey, "Tragic Voice: The Great Singing Movements of the Sixties" (Evaluation of the Civil Rights Movement Conference, Smithsonian Institution, Jan, 30–Feb. 3, 1980).

93. Bremer, *America,* 105. There is little or no evidence supporting the view that slaves gave up dancing on becoming Christian; it is a view, in fact, that has little basis in slave action when slaves were alone or in the company of that rare white who seemed non-threatening.

94. Bremer, *America,* 279; Higginson, *Black Regiment,* 41.

95. Bremer, *America,* 280.

96. Thompson, *Four Moments,* 149.

97. Frederick Law Olmsted, *A Journey in the Back Country* (New York: Schocken Books, 1970), 90 (originally published in 1860).

98. Frederick Law Olmstead, *The Cotton Kingdom* (New York: Knopf, 1953), 240-41 (originally published in 1861).

99. Ibid., 242.

100. Ibid., 243.

101. Ibid., 244–45.

102. Ibid., 245–46.

103. Ibid., 246.

104. Ibid.

105. William Wells Brown, *My Southern Home* (Upper Saddle River, N.J.: Gregg Press, 1968), 191 (originally published in 1880).

106. Ibid., 192.

107. Ibid., 193.

108. Ibid., 194.

109. Ibid.

110. Georgia Writers' Project, *Drums and Shadows,* 127–28, 131, 186–87.

111. Ibid., 159.

112. Herskovits, *Myth,* 133; Georgia Writers' Project, *Drums and Shadows,* 174.

113. Roscoe Lewis, *The Negro in Virginia* (New York: Arno Press, 1969), 89.

114. Ibid., 90. When slave fiddlers called figures, slaves most commonly responded with African figures, mainly dances in which animal movements were emulated. Fiddlers who called for whites in the big house certainly elicited different responses from blacks, who usually responded with African dance when not mocking white dance movements. Such a fiddler was Louis Cave: "Chile, he sho' could strung dat fiddle. Never did do much work . . . he used to play and' call de figgers 'long as dere was anyone on de floor. Chile, when I was a girl guese I'd ruther dance dan eat." When a slave danced "on de spot," someone might take "a charred corn-cob an' draw a circle on de flo', den call one arter de odder up an' dance in de circle. Effen yo' feet tetch de edge you is out." This dance, more than most, may have called for extra effort, since the circle was drawn on the floor, its sacred significance inspirational. Ibid., 91.

115. Ibid., 93.

116. Ibid.

117. Ibid. The balancing of objects on the head, a skill not peculiar to Africans but as characteristic of them as of any people—widespread in black Africa but not in Europe—persisted throughout slavery and carried over into the postslavery era. That skill, which seemed particularly characteristic of women but was by no means confined to them, was manifested in scenes of everyday life three-quarters of a century after slavery: an enormous basket of flowers on the head of a hat-wearing, middle-aged woman, her eyes shaded from the sun; an elderly woman carrying, in pyramid fashion, two large metal containers on her head while holding a third in her right hand—she also carries a purse that hangs from her right forearm—as she looks out from the page unperturbed; and a large woman, her left hand on her hip, her hair braided, stands before a wooden fence, an enormous straw basket on her head. See Doris Ulmann, *The Darkness and the Light* (Millerton, N.Y.: Aperture, 1974), 21, 42, 46. Not surprisingly, in the same masterly photographic essay, one finds a tombstone with the inscription "Hackless Jenkins, June 15, 1878 to June 23, 1926" and a mound on which there are jars, cups, glasses, a water pitcher, and other intimate objects of the deceased. Ibid., 60.
118. Dougald MacMillan, "John Kuners," *Journal of American Folk-Lore* 39 (Jan.–March 1926): 54–55.
119. Ibid., 54.
120. Talbot, *Southern Nigeria,* 760–61.
121. Ibid., 761.
122. Joshua Leslie, "Among the Yoruba" (unpublished MS). Leslie's observations are supported by Herskovits's; this is a measure of the continuing force of the Egun masquerade in West Africa today. "In Nigeria, the Egungun go masked about the streets; there are no attendants for the masked figures, who themselves carry whips, chastise those . . . who do not show them the proper respect." Herskovits, *Dahomey,* 2:246.
123. Herskovits, *Dahomey,* 1:246–47. "The importance of women as singers of songs is a Dahomean innovation . . . On the other hand, the costuming, and, it is said, many of the songs, are Nigerian. Certainly the concept of the Egu as a power emanating from the spirits of the dead has been taken over directly from Nigeria." Ibid., 247.
124. Talbot, *Southern Nigeria,* 763. Although John Kunering was mainly associated with Christmas in North America, some scholars contend the ceremony was performed at other times as well. "This in no manner detracts from the fact that it originally was confined to a period which marked the close of the year, but opens an avenue of study relative to trait culture dissemination and change in social significance." Ira De A. Reid, "The John Canoe Festival: A New World Africanism," *Phylon* 3 (1942): 351.
125. Edward Warren, *A Doctor's Experiences on Three Continents* (Baltimore: Cushings and Baily, 1885), 201.
126. Ibid., 200.
127. Ibid., 201.
128. Ibid.
129. Ibid., 201–2.
130. Ibid., 202.
131. Douglass, *Life and Times,* 54–55.
132. Warren, *A Doctor's Experiences,* 203.
133. Ibid., 200.
134. The music historian Eileen Southern, who has deeply researched black culture, is an exception to the rule in her findings regarding slave ceremony in the North during the colonial period and in her conclusions regarding the African character of much of that

ceremony then and later. See Southern, *The Music of Black Americans* (New York: Norton, 1971), chaps. 1 and 2.

135. Hubert H. S. Aimes, "African Institutions in America," *Journal of American Folk-Lore* 18 (Jan.–March 1905): 15.

136. Orville H. Platt, "Negro Governors," *Papers of the New Haven Colony Historical Society* 6 (1900): 319; Aimes, "African Institutions," 98; Lorenzo Greene, *The Negro in Colonial New England* (New York: Atheneum, 1968), 36 (originally published in 1942).

137. Aimes, "African Institutions," 15. Lorenzo Greene is one of the few historians to write about the "Negro Governor." In fact, he does so in some detail. See Greene, *Negro in Colonial New England,* 249–55. For a more recent treatment of this ritual, see Joseph P. Reidy, "Negro Election Day and Black Community Life in New England, 1750–1860," *Marxist Perspectives* 1 (Fall 1978): 102–17.

138. Quoted in Platt, "Negro Governors," 324.

139. Jane De Forest Shelton, "The New England Negro: A Remnant," *Harper's Monthly Magazine,* March 1894, 537.

140. Platt, "Negro Governors," 324.

141. Quoted ibid., 331. Rhode Island masters "foresaw that a sort of police managed wholly by the slaves would be more effectual in keeping them within the bounds of morality and honesty, than if the same authority were exercised by the whites." Quoted ibid. Thus, a compromise in some respects mutually beneficial was effected between slave and master as a result of the Negro governor practice. The relative mildness of slavery in New England provided crevices that were exploited by blacks in the interest of values proper to them in certain areas—in ceremonies and in personal contact.

142. Ibid., 322–23.

143. Aimes, "African Institutions," 20.

144. Quoted ibid.

145. Quoted in Platt, "Negro Governors," 326.

146. Aimes, "African Institutions," 20.

147. Dr. James Eights, "Pinkster Festivities in Albany Sixty Years Ago," *Collections on the History of Albany,* vol. 2 (Albany, 1867), 323.

148. Ibid., 324.

149. Ibid., 325.

150. Ibid.

151. Ibid., 325–26.

152. Ibid., 326.

153. Higginson, *Black Regiment,* p. 41.

154. Ibid.

155. Ibid., 47; Melville writes of the cook in *Redburn,* one Mr. Thompson, that he "sat over his boiling pots, reading out of a book which was very much soiled and covered with grease spots. . . . I could hardly believe my eyes when I found this book was the Bible." Herman Melville, *Redburn* (New York: Penguin Books, 1976), 137 (originally published in 1849).

156. Higginson, *Black Regiment,* 46-47.

157. Ibid., 45, 55.

158. Ibid., 44–45. "Give these people their tongues, their feet, and their leisure, and they are happy," observed Higginson. "At every twilight the air is full of singing, talking and clapping of hands in unison. . . ." Since he did not grasp the substance of their religious belief, it is not surprising that Higginson, whose intelligence and sensitivity on matters of black culture were superior to that of most of his contemporaries, believed the memories of the

blacks around him "a vast bewildered chaos of Jewish history and biography; and most of the great events of the past, down to the period of the American Revolution, they instinctively attribute to Moses." As principled and faithful a friend of blacks as he could comment. "They seem the world's perpetual children, docile, gay, and lovable, in the midst of this war for freedom on which they have intelligently entered." Ibid., 36–38, 44, 45, 49, 51. Little did he realize that their tales of greatest depth—he had heard only those in a humorous vein—contained attacks on oppression sharper than anything managed by the keenest and most sympathetic intellectuals in the North. Melville, *Redburn,* 137–38.

159. Edward Channing Gannett, "The Freedom at Port Royal," *North American Review* 101 (1865): 10.

160. Ibid., 9. The protracted praying and self-examination resembles, in the context referred to by Gannett, the praying of the Egungun mentioned by Talbot in his discussion of the Nigerian ceremony to which John Kunering may well have been related. See Talbot, *Southern Nigeria,* 761.

161. Gannett, "Freedman," 9–10.

162. Charlotte Forten, *The Journal Charlotte L. Forten* (New York: Dryden Press, 1953), 149, 151.

163. Forten, "Life on the Sea Islands," *Atlantic Monthly,* May 1864, 593.

164. Ibid., 594.

165. Ibid., 592; Gannett, "Freedmen," 7.

166. Forten, "Sea Islands," 593; Leslie and Stuckey, "Death of Benito Cereno," 290.

167. Forten, "Sea Islands," 593–594.

168. Higginson, *Black Regiment,* 136. Higginson noted, "The habit of carrying bundles on the head gives them erectness of figure, even where physically disabled. I have seen a woman, with a brimming water-pail balanced on her head, or perhaps a cup, saucer, and spoon, stop suddenly, turn round, stoop to pick up the missile, rise again, fling it, light a pipe, and go through many evolutions with either hand or both, without spilling a drop." Ibid., 52. The dignified demeanor of the laundress is not unrelated to the manner in which Negro "kings" and "governors" conducted themselves in parades in New England and New York State and in the West Indies.

169. Bremer, *America,* 114–15.

170. Ibid., 119; Herskovits, *Dahomey,* 214. Had Bremer been unobserved in the tent in which the slaves were beating their breasts, she undoubtedly would at some point have witnessed the ring ceremony, so prevalent was the ceremony in Georgia during the slave era. And while sacrifices of animals were not unknown in American slavery, that practice was severely curtailed in the new environment because the master did not tolerate the killing of animals for such purposes. For abundant evidence of the ring ceremony in Georgia during slavery see Georgia Writers' Project, *Drums and Shadows.* Human sacrifice, associated with the ring ceremony in Dahomey and elsewhere in Africa, came to an abrupt end in North American slavery, for the lives of Africans were no longer spared or taken according to traditional practices, since the basis for such practices was shattered by property relations.

171. Bremer, *America,* 119.

172. Lyell, *Second Visit,* 270.

173. Ibid.

174. John Michael Vlach, *The Afro-American Tradition in Decorative Arts* (Cleveland: Cleveland Museum of Art, 1978), 47.

175. Ibid.

176. Ibid.

177. Ibid. Anne Spurgeon further illumines Bakongo dimensions of the quilt, noting of its upper left corner that it is "of a darkened diamond shape, with sun-like figures glowing at the

four corners of the diamond. There are two cross shapes above this image, and below it are the figures of four humans in a semi-circle, and another sun-image with some sort of ray extending out of it. Both the crosses and the diamond signify the life cycle, and are a comment on the human figures below." Regarding the lower right-hand corner of the quilt, Spurgeon writes that it "is a scene from the crucifixion of Jesus Christ, with the two thieves hanging from crosses on either side and below him. Above the Christ figure, there is a line which connects a bright sun at the left to a dark one at the right—the path from day to night, or from life to death. This is a complex religious symbol, which is a very clear physical example of the mixture of newly acquired and long retained spiritual understanding." See Spurgeon, "African Religious Culture."

178. Vlach, *Decorative Arts,* 47.
179. Payne, *Recollections,* 253–54.
180. Ibid., 92–94.
181. Payne further notes that the ring practices "vary somewhat in different localities," which helps explain differences reflected in the New Orleans African Church, where jumping was the cardinal feature and the more common form of expression of that ceremony. That improvisation was a feature of the shout guaranteed some variation from locale to locale. Ibid., 254–55.
182. Ibid., 256.
183. Ibid., 254.
184. Ibid., 255–56. It is especially ironic that Payne, believing that the ceremony that so offended him "far from being in harmony with the religion of the Lord Jesus Christ . . . antagonizes his holy religion," failed to realize that the faith of Africans helped them, in the spirituals, give expression to Christianity on a level that has yet to be surpassed over the past two centuries. See W. E. B. Du Bois, *Black Reconstruction* (New York: Russell and Russell, 1935), chap. 5.
185. Stearns, *Story of Jazz,* 13.
186. Ibid., 59–60.
187. Ibid., 14
188. The author saw Monk dance at the Five Spot in New York in the 1960s.
189. Clifton Joseph Furness, "Communal Music among Arabians and Negroes," *Musical Quarterly* 16 (1930): 47–48.
190. Anne M. Spurgeon, "From the Wellspring of Africa: African Spirituality in Afro-American Culture" (Senior thesis, Northwestern U., 1986), 22.
191. Furness, "Communal Music," 47–51. Spurgeon writes,

> Maum Hester was quite sure that the sun would carry word of her actions that day to the world of the dead and of the ancestors, where Jesus waited to sit in judgment over her behavior. She achieved this communication with the other world by dancing the circle dance and chanting her phrase until it became almost a song. It is very significant that it was the sun which served as the portal between two worlds, through which was passed the record of her deeds. She refers to the apparent motion of the sun over the earth as "shoutin," showing that she sees a parallel between the circle of the ringshout and the daily cycle of the sun—the four moments of the sun.

Spurgeon, "African Spirituality," 23.
192. Zora Neale Hurston, *The Sanctified Church* (Berkeley: Turtle Island, 1981), 103. This volume was published posthumously.
193. James Baldwin, *Go Tell It on the Mountain* (New York: Dell, 1952), 14–15.

Gullah Attitudes Toward Life and Death
Margaret Washington Creel
Historian

Margaret Washington Creel is the author of the influential: "A Peculiar People": Slave Religion and Community among the Gullahs *(1988). She was an adviser to the PBS Series* Africans in America. America's Journey through Slavery. *She is currently professor of history at Cornell University.*

The coastal region of South Carolina, bounded on the north by Georgetown and on the south by Port Royal and St. Helena Sound, is the land of the Gullah slave population. Halfway between Charleston and Savannah a fringe of fertile islands borders these coastal lowlands and stretches out into the arms of the sea. Here, as slaves, the most isolated Gullah people lived, first cultivating indigo and later the famous long-staple fine-quality cotton. More significantly, the Gullahs created a distinct, original African-American cultural form.[1]

Diversity of African ethnic origins was limited in the Sea Island region because Carolina planters paid particular attention to the geographical sources of their black cargoes. White Carolinians preferred Gold Coast Africans, but they were difficult to obtain because West Indian sugar planters usually got first choice. Still, the first African-Carolinians were probably of Gold Coast origin (Tshi speaking), since West Indian planters who settled the colony brought about a thousand slaves with them. Next in demand were Africans from the Kongo-Angola area. But in 1739, when African-born Angolans rose up against Carolina masters, slaves from this region were no longer so desirable. Following the 1739 Stono Rebellion a nonimportation act was in effect for ten years.[2] Afterward a preponderance of Africans from the Windward Coast (Sierra Leone and Liberia) was imported. Many of these slaves went to the Sea Islands during a period of extensive settlement and agricultural expansion twenty-five years before the War for Independence. The postwar years witnessed another period of massive importations, and the Kongo-Angolan region once again supplied the majority of Africans to slave coffles. Some of them peopled the Carolina low country, but an even larger number went to up-country plantations and to planters in states refusing to import.[3]

Thus some cultural homogeneity was retained as Africans passed from the Old World to the New. In the Sea Island region of South Carolina, cultural similitude was coupled with relative isolation and resulted in a tendentious process of African provenance, American acculturation, and intergroup socialization.[4] The prevalence of Tshi

Margaret Washington Creel, "Gullah Attitudes Toward Life and Death," in Africanisms in American Culture, *edited by Joseph E. Holloway, pp. 69–97 (Bloomington: Indiana University Press, 1990).*

names in Gullah Creole language certainly indicates Ashanti and Fanti influence and supports the "hearth area" concept, emphasizing the lasting effects of first "settlers" whose influence far exceeds their numbers. But evidence demonstrates that the dominant African presence in the Sea Island region derives from the Kongo-Angolan and Windward Coast ethnic groups.[5]

Kongo-Angola was the home of Bakongo civilization and Bantu-speaking peoples whose language is Kikongo.[6] Kikongo linguistic presence in Gullah Creole is demonstrative. Gullah *ndoko* is Bobangi (Kikongo), meaning "a bewitching that is said to cause illness." *Ndoko* is also a version of what in Kikongo is *ndoki,* meaning sorcerer or witch. Also the Gullah name *n'zambi* is Kikongo for God. Many scholars even suggest that the name Gullah is a shortened form of Angola. The Central African Mbundu ruler was called the Ngola, from which the Portuguese named the colony. There is obvious similarity between Ngola and Gullah (which went through various spellings).[7] But equally significant and generally overlooked is the African influence from the Windward Coast region.

Gola (sometimes spelled Goulah) is the name of a large group of Africans from the Liberian hinterland. Golas were heavily preyed upon by neighboring Mende, Vai, and Mandingas, and were imported into the Sea Island regions of South Carolina and Georgia at the height of rice and indigo cultivation. Africans from Upper Guinea (Gola, Vai, Mende, Kissi, Kpelle, and so on) shared a common socioreligious bond that provided a certain cultural uniformity through mandatory secret societies.[8] Names related to these societies appear in Gullah Creole.

Lorenzo Turner wrote extensively on African influences in Gullah Creole but identified no Gola language terms. As P. E. Hair notes, however, the majority of Turner's Gullah words in stories, songs, and prayers are Mende and Vai, and the Sierra Leone–Liberian influence is also prominent in Turner's list of personal names. Hair further believes that Turner missed these relationships because "no dictionary or informant" from this region "was available." Several Gullah personal names identified by Turner and listed with West African equivalents relate to Windward Coast secret societies. For example, Turner lists Gullah *beri* and *berimo* as Vai, stating that these words refer to "a branch of the society known as pora, a 'ceremonial rite.'" The Gullah name *pora* Turner determines is Mende, meaning "the great secret society of men." These relationships appear correct. *Beri* is one name used to refer to the secret society institution found in the Sierra Leone–Liberian region, and *Poro* is the more generally used name for the same male organization. Similarly, Turner's African equivalent for the Gullah name *zo* is a Vai term, "the wearer of the mask in Sande Society." *Sande* was the most common name (Bundu was another) describing the mandatory female secret society of the Upper Guinea region. Among these groups, secret society leaders, who hid behind masks, were the spiritual leaders called *zo.*[9]

The purpose of this essay is threefold: to offer some original interpretations of Gullah attitudes toward life and death, to suggest how an African cosmological and ontological heritage could impact the Gullah culture, and to show how the Gullahs forged African Christianity into a liberation struggle.

Little attention was focused on Gullahs in antebellum days, and much of their early cultural history appeared lost. During the post–Civil War era and the early twentieth century, however, Gullahs became the focal point of a large body of research, writing, and fictional literature. Although much of this literature is filled with sociological bias, the studies of Gullah music, folklore, linguistic patterns, and life-style reveal a North American example of African retentions within black society.[10] Several more recent works on Gullah culture have been published.[11] Yet the cultural realm that provides some of the clearest examples of African-American syncretism among Gullahs has received little attention. For indeed, the sphere of "things of the spirit" reveals how Gullahs synthesized the old and new into African-American. Despite the paucity of published material on the Gullahs' spiritual beliefs,[12] most observers who studied or lived among the Gullahs attest to religion's importance in Gullah life. Gullah African Christianity was a vital folk religion, filled with peculiar patterns of beliefs linking them with their traditional past. The Gullahs' original interpretation of religion included viewing spirituality as a means of communal harmony, solidarity, and accountability.

Christian proselytization of Lowcountry slaves did not seriously begin until 1830. The primary motive of this instruction was to use Christianity as a conservative element in plantation life and slave conduct. Sporadic and intermittent exposure to Christianity occurred during the colonial and early national periods. But Methodist missionaries sent among the Gullahs in the 1830s provided their first organized exposure to Christianity.[13] Later, Baptist planters dominating the region took over this activity. Their efforts consisted chiefly of occasional preaching on plantations and building plantation praise (or pray's) houses,[14] mainly to keep slaves on numerous estates from mingling. Even today praise houses are found on some plantations. The desire to cloister the slaves actually encouraged them to fashion their own version of Christianity more suited to their circumstances. And this was done under the "watchcare" of black elders ostensibly responsible to white deacons. The fulcrum of the bondspeople's folk religion was spiritual and psychological autonomy. Baptist planters unwittingly contributed to its continued development. Hence, while energetic Methodist missionaries were somewhat influential among Gullahs up until 1844, most slaves united with the white Baptist church through the praise house. But the majority never saw the inside of Baptist churches until the Civil War.[15] Thus memories of African social and spiritual traditions were often nestled within Christianity but were still making a forceful impact on Gullah life, thought, and culture.

An African world view, an African theory of being, and some African customs were significant in Gullah religious tendencies and communal existence. These features of Africanity sometimes superseded, sometimes coexisted with the Christian influence. Elements of syncretism were especially pronounced in Gullah attitudes toward life and death. The African traditional world view was consonant with the idea that in a cohesive and integrated society each member had a place. This was true even though traditional religion, unlike Christianity, was not primarily an individual experience. Emphasis was on total well-being of the community of which an individual was only a part. For the Africans—and this was also true for the Gullahs—religion was a process of total immersion. Spiritual concerns could not be set apart from secular or communal ones. Religion assumed a meaning outside of a "holy" building, a "sacred" day of the week, or a set of dogmas and creeds to be accepted at face value. In the traditional world view, spirituality affected one's whole system of being, embracing the consciousness, social interactions and attitudes, fears and dispositions of the community at large. As John Mbiti expressed it,

> in traditional society there are no irreligious people. To be human is to belong to the whole community, and to do so involves participating in the beliefs, ceremonies, rituals and festivals of that community. A person cannot detach himself from the religion of his group, to do so is to be severed from his roots, his foundation, his context of security, his kinships and the entire group of those who make him aware of his existence. To be without one of these corporate elements of life is to be out of the whole picture. Therefore, to be without religion amounts to a self-excommunication from the entire life of society, and African peoples do not know how to exist without religion.[16]

In traditional African society, codes of ethics also stemmed from religiosity. Moral defects were spiritual flaws as well as character blights. Individuals were guided by the ethics characteristic of God, the ultimate upholder of moral order. Ancestral patriarchs, matriarchs, diviners, the living dead, and other spirits were daily guardians of human behavior. Punishments and retribution for breaches in morals and ethics were not the province of a future world judge but were dealt with on earth.[17] Thus, although Africans were not adherents of the Christian concept of a future tribunal, they believed that evil activities and failure to obey social regulations warranted earthly censure and punishment according to the degree of the depravity. This was perhaps a more efficient method of controlling deviant social behavior, since immediate repercussion and ostracization from society were more realistic threats than fear of a remote world beyond.

Inherent in an African world view with religion foremost as a unifying force was an anthropocentric philosophy. John Mbiti, an adherent of this point of view, divides the categories of African ontology into five parts: God as the ultimate explanation of the genesis and sustenance of all things; spirits, made up of superhuman beings and the spirits of those who died long ago; humans, including those who are alive and those about to be born; animals and plants, or the remainder of biological life; and phenomena and objects without biological life.[18]

While God is the apex in this African theory of being, humankind is the center, as everything is viewed in relation to life. This anthropocentric approach also expresses affirmation of life as ontological categories of human existence and environments integrate, from the highest to the lowest form of being. Human spiritual activity encourages justification, preservation, protection, and enrichment of life. God is a supreme all-knower who explains creation and provides a model of virtue. Lesser spirits are intermediaries, representing an assurance of human perpetuity beyond the grave. While human actions represent confirmation that earthly life is the nucleus of existence, the recognition of ancestors and tributes to lesser gods represent the Africans' endeavor to have an impact on the natural and supernatural processes believed to govern life and death.

Relationships between the pivotal position of humanity and spirituality in African ontology are demonstrated in general concepts regarding life on individual as well as on communal levels. Religion accompanied one from conception to physical death and in the afterlife. Significant events in individual life activities were enveloped in beliefs and rites with deep spiritual connotations: each person's introduction into various states of life was accompanied by a sacred observance. Marriage rites were festive, socioreligious commemorations of human life and community longevity. African women's participation in numerous religious ceremonies was to ensure bringing healthy children into the world. The fate of the unborn was in the care of spiritual beings and forces. When only a few days old an infant was honored with a naming ceremony and was blessed by the priest who invoked God to direct the child through a life of good habits and industry and toward a meaningful occupation. At childhood's end a sacred rite expressed appreciation for care received from God and the spirits. Upon entrance into puberty, the send-off into the bush for initiation was a sacred and spiritually charged event. After initial bush training, a religious commemoration welcomed the neophyte into the community as a citizen. Death called for a sacred send-off of major proportions. This passage into the unseen (but not remote) spiritual world was the climax of one existence, which continued through contact with the living, and the beginning of another.[19]

African religion and spiritualism thus emphasized a celebration of human life. To live fully and robustly, to be esteemed by the community, was basic to African thinking and was incorporated into Africans' particular ontology. Sacred observances were often a fusion of the festive and the solemn. But their meanings to community living and social responsibility reveal the seriousness of the services. That which threatened the will to live, this "vital force," was dangerous to the individual and hence to society. Inhabitants of the spiritual world were the guardians of life, appealed to in periods of crisis, such as illness, environmental disaster, and the malice of others, or under normal stress of adult life. Often spiritual forces were placated as a precautionary measure for the preservation of the person, the clan, the village, and the ethnic group.

An underlying and dynamic force operative in Gullah folk religion and spirituality was rooted in an African world view. Some pristine elements of traditional religious thought that remained with Sea Island slaves, although not inconsistent with Christianity, largely account for the vigor of their African-American culture.

During the Civil War some observers were appalled at what they interpreted as resignation among Sea Island slaves. A northern teacher, Arthur Sumner, wrote from St. Helena Island in 1863: "I am astonished that they should be fit to live after such generations of mere animal life. A higher race would have lost all moral sense."[20] Even one of the Gullahs' staunchest Yankee advocates, Elizabeth Botume, remarked that "the patience of the freed people in sickness was so general and remarkable, it seemed like apathy."[21] This attitude might be attributable to the Gullahs' affiliation with the fatalistic features of Christianity. Yet it also came from the sense of protection that spiritual association offered, since religious and community membership together forged social ties, strengthening the Gullahs' resolve and their belief in collective survival. Thomas Wentworth Higginson, Civil War commander of the First South Carolina Volunteers composed mainly of Gullah men, was "surprised" to find the black soldiers so little demoralized. He attributed it to religion:

> I learned to think that we abolitionists had underrated the suffering produced by slavery among the negroes, but had overrated the demoralization. Yet . . . it must be admitted that this temperament, born of sorrow and oppression, is far more marked in the slave than in the native African.[22]

Higginson recognized the significance of slave religion. But the personality and "religious temperament" of Gullahs owed much to a non-Christian tradition and hence was not as much "born of sorrow and oppression" or as foreign to the "native African" as he imagined. If traditional African religion celebrates and affirms human life, with God as the apex of being and humankind as the center or pivotal point, it could also function thusly for Gullah slaves in the New World. On the conscious level, perhaps, the pillar of their faith rested on an association with Christ. But this faith may primarily have helped shape their Old World thinking into an organized, plausible New World perception. Paul Radin insightfully wrote that the Christian God provided the African-American slaves with a "fixed point," and rather than being converted to God they converted God to themselves.[23] The Gullahs converted Christianity to their African world view, using the new religion to justify combating objective forces, to collectively perpetuate community-culture, and as an ideology of freedom. Thus it was less a case of Christianity instilling a sense of resignation because of beliefs in future rewards than of an African philosophical tradition being asserted in the slave quarters.

Life on earth was not negated by Gullahs, as is illustrated by their desire for freedom and their capacity to create. Freedom was a continuous topic of conversation among them.[24] It was often expressed thematically in Gullah spirituals. While spirituals appear to be a portent of heavenly futurity in a Christian sense, the ambiguity in many Gullah "prayer songs" implies otherwise. Double meanings and surrogates abound in them. For example:

Jesus made de blind see,
Jesus made de cripple walk,
Jesus made de deaf to hear.
Walk in, kind Jesus!
No man can hinder me.[25]

When northern teacher Laura Towne heard this impressive spiritual she believed that the refrain "No man can hinder me" meant that "nothing could prevent access to Jesus."[26] Yet Charles Nordhoff, a journalist sent to Port Royal in 1863 to write about the freedpeople, heard the song and attributed to it "an aspiration for liberty."[27] Nordhoff was probably closer to the mark. Some observers reported that the phrase was sung as "No man can hinder *we.*" Certainly both interpretations have an element of truth—a combination of mystical belief in the miraculous powers of the Christian God, a deep sense of pride that was a heritage of the Gullahs' African past, and feelings of nationalism developed over generations as similar social and cultural traditions merged under slavery, creating one people with common interests, ambitions, and beliefs.

The Gullahs' Marseillaise was the spiritual "New Jerusalem":

De talles' tree in Paradise
De Christian calls de Tree ob Life,
An' I hope dat trumpet blow me home
To my New Jerusalem.

Blow Gabriel! Trumpet, blow louder, louder!
An I hope dat trumpet blow me home
To my New Jerusalem!

Paul and Silas jail-bound
Sing God's praise both night and day,
An' I hope dat trumpet blow me home
To my New Jerusalem![28]

This song was triumphant not tragic and was a favorite Gullah "shout" song. Thus it was not sung with a "heby heart" or a "troubled speerit." When a freedman named Maurice, who had been blinded by his master in a fit of rage, sang "New Jerusalem" at the praise house his mind turned toward heaven and gaining his sight in a future world. But when the freedpeople sang "New Jerusalem" at the Emancipation Jubilee on New Year's Day in 1866 their earthly future and enthusiasm for long-awaited freedom filled their thoughts and expectations. The tree of life was apparently the tree of liberty, as paradise was a land free of bondage. The meaning behind the spiritual was not lost on Elizabeth Botume. She wrote:

> The streets of the city were filled with happy freed people. According to their spiritual, they had "fought for liberty," and this was their "New Jerusalem," of which they so often sang. Even the poorest, and those most scantily clothed, looked as if they already "walked that golden street," and felt "that starry crown" upon their uncovered hands. It was indeed a day of great rejoicing, and one long to be remembered. These people were living their "New Jerusalem."[29]

God, personified as Jesus, and an African world view offered the Gullahs an explanation for life and provided a model of virtue. Gullah religion contained a fervent zest for life, and the cornerstone of their faith was a confidence that freedom on earth would come to them or their progeny.

Gullahs, as realists, did not accept all religious teachings imposed upon them and were not beguiled by stealthy attempts to "make them better slaves." From their African heritage Gullahs possessed a proclivity for rising above their near-tragic situation for the sake of community. That was more important than blindly striking out and possibly committing racial suicide. Gullahs also considered the issue of insurrection in practical terms. They believed that successful armed rebellion was impossible. Still, the Gullahs were not without great courage. Men, women, and children risked their lives for freedom when the Union Army occupied part of South Carolina. Gullah soldiers also served in that army under the most unfair circumstances. Furthermore, Gullahs did not merely survive and persevere. They taxed creative talents to a maximum by developing a community, perhaps seeing that as one way to maintain their dignity. This development of a community may be the truest example of their valor and vitality. Gullahs maintained a passionate love of humanity and confronted the masters without motives of revenge. Yet they also displayed a keen sense of revolutionary rationalism through a calm realization that masters and slaves were natural enemies. In observing the Gullahs' capacity to endure pain and their tendency to transcend individual situations, the surgeon in Higginson's black regiment referred to them as "natural transcendentalists."[30] While that is true to some extent, perhaps a more accurate characterization is that these African-American slaves were natural humanists who believed in the integration of the human personality on a collective level, placing cultural considerations first, sometimes at the expense of practical, personal ones.

While the African tradition from which the Gullahs were descended emphasized the preservation, protection, and enrichment of life, the phenomenon unifying this anthropocentric philosophy was religion. Hence it is not difficult to understand why Gullah life was expressed from an essentially religious perspective. Christianity and traditional African religion combined, providing the Gullahs with an ideology of freedom and a lofty, mystical explanation of their existence as a people. The optimism present in traditional West African religion and spiritualism provided a necessary ingredient in the creation of Gullah culture. Slavery did not erode the African sense of pride, the love of home and family. Yet how long could these attributes alone sustain cultural life among slaves, no matter how their spirits struggled against degradation? Christianity offered cohesion of a kind needed to develop a homogeneous people. The heritage from Upper Guinea and from the Bakongo tradition also inspired social cohesion.

The Upper Guinea region of Africa (Senegal, Gambia, Sierra Leone, and Liberia) contained a multiplicity of ethnic groups, mixed kinship systems, and languages. Non-Moslem societies there did not possess high degrees of political centralization. Nor were community groups usually as large or territorial holdings as extensive as those in the Niger Delta or Western Sudan. Yet early explorers, travelers, and traders were struck by what H. Baumann called distinctive culture circles on the West African coast. Upper Guinea exemplifies Baumann's conceptual framework. There peoples historically had common cultural features, the most significant being secret societies that regulated the social, political, and, to some extent, economic life of the communities. The Poro (or Beri) society for men and the Sande (or Bundu) society for women were almost universal and, where they existed, always mandatory. The area of the "Poro Cluster" on the inland African coast included the Lokko, Temne, Kono, Mende, Bullom, Krim, and Limba in Sierra Leone. On the Malguetta Coast (today Liberia), Poro and Sande groups included the Gola, Vai, De, Kpelle, Kissi, Gbande, Belle, Loma, Mano, Gio Ge, Bassa, and Kru. Sixteenth-century Portuguese traders observed similarities among various groups belonging to these associations. Affinity was so strong that traders viewed these people as one society. They dressed alike, had the same system of justice, and understood each other. Although they lacked political centralization, these groups possessed social homogeneity through their common secret societies. Ostensibly these societies were a way of training youth. They introduced all members into adulthood after isolating them from the community for years in a special "sacred grove."[31]

While Poro and Sande represented transformation from childhood to citizenship, membership was much more than a puberty rite of passage. Sylvia Boone writes that "Sande is a socially consolidating force," and "a religion with the power to make life good and to inspire the highest aspirations among its members." According to Kenneth Little, Poro's function as a puberty rite was secondary to the main one, "to impress upon the new member the sacredness of his duty to the Poro" and hence to the community. To this end the youths underwent a *travel,* a series of terrifying dreams in which they were symbolically eaten by the Poro or Sande spirit—the devil—and were then reborn by the same spiritual force. Once rebirth in the bush occurred, each individual was bound to the society and vowed to uphold secrecy of the initiation and to abide by Poro-Sande authority. Allegiance was no longer to parents and kin but to the secret society as foremost arbiter. Thus Poro-Sande instituted a regulatory process with sociopolitical duties implemented to fulfill collective and societal goals. The Poro council was supreme. It stopped village quarrels, tried and condemned social criminals, intensified holiday spirit, and gave permission to declare war. Although the chief was the nominal ruler, real power rested with the council, which was composed of senior members of both Poro and Sande societies and could even depose a chief. Thus the secret society functioned as the primary psychological and physical coercive agent for the common good. The institution's power, however, was derived from its affinity with the spirits and from other religious manifestations. Poro-Sande was law. Poro-Sande was order. And Poro-Sande came from God.[32]

No aspect of West African life was completely secular, and Poro-Sande sociopolitical power symbolized relationships between the sacred and the temporal. The foundation of Poro-Sande prerogative was mystical in nature, since the institution was considered to be made by God. Thus Poro-Sande spiritual significance was pervasive. Spirits dwelled in the sacred grove; among them were ancestral spirits, bush and water spirits, spirits of associations, and Poro-Sande spirits all with particular functions. Ancestral spirits, for example, explained life after death, were concerned with family and the larger group's well-being, and were protectors. Poro-Sande spirits, of whom the "bush devil" was the most important, were worldly representations of supernatural forces, personifying the will of God and mysteries of life. While other spirits in the pantheon were of the unseen world, Poro-Sande spirits represented the supernatural sphere and earthly manifestations of supernatural power. All spirits remained hidden behind masks, and the chief spiritual leader's identity was an especially guarded secret. The leader's authority was intergroup, and his or her standing was recognized even in distant chiefdoms where a language barrier existed. Bush initiates were often taken from several surrounding villages, adding to the strength of communal regulation and superseding immediate kinship ties.[33]

Hence one aim was spirit control, mainly through ceremony, ritual, meditation, medicine, and exclusive contact. Essentially, as Harley writes, Pro-Sande was a means of reducing the pervading spirit world to an organization in which humans might become spirits and take on "godhead." This transformation allowed secret society religious leaders to "contact the spirit world and interpret it to the people." The initiates' capacity to withstand the sacred bush experience and uphold its secrets extended functionally into the secular realm. Society was organized around allegiance to and belief in the power of Poro and Sande. Reverence for the symbolically sacred led to obedience, accountability, and respect for what was generally its identical secular arm, the Poro council.[34]

Nearly all Africans brought to America came from groups that practiced some type of initiation process. While none contained the distinctive structurally inclusive elements of Poro and Sande, one can still argue for the tenacity of the practice. The bush experience was a shared memory instilling loyalty, bonds of attachments, and unity that neither Christianity nor Islam could destroy, even today.

In the antebellum period Methodist missionaries found some Gullahs "professing" Christianity and nearly all of them organized into "black societies." "The society exerts its influence against us which is remarkably strong," wrote one missionary in 1844.

"This 'society' is altogether in the hands of the colored people who are actively engaged against us."[35] Thus Gullahs struggled to exercise spiritual and communal independence and missionaries attempted to fragment black control. Another Methodist wrote to the *Southern Christian Advocate* in 1846, bemoaning the "deplorable exhibition of pseudo religion" among the slaves on large plantations in coastal South Carolina:

> The superstitious notions prevalent here and there . . . probably . . . reflects . . . more ancient superstitions, handed down by tradition and propagated by so called *leaders,* who prior to the preaching of the gospel by . . . the missionaries . . . wielded a fearful amount of spiritual influence among their followers, and the negro communities of the plantations generally. And it is with remarkable tenacity these superstitious actions still maintain their hold in spite of a better teaching. Instead of giving up their visionary religionism, embracing the simple truth . . . our missionaries find them endeavoring to incorporate their superstitious rites with a purer system of instruction, producing thereby a hybrid, crude, and undefinable medley of truth and falsehood.[36]

Unlike Methodist missionaries, Baptist planters did not try to destroy the black societies but organized them into plantation churches. "Subsidiary to the church," wrote Civil War observer Edward Channing Gannett, "are local 'societies,' to which 'raw souls' are admitted after they have proved the reality of their 'strivings.'" Gullah slaves rarely saw the inside of a white church prior to their taking them over when owners fled during the Civil War. Gullahs embraced Christianity through praise house membership and maintained complete loyalty to these "invisible institutions" in both a spiritual and communal sense. Elders and members scrutinized personal behavior, and the praise house functioned as a religious court. Plantation membership and praise house membership were synonymous and were termed "catching sense." According to Patricia Guthrie, who did field work in the Sea Islands, "entrance into the religious and politico-jural domains parallels the time when plantation membership becomes fully realized," and in antebellum days joining the praise house formally expressed initiation into the plantation domain of the bondspeople. An individual was no longer only a household member but was also a citizen of the slave quarters through church membership. Personhood was attained through praise house membership, and all members answered to its religious court whenever internal discord arose. Praise house law was "just law," and membership demanded that disputes be settled within its jurisdiction. The "unjust law" was white law or forces outside praise house authority. Harmony, morality, justice, leadership, and dignity were upheld by the praise house. Thus plantation societies were the nucleus of the Gullah socioreligious community, perhaps just as the West African secret society was the communal and spiritual center of village life.[37]

Gullah methods of admission to church membership further demonstrate the relationship to secret society initiation. The time between an expressed desire to become a Christian and acceptance by the elders of one's religious experience was called "seekin'." It was a time when "raw souls" began their "striving." The phrase "to seek Jesus" was introduced to bondspeople by Methodists, but the seekin' process represents a Gullah interpretation. Gannett noted: "This 'striving' is a long process of self-examination and solitary prayer 'in the bush,' and so unremitting must be the devotion during this stage that even attendance at school is thought to interfere with the action of the spirit." Seekin' began with a personal decision not devoid of community pressure, followed by the choosing of a lifelong "spiritual parent," usually a female elder pointed out in a dream. The spiritual parent taught the seeker correct conduct and "how to pray." A seeker shunned social contact and went into "de wilderness" for prayer, solitude, and meditation. Night vigils (usually unapproved by plantation authority) were common, occurring in graveyards, cotton or cornfields, and marshes. Seekers often prayed to nature objects.[38]

The most important indication of spiritual transformation was the vision or *travel* as interpreted by the spiritual parent. "This word *travel*," wrote one Methodist missionary, "is one of the most significant in their language, and comprehends all those exercises, spiritual, visionary and imaginative which make up an 'experience.' " While the *travel* might differ in some things, "in others they all agree. Each seeker meets with warnings—awful sights or sounds," and has a vision of a white man who warns and talks with the seeker and eventually leads the seeker to the river. The spiritual parent decides when "de trabbel" is complete and when the seeker is ready to be presented to the praise house. The praise house elder and his committee further examine the candidate, asking spiritual and communal questions and finally approving baptism. Following baptism and church fellowship, new members engaged in a "ring shout." This counterclockwise dance involves people moving around in a circle, rhythmically shuffling their feet and shaking their hands while bystanders outside the ring clap, sing, and gesticulate. This religious circle dance is a spiritual outpouring which symbolizes community integration.[39]

The mystical nature of the Gullahs' conversion and its importance in community accountability has African antecedents. Sterling Stuckey argues that "movement in a ring during ceremonies honoring ancestors" was an integral part of life in central areas of Africa. According to Stuckey, the circle ritual of Bakongo peoples was "so powerful" and elaborate" that it "gave form and meaning to black religion and art." Community initiation through spiritual metamorphosis, symbolic death, and rebirth in "de wilderness" or "the bush" was germane to both societies. The role of slave women in seekin' correlates to the influence of female altar parents in African secret society. The head of the Sande society also wore white. Additionally, once African neophytes returned to the village they were given a water burial and new clothing, just as Gullah Christian seekers were baptized in old clothes and dressed in their "best" afterward for their communion and fellowship service.[40] Both processes, of a journey into the world of the ancestors (i.e., death) and subsequent return, represented an end of individualistic tendencies inimical to group interests. Both initiates were in the power of a spiritual leader who would not condone or overlook frailties. In each case the initiate or seeker entered into a state of wildness, helplessness, and irresponsibility, having no social sense. Guided by the altar parent, a physical, mental, and moral test was undergone to prove the individual's worth. In Africa, if transformation was not evident, the initiate did not return. In both societies, initiation represented efforts either to transcend what could not be controlled or to control elements of human variance and division.

Like Islam and Christianity, traditional African religions adhered to monotheism, though for non-Moslem Africans the Supreme Being or Sky God had many names. Akan-Ashanti referred to God as Onyame. Bantu peoples called God Nzambi. Among the Mende God was Ngewo and to the Gola, Daya. The Supreme Deity was generally considered omniscient and omnipotent, the creator of all life forms. God represented the highest values—kindness, justice, sincerity, and mercy. Thus in African perceptions God was no fomentor of mischief or ill will. Unlike Jehovah, the African God was not to be feared, and no prayers needed to be offered. Evil came from other sources, not the Creator. Although God was not accorded worship through libation and was invisible, allegiance was rendered, and the deity's ultimate power over humans was recognized. "Nzambi possesses us and eats us" or "He is gone, Nzambi has willed it," were central themes in some Bakongo proverbs and songs.[41]

Belief in afterlife was integral to traditional African religion. But Africans did not view the future world with fear nor as a place of dispensations for rewards and punishments in a Christian sense. In this land of the dead, where life continued, there was no sickness, disease, poverty, or hunger. But underworld inhabitants retained the positions of their earthly hierarchy. Death was a journey into the spirit world, not a break with life or earthly beings. The idea of the perpetuity of life through time, space, and circumstance was common to African religious culture, and the complexity of this belief system is typified by Bakongo cosmology and concepts of the four moments of the sun. Using the sun through its course around the earth, the Bakongo pointed out the four stages that make up one's life cycle: rising (birth, beginning, or regrowth), ascendancy (maturity and responsibility), setting (death and transformation), and midnight (existence in the other world and eventual rebirth). Life was a continuum, and the sign of the four moments of the sun symbolized "spiritual continuity and renaissance" through a spiral journey. The crossing of the four solar moments, though similar to the Greek cross and the Christian cross, was not introduced to the Bakongo by early Christianity. Long before the arrival of Europeans this geometric statement, the Kongo cruciform, adorned funerary objects and in other ways reflected Bakongo aesthetic perceptions of their relationship to the world. Robert Farris Thompson and Joseph Cornet brilliantly demonstrated this fact through Bakongo visual traditions in Africa and the New World.[42]

Belief that one's spirit consciously exists after death was also common. "New" Africans, once they learned English, found reinforcement, in Christian principles taught by white ministers, of the belief that everyone possessed a soul apart from one's human form, with its own destiny. In certain ways African concepts were more complicated.

Bakongo peoples probably had the most elaborate and complex system of afterlife beliefs, and these beliefs were central to their religious traditions. Humans were double beings, consisting of an outer and inner entity. Each entity in turn had two parts. One part of the outer being, the shell, was visible. After death it was buried and rotted. The second part was invisible and could be "eaten" by bad medicine, *kindoki*, but helped by good medicine, *minkisi*. The inner being's two parts were both necessary for continued existence. One signified personal life and, although expressions differed among groups, there was continuity in meaning. Some Bakongo peoples expressed the personal entity as *kivuumunu* (breathing). *Kivuumuni* was the agent of life and breath, hidden and protected from bad medicine. Death could not destroy it. The second part of the inner being, the *belly,* was different. It took food, which had to be provided for the entity to continue living. Both contributed to continued existence, one through breath and the other through nourishments. In the world of *mpemba* (land of all things white), the dead, through powers commensurate with the goodness of their previous earthly life, are expunged of earthly acquired impurities and reenter the world as reincarnated spirits (in grandchildren) or as immortal *simbi* spirits. Notions of the afterlife practiced by Bakongo peoples and their neighbors and reinforced by similar beliefs among other Africans parallel some Gullah "Christian" ritualistic customs of death and burial.[43]

Gullahs attached a tremendous significance to death, but there was little evidence of apprehension at the prospect of dying. Slaves lived in the presence of death constantly and seemed to feel that the phenomenon was as much a part of living as their continuous labor. That they often reflected on the subject is evident in their spirituals. Yet these songs do not indicate that Gullahs thought of death with fear, foreboding, or morbidity. Perhaps it was partly this stoicism in the face of earthly demise that some observers viewed as resignation or the effects of demoralization. All African ethnic groups believed in life beyond physical death. Possibly Gullahs retained the West African bush-initiation experience in their attitude toward death. This idea of a symbolic journey to the world of the dead and a triumphant return might explain the Gullahs' ability to transcend feelings of dread about death and to disavow its ultimate power over them. But perhaps an equally strong influence was the Bakongo, since these societies had the most elaborate afterlife beliefs. In the four moments of the sun, earthly death, the setting of the sun, is only the third moment. Thus death was not the end of life nor the cemetery a final resting place; it was a door *(mwelo)* between two worlds. The fourth moment is midnight on earth, when the sun is shining on the world of the dead. There rebirth takes place.[44]

No matter what the unconscious motivation, however, what many considered to be a weakness among these bondspeople was actually a source of strength. They overcame a fear of death in light of the reality of its dominant presence among them and through their realization that they, more than most other people, were often powerless to alter its course. Thus while Gullahs did not shrink from death they were aware of the degree to which their lives were exploited and of the oppression that often caused an untimely end to life.

The depth of their understanding was sometimes grippingly demonstrated. Teacher William Allen was struck by how much the children sang of pain and death. Little "Margaret" came to the well to draw her pail of water. Putting it on her head, she walked off singing, "Shall I die—shall I die." She was followed by Tom and Abraham, "galloping along on bamboo horses and shouting, 'my body rock 'long feber.'"[45]

Charlotte Forten was much affected by one of the hymns which she heard Gullah children singing:

> *I wonder where my mudder gone;*
>   *Sing, O graveyard!*
> *Graveyard ought to know me;*
>   *Ring, Jersusalem!*
> *Grass grow in de graveyard;*
>   *Sing, O graveyard!*
> *Graveyard ought to know me;*
>   *Ring, Jerusalem!*

"It is impossible," Forten wrote, "to give any idea of the deep pathos of the refrain, 'Sing, O graveyard,'"[46] The pathos is there certainly, but the sense of hope, so characteristic of the Gullahs, is also present in the words "Grass grow in de graveyard." This statement might indicate that in the Bakongo tradition, although there was death, there was also life and rebirth. The refrain "Graveyard ought to know me" might refer to the slaves' previous journey to the world of the dead as "seekers." The phrase might also recognize the omnipresence of death among the slaves.

Another spiritual expressed a sense of optimism and a superior attitude toward death:

> *O Massa Death,*
> *He's a very little man,*
> *He goes from door to door;*
> *He kills some souls,*
> *And he woundeth some.*
> *Good Lord remember me;*
> *Good Lord remember me;*
> *Remember me as the years roll round,*
> *Good Lord, remember me.*[47]

In Christian belief the finality of death was often negated. One of the most appealing aspects of Christianity for Gullahs was the expectation of a better life after death. This afterlife was not visualized in the African sense, which held that an individual's status would not differ from one's mortal position. Instead, Gullahs strongly adopted the Christian concept of heaven, where all "true believers" would sit on "Christ's right side." For obvious reasons this was the tenet of Christianity they cherished most. While their African world view encouraged Gullahs to take a positive attitude toward life, through the Christian influence they expected a better life as payment for their suffering. As one person expressed it:

> De harder me cross to bear down here de better I go be prepare to tek me place in dat Happy Land where all is 'joicin, an' when I git dere, I want de Lord to say, "Ophelia . . . come an' rest wid de elect ob de Lord!"[48]

There was little in the prayers or songs of the Gullahs to indicate they feared the tribunal expected to reward the "faithful" and damn the "sinners." Thus they disregarded that portion of their religious instruction that strenuously emphasized a judgment day when "every theft or falsehood" would be brought to light and held against them. What was more important to the Gullahs was a change in their conditions. A Baptist slave master, Daniel Pope, asked Marcus, the praise house elder, whether the Gullahs really believed Christ wanted "black nigger in heben." But so were the slaves convinced that the "Kingdom of God" would have almost no white subjects. Gullah Christianity was one of recompense. Slaves accepted the Christian doctrine of eternal life but modified it so that heaven was an exclusive place, primarily available to sufferers of the right hue, as expressed by a former slave:

> It is impossible to reconcile the mind of the native slave to the idea of living in a state of perfect equality, and boundless affection with white people. Heaven will be no heaven

to him, if he is not to be avenged of his enemies. I know, from experience, that these are fundamental rules of his religious creed; because I learned them in the religious meetings of the slaves themselves. A favorite and kind master or mistress may now and then be admitted into heaven, but this rather as a matter of favor, due to the intercession of some slave, than as a matter of strict justice to the whites, who will, by no means be of an equal rank with those who shall be raised from the depths of misery, in this world.

The idea of a revolution in the conditions of the whites and the blacks, is the cornerstone of the religion of the latter; and indeed it seems to me, at least, to be quite natural, if not in strict accordance with the precepts of the Bible.[49]

Although the Gullahs did not fear death, they recognized its power, and the passing of one of their number had a profound effect on the community. Methodist missionaries observed this effect and often tried to use the drama of death among the Gullahs to "bind them to the cross."[50] But while the Gullahs' perception of life after death was essentially of Christian origin, many practices associated with the dying and the dead were derived from African antecedents.

When death was expected the plantation community members felt compelled to enter into the spirit of the event and vicariously involve themselves in the death throes of the individual. Otherwise, when their time came they might have to face the ordeal alone, or the deceased, dissatisfied with the sendoff, might return and bring evil. The dying person was surrounded by the community, which offered comfort and support. "We got tuh help him cross de ribber," the Gullahs would say. Friends of the dying were expected to bring gifts even though the sufferer could not use them. Such offerings were usually edibles "tuh taste de mout'," but never flowers. Singing, praying, and pious conversation filled the cabin nightly. It was not a solemn time, unless sad or obscure circumstances caused the death, but rather was somewhat cheerful, and the subject of death itself was not neglected. Everyone was expected to hold forth as part of the ritual of coaching the dying person to report a heavenly visit or some other evidence of "dying good." When the sufferer drew the last breath, everyone present gave a loud shriek as notification that another soul "done crossed ober." Many northern teachers were repulsed at the Gullah "death-watch":

This practice of sitting up all night with the dying, H. W. [Harriet Ware] justly enough condemns as "heathenish." The houses cannot hold them all, of course, and they sit round out-of-doors in the street, the younger ones often falling asleep on the ground, and then they "hab fever."

But of course it was useless to expostulate with them; to their minds the omission of the watch would be a mark of great disrespect.[51]

Like their African forebears, Gullahs believed in the presence of evil almost as much as they believed in the forces of good, and their attempts to please both God and the "powers of darkness" explain much about their customs regarding death. Although Gullahs professed to believe that God "called" his servants to heaven, they still viewed death as an instrument of the powers of darkness. Thus night vigils, singing, praying, and preaching around the bedside of the dying were supposed to strengthen the dying as they "passed death's door." The loud shriek as the last breath was drawn was a formal announcement of the death, but it also "scares off the spirits of hell who are always lurking around to get possession of another soul."[52]

Gullahs believed that one could not always know whether demise had come through natural causes because "God called," which was a "good" death, or by witchcraft, a "bad" death. That was also true of many African peoples. Among those of the Windward Coast, death was said to come to people because God or the ancestors wanted them or because of witchcraft. Among the Bakongo the concept of a bad or a good death was also important. A bad death would be indicated if the sick person quarreled with those present, had severe pains, or suffered a prolonged death agony. If a person could not speak properly when dying or turned his or her head toward the wall, a bad death was also suspected. A bad death meant a person was "shot with nkisi-guns" and was considered an *ndoki,* or witch. A good death was a calm ordeal, peaceful and easy, with the person lying on his or her back.[53]

Though Gullah attitudes about good and bad deaths were infused with African customs, the death watch was viewed in a Christian context. An individual was said to "die good" by praying out loud, reporting a heavenly vision, or giving some evidence that peace had been made with God on the deathbed. A pious life counted for little if such things were not observed. Nor did an evil life mean damnation if the dying could satisfy spectators with an appropriate heavenly vision. What was probably more important to Gullahs was that the deceased be at peace with the world, assuring the community that he or she was not a witch or bewitched and would not return to "haant" the living.[54]

Spirits destined for hell did not actually go there until judgment day, according to Gullahs. Instead these "on-easy speerits," having no resting place, roamed the earth and tormented the living. Some Gullahs believed that good spirits went straight to heaven, but most seemed to think that even these spirits remained on earth, close to the place of their burial. Unlike those who "died bad," good spirits would normally not harm the living; nor would they roam. They appeared only in dreams, giving messages and warnings to the living. Thus Gullahs had a real concern for coaxing an individual to "die good" and a real superstition about those who "died bad." The slaves devised various mechanisms of defense against the latter spirits.[55]

Much of the Gullah attitude toward death and belief in spirits was inherited from the African respect for and honor of the living dead and from the African belief in the power of sorcery. Consider a description of death among the Mende:

> When a dying man is panting for breath, the Mende say "Taa ha ha yiyei le ma" ("he is climbing the hill of death"). As soon as death is announced, the members of the family all begin to wail. The body of the deceased is then washed, and messages are sent to call the absent members of the family. . . . Members of the family will bring money, cloth, wine and rice as their contribution towards the funeral expenses. . . . On the fourth day for a man (the third day for a woman), the "crossing-the-river" ceremony takes place. . . . If these ceremonies are not properly performed, the evil will fall on those responsible.

Similarly, for Temne people the underlying idea of funeral rites is to appease the spirits of the dead so they will not trouble the living. Mende also believe that separation of good and bad people takes place after crossing the river. While there is no clear-cut idea as to who bad people are, they are chiefly thought of as those who dealt in bad medicine or witchcraft. These evil ones in their spirit form will vent their feelings by sending disease and will haunt the living and take possession of them. Among the Bakongo the curse of the dying is much dreaded, especially that of a relative, for the deceased will soon enter the spirit world. A dying person may admonish those around to take care of his or her affairs. "If you do not, I shall fetch you, and you will not become old here on earth." The dying one may also request the living to "wrap me well in the cloth that I leave" and may insist that the living hold many lamentations after the death and care for the deceased's family. If not properly buried the deceased might bring *kindoki* (evil).[56]

A curious example of the application of both African and Christian practices among the slaves is provided by a former South Carolina bondsman. A good-looking and popular slave girl named Mary died after a lingering illness of a few months. The slaves on the surrounding plantations were sure that Mary had been conjured (poisoned) by a rival in a love triangle. The plantation proprietor, a Methodist minister, had Mary treated by his brother, a practicing physician. While the white doctor was attending Mary the slaves appealed to their own doctor, a plantation slave, who also treated the young woman. But Mary died and, according to the author, her funeral—which, in line with tradition, took place at night—"was the largest ever held in all that region of the country":

> The coffin, a rough home-made affair, was placed upon a cart, which was drawn by an old Gray, and the multitudes formed in a line in the rear, marching two deep. The procession was something like a quarter of a mile long. Perhaps every fifteenth person down the line carried an uplifted torch. As the procession moved slowly toward "the lonesome graveyard" down by the side of the swamp, they sung the well-known hymn of Dr. Isaac Watts:

> *When I can read my title clear*
> *To mansions in the skies,*
> *I bid farewell to every fear*
> *And wipe my weeping eyes.*

Mary's baby was taken to the graveyard by its grandmother, and before the corpse was deposited in the earth, the baby was passed from one person to another across the coffin. The slaves believed that if this was not done it would be impossible to raise the infant. The mother's spirit would come back for her baby and take it to herself.

After this performance the corpse was lowered into the grave and covered, each person throwing a handful of dirt into the grave as a last farewell act of kindness to the dead, and while this was being done the leader announced that other hymn by Dr. Watts:

> *Hark! from the tomb a doleful sound*
> *My ears, attend the cry;*
> *Ye living men, come view the ground*
> *Where you must shortly lie.*

> . . . A prayer was offered. . . . This concluded the services at the grave. No burial or commital service was read. At a subsequent time, when all the relatives and friends could be brought together a big funeral sermon was preached by some of the antebellum negro preachers.

The presence of a plantation slave "doctor" is reminiscent of the Bakongo priest, *nganga,* who employed life-affirming *nkisi* to heal and ward off *kindoki.* The charm did not work for the plantation slave, and the large funeral turnout may represent the people's desire to protect themselves from whatever evil had caused Mary's death as well as to express their respect. Passing the woman's baby back and forth over her coffin was a well-known Gullah graveside custom. "Dead moder will hant de baby," Gullahs explained, and "worry him in his sleep." A similar custom among the Bakongo women was crossing back and forth over the graveside of a woman who died in childbirth, hoping that such a fate would not befall them. Singing at the grave was also part of the Bakongo sendoff. The funeral, a lavish affair, would take place when all members of the clan could gather and enough food could be collected.[57]

Thus besides the Christian version of immortality there were elements of African tradition that accounted for the Gullahs' attitude toward death, as indeed it did their philosophy of life. Not only was the existence of deceased spirits central to African ontology, but these beings also constituted the largest group of religious intermediaries. Hence Africans viewed death as perhaps the most important rite of passage rather than as the end of life. Death was a momentous transition, requiring demonstrative evidence that the physical presence of the deceased would be missed. But it was just as necessary to celebrate this passage into the spirit world in a manner indicating a continued existence. Africans believed that the spirit that survived the body was conscious of all earthly events and had the power to exercise influence over the destiny of the living. Consequently, the death of a clan member was observed with greatest respect, and the death commemoration was expressed collectively.[58]

Ancestors retained their normal human passions and appetites, which had to be gratified in death as in life. Ancestors felt hunger and thirst. They became angry or happy depending on the behavior of their living "children." The living dead were vindictive if neglected but propitious if shown respect. Just as filial loyalty prevents one from allowing a parent to go hungry, "so must food be offered to the ancestors." Among the Bakongo, food was put out immediately after the burial and palm wine poured over the grave. Survivors believed the deceased would eat the food and bless those who placed it there.[59]

Among the Gullahs, even for one who "died good" the spirit could not rest if something had been left behind which it desired. Observers noted that Gullahs and other African-Americans placed articles on new graves. These objects were usually personal belongings, broken pottery and porcelain, playthings, lighting utensils, objects pertaining to medicine, food, and water. According to the antebellum memories of Telfair Hodgson, a number of her father's slaves came directly from Africa. Their graves were "always decorated with the last articles used by the departed, and broken pitchers, and broken bits of colored glass were considered even more appropriate than the white shells from the beach nearby." Sometimes the slaves also carved "wooden figures like images of idols" or put a "patchwork quilt" on the grave. One twentieth-century investigator, Samuel Lawton, was told by a number of Sea Island ministers that it was also a common custom to bury articles along with the dead:

You must not think that just because you do not find anything on those graves that the relatives did not put some things in there. It is most likely that they have a number of things buried with the body. I have often, at the burials I have conducted, seen the relatives pour hamper baskets full of things right down on top of the coffin before the dirt is shoveled into the grave.[60]

The custom of putting objects both in and on top of graves can be traced to African origins. The Ovimbundu place such articles as baskets, gourds, and instruments used in the burial on top of grave sites. People in the Kongo were said to "mark the final resting-places of their friends by ornamenting their graves with crockery, empty bottles, old cooking-pots, etc." Many ethnic groups of the Windward Coast believed it necessary to provide the dead with various gifts, domestic articles, and clothing to use in the life beyond the grave. Such articles, along with food and water, would be left at the grave, and it was believed that the spirit of the deceased would come and claim them.[61]

Of the two spirits the Gullahs believed in, it was the "trabblin" spirit rather than the heaven-going spirit that caused the greatest concern. The reasons given for grave adornment clearly indicate the African precedent. One informant related:

Yo' see, suh, everybody got two kinds ob speerits. One is der hebben-goin' speerit. . . . Den dere is de trabblin' speerit. De hebben-goin' speerit don't gib you no trouble, but de trabblin' speerit, 'e be de one dat gib you worriment. E come back to de t'ings 'e like. E try fur come right back in de same house.[62]

Similarity of beliefs and motives regarding grave adornment is best illustrated by the types of articles found on graves in the Sea Islands. Such objects as partially filled medicine bottles, mirrors, broken pitchers, saucers and cups, mayonnaise jars, cold cream, tobacco, and black pepper were commonly placed on graves. Seashells were also commonly placed on graves. Other personal items included shaving brushes, toothbrushes, combs, and belt buckles. Twelve Gullah ministers reported to Samuel Lawton that other articles of food, such as grapes, oranges, apples, bananas, bread, and cake, were often placed on graves and soon eaten by animals and birds. Further efforts to satisfy the spirits of the dead included pouring water on the grave during a drought. This custom could have been for the purpose of quenching the thirst of the spirit so that the dead would not disturb the living by seeking water.[63]

Gullah decoration of graves indicates a firm belief in the return of ancestors from the world of the dead. Offerings on graves were statements of homage, and in these graveyards one finds the strongest expressions of African-inspired memories. Many objects are associated with or used to hold water. In Bakongo religion, deceased ancestors became white creatures called *bakulu,* who lived in the land of all things white. This village of the dead was located under riverbeds and lakes. The white spiritual transparency of *bakulu* allowed them to return to the world of the living undetected. Seashells used on Gullah graves, for instance, are an important theme in Bakongo metaphysics. One Bakongo prayer that addresses the shells states: "As strong as your house, you shall keep my life for me. When you leave for the sea, take me along, that I may live forever." The essence of this prayer is recaptured by the late Bessie Jones of St. Simons Island, Georgia: "The shells stand for the sea. The sea brought us, the sea shall take us back. So the shells upon our graves stand for water, the means of glory and the land of demise."[64]

Just as seashells and pottery express immortal existence and the significance of a water underworld, so the glittering, iridescent mirrors and porcelain on Gullah graves reflect the light that represents the spirit. These objects, like water when struck by sunlight, are intimations of the flash of the separated spirit in symbolized flight. Mirrors, lamps, porcelain, and glass are spirit-embodying once they are placed on the graves. Their presence keeps the spirit away from the living. The significance of spiritual proximity in brilliance gave rise to the Bakongo custom of lighting bonfires on graves to lead one's soul to the other world. Similarly, Gullah torchlight burials may have a deeper meaning than simply lighting the path. Certainly the presence of lamps on African-American graves indicates that perhaps this was a means of lighting the way to the world beyond and keeping away the deceased's spirit. Furthermore, the decorations imply the deceased's entrance into the fourth moment, a spiritual existence where all is light and brilliance. Breaking pottery and porcelain was perhaps not done to prevent theft, as some researchers believe, but may indicate the deceased's break with earthly life.[65]

Another interesting continuity between Gullah and African traditions in regard to burial is the positioning of the deceased. In central West Africa the coffin is placed so that the deceased faces eastward. Folklorist Elsie Parsons noted that Gullah graves were "invariably dug east to west, with the head to the west." Thomas Higginson wrote in his diary of a "very impressive" funeral for two black soldiers in his regiment. Just before the coffins were lowered "an old man whispered to me that I must have their positions altered—the heads must be towards the west." Higginson complied without asking why. Gullahs and Africans shared a concept of the cosmos. The world followed the sun from east to west.[66]

The deity empowered Upper Guinea peoples through Poro-Sande, gave *minkisi* to the Bakongo, and transformed the ancestors into spiritual guardians. Hence God was not only a Supreme Spirit but a lawgiver as well. The supernatural existence of Poro-Sande was thus ordained and the pantheon of Poro-Sande spirits, through association with God, decreed laws and set standards and modes of behavior, worship, and customs. The "captured spirit" in each *nkisi* was incarnated power sent directly from Nzambi (similar perhaps to the Christian Holy Ghost). Ancestors were the emissaries of the withdrawn Supreme Deity. This idea of the remoteness of God, noted by writers and observers, is disputed by some recent African scholars. Still, both sides of the debate acknowledge the presence of a Supreme Deity in African spiritual concepts, and that God had agents through which divine will was dispensed. This provided a linkage of spiritual virtue with communal responsibility. The attributes of God corresponded with characteristics of harmony and social order, the antithesis of bush living, which was a wild, antisocial state of consciousness.

Similarly, Gullahs who accepted Christianity associated community socialization with religious piety. The laws of God were synonymous with correct conduct toward other members of the slave quarters. In maintaining this African socioreligious connection in the American ambiance, bondspeople operated on an internal logic that excluded planters, overseers, even white Christian ministers. A parallel existed between the structural configuration of what became Gullah folk religion and the composition of social order in the quarters. African and Gullah theories of being are related. In both, God (Jesus for the Gullahs) was the apex, representing honor, constancy, harmony, and perfection, while humanity occupied the center, ever striving to be godlike through a sense of community, kinship, and cooperation. In addition, the good and bad of the spirit world existed in both traditions, although it was far more complex for Africans than for Gullahs. These beings included superhumans, animals, and objects without biological life. Gullahs applied the African ontology, adapted Christianity and bondage to it, and created a religion that employed spirituality as a means of self-preservation and as a vital component of community life.

It is, then, to the Gullahs' credit that, though circumstances prevented their rising up against slavery physically, they did not succumb to white cultural domination. Instead, the Gullahs successfully rose above deceptive aspects of their Christian instruction while assimilating certain other attributes that were serviceable and syncretistic with African culture. In bondage, Gullahs achieved elevation through personal culture and the molding of community values. The edifying qualities of Gullah African-Christian folk religion must be seen as having contributed much to that achievement.

Notes

1. Mason Crum, *Gullah: Negro Life in the Carolina Sea Islands* (Durham, N.C.: Duke University Press, 1940), 3, 19–22, 78. Paul Quattlebaum, *The Land Called Chicora* (Gainesville: University of Florida Press, 1956), 86–88. Margaret Washington Creel, *"A Peculiar People": Slave Religion and Community-Culture among the Gullahs* (New York: New York University Press, 1988), passim.
2. Peter H. Wood, *Black Majority: Negroes in Colonial South Carolina from 1670 through the Stono Rebellion* (New York: Knopf, 1974), 131, 301–4, 333–41.
3. Elizabeth Donnan, *Documents Illustrative of the History of the Slave Trade to America, 4, The Southern Colonies* (Washington, D.C.: Carnegie Institution, 1935), and "The Slave Trade into South Carolina before the Revolution," *American Historical Review* (1927–28) 33:807–8, 816–17. Converse Clowse, *Economic Beginnings in Colonial South Carolina, 1730–1760* (Columbia: University of South Carolina Press, 1971), 206, 230–32. Philip Curtin, *The Atlantic Slave Trade: A Census* (Madison: University of Wisconsin Press, 1969). W. Robert Higgins, "The Geographical Origins of Negro Slaves in Colonial South Carolina," *South Atlantic Quarterly* (1971) 70:42–43. Creel, *"A Peculiar People,"* 29–30, 37.
4. The same is true of the Georgia Sea Island region, home of the "Geechee" slave population; see Creel, *"A Peculiar People,"* 17–19.
5. Lorenzo Turner, *Africanisms in the Gullah Dialect* (New York: Arno Press, 1968; reprint of 1949 edition). Donald R. Kloe, "Buddy Quow: An Anonymous Poem in Gullah-Jamaican Dialect Written circa 1800," *Southern Folklore Quarterly* (June 1974) 38(2):82–84. Wilbur Zelinsky, *The Cultural Geography of the United States* (Englewood Cliffs, N.J.: Prentice-Hall, 1973), 20–21. Wood, *Black Majority,* 333–41. Curtin, *Atlantic Slave Trade,* 30–36, 44–45, 134–35, 411. Creel, *"A Peculiar People,"* 29–44, 329–34. Daniel Littlefield, *Rice and Slaves: Ethnicity and the Slave Trade in Colonial South Carolina* (Baton Rouge: Louisiana State University Press, 1981).

6. The spelling of Kongo with a *K* instead of a *C* is used by some Africanists. It refers to the traditional, unitary civilization and way of life of Bakongo peoples. The *C* spelling represents the political shift that occurred with white colonial penetration and partition in Central Africa. Traditional Kongo civilization includes modern Bas-Zaire, neighboring Cabinda, Congo-Brazzaville, Gabon, and Northern Angola. The ancient civilization was once under the suzerainty of the kingdom of Kongo. The language is KiKongo, although dialects vary widely in this Bantu-speaking area of Africa. The numerous ethnic groups and some neighboring ones share cultural and religious traditions. They also share memories of the trials and tears left in the wake of centuries of transatlantic slave trading and subsequent colonial exploitation. John M. Janzen and Wyatt MacGaffey, *An Anthology of Kongo Religion: Primary Texts from Lower Zaire* (Lawrence: University of Kansas Publications in Anthropology, no. 5, 1974), 1–3. Robert Farris Thompson and Joseph Cornet, *The Four Moments of the Sun: Kongo Art in Two Worlds* (Washington, D.C.: National Gallery of Art, 1981), 27. Robert Farris Thompson, *Flash of the Spirit: African and Afro-American Art and Philosophy* (New York: Vintage Books, 1983), 103. Wyatt MacGaffey, *Custom and Government in the Lower Congo* (Berkeley: University of California Press, 1970), 11.

7. Turner, *Africanisms in Gullah,* 63, 136, 138, 151, 189, 194. Winifred Vass, *The Bantu Speaking Heritage of the United States* (Los Angeles: UCLA, Center for Afro-American Studies, 1979), 31.

8. *Southern Christian Advocate,* December 22 and 29, 1843. Creel, *"A Peculiar People,"* 29–44.

9. P. E. Hair, "Sierra Leone Items in the Gullah Dialect of American English," *Sierra Leone Language Review* (1965), 4:79–84, 89–93. Turner, *Africanisms in Gullah,* 63, 150, 189. Creel, *"A Peculiar People,"* 17–19.

10. For an extensive bibliography on works about Gullahs and the need for more modern approaches, see Mary A. Twining, "Sources in the Folklore and Folklife of the Sea Islands," *Southern Folklore Quarterly* (1975) 39:135–50. In 1980 the *Journal of Black Studies* devoted an entire issue to Sea Island culture, edited by Twining and Keith E. Baird.

11. See Willie Lee Rose, *Rehearsal for Reconstruction: The Port Royal Experiment* (Indianapolis: Bobbs-Merrill, 1964), and, more significant, Charles Joyner, *Down by the Riverside: A South Carolina Slave Community* (Urbana: University of Illinois Press, 1984), and Patricia Jones-Jackson, *When Roots Die: Endangered Traditions on the Sea Islands* (Athens: University of Georgia Press, 1987).

12. The current exception is Creel, *"A Peculiar People."*

13. Charles C. Pinckney, *An Address delivered in Charleston before the Agricultural Society of South Carolina, at Its Annual Meeting, 18th August,* 1829 (Charleston, S.C.: A. E. Miller, 1829). Charles C. Jones, *The Religious Instruction of the Negroes in the United States* (New York: Negro Universities Press, 1969; reprint of 1842 edition), 70–71. William Wightman, *Life of William Capters, including an Autobiography* (Nashville, Tenn.: J. B. McFerrin, 1858), 291–92. Luther Porter Jackson, "Religious Instruction of Negroes, 1830–1860," *Journal of Negro History* (1930) 15:83–84. James O. Andrew, "The Southern Slave Population," *Methodist Magazine and Quarterly Review* (1831) 13:315–21.

14. Most sources refer to the Sea Island plantation churches as praise houses because northerners living among and writing about the Gullahs adopted this spelling. But the term *pray's house* is used to signify its function as a place of prayer on the plantations—hence a house of prayer. The Gullahs' pronunciation of the flat *a* and their failure to pronounce the last syllable on many words probably explains why no difference between *pray's* and *praise* was detected. Yet according to Samuel Lawton, who interviewed Sea Island blacks, many of them former slaves, Gullahs called the plantation churches either "pray house," without the *s* sound, or they pronounced the two syllables very distinctly, "pray-ers house," and stated

that it was "Way oner go fur pray." Lawton also observed that the Gullahs freely changed verbs into nouns without adding the extra ending. Thus, at the meeting house, "One pray, Den Annuder lead a pray'—Dat mak' two pray's" Lawton's argument is reinforced by Patricia Guthrie's more recent field work in the 1970s. According to Guthrie, "Praise houses are also known locally and in the literature as prayer and pray houses." The Gullahs' mastering of double meaning may also inform the discussion. They often asked white northerners to "jine praise wid we." Also their anthem, "New Jerusalem," stated, "Sing God praise both night and day." Thus the Gullahs went to the meeting house to praise *and* pray. Samuel Lawton, "The Religious Life of Coastal and Sea Island Negroes," Ph.D. dissertation, George Peabody College for Teachers, 1939, 54–56. Patricia Guthrie, "Praise House Worship and Litigation among Afro-Americans on a South Carolina Sea Island," paper, Sixth Annual Martin Luther King Lecture Series, Purdue University, February 21, 1980, 1.

15. William Pope, Sr., to William E. Baynard, Esq., January 8, 1834, and James Sealy to William E. Baynard, Esq., January 8, 1834, Historical Society South Carolina Conference, Methodist Church Archives, Wofford College, Spartanburg, S.C. *Christian Advocate and Journal,* January 31 and June 20, 1834; July 22, 1836. *Southern Christian Advocate,* June 26, 1840; June 26, 1843; April 8, 1842; February 16, 1844; September 29, 1843. James H. Cuthbert, *Life of Richard Fuller, D.D.* (New York: Sheldon, 1879), 81–106. James W. Busch, "The Beaufort Baptist Church," Beaufort County Historical Society paper, Beaufort, S.C., Township Library, n.d., 14–16. Minutes, Savannah River Baptist Association, Baptist Collection, Furman University, Greenville, S.C. Minutes, Beaufort Baptist Church, Baptist Collection, 271–74 and passim. George P. Rawick, *The American Slave: A Composite Autobiography.* 2, *South Carolina Narratives* (Westport, Conn.: Greenwood Press, 1972 reprint), pt. 1, 274; pt. 2, 185. Diary of Laura M. Towne, 15, Penn School Papers, vol. 1, Southern Historical Collection, University of North Carolina, Chapel Hill.

16. John S. Mbiti, *African Religions and Philosophy* (New York: Praeger, 1969), 1–5, 15. James L. Sibley and D. Westermann, *Liberia Old and New* (London: James Clarke, 1928), 187–88. Willie Abraham, *The Mind of Africa* (Chicago: University of Chicago Press, 1962), 52. Robert T. Parsons, *Religion in an African Society* (Leiden: E. J. Brill, 1964), 173–76, 179, 183–85. Geoffrey Parrinder, *Religion in Africa* (Middlesex, England: Penguin, 1969), chaps. 2–6. Placinde Tempels, *Bantu Philosophy,* trans. from French by Colin King (Paris: Presence Africaine, 1959). MacGaffey, *Custom in Lower Congo,* 261–62.

17. Mbiti, *African Religions,* 210–13. Abraham, *Mind of Africa,* 106. Sibley and Westermann, *Liberia,* 190–91. Parsons, *Religion in an African Society,* 174, 183–84. W. T. Harris and Harry Sawyerr, *The Springs of Mende Belief and Conduct* (Freetown: Sierra Leone Press, 1968), 103–5. Parrinder, *Religion in Africa,* 41, 81–89. Tempels, *Bantu Philosophy,* chaps. 5 and 6. Jahnheinz Jahn, *Muntu: An Outline of Neo-African Culture,* trans. from German by Marjorie Greene (London: Faber, 1961), 110, 114–17. Kwabena Amponsah, *Topics on West African Traditional Religion* (Accra, Ghana: McGraw-Hill, 1974), 70–80. Kofi Asara Opoku, *West African Traditional Religions* (Jurong, Singapore: FEP International Private, 1978), 152–60.

18. Mbiti, *African Religions,* 2–16. Despite the exalted modern application of *ontology* in its reference to abstract being, the word originally referred to that which belongs to existent finite being; see Walter Brugger, ed., *Philosophical Dictionary,* trans. from German by Kenneth Baker (Spokane, Wash.: Gonzaga University Press, 1972), 301–2. With regard to African culture and spirituality, the concept of being cannot be restricted to the physiological as opposed to the psychological or fantastic sphere.

19. Thompson and Cornet, *Four Moments of the Sun,* 27–99. Tempels, *Bantu Philosophy,* 64–66. Jahn, *Muntu,* 121–27. Sibley and Westermann, *Liberia,* 187–202. Abraham, *Mind of Africa,* 48–49, 52, 59–62. Parsons, *Religion in an African Society,* 174–93. Harris and Sawyerr, *Mende Beliefs,*

117–21, 123–24. Mbiti, *African Religions,* 15–16, chaps. 11–14. Parrinder, *Religion in Africa,* 78–83. Opoku, *West African Religion,* 91–139. Amponsah, *Topics on Traditional Religion,* 48–68.

20. Arthur Sumner to Lt. Joseph H. Clark, January 23, 1863. Penn Papers, vol. 4, Southern Historical Collection, University of North Carolina, Chapel Hill.

21. Elizabeth Hyde Botume, *First Days amongst the Contrabands* (New York: Arno Press, 1969; reprint of 1893 edition), 218.

22. Thomas W. Higginson, *Army Life in a Black Regiment* (New York: Collier, 1962 reprint of 1870 edition), 231–39.

23. Paul Radin, "Status, Phantasy, and the Christian Dogma," in *God Struck Me Dead: Religious Conversion Experience and Autobiographies of Negro Ex-slaves* (Nasvhille, Tenn.: Social Science Institute, Fisk University, 1945), i–ix.

24. John W. Blassingame, ed., *Slave Testimony: Two Centuries of Letters, Speeches, Interviews and Autobiographies* (Baton Rouge: Louisiana State University Press, 1977), 377. Dorothy Sterling, *Captain of the Planter: The Story of Robert Smalls* (Garden City, N.Y.: Doubleday, 1958), 32–33. Mary Ames, *From a New England Woman's Diary in Dixie* (New York: Negro Universities Press: reprint of 1906 edition), 45.

25. Charlotte Forten, "Life on the Sea Islands," *Atlantic Monthly,* May 1864, 588.

26. Rupert Holland, ed., *Letters and Diary of Laura M. Towne* (New York: Negro Universities Press, 1969; reprint of 1912 edition), 26.

27. Charles Nordhoff, "The Freedman of South Carolina," in *Papers of the Day,* ed. by Frank Moore (New York: C. T. Evans, 1863), 10.

28. Higginson, *Army Life,* 192. Botume, *Amongst the Contrabands,* 204. Forten, "LIfe on the Sea Islands," 672.

29. Botume, *Amongst the Contrabands,* 204.

30. Higginson, *Army Life,* 235–38, 267–76.

31. Walter Rodney, *A History of the Upper Guinea Coast,* 1545–1800 (Oxford, Clarendon Press, 1970), 32–33, 65–67. Kenneth Little, "The Political Function of the Poro," pt. 1, *Africa* (October, 1965) 35:349–56; *The Mende of Sierra Leone* (London: Routledge & Kegan Paul, 1951), 7–8, 240–42; and "The Poro Society as Arbiter of Culture," *African Studies* (March 1941) 7:1. Nicholas Owen, *Journal of a Slave Dealer: A View of Some Remarkable Axedents in the Life of Nicholas Owen on the Coast of Africa and America from the Year 1746 to the Year 1757* (London: George Routledge, 1930), 30–31. John Matthews, *A Voyage to the River Sierra Leone* (London: Frank Cass, 1966; reprint of 1788 edition), 82–83. Warren L. d'Azevedo, "The Setting of Gola Society and Culture: Some Theoretical Implications of Variation in Time and Space," *Kroeber Anthropological Society Papers* (Berkeley: University of California, 1959), 43–45, 67–68. M. McCulloch, *Peoples of Sierra Leone* (London: International African Institute, 1950), 29–37, 68–69, 81–82, 93. George W. Harley, "Notes on Poro in Liberia," *Papers of the Peabody Museum of American Archaeology and Ethnology* (1941) 19:6. Sibley and Westermann, *Liberia,* chaps. 5–9. Folkways Research Series, *Tribes of the Western Province and the Denwoin People* (Monrovia: Department of Interior, 1955), 17, 24–32. Parsons, *Religion in an African Society,* 140–51.

32. Mark Hanna Watkins, "The West African 'Bush' School," *American Journal of Sociology* (1943) 48:667–71, 674–75. Sylvia Boone, *Radiance from the Waters: Ideals of Feminine Beauty in Mende Art* (New Haven, Conn.: Yale University Press, 1986), 13–18. Little, "Political Function of the Poro," pt. 1, 357–58; "The Role of Secret Society in Cultural Specialization," *American Anthropologist* (1949) 51:200–205; and "Poro as Arbiter of Culture," 1, 4–6, 9–10. Richard Fulton, "The Political Structures and Functions of Poro in Kpelle Society," *American Anthropologist* (1972) 74:1222–23. Sibley and Westermann, *Liberia* 176–86, 217–36. Folkways Research Series, *The Traditional History and Folklore of the Gola*

Tribe in Liberia, 2 (Monrovia: Department of Interior, 1961), 10–12, 16–22. S. N. Eisentadt, "Primitive Political Systems: A Preliminary Comparative Analysis," *American Anthropologist* (1959) 61:202–3, 208. Warren d'Azevedo, "Common Principles of Variant Kinship Structures among the Golas of Western Liberia," *American Anthropologist* (1962) 64(3):513–14, and "Gola Society and Culture," 70–76.

33. Little, *The Mende,* 226–27, 240–47; "Poro as Arbiter of Culture," 3; and "Secret Society in Cultural Specialization," 199–201. Fulton, "Functions of Poro in Kpelle Society," 1226–28. Harley, "Notes on Poro," 3–9, 11–12, 29–31.

34. Harley, "Notes on Poro," 7.

35. "Origin of the Colored Societies," Minutes, Beaufort Baptist Church, October 7, 1859, 12, Baptist Collection, Furman University, Greenville, S.C. *Christian Advocate and Journal,* January 31, 1834; November 20, 1835; July 22, 1836. *Southern Christian Advocate,* May 1, 1840; April 8, 1842; June 26, 1843; February 16, 1844; October 30, 1846.

36. *Southern Christian Advocate,* February 16, 1844; October 30, 1846.

37. Edward Channing Gannett, "The Freedman at Port Royal," *North American Review* (July 1865) 101:9. Thomas J. Woofter, *Black Yeomanry* (New York: Henry Holt, 1930), 243–54. Lawton, "Religious Life," 62–63, 69–72. Guthrie, "Praise House Worship and Litigation," 1, and "Catching Sense: The Meaning of Plantation Membership on St. Helena Island, South Carolina," Ph.D. dissertation, University of Rochester, 1977, chaps. 4 and 5.

38. *Southern Christian Advocate,* April 18 and July 28, 1843; October 30, 1846; October 30, 1847; September 6, 1859. Gannett, "Freedmen at Port Royal," 9. Jenkins Mikell, *Rumblings of the Chariot Wheels* (Columbia, S.C.: The State Company, 1923), 137–39. Higginson, *Army Life,* 194–95. Elsie Clews Parsons, *Folk-Lore of the Sea Islands of South Carolina* (Cambridge, Mass.: American Folklore Society, 1923), 204–5. Diary of William F. Allen, William F. Allen Family Papers, 1775–1937, State Historical Society of Wisconsin, Madison, 155. Charles A. Raymond, "The Religious Life of the Negro Slave," *Harpers New Monthly Magazine* (October 1863) 27:680–81. Botume, *Amongst the Contrabands,* 254–55. Seekin' may also have been practiced by other African-American slaves; see Raymond, 680–82.

39. *Southern Christian Advocate,* October 30, 1846; October 30, 1847. Towne Diary, 52. Gannett, "Freedmen at Port Royal," 10. Sterling Stuckey, *Slave Culture: Nationalist Theory and the Foundations of Black America* (New York: Oxford University Press, 1987), 85–90. Creel, *"A Peculiar People,"* 297–302.

40. Stuckey, *Slave Culture,* 11, 13–16, 89–90. Watkins, "'Bush' School," 66–67. D'Azevedo, "Kinship Structures among the Golas," 505. Harris and Sawyerr, *Mende Belief,* 47–49. M. C. Jedrej. "Structural Aspects of a West African Society," 136; Carolina H. Bledsoe, "Stratification and Sande Politics," 143–45; Svend Holsoe, "Notes on the Vai Sande Society in Liberia," 97–107; and Warren d'Azevedo, "Gola Poro and Sande: Primal Tasks in Social Custodianship," 98–104, all in *Ethnologische Zeitschrift Zurich* 1 (1980). Towne Diary, 52. David Thorpe to John Mooney, January 25, 1863, Dabbs Papers, Thorpe Series, Southern Historical Collection, University of North Carolina, Chapel Hill.

41. Opoku, *West African Traditional Religion,* 14–29. Amponsah, *Topics on West African Religion,* 20–30. J. B. Danquah, *The Akan Doctrine of God: A Fragment of Gold Coast Ethics and Religion* (London: Lutterworth Press, 1944), 30–42. Sibley and Westermann, *Liberia,* 192–97. Folkways Research Series, *History of Gola Tribe,* 1–5. Harris and Sawyerr, *Mende Belief,* 2–13, 119–20. Karl Laman, *The Kongo* (Uppsala: Studia Ethnographica Upsaliensia, 1962) 3:1–2, 53–63. Georges Balandier, *Daily Life in the Kingdom of Kongo, from the Sixteenth to the Eighteenth Century,* trans. by Helen Weaver (London: George Allen & Unwin, 1968), 244–45. Edwin Smith, ed., *African Ideas of God* (London: Edinburgh House

Press, 1950). Beryl L. Bellman, *Village of Curers and Assassins: On the Production of Fala Kpelle Cosmological Categories* (The Hague: Mouton, 1975), 129–30.

42. Parrinder, *Religion in Africa,* 26. Mbiti, *African Religions,* 159–62. Jahn, *Muntu,* 109–14. Janzen and MacGaffey, *Anthology of Kongo Religion,* 34. Thompson and Cornet, *Four Moments of the Sun,* 27–28, 42–47, 134 n. 50, and passim. Thompson, *Flash of the Spirit,* 103–58. Balandier, *Daily Life in Kongo,* 245–49.

43. Laman, *Kongo* 3:1–6, 216–18. Thompson and Cornet, *Four Moments of the Sun,* 43.

44. Thompson and Cornet, *Four Moments of the Sun,* 27.

45. Allen Diary, 96.

46. Forten, "Life on the Sea Islands," 666.

47. Nordhoff, "Freedmen of South Carolina," 4.

48. *Southern Christian Advocate,* July 7 and August 11, 1843; January 19, 1844; August 20, 1847; May 5, 1844. South Carolina Folklore Project 1655, D-4-27, W.P.A. Collection, South Carolina Library, University of South Carolina, Columbia.

49. Towne Diary, 26. James Ball, *Fifty Years in Chains, or the Life of an American Slave* (New York: H. Dayton, 1860), 150.

50. *Southern Christian Advocate,* July 7, 1843.

51. Elizabeth Ware Pearson, *Letters from Port Royal* (New York: Arno Press: reprint of 1906 edition), 253–54. Towne Diary, 64, 75. Folklore Project 1655 D-4-27.

52. Pearson, *Port Royal,* 252. Irving E. Lowrey, *Life on the Old Plantation* (Columbia: University of South Carolina Press, 1911), 81–83. Folklore Project 1655 and 1855, D-4-27. T. W. Richardson to Rev. George Whipple, September 14, 1863. American Missionary Association Papers.

53. Harris and Sawyerr, *Mende Belief,* 31–32. Laman, *Kongo* 2:85.

54. Folklore Project 1655 and 1855, D-4-27A, 27B. Janie G. Moore, "Africanisms among Blacks in the Sea Islands," *Journal of Black Studies* (June 1980) 10(41):476–77. John M. Vlach, *The Afro-American Tradition in Decorative Arts* (Cleveland: Cleveland Museum of Art, 1978), 139–40. Parsons, *Folk-Lore of the Sea Islands,* 213–14.

55. Parsons, *Folk-Lore of the Sea Islands,* 213–14.

56. Harris and Sawyerr, *Mende Belief,* 31–32, 89. McCulloch, *Peoples of Sierra Leone,* 74. W. C. Willoughby, *The Soul of the Bantu: A Sympathetic Study of the Magico-Religious Practices and Beliefs of the Bantu Tribes of Africa* (Westport, Conn.: Negro Universities Press, 1970; reprint of 1928 edition), 86–87. Laman, *Kongo* 2:84.

57. Lowrey, *Old Plantation,* 83–87. Laman, *Kongo* 2:88–92. Moore, "Africanisms in the Sea Islands," 473–76. Parsons, *Folk-Lore of the Sea Islands,* 213. Thompson, *Flash of the Spirit,* 117. John H. Weeks, *Among the Primitive Bakongo* (London: Seeley Service, 1914), 267–68.

58. Mbiti, *African Religions,* 149. Ellis, *Negro Culture in West Africa,* 70–71. Harris and Sawyerr, *Mende Belief,* 14, 50. Laman, *Kongo* 2:95–96.

59. Harris and Sawyerr, *Mende Belief,* 14. Laman, *Kongo* 2:95–96.

60. Lowrey, *Old Plantation,* 85–86. Folklore Project 1655 and 1855. D-4-27. Vlach, *Afro-American Decorative Arts,* 139–40. H. Corrington Bolton, "Decoration of Graves of Negroes of South Carolina," *Journal of American Folklore* (July–September 1891) 4:214. "Notes and Documents: Antebellum and War Memories of Mrs. Telfair Hodgson," Sarah Hodgson Torian, ed., *Georgia Historical Quarterly* (December 1953) 27(4):352. Virginia C. Holmgren, *Hilton Head: A Sea Island Chronicle* (Hilton Head, S.C.: Hilton Head Publishing, 1959), 63. Lawton, "Religious Life," 196.

61. Wilfred Hambly, *The Ovimbundu of Angola* (Chicago: University of Chicago Press, 1934), 288. Laman, *Kongo* 2:92–95. Bolton, "Decoration of Graves," 214. Thompson and Cornet, *Four Moments of the Sun,* 181–91. Folkways Research Series, *Tribes of the Western Province,*

25, 27, McCulloch, *Peoples of Sierra Leone,* 74.

62. Lawton, "Religious Life," 214.

63. Ibid., 217. Vlach, *Afro-American Decorative Arts,* 143. Thompson, *Flash of the Spirit,* 132–46. Elizabeth Fenn, "Honoring the Ancestors: Kongo-American Graves in the American South," *Southern Exposure* (September-October 1985) 28:44–45. Hodgson, "Antebellum and War Memories," 352.

64. Vlach, *Afro-American Decorative Arts,* 143. Laman, *Kongo* 3:21, 37. Thompson and Cornet, *Four Moments of the Sun,* 198.

65. Thompson, *Flash of the Spirit,* 139–42. Thompson and Cornet, *Four Moments of the Sun,* 183. Vlach, *Afro-American Decorative Arts,* 141. Laman, *Kongo* 2:95, writes that "the porcelain articles may comprise mugs (with holes knocked in bottom), to prevent their being stolen."

66. Vlach, *Afro-American Decorative Arts,* 147. Parsons, *Folk-Lore of the Sea Islands,* 215. Higginson, *Army Life.*

A Wild African Tribe
William S. McFeely
Historian

William S. McFeely is author of Frederick Douglass *(1991), the Pulitzer Prize–winning* Grant: A Biography *(1981), and* Yankee Stepfather: General O.O. Howard and the Freedman *(1968). He recently edited the revised edition of* The Narrative of The Life of Frederick Douglass: Authoratative Text, Contexts, Criticism *(1997) with William L. Andrews. He is currently the Abraham Baldwin professor of humanities at the University of Georgia.*

Sapelo—the accent is on the first syllable—is one of the large low-lying barrier islands that stretch along the South Carolina coast and the 110 miles of the Georgia coast. From the mainland—the "other side" to the islanders—it is a remote dark stretch on the horizon, barely visible beyond nearer would-be islands—rounded anchored floating rafts of dense, tall grass—through which a channel of seawater snakes its way to find a habitable island shore.

• • •

William S. McFeely, "A Wild African Tribe," in Sapelo's People. A Long Walk into Freedom *[1994], p. 13, pp. 44–58, 181–182 (Reprint, New York: Norton, 1995).*

No one talks about slavery today on Sapelo. But it is the dead past that is not dead. It slumbers silently on the island as it does all over the South. Only the worst of the haters of the slaves' descendants would want it awakened, and the long decades of overcoming have not prevented slavery's shadow from spreading darkness.

Here on Sapelo there was slavery of the classic North American sort. Over vast stretches of the island, woodlands were cleared and marshes drained by slaves laboring on the Spalding plantation. Money crops—rice, sugar, and cotton—were planted, cared for, and harvested. There is almost no one in Hog Hammock today who is not a descendant of these very slaves. The slave past is, however, too many generations back for there to be much more than the uneven recollection of a great-grandmother's stories when someone does talk about the "slavery days."

This island is unlike other places in the South where, fortunately, the records of slavery have been preserved. Of Sapelo there are few documents that yield a picture of the lives of the people who lived and worked here. We know from Thomas Spalding's own writings, those of his grandson, and accounts of visitors what work was done here; we do not know precisely which people did what, nor, more important, what they thought about as they labored.

What we do have is another, singular, hold on these people. We know their names. I had the good fortune of talking with Glasco Bailey, Matty Carter, and Allen Green right there in Hog Hammock, of meeting Bankses, Grovners, Walkers, Wilsons, and Johnsons. And, thanks to the astonishing genealogical work of Mae Ruth Green, I can know them in another way; doing assiduous research, she traced the lineage of these families—and more—to forebears who were slaves.

When names emerge, slavery ceases to be an institution, a labor system, an evil, a way of life—an abstraction—and becomes, instead, a populated time. Sapelo is an island whose people have names. We know Carolina Underwood and his wife, Hannah; we know not only that they were born in Africa, but that "deh bote Ibos," an agricultural people who lived just above the delta of the Niger River in what is now Nigeria.[1] That they were from the same (large) region might suggest that they had been together when enslaved and stayed together through all the transactions that ended with their being brought to Sapelo. It is far more likely that like other lonely people seeking some hold on a terrifying world, they discovered they shared a language.

Hannah Underwood knew, with considerable precision, where in Africa she was from and how she was taken. As her granddaughter Julia Grovner reported: "Muh gran, she Hannah. . . . she tell us how she brung yuh. . . . she wid huh ahnt who wuz diggin peanuts[2] in duh fiel, wid uh baby stop on uh [the aunt's] back. Out uh duh brush two wite mens come. . . . Dey led um in tuh duh woods, weah deah wuz ud-duh chillun dey done ketched an tie up in saks. Duh baby an Hannah wuz tie up in sacks lik duh udduhs an Hannah nebuh saw huh ahnt agen an nebuh saw de baby agen. Wen she wuz let ou uh duh sack, she wuz on boat an nebuh saw Africa agen."[3]

Brought through the steps of the slave trade, Hannah found herself in the pens of the Charleston slave market where Thomas Spalding bought many of his Sapelo slaves. She never yielded her Ibo identity. Whatever her work, the Spaldings were not permitted to forget the origin of the woman who was doing it. In a reminiscence forty years after Hannah and her husband died, a relative of the Spaldings referred to—

identified—her as the "old 'Yebo' nurse, Maam Hannah."[4] The Underwoods shared each other's lives into extreme old age. They died—together—in 1871. Their house caught fire and they were too infirm to move; one of Thomas Spalding's grandsons (whose father Hannah probably had nursed) carried them out, but they died of their burns.

Twentieth-century grandchildren of the Underwoods had, in these family stories, ties to a long African past, and Sapelo grandchildren had a long American past as well. To sit on Hicks Walker's porch and watch his large, sure hands tie the delicate knots of a beautiful throwing net for island fishing is to visit with the son of Gib Walker, a "longshoreman" (according to the 1910 census) and himself the son of Alexander Walker, a farmer. Alexander, having reached voting age, registered to vote in 1877, as did his father, Charles Walker, who had been going to the polls since 1867—after having lived as a slave for sixty years. A lot of history sits with you on Sapelo.

It is hard to reach back beyond Sapelo memories to Africa, or even to the Bahamas, although a legend of a ship coming from the islands is still alive. There are now only the shards of recollections of Bilali and Carolina and Hannah Underwood. As for other descendants of immigrants whose coming was so long ago, it is hard to give some ancient, distant home meaning. Among a few of the younger members of the community there has been a conscious effort to achieve that meaning.

With the simultaneous rise of the independent black African states and the civil rights movement, there was a powerful drive here in America to establish an African identity, to construct a connection to an African past. Like other Americans who have found an ethnic linkage forced, some travelers to Africa found that pillar of the past to be hollow. What they observed might be intellectually compelling, but they had to admit (usually to themselves) that they were observing as strangers.

And yet, in a basic way, the connection does matter. Frederick Douglass knew he stuck out like a sore thumb on most of the prosperous white streets of America (and rather enjoyed the fact), but, somewhat to his surprise, he found it reassuring to see on the clamorous, busy docks of Cairo that most of the people of an admixture of races looked more or less the way he had when he worked on Baltimore and New Bedford docks as a young man. He was, even as he watched from an upper deck, part of a crowd and not apart from it. So too, Cornelia Bailey tells of arriving in Sierra Leone a decade ago and "being at home."

On the other hand, when a scholarly linguist comes to Hog Hammock from Sierra Leone, as Salikoko Mufwene recently did, he can't count too heavily on being of the family. In appearance, he may, at first glance, seem a candidate for kinship. But when, in crisp precision, the linguistic queries are put forward, he finds to his amusement—and frustration—that he's just one more of the seemingly endless procession of curious visiting anthropologists—professional and amateur—asking damn fool questions.

Cornelia Bailey, not only with her trip to Africa but also with her willingness to suffer any fool as long as she can champion Hog Hammock, is an exception to her neighbors. They are not as assertive; even if there were means it seems unlikely that there would be curiosity sufficient to make most of the island's people pack a bag for Africa.

For Cornelia's neighbors the remembered memories, the stories, are all on the Hog Hammock side of the ever-ominous Atlantic Ocean. It is not for crossing or even troubling with save when it rises in a storm. Oceans are for romantics. Sardine-packed sunbathers and solitary walkers crave its edges, are drawn to it, into it. Men who must go to sea to fish or to wrench vessels from one coast of an ocean to another are required to confront and try to master its power, to hold its surface. Some of them secretly know the romance; adventurers who choose the encounters surely do.

Sapelo's people know their ocean differently. On one hand, it is simply there—to be ignored; on the other, it echoes a remote, real past. Africa is on its other side. Sapelo forebears were survivors of the terrible voyages from Africa to America, the Middle Passage, of the dragging from a home and of the cramming into the holds of slavers to endure the torture of an ocean crossing. Their fellow slaves-to-be who did not endure were, dead or dying, thrown into the sea. The ships took those who lived into New World ports. Many who eventually were sold to sea island planters were taken first to the Bahamas, sold, and driven to work. Then, to be sold again, were shipped to Charleston. There as well as in the Bahamas earlier, Thomas Spalding or his agent bought Sapelo's people, who were walked and ferried onto the island. Spalding made them clear his forest, work his fields; they in turn—and not out of choice—made his island their home. Their bitter adopted home.

But their birthplace won't allow itself to be forgotten. There was for Cornelia a reaching for roots, but danger lurks in such memories. Reinventing the original African leave-taking and the American arrival—as well as the voyage between—is an exercise in pain. Something of the terror of the Middle Passage emerges in the prose of a white man who knew the island as a boy and wrote of it eighty years later. Charles Spalding Wylly tells—without names—of the experiences of the first American generation of his grandfather's slaves. Wylly recounts the visit to the island of "Captain Swarbreck, retired, master and owner of the good ship 'Ann.'" He "had spent near fifty of his sixty years in 'trading and voyaging' from the west coast of Africa to Brazil, Cuba and the West Indies.[5]

"Very various in kind and character had been the cargoes carried—palm oil, rare woods, mahogany, ebony, with a little 'dust' from where Bishop Heber tells us, 'Africa's sunny fountains roll down their golden sands,' had of late been most common. In earlier days and past years, cargo after cargo had been listed as 'live stock' and great profits had been credited to the captain's books upon their safe arrival in Havana, Charleston, or Rio. His true nature had been a most kindly one and he hated the whole business, but 'trade is trade,' and if the ship 'Ann' were out of it the barque 'Polly' would be in it. So when forcing the 'Ann' with heavy press of sail with *stock* that moaned, even died, from overcrowding, the captain said to himself: "The more I load and the quicker I sail, the sooner it will be over and I can quit and lay up in a snug harbor with money enough to live on, and leave to those who bought of me the awaiting of the 'scourge one day or another' to return to their children or their children's children."[6]

The snug harbor found by Swarbreck and his wife was Burbon, a place on the northwestern side of Sapelo once owned by a Frenchman and not much later sold to the Spaldings. That family, profiting from the stock "bought of me," knew not yet of any scourge, and the Spaldings expressed their distaste for the former master of a slaver and his wife only with ostracism. As Wylly told it, "The social position, the education, the birth and tastes of the [Swarbrecks] made it impossible that there should be much intercourse."[7]

Wylly's perspective, not surprisingly, remained focused on his family as he wrote: "I think it may gratify curiosity to tell in what manner these men and women fresh from Africa would with any safety be taken into the life of a family where in all probability there were not three white men to three hundred of their own race."[8] As Wylly begins his account of the arrival of the Sapelo people, he proves that the Spalding place was a classic plantation not in terms of its large size and its cotton crop, but in the fact that, like all other Southern plantations, it was not precisely like any other.

As they brought African slaves onto the remote island, the Spaldings did so according to a plan. They sought safety in the face of great outnumbering. But if there was fear in the big house, a description of that plan hints as well at the terror of those enslaved in Africa, forced into the stinking holds of slave ships, like Swarbreck's, for the Middle Passage, and then driven from those ships and into the slave pens of the Charleston market. Already separated from family and other familiar people, having seen their fellow cargo, dead and no longer of value, thrown into the sea, these were the survivors. Unable to communicate with most of the other people in the pens and shouted at in a language wholly alien, they can scarcely have imagined what would be their fate.

If that fate was to be bought for Sapelo, they would have been herded onto a packet with about forty other people: "slaves were seldom bought at one time in a larger number than fifty, the sexes being generally equal." The purchase, Wylly recalled, "would probably be ten men, ten women, fifteen boys from twelve to fifteen years of age, and the same of girls." Spalding's credit was good; he paid one hundred dollars, and up, for the people—half in cash, half twelve months later, if, leanly fed, they proved to be as healthy as represented. "They were a perishable commodity and were subject to glut."[9]

The "merchandise," carefully chosen in the Charleston market, was ferried to Sapelo and driven onto the landing. There someone had to be able to talk to each of these miserable newcomers, sullen or shaking. Neophytes were matched with those already "seasoned": "Here always would be found a number of men and women acquired in former years who belonged to the same race, frequently of the same tribe and speaking the same dialect, or at least capable of making themselves understood."[10] Slaves already on Sapelo most probably were lined up at the island's dock and, as they found their voices responded to, given the task of sorting the new people. Then, according to Thomas Spalding's careful scheme for establishing units of slaves of a size appropriate to observation and discipline, one man, "chosen for his ability to command and fluency in speech, would be given the ten men, with the right of issuing food when and where he pleased, or to retain it and not call for the daily ration."[11] Not too subtly, a hierarchical structure based on the power of food, of life, was established among the slaves; more subtly, the manipulation of established people into imposing the discipline of masters was achieved, along with the indoctrination of the newcomers.

"To a woman with the same gifts the ten women would be assigned, and to a third [person] the boys and girls," wrote Wylly. Then he added, with considerable ambiguity, "Frequently they were divided between two of different sexes, this being governed by the ages." What was the chronicler driving at—or past? Were the younger children given to a woman and the older to a man? We are told later that instruction in manual labor came only months later, so why the division? It is not possible to tell, but, Wylly reports, "the birth rate" of the Sapelo slaves "was phenomenal," and he asserts that the chief reason was "the youth and the equality in the number of the sexes."[12] In all purchases not only healthy workers but prospective childbearing appears to have been in the buyer's eye. Hannah Underwood is reported to have borne twenty-two children.

Wylly, adopting the familiar metaphor of slavery as a school, asserted that the "education thus started progressed rapidly." The pupils were segregated, men from women and both from children, and taught plantation discipline. "The reward was good food, . . . bread or its substitutes, such as rice and hominy, . . . was issued daily at the barns on the call only of the preceptor. He lived with them, talked and walked with them. . . . Fish, crabs and such stuff they caught for themselves under the eye and teaching of their constant guide [who was released from other labor] and watchful guard.

"After a tutelage of perhaps three to five months they were assigned to work requiring not skill but manual strength, such as gathering shell for the burning of lime, the mixing of sand, lime, and shell into concrete [the famous tabby]—in the mortar beds— still under the eyes of their teacher—and transferring in hand-barrows of the concrete to the moulds which were slowly growing into the walls of house, stable, or barn.

"In twelve months they were generally . . . 'tamed,' and had acquired enough of the English language to be understood and to understand when spoken to. Then, and not until then, did their master begin to notice their personal qualities and abilities and assign them to duties which they were best fitted for."[13] The Spaldings had created the fiction that these people had no past, that their lives began in the school of slavery which brought them from unintelligibility to the possession of personality and of an understanding sufficient to undertaking of specific tasks.

The carefully orchestrated indoctrination plan did not always work. A much-garbled legend told to explain "Behavior" as a place-name has "a considerable number of negroes belonging to a wild African tribe" rebelling against the mentors to which they were assigned. They bolted and "betook themselves to the woods." As the story goes, "Mr. Spalding permitted them to remain unmolested for three weeks and then took an interpreter and went to see them, making promises of beef and other food if they would come to the plantation and join other slaves."[14] These negotiations, in which Spalding apparently depended on coaxing (and perhaps threats and warnings of starvation) rather than outright force, were designed to alter the "behavior" of these "wild" Africans and bring them within the plantation's civil order.

It is difficult to reconstruct just how the Spalding plan of indoctrination, of behavioral control, played out. His grandson, not surprisingly, insists that "no cruelty of any kind was practiced or relied upon." He even contended that "in this early stage of plantation life on the seacoast was to be found the happiest form of peasant life that the country could offer."[15] The period he was referring to was the nineteenth century's first decade, when the importation of slaves was still legal and when Thomas Spalding was purchasing these people. For Charles Wylly this was the "early and almost initiative stage . . . in the evolution of the rudest and most primal form of men into a higher state of civilization before there had been born into him a love of personal rights, not physical freedom." (For Wylly, slavery, *"in its first stage,"* was not "an unmitigated evil. It is an apprenticeship through which a race becomes worthy of freedom. The wrong is in its continuation after the man or race has become worthy of freedom.")[16]

The desperate attempt of the Behavior slaves to establish a maroon—a secret place of refuge for slaves (or others) escaping authority—right on the island makes clear that all was not as tranquil as Wylly contends. An island, of course, has its moat, but a swimmer with any proficiency at all could swim to the uninhabited Blackbeard Island to Sapelo's north. Still, even the most defiant slave might have hesitated with warnings of no fresh water, plenty of poisonous snakes, and no food other than the immensely prolific oysters and mussels.

The newly arrived "wild" slaves were not the only ones who wanted out; in 1807 Thomas Spalding offered a twenty-dollar reward for the return of Landau, a slave bought from one of the Frenchmen who had lived on Sapelo. The runaway was "a Negro Man . . . about five feet nine inches high, stout and well made, pleasing countenance, speaks both French and English, about forty-five years of age." The slave bore the brand (applied by the previous owner) "S24" on his chest; he was said "to be lurking about the city of Savannah or Sapelo main."[17]

There is, then, no way to take a clear measure of the psychological stress of either the terrified slaves newly from Africa and unable to comprehend what was being done to them or the veterans who knew—in at least two languages—all too well. But we can make out the contours of the unusual structure of the Sapelo communities. The new slaves were young: "vessels seldom shipped 'merchandise' younger than fifteen, or older then twenty-three or twenty-four." After 1810, Spalding allegedly bought no slaves; he didn't need to: "plantation books in 1840 and 1851 used to show for four hundred souls annual births of sixty, seventy and eighty; death, five, six and seven." By the time he made his last will, he had "given to my two sons and four married daughters over one thousand negroes."[18]

Thomas Spalding sought in "the management of slave property—to make them a serf peasantry."[19] He did so perhaps in part to work past his great-grandfather's passionate demand that there never be slavery in Georgia. In 1738, "John Mackintosh Moore" and seventeen other residents of "New Inverness" (Darien) petitioned Governor James E. Oglethorpe to reject the request of "our Neighbors of Savannah . . . for the Liberty of having Slavery." To no avail, these Scotsmen wrote: "It's shocking to human Nature, that any Race of Mankind, and their Posterity, should be sentenced to perpetual Slavery; nor in Justice can we think otherwise of it, than they are thrown amongst us to be our Scourge one Day or another for our Sins; and as Freedom to them must be as dear as to us, what a Scene of Horror must it bring about! And the longer it be unexecuted, the bloody Scene must be the greater."[20]

If this echo from his mother's family sounded in his conscience we do not know; more surely, Thomas Spalding, with his sense of being responsible for a structured hierarchical society, found it comfortable to think of his slaves as serfs. This antique antidemocratic doctrine he made square with his concepts of a modern, scientific, agricultural enterprise. On his domain, he sought to establish "a peonage belonging to the soil and the family."[21] In this, in part, he and they succeeded. The Sapelo people still hold to place and family.

In writing of the feeding of newcomers, Wylly reported that they were fed from barns, not from one barn. Similarly, a contributing factor to the high birthrate was "a division of the families into settlements or villages."[22] Beginning as a safe and orderly way of introducing slaves onto his remote island, Spalding encouraged family formation in family-oriented villages, the hammocks. Newly arrived slaves were assigned to a strong disciplined man or woman and under that tutelage brought into the village. These family villages remain today in the memory of the hammocks now left behind, and in the churches, the First African Baptist, which was moved from Raccoon Bluff, and St. Luke's, founded in 1884 in Hog Hammock. People move freely from one church to another in the alternately scheduled services, but it is still true that Julius Bailey and the Carters, Hillerys, and Dixons are St. Luke's; the Greens, Bankses, and Cornelia Bailey are First African Baptist.

Whatever the toll on the newly arrived slaves, on those who were required to train them (and who elected to comfort them)—on people enslaved, Spalding's scheme engendered a sense of community solidarity that is still in place. It is nearly two hundred years since Africans fierce with grief made their hammocks their own. There the wild African tribe made of itself a people. A people visible; coming up on the Meridian dock there can be no mistaking a person's belonging. The mark is there in the set of the jaw and the weight of the head, in the stature and gait of the old men as they take their seats on either of the church's deacon's bench, in Cornelia Walker Bailey as she strides up the gangway.

But color even more than physical structure is Sapelo's true ensign. It is distinctive, even unique. It is theirs. Argene Grovner, eight generations from Africa, is its Rembrandt canvas; the boatman's face outdoes Nathaniel Jocelyn's *Cinque* and Thomas Eakin's *Negress;* his is our most richly colored American face. A brush would want a daub from almost every pigment on the pallet to do justice to his rich burnish of brown, blue-black, red, and gold. Grovner's forehead, turned to the light as he deftly tends to the lines that make the boat secure, is a magnificent banner of defiant African memory.

Notes

1. *Drums and Shadows,* 163. The census taker in 1870 recorded "Guinea" as the place of birth of both Carolina and Hannah Underwood. This could be accurate, or it could be an example of the frequent use of "Guinea" as a name for anywhere in Africa that African Americans came from. There are other explicit statements that the Underwoods were Ibo.
2. It is likely that the "peanuts" were bambara ground nuts.
3. *Drums and Shadows,* 163.
4. Ellen Barrow Spalding to Charles Wylly, August 1914, in Robert L. Humphries, ed., *The Journal of Archibald C. McKinley* (Athens: University of Georgia Press, 1991), p. 242.
5. Wylly, "Story of Sapeloe," p. 31.
6. Ibid., p. 31.
7. Ibid., p. 37.
8. Ibid., p. 39.
9. Ibid.

10. Ibid.
11. Ibid.
12. Ibid., p. 42.
13. Ibid., p. 40.
14. Wylly quoting H. E. Coffin's record of a conversation the two held in December 1913, ibid., 146.
15. Ibid., pp. 39, 41.
16. Ibid., p. 41.
17. Coulter, *Thomas Spalding,* p. 82.
18. Wylly, "Story of Sapeloe," p. 42.
19. Ibid., p. 23.
20. John Mackintosh Moore, *et al.,* to James Oglethorpe, January 3, 1738–9, in Allen D. Candler, comp., *Colonial Records of Georgia* (Atlanta: Franklin Printing and Publishing, 1905), 3: pp. 427-28.
21. Wylly, "Story of Sapeloe," p. 23.
22. Ibid., p. 42.

Suggested Reading

Booth, Nowell S., Jr. "Time and Change in African Traditional Thought." *Journal of Religion in Africa* 7 fasc. 2 (1975): 81–91.

Creel, Margaret Washington. *"A Peculiar People": Slave Religion and Community Among the Gullahs.* New York: New York University, 1988.

Fenn, Elizabeth A. "Honoring the Ancestors: Kongo-American Graves in the American South." *Southern Exposure* 28(September-October 1985); 42–47.

Hall, Robert L. "Religious Symbolism of the Iron Pot: The Plausibility of a Congo-Angola Origin." *The Western Journal of Black Studies* 13(3) (1989): 125–129.

Herskovits, Melville. *The Myth of the Negro Past.* Boston: Beacon Press, 1958.

Holloway, Joseph E., ed. *Africanisms in American Culture.* Bloomington: Indiana University Press, 1990.

Idowu, E. Bolaji. *African Traditional Religion. A Definition.* Maryknoll, N.Y.: Orbis Books, 1973.

Ingersoll, Ernest. "The Decoration of Negro Graves." *Journal of American Folklore* 4(1892): 68–69.

Janzen, John M., and Wyatt MacGaffey. *An Anthology of Kongo Religion: Primary Texts from Lower Zaire.* Lawrence: University of Kansas, Publications in Anthropology, No. 5, 1974.

King, Noel Quinton. *African Cosmos: An Introduction to Religion in Africa.* Belmont, Calif.: Wadsworth, 1986.

Levine, Lawrence. *Black Culture and Black Consciousness.* New York: Oxford University Press, 1977.

Mbiti, John S. *African Religions & Philosophy* [1969]. Reprint, London: Heinemann, 1988.

———. *The Prayers of African Religion.* Maryknoll, N.Y.: Orbis Books, 1975.

Nichols, Elaine, ed. *The Last Miles of the Way: African American Homecoming, 1890–Present.* Columbia: South Carolina State Museum, 1989.

Parrinder, Geoffrey. *African Mythology.* London: Paul Hamlyn, 1967.

Pennington, Dorothy. "Time in African Culture." In *African Culture: The Rhythms of Unity,* edited by Molefi Kete Asante and Kariamu Welsh Asante. Westport, Conn.: Greenwood Press, 1985: 123–139.

Pitts, Walter, "Like a Tree Planted by the Water. The Musical Cycle in the African American Baptist Ritual." *Journal of American Folklore* 104(413) (1991): 318–340.

Raboteau, Albert J. *Slave Religion: The "Invisible Institution" in the Antebellum South*. New York: Oxford University Press, 1978.

Sobel, Mechal. *Trabelin' On: The Slave Journey to an Afro-Baptist Faith*. Westport, Conn.: Greenwood Press, 1979.

Thompson, Robert Farris with Joseph Cornet. *The Four Moments of the Sun*. Washington, D.C.: National Gallery of Art, 1981.

———. *Face of the Gods: Art and Altars of Africa and the African Americas*. New York: Museum for African Art, 1993.

———. *Flash of the Spirit: African and Afro-American Art and Philosophy*. New York: Random House, 1983.

Wahlman, Maude Southwell. "Gifts of the Spirit: Religious Symbolism in Afro-American Arts." In *Gifts of the Spirit*. Asheville, N.C.: Southern Highland Handicraft Guild, 1984.

Zahan, Dominique. *The Religion, Spirituality, and Thought of Traditional Africa* [1970]. Translated by Kate Ezra and Lawrence M. Martin. Reprint, Chicago: University of Chicago Press, 1979.

Chapter 2

MOVEMENT OR DANCE

"Movement or Dance" begins, as did Vincent Harding's *There Is a River,* with some professional, but certainly no scholarly, risk-taking. Wilson Harris, the author of the first essay in this chapter, "The Limbo Dance and History, Fable, and Myth in the Caribbean and Guianas," is a noted West Indian writer[1] who is much involved in discussions about the role of aesthetics and imagination in understanding history and giving it meaning. His work as a literary scholar complements that of historian Sterling Stuckey, especially as that work is reflected in Stuckey's collection of essays, *Going Through the Storm. The Influence of African American Art in History,* which shows how history is informed by aesthetics.[2]

Harris uses insights gleaned from mythology, fable, and folklore—disciplines that predate history as an intellectual endeavor and also the social sciences—to suggest that African dances of the diaspora, and in this instance what has become the carnival limbo dance of the Caribbean and Guianas, were *possibly* born as the (creative) response of

---

1 Wilson Harris is an important Caribbean writer and critic on Caribbean culture who started his career as a government land surveyor. His biographical sketch in *Contemporary Authors* makes the point that his work on the utilitarian uses of "art as imagination" is informed by his working knowledge of the physical and topographical landscapes and cultural boundaries of his homeland and has been applied to his literary study. It can be seen in the extended monograph he wrote, based on the essay *History, Fable and Myth in the Caribbean and Guianas,* which was published as a pamphlet in 1994 by Calaloux Publications (Wellesley, MA 02181-0012). Harris's work includes *The Womb of Space: The Cross-Cultural Imagination* (Contributions in Afro-American and African Studies, No. 73) (Westport, Conn.: Greenwood Press, 1983); *Fossil and Psyche* (Austin: University of Texas, African and American Studies & Research Center, 1974); *Tradition, the Writer and Society: Critical Essays* (London: New Beacon, 1967); and *The Guyana Quartet,* which includes the novels *Palace of the Peacock, The Fair Journey of Oudin, The Whole Armour,* and *The Secret Ladder* (London: Faber, 1989). A biography of Harris published in 1986 by Sandra E. Drake is entitled, *Wilson Harris and the Modern Tradition: A New Architecture of the World* (Westport, Conn.: Greenwood Press).

Of his work, critic Hena Maes-Jelinek, quoted in *Contemporary Authors,* has written, "Two major elements seem to have shaped Harris's approach to art and his philosophy of existence: the impressive contrasts of the Guyanese landscapes . . . and the successive waves of conquest which gave Guyana its heterogeneous population polarised for centuries into oppressors and their victims. The two, landscape and history, merge in his work into single metaphors, symbolising man's inner space saturated with the effects of historical—that is, temporal—experiences" (p. 215).

2 *Going Through the Storm. The Influences of African American Art in History* (New York: Oxford University Press, 1994).

movement—on the part of captive Africans on slaver ships. The idea of a "limbo" dance, dance employing the word "limb," could suggest movement of the human body (made chattel) in opposition to the historical immobility of human limbs that resulted from cramped decks and underdecks on slaver ships that were filled to capacity with "black gold" or human "captives" during the Middle Passage. In order to move, in order to exercise their limbs and bodies, in order to survive, African captives had to contort themselves in various ways to find room, often futilely, for themselves in the limited and restricted spaces while floating between Europe and America.

If we follow where Harris leads, the contortions and manipulations of *festival* limbo dance can be seen as a celebratory commemorative response to that aspect of slave trading many, but of course not all, survived. It was an inversion of reality: the creative move to make horror into celebration and even a game.

Out of adversity has often come, and possibly did in this case in the form of the limbo dance, an art form. More importantly for Harris and for this anthology, is that this creative form is to be attributed not to the Old Worlds of Africa or Europe but to the still being created world of the (African) Americas. Although the dance or the gymnastics of limbo is historically particular to the Caribbean rather than to North America, Harris's paradigm is still useful to the schema of *How Sweet the Sound*. He makes a case, using movement or dance as an example, that Western historians (black and white) have too easily subscribed to the idea that all cultural manifestations and social formulations by black peoples in the Americas are due to the actions, good or bad, of either Europe or a traditional continental African past. That is to say, they are not perceived to be attributable to those who survived the Middle Passage or to their descendants who created a creole culture and society out of three traditions—African, European, and (indigenous) American. That belief and any subsequent practice of the writing of the history of the Americas that attributes everything "African American" almost entirely to violence and victimization has led, according to Harris, to exploitation as the muse of African American culture. This view of African diasporic history would negate and devalue even the possibility that African captive peoples, having a genius for survival, employed adaptation, innovation, and improvisation[3] into all phases of their daily living in the Western Hemisphere. That in fact, out of the imposition of victimization may have come also transcendence.

Harris posits the idea, in this provocative excerpt from a longer critical review of American cultural forms and origins,[4] that these early African Americans (in the Caribbean) made adaptations or changes to their particular circumstances as a result of enslavement, so they could survive and then possibly ameliorate their lives and even transform or change their new social context. They might even, along the way, transform aspects of the dominant societies that created and perpetuated slavery and discrimination into those that are more humane and more livable. These Africans may have brought

---

[3] The employment of adaptation of self or environment; innovation, the creation of new elements or the bringing of different elements from one's past into a new horrific social context like slavery; and improvisation, changing and embellishing for the greater welfare, text and context, I believe are basic principles that enslaved persons in the Americas used for their survival.

[4] *History, Fable and Myth in the Caribbean and Guianas* (Wellesley, Mass.: Calaloux Publications, 1994).

new elements into the dominant society, that is, cuisine, idiom in language, and new ways of looking at the world (i.e., communally and spiritually rather than competitively or materially) or brought a different spin to reality sounding from the American Revolutionary era, if not before, the discordant notes between democratic principles as enunciated in such a founding American document as the Declaration of Independence and the reality of the evolving United States as slavocracy—improvising to make the liberatory tune not only sound true but ring true.

He builds on the idea, presented in Chapter 1 on cosmology, that the exploited Africans were more than victims although surely victimized. They were also proactive in overcoming that victimization, if not at some point in history even mocking it. The mocking may even be seen in the limbo dance itself where the accompanying sung carnival question is, "How low can you go?" Along with the limbo, which Harris speculates is evolved from Middle Passage exercise and movement, is the revitalizing of the *anancy,* the spider god of African and African American folktales, that in African diasporic folklore traveled with "the people" on the Middle Passage. The *anancy,* in the contemporary festival and carnival, may also have grown long limbs and now is represented by a carnival dancer on tall stilts looking down on those watching him move freely and grandly. It may be the case, Harris speculates, that movement or dance, possibly including the limbo, are further examples of the adaptation and innovation coming from the suffering brought by servitude. If this is so, movement/dance, the "new" home/land still with neither roof nor walls, become pillars of African American culture, a part of a "new architecture."

Using the imagery or symbol of the limbo dance, now an integral part of Jamaican and Trinidadian carnival festivities, could provide not only a paradigm for diasporic aesthetics, which are a response to adversity, but may also visualize some of what African captives experienced during the Middle Passage: the crowding, the cramping, the contortions. This is in combination with *anancy* or spider tales—bringing known and familiar context to a new and especially horrific reality. The *anancy,* the metaphoric spider, has multiple limbs and lives in small corner spaces. But there is more to the animal. The *anancy* is a trickster who may not always be what it seems. Africanist Ivan Van Sertima, in Linda Goss and Marian E. Barnes's anthology, *Talk That Talk. An Anthology of African American Storytelling,*[5] discusses the rabbit, wolf, tortoise, monkey, and lion as representing the human world, in both African and African American folklore. He creates a paradigm in which the political and socially disempowered, like those in the animal world who have little physical strength, rely on intellect and wit, which are perceived as higher powers. They also use wit and ingenuity and the art of masquerade or masking (hiding one's true feelings or intentions) and an ability to mislead or misdirect in word and action. All this not only to critique society, invert power relationships, and create mischief—but to survive. Van Sertima sees these animals, with human qualities, as revolutionaries in combat with the domineering lion that represents white hegemonic society. By this he means that the rabbit, tortoise, monkey, and *anancy* meet adversity and attempt, even succeed, in overturning it often in mocking and humorous ways. Citing

---

5 *Talk That Talk. An Anthology of African American Storytelling* (New York: Simon & Schuster/Touchstone, 1989).

Harris's novel, *Companions of the Day and Night,*[6] which Van Sertima explains places the *anancy* as god of consciousness and power, he writes then in "Trickster, The Revolutionary Hero,"

> He is a god in the sense that all the creations of the world through which he *moves* [emphasis mine] seem also to *move* [emphasis mine] through him. They are not separate or divisible from him. They are extensions and complements of his own, the limbs and organs of one body of which he is the heart and brain, the center of consciousness. . . . That is what I intend to imply when I speak of the freedom and power of a god. The object of this highly imaginative exercise is to demonstrate the capacity of the human spirit and substance to *recreate* [emphasis mine] itself, to feel its way toward a consciousness that breaks down and breaks through apparently fixed and frozen, partial and polarized, states of being and belief. The revolution implied here is a revolution of the imagination, a revolution in consciousness, a fundamental revision and reassessment of static and ritualized modes of seeing, thinking, feeling, which may afflict a whole civilization. . . . This is, in effect, the ultimate conflict between man's *freedom* to remake himself and the world he has already made, which *imprisons* him in the tightly woven fabric by its ritualized reflexes, ideologies, and institutions.[7]

Van Sertima gleans from Harris's work a revolutionary "principle" that will "*re-root* that world, . . . to point the way forward to a new course, a new possibility, a new human person."[8] In a way, Van Sertima has defined improvisation (coming out of the jazz lexicon) that is an always evolving amelioration—to make better—to create new potentialities from a basic narrative.

Harris's work in this essay is a challenge to historians and social scientists alike to look not only to art but to imagination and also to African Americans and their predecessors, the African captives themselves *away* from the ancestral homeland, for the source of the creativity that has allowed them and their descendants to survive. His paradigm shows linkages between Africa and the African Americas and both the extensions (embellishments) and improvisations that Africans/African Americans have placed on traditional African and European traditions in the arts, spirituality, and thought. Harris uses the idea of the limbo dance, possibly coming from the "remembered" experience of the exercising of cramped human limbs on slaver ships, as the necessary "gateway" that connects the Middle Passage to both Africa and the Americas. Using the "imagination of the arts" to inform history by expanding, in a responsible way, the known facts of history may reveal the *meaning* and *truth* of human experience and potential beyond the scientific facts and evidence of the social sciences.

Harris's essay is about an American art form that is an inversion of the historical cramping and packaging of human "cargo" shackled together and barely able to move. It is an inversion coming out of a "state of limbo" where one is in the process of "becoming," being no longer one thing (African) nor yet another (American)—where one is really a "gateway" person. The concept of inversion, of turning reality upside down and

---

6 *Companions of the Day and Night* (London: Faber, 1975).

7 Ibid., p. 109.

8 Ibid., p. 110.

finding other sources of power through the process, as can be seen in contemporary carnival festivals including Mardi Gras in Louisiana and also in the election and Pinkster festivals,[9] is an intriguing way of (re)membering the horrors of the Middle Passage and all that came subsequent to it such as enslavement and racial discrimination. Harris's (speculative) essay is a challenge to go beyond the human limitations of history itself, or the parameters of time and space, events and persons, to find in the text—instead of control and domination—meaning and understanding.[10] The limbo, in fact African American movement/dance aesthetic, should be seen not as reaction to the dynamics of European history that create an Atlantic slave trade but as mythically, if not historically, creative, innovative, life-affirming African/African American response that transcends, rises above, mocks, and even makes celebratory human efforts and initiatives toward survival.

Olly W. Wilson, in "The Association of Movement and Music as a Manifestation of a Black Conceptual Approach to Music Making," and Robert Farris Thompson, in "An Aesthetic of the Cool: West African Dance," introduce an historical approach to the concept of movement or dance.[11] In doing so, Wilson and Thompson provide connections between African American and African forms of music making, which is conceptualized holistically and includes both sound and motion. These essays discuss such concepts as "call and response," the indivisibility of time, and the concept of the "affective" power of music. That power, in music and in African-derived existence, is a life force that, in Wilson's words, can "make things happen."[12]

In Europe, music has been compartmentalized and associated more with sound than movement. In fact, movement or dance is not often considered *text*—or a way of speaking. But in this chapter, movement or dance is part of the rhythm of the universe taking on the function of the drum: to speak, to send a message. It is associated with *nommo,* or "the spoken word," and thus is part of the oral heritage of African peoples. Movement or dance is, in an African context, sound, gesture, prayer, message, and as

---

9 Articles on election, coronation, and festival celebrations include Ira De A. Reid, "The John Canoe Festival. A New World Africanism," *Phylon* 3(4) (1942): 349–370; Sterling Stuckey, "The Skies of Consciousness: African Dance at Pinkster in New York: 1750–1840," in *Going Through the Storm. The Influence of African American Art in History* (New York: Oxford University Press, 1994), pp. 53–80; and "Negro Election Day and Black Community Life in New England, 1750–1860," *Marxist Perspectives* (Fall 1978): 104–117; Melvin Wade, "'Shining in Borrowed Plumage': Affirmation of Community in the Black Coronation Festivals of New England (c. 1750–c. 1850)," *Western Folklore* 40(3) (1981): 211–231; and William H. Wiggins, Jr., *O Freedom: Afro-American Freedom Celebrations* (Knoxville: University of Tennessee Press, 1987).

10 Molefi Kete Asante, *The Afrocentric Idea* (Philadelphia: Temple University Press, 1987).

11 There are several important texts, of varying levels of sophistication, that place African American dance within an historical context and connect culturally the African Americas (with one another) with the African continent. They include Joyce Aschenbrenner, *Katherine Dunham. Reflection on the Social and Political Contexts of Afro-American Dance,* in *Dance Research Annual XII,* edited by Patricia A. Rowe (New York: CORD, Inc. 1981); Lynne Fauley Emery, *Black Dance from 1619 to 1970* (Palo Alto, Calif.: National Press Books, 1972); Katrina Hazzard-Gordon, *Jookin': The Rise of Social Dance Formation in African-American Culture* (Philadelphia: Temple University Press, 1990); Richard A. Long, *The Black Tradition in American Modern Dance* (New York: Rizzoli, 1989); Marshall and Jean Stearns, *Jazz Dance. The Story of American Vernacular Dance. (A History of Dancing to Jazz, from Its African Origins to the Present)* [1964] (Reprint, New York: Schirmer Books, 1968); and Edward Thorpe, *Black Dance* (Woodstock, N.Y.: Overlook Press, 1990).

12 Olly W. Wilson, "The Association of Movement and Music as a Manifestation of a Black Conceptual Approach to Music Making," *African Forum,* 2(2) (1966): 99.

A Tuskegee Institute marching band that illustrates the connections between music and movement and how, at the Historically Black College and University, the marching band was used to identify the spirit of the individual institution and its marching, musical, and costume styles.

such an important aspect of human existence and survival. Music with dance was a method of maintaining a connection to African culture and heritage, which are oral in nature. What the supporters of slavery did not see was that the human body, for African peoples, served a similar purpose. Singing and dancing were not only allowed but encouraged. Those observing these activities did not see that they were power forces being expressed; they did not understand that this music making of clapping, swaying, shuffling, and using the chest and thighs as skin to be drummed were the muted and persistent calls for liberation. Sound with motion and its influence on liberatory movement, beginning with the humming and singing of the spirituals, would continue through the civil (human) rights movement of the 1960s. Linked arms of black and white people facing fire hoses and growling police dogs—yet marching and swaying to the words of "We Shall Overcome"—were powerful and are still powerful visual American images. Although music making is surely aesthetics or art, it served and still serves the black community as a creative life force—a source of energy for a community that could have been expected to have low supplies of both energy and spirit. Music making would direct the African American community to transcend the possibility of no possibilities—for itself and even its distant progeny.

Music making was/is not a singular experience. It transcends time and space boundaries and encompasses what are often considered disparate elements, embracing not only dance but instrumental and vocal music including the singsong of the black preacher's sermon noted in Pearl Primus's essay in *The Dance Encyclopedia* and as revealed in the plastic arts and ritualistic drama with masks and masquerades. Movement as creative life force and energy is fuel for the emotions, a form of human expression that "makes things happen."[13] The "motor responses" are not only part of performance or drama but are an integral part of home and work life. In fact, they are an aspect of work that contributes not only to productivity but also creates community. There is a shared sense of common endeavor and unity to be found in the singing of work songs and in the rhythms that are shared to keep the work going, especially, historically, in the cotton fields or on the prison work gang, or in the laying of railroad track. In much the same way, the preacher's words—Primus tells us—are supported if not even created by the responses of congregations that play an active role in the rituals of the black church service. Music making is all that Africans brought with them and that they not only could all share but also all claim as uniquely their own. Once in the Americas it became fuel for their lives, a source of and for survival and the foundation of their community. It was clearly highly portable—the tools of survival and amelioration always accompanied the people.

Robert Farris Thompson adds another dimension to this discussion of movement and dance by discussing the philosophical and ethical aspects of African dance—concepts of beauty, of balance and moderation in life—of "right living." This is sometimes called "the cool," a concept well known within the jazz lexicon or vocabulary.[14] From his definition of prayer as "space for moving and shouting with the spirits,"[15] Thompson further associates dances of the cool with "a kind of prayer."[16] Dances of the cool have a spiritual context and are juxtaposed with what is considered "hot," that associated with intemperateness, pain, with what is bitter rather than with what is sweet. In his essay here, Thompson writes, "It is cool to sweeten hurt with song and motion; it is hot to concentrate upon the pain."[17] Borrowing from African cosmology, he reminds us that water is a symbol of coolness. This is consistent with Katherine Dunham's belief that the sweat, coming from physical exertion, exercise, movement/dance, is part of a purifying process, like African rituals of total immersion and the Christian baptism.

Pearl Primus, the late dancer/choreographer and anthropologist, in her brief but eloquent "Primitive African Dance and Its Influence on the Churches of the South,"

---

13 Marching is also an aspect of African American sound and motion. (See also Lea and Marianna Seale's article, "Easter Rock: A Louisiana Negro Ceremony," *Journal of American Folklore* 55(218) (October–December 1941); pp. 212–218. For example, there is the marching band of Historically Black Colleges and Universities. These famous bands perform during halftime and are ritual and performance in their own right, with signs of community that include the display of school colors and letters, and fancy and intricate dance steps and formations that distinguish one institution from another and create institutional reputations for musical virtuosity. There is also the step dance of the black Greek letter societies. An interesting article on the latter is Elizabeth C. Fine's "Stepping, Saluting, Cracking, and Freaking. The Cultural Politics of African-American Step Shows," *The Drama Review* 35(2) (1991): 39–59. Sound and motion also play a role in chronicling the life of persons who have passed on by moving through the places and spaces they inhabited and frequented—with a last tune. See Jules L. Cahn, "The Jazz Funeral," in the special double issue ("Older, Wiser, Stronger") in *Southern Exposure* 13(2–3), (1985): 128–129.

14 Robert Farris Thompson also discusses what he terms "dances of derision," which critique society and often call for change in "An Aesthetic of the Cool: West African Dance," *African Forum* 2(2), (1966):86.

15 In Robert Farris Thompson, *Face of the Gods: Arts and Altars and the African Americas* (New York: Museum for African Art, 1993), p. 81.

16 Robert Farris Thompson, "An Aesthetic of the Cool," p. 99.

17 Ibid., p. 86.

builds on Thompson's discussion of African religions as "danced faiths."[18] Her discussion is about the black preacher and the congregation engaged in "call and response," and the ritual of sound and motion involved in the black sermon where words often appear to be sung and to have the percussive vocal sounds found in the work songs of black men swinging hammers and picks while building America's railroads. Primus sees Africa and the Caribbean as sources of black church ritual and dance that includes the booming of the preacher's voice, which is reminiscent of the drum, and his *total* body movements including hand gestures, facial expressions, movements, and dancing in the freer areas of the church sanctuary—the open spaces around and in front of the pulpit, and in the aisles. Involved also in this ritual is *nommo,* or word, which represents water and purification. The preacher, with his words and motions, plays the role of Harding's warrior-preacher depicted in *There Is a River.* He is the leader of the community (or in this case of the congregation), and his voice and message, his chanting and singing—forms of spiritual expression—lead not only to freedom of expression but to political freedom and liberation. The excerpt here from "Easter Sunrise Sermon" by Rev. W. T. Goodwin, as transcribed by Peter Gold from an original recording done by Gold and Harriet Yurchenco, visualizes with words that dance is the verbal and physical choreography between a preacher and his congregation.[19]

---

[18] Ibid.

[19] Rev. W.T. Goodwin, "Easter Sunrise Sermon." Transcriptor, Peter Gold. *Alcheringa* 4 (Autumn 1972): 1–14. See also Patricia Jones-Jackson, "Let the Church Say 'Amen': The Language of Religious Rituals in Coastal South Carolina," in *The Crucible of Carolina. Essays in the Development of Gullah Language and Culture,* edited by Michael Montgomery (Athens: University of Georgia Press, 1994), pp. 115–132.

The Limbo Dance and History, Fable, and Myth in the Caribbean and Guianas

Wilson Harris
Writer/Critic

Wilson Harris writes about Caribbean culture especially that of Guiana. His previous work as a government land surveyor—and his interest and knowledge of the physical and topographical landscapes of his homeland and the Caribbean in general—informs his writing. His imaginative and nonfiction works include the set of four novels collectively titled The Guiana Quartet *(1985),* The Womb of Space: The Cross-Cultural Imagination

---

Wilson Harris, "History, Fable, and Myth in the Caribbean and Guianas," Caribbean Quarterly *16 (2) (1970): 1–32. 1–32.*

(1983), Fossil and Psyche *(1974), and* Tradition, the Writer and Society: Critical Essays *(1967). In 1992,* The Radical Imagination: Lectures and Talks by Wilson Harris, *edited by Alan Riarch and Mark Williams was published. Harris has taught at the University of Texas at Austin, Yale University and, was Regents' Lecturer at the University of California. He has also held positions in Canada, England, Australia, and at the University of the West Indies.*

• • •

There are two kinds of myths related to Africa in the Caribbean and Guianas. One kind seems fairly direct, the other has clearly undergone metamorphosis. In fact even the direct kind of myth has suffered a "sea-change" of some proportions. In an original sense, therefore, these myths which reflect an African link in the Caribbean are also part and parcel of a native West Indian imagination and therefore stand, in some important ways I feel, in curious rapport with vestiges of Amerindian fable and legend. (Fable and myth are employed as variables of the imagination in this paper.)

Let us start with a myth stemming from Africa which has undergone metamorphosis. The one which I have in mind is called limbo. The limbo dance is a well known feature in the Carnival life of the West Indies today though it is still subject to intellectual censorship as I shall explain as I go along in this paper. The limbo dancer moves under a bar which is gradually lowered until a mere slit of space, it seems, remains through which with spread-eagled limbs he passes like a spider.

Limbo was born, it is said, on the slave ships of the Middle Passage. There was so little space that the slaves contorted themselves into human spiders. Limbo, therefore, as Edward Brathwaite, the distinguished Barbadian born poet, has pointed out is related to anancy or spider fables. If I may now quote from ISLANDS the last book in his trilogy—

> *drum stick knock*
> *and the darkness is over me*
> *knees spread wide*
> *and the water is hiding me*
> *limbo*
> *limbo like me*

But there is something else in the limbo-anancy syndrome which, as far as I am aware, is overlooked though intuitively immersed perhaps in Edward Brathwaite's poems, and that is the curious dislocation of a chain of miles reflected in the dance so that a re-trace of the Middle Passage from Africa to the Americas and the West Indies is not to be equated with a uniform sum. Not only has the journey from the Old World to the New varied with each century and each method of transport but needs to be reactivated in the imagination as a limbo perspective when one dwells on the Middle Passage: a limbo gateway between Africa and the Caribbean.

In fact here, I feel, we begin to put our finger on something which is close to the inner universality of Caribbean man. Those waves of migration which have hit the shores of the Americas—North, Central and South—century after century have, at various times, possessed the stamp of the spider metamorphosis in the refugee flying from Europe or in the Indentured East Indian and Chinese from Asia.

Limbo then reflects a certain kind of gateway or threshold to a new world and the dislocation of a chain of miles. It is—in some ways—the archetypal sea-change stemming from Old Worlds and it is legitimate, I feel, to pun on limbo as a kind of shared phantom limb which has become a subconscious variable in West Indian the-atre. The emergence of formal West Indian theatre was preceded, I suggest, by that phantom limb which manifested itself on Boxing Day after Christmas when the ban on the 'rowdy' bands (as they were called) was lifted for the festive season.

● ● ●

It has taken us a couple of generations to begin—just begin—to perceive, in this phenomenon, an activation of subconscious and sleeping resources in the phantom limb of dis-membered slave and god. An activation which possesses a nucleus of great promise—of far-reaching new poetic synthesis.

For limbo (one cannot emphasise this too much) is not the total recall of an African past since that African past in terms of tribal sovereignty or sovereignties was modified or traumatically eclipsed with the Middle Passage and within generations of change that followed. Limbo was rather the renascence of a new corpus of sensibility that could translate and accommodate African and other legacies within a new archi-tecture of cultures. For example the theme of the phantom limb—the re-assembly of dismembered man or god—possesses archetypal resonances that embrace Egyptian Osiris, the resurrected Christ and the many-armed deity of India.

In this context it is interesting to note that limbo—which emerges as a novel re-assembly out of the stigmata of the Middle Passage—is related to Haitian vodun in the sense that Haitian vodun . . . also seeks to accommodate new Catholic features in its constitution of the muse.

It is my view—a deeply considered one—that this ground of accommodation, this art of creative coexistence—pointing away from apartheid and ghetto fixations— is of the utmost importance and native to the Caribbean, perhaps to the Americas as a whole. It is still, in most respects a latent syndrome and we need to look not only at limbo or vodun but at Amerindian horizons as well—shamanistic and rain-making vestiges and the dancing bush baby legends of the extinct Caribs which began to haunt them as they crouched over their campfires under the Spanish yoke.

Insufficient attention has been paid to such phenomena and the original native capacity these implied as omens of re-birth. Many historians have been intent on in-dicting the Old World of Europe by exposing a uniform pattern of imperialism in the New World of the Americas. Thus they conscripted the West Indies into a mere adjunct of imperialism and overlooked a subtle and far-reaching renascence. In a sense therefore the new historian—though his stance is an admirable one in debunking imperialism—has ironically extended and reinforced old colonial prejudices which cen-sored the limbo imagination as a 'rowdy' manifestation and overlooked the complex metaphorical gateway it constituted in rapport with Amerindian omen.

Later on I intend to explore the Amerindian gateways between cultures which began obscurely and painfully to witness (long before limbo or vodun or the Middle

Passage) to a native suffering community steeped in caveats of conquest. At this point I shall merely indicate that these gateways exist as part and parcel of an original West Indian architecture which it is still possible to create if we look deep into the rubble of the past, and that these Amerindian features enhance the limbo assembly with which we are now engaged—the spider syndrome and phantom limb of the gods arising in Negro fable and legend.

I used the word 'architecture' a moment or two ago because I believe this is a valid approach to a gateway society as well as to a community which is involved in an original re-constitution or re-creation of variables of myth and legend in the wake of stages of conquest.

First of all the limbo dance becomes the human gateway which dislocates (and therefore begins to free itself from) a uniform chain of miles across the Atlantic. This dislocation or interior space serves therefore as a corrective to a uniform cloak or documentary stasis of imperialism. The journey across the Atlantic for the forebears of West Indian man involved a new kind of space—inarticulate as this new 'spatial' character was at the time—and not simply an unbroken schedule of miles in a log book. Once we perceive this inner corrective to historical documentary and protest literature which sees the West Indies as utterly deprived, or gutted by exploitation, we begin to participate in the genuine possibilities of original change in a people severely disadvantaged (it is true) at a certain point in time.

The limbo dance therefore implies, I believe, a profound art of compensation which seeks to re-play a dismemberment of tribes (note again the high stilted legs of some of the performers and the spider-anancy masks of others running close to the ground) and to invoke at the same time a curious psychic re-assembly of the parts of the dead god or gods. And that re-assembly which issued from a state of cramp to articulate a new growth—and to point to the necessity for a new kind of drama, novel and poem—is a creative phenomenon of the first importance in the imagination of a people violated by economic fates.

One cannot over-emphasise, I believe, how original this phenomenon was. So original it aroused both incomprehension and suspicion in the intellectual and legal administrations of the land (I am thinking in particular of the first half of the twentieth century though one can, needless to say, go much farther back). What is bitterly ironic—as I have already indicated—is that present day historians in the second half of the 20th century—militant and critical of imperialism as they are, have fallen victim, in another sense, to the very imperialism they appear to denounce. They have no criteria for arts of originality springing out of an age of limbo and the history they write is without an inner time.

• • •

I believe that the limbo imagination of the folk involved a crucial inner re-creative response to the violations of slavery and indenture and conquest, and needed its critical or historical correlative, its critical or historical advocacy. This was not forthcoming since the historical instruments of the past clustered around an act of censorship and of suspicion of folk-obscurity as well as originality, and that inbuilt arrogance or suspicion continues to motivate a certain order of critical writing in the West Indies today.

• • •

As such the very institutions of the day will become increasingly rigged by fear and misgiving and political deterioration is the inevitable corollary. And this indicates to me that in the absence of a historical correlative to the arts of the dispossessed some kind of new critical writing in depth needs to emerge to bridge the gap between history and art. Denis Williams stated the dilemma very effectively in *Image and Idea in the Arts of Guyana* (The Edgar Mittelholzer Memorial Lectures second series January 1969, published by the National History and Arts Council of Guyana). I now quote—

"Yet the first fact of the Caribbean situation is the fact of miscegenation, of mongrelism. What are the cultural implications of this mongrel condition? It is important to have experienced the homogeneity, richness, the integrity of the racially thoroughbred cultures of the Old World in order properly to take the force of this question. It is important if only as a means of discriminating between our condition and theirs, of assessing the nature and status of our mongrel culture when contrasted with the cultures of the thoroughbred, of realising the nature and function of the ancestor as he determines our cultural destiny. For we are all shaped by our past; the imperatives of a contemporary culture are predominantly those of a relationship to this past. Yet in the Caribbean and in Guyana we think and behave as though we have no past, no history, no culture. And where we do come to take notice of our history it is often in the light of biases adopted from one thoroughbred culture or another, of the Old World. We permit ourselves the luxury, for one thing, of racial dialectics in our interpretation of Caribbean and Guyanese history and culture. In the light of what we are this is a destructive thing to do, since at best it perpetuates what we might call a filialistic dependence on the cultures of our several racial origins, while simultaneously inhibiting us from facing up to the facts of what we uniquely are."

I would now like to resume the earlier thread of my argument in the dance of the folk—the human limbo or gateway of the gods which was disregarded or incomprehensible to an intellectual and legal and historical convention. I had begun to point out that, first of all, the limbo dance becomes the human gateway which dislocates (and therefore begins to free itself from) a uniform chain of miles. In this context I also suggested that the gateway complex is also the psychic assembly or re-assembly of the muse of a people. This brings me now to my second point about limbo, namely, that it shares its phantom limb with Haitian vodun across an English/French divide of Caribbean cultures. This is a matter of great interest, I believe, because Haitian vodun is more directly descended from African myth and yet—like limbo which is a metamorphosis or new spatial character born of the Middle Passage—it is also intent on a curious re-assembly of the god or gods. Therefore I ask myself—is vodun a necessary continuation of a matrix of associations which had not fulfilled itself in the Old World of Africa? If so that fulfilment would be in itself not an imitation of the past—much as it is indebted to the past—but a new and daring creative conception in itself.

If Haitian vodun is a creative fulfilment of African vodun one must ask oneself where do the similarities and differences lie. The basic feature they hold in common lies in 'possession trances'—trance features, I may add, which are not the case with limbo.

• • •

I would like . . . to give my definition of Haitian vodun which appears in *Tradition, the Writer and Society* (New Beacon Publications 1967) as this will help me, in parenthesis, to unravel certain similarities and differences in African and Haitian vodun and to look back afresh at the significance of the human limbo gateway.

"Haitian vodun or voodoo is a highly condensed feature of inspiration and hallucination within which 'space' itself becomes the sole expression and recollection of the dance—as if 'space' is the character of the dance—since the celebrants themselves are soon turned into 'objects'—into an architecture of movement like 'deathless' flesh, wood or stone. And such deathless flesh, wood or stone (symbolic of the dance of creation) subsists—in the very protean reality of space—on its own losses (symbolic decapitation of wood, symbolic truncation of stone)) so that the very void of sensation in which the dancer begins to move, like an authentic spectre or structure of fiction, makes him or her insensible to all conventional props of habit and responsive only to a grain of frailty or light support."

"Remember at the outset the dancer regards himself or herself as one in full command of two legs, a pair of arms, until, possessed by the muse of contraction, he or she dances into a posture wherein one leg is drawn up into the womb of space. He stands like a rising pole upheld by earth and sky or like a tree which walks in its shadow or like a one-legged bird which joins itself to its sleeping reflection in a pool. All conventional memory is erased and yet in this trance of overlapping spheres of reflection a primordial or deeper function of memory begins to exercise itself within the bloodstream of space.

"Haitian vodun is one of the surviving primitive dances of sacrifice, which, in courting a subconscious community, sees its own performance in literal terms—that is, with and through the eyes of 'space': with and through the sculpture of sleeping things which the dancer himself actually expresses and becomes. For in fact the dancer moves in a trance and the interior mode of the drama is exteriorized into a medium inseparable from his trance and invocation. He is a dramatic agent of subconsciousness. The life from within and the life from without now truly overlap. That is the intention of the dance, the riddle of the dancer."

"The importance which resides in all this, I suggest, is remarkable. For if the trance were a purely subjective thing—without action or movement—some would label it fantasy. But since it exteriorizes itself, it becomes an intense drama of images in space, which may assume elastic limbs and proportions or shrink into a dense current of reflection on the floor. For what emerges are the relics of a primordial fiction where the images of space are seen as in an abstract painting. That such a drama has indeed a close bearing on the language of fiction, on the language of art, seems to me incontestable. The community the writer shares with the primordial dancer is, as it were, the complementary halves of a broken stage. For the territory upon which the poet visualizes a drama of consciousness is a slow revelation or unravelling of obscurity—revelation or illumination within oneself; whereas the territory of the dancer remains actually obscure to him within his trance whatever revelation or illumination his limbs may articulate in their involuntary theme. The 'vision' of the poet (when one comprehends it from the opposite pole of 'dance') possesses a 'spatial' logic or 'convertible' property of the imagination. Herein lies the essential humility of a certain kind of self-consciousness within which occurs the partial erasure, if nothing more, of the habitual boundaries of prejudice."

I have quoted rather extensively here from my previous essay because I think this may help us to see . . . that while the trance similarity is clear, the functions have begun to differ. Haitian vodun—like West Indian and Guianese/Brazilian limbo—may well point to sleeping possibilities of drama and horizons of poetry, epic and novel, sculpture and painting—in short to a language of variables in art which would have a profoundly evolutionary cultural and philosophical significance for Caribbean man.

• • •

It is my assumption, in the light of all the foregoing, that a certain rapport exists between Haitan Vodun and West Indian limbo which suggests an epic potential or syndrome of variables. That epic potential, I believe, may supply the nerve-end of authority which is lacking at the moment in the conventional stance of history.

But we need to examine this with the greatest care in order to assess and appreciate the risks involved.

In the first place the limbo imagination of the West Indies possesses no formal or collective sanction as in an old Tribal World. Therefore the gateway complex between cultures implies a new catholic unpredictable threshold which places a far greater emphasis on the integrity of the individual imagination. And it is here that we see, beyond a shadow of doubt, the necessity for the uncommitted artist of conscience whose evolution out of the folk as poet, novelist, painter is a symbol of risk, a symbol of inner integrity.

With African vodun—as we have seen—the integrity of the tribal person was one with a system which was conservative and traditional. There was no breath of subversion—no cleavage in the collective. History and art were one medium.

With Guyianese/West Indian limbo that cleavage is a fact and the rise of the imaginative arts has occurred in the face of long-held intellectual and legal suspicion. Therefore the rise of the poet or artist incurs a gamble of the soul which is symbolised in the West Indian trickster (the spider or anancy configuration). It is this element of tricksterdom that creates an individual and personal risk absolutely foreign to the conventional sanction of an old Tribal World: a risk which identifies him (the artist) with the submerged authority of dispossessed peoples but requires of him, in the same token, alchemic resources to conceal, as well as elaborate, a far-reaching order of the imagination which, being suspect, could draw down upon him a crushing burden of censorship in economic or political terms. He stands therefore at the heart of the lie of community and the truth of community. And it is here, I believe, in this trickster gateway—this gamble of the soul—that there emerges the hope for a profoundly compassionate society committed to freedom within a creative scale.

I would like to re-emphasise the roles of "epic" and "trickster". The epic of limbo holds out a range of variables—variables of community in the cross-cultural tie of dispossessed tribes or families—variables of art in a consciousness of links between poetry and drama, image and novel, architecture and sculpture and painting—which need to be explored in the Caribbean complex situation of apparent "historylessness". And furthermore in the Americas as a whole, it would seem to me that the apparent void of history which haunts the black man may never be compensated until an act of imagination opens gateways between civilisations, between technological and spiritual apprehensions, between racial possessions and dispossessions in the way the Aeneid may stand symbolically as one of the first epics of migration and resettlement beyond the pale of an ancient world. Limbo and vodun are variables of an underworld imagination—variables of phantom limb and void and a nucleus of stratagems in which limb is a legitimate pun on limbo, void on vodun.

The trickster of limbo holds out a caveat we must reckon with in our present unstable situation. It is the caveat of conscience and points to the necessity for a free imagination which is at risk on behalf of a truth that is no longer given in the collective medium of the tribe. The emergence of individual works of art is consistent with—and the inevitable corollary of—an evolution of folk limbo into symbols of inner cunning and authority which reflect a long duress of the imagination.

• • •

CONTINUITY AND DISCONTINUITY

So far we have been looking at a cleavage between the historical convention and arts of the imagination in the Caribbean. I have suggested that the historical convention remains a stasis which possesses no criteria for assessing profoundly original dislocations in the continuous pattern of exploiter/exploited charted by the historian. As such the West Indies—history-wise—appear to me to be little more than an adjunct of imperialism. It has become essential, I feel, to assess dislocations which point away from the straitjacket of convention. These, I have sugested, may be perceived in areas of folk obscurity such as Negro limbo or phantom limb of the dismembered god and slave, in aboriginal features at which we have also been looking, and in the rise of the individual artist and imagination in the West Indies today. . . .

The Association of Movement and Music as a Manifestation of a Black Conceptual Approach to Music Making

Olly W. Wilson
Musicologist

Olly W. Wilson teaches in the Department of Music at the University of California at Berkeley. He is also the author of "The Significance of the Relationship between Afro-American Music and West African Music," Black Perspective in Music *2 (Spring 1974):3–22.*

The relationship between African and Afro-American music has been an intriguing question for almost as long as individuals have been aware of the existence of strong musical cultures of Black people on both sides of the Atlantic. The full nature of that relationship has never been adequately examined however. The comparative studies that exist tend to make comparisons on the basis of the presence or absence of specific musical characteristics.[1] Hence the common occurrence of such well-known African musical characteristics in Afro-American music such as antiphony (call-and-response patterns), pentatonic (5 tone) scales, and "offbeat phrasing of melodic accents" are usually cited as examples of the interrelationship of the musics. While this approach is certainly necessary and valuable as far as it goes, it is inadequate in expressing the full nature of the relationship of African and Afro-American music. This is so because it deals with foreground aspects of the music and not the guiding background factors which determine the presence of these foreground features.

The artistic output of any culture reflects the collective cultural attitudes and values of that culture. Western art reflects attitudes toward time and space which are the result of peculiar developments in Western society. The artist who sets out to create brings certain conceptual approaches with him to his task which are the result of his cultural nuturement. He decides to write a piece of music with a beginning, middle and end which he assumes will be listened to as a process which occurs within the dimensions of linear time.[2] Because these aspects of the musical event seem to be so basic, the Westerner assumes that they are universal and takes them for granted. It is these assumed aspects of the musical experience that form his basic conceptual approach to the process of either making or experiencing music. Therefore, an analysis

Olly W. Wilson, *"The Association of Movement and Music as a Manifestation of a Black Conceptual Approach to Music Making," in* Report of the 12th Congress, American Musicological Society (London, 1981), *pp. 98–105.*

of the foreground aspects of the music will not only be enhanced by an understanding of these background factors, but the total musical experience cannot be adequately probed without taking them into consideration.[3]

Sub-Saharan African Peoples have a conceptual approach to the process of music making which is a reflection of their collective cultural experiences. It includes many dimensions. Among these is the affective power of music, that is, the belief that music is a force capable of making something happen. It also includes the attitude that the musical experience is most properly part of a multi-media one in which many kinds of collective human output are inextricably linked. Hence, a typical traditional ceremony will include music, dance, the plastic arts (in the form of elaborate masks and/or costumes) and perhaps ritualistic drama. There are many other aspects of this basic conceptual approach, some of which are operative but undiscovered at this point.[4]

The relationship of African and Afro-American music is based upon the retention to a large degree of African conceptual approaches to music making. The retention of these attitudes and the values they reflect provides us with a viable framework to analyze relationships between African and Afro-American music as well as between various types of African music. The commonly retained core is a set of attitudes which are revealed in the manifestations of specific foreground musical characteristics.[5] I wish to concentrate in this paper on one aspect of this conceptual approach. That aspect is the relationship of music and body movement.

In traditional sub-Saharan musical cultures body movement must be seen as an integral part of the music making process. Although it is true that physical motion, especially as dance, frequently accompanies music in many cultures, in most instances that physical activity is extrinsic to the act of making music. That is, it is seen as something which accompanies the musical experience, something which is not absolutely necessary in order for the music to exist. In sub-Saharan cultures, conceptually, the two activities are viewed as interrelated components of the same process.[6] The Western conceptual assumption of a division between consciously organized sound (music) and movement associated with that sound (dance) usually does not exist here. That is why in many traditional music making situations the dancers and the musicians frequently are one and the same. An example of a common performance practice which reflects this conceptual view is the elaborate physical body movement characteristically associated with playing musical instruments. The Yoruban *dun dun* player moves his arms, head, shoulders, feet, and legs as he performs a praise song for an elder of the community during a festive occasion. It is important to note that those movements are not capricious gestures of ecstasy, but are actions necessary to produce a particularly desired effect from the musical performance. The movement is part of the music making process and therefore intrinsic to the music.

Scholars of African music, while not formulating the concept in these terms, have long been aware of the special relationship between physical body motion and music in African cultures.

John Blacking, speaking of Venda music, says:

"Venda music is founded not on melody, but on a rhythmical stirring of the whole body of which singing is but one extension. Therefore, when we seem to hear a rest between two drumbeats, we must realize that for the player it is not a rest: each drumbeat is the part of a total body movement in which the hand or a stick strikes the drum skin."[7]

Kwabena Nketia, in the *Music of Africa,* devotes a chapter to the "Interrelations of Music and Dance." Among the points he makes are the following:

"Although purely contemplative music, which is not designed for dance or drama, is practiced in African societies in restricted context, the cultivation of music that is integrated with dance, or music that stimulates affective motor response, is much more prevalent. For the African, the musical experience is by and large an emotional one: sounds, however beautiful, are meaningless if they do not offer this experience or contribute to the expressive quality of a performance."[8]

And later on, in discussing response to music, the importance of physical body motion is emphasized:

"Affective response to music may be shown outwardly in verbal or physical behavior. The values of African societies do not inhibit this: on the contrary, it is encouraged, for through it, individuals relate to musical events or performing groups, and interact socially with others in a musical situation. Moreover, motor response intensifies one's enjoyment of music through the feelings of increased involvement and the propulsion that articulating the beat by physical movement generates."[9]

Finally Rose Brandel, in discussing work songs of Central Africa, states:

"The paddler who flexes his arms and bends his body in a symmetrical, purposeful rhythm begins to identify himself with the sounds and feel of paddling. The paddle cuts the water; the water swishes; his hands grip the handle of the paddle sending it forward, around, and back in some time relationship to the cutting and swishing; his muscles stretch and his bones may creak; the boat has a myriad of motions and counter-motions; all in some interrelated complex of rhythm which causes him to hear and sing something that seems to flow with the rhythm. The paddler's song comes into being."[10]

Another common example of this phenomenon is in the usage of various sound producers on the body of dancers in traditional societies. These sound makers, usually of the arm, ankle, or waist rattle variety with their characteristic "buzzy" sound, are important components of the normal musical ensemble. The sound that they produce is determined by the nature of the movements the dancers make. Therefore, the movements of the dancers have two dimensions—one as dance, and another as means of producing an important component of the music. Obviously these functions are inextricably linked. The dance is the music and the music is the dance.

There are other examples of this phenomenon, but the above cited examples (which are found throughout sub-Saharan Africa) will suffice to support my thesis that motion and music are viewed as interacting aspects of the same act in the traditional African cultures.

This attitude is an important part of the approach to making music which the "African exiles" brought with them as subliminal cultural baggage when they came to the Western Hemisphere. It thus provides us with an insight into the rationale for certain choices which were collectively made in the development of early Afro-American music. In the course of my paper I will illustrate this by focusing upon three developments in early Afro-American music.

These three developments are the association of movement and music in religious Afro-American music, the association of movement and music in the work song, and the involvement of Blacks in marching bands from the colonial period up to the present. Each of these developments will be analyzed as a reflection of a peculiar Afro-American conceptual approach to music making in which physical body motion is viewed as intrinsic to music.

The first development in Afro-American music history that reflects the presence of this motion and music concept is the adoption of Christianity by large numbers of Blacks. Prior to 1740, the number of Blacks who had adopted Christianity was relatively small. However, by 1830, the number of Blacks who professed belief in Christianity was a significant percentage of the total Black population in the United States.[11] In the interim, not only were large numbers of Blacks converted to the Methodist and Baptist Protestant denominations, but the earliest independent Black churches were established.[12]

There are a number of interrelated factors which explain this phenomenal development, but one which is frequently overlooked is the fact that several aspects of the common form of worship used by the Protestant revivalist movement in the United States at that time were consonant with several traditional West African practices. From about 1740 through 1830, America was caught up in what has been subsequently called "The Great Awakening" or the first great evangelical movement.[13] This revivalist trend, which grew out of the evolvement of Methodism in Europe, with its emphasis on "Christ as a personal savior" and outward individual expressions of spiritual intensity, struck a responsive chord with the Black masses that were initially on the periphery of these rural "great camp meetings."[14] One of the reasons why these services of religious fervor were so appealing to Blacks was because of their own internalized positive attitudes toward outward physical expressions of spiritual zeal. Moreover, because the ideal of the revivalist movement supported individual expressions of religious fervor, the revivalists' attitude toward physical motion as part of the religious experience was more tolerant than that of older non-revivalist religious denominations in the 18th century. As a result, the Blacks who subsequently formed a large part of the great camp meetings began to adopt Christianity in large numbers because within this milieu, their predilection for combining physical body motion with music in the form of rhythmical hand clapping, foot patting, head bobbing, rocking back and forth, and even dancing could not only be pursued with impunity, but was, at least philosophically, if not always in practice, encouraged. Christianity as practiced by the revivalist Methodist and particularly the non-hierarchical Baptist thus provided Black Americans an institution in which musical practices based on "reinterpreted" African concepts of music making could be pursued. Thus Herskovits's conditions for "cultural syncretism" appear to be met here.[15] Hence, the probability of the "reinterpreted" African practice being retained was increased.

There are numerous accounts of the association of physical body movement and music in chronicles of the early Afro-American music. Before the mass conversions of slaves, Rev. Morgan Godwin, who arrived in York Country, Virginia in 1665, complained of the religious dance of the then non-Christian slaves:

". . . nothing is more barbarous and contrary to Christianity, than their . . . Idolatrous Dances and Revels; in which they usually spend the Sunday . . . And here, that I may not be thought too rashly to impute Idolatry to their Dances,my conjecture is raised upon this ground . . . for that they use their Dances as a means to procure Rain; Some of them having been Known to beg this liberty upon the Week Days, in order there unto."[16]

Later,

"Alexander Hewatt noted in 1779 that in South Carolina 'the Negroes of that country, a few only excepted, are to this day as great strangers to Christianity, and as much under the influence of Pagan darkness, idolatry, and superstition, as they were at their first arrival from Africa . . .' He was particularly disturbed that Sundays and 'Holidays are days of idleness . . . in which the slaves assemble together in alarming crowds for the purposes of dancing, feasting and merriment.'"[17]

Perhaps the most thorough contemporaneous discussion of the usage of physical body motion in early Afro-American religious music is found in the frequently quoted book by the Methodist evangelist John Watson, published in 1819. The book, entitled *Methodist Error or Friendly Advice to Those Methodists Who Indulge in Extravagant Religious Emotions and Bodily Exercises,* complained about musical practices of Blacks in the Philadelphia Conference:

"In the blacks' quarter, the coloured people get together, and sing for hours together, shout scrapes of disjointed affirmations, pledges, or prayers, lengthened out with long repetitious choruses. These are all sung in the merry chorus-manner of the southern harvest field, or husking-frolic method, of the slave blacks; and also very greatly like the Indian dances. With every word so sung, they have a sinking of one or the other leg of the body alternately; producing an audible sound of the feet at every step, and as manifest as the steps of actual negro dancing in Virginia & co. If some, in the meantime sit, they strike the sounds alternately on each thigh . . . the evil is only occasionally condemned and the example has already visibly affected the religious manners of some whites."[18]

In one paragraph, Watson provides evidence of the distinctiveness of early Black religious musical practices, the utilization of a myriad of physical body motions associated with music from body percussion to a shuffling dance, and the fact that these "indulgences" in bodily exercises were beginning to influence white Methodists—all clear testimony of the continuation of African behavioral patterns within the context of Protestant revivalism.

The literature on early Afro-American Christianity also contains frequent references to the association of movement and music in the form of religious dancing in general, and the "ring shout", or "runnin sperichil", in particular.[19] Raboteau devotes a large segment of his work on early Afro-American religion to a review of 18th and 19th century accounts of religious dancing which he demonstrates was very widespread.[20] Of particular note is his quote (originally cited by Herskovits) of a comparison of ecstatic religious behavior in Northern Ireland with that of Kentucky. The quote states:

"I wish in closing to call attention to the difference in type of the automations of Kentucky and Ulster. In Kentucky the motor automations, the voluntary muscles in violent action, were the prevailing type, although there were many of the sensory. On the other hand, in Ulster the sensory automations, trance, vision, the physical disability and the sinking of muscular energy were the prevailing types, although there were many of the motor."[21]

The distinction in kinds of ecstatic behavior led Herskovits to state that:

"It is just in the forms of motor behavior remarked on as characteristics of the 'automations' of the (white) Kentucky revivals that aboriginal modes of African worship are to be marked off from those of Europe."[22]

Finally, John and Alan Lomax concluded the following after their experience of observing ring shouts which persisted in the 20th century:

"We have seen shouts in Louisiana, in Texas, in Georgia and the Bahamas; we have seen vaudou dancing in Haiti; we have read accounts of similar rites in the works upon Negro life in other parts of the Western Hemisphere. All share basic similarities: (1) the song is 'danced' with the whole body, with hands, feet, belly, and hips; (2) the worship is, basically, a dancing singing phenomenon; (3) the dancers always move counter-clockwise around the ring; (4) the song has the leader-chorus form, with much repetition, with a focus on rhythm rather than on melody, that is, with a form that invites and ultimately enforces cooperative group activity; (5) the song continues to be repeated from sometimes more than an hour, steadily increasing in intensity and gradually accelerating until a sort of mass hypnosis ensues . . . This shout pattern is demonstrably West African in origin."[23]

Although the Lomaxes were discussing ring shouts performed in the 20th century, their description of common characteristics of these dances appears to be applicable to 18th and 19th century religious dances as well.

The point to be made here is that the basic conceptual approach to music making Blacks brought with them from Africa found a responsive environment in the form of worship practiced in the evangelical meetings. Because of this, it spawned a tradition of important music in Afro-American history. The Black spiritual developed because it was possible in this form of music to fulfil the basic criteria of the association of body movement and music. Therefore, the musical experience became an important factor in attracting large numbers of Blacks to Christianity. It must be noted here that this analysis suggests that a major motivation of Blacks in the adoption of Christianity was the form of worship possible in that religion at that historical moment: a form of worship which, from a behavioral pattern point of view, was consonant with traditional West African practice. This is not to suggest that this factor was the only one which contributed to this development. Obviously, there were a number of interrelated factors which contributed to that development, but the factor of patterned behavior within the context of musical performance is one which is frequently overlooked. In a comparative analysis of African and Afro-American "spirit possession", another distinct form of behavior commonplace within the context of a religious musical experience, several scholars point out that a proper analysis must take into account a comparison of the following two factors: (a) "the faith-context" or theological interpretation and meaning "in which the possession experience occurs"; and (b) "the patterned style of outward response by which the ecstatic experience is manifest."[24] After discussing the considerable differences between the African and the Afro-American faith-context, Raboteau makes the following statement regarding behavior patterns:

> "It is in the context of action, the patterns of motor behavior preceding and following the ecstatic experience that there may be continuity between African and American forms of spirit possession. While the rhythms of the drums, so important in African and Latin American cults, were by and large forbidden to the slave in the United States, handclapping, foot patting, rhythmic preaching, hyperventilation, antiphonal (call and response) singing, and dancing are styles of behavior associated with possession both in Africa and in this country."[25]

Although Raboteau was specifically discussing spirit possession, his comments regarding general behavioral patterns could also be applied to the continuity between African and Afro-American religious music; that is, although the specific theological context, as well as the specific music differs, the general musical behavioral patterns are very similar. Put another way, the two musical practices share the same general behavioral patterns in the process of music making, though the specific manifestations of that shared conceptual approach vary in detail.

The approach to music making in which body movement is seen as an integral part of the musical process is also illustrated in other forms of Afro-American music. The work song is a vivid example of this.

In these songs, as in the African context, the physical activity of work is incorporated as a means of making the song, and conversely, the song is part of the work. This relationship is different from the "whistle or sing while you work" practice which one finds in many cultures. In the latter case, the song of the whistler accompanies the work activity and may indirectly assist the work by drawing attention away from the laborious task. In the former case, however, the physical activity of the work is a means of producing the music itself. It is part of the music making process. Janheinz Jahn, in discussing African work song within his exposition of the Bantu philosophical system, gives perhaps the most provocative analysis of the relationship of the work to the song:

> "Song and dance do not have the purpose of lightening the work, but in song and dance Nommo is doing the real work, and conjuring up the latent forces of nature, while the work itself is only an addition. The meaning of the work lies in the song and dance; they are not a purposive means for the end of lightening the work, even though their influence has that effect. The song is not an aid to the work, but the work an aid to the song."[26]

Independent of whether or not one agrees completely with Jahn's analysis, it is instructive to note that his assertion is based upon an assumption of the inextricable association of physical movement with music. The physical movement of the work is viewed as a component of the music. The Afro-American work song frequently reflects this relationship. For example, listen to Leadbelly's performance of the popular work song "Take this Hammer". Note here that the sound of the hammer is part of the song. It is absolutely essential. That is why folk singers find it necessary to simulate the sound of the hammer when the song is sung outside of its original functional context. The first line of the song is not "Take this hammer . . .", but "Take this hammer—*pow!*" Thus, the music making activity is also a work activity. Hence, the work is not only facilitated by the music, but becomes part of the music.

Another development in Afro-American history which reflects the concept of physical body motion as an integral part of the music making process is the long association of Americans of African descent with marching bands. From as early as the Revolutionary War up to the present, Black people in the United States have been associated with the marching traditions. Chroniclers of the Revolutionary War cite many examples of the involvement of slaves and free blacks with martial music. Eileen Southern in *The Music of Black Americans* cites a "Virginia Act of 1776 (which) specifically stated that Blacks 'shall be employed as drummers, fifers, or pioneers.'"[27] She also indicates that although there is:

> ". . . little on record in regard to black army musicians in the War of 1812 . . . more black musicians must have been active during the war because of the number of all-black brass bands that began to appear soon after the war—especially in New Orleans, Philadelphia, New York and sections of New England. After the war, for example, the Third Company of Washington Guards (Philadelphia) organized a Negro band under the leadership of Frank Johnson that was destined to become internationally famous. Johnson, a Negro, earned for himself a reputation as 'one of the best performers on the bugle and French horn in the United States.' The black musicians who composed the military bands of the early nineteenth century undoubtedly acquired their training—as well as their instruments—during the War of 1812."[28]

The activities of Black military bands during the Civil War have been well documented. James Monroe Trotter, himself a member of a black regimental band during the war, and the esteemed author (in 1878) of the first biographical history of either Black or white American music, *Music and Some Highly Musical People,* wrote the following in an article entitled "The Schoolmaster in the Army":[29]

> "In quite a number of the colored regiments military bands were formed, and under the instruction of sometimes a band teacher from the north, and at others under one of their own proficient fellow-soldiers, these bands learned to discourse most entertaining music in camp, and often by their inspiring strains did much to relieve the fatigue."

Trotter, in *Music and Some Highly Musical People,* Colonel Thomas Wentworth Higginson in his *Army Life in a Black Regiment,* Eileen Southern in *The Music of Black Americans,* as well as numerous others, provide copious documentation of the widespread involvement and excellence of Black military bands during the Civil War.

The period from the end of the Civil War up to the end of World War I was one in which Black brass bands enjoyed a high point. Perhaps as a result of the influence of the French military tradition, throughout the entire former Louisiana Territory brass bands were highly involved in this popular American pastime. Indeed, the important development of the musical genres of ragtime and early traditional jazz (both of which developed during this period), were profoundly influenced by the involvement of Blacks in brass marching bands.[30] On the east coast during World War I, there were a number of outstanding Black infantry bands with James Reese Europe's world famous 369 Infantry band setting the standard.

Finally, during more recent times, Black military bands, drum and bugle corps, and college and university marching bands continue to be in the forefront of the American marching band tradition. Of particular note in the last fifteen years is the role played by Black college and university marching bands in revolutionizing the spectacle of football half time shows.[31] Clearly then, from the time of the Black fifers and drummers of the Revolutionary War, through that of the internationally acclaimed bands of Frank Johnson[32] and James Reese Europe, up to the contemporary "Marching One Hundred" of Florida A.&M. University, the Black presence in the American marching band tradition has been significant.

I suggest that the long tradition of Black marching bands is a reflection of an African and Afro-American conceptual approach to music making. The very nature of marching and making music is one in which the ideal of music and motion as complementary facets of the same process may be realized. In most marching music, the process of marching becomes a component of the music. The physical act of the synchronized steps of a massed group of marchers, and the resultant regular tactus it produces, provides a basic periodic pulsation, in the framework of which the band plays music. This regular pulsation, the basis of the rhythmic foundation of the music, is thus literally produced by the act of marching. Hence, motion is an inextricable aspect of the music. I suggest that, given their particular cultural bias regarding motion and music, Americans of African descent would be particularly attracted to this mode of music making. The historical evidence seems to corroborate this view.

In summary, my basic hypothesis is that African and Afro-American music reflect underlying conceptual approaches to the process of music making. Further, that one of these conceptual approaches, the peculiar association of motion and music, provides us with a framework within which to focus our analysis of the historical development of the music, as well as of specific foreground features. It is this conceptual background which functions as the constant, the core of "African roots of music in the Americas" which is retained, although the outer features of the music may change. For example, Afro-American work songs may differ from African work songs, though the nature of the role of work in both kinds of the songs is the same. What has been retained is a basic approach to the role of work and music.

Although I have concentrated here primarily on developments in early Afro-American music, there is evidence that this conceptual approach is equally operative in contemporary Afro-American music. Several writers on contemporary Afro-American music, while not dealing with the subject in the terms put forth in this paper, address the question of physical motion and music. For example, A.B. Spellman discusses the role of movement in the performance of a specific jazz artist,[33] and Charles Keil mentions it as part of the ritualized performance of the popular blues singer.[34] Moreover, although no systematic analysis of its role has been made, the well-known physical movement of contemporary jazz, soul, blues and gospel performers suggests that this principle is still very much intact.

Notes

1. Among these studies are Harold Courlander, *Negro Folk Music U.S.A.* (New York, 1963); Alan Merriam, Whinery and Fred, "Songs of a Rada Community in Trinidad," *Anthropos* 51 (1956); John Roberts, *Black Music of Two Worlds* (New York, 1972); Gunther Schuller, *Early Jazz* (New York, 1968); Richard Waterman, "African Influence on the Music of the Americas." *Acculturation in the Americas,* ed. Sol Tax (Chicago, 1952). A summary of most of these studies as well as the outline of a different approach to the problem may be found in Olly Wilson, "The Significance of the Relationship between Afro-American Music and West African Music." *The Black Perspective in Music* II. No. 1, ed. Eileen Southern (New York, 1974). In addition to the above there are other comparative studies between specific genres of Afro-American music and African music. Among these are Paul Oliver, *Savannah Syncopators* (London, 1970), and the chapter entitled "Blues, Residual African Elements in North America," in Janheinz Jahn, *Muntu* (New York, 1961).

2. There are, of course, exceptions to this basic assumption, particularly since 20th century developments in Western music.

3. For a further discussion of the role of culture in framing aesthetic values see Leonard B. Meyer, *Music, the Arts, and Ideas* (Chicago, 1967) and Alan Merriam, *The Anthropology of Music* (Evanston, Ill., 1964).

4. See Robert Plant Armstrong, *The Affecting Presence* (Urbana, Ill., 1971) and Janheinz Jahn's *Muntu* for a complete discussion of African aesthetics.

5. The reader may wish to consult Melville Herskovits's monumental *Myth of the Negro Past* (Boston, 1958) for a thorough study of African retentions in the Western Hemisphere. Of special relevance to us is his "theory of reinterpretation" in which he asserts that "African-exiles" reinterpreted traditional African cultural patterns to conform to their new social situation, while retaining a core of essentially African values. He states on pages 141–142 of *Myth* that a "principle of disregard for outer form while retaining inner values is characteristic of Africans everywhere" and is "the most important single factor making for an understanding of the acculturative situation."

6. See chapter 18 entitled "Interrelations of Music and Dance" in J.H. Kwabena Nketia, *The Music of Africa* (New York, 1974).

7. John Blacking, *How Musical is Man* (Seattle and London, 1973), p. 27.

8. Kwabena Nketia, *The Music of Africa, op. cit.,* p. 206.

9. *Ibid.,* p. 207.

10. Rose Brandel, *The Music of Central Africa* (The Hague, 1961), p. 33.

11. Al Raboteau, *Slave Religion: "The Invisible Institution" in the Ante-Bellum South* (New York, 1978), p. 66.

12. The Bethel A.M.E. church was founded in Philadelphia in 1794. Several other Black churches were founded during this period.

13. See Gilbert Chase, *America's Music, from the Pilgrims to the Present* (New York, 1955) for a further discussion of music in the "Great Awakening."

14. Eileen Southern, *Readings in Black American Music* (New York, 1971), Gilbert Chase, *America's Music* (New York, 1955), and Portia Maultsby, *Afro-American Religious Music: 1618–1861* (Ph.D. dissertation, University of Wisconsin, 1974) all discuss the extent of Black involvement in the revivalist movement.

15. See Herskovits, *Myth of the Negro Past*. According to Herskovits, "cultural syncretism" may take place when there is enough similarity between dissimilar cultures to allow for the reinterpretation and retention of a particular cultural practice within the new cultural milieu. What results is a reconciliation or merger of the two cultures in terms of that particular practice.
16. Morgan Godwin, *The Negro's and Indian's Advocate* (London, 1680), cited by Dena J. Epstein, "African Music in British and French America," *The Musical Quarterly* LIX (1973), pp. 79–80.
17. Alexander Hewatt, *An Historical Account of the Rise and Progress of the Colonies of South Carolina and Georgia* (London, 1779), II, pp. 100, 103 (cited by Epstein, *op.cit.,* p. 81, and Raboteau, *Slave Religion,* p. 94).
18. John Watson, *Methodist Error* (Trenton, N.J., 1819) pp. 28–31, cited by Eileen Southern, *Readings, op.cit.,* pp. 62–64.
19. See Southern, *The Music of Black Americans* (New York, 1971), pp. 160–162.
20. See Raboteau, *Slave Religion, "The Invisible Institution" in the Ante-Bellum South,* pp. 68–72.
21. Frederick Morgan Davenport, *Primitive Traits in Religious Revivals* (New York, 1917), pp. 92–93. Cited by Herskovits, *Myth* pp. 230–231; Raboteau, *Slave Religion,* p. 60.
22. Herskovits, *Myth,* p. 231.
23. John A. Lomax and Alan Lomax, *Folksong U.S.A.* (New York, 1947), p. 335.
24. Raboteau, *Slave Religion,* p. 63.
25. *Ibid.,* p. 65.
26. Janheinz Jahn, *Muntu,* p. 224. Jahn explains Nommo as "the life force, which produces all life, which influences 'things' in the shape of the word" (p. 124).
27. Eileen Southern, *Music of Black Americans,* p. 74.
28. *Ibid.,* p. 77.
29. Published in Joseph T. Wilson, *The Black Phalanx: A History of Negro Soldiers of the United States* (Hartford, Conn., 1887), pp. 505–507, cited by Robert Stevenson in "America's First Black Music Historian," *Journal of the American Musicological Society* XXVI (1973), pp. 383–404.
30. See Gunther Schuller, *Early Jazz,* especially the chapter entitled "The Beginnings"; Rudi Blesh, *They All Played Ragtime* (New York, 1958); and Russ Russel, *Jazz Style in Kansas City and the Southwest* (Berkeley, 1971).
31. During the 1950's, Black university marching bands, led by the Florida A.&M. University "Marching One Hundred," began to march at a very fast cadence ($\quarternote$ = ca. 240), and to use popular rhythm and blues songs as part of their repertoire. Following the first appearances of these bands on National television during the half time shows of the National Football League Championship and All Star Games, this marching style became part of the standard practice of university marching bands all over the country.
32. See Eileen Southern's article "Frank Johnson of Philadelphia and His Promenade Concerts" in *The Black Perspective in Music* V, 1 (1977), pp. 3–29, for a thorough discussion of Frank Johnson's widely acclaimed concerts in London and Philadelphia. Robert Stevenson in his article "America's First Black Music Historian" also discusses Frank Johnson's illustrious career.
33. A.B. Spellman, *Black Music. Four Lives in Jazz* (New York, 1966).
34. Charles Keil, *Urban Blues* (Chicago, 1966).

An Aesthetic of the Cool: West African Dance
Robert Farris Thompson
Art historian

Robert Farris Thompson's work includes Face of the Gods: Art and Altars and the African Americas *(1993), the influential* Flash of the Spirit: African and Afro-American Art and Philosophy *(1983),* The Four Moments of the Sun: Kongo Art in Two Worlds *(1981),* African Art in Motion *(1974), and* Black Gods and Kings *(1971). Thompson is currently professor of African and Afro-American Art history at Yale University.*

The scope of this article[1] will be restricted to West Africa, for this sector is one of the few in tropical Africa (East Africa is, to a lesser extent, an exception) where a cohesive musical geography, so to speak, has been isolated.[2] For many reasons, of which I shall give but three, the traditional Guinea Coast choreographies deserve study: West African dances are key documents of aesthetic history; they are nonverbal formulations of philosophies of beauty and ethics and they furnish a means of comprehending a pervasive strand of contemporary American culture.

To take up the last point first, let me say at once that Americans fail to understand the rock-and-roll of their children because of their ignorance of black artistic traditions, which even blue-eyed youngsters seem to have absorbed. In general, American whites still seem to restrict their most genuine singing to the shower, their best dancing to the cabaret or club, and their worship to a weekly remembrance. By contrast, members of Negro sanctified churches sing, worship, and dance in their pews.

Similarly, African traditional cults are *danced faiths,* worship converted into sound and motion, performed in the open air. The alfresco emphasis, in fact, may well explain why with few exceptions—Zimbabwe is one—large-scale religious architecture is absent south of the Sahara.[3] Black religions are instruments of moral edification *and* entertainment, excitement *and* decorum;[4] consequently, African devotees blend the sacred with the profane, night after night, day after day. If, while observing an American Negro descendant of this tradition, we are surprised when B. B. King pauses in the middle of his blues to deliver a sermon of the cool,[5] we are admitting an inadequate understanding of the aesthetic history of the Negro. One approach to this history lies in the study of West African dances. The traditional choreographies of tropical Africa constitute, I submit, complex distillations of thinking, comparable to Cartesian philosophy in point of influence and importance.

Robert Farris Thompson, "An Aesthetic of the Cool: West African Dance," African Forum *2 (2)
(1966): 85–102.*

The equilibrium and poetic structure of traditional dances of the Yoruba in western Nigeria, as well as the frozen facial expressions worn by those who perform these dances, express a philosophy of the cool, an ancient, indigenous ideal; patience and collectedness of mind. Yoruba myths relate tales of disjunction, of the dangerous jarring of elements that had been in balance, of the near-destruction of mankind by breach of trust. In one myth, the Yoruba god of divination locates the mediating principle in cool water; in another, a powerful man named Agirilogbon locates the mediating principle in a cool, healing leaf.[6] There is nothing arbitrary about these myths: They all posit water, certain leaves, and other items as symbols of the coolness that transcends disorder and without which community is impossible. Ask a traditional member of this populous African society, "What is love?" and he may tell you, as one told me, "Coolness."

The last words spoken by Malcolm X were: "Now brothers! Be cool, don't get excited."[7] Was this sheer coincidence? I think it is permissible to sound the idiom of Harlem (which has been appropriated by much of white America) for possible relationships with West African thinking. Perhaps one reason many American Negroes sing a sad song happy and some whites sing it sad is that the Negro is an heir to an aesthetic of the cool and the latter is not. It is cool to sweeten hurt with song and motion; it is hot to concentrate upon the pain.

Marshall McLuhan argues that literacy heats up the eye at the expense of the other senses.[8] When a Yoruba chief explains that men dance to keep the town cool, one might use McLuhan's concepts to analyze the significance of the chief's remark: Dancing returns consciousness to a ratio between the senses—feet touch earth, ears hear drumming, eyes study gesture. Since dance also interrelates the arts themselves, we recognize the urgent need, in speaking of black choreography in Africa, to maintain the ratio between music and dance, and the more we project the findings of ethnomusicologists into the study of West African dance the more we learn. Adeleye, an informal oral critic of traditional dance in the village of Ajilete in western Nigeria, stresses that an excellent dancer "hears [comprehends] the drum and makes the whole body dance," which succinctly summarizes the involvement Africans relish and the balance between musical and choreographic expression they seek to strike.

Although dance structure may be broadly related to musical structure everywhere in the world, the special African instance of the problem arrests our attention, for we are attempting to discern some broad structural traits of West African dance in relation to dominant West African musical precepts. These seem joint bearers of a dynamic sensibility; both seem to fuse energy and decorum in a manner that confounds the either/or categories of Western thinking.

Another reason for the relationship is that the gross characteristics of African dance have been more or less documented in word descriptions over the years by people who are ignorant of precise movement analysis. Nuances of gesture and dynamics require a painstaking translation of filmed sequences into the objective medium of labanotation, a system of dance notation that has become the archival lingua franca of the modern world of choreography. Although these difficult prescriptions are, happily, being met by Joann Kealiinohomoku at Indiana University and Nadia Chilkovsky Nahumck of the University of Pennsylvania, most of us still depend upon word descriptions—and these are very gross. But to throw them away in favor of an exclusive parlance of notation might well prove as controversial as an exclusive reliance upon written (as opposed to oral) tradition in the writing of African history. The felicitous research of the future will probably involve a cooperation between labanotaters and other observers of African dance, much as African historians have learned to marshall oral and archival data together.

Music and dance, of course, evince some traits peculiar to themselves. Such self-logics, for example, include timbre (as to music) and footwork (as to dance). Except as a metaphor, it would be difficult to portray a formal correspondence between these two phenomena. Yoruba, for example, clearly mark the distinction between music and dance with separate words, respectively *orin* and *ijó*. But we are concentrating on dance music—that is, music which has regular pulsations—since it would be pointless to study the structure of music not specifically intended for the dance, such as certain dirges in Ghana that are metrically free, rhythmically relaxed, and lacking a steady beat.[9]

From the point of view of dance, West Africa is as historically suggestive as it is rich in musicological description. The Guinea Coast lay astride the area of intensive slaving that resulted in the forced transference of the music and dances of the area to the New World. African-influenced dances, where they appear in the Americas, seem to furnish means of testing assertions about the "parent stock." If one believes that West African dances are multimetric in nature, for example, the demonstration that some forms of Afro-Cuban dancing are also founded upon the simultaneous use of one or more meters (in addition to the basic time signature of the music) might strengthen the assertion.

Four shared traits of West African music and dance are suggested here, together with a fifth, which, although nonmusical, seems very relevant. These shared characteristics appear to be the following: the dominance of a percussive concept of performance; multiple meter; apart playing and dancing; call-and-response; and, finally, the songs and dances of derision.

The first phrase, which is Alan Merriam's—the dominance of a percussive concept of performance—describes a core element.[10] In the Western classic symphony, two tympani are outnumbered by some forty-three melodic instruments, which is symptomatic of an ascendancy of harmonic and melodic concepts and the relative unimportance of percussive traditions. But in tropical Africa even instruments outside the membranophone and idiophone classes will be played with percussive bias instead of in ways soft and legato. Africans do not traditionally bow fiddles legato, but pluck them energetically, with vigorous attack.[11] So striking is this emphasis upon percussive musical diction (which has to do with aesthetic choices and not the inevitable use of a drum or even hardwood sticks) that I am tempted to designate West Africa as a percussive culture. In fact, heaven itself has been portrayed by a West African poet in terms of percussive display and onomatopoeia:

> Let the calabash
> Entwined with beads
> With blue Aggrey beads
> Resound
> Let the calabash resound
> In tune with the drums

Mingle with these sounds
The clang of wood on tin:
Kentensekenken
Ken-tse ken ken ken[12]

In the West African world, it is one of the dancer's aims to make every rhythmic sub-tlety of the music visible.[13] When the master drummer of the Ijebu Yoruba rises in level of pitch, during a ceremony for the waterspirit named Igodo, the master dancer is said to rise, correspondingly, upon his toes. When a Thundergod drum choir of the Egbado Yoruba plays music expressive of the hot-tempered God of Iron, the master dancer immediately becomes explosive in her gestures to maintain an appropriate balance with the emotional coloring of the percussive patterns being rendered.

Surface appreciation of such procedures may mask the fact that it is West African *dancing* that is percussive, regardless of whether or not it is expressed with a striking of one part of the body against another (the chest whacking with the hands of Dahomean *Kpe*) or with stamping patterns and rattles. Percussive flavoring governs the motion of those parts of the body that carry no weight—the gestures—as well as the steps that do. Unsurprisingly, a good drummer in West Africa is a good dancer, and vice versa, although the degree of specialty and professionalism varies with each individual.

The mnemonic retention of dance steps shares the same verbal basis of drummers who are attempting to impart the memory of a given drum pattern to an apprentice drummer. This verbal basis often consists of drum syllables:[14] They are used when a dancer wishes to speak out the drum or bodily rhythms of a particular dance in order to make clear the duration of the gestures and steps and the contrasts with which a particular movement is built. To return to the master dancer of Ajilete, Nigeria, we note that she pays close attention to the syllables enunciated by the drums, and when she hears the pattern *gẹrẹ gẹrẹ gẹrẹ gẹkan*, she swings her hands across her body during the first six syllables. Each time the last two syllables sound, she draws her hands up to her breasts with a simultaneous inhalation of breath.[15]

Thus, West African dances are *talking dances,* and the point of the conversation is the expression of percussive concepts. This gift reappears in the Negro New World: Marshall and Jean Stearns have informed me that tap dancers sometimes spell out their ideas with syllables, in the West African manner, and I have observed similar instances among New York's Afro-Cuban dancers. Perhaps the absorption of this tradition has sharpened the exceptional mambos of James Evans, one of the finest Negro dancers of New York:

> Over the years Evans has worked out a "semaphoric" mambo that is his own, a means of metrically conversing with his hands. Unlike the handwork in certain Polynesian dances, Evans' is only occasionally pictorial; it is his aim to capture and describe percussion, not specific images, and the extent to which he succeeds is perhaps best summarized by [Hoyt Warner] who once shouted to him "You *caught* that riff."[16]

Warner, a young white mathematician and amateur of mambo, meant that the music indicated a sudden repeated phrase and that Evans had convincingly translated the iteration into motion.

Instead of emphasizing the expression of West African dance (and its derivatives) in terms of taps and rattles, clapping and stamping, it would seem far more penetrating to say that it is West African dancing itself that is percussive. The vigor and the attack of the idiom can be so subtly elaborated as when Ohori Yoruba open and close their shoulder blades in time to a mental gong.

Multiple meter, the second trait, is a well-documented element of West African music. The phrase means the simultaneous execution of several time signatures, not unlike the sounding of the ¾ of the waltz and the ⁴⁄₄ of jazz at the same time,[17] survivals of which enliven the Negro barrios of the Americas. Polymeter in the West African manner turns up in the urban music of the Spanish-speaking segments of the United States. A pleasing example has been recorded by Mongo Santamaría, wherein two types of drum establish parallel lines of ⁴⁄₄ time with machine-gun celerity while another type of drum lays down a ⁶⁄₈ at a slow tempo.[18]

Multiple meter qualifies much West African dancing as a mirror image. A useful theoretical introduction to the problem was established in 1948 by Richard Alan Waterman:

> The dance of the West African is an essay on the appreciation of musical rhythms. For the performance of a good dancer the drums furnish the inspiration, in response to which the thread of each rhythmic element contributing to the thunderous whole of the percussion *gestalt* is followed in movement without separation from its polyrhythmic context.[19]

Waterman describes a maximum instance. The dancer picks up each rhythm of the polymetric whole with different parts of his body; when he does so, he directly mirrors the metric mosaic. But it is important to note that in many instances West Africans find it convenient to dance to only one rhythm, or to shift from two basic pulsations in their footwork to three (as in a kind of Ewe virtuoso dancing), or to follow three mental pulsations while the gong player actually strikes four. In other words, there are minimum instances of multimetric dancing to oppose against the full expression described by Waterman.

In this context, the notion of balance is not only a canon of West African dancing but an aesthetic acid test: The weak dancer soon loses his metric bearings in the welter of competing countermeters and is, so to speak, knocked off balance, as if a loser in a bout of Indian wrestling. Multiple meter is, in brief, a communal examination of percussive individuality.

Bertonoff defines multimetric dancing as bodily orchestration:

> The Ewe dances are the most fervent among all the Ghanaian tribes, for in them the body moves as though it were orchestrated. The various limbs and members, head, shoulders, and legs are all moving simultaneously but each in a rhythm of its own. The main movement is carried out at dizzying speed by the elbows. The motion resembles that of the wings of an injured bird, yet it is as light and easy as the swaying of a fish's fins.[20]

I suspect dancers from different African societies choose different parts of the body for emphasis within the polymetric whole. We know that the rhythmic emphasis of West African music shifts back and forth from meter to meter, and the parts of the dancer's body that reflect these shifts may also constitute major determinants of local styles.

On the northwest "verge" of Ghana, at Lawra, Bertonoff documented a second manifestation of multiple meter. The movement was actually the seated "dance" of the musician playing a xylophone:

> He held a stick in each hand, and the rhythm of the left hand was opposed to that of the right. His head was moving in a third rhythm between the strokes. It seemed to me that the soles of his feet were also on the move and giving the rhythm and counter-rhythm an interpretation of their own. During the dance the feet interpret the rhythm according to which the other parts of the body are moving.[21]

The last observation is interesting. Implied is a notion of the dancer monitoring the rhythmic *donnée* of the music with his feet while with other parts of his body he duplicates or comments upon the polymeters of the music. The metric "given" of the music in West Africa is normally the accents of a gong. Significantly, A. M. Jones, who has also briefly studied Ewe dancing, finds that in the *Adzida* club dance ("very popular in Eweland") the foot and hand movements are staggered, though the feet are in phase with the gong. It should be noted, however, that Jones's careful notation shows the bell pattern in $^{12}/_8$ time, the feet in $^3/_4$; thus, even though the dancer follows the organizing meter of the music with his feet, he has executed a statement at metrical variance from it.

The notion of the feet interpreting the foundation beat of gongs finds an interesting corroboration among the Tiv of central Nigeria. Laura Bohannan reports a confrontation with informants who insisted that she dance at a wedding to prove her solidarity with the relevant family: "'Teach me then,' I retorted. Duly, she and the other senior women began my instruction: my hands and my feet were to keep time with the gongs, my hips with the first drum, my back and shoulders with the second." [22] Whenever Mrs. Bohannan subsided into an "absent-minded shuffle," indignant old women promptly poked her in the ribs and commanded "Dance." Thus, in at least one Tiv society, the articulation of multiple meter seems to amount to protocol.

Cult and secular dancing among the Negroes of Cuba evinces some multimetric dancing. Rumbaists, for example, sometimes introduce a passage of $^6/_8$ elbow-work at a fast tempo in opposition to the basic $^2/_4$ or $^4/_4$ pulsations marked by their footwork. Señor Julito Collazo, an excellent dancer of an entire range of Cuban cult dances, told me that "there have been many times when I was dancing rumba with or against the $^2/_4$ of the music when I varied my steps by adding passages of Cuban-Ibibio style in $^6/_8$ time." Whenever this happened, his steps were immediately at variance with the basic beat.

The third trait is apart playing and dancing. And perhaps the best way to gain an insight into the dissection of experience that affects Western life may be to study the physical movements of the musicians of a classic symphony orchestra. The violin section is seated in ordered rows; and when the violinists are observed in profile, their silhouettes, a repeated pattern of human figures seated stiffly erect, form a kind of step-fret series. At the sign of the conductor's baton, more than a score of violinists take up their instruments and, holding them against their chins, bow-and-finger them in unison; as they do so, their restricted action hovers like a nimbus over the more-or-less motionless body. Action has been restricted, essentially, to the right arm and to the fingers and wrist of the left hand, although the body may sway somewhat.

In dramatic contrast to this remarkable compression of motion, West African musicians move the whole trunk and head, whether seated or standing, in response to the music. West African musicians dance their own music. They play "apart" in the sense that each is often intent upon the production of his own contribution to a polymetric whole. The members of a drum choir of three do not strike the skins of their instruments in unison. At least one—normally the master drummer—creates pleasing clashes with the rhythmic structure of his helpers; he departs from their text, as it were, and improvises illuminations. "Apart playing" defines much of the production of music in West Africa whereas "synchronous" playing defines much of the music of the West. (But certainly not all: "Classic" compositions come to mind wherein the clarinets may do something different from the violins.) Africans unite music and dance but play apart; Europeans separate dance and music but play together. As A. M. Jones notes: "With Western music deliberate synchrony is the norm from which our music develops; that is why it is possible for one man with a baton to conduct a whole orchestra."[23] Playing apart, on the other hand, grants the West African space in which to maintain his own private or traditional meter and to express his own full corporeal involvement in what he is doing.

A close inspection of dance modes in West Africa will reveal that "apart dancing" is as important a part of choreographic custom as "apart playing." It is one of the more striking traits of sub-Saharan dance,[24] and it is one of the few dance constituents that European outsiders consistently identified in verbal descriptions. F. de Kersaint-Gilly noted in 1922: "In Negro Africa—I have spent time among Bakota and among various societies of West Africa—man and woman never put their arms around each other while dancing, as we generally do in France."[25]

Apart dancing is not correlated with the apart playing of instruments in the sense of absence of body contact. The unity which the musicians and dancers share seems, rather, to constitute a constellation of solo and chorus performances. The master drummer (or drummers) plays alone, intent upon improvisation; the master dancer (or dancers), intent upon following or challenging these improvisations, also dances alone. And the drum chorus and the dancing chorus interact by repetitive patterns, which means that a certain amount of performing together balances the apartness. But the critical fact seems to be this: West Africans perform music and dance apart the better to ensure a dialog between movement and sound.

Dancers of the classic ballet do not touch either, as a rule, but these dancers are governed by a single metrical reference and, moreover, dance together in the sense that all their actions are governed by identical demands of pictorial legibility—which is to say that their *pliés* and *tours en l'air* must project crisply across row upon row of seated spectators. Considering the literary bias of the West, this tendency was inevitable. (Modern dance, in which apart playing and dancing are not uncommon, might be described as a dramatic break with this tendency, comparable with Cézanne's shift from representation to expression; but to what extent African influence and/or independent inventions shaped this revolution cannot be estimated in this article.) Africans seem to dance with full muscular actions so palpably syllabic that one can scarcely fail to comprehend the sense of linguistic community that pervades the whole. To dance with arms enlaced around the partner, in the manner of pre-jazz Western ballrooms, lessens the opportunity to converse. Even when Africans dance together, as in certain performing pairs of Abomey, they are actually operating apart to achieve a playing of hand movements against hips, something not possible were their hands locked in an embrace. Nor could their hands find individual metric inspiration were the members of the percussive choir similarly locked into a single metrical scheme. To recapitulate, West Africans and Afro-Americans dance apart and play apart to liberate their attention, as it were, for continuous conversation between motion and music, instead of specializing in purely musical or choreographic activity.

The fourth trait of West African music and dance is a special form of antiphony, wherein a caller alternates his lines with the regularly timed responses of a chorus; it is the formal structure of indigenous singing,[26] and it is known as call-and-response. The important fact is that the caller frequently overlaps or interrupts the chorus. Antiphony exists the world over, but nowhere else in the world does the overlapping of the phrases of leader and followers so consistently occur. Are there similar patterns in the dance? Yes. J. Van Wing summarized the dances of the important Bakongo peoples of what is now the Democratic Republic of Congo (Kinshasa): "There are always two bodies or two groups of bodies in movement: a solo dancer in front of a group, or an individual before another in a group, or an individual before another in a couple, or two groups placed in front of the other. They perform periodic movements that are like questions and responses."[27]

Similar patterns appear in the world of Spanish Harlem ballrooms, where Puerto Ricans improvise constantly varying steps—dancing apart while their partners maintain a recurrent movement. These men "interrupt" the movement of their women in a call-and-response manner, for they begin a new step or flourish considerably before their partners have finished the execution of their basic movements. In Ushi, an especially musical Ekiti Yoruba village, my wife and I observed a lead dancer improvise patterns that consistently began before a "chorus" had finished its "refrain," which consisted of swinging the ends of their head-ties in concerted rhythm, first to the right, then to the left, over their wrists.

The fifth trait, a nonmusical element, is the moral function of the songs of social allusion and the dances of derision. "In West Africa," Laura Boulton writes, "songs are frequently used as an important moral agent in the community. Songs of satire are very powerful because there is no punishment an African dreads more than being held up to the ridicule of his fellow men."[28] (A wealth of similar examples may be found in Alan P. Merriam's *Anthropology of Music*.) Although we are, of course, referring to *content* rather than to form or style—a different analytic level—we intend to illustrate briefly, in the conclusion, that a relationship between content and style is best displayed by singers' deliberately distorting their voices when singing in traditions noted for moral allusion and inquisition.

The dance of derision, the choreographic correlate of the song of allusion, is a striking trait of much West African dancing. Even in Zululand, outside the purview of West Africa, derision dances are found and have been described by Kaigh as "dances of domestic oddities":

They dance after any event, white or black, which takes their fancy. I have seen danced imitations of myself and party too veracious to be flattering, or even comfortable. After I had lost a steeplechase by being thrown from the horse my boys danced the accident so faithfully that I came away a sadder, if not a wiser clown. The boy who took the part of me was most embarassingly accurate as to detail.[29]

Pride and pretension are as much a target of the African dancer as they are of the singer of allusion. Surprisingly, the connection between the arts in this regard has not, to my knowledge, been pointed out. The former colonial authorities of what is now the Republic of Zambia were aware of the potentialities of African derision dancing, or so Chapter 120, Section 7, of the former laws of that area implies: "No person may organize or take part in any dance which is calculated to hold up to ridicule or to bring into contempt any person, religion, or duly constituted authority."[30] This apparent characteristic was noted in 1825 by Captain Hugh Clapperton, who witnessed a dance, evidently danced at his expense, at Old Ọyọ, the ancient imperial capital of the Yoruba Peoples.[31]

Dances of derision in the Negro world are legion. Camille Poupeye mentions them in the Bamako area of Mali and calls them "satires in action,"[32] and S. F. Nadel has described one instance at Bida in northern Nigeria. I have observed over the last ten years Puerto Rican dancers mock fatuous or eccentric dancing with cruelly accurate movements in New York City. The dance of derision brings home the fact that Africans and Afro-Americans are interested not only in force and the affirmation of fertility in their controlled energetic dancing, but also with ethics and right living. The man who misbehaves may not only have to "face the music," as in the "signifying songs" of the old-time New Orleans Negroes, but he may also have to face the movement.

To summarize these points with the help of a Yoruba critic: One cultivator—criticizing a dance by members of a society which performs during the installation of the king of the Anago town of Ipokia and during the funerals of its members—said: "This dance is aesthetically pleasing [ijó nã wù mi dãdã] because the legs and all parts of the body are equal" [nítorípé ẹ sẹ tó ngbe àti gbogbo ara dógba]. The key word is dógba, which means in Yoruba "is symmetrical." The native connoisseur of artistic motion had put his finger on one of the most important canons of West African dance—balance.

The point of one form of Ibo dancing in Nigeria, for example, is to infuse the upper torso and the head with violent vibrations without losing an overall sense of stability. In this case, equilibrium is shown by the relatively motionless extension of the open palms in front of the dancer, almost at arm's length, each palm at an equal distance from the body. And, moreover, despite the ferocity of the "shimmying" of the upper frame, the shuffling feet of the dancer indulge gravity and thus convey balance. When West Africans shuffle—and most of them do in their traditional dancing (although there are dances galore in which dancers, especially men, break the bonds of gravity with special leaps and other gravity-resistant motions)—their bodies are usually bent forward, toward the stabilizing earth. They maintain balance. And balance is cool.

A further case in point: A gifted Egbado Yoruba dancer maintains the whole time she dances a "bound motion" in her head, thus balancing a delicate terracotta sculpture on her head without danger, while simultaneously subjecting her torso and arms to the most confounding expressions of raw energy and force. It is not difficult to find similar instances of control in other African dances. Thundergod devotees, for instance, sometimes dance with a burning fire in a container coolly balanced on the top of their heads. Coolness in the sense of control and symmetry seems a metaphor of the spiritual. And this is not to mention the manifold secular manifestations of this basic tendency—for example, Africans traveling while balancing even ink wells and sheets of paper on their heads or African wrestlers defeating their opponents not by "pinning" them to the ground in the Western manner, but by knocking them off balance.

From this cultural background a philosophy of music and dance seems to emerge. In the case of the dominance of a percussive concept, one is talking about the vigorous involvement of the whole body (the performances of the aged continue to provoke the amazement of Western observers). The vibrations may be subtle but they are diffused throughout the body. This trait might be compared with Yoruba ephebism or the deliberately youthful depiction of the human frame in sculpture.[33]

Old age is rare in West African sculpture. Its depiction seems restricted to situations of satire, psychological warfare, and moral vengeance. The dignity of the Yoruba dancer's facial expression might be profitably compared with the ephebistic (youthful) flawless seal of most Yoruba sculpture. In both cases, in any event, indigenous critics of art may characterize the dignity of the respective expressions as "cool." When Tiv (in northern Nigeria) dance satirically, as in the *Ngogh*[34] dance making fun of swollen bodies, the flawless seal shatters and faces become twisted with exaggeration and grimaces. But in the aggregate, West Africans dance with a mixture of vigor and decorum.

Multiple meter essentially uses dancers as further voices in a polymetric choir. The conversation is additive, cool in its expressions of community. The balance struck between the meters and the bodily orchestration seems to communicate a soothing wholeness rather than a "hot" specialization. The implications of dialog in apart performing have been discussed. Call-and-response is a means of putting innovation and tradition, invention and imitation, into amicable relationships with one another. In that sense it, too, is cool. Finally, the dance of derision sometimes breaks these rules in order to mime the disorder of those who would break the rules of society.[35] Yoruba moral inquisitors do not really dance; they loom. Their shapes, their cries, their motions are unearthly, meant to startle, meant—quite literally—to frighten the hell out of people.

The dance of derision attests that although most West African dances exist as concrete metaphors of right living, some Africans do cheat, steal, and kill. Terrible events occur in West Africa not because the inhabitants lack moral control (their dances make this clear), but because thus far no society on earth has ever completely satisfied or embodied a definition of ideal behavior.[36]

When Christians go to war (instead of turning the other cheek), they have the effrontery to do so within a system of ethics that imparts the promise of redemption. But when an African, finding his security threatened, kills his neighbor, depressingly large segments of the Western world believe that he does so instinctively, without any moral check whatsoever. But an increasing familiarity with the ideal of the cool, documented by the nonverbal "texts" of the dance, will reveal a fact of moral equality. Should Westerners, white and black alike, forsake comfort and estimate the meaning of the words that are made flesh in the dances of the Guinea Coast, they might find our double standards intolerable. They might even detect logical inconsistencies when they observe that the murder of Greek by Turk, of Turk by Greek, on Cyprus is described as an "historical conflict," but that the murder of Ibo by Hausa, and Hausa by Ibo, in Nigeria is described with horror as a "reversion to savagery."

The time-resistant dances of the cool form a kind of prayer: May humanity be shielded from the consequences of arrogance and the penalties of impatience.

Notes

1. It is a pleasure to acknowledge the support of the Ford Foundation, which enabled me, as a Fellow of the Foreign Area Training Program, to study Yoruba sculpture and dance in Nigeria and Dahomey from October, 1962 to January, 1964. I should also like to thank warmly the Councilium for International Study at Yale for a grant which enabled me to continue these studies in Nigeria during the summer of 1965. The sympathy and advice of Leonard Doob is especially noted in this regard. I have also profited from correspondence with Alan P. Merriam, Chairman of the Department of Anthropology, Indiana University, and with Judith Lynne Hanna, of the Center for Research in Social Systems at the American University. Vincent Scully was kind enough to read portions of a first draft of this paper and made, as did Merriam and Hanna, many relevant criticisms. Finally, I should like to thank John Davis for encouraging this brief study.

2. Alan P. Merriam, "African Music" in *Continuity and Change in African Cultures,* ed. William R. Bascom and Melville J. Herskovits (Chicago: University of Chicago Press, 1959), p. 76.

3. See Julius Glück, "Afrikanische Architektur," *Tribus,* VI (1956), 65.

4. For example, see Robin Horton's "The Kalabari Ekine Society: A Borderland of Religion and Art," *Africa* (April, 1963).

5. Transcribed by Charles Keil in his *Urban Blues* (Chicago: University of Chicago Press, 1966), p. 98. A slightly variant version may be heard on ABC-Paramount 509, *B. B. King Live at the Regal.*

6. As to a Yoruba myth concerning water as symbol of reconciliation, see the excellent vernacular source *Ijala: Are Ode,* by Oladipo Yemitan (Ibadan: Ibadan University Press, 1963), pp. 4–6. As to a Yoruba myth concerning leaves, see J. O. George, *Historical Notes on the Yoruba Country* (Lagos: 1895), pp. 62–63. Here the agency of reconciliation was "the leaf of a tree called *Ewe-Alasuwalu,* a leaf that is capable of remodeling a man's evil character. . . . Agirilogbon took it out of the . . . bag of deep mystery, healed all the people, and stopped the calamity."

7. See *Time,* "Death and Transfiguration," March 5, 1965, p. 23.

8. McLuhan's *Understanding Media: The Extensions of Man* (New York: McGraw-Hill, 1965) is a richly aphoristic text suggestive, by means of a jumpy, electric style, of its subject matter. McLuhan observes that "a hot medium is one that extends one single sense in high definition" (p. 22). He seems to feel that the rise of the concept "cool" (and, symptomatically, he quotes Jack Paar) is caused by the mass media. My own view is historical: I think the philosophy of the cool existed, in one form or another, in Negro-American culture long before the time of the telephone, radio, and television. The fact that American Negroes have been noted for their dancing since the coming of their ancestors to these shores seems to suggest the historical basis of the importance of "not losing one's cool" in their world view. This is in the nature of theory, of course. Much sharpening of issues and further research is needed.

9. Yet motion in response to the dirge is not uncommon. See J. H. Nketia, *Funeral Dirges of the Akan People* (Achimota: 1955), p. 10.

10. Merriam has enriched our understanding of the interrelationship between percussion music and the dance of tropical Africa. His notions about music clearly inspired my own statement that it is African *dancing* that is percussive, regardless of the presence or absence of

percussion. In this regard, it is interesting to look at an observation made shortly after the turn of the century by the Duke of Mecklenburg apropos of Watutsi in his *In The Heart of Africa* (London: Cassell and Co., 1910), p. 60: "There was no musical accompaniment to the majority of the eleven different kinds of dance which we observed, such as is usual with all the terpsichorean exercises of the Negro people. In spite of this, however, there was no lack of rhythm."

11. Alan P. Merriam, "The African Idiom in Music," *Journal of American Folklore,* April–June, 1962, p. 127.

12. Francis Ernest Kobina Parkes, "African Heaven," in *New World Writing No. 15* (New York: Mentor, 1959), pp. 230–232.

13. Marshall Stearns, "Is Modern Jazz Dance Hopelessly Square?" *Dance,* June, 1965, p. 33.

14. An excellent discussion of the verbal basis of Akan drumming may be found in Nketia's *Drumming in Akan Communities of Ghana* (London: Thomas Nelson and Sons, 1963), pp. 32–50. In addition, an interesting colloquium, "Drumming Syllables in Five Traditions: South India, Colonial North America, Arabic Countries, Japan, and West Africa," held at the New England Chapter Meeting of the American Musicological Society at Boston University on March 5, 1966, furnished fresh insights into similar practices in other parts of the world. For example, in South India, as among Yoruba, syllables ending in nasalization are sustained. And both Yoruba and Colonial North Americans seem to choose the consonant *k* (*que,* actually, in the orthography of the latter instance) to represent heavy beats. Compare, also, the Akan phrase "tiri tiri *kon*" with the American Colonial "ratama*que*."

15. I am especially beholden to Perk Foss for assisting in many ways the field documentation of Yoruba dancing at Ajilete in April, 1966.

16. Robert Farris Thompson, "Portrait of the Pachanga," *Saturday Review,* October 28, 1961, p. 54.

17. Richard Alan Waterman, "African Influence on the Music of the Americas" in *Acculturation in the Americas,* ed. Sol Tax (Chicago: University of Chicago Press, 1952). This article is a landmark in the literature of Africanist ethnomusicology.

18. Some Afro-Cuban musicians maintain that the secret of their music is an opposition of two pulsations against three. This understates, in my opinion, a rich tradition of multiple meter.

19. Richard Alan Waterman, "Hot Rhythm in Negro Music," *Journal of the American Musicological Society,* Spring, 1948, p. 4.

20. Deborah Bertonoff, *Dance Towards The Earth* (Tel Aviv: Alytiros, 1963), p. 46.

21. Bertonoff, pp. 189–190.

22. Laura Bohannan, *Return to Laughter* (Garden City, New York: Doubleday and Co., 1964), p. 123.

23. A. M. Jones, *Studies in African Music* (London: Oxford University Press, 1959), I, p. 193.

24. The phrase "apart dancing" is my own. Marshall Stearns phrases the mode another way: "solo dancing—the universal way of dancing in Africa." See Marshall and Jean Stearns, "Profile of the Lindy," *Show,* October, 1963, p. 112.

25. F. de Kersaint-Gilly, "Notes sur la danse en pays noir," *Bulletin du comité d'études historiques et scientifiques de L'Afrique occidentale française,* January-March, 1922, p. 80.

26. See Alan Merriam, album notes, *Africa South of the Sahara,* Ethnic Folkways FE 4503.

27. J. Van Wing, "Les Danses Bakongo," *Congo: Revue générale de la colonie belge,* July, 1937, p. 122.

28. Laura Boulton, album notes, *African Music,* Ethnic Folkways 8852.

29. Frederick Kaigh, *Witchcraft and Magic of Africa* (London: Richard Lesley and Co., 1947), p. 26.

30. Quoted in J. Clyde Mitchell, *The Kalela Dance* (Manchester: Rhodes-Livingston Papers, 1956), p. 12, note 5.

31. Captain Hugh Clapperton, *Journal of a Second Expedition into the Interior of Africa* (London: John Murray, 1829), p. 55.
32. Camille Poupeye, *Danses dramatiques en théâtres exotiques* (Brussels: Le Cahiers du Journal des Poètes, 1941), p. 109.
33. See Robert Farris Thompson, "Yoruba Artistic Criticism," paper read at the Conference on the Artist in Traditional African Society, Lake Tahoe, May, 1965.
34. I acknowledge with many thanks a personal communication, dated February 1, 1966, from Charles Keil, who, writing from the field, informed me of the *Ngogh* dance and other items of Tiv traditional choreographies.
35. In a future volume, I shall intensively analyze the problem of the anti-aesthetic in African art, dance, and music.
36. It is convenient for some Westerners to note this basic fact only outside their culture. Thus, in the *New York Times* of October 9, 1966, we read, p. 10E: "Asia where nations preach morality and respect force."

Primitive African Dance and Its Influence on the Churches of the South
Pearl Primus
Dancer, Choreographer, Teacher, Anthropologist

Pearl Primus (1919–1994) was director of black studies at the State University of New York, director of Performing Arts Center in Monrovia, Liberia (1959), and along with her late husband, dancer Percival Borde, she founded a dance school in New York City. During her career, which began with a biology degree and eventually a doctorate in anthropology in 1978, she was part of the National Youth Administration (NYA). As a result of working as an understudy in a NYA dance group, she received a scholarship with New York's New Dance Group. Finally abandoning her desire to become a physician because of difficulty in securing lab work due to racism, Primus turned to dance as a career.

The 1944 entry in Current Biography *said of her work that it was "not a form of entertainment but a method of education, a means of communicating to others her deep emotional and intellectual feeling about democracy and about the Negro as a race and as a member of the society in which he lives." Her repertoire includes* Strange Fruit, The Negro Speaks of Rivers, Slave Market, Rock David, *and* African Ceremonial.

Pearl Primus, *"Primitive African Dance and Its Influence on the Churches of The South," in* The Dance Encyclopedia, *compiled and edited by Anatole Chujoy (New York: A.S. Barnes, 1949), pp. 387–389.*

On my trips south of the Mason and Dixon line in 1944 I discovered in the Baptist Churches the voice of the drum—not in any instrument, but in the throat of the preacher. I found the dynamic sweep of movement through space (so characteristic of Africa) in the motions of minister and congregation alike. I felt in the sermons the crashing thunder dances of Africa and I was hypnotized by the pounding rhythm of song. Did the dance which the slaves brought to America and which disappeared under pressure of their masters break through disguised in the freedom of their church?

In Africa the dance was at one time all important. With very few exceptions the social, political, religious and esthetic life of the village centered in the dance. It expressed the very pulse of communal living and was an accurate mirror of the psychology of the people. Today this does not exactly hold true. The fight to exist has become so great (except in sections where the pressure of modern life has not quite penetrated) that dance is not what it used to be.

Even so, there is no audience, as such, in Africa. In dances where trained performers may begin or end a dance, the entire group at one time or another actually takes part in the activity. In certain solo dances the crowd acts as inspiration—cheering, singing and clapping hands in time to the rhythm of the drum.

The drums control the dancer. And even if to untrained eyes his movements seem wild, he is exacting of his body a precision unsurpassed in any other culture. His movements for the most part are large. All the big muscles of the torso are used. The subtlety comes not in gesture but in the invisible tie between drum and dance.

The actual dance steps range from a simple walk to the most amazing and precisely executed acrobatic miracles. At the peak of his dance, the dancer may move like a snake or spring into the air and land on the base of his spine, bouncing up and down like a rubber ball.

The subject matter of the dance includes birth, death, puberty rites, marriage, hailing a new chief, discovering evil spirits, praying for rain, sun, strong children, good harvesting, good hunting, victory in warfare, success in love, revenge, protection of the gods, forgiveness of the gods, honoring the ancestors, and play.

Dancing in the churches in the south, though it is not called dance, resembles what I know of Africa so closely, I can say with conviction that the people brought here centuries ago from the gold coast and other parts of West Africa preserved the dance in their religious expressions.

Forbidden by their masters to meet for any purpose other than religious or even to dance and sing the songs of their old country, the slaves' tortured cries emerged disguised in Spirituals and Shout songs. Both of these were accompanied by rhythmic movement.

Glance for a moment at a cross section of a slave plantation—first generation. Is it impossible to conceive chieftains, witch doctors, dancers, warriors, hunters, stone, ivory, wood carvers, men who worked in clay, copper, bronze—women who wove cloth from tree and vegetable fibers—children studying for their place in the tribal set-up—jesters—story tellers and, above all, drummers?

But on one plantation the tribes were so mixed, so scattered as to have no common language. Three emotions were universal: 1. deep unhappiness, 2. anger, 3. feeling of rebellion. When they were permitted to meet in the Christian Church, these emotions burst forth in forms similar to those heard and seen in Africa.

The preacher chosen from among them, a man of tremendous strength and intelligence, committed whole parts of the Bible to memory and, using the techniques of both witch doctor and dancer, galvanized his congregation and rocked the doors of heaven and hell with his message. "It was through him that the people of diverse languages and costumes were given their first sense of unity and solidarity . . . He loved the sonorous mouth-filling, ear-filling phrase because it gratified a highly developed sense of sound and rhythm in himself and his hearers."[1]

The voice of the preacher was the voice of the drum—deep, hypnotizing—booming, racing, slowing down—sweet, like bells—controlled and yet wild.

I have heard this voice take on some of the most intricate of the African rhythms and have seen the speaker's body become the plucked strings of a bass fiddle—vibrant and electric!

I have seen him pace the full length of the pulpit, arms swaying, head shaking. I have seen him turn, like a ballet dancer, to express creation and jump like a demon possessed to tell of the judgment day. As James Weldon Johnson once wrote: "His eye is to the telescope of eternity and he looks on the paper walls of time. His imagination is turpentined and perpetual motion is in his arms. He is filled with the dynamite of power. He is anointed with the oil of salvation and his tongue is set on fire."[2]

The audience, psychologically removed from their environment, would absorb this figure before them and memory, mixed with a basic unhappiness, would dictate strange reactions. This seems to be the general pattern. First the shaking of the head, slowly, side to side. Then faster, emphasizing the sharp repudiation of reality. Then violent trembling in the body, starting like the mutterings of a volcano—growing, growing—tossing back and forth till suddenly passion bursts like a bomb—tearing the voice with its heat, stamping the feet madly to the earth, beating the arms convulsively upward.

Such close resemblances to African rhythm and steps cannot be coincidental. Many of these people will tell you they have never danced in their lives. (As a matter of fact, many are forbidden by the church to indulge.) Yet to watch them in the ecstasy of religious movement is to experience dance in its most primitive and moving form.

Congregation and preacher fuse. There is no spectator. From the little old lady sitting with closed eyes in the corner, tapping her dried up fingers lightly on her fan, to the dynamo chanting the sermon, all have become one.

These gatherings in the church were the all important function of the society, and the message of freedom which could not be preached boldly found outlet in the chanting and dancing of the people.

In emotional impact, group reaction, rhythms, tempos, actual steps and the exact precision with which they were done, dance in the Southern Baptist Churches so closely resemble the dance in Africa as to leave no doubt in the mind that the American form emerged from the African.

Notes

1. James Weldon Johnson, *God's Trombones*—Preface.
2. Ibid.

Total Transcription of a Sermon-Poem
REV. W. T. GOODWIN
United Methodist minister

At the time of the recording of this sermon-poem, Rev. W. T. Goodwin preached on John's Island in South Carolina. Following is an excerpt from his Easter Sunday sermon of 1971.

i don't KNOW in St. JAMES this MORning m m ᵐ m m m m 8

         a a a

           a

          a ahhhhhhhhhhhhhhhhhhhh 16

THIS MAY be the LAST TIME y e s s i r !

                y e h h -

              o h y e h !

on this EASter MORning   o   o oh
h h h   4   l o r d 15

MAY be the LAST TIME we'll ALL SING toGEther y e s s i r !

       l a s t t i m e !
MAY be the LAST TIME o h l o r d ! we will pray toGEther y e s !

                  o h
              o h   o
         o h   o   o h h h -

Rev. W. T. Goodwin, "Total Transcription" of a Sermon-Poem, Peter Gold, transcriptor, from an original recording by Gold and Henrietta Yurchenco, Alcheringa *4 (Autumn 1972): 1–14.*

MAY be the LAST TIME y e s   s i r !   we'll KNEEL toGEther ^{y e s !}

hhhhhhhhhh 17   yehhhhhhhhhhhhhhhh ^{y e   e   e   e h h h -}
                                                            2

but I DON'T KNOW this MORning ^{oh yeh!}

hhhhhhhhhhhhhhhhhhhhhhhhhh 15   ohhn 2

MMMMMMM my GOD HAVE MERCY y e s   l o r d !

I'M COming DOWN HERE

          e ^{esss 21}

yes ye

BUT ONE DAY one DAY o n e   d a y   y e h !

DEATH gonna SHAKE MY HAND o h h h   5

I'M   SO   GLAD mm mmmm 7

IN the JUDGment MORning   y e s !

y e s
lord 7

I'M gonna SHAKE OFF this MORtal BOdy   y e s !

PUT ON immorTAlity   a h a !

a a
ahhh 7

y e h !   y e h !
GOnna be CAUGHT UP SOME WHERE
preacher slaps lecturn

yes sir!
to MEET my GOD in the AIR
ye
ehhh 7

SOME BOdy SAID in the MORning y e h !
                                 y e h h 2

I'M gonna MOVE on up a little HIgher y e s s i r !
                                      y e h h 2

I'm gonna MOVE y e s ! on UP a little HIgher y e h !
                                                w e l l 5
                                                y e h h 2

gonna TALK with old man DAniel o h y e h !
                                 y e h h 2

                                 preacher slaps lecturn

                                                          y e s y e
SOME BOdy SAID I'm gonna MOVE on up a little HIgher m m   e s s s 10
         m m m   m m m m m m m m m m m m m m m m m m 9   m m m m
           m

gonna TALK with the POOR and the twenty ELders y e s !
m m m m m m m m m m 7   y e h h 2

ah yes!

gonna MOVE on UP a little HIgher   yes!

y e
        e
           e s
                l o r d   15   preacher claps hands

                                              s i t   d o w n !   y e s !

SOME BOdy gonna say SIT DOWN d o w n !   for a WHILE y e
                                                              e
                                                               e h
                                                                 l o r r -
                                        preacher claps hands

              s i t   d o w n !

just SIT down SERvant   y e h !
r r r r r r r r r r r d 15   preacher claps hands

    a h h h s !   y e s !

AH SIT DOWN and REST a little WHILE preacher claps hands
                          y e
                               e
                                 e
                                   e   e h
                                        l o r d   18

                    preacher claps hands

but you SAY no NO   preacher slaps lectern   y e s !

                                                n o !

i CAN'T sit DOWN preacher slaps lectern twice, c a n ' t   s i t   d o w n !
              o o o o -
         o o o o
w o o o

I'VE got a FAther I'm looking FOR   y e s   s i r !   y e h ¡
                                              2 hand claps from congregation
o o o o   o o o o o o o o o o o o o o o o o o o o o o o o o o o o 22

                    a n d   a   m o m m a   o v e r   t h e r e   t o o ,   y e s !
I wanna SEE my FAther

        hand claps from congregation,
for the LAST TIME   y e s !
                        y e   h e s
                                l o r d 11

i wanna SHAKE HANDS with my FAther J e s u s !   y e s !

                                        w e l l 2

SOME BOdy said y e s ! SIT DOWN   y e s !
                                       y e   e   e h
                                                l o r r -

and REST a little WHILE y e h h 3
r r r r r r r r r r r r r r r r r r r r r d 15

hand claps from congregation

i said NO NO NO ah   n o !   preacher slaps lecturn

c a n ' t   s i t   d o w n !

i CAN'T sit DOWN   y e h h -

I GOnna see my MOther   m y   m o t h e r   y e s !

h h h h h h h   4   o h   y e s s   1

y e s !   O . K . !

i got a MOther who's GONE from beFORE   y e s   s i r !

my DEAR old mo^THER   y e h !   y e s !

m   m

m

m m m m -

y e h !

mother's bragging!

y e s

SOME BOdy said if I could HEAR MY MOther   lord 7

m m m m m m m m m m m m m   15

                       y e s !   w o o !
i SAY aGAIN
                  y e   e   e h h h   8

                          I ' l l   b e !
HOW HAPPY it would BE   y e
                                    e h h h   7

I'm gonna SHAKE HANDS with my MOther preacher claps hands y e
                                                                e h h h   7

                                              y e s !
I'm gonna SHAKE HANDS with my FAther   y e h h   2
                     o o o o o o o o o o o o o o o o o o o o -
          o o o o
w o o o

ah WHERE are you GOing this mor NING ?   o h   y e h !
o o o o o o o o   23   y e
                                                   e   e s s s   19

I'm GOing to SEE my JEsus   Jesus! yeh!
                                 y e h h   5

I'm gonna y e h !   SEE Mary's BAby _{y e s !} preacher claps hands
m m m m 2

the LIly of the VAlley ^{y e s !}

the m o r n i n g s t a r !
the BRIGHT and the MORning STAR   preacher claps hands

ah SOME BOdy SAID this MORning ah m m m m -

THERE gonna be WAter there o h y e s !
m m m m m m m m m m m m m m m m m m m m m m 8

y e h !   y e h !
gonna BE FREE there GOOD y e h ! for the STEEring of the NAtion
y e   7
e h h h
7

AH WILL you be THERE?   y e h !

                             y e h h -

                 hand claps from congr.
AH WILL you be THERE church?   y e h !
h h h h h h h   3   y e   e s
                                                       l o r r -

claps from congr.   claps from congr.   claps from congregation
          i WONder WILL you BE there?   o h   y e h h   1
      r r r r r r r r r r d   1 5

                                        y e h ! !
ah LET me see your HAND this MORning
                           y e s   o h   y e s s 6
                              l o r d   1 2

ah WILL you be THERE?   y e s ! ! y e h ! !
                          o h h
                              y e
                                 s
                                     l o r r -

WILL you be THERE?   y e s ! !   y e s ! !
r r r r r r r r d   2 0

gonna be a great big day!!

WILL you be THERE?   yes lord!

preacher claps hands

WILL you be THERE this MORning? oh yeh!

yes

lorrrrrrrrrrrrrrrrrrrd 7

preacher claps hands   Christ!

AH LET me see your HANDS

preacher claps hands

I just wanna be THERE   yes! oh yes!

i WANT you to reMEMber this MORning ye ehhh7

mm

mmmmmmmmmmmmmmmm 7

that I have TRIED to DO my BEST DOWN HERE that's allright! yes!

IF YOU GO beFORE   i DO   yes!   ha ha!
                 yes sir!
              ohhhhhhhhh 4

DON'T- - - - -   oh yes!
                    o   o   oh
                               yehh 15

DON'T- - - - -   yes! yes!
                   yehh 2

preacher claps hands   when I GET THERE   yes! woo!

I wanna BE THERE   yes!
            oh
                yes
                    lorr-

I AM LORD of GOD   preacher claps hands y e s !
rrrrrrrrrrrd 14

preacher claps hands   ah KING of KINGS y e s !

                m m m m m m m m m m m m m m m -
        m

      m

                     G o d !

and LORDS of GOD   o h y e s !

m m m m m m m m m m m m m m m 13

NOTE ON THE "TOTAL TRANSCRIPTION" OF A SERMON-POEM BY REVEREND W. T. GOODWIN. Like the Siberian Shaman through whom the spirit world speaks directly to the people, the southern Black preacher communicates certain vital and otherwise unobtainable information through the medium of the sermon. In both cases the performances are combinations of vocal, musical and dramatic cues within which the messages are couched and to which the audiences respond.

Reverend W. T. Goodwin, whose sermon is transcribed here, is a United Methodist preacher on John's Island, South Carolina. He is the link between his congregation and two worlds outside their immediate reach: a heavenly realm, especially for those older people who attend church in order to attain salvation; and an earthly realm, especially for the younger ones who attend church for social and moral guidance.

The organization of the sermon reflects this two-part role. The initial section, consisting of a rather low-key delivery, advocates social change and specifies certain moral values. The latter section is geared to eliciting an excited emotional response. For those more conservative members of the congregation this catharsis-oriented section counterbalances the possibly distressing message in the first section. The transcription, above, is of the latter part of Goodwin's sermon from the 1971 Easter Sunrise Service in St. James Church.

The meaning of the sermon is not found exclusively in its poetic content, because the nature of the congregation's responses affects the way in which the preacher combines his verbal, musical and kinesic symbols, his total performance. There seem to be two degrees of response. The first is the standard type of response coming at the end of each of the preacher's phrases. These are verbal cries such as "yes!" or "oh yeh!", and musical responses or moans. As the parishioner is "moved by the spirit" he will tend to respond at the very moment in which his emotions spill over and can no longer be contained. So, there are places where the moans and verbal cries come in during the sermon phrases.

But the preacher, his words, tone of voice and physical gestures, are not the only stimuli to the parishioner's cathartic release. This state is also built up by the emotional level of others responding and through his own participation in events leading up to the preacher's performance: the singing of spirituals and the response to numerous prayers intoned by lay preachers or ordinary members of the congregation. The sermon is the culmination of an ever ascending emotional spiral which satisfies those who need to feel the sense of coming closer to God, and those who need essential information for the maintenance of their lives.

KEY TO THE TRANSCRIPTION:

Large type indicates phrases of the sermon. Upper case indicates stressed syllables, lower case, unstressed syllables. Diagonal syllables indicate a jump of a major third from the basic C sharp pitch of the sermon. - - - - - indicates an unintelligible word.

Small type indicates responses by the congregation. Words or phrases followed by exclamation points indicate a verbal response. Words or nonsense vocables followed by a number indicate a sung response. They are presented in the contour which the melody follows. The numbers refer to the musical transcription.

A MUSICAL KEY TO SUNG RESPONSES IN "EASTER SUNRISE SERMON"

Suggested Reading

Adamczyk, Alice J. *Black Dance. An Annotated Bibliography*. NY: Garland Publishing, Inc., (1989).

Brown, Cecelia R. "The Afro-American Contribution to Dance in the United States." *Negro Heritage* 14 (1975): pp. 63–69.

David, Jonathan. "The Sermon and the Shout: A History of the Singing and Praying Bands of Maryland and Delaware." *Southern Folklore,* vol. 51, no. 3, (1994): pp. 241–263.

Fernett, Gene. *Swing Out. Great Negro Dance Bands* Midland, MI: The Pendell Publishing Company (1970).

Floyd Jr., Samuel A. *The Power of Black Music. Interpreting Its History From Africa to The United States*. NY: Oxford University Press (1995).

Frank, Rusty E. *TAP! The Greatest Tap Dance Stars and their Stories, 1900–1955*. NY: De Capo Press, Rev. Ed. (1994).

Friedland, LeeEllen. "Disco: Afro-American Vernacular Performance." *Dance Research Journal,* vol. 15, no. 2, Spring 1983: pp. 27–35.

Giordano, Gus. *Anthology of American Jazz Dance*. Evanston, IL: Orion Publishing House (1975).

Hollenweger, Walter J. "Danced Documentaries: The Theological and Political Significance of Pentecostal Dancing," *Workship and Dance* edited by J.G. Davies. Birmingham, England: University of Birmingham (1975): pp. 76–82.

Hurston, Zora Neale. *The Sanctified Church*. Berkeley, CA: Turtle Island (1983).

Jackson, Irene. *More than Dancing: Essays on Afro-American Music and Musicians.* (Contributions in Afro-American and African Studies, No. 83) Prepared under the auspices of the Center for Ethnic Music, Howard University. Westport, CT: Greenwood Press (1985).

Jahn, Janheinz. *Muntu. African Culture and the Western World*. NY: Grove Weidenfeld (1989 [1961]).

Jones, Bessie and Bess Lomax Hawes. *Step It Down. Games, Plays, Songs, and Stories from the Afro-American Heritage*. NY: Harper & Row, Publishers (1987 [1972]).

Niles, Lyndrey A. "Rhetorical Characteristics of Traditional Black Preaching." *Journal of Black Studies,* September 1984: pp. 41–52.

Pitts, Walter, "Like a Tree Planted by the Water. The Musical Cycle in the African American Baptist Ritual." *Journal of American Folklore,* vol. 104, no. 413, Summer 1991: pp. 318–40.

Szwed, John F. and Morton Marks. "The Afro-American Transformation of European Set Dances and Dance Suites." *Dance Research Journal,* vol. 20, no. 1, Summer 1988: pp. 29–36.

Vogel, Susan Mullen. *Aesthetics of African Art*. (Photographs by Mario Carrier. The Carlo Monzino Collection) NY: The Center for African Art (1986).

SELECTED VIDEOS, FILMS, CD-ROMS, AND SLIDES

CINEMA GUILD

Dance on the Wind. Profile of dancer Eno Washington. Marty Frame, Ivor Miller, Jeremy Brecher,

and Jill Cutler. Cinema Guild. Color. VHS Video. 30 mins. 1994.
Steppin'. Jerald B. Harkness. Color. Video. 56 mins. 1992.

VITOPHONE

All-Colored Vaudeville Show. Nicholas Brothers. Vitaphone. Short subject. September 6, 1935.
Reb Spikes Band. Four unknown Black tap dancers. Vitaphone (1 reel). October 17, 1927.

OTHERS

Alvin Ailey: Memories and Visions. Phoenix, 1975. 52 minutes.
Don't Gamble with Love. The Nicholas Brothers. Uncredited. Columbia. February 15, 1935.
The Emperor Jones. Harold Nicholas. United Artists. September 9, 1933.
Harlem After Midnight. Uncredited tap and chorus line. Micheaux Pictures. 1935.
Harlem Is Heaven. Bill Robinson and Chorus tap. Lincoln. 1932.

DANCE HORIZON VIDEOS

Dance Black America. D.A. Pennebaker, Chris Hegedus, producers. Pennebaker Associates. Color. Video. 87 mins. 1990.

Chapter 3

SPACE AND PLACE

How Sweet the Sound has discussed issues of space and place, the idea of a new home/land, in terms of the circle specifically the ringshout,[1] and orality in terms of movement or dance. Due to the dislocation of millions of Africans, the circle and movement (dance) have constituted the country or nation in the Americas for black people. In terms of spatial institutions, the most prominent community architectural structure was an "invisible" one—the roof-less and wall-less evolving black church with its focus on water and water rites,[2] makeshift altars made of trees, and the woods as (and for) sanctuary. These constructions were made out of the essence of African American culture and memory rather than of stone, wood, or brick. But they were the building blocks of the African American community. They were spiritual and natural (and cultural rather than concrete) places of shelter and refuge. They were the foundations of the vernacular and oral traditions in African America that constituted firmament.

A Dogan creation story[3] about *nommo* or *nummo* and the concept of shelter as raiment and covering is instructive. In the Christian tradition, the Word came from God and was made flesh in the Christ. In Dogon cosmology, *nummo,* the "life force" of the world, is the child of God and earth. From *nummo* comes motion and energy (as in movement/dance) and the foundation of that life force is water (and light: "the truth is the light of the world") and the Word that is spiritual. Remembering Katherine Dunham's connection of motion with moral sense and Margaret Washington Creel's discussion of the ringshout (sacred dance) informing the architecture of community "moral order," we see "the cool" power[4] of space and place in the circle of community and in the ringshout, in geographic separation whether it is the establishment of the black church, the Historically Black Colleges and Universities, in the nineteenth- and twentieth-century

---

[1] See the Introduction and Chapters 1 and 2 of this volume on the significance of the circle and ringshout to African American culture and history.

[2] See Walter Pitts's "Like a Tree Planted by the Water. The Musical Cycle in the African American Baptist Ritual," *Journal of American Folklore* 104, (413) (1991): 318–340.

[3] See Geoffrey Parrinder's *African Mythology* (London: Paul Hamlyn, 1967), pp. 23–24, 27, 46, 48, 62, 76.

[4] See Robert Farris Thompson's discussion of "the cool" in Chapter 2, "Movement or Dance."

migrations of black people, or the founding of all-black towns. In opposition was the politics of space on slaver ships, on auction blocks, in barracoons,[5] on plantations, in the slave quarters, in legally sanctioned segregated neighborhoods, in the inner-city and red-lined suburbs, and in the placing of African peoples on the lower end of the human-made race or color line.

By the Word becoming flesh, it also becomes "place." *Nummo,* the twins and also the first blacksmith, the magic worker with anvil and forge, took fibers, tied them into bundles, and clothed the world. According to Geoffrey Parrinder's recounting of the Dogan creation story, the fibers were "moist and full of the essence of the *Nummo* spirits. By means of this clothing the Earth obtained a language . . ." and "the power of speech" was born.[6] By extension, the Word is also shelter and a space/place for life, worship, human growth and potentiality, including intellectual and spiritual, and the way persons express themselves, not only individually but culturally as a community. In this chapter a variety of spaces and places and ways of interpreting them are illustrated[7] as well as a variety of disciplines through which to discuss them in the context of cultural history. In addition to the historian, and her tools, are anthropologist, folklorist, and landscape architect. Along with issues of geography, architecture, and social politics is material culture (the stuff that goes into these structures or places, for example the contents of the spirit yards and of traditional southern black burial grounds); and behind the *now* walled and roofed constructions are the philosophy and vision that went into them.

In "Space and Place," a period in African American and American history not often discussed in terms of black people—the colonial era—is discussed. In this case, it is Spanish colonial Florida in the seventeenth and eighteenth centuries. Some Africans/Americans in the British colonies of South Carolina and Georgia fled, as did these fugitives, and like the maroons[8] sought refuge away and apart (but with each other) from those who would deny them freedom. Also discussed is how space and place defined a young man's character and made him the adult he was to become by his maintaining cultural values for a lifetime even when no longer living in the space/place where he grew up; the spiritual functions of spaces and places, which, to the undiscerning eye, masquerade as "something else"; and the building of an institution

---

5 A barracoon is a cagelike structure that was used to contain African captives, as if they were animals, when they arrived in the Caribbean.

6 Geoffrey Parrinder, *African Mythology,* pp. 23–24.

7 Space and place can both relate to communities, parks and squares, spirit yards, and rooms in a house. Place, however, can also pertain to stages in life, for example in the essay "Poor People Done It Like That," about Philip Simmons's maturation on Daniel Island and placement on the economic scale.

For a palpable sense of the meaning and significance of space and place, see Toni Morrison's *Beloved* (New York: A Plume Book [Penguin Group], 1988) and especially pp. 162–165 where the main character, Sethe, is losing her safe haven and must take drastic action to "save" her children. Also, see *Journey to "Beloved"* by Oprah Winfrey (New York: Hyperion, 1998) and the movie *Beloved* directed by Jonathon Demme.

8 Maroons in the Caribbean were African captives who escaped to the mountains and established self-sustaining, separate communities. They were slave fugitives who escaped enslavement and lived among themselves. Some of their descendants still live in these mountain enclaves. There were also maroons in what is now the United States. These fugitives also attempted escape but were often captured. See Richard Price, ed., *Maroon Societies. Rebel Slave Communities in the Americas* (New York: Anchor Books, 1973).

of black higher education that incorporates not only physical landscape, reflecting social realities and natural land contours, but one man's mental vision for his community. Through these essays, you will see connections between Africa, the Caribbean, and the United States. These particular spaces and places were selected because they reflect states of mind and thought, as well as states of being in African American culture.

John Michael Vlach, anthropologist/folklorist, has been an important contributor to African/American vernacular culture. His research includes folklore and architecture[9] that can be seen as a special language, a language of existence whether on an isolated Sea Island or in a shotgun house, a casket, or a burial ground. Two examples of his writing are included here. The first, "Shotgun Houses," reflects the communal concept of traditional black life in Africa, the Caribbean, and culminating in the United States. It is a discussion of community: the collective relationship of persons within the house and their relationship to the outside world beyond the front porch.

The shotgun house is still seen in the South. It gets its name, at least, from its form: if you shoot a pistol from the front door, straight ahead, the bullet should fly unobstructed, straight through an open back door to the outside. The central interior of the house is hall space with rooms on each side. Vlach describes basic shotgun houses as "small, . . . rectangular buildings, one room wide."[10] There is some controversy about its origin, however.[11] Robert Farris Thompson sees it as an architectural structure whose prototype is a house from sixteenth-century Africa. This would appear to support Vlach. Others see it as an African American creation from the Caribbean. Wherever it is from, it is a creation of African peoples (and possibly with adaptations from indigenous Americans),[12] and it reflects Africanist cosmology in the sense that it is meant to be a shared space, where there is intimate social interaction, rather than a floor plan for privacy. It is also adaptable: it can be a duplex or have a second story built on its rear side. Vlach makes an eloquent statement about architecture and also about the shotgun house as Africanist space:

> We are only now beginning to understand that humankind possesses an internal architecture of ideas, that we have architecture without building. With space as our only medium, we are constantly constructing invisible barriers, walls, and fences behind which we conduct our daily rituals of conversation, greeting, intimacy, and personal encounter

---

[9] John Michael Vlach, *The Afro-American Tradition in Decorative Arts* (Cleveland: Cleveland Museum of Art, 1978); "Arrival and Survival: The Maintenance of an Afro-American Tradition in Folk Art and Craft," in *Perspectives on American Folk Art,* edited by Ian M. G., Quimby and Scott T. Swant (New York: W.W. Norton, 1980), pp. 177–217; *Back of the Big House. The Architecture of Plantation Slavery* (Chapel Hill: University of North Carolina Press, 1993), The Fred W. Morrison Series in Southern Studies; and *By the Work of Their Hands. Studies in Afro-American Folklore* (Charlottesville: University Press of Virginia, 1991).

[10] "Shotgun Houses," *Natural History,* Vol 86 (February 1977): 51.

[11] There has been controversy about the origins of the shotgun house, for example whether it is diasporic, and if so what is the extent of indigenous contributions, or is it directly of African tradition or a mixture of both. Robert Farris Thompson, in his chapter, "From Ancient Loango to Twentieth-Century North America: Roots of the Yard Show," does include a graphic that indicates a structure Thompson sees as a prototype to the shotgun house that has been found in the United States. It is reproduced from Olfert Dapper's *Description de l'Afrique,* 1668 (Thompson, p. 74).

[12] "Shotgun Houses," p. 53.

Charleston artisan Philip Simmons at his forge practicing the traditional African craft of ironwork.

. . . [a shotgun house] is a house in which there is a focus on communal activity; it is an architecture of intimacy.[13]

Vlach's second essay is about Philip Simmons, blacksmith and worker in iron, excerpted from his book *Charleston Blacksmith: The Work of Philip Simmons.*[14] Here Vlach discusses geography and character, in this case that of Daniel Island, a Sea Island off the Charleston, South Carolina, mainland. Philip Simmons is responsible for much of the contemporary ornamental ironwork in the city of Charleston, where he lived and worked

---

13 Ibid., p. 56.

14 "Poor People Done It Like That," in *Charleston Blacksmith. The Work of Philip Simmons,* revised ed. (Columbia: University of South Carolina Press, 1992) pp. 1–10.

as an adult, and Vlach has followed Simmons's life and career. Simmons was an islander and lived with his grandparents in a house built by his grandfather. Vlach uses space and place not only in geographical terms but as stages of an adult's maturation. Daniel Island is a physical environment revolving around subsistence living, based on agriculture and fishing, which in turn heavily depends on the seasons and weather. When there were no agricultural tasks for the young Philip to help with, he would go to Charleston where his parents worked for others, rather than for themselves or their neighbors, and attend school. His "place" on Daniel Island, as a child and young man, was to emulate the work of his grandfather and internalize the work ethic and sense of community responsibility of his grandmother and grandfather. As he matured, the work of agriculture and fishing became more diversified and more demanding physically. There was a natural order to his maturation, to the activity on the island, to the guidance he received from his elders, to the communal rhythms of island life where everyone was poor but interdependent. On Daniel Island, work was around the clock, and it is there Philip Simmons learned a life of "action" explained to Vlach as "Poor People Done It Like That."[15]

When it was not possible to farm or fish, the elder Simmons still worked. He built his own home. There is reason to believe he also built them for others as well as a variety of other buildings around the island. He was not a "professional"—it was something he *had* to learn how to do, being poor in money. He also did carpentry, and Simmons remembered that his grandfather made caskets. From that latter activity especially, Philip Simmons learned the importance of respecting the spaces of other people, for surely a casket is a space for residing in (staying in)—it is another room, an eternal shelter for the raiment that is the human body. Vlach writes,

> The importance of funerary rites in the Sea Island tradition required that the remains of the deceased be lavished with as much ceremony and finery as possible. To give anything less than one's best effort would be to invite the fury of the spirit of the deceased person. . . . Philip . . . lent a hand [in the making of caskets] and learned some basic lessons about making objects, about attention to detail, about the responsibility of the craftsman to his client.[16]

Daniel Island provides a catalog of Sea Island symbols. They include the language of Gullah, which always influenced Simmon's speech and marked him as an outsider in Charleston, although he lived there all his adult life; the mortar and pestle representing the pounding of rice and Sea Island rice culture; coiled-grass baskets; clapboard houses; dirt yards immaculately swept, where for aesthetic reasons, no grass is allowed to grow; and men and women carrying "loads" on their heads.

Historian Jane Landers, in "Gracia Real de Santa Teresa de Mose: A Free Black Town in Spanish Colonial Florida," describes African American slave fugitives from South Carolina and Georgia who took a page from maroon history by leaving an unfriendly colonial power (the British) for refuge among other like-minded fugitives—among the

---

[15] Ibid.

[16] Ibid., p. 5.

Spaniards. They lived within a fortress environment under the protection of Spanish militia, which included not only their own numbers but their own leadership as well, and under the protection of the Catholic Church through the 1693 edict that granted sanctuary to fugitive converts. Fort Mose (1738–1763), actually two fortresses after the burning of the first, is currently being excavated by archaeologists on a remote island, now under water, two miles from St. Augustine. It was "America's first legally sanctioned free black community." Those working on resurrecting its (his)tory and collecting what physical evidence may exist, see it as "a powerful alternative image to slavery as the dominant theme in African-American history."[17] Although it may or may not be an alternative image to slavery, it *is* an alternative way of looking at enslaved persons who became fugitives, persons who did not quietly accept servitude. This tradition of protest, of course, started on the slaver ships themselves. Inhabitants of Fort Mose sought freedom and the opportunity to fight those who denied it to them. In escaping from South Carolina and Georgia, to the Spanish, they were making a conscious distinction and choice between two colonial powers and their respective spaces and places. By living among the Spanish, the refugees were treated (relatively) like human beings, and allowed legal and church-sanctioned marriages and family life upon their conversion to Roman Catholicism. This is not to say that life was perfect, but they were "free." Fort Mose benefited the Spanish as well. It was a poke in the eye of the British, their competition in the "New World," and Fort Mose constituted a buffer zone between the British and St. Augustine.

Landscape architect Kendrick Ian Grandison takes us to the "Black Belt" of Alabama after Reconstruction in his essay "From Plantation to Campus: Progress, Community, and the Lay of the Land in Shaping the Early Tuskegee Campus." Grandison presents more than just the story of the geographic and architectural (and controversial) historically black college (university), child of an industrial education movement in black higher education started by Booker T. Washington's alma mater Hampton Institute (now Hampton University).[18] It is also an example of power inversion and a reflection of one man's mental landscape. The Black Belt was the center of the economy of the slavocracy, the Kingdom of Cotton. Tuskegee, in fact, was built on a former plantation, but its occupants were not enslaved either by slavery or sharecropping—they were students of industrial education (which at the time was the rage for both black and white institutions) and of life. The space that had previously grown cotton, through the unpaid labor of black people, would now grow what the South feared the most—black minds and intellect. Tuskegee, sometimes known as "Booker T. Washington City," became a

---

17 Darcie MacMahon and Kathleen Deagon, "Legacy of Fort Mose," *Archaeology* (September/October 1996): 54–58.

18 According to Rev. Anson Phelps Stokes's *Tuskegee Institute, The First Fifty Years. Being the Founder's Day Historical Address. Delivered April 14, 1931, at the Semi-Centennial of the Institute's Founding. With Additions, Notes, and Appendices.* (Tuskegee: Tuskegee Institute Press, 1931), those institutions that eventually became historically black colleges and universities are Voorhees Industrial School and Utica Normal & Industrial Institute. Also consulted was an unpublished manuscript by Nancy-Elizabeth Fitch with research assistance by Gillian Johnson, for the Institute for Independent Education in Washington, D.C., entitled "A Chronological Listing of Institutions of Higher Education That Became Historically Black Colleges and Universities and the Institutions That Made Them" (Summer 1988), under the auspices of the U.S. Equal Employment Opportunity Commission.

powerful force in the black community. It was a laboratory in which to test a man's vision of the potentiality of the South and of the black man (and woman) and black youth, together with their white neighbors, rebuilding the region after the ravages of the War Between the States.

This article and another by Grandison not included here, "Landscape of Terror: A Reading of Tuskegee's Historic Campus,"[19] show the parallel evolution, and growth into reality, of the mental landscape of Washington and the physical landscape of rural Tuskegee. How Washington reconciled the principles of self-help, autonomy, and community building. At the same time there was a hostile white Tuskegee community concerned about educated black people no longer useful to them as cheap labor and potentially a political/social threat as well.[20] Washington built an educational empire on what had been a "waste place"[21] and transformed it and his students into black success stories. Just as Thomas Jefferson created Monticello and the University of Virginia to reflect enlightenment principles and classical structures, Booker T. Washington's "city" was to reflect the entrepreneurial spirit of black people, which would, he hoped, lead to their economic self-sufficiency.

The "yard" in Grey Gundaker's "Tradition and Innovation in African-American Yards," as the burial ground is another example not only of a spiritual space/place but of black expressive culture. It is also, like Booker T. Washington's "waste place," a place of renewal and regeneration. Creation of these spirit yards is called "decorating," "dressing," and "working" the yard, and they are dedicated to the ancestors, possess the power to protect those who tend them, just as the guardian posts outside an African home do, and are an example of masquerade, for these power places are not recognized by outsiders as things of the spirit. In their masquerade, they are seen as "junk" and the "discards" of life.[22] Gundaker writes about her understanding of the meaning of "dressing a yard":

> [T]ransforming the functions and meaning of objects and the whole site, not mere surface decorating. . . . "It's just castoff stuff people throw away [quote from sculptor Charlie Lucas]. Like people who've been cast off, and everybody thinks they're worth nothing. I've been there. Beat up, broken, down at the bottom. But I had this dream in my head, and that made me more than a piece of junk," . . . Junk is the emergent stuff of rebirth.[23]

---

[19] Kendrick Ian Grandison, "Landscapes of Terror: A Reading of Tuskegee's Historical Campus," in *Geography of Identity,* edited by Patricia Yaeger *Ratio* (Ann Arbor: Institute for the Humanities; University of Michigan Press 5, 1996), pp. 334–367.

[20] See Booker T. Washington's autobiography, *Up From Slavery,* in *Three Negro Classics,* edited by John Hope Franklin (New York: Avon, 1969), and Chapters 2 and 5 in Ralph Ellison's novel *Invisible Man* (New York: Random House, 1952). The latter provides brief descriptions of an institution patterned after Tuskegee. See also Houston A. Baker's interesting discussion in *Modernism and the Harlem Renaissance* (Chicago: University of Chicago Press, 1987) and his views on the contributions of W. E. B. Du Bois and Booker T. Washington to the development of the concept of modernism in the United States.

[21] Kendrick Ian Grandison, "From Plantation to Campus: Progress, Community, and the Lay of the Land in Shaping the Early Tuskegee Campus," *Landscape Journal* 15 (1) (1996): 11.

[22] Grey Gundaker, "Tradition and Innovation in African-American Yards," *African Arts* (April 1993): 60.

[23] Ibid., p. 59.

The Magee House in Canister, New York which was a way station on the Underground Railroad used to assist fugitive slaves walking to freedom in the North or to Canada.

Gundaker later cites Melville Herskovits, specifically speaking of the Dahomean *vodu,* who writes of the spirit that is "localized" and "while philosophically conceived as existing everywhere in space, must also have definite places to which it can be summoned, where it can be commanded . . . , and from which it can go forth to achieve those things desired of it."[24]

---

[24] Ibid., p. 61.

Shotgun Houses

John Michael Vlach
Folklorist

John Michael Vlach is a prolific author and writes about American and African American rituals, vernacular, architectural, and material culture. Vlach's work includes Back of the Big House: The Architecture of Plantation Slavery *(1993),* By the Work of Their Hands: Studies in Afro-American Folklore *(1991),* The Afro-American Tradition in Decorative Arts *(1978). He is professor and director of the Folklore program at George Washington University.*

Old buildings can tell us a great deal. In many cases, they are the only records left of the aspirations and experiences of those who lived before us. If we care at all about the day-to-day life of the past in which our present society began to take shape, we should examine those unpretentious, often derelict structures that sit beside seldom-traveled roads. Should we be sensitive enough to regard these castoffs as the products of effort and hope, we might discover a new pathway to an understanding of ourselves.

The rich insights that may reward further searching are illustrated by the story of a humdrum little house often called a "shotgun shack." An architectural saga that began centuries ago in Africa lies enfolded in its shingles and tar paper. Shotgun houses are rather common in the United States, and for this reason, do not usually attract the attention of the passerby. In their most basic form, they are small, usually rectangular buildings, one room wide (no more than 12 feet across); three rooms deep, all connected to each other; and with doors at each end. One supposed reason for their name is that pellets from a shotgun fired through one of the outside doorways could allegedly pass through the entire building without doing any damage.

Today, shotgun houses, common in both rural and urban areas, are most often seen in mill towns, cotton and sugar plantations, lumber camps, railroad construction sites, and around oil fields. Traditionally built in this country to house large numbers of workers, they are found from Chicago to the gulf coast and from North Carolina to California.

Their wide distribution during this century makes their history difficult to unravel. Several clues in the American cultural pattern, however, point to Louisiana as the place of origin, in this country, for the shotgun house. Along some stretches of the Mississippi River in Louisiana and in the state's bayou country, no other house form

John Michael Vlach, "Shotgun Houses," Natural History *86 (February 1977): 51–57.*

exists. Large numbers of these buildings, many dating back to the last century, are also found in New Orleans, Vicksburg, Memphis, Saint Louis, and Louisville, all river towns first established by settlers as they penetrated the country's interior along its larger waterways.

Architectural historians have thought that the long, narrow form of the New Orleans shotgun house was a reflection of nineteenth-century land pressures, which shaped city lots into narrow, rectangular sections. While it is true that the shotgun plan fit well into the city's urban context, houses of other shapes were also built on these lots. Indeed, the shotgun was not as wide as the usual city lot and was therefore not so restricted by lot size as were some of the large French Creole dwellings. Thus the boundaries set by the city surveyor cannot entirely account for the form of shotgun houses. The proliferation of shotguns in New Orleans suggests an earlier origin based on motivations other than functional ones.

The basic shotgun form is very adaptable. A number of alternate designs in New Orleans suggest that the shotgun house had a long formative period. Such variations were probably a response to conditions not anticipated when the basic shape was first used.

One variant, the double shotgun, developed as early as 1854 and was composed of two single shotgun houses built side-by-side under one roof. Builders also expanded shotgun houses vertically to create "camel-back" or "humpback" houses. In these buildings the last rooms were two stories high, thus producing a hump. The double shotgun was also modified by the creation of a second-story rear addition. The development of porches produced yet another variation. Dwellings known as "north shore" houses had wide verandas on three sides. Most of these were built in the piney woods region along the north shore of Lake Pontchartrain, where many wealthy white residents of New Orleans spent the summer months.

Shotguns of this latter type were built in New Orleans as early as 1832. In addition to early dates of construction, variations on the basic shotgun design also suggest antiquity by the very fact of their existence. The long history of the double shotgun, the single and double camel-backs, and the north shore houses provides strong evidence for assuming that the basic single shotgun originated in the first quarter of the nineteenth century. Sporadic documents provide evidence that shotgun houses were sold in the 1830s. These houses were probably built at least fifteen or twenty years earlier.

The origin of the shotgun house lies in the history of New Orleans's black community. In 1803 there were 1,355 free blacks in the city, many of whom were active and successful in a variety of trades. The size of the community was greatly increased in 1809 by the immigration of approximately 2,100 Haitian mulattoes, who first emigrated to Cuba but were later forced off the island by anti-French sentiment. At the same time, a like number of slaves arrived from Haiti, including many who were relatives of free blacks. By 1810, blacks outnumbered whites in New Orleans, 10,500 to 4,500. Such a population expansion necessitated new housing. As many of the carpenters, masons, and inhabitants were Haitian, it was only natural that they modeled their new homes on those they had left behind.

Even today, many Haitian dwellings closely resemble the single shotgun houses of New Orleans; in some cases, they are identical. More importantly, they share the same set of secondary characteristics. Room sizes are comparable: dimensions average 12 by 14 feet in New Orleans and 12 by 12 feet in Port-au-Prince, the capital of Haiti. Ceiling heights are about 12 feet in both cities. Patterns of internal partitioning are also shared. The first two rooms may be converted into, or treated as, one large room. House façades in Port-au-Prince and New Orleans frequently have two tall frontal openings that serve as either doors or windows. Furthermore, shotgun houses in both cities carry a large amount of decoration on their fronts, while the sides are neglected.

In Port-au-Prince, shotgun houses were an alternative to Creole houses. This latter type of building was based on Norman houses and was used primarily by French colonials. Although there are some similarities in plan to a Creole house type, the shotgun appears to have developed independently, occurring in those areas that were formerly under the exclusive control of the free blacks. Consequently the shotgun house is most frequent in southern Haiti near Port-au-Prince and rarely appears in the north, the area dominated by the former colonial capital, Cap-Français (now Cap-Haïtien).

The long association of free Haitian blacks with the shotgun house type is suggested by the way in which they clung to the design in the late nineteenth century. Even when the Neo-Gothic style—with its spires and lacy trim—was brought to Port-au-Prince from Europe, the narrow shotgun house design was retained as the core of the new architecture, with the new elements draped over the outside of the older form. This tenacious conservatism indicates that Haitian blacks had become accustomed to the shotgun form, retaining internal familiarity while bowing to stylish fashion.

The shotgun houses of Port-au-Prince, however, have as a local antecedent the dwellings constructed by slaves brought from Africa to Haiti in the early eighteenth century when a strong plantation economy began to develop.

The architectural style of plantation housing in Haiti developed from the interaction of the indigenous Arawak Indians, the French colonials, and the slaves. The Arawaks lived in both round and rectangular houses. The rectangular type, called a *bohio,* was very much like the shotgun in form, but was significantly different in that it had only one room. In the seventeenth century, French settlers copied this building for their own dwellings. The first Frenchmen in Haiti were groups of vagabonds who for almost a century lived a hunting-and-gathering existence while plundering and raiding the sea lanes of the Caribbean. They had no need for a more substantial house form than the *bohio;* thus it remained a familiar dwelling long after the settlers had killed off the Arawaks.

When the slaves built their plantation dwellings, they used the form of the *bohio,* but made it a two-room structure. These houses, constructed of wattle and daub with thatched roofs, were one story high, one room wide, and two rooms deep, had a frontward-facing gable, and usually measured 10 by 20 feet. Today, parts of the southern Haitian countryside are dotted with similar buildings. The stable size of these rural dwellings represents more than two centuries of building custom. Urban shotguns and their rural prototypes can thus be linked in a continuum since they are of the same type. But for the origins of this house form, which evolved after the eighteenth-century influx of slaves, we must look to west Africa.

During the entire slave period, many of the Africans who were taken to Haiti came from southwestern Nigeria, an area dominated by the Yoruba. The houses of the

Yoruba, like those in most of western and central Africa, are extremely similar, in spatial terms, to rural shotguns in Haiti. The basic Yoruba house is a two-room module measuring 10 by 20 feet. This unit is variable in its orientation; either the long side or the gable may face the front. With the doorway on the gable end, the house is a true shotgun. The Yoruba slaves probably continued to use their customary buildings after they arrived in Haiti; they had only to make a minor adjustment to preserve their preferred house form and simultaneously satisfy the demands of plantation owners. Furthermore, the similarity between Yoruba houses and other houses in western Africa allowed other African peoples to accept the Haitian shotgun as their own.

The two-room dwelling is the core of many Yoruba houses, and the continuous use of the 10- by 20-foot unit suggests that it is a basic premise of design in Yoruba architectural traditions. Entire compounds are fashioned by grouping two-room units together. The compound, the domain of the extended family, is a large rambling structure with many rooms arranged around an open courtyard or a small impluvium.

Compounds are called *agbo ile* in Yoruba, literally "a flock of houses." This term suggests something of the process by which these houses evolved. Compounds, some of which are said to be more than 300 years old, are the conglomerate result of individual family segments building all their dwellings in one place, using the same kinds of housing units they would have built separately, but in this case, constructing the units in accordance with a communal living pattern.

The odyssey of the shotgun house from Africa to the United States is long and complex. African architectural concepts provided the central, formative influence for plantation houses in Haiti. These concepts, together with features borrowed from house forms used by Indians and Europeans, were incorporated into the rural Haitian shotgun. The long association of blacks with the house form was not severed when slaves were granted their freedom. The mulatto class took the mud-and-thatch house and, by changing the techniques of construction, transformed it into a stylish city dwelling. But their changes did not alter the plan of the building. The internal pattern remained familiar. The shotgun form became for the free Haitian black a physical symbol of independence. And when Haitian blacks were forced to migrate to New Orleans, they retained the basic form.

The importance of the odyssey from the Caribbean and western Africa lies in the African influence that the shotgun house displays in this country. Here, the shotgun is common in black areas and hence is Afro-American by virtue of its users. But in some regions, like Bayou Lafourche in Louisiana, it is the dominant house type used by whites. Although there may be two shotgun traditions—one black and one white (in the latter, the buildings are wider)—both are clearly derived from a single house form.

Although the term shotgun may be related to the door arrangement of the houses and the idea that shotgun pellets fired through the house will meet no obstruction, the name may have also originated from western African languages. Several words commonly used in New Orleans came from western Africa. *Voodoo,* derived from the Fon word for the god Vodun, is a prominent one. In southern Dahomey, the Fon area, the term used to describe houses is *to-gun,* "place of assembly." The description, probably used in New Orleans by Afro-Haitian slaves, was misunderstood and then reinterpreted as shotgun.

But what significance could this house type have for the black community? We are only now beginning to understand that humankind possesses an internal architecture of ideas, that we have architecture without buildings. With space as our only medium, we are constantly constructing invisible barriers, walls, and fences behind which we conduct our daily rituals of conversation, greeting, intimacy, and personal encounter. In black neighborhoods there is often a great degree of tactility in the way people interact. Touching—hands on shoulders, slapping of knees, extensive ritualized handshakes—is common. There is a type of physical intimacy that is measurably absent in the face-to-face encounters in many white communities.

A tradition for this physical closeness is implicit in the shotgun house plan. The series of small rooms, usually joined without hallways, forces family members in one of two directions—into contact with each other or out to the porch and street. When many shotguns are put side by side, as in a plantation arrangement or a city block, interaction with neighbors is as frequent as involvement with one's family. I once asked a group of black women in New Orleans to define a shotgun house. Their collective reply was. "A shotgun house is a house without privacy." But in positive terms, it is a house in which there is a focus on communal activity; it is an architecture of intimacy.

This attitude has its counterpart in western Africa where the communal compound is generally dominant. The many rooms of this building type provide a spatial realm in which a hundred or more family members can interact communally or where small segments of the family can be together. In this way priorities for public and private intimacy are satisfied. While the shotgun house differs greatly in form from a Yoruba compound, in philosophy, a neighborhood of shotgun houses is identical to a compound. The shotgun house thus serves today as a vessel in which an alternative black tradition, an etiquette of involvement, has been maintained. The shotgun house is a physical expression of an Afro-American state of mind.

"Poor People Done It Like That"
John Michael Vlach

Across the Cooper River from Charleston there stands on the shore a dense thicket of trees. This forest is interrupted by stretches of lush green marsh grass. The vast foliage of leaf and blade gives the impression that a broad expanse of land lies beyond. But it is just an impression, for what you see is only Daniel Island, a small dot of soil in the South Carolina low country. Surrounded by the Cooper and Wando rivers and a series

John Michael Vlach, "Poor People Done It Like That," in Charleston Blacksmith. The Work of Philip Simmons *(rev. ed) (Columbia: University of South Carolina, 1992) pp. 1–10.*

The city of Charleston and the Daniel and James Sea islands.

of interlinked swamps and creeks, it is technically an island. At the threshold of one of the oldest cities in the United States, the island's watery boundaries have kept it astonishingly isolated. Even now only one very roundabout road provides access. Daniel Island was once plantation land owned by Robert Daniel of Barbados, a colonial governor of South Carolina, and it has remained farm land ever since the end of the seventeenth century. It was here on a small holding, in 1912, that Philip Simmons was born. Destined to become a blacksmith, he was first an islander who learned the ways of the farm and the river. For more than half a century he has lived in Charleston and could rightly claim the cosmopolitan character of that city. Yet when asked about his origins, he is quick to say:

> I came from Wando, Daniel's Island. That's is in Wando and Wando is in Berkeley County. I born in Wando, up there in Wando. That's just near Cainhoy.

Philip led the life of a Sea Island farmer and fisherman for his first thirteen years. He stayed on the island constantly until he was eight years old. It was then that he first saw Charleston.

> At that particular time children, student in school, then they [didn't] start school until they were seven years old. Now it is six but then it was seven. My seventh year—birthday— I went to school, start to school. I went to school one year in Berkeley County and the next year the teacher didn't come. The money—the budget—they didn't get up the budget for 'em. At that time it was a little slow gettin' that money. Money was scarce so the teacher didn't come early that year. They came about two months later. So my granddaddy send me here to Charleston.

But when summer came he returned to the island.

> Used to work with my granddaddy in the country, fish and farming. I made a living off that. I helped buy all my clothes to come to school to Charleston. When I come to Charleston to go to school in September I got all my clothes and everything I need. During the summer months I work and I made enough money. . . . Let me say every year until I was thirteen, I went back in the country and farm with my grandparents and fish.

So every day for his first eight years, and during summer for the next five, Philip acquired the rural values of a Sea Islander. His great-grandparents had once been slaves, and they told him about those days in bondage. He learned that the work was hard then and learned from his grandparents that conditions had remained hard. He came to know and prefer a busy life full of chores and tasks, a routine that he has never abandoned. It was his Sea Island upbringing that helped establish his current motto: "I like action."

The house in which Philip was born was fairly typical for the black residents of the region. It was a small frame dwelling with a lean-to shed across the rear; the whole building contained four rooms. There was an attic above that could have been used for a sleeping room, but the space was only used for storage. The house was sided with handriven clapboards. This dwelling, while quite ordinary, was particularly important to Philip because his grandfather had built it.

> Our house was made out hand clapboard you get out of the woods. No mill work at all attached to it. My grandfather built it. He was everything. He was a poor man. He wasn't a professional. He built his own house, wasn't a professional house builder. He wasn't a professional fisherman. He wasn't a professional farmer. But that's the thing that he done.

While Philip admired the effort and resourcefulness of the builder, we might further marvel at the continuity of architectural tradition. Those tiny frame houses were more than an element of the Anglo-American plantation era. They were survivals of an Afro-Caribbean plan first used in Barbados, the immediate homeland of the first black settlers in the Sea Islands. Houses of this type were built in the general area until very recently. We may only conjecture at this point on the importance of Sea Island architecture on Philip's upbringing, but consider the scenes of family life in close quarters. One is never far away from anyone; one hears most of what goes on; one's sense of self is secondary to one's sense of family or group. We might conclude that an individual's character will be profoundly shaped by such circumstances, and we will eventually see that some aspects of Philip's personality, particularly his devotion to his family and the members of his church, can perhaps be traced back to the small clapboard house on Daniel Island.

The larger room in the house was sparsely furnished with a table and a few chairs that Philip's grandfather made. It was a lean existence, a life of poverty but not debilitating poverty. His folks didn't have much money, but they were skillful and made do well enough.

> Back then they didn't have a way to cook . . . especially the poor ones. They cook on fire. The rich people, they use these different [fireplace] cranes and stuff. That was modern for them at that time. But we had to go 'bout it the old way. Right down there, put the potatoes in the ashes. And you could bake potato, man! Take it off and brush the ashes and once you peel it you think it was cook in the oven. Rich people had those cranes. Poor people couldn't afford it. Had to put bricks on the two sides. Couldn't afford dog iron. Bricks on two sides. Put your stuff on there. You burn the ashes, you burn the coals. You burn the wood while he green, and after it burn a certain time, he get red and it coal. Then you put your pot on there. Brother it cook right. Oh, it cook nice! Then you put some that coals on the side and poor people done it like that. That's the way my grandmother done it.

Philip cherishes the hours spent in his grandmother's kitchen. He says, "And you see I glad for that experience."

Philip's memories of his "Dan's Island" days are of course vague for the first six years: "You can't remember nothin' much before the age of six anyhow." But we can piece together a broad outline of daily life in the Sea Islands which would reasonably approximate his experience. His grandfather was a farmer and had to match his actions to the shifts in climate and season. There was spring planting, summer weeding, fall harvest, and winter "lay by." As a tiny lad, Philip followed his grandfather about and watched him perform his usual chores. Maybe Philip even got in the way. He remembers that his grandfather raised "all kinds of vegetables like corn, beans, and cotton—he planted a lot of cotton. Especially he'd plant stuff for the household. He'd plant enough for the market. That's the only way we had to live."

The farm was small, not more than thirty acres, as was the common Sea Island pattern. The farmstead was thus mainly an oversized kitchen garden intended to produce the staples for a year's self-sufficiency. Extra truck crops, if there were any, could be sold in the Charleston market. These were beans and cucumbers. Animals were kept too: usually chickens, a hog or two, and a solitary milk cow. During the first decade of the twentieth century, draft animals—oxen, mules, or horses—were used to pull plows, but only sporadically. Deep turning of the sandy soil was just then being introduced into the Sea Islands. This innovation in tillage did not completely displace the tradition of hoe cultivation, the method of their African forebears, which the islanders retained from plantation days. They used heavy hoes with broad blades hafted on thick saplings. Those hoes weren't at all delicate like our modern garden hoes. They were tools to give shape to the land, the prods that stirred the tired soil into producing one more year's sustenance. Heavy, rough, and crude, they were not for children to use. No doubt Philip watched his grandparents from the edge of the field as they raised their greens, potatoes, corn, beans, and rice.

Philip's grandmother was no stranger to field work. Like most Sea Island women, she was not housebound and consequently took a place in the garden patch along with her husband. With a bandana around her head and dressed in a loose-fitting blouse with the sleeves rolled up and a long skirt tied with a string at the hips, she toiled both in the fields and the kitchen. Thus it was that Philip had two models for action. When he was a child, everyone worked all the time and worked hard at the same jobs. For the rest of his life he would know and prefer no other way of living than working full time, all the time.

One of Philip's first memories of farming tasks involved the use of a mortar and pestle. The mortar was a section of an oak trunk standing about three feet high and measuring fifteen inches across. Philip's grandfather had hollowed out a section of the top with his axe and by controlled burning. At age six Philip was too short to work at the mortar. He had to stand on top of a box to look inside, and he wasn't strong enough to lift the regular pestle. Nevertheless, he was allowed to play at "mashin' the corn." The pestle, a wooden pole with two blunt ends, was too big for Philip's little hands, so his grandfather made a small one for him to use. When his grandmother prepared corn or rice, Philip could then take part in the work. He made his contribution, even though it certainly couldn't be regarded as a full share. The cooperative use of two pestles was not uncommon in the Sea Islands; the husking of rice was often done by two people working in unison.

As he became older, he abandoned his small pestle. Philip regarded it as a toy, a plaything. He threw it away without regret when he found that he could master the implement his grandparents regularly used. Not only was it bigger, it was a more specialized tool. One end was broad and blunted into a dull roundness through its many collisions with the mortar. The other end was kept wedge-shaped like a broad chisel. This pestle was a proper rice-husking tool. While the Simmonses' farm had little acreage given to rice, rice was a major staple in the diet. It had been an element of the regional cuisine for the low country since 1690. The blunt end of the pestle was used for cracked rice, since it was the smashing end; the pointed end produced whole grain rice. In either case, the husk of the rice was separated from its kernel. Once the husking was completed, the two parts of the rice grain lay jumbled in the mortar and further cleaning was required. This phase was done with a round, traylike, coiled-grass basket called a fanner. The contents of the mortar were placed in the fanner and tossed gently into the air, allowing the lighter husks to blow away. Philip claims never to have "flapped the rice," but he saw it done many times.

Reaching the age of seven, Philip started to school. It was a one-room school for the black children on Daniel Island and, as he remembers, it only lasted for three months—just enough time to learn the alphabet, some numbers, and how to write his name. This left most of the year free to do farm work. Many of his chores involved carrying and hauling. While he was never charged with milking the cow, he certainly had to carry its feed and at times take the milk pail to the house. His grandmother usually fed the chickens, but he would do that too. Occasionally it was his job to carry slops to the hogs, and it always was his job to gather up the firewood.

At the age of eight, Philip was given the task of carrying "dinner" to the working people in the fields. The annual field cycle first involved enriching the soil, usually following the local practice of spreading a natural compost of marsh mud mixed with manure and working it into the ground with hoes. Planting would be finished by April, and throughout the spring and summer weeding required constant vigilance. As the bean plants matured they were picked as needed and the small crop taken to the house for supper. The other vegetables—the peas, tomatoes, collards, and okra—were harvested in their turn. With the coming of fall, the potatoes were dug up and banked near the house to be used through the winter. There were certain slack periods in the growing process when the field did not require immediate attention, but there was never a time when there was nothing to do. The household chores were constant and tended to fill the momentary lulls in Philip's routine.

Beyond the tasks of field and house, Philip also gave a hand to his grandfather's carpentry. William Simmons's skills as a joiner were apparently valued in the Daniel Island community. He built his own house; he may have built houses for others. If he could build a house, it is likely that he also built barns, sheds, smokehouses, and other structures. Such buildings were part of the architectural repertoire of Daniel Island, and William Simmons may have been one of the carpenters responsible for their construction. What Philip remembers best, however, is that his grandfather made caskets. These were fashioned with milled pine boards and formed into an elongated six-sided box. The angles were tricky to figure, and the joinery had to be precise. The importance of funerary rites in the Sea Island tradition required that the remains of the deceased be lavished with as much ceremony and finery as possible. To give anything less than one's best effort would be to invite the fury of the spirit of the deceased person. The wooden caskets were simple and unadorned, yet they were a fine display of the country carpenter's skill. Philip helped to steady the boards as they were sawn. He searched for the tool that his grandfather called for. He braced his weight against the sides as they were nailed or screwed together. In short, he lent a hand and learned some basic lessons about making objects, about attention to detail, about the responsibility of the craftsman to his client.

When there was no demand for carpentry and the fields could be left untended (particularly after the potatoes had been dug up), William Simmons became a fisherman. Indeed, throughout the entire Sea Island chain running from Georgetown, South Carolina, to northern Florida, fishing in the rivers and creeks has always served as a means of supplementing the diet. Myriad species of water creatures are caught, including bass, perch, trout, salmon, flounder, croaker, shrimp, clams, oysters, crabs, and turtles. On Daniel Island there were two main types of fishing, line fishing and shrimping. Speaking of his grandfather, Philip recounts this pattern:

> He farmed part of the season, and the other part after harvesting, then he fished . . . he done shrimp. He catch shrimp for a living, fish for a living. Bring it to the market here [in Charleston]. You see where the main city market is over here; it's the same market we brought out produce like fish and shrimp. . . . We fish with line and net. Most times we'd fish for pleasure. We'd use the line. Commercial fishing for the market we'd use the net.

Cast net we'd call it. Cast net and fish line. We cast net one tide, we'd sit down and we'd fish the other tide. Well, when it don't run in the net, we use the fishing line. We didn't use the fish pole and cane then, rod and reel. Weren't no rod and reels then.

It was only natural that a farmer from Daniel Island would bring shrimp to Charleston. The city is clearly visible from the mouth of the Wando River, which was the major fishing area. A good hour's row across the Cooper offered a reward of much-needed cash from hungry Charlestonians, who have long considered the rice and shrimp concoction they call "shrimps creole" an indispensable part of their cuisine.

The shrimping business is now highly industrialized, with trawlers grabbing virtually all of the coastal catch. Yet in the creeks and shallows amid the islands, shrimp can still be caught with the centuries-old cast net. This type of net is known both in Africa and the Caribbean, and Sea Islanders have fished with it since the eighteenth century. The net is conical in shape, with its outer edge or "foot" weighted with lead shot "bullets." Draw lines run from the foot to the center where they are spliced into a hand line. When the net is thrown, it unfurls to its full diameter over the water and then sinks, trapping the shrimp below it. There are several techniques for throwing the net. In one approach a portion of the net is held in the mouth to help spread the net quickly to its fullest dimensions as it is thrown. Precise hand-mouth coordination is required for a proper release. Philip comments:

I can throw it, yes I can throw it. . . . Some people put it in he mouth and some don't. Those expert don't put 'em in they mouth. They could throw it without puttin' it in their mouth. Hand line in one hand and net in the other. Throw it and spin it. Yeah, it's an art in doin' it. You throw it right, hold it right, throw it right, it'll open.

Philip learned to throw a cast net from his grandfather, who could also make them. While Philip never learned to "knit net," he did discover that there was a native taxonomy which varied with the size of the mesh. The larger openings identified a "rich man's net." The rationale for this name was that the larger openings allowed some of the small shrimp to escape and "rich folk" didn't want to go through the trouble of cleaning the morsel-sized shrimp anyway. The poor man, on the other hand, with many mouths to feed, must capture as much as he can with every cast. Hence, his net has a fine mesh through which no shrimp can escape.

On a subsistence farm nearly everything produced is consumed. When the Sea Island farmer turned to the waterways, the same attitude prevailed. Industriousness in both lines of work could, however, provide a surplus, as it did for William Simmons. Extra vegetables and extra shrimp could be sold in the Charleston market. With the money gained he was able to buy a wood-burning stove, which transformed the food-preparation customs from those of the plantation slave to those of a freedman. This change occurred around 1919, half a century after slavery. At this time he also thought it wise that his grandson get a good education. It was clear to him that the brief and interrupted appearances made by the teacher at Daniel Island were not enough. Thus, in the fall of 1920, Philip was sent to Charleston to live with his parents and to go to school for eight months of the year—a proper education.

Philip was rowed over to Charleston and disembarked at the foot of Calhoun Street, a docking point for many Sea Island boats or *bateaux* as they were called. From there it was only a few blocks to the house on Vernon Street where Philip would live for the next three years. The move to the city was exciting for Philip. Imagine the vast difference between a city like Charleston, teeming with people, and the few clusters of tiny farm houses on Daniel Island. In Charleston there were paved roads, sidewalks, parks, multistory houses, office buildings made of stone, and ships at the wharves—and there were thousands and thousands of people. All of them were new and strange to Philip. On the island everyone had a clear identity; in Charleston the procession of strangers was endless. Adventure thus lay around every corner, particularly in the area surrounding Philip's house. Charleston was a bustling port city, and Philip was but two blocks from the waterfront where, in the 1920s, one could still see three-masted schooners and all manner of steamships. Wagons pulled by horses were still the order of the day, and drivers constantly urged their burdened teams back and forth between the docks and the warehouses. Many service trades were also located along the river, and Philip would spend hours with the cobbler, the pipefitter, the shipwright, the cooper, and other craftsmen.

Exciting though the city was, it remained only a temporary home. Philip was still a country boy and may have been prone to follow his grandmother's warning, "There time to see and not see, time to know and not know," which promoted a cautious, reticent view of life. He was happy when summer came and he could return to Daniel Island. Until about the age of eleven he was most comfortable with the regimen of the fields. The quest for shrimp and sea bass he saw as sport. Yet both endeavors were an economic necessity. The money Philip earned in the summer helped get him through the school year. During the rest of the year, in Charleston, he did odd jobs to supplement the money his mother made as a domestic helper. He shined shoes or sold newspapers, but these jobs were not important enough to keep him off the island.

Between the ages of eleven and thirteen Philip's role on the farm and in the boat increased tremendously. He was under less supervision and was expected to perform more responsibly, almost at the level of an adult. He worked the same hours as his grandfather, getting up at dawn and returning to the house at dusk. Philip's main memories are of the rush to harvest Irish potatoes before he returned to Charleston for school. Rows of plants had to be turned in order to unearth the knotty clumps of potatoes. Then Philip had to gather up the potatoes, shake the dirt off them, and carry them back to the house, where they would be stored. He took over other crops too: the corn, the sweet potatoes, and the beans. He learned more and more about plant cultivation and animal care, and if he had continued to return to Daniel Island beyond his thirteenth summer, he might have remained a farmer.

The impact of Philip's Sea Island childhood was particularly significant in terms of his sense of ethnic and regional identity. While he has lived and worked in the black community of Charleston most of his life, his first seven years were spent almost exclusively in the presence of blacks. White people rarely came to Daniel Island and then were seen only at the store in Cainhoy. Other than in trips to the Charleston market, Philip lived among immediate family, lesser kin and familiar neighbors who were all farmers as well as members of the same race and social class. They shared the same island setting; all knew nature intimately and had the same concerns produced by the fickleness of weather or shifts in the season. Foodways were so uniform from one household to another that all ate the same basic diet, which, by Philip's account, tended to concentrate on grits and rice. Moreover, on the basis of food-preservation customs, he can separate the residents of Yonges, Wadmalaw, and Daniel Islands; on other islands, "they canned," while on his island "they dried" their foodstuffs. His favorite dish remains one that his grandmother made, okra soup with dried shrimp in it. This should then be poured on top of a plateful of rice cooked "Geechee style, so dry that each grain fall apart."

It is the widely shared experience of the islanders and specific eating habits that cause Philip to identify himself first as a Geechee, a local term for a Sea Islander:

> Well, Geechee [people] mostly like rice and most of the people come in see you eating a lot of rice, they call you Geechee. So I'm a colored, black Geechee.

In the social context of Charleston, which has long maintained a distinct black subculture of its own tied to a history of urban servitude, manumission, and the independence of free black tradesmen, to identify oneself as Geechee is to confirm one's status as an outsider. But Philip feels no shame or anxiety about this circumstance. As we have noted before, he is "glad for that experience." He considers rural life a good training with many hardships that have made him appreciate more fully the successes he has earned in Charleston.

But even more than identity, his island days provided links to some of the oldest elements in the black culture of the Carolina low country. One very important aspect of Sea Island tradition is found in his speech pattern. Philip's speech is profoundly influenced by the rhythms and sounds of Gullah, the African-based creole spoken in the islands. Over the years since he left Daniel Island the Charleston version of black English and his deliberate attempts to learn "proper English" in school have modified his usage pattern, but the inflectional aspects of Gullah remain. Philip acknowledges that "that ol' Geechee" comes out now and again when his sentences tend to rise tonally for emphasis, what he calls "gainin' up." Creolists would no doubt perceive certain distinct Gullah grammatical forms such as unconventional pronoun usage or sentences with serial verbs, but it is enough for the present to recognize that after an absence of fifty years from Daniel Island Philip still speaks a form of Gullah.

The things he confronted daily on his grandparents' farm—the mortar and pestle, the coiled-grass baskets, the cast nets, the house itself—constitute a physical statement of tradition as old as Sea Island speech. Each was used in the plantation era and can be traced historically to an African genesis. Philip was, however, not conscious of this heritage; for him the immediate history of his grandparents and great-grandparents was more significant. He, in fact, finds it exotically interesting that elements of his life can be traced back to Africa. His usual comment on such matters is, "Well, poor people had to do it that way." It is nonetheless important that there were Africanisms in his early experiences, for they can be interpreted as a prime statement of the cultural conservatism of his background. The artifacts which surrounded him were old in form and concept. Philip today places high value on items made "the old-fashioned way." There can be no denial that from his first days old ways were considered the best ways.

Certain patterns of behavior with which he was in daily contact are also traceable to Africa. In some cases the yard around the house was treated as an extension of the building. The dirt was swept regularly as if it were floor space. The soil was packed hard and no grass was allowed to grow, in contrast to the usual European pattern. Work was often done communally; tasks were shared when possible. Whether weeding the cotton, digging the potatoes, or smashing the corn in the mortar, the islanders preferred not to work alone. Cultivation was generally done with a hoe, not just because folks were too poor to afford traction animals: if hoes were used more people could join in. Chanting as they worked, a monotonous job became more enjoyable.

If patterns in residence and labor are not enough to signal a sense of alternative cultural order, consider the habit of carrying loads on one's head. This practice on the part of both men and women is seen occasionally today in the low country. In the 1920s and 1930s it was so common as to be unremarkable. Since no one has reported even a single white farm wife carrying her supper greens back to the house on her head, we must consider the practice another source of black Sea Island identity. Having lived with all of these behavioral traditions, Philip would forever have a clear sense of his roots. The way of his grandparents was definitely the Sea Island way, the black way, the old-fashioned way. The links even to an African past are there too, even if not consciously acknowledged.

In the 1920s and 1930s many black people left their Sea Island homes to go to cities all along the Atlantic coast. Many went to New York. Relatively few came to Charleston, mainly because there were few well-paying jobs. Philip had been migrating back and forth across the Cooper River for six years when he became a permanent Charleston resident. Intrigued by ironwork, he decided to become a blacksmith in the city, but he would never shake his country origins. The influences of the islands even today shape his point of view. With that in mind we can well imagine how much of an islander he was when he first stood at the door of Peter Simmons's blacksmith shop.

Gracia Real de Santa Teresa de Mose: A Free Black Town in Spanish Colonial Florida
Jane Landers
Historian

Along with Kathleen Deagan, Jane Landers has worked on the Fort Mose archaeological project of the Florida Museum of Natural History. She is also the author of "Spanish Sanctuary: Fugitive Slaves in Florida, 1687–1790," Florida Historical Quarterly *62 (September 1984): 296–313. Landers currently is assistant professor in the Department of History at Vanderbilt University.*

Jane Landers, *"Gracia Real de Santa Teresa de Mose: A Free Black Town in Spanish Colonial Florida"* (American Historical Review, *95 [1] February 1990): 9–30.*

For too long, historians have paid little attention to Spain's lengthy tenure in the South.[1] As a result, important spatial and temporal components of the American past have been overlooked. Recent historical and archaeological research on the free black town of Gracia Real de Santa Teresa de Mose, located in northeast Spanish Florida, suggests ways in which Spanish colonial records might illuminate these neglected aspects of the Southern past.[2] Because of this black town's unusual origins and political and military significance, Spanish bureaucrats documented its history with much care.

Gracia Real de Santa Teresa de Mose, hereafter referred to as Mose, was born of the initiative and determination of blacks who, at great risk, manipulated the Anglo-Spanish contest for control of the Southeast to their advantage and thereby won their freedom. The settlement was composed of former slaves, many of West African origin, who had escaped from British plantations and received religious sanctuary in Spanish Florida. Although relatively few in number (the community maintained a fairly stable size of about 100 people during the quarter-century between 1738 and 1763, while St. Augustine's population grew from approximately 1,500 people in the 1730s to approximately 3,000 by 1763), these freedmen and women were of great contemporary significance.[3] By their "theft of self," they were a financial loss to their former owners, often a serious one.[4] Moreover, their flight was a political action, sometimes effected through violence, that offered an example to other bondsmen and challenged the precarious political and social order of the British colonies. The runaways were also important to the Spanish colony for the valuable knowledge and skills they brought with them and for the labor and military services they performed.[5] These free blacks are also historiographically significant; an exploration of their lives sheds light on questions long debated by scholars, such as the relative severity of slave systems, the varieties of slave experiences, slave resistance, the formation of a Creole culture, the nature of black family structures, the impact of Christianity and religious syncretism on African-American societies, and African-American influences in the "New World."[6]

Although a number of historians have alluded to the lure of Spanish Florida for runaway slaves from the British colonies of South Carolina and Georgia, few have examined what became of the fugitives in their new lives or the implications of their presence in the Spanish province.[7] The Spanish policy regarding fugitive slaves in Florida developed in an ad hoc fashion and changed over time to suit the shifting military, economic, and diplomatic interests of the colony as well as the metropolis. Although the Spanish crown preferred to emphasize religious and humane considerations for freeing slaves of the British, the political and military motives were equally, if not more, important. In harboring the runaways and eventually settling them in their own town, Spanish governors were following Caribbean precedents and helping the crown to populate and hold territory threatened by foreign encroachment.[8] The ex-slaves were also served by this policy. It offered them a refuge within which they could maintain family ties. In the highly politicized context of Spanish Florida, they struggled to maximize their leverage with the Spanish community and improve the conditions of their freedom. They made creative use of Spanish institutions to support their corporate identity and concomitant privileges.[9] They adapted to Spanish values where it served them to do so and thereby gained autonomy. They also reinforced ties within their original community through intermarriage and use of the Spanish mechanism of godparenthood *(compadrazgo)*. Finally, they formed intricate new kin and friendship networks with slaves, free blacks, Indians, "new" Africans, and whites in nearby St. Augustine that served to stabilize their population and strengthen their connections to that Hispanic community.[10]

That runaways became free in Spanish Florida was not in itself unusual. Frank Tannenbaum's early comparative work shows that freedom had been a possibility for slaves in the Spanish world since the thirteenth century. Spanish law granted slaves a moral and juridical personality, as well as certain rights and protections not found in other slave systems. Among the most important were the right to own property, which in the Caribbean evolved into the right of self-purchase, the right to personal security, prohibitions against separating family members, and access to the courts. Moreover, slaves were incorporated into the Spanish church and received its sacraments, including marriage. Slaves in the Hispanic colonies were subject to codes based on this earlier body of law.[11] Eugene Genovese and others have persuasively argued that the ideals expressed in these slave codes should not be accepted as social realities, and it seems obvious that colonials observed these laws in their own fashion—some in the spirit in which they were written and others not at all.[12] Nevertheless, the acknowledgement of a slave's humanity and rights, and the lenient attitude toward manumission embodied in Spanish law and social practices, made it possible for a significant free black class to exist in the Spanish world.[13]

Although the Spanish legal system permitted freedom, the crown assumed that its beneficiaries would live among the Spaniards, under the supervision of white townspeople *(vecinos)*. While the crown detailed its instructions regarding the physical layout, location, and function of white and Indian towns, it made no formal provisions for free black towns. But Spanish colonizers throughout the Americas were guided by an urban model. They depicted theirs as a civilizing mission and sought to create public order and righteous living by creating towns. Urban living was believed to facilitate religious conversion, but, beyond that, Spaniards attached a special value to living a *vida política,* believing that people of reason distinguished themselves from nomadic "barbarians" by living in stable urban situations.[14] Royal legislation reflected a continuing interest in reforming and settling so-called vagabonds of all races within the empire. The primary focus of reduction efforts was the Indians, but, as the black and mixed populations grew, so too did Spanish concerns about how these elements would be assimilated into "civilized" society. The "two republics" of Spaniards and Indians gave way to a society of castes, which increasingly viewed the unforeseen and unregulated groups with hostility. Spanish bureaucrats attempted to count these people and to limit their physical mobility through increasingly restrictive racial legislation. Officials prohibited blacks from living unsupervised or, worse, among the Indians. Curfews and pass systems developed, as did proposals to force unemployed blacks into fixed labor situations.[15] The crown also recognized with alarm the increased incidence of *cimmaronage,* slaves fleeing Spanish control. Communities of runaway blacks, mulattos, Indians, and their offspring were common to all slaveholding societies, but they challenged the Spanish concept of civilized living, as well as the hierarchical racial and social order the Spaniards were trying to impose. Despite repeated military efforts, the Spaniards were no more successful than other European powers at eradicating such settlements.[16]

Paradoxically, it was in this context of increasing racial animosity that Spanish officials legitimized free black towns. These towns appeared in the seventeenth and eighteenth centuries in a region described by one scholar as the "Negroid littoral"—the sparsely populated and inhospitable coastal areas of the Caribbean.[17] Faced with insurmountable problems and lacking the resources to "correct" them, the Spanish bureaucracy proved flexible and adaptable. When maroon communities such as those described by Colin Palmer and William Taylor in Mexico were too remote or intractable to destroy, the Spaniards granted them official sanction.[18] The Spanish governor of Venezuela once chartered a free black town to reward pacification of lands held by hostile Indians.[19] Mose was established as a buffer against foreign encroachment and provides a third model of free black town formation.[20]

The experience of the residents of Mose was in many ways shaped by Caribbean patterns. Declining Indian populations, a Spanish disdain for manual labor, and the defense requirements of an extended empire had created an early demand for additional workers. Blacks cleared land and planted crops, built fortifications and domestic structures, and provided a wide variety of skilled labor for Spanish colonists. By the sixteenth century, they had become the main labor force in Mexican mines and on Caribbean plantations. Also by that time, the Spanish had organized them into militia companies in Hispaniola, Cuba, Mexico, Cartagena, and Puerto Rico.[21] In Florida, too, Spaniards depended on Africans to be their laborers and to supplement their defenses. Black laborers and artisans helped establish St. Augustine, the first successful Spanish settlement in Florida, and a black and mulatto militia was formed there as early as 1683.[22]

Florida held great strategic significance for the Spanish: initially, for its location guarding the route of the treasure fleets, later, to safeguard the mines of Mexico from the French and British. The colony was a critical component in Spain's Caribbean defense, and, when British colonists established Charles Town in 1670, it represented a serious challenge to Spanish sovereignty.[23] No major response by the weakened Spanish empire was feasible, but, when the British incited their Indian allies to attack Spanish Indian missions along the Atlantic coast, the Spaniards initiated a campaign of harassment against the new British colony. In 1686, a Spanish raiding party including a force of fifty-three Indians and blacks attacked Port Royal and Edisto. From the plantation of Governor Joseph Morton, they carried away "money and plate and thirteen slaves to the value of [£]1500." In subsequent negotiations, the new governor of Carolina, James Colleton, demanded the return of the stolen slaves as well as those "who run dayly into your towns," but the Spaniards refused.[24] These contacts may have suggested the possibility of a refuge among the enemy and directed slaves to St. Augustine, for, the following year, the first recorded fugitive slaves from Carolina arrived there. Governor Diego de Quiroga dutifully reported to Spain that eight men, two women, and a three-year-old nursing child had escaped to his province in a boat. According to the governor, they requested baptism into the "True Faith," and on that basis he refused to return them to the British delegation that came to St. Augustine to reclaim them.[25] The Carolinians claimed that one of Samuel de Bordieu's runaways, Mingo, who escaped with his wife and daughter (the nursing child), had committed murder in the process. Governor Quiroga promised to make monetary restitution for the slaves he retained and to prosecute Mingo, should the charges be proven.[26] Quiroga housed these first runaways in the homes of Spanish townspeople and saw to it that they were instructed in Catholic doctrine, baptized and married in the church. He put the men to work as ironsmiths and laborers on the new stone fort, the Castillo de San Marcos, and employed the women in his own household. All were reportedly paid wages: the men earned a peso a day, the wage paid to male Indian laborers, and the women half as much.[27]

Florida's governors enjoyed considerable autonomy. Their dual military and political appointments, the great distance from the metropolis, and an unwieldy bureaucracy contributed to their ability to make their own decisions. In unforeseen circumstances, they improvised. But, as fugitives continued to filter into the province, the governors and treasury officials repeatedly solicited the king's guidance. Eventually, the Council of the Indies reviewed the matter and recommended approving the sanctuary policy shaped by the governors. On November 7, 1693, Charles II issued the first official position on the runaways, "giving liberty to all . . . the men as well as the women . . . so that by their example and by my liberality others will do the same."[28]

The provocation inherent in this order increasingly threatened the white Carolinians. At least four other groups of runaways reached St. Augustine in the following decade, and, despite an early ambiguity about their legal status, the refugees were returned to their British masters only in one known example.[29] Carolina's changing racial balance further intensified the planters' concerns. By 1708, blacks outnumbered whites in the colony, and slave revolts erupted in 1711 and 1714. The following year, when many slaves joined the Yamassee Indian war against the British, they almost succeeded in exterminating the badly outnumbered whites. Indians loyal to the British helped defeat the Yamassee, who with their black allies headed for St. Augustine. Although the Carolina Assembly passed harsh legislation designed to prevent further insurrections and control the slaves, these actions and subsequent negotiations with St. Augustine failed to deter the escapes or effect the reciprocal return of slaves. British planters claimed that the Spanish policy, by drawing away their slaves, would ruin their plantation economy. Arthur Middleton, Carolina's acting governor, complained to London that the Spaniards not only harbored their runaways but sent them back in the company of Indians to plunder British plantations. The Carolinians set up patrol systems and placed scout boats on water routes to St. Augustine, but slaves still made good their escapes on stolen horses and in canoes and piraguas.[30]

In 1724, ten more runaway slaves reached St. Augustine, assisted by English-speaking Yamassee Indians. According to their statements, they were aware that the Spanish king had offered freedom to those seeking baptism and conversion.[31] The royal edict of 1693 was still in force, and Governor Antonio de Benavides initially seems to have honored it. In 1729, however, Benavides sold these newcomers at public auction to reimburse their owners, alleging that he feared the British might act on their threats to recover their losses by force. Some of the most important citizens of St. Augustine, including the royal accountant, the royal treasurer, several military officers, and even some religious officials, thus acquired valuable new slaves.[32] Others were sold to owners who took them to Havana. In justifying his actions, Benavides explained that these slaves had arrived during a time of peace with England and, further, that he interpreted the 1693 edict to apply only to the original runaways from the British colony.[33]

Several of the reenslaved men were veterans of the Yamassee war in Carolina, and one of these, Francisco Menéndez, was appointed by Governor Benavides to command a slave militia in 1726. This black militia helped defend St. Augustine against the British invasion led by Colonel John Palmer in 1728, but, despite their loyal service, the Carolina refugees still remained enslaved.[34] Meanwhile, the Spaniards continued to send canoes of Carolina fugitives and Yamassee Indians north in search of British scalps and live slaves. Governor Middleton charged that Governor Benavides was profiting by the slaves' sale in Havana, a charge that seems well founded.[35]

Perhaps in response to continued reports and diplomatic complaints involving the fugitives, the crown issued two new edicts regarding their treatment. The first, on October 4, 1733, forbade any future compensation to the British, reiterated the offer of freedom, and specifically prohibited the sale of fugitives to private citizens. The second edict, on October 29, 1733, commended the blacks for their bravery against the British in 1728; however, it also stipulated that they would be required to complete four years of royal service prior to being freed. But the runaways had sought liberty, not indenture.[36] Led by Captain Menéndez of the slave militia, the blacks persisted in attempts to secure complete freedom. They presented petitions to the governor and to the auxiliary bishop of Cuba, who toured the province in 1735, but to no avail.[37] When Manuel de Montiano became governor in 1737, their fortunes changed. Captain Menéndez once more solicited his freedom, and this time his petition was supported by that of a Yamassee cacique named Jorge. Jorge related how Menéndez and three others had fought bravely for three years in the Yamassee rebellion, only to be sold back into slavery in Florida by a "heathen" named Mad Dog. Jorge condemned this betrayal of the blacks whom he stated had been patient and "more than loyal," but he did not blame Mad Dog, for he was an "infidel" who knew no better. Rather, he held culpable the Spaniards who had purchased these loyal allies.[38] Governor Montiano ordered an investigation and reviewed the case. On March 15, 1738, he granted unconditional freedom to the petitioners. Montiano also wrote the governor and captain general of Cuba, attempting to retrieve eight Carolinians who had been taken to Havana during the Benavides regime. At least one, Antonio Caravallo, was returned to St. Augustine, against all odds.[39]

Governor Montiano established the freedmen in a new town, about two miles north of St. Augustine, which he called Gracia Real de Santa Teresa de Mose.[40] The freedmen built the settlement, a walled fort and shelters described by the Spaniards as resembling thatched Indian huts. Little more is known about it from Spanish sources, but later British reports add that the fort was constructed of stone, "four square with a flanker at each corner, banked with earth, having a ditch without on all sides lined round with prickly royal and had a well and house within, and a look-out." They also confirm Spanish reports that the freedmen planted fields nearby.[41] The town site was said to be surrounded by fertile lands and nearby woods that would yield building materials. A river of salt water "running through it" contained an abundance of shellfish and all types of fish.[42] Montiano hoped the people of Mose could cultivate the land to grow food for St. Augustine, but, until crops could be harvested, he provided the people with corn, biscuits, and beef from government stores.[43]

Mose was located at the head of Mose Creek, a tributary of the North River with access to St. Augustine, and lay directly north of St. Augustine, near trails north to San Nicholas and west to Apalache. For all these reasons, it was strategically significant. Governor Montiano surely considered the benefits of a northern outpost against anticipated British attacks. And who better to serve as an advanced warning system than grateful ex-slaves carrying Spanish arms? The freedmen understood their expected role, for, in a declaration to the king, they vowed to be "the most cruel enemies of the English" and to risk their lives and spill their "last drop of blood in defense of the Great Crown of Spain and the Holy Faith."[44] If the new homesteaders were diplomats, they were also pragmatists, and their own interests were clearly served by fighting those who would seek to return them to chattel slavery. Mose also served a vital objective of Spanish imperial policy, and, once Governor Montiano justified its establishment, the Council of the Indies and the king supported his actions.[45]

Since Spanish town settlement implied the extension of *justicia,* the governor assigned a white military officer and royal official to supervise the establishment of Mose. Mose was considered a village of new converts comparable to those of the Christian Indians, so Montiano also posted a student priest at the settlement to instruct the inhabitants in doctrine and "good customs."[46] Although the Franciscan lived at Mose, there is no evidence that the white officer did. It seems rather that Captain Menéndez was responsible for governing the settlement, for, in one document, Governor Montiano referred to the others as the "subjects" of Menéndez. The Spaniards regarded Menéndez as a sort of natural lord, and, like Indian caciques, he probably exercised considerable autonomy over his village.[47] Spanish titles and support may have also reinforced Menéndez's status and authority. Whatever the nature of his authority, Menéndez commanded the Mose militia for over forty years, and his career supports Price's contention that eighteenth-century maroon leaders were military figures well-versed in European ways and equipped to negotiate their followers' best interests.[48]

As new fugitives arrived, the governor placed these in Menéndez's charge as well. A group of twenty-three men, women, and children arrived from Port Royal on November 21, 1738, and were sent to join the others at the new town. Among the newcomers were the runaway slaves of Captain Caleb Davis of Port Royal. Davis was an English merchant who had been supplying St. Augustine for many years, and it is possible that some of the runaways had even traveled to St. Augustine in the course of Davis's business. Davis went to the Spanish city in December 1738 and spotted his former slaves, whom he reported laughed at his fruitless efforts to recover them.[49] The frustrated Davis eventually submitted a claim against the Spanish for twenty-seven of his slaves "detained" by Montiano, whom he valued at 7,600 pesos, as well as for the launch in which they escaped and supplies they had taken with them. He also listed debts incurred by the citizens of St. Augustine. Among those owing him money were Governors Antonio Benavides, Francisco Moral Sánchez, and Manuel de Montiano, various royal officials and army officers, and Mose townsmen Francisco Menéndez and Pedro de Leon.[50] There is no evidence Davis ever recouped his losses.

In March 1739, envoys from Carolina arrived in St. Augustine to press for the return of their runaway slaves. Governor Montiano treated them with hospitality but referred to the royal edict of 1733, which required that he grant religious sanctuary.[51] In August, an Indian ally in Apalache sent word to Montiano that the British had attempted to build a fort in the vicinity, but that the hundred black laborers had revolted, killed all the whites, and hamstrung their horses before escaping. Several days later, some of the blacks encountered the Indians in the woods and asked directions to reach the Spaniards.[52] The following month, a group of Angola slaves revolted near Stono, South Carolina, and killed more than twenty whites before heading for St. Augustine. They were apprehended before reaching their objective, and retribution was swift and bloody. But officials of South Carolina and Georgia blamed the sanctuary available in nearby St. Augustine for the rebellion, and relations between the colonies reached a breaking point.[53] With the outbreak of the War of Jenkins' Ear, international and local grievances merged. In January 1740, Governor James Oglethorpe of Georgia raided Florida and captured Forts Pupo and Picolata on the St. John's River west of St. Augustine. These initial victories enabled Oglethorpe to mount a major expeditionary force, including Georgia and South Carolina regiments, a vast Indian army, and seven warships for a major offensive against the Spaniards.[54]

The free black militia of Mose worked alongside the other citizenry to fortify provincial defenses. They also provided the Spaniards with critical intelligence reports.[55] In May, one of Oglethorpe's lieutenants happened across five houses occupied by the freedmen and was able to capture two of them.[56] Unable to protect the residents of Mose, Governor Montiano was forced to evacuate "all the Negroes who composed that town" to the safety of St. Augustine. Thereafter, the Mose militia continued to conduct dangerous sorties against the enemy and assisted in the surprise attack and recapture of their town in June.[57] The success at Mose was one of the few enjoyed by the Spaniards. It is generally acknowledged to have demoralized the combined British forces and to have been a significant factor in Oglethorpe's withdrawal. British accounts refer to the event as "Bloody Mose" or "Fatal Mose" and relate with horror the murder and mutilation (decapitation and castration) of two wounded prisoners who were unable to travel. They do not say whether Spaniards, Indians, or blacks did the deed. Although Spanish sources do not even mention this incident, atrocities took place on both sides. Both Spanish and British authorities routinely paid their Indian allies for enemy scalps, and at least one scalp was taken at "Moosa," according to British reports.[58]

Cuban reinforcements finally relieved St. Augustine in July. Shortly thereafter, Oglethorpe and his troops returned to Georgia and Carolina.[59] Governor Montiano commended all his troops to the king but made the rather unusual gesture of writing a special recommendation for Francisco Menéndez. Montiano extolled the exactitude with which Menéndez had carried out royal service and the valor he had displayed in the battle at Mose. He added that, on another occasion, Menéndez and his men had fired on the enemy until they withdrew from the castle walls and that Menéndez had displayed great zeal during the dangerous reconnaissance missions he undertook against the British and their Indians. Moreover, he acknowledged that Menéndez had "distinguished himself in the establishment, and cultivation of Mose, to improve that settlement, doing all he could so that the rest of his subjects, following his example, would apply themselves to work and learn good customs."[60]

Shortly thereafter, Menéndez petitioned for remuneration from his king for the "loyalty, zeal and love I have always demonstrated in the royal service, in the encounters with the enemies, as well as in the effort and care with which I have worked to repair two bastions on the defense line of this plaza, being pleased to do it, although it advanced my poverty, and I have been continually at arms, and assisted in the maintenance of the bastions, without the least royal expense, despite the scarcity in which this presidio always exists, especially in this occasion." He added, "my sole object was to defend the Holy Evangel and sovereignty of the Crown," and asked for the proprietorship of the free black militia and a salary to enable him to live decently (meaning in the style customary for an official of the militia). He concluded that he hoped to receive "all the consolation of the royal support . . . which Christianity requires and your vassals desire." Several months later, Menéndez filed a second, shorter petition.[61] It was customary for an illiterate person to sign official documents with an X, and for the notary or witnesses to write underneath, "for _____, who does not know how to write." Both these petitions, however, were written and signed in the same hand and with a flourish, so it would seem that at some point Menéndez learned how to write in Spanish—perhaps when he was the slave of the royal accountant whose name he took.[62] Despite his good services, appropriate behavior and rhetoric, there is no evidence of a response, and the noted royal parsimony made such payment unlikely.

Nevertheless, the runaways from Carolina had been successful in their most important appeal to Spanish justice—their quest for liberty. Over the many years, they persevered, and their leaders learned to use Spanish legal channels and social systems to advantage. They accurately assessed Spain's intensifying competition with England and exploited the political leverage it offered them. Once free, they understood and adapted to Spanish expectations of their new status. They vowed fealty and armed service, establishing themselves as vassals of the king and deserving of royal protection. Governor Montiano commended their bravery in battle and their industry as they worked to establish and cultivate Mose. They were clearly not the lazy vagabonds feared by Spanish administrators, and the adaptive behavior of Menéndez and his "subjects" gained them at least a limited autonomy.

Such autonomy is evident in both the black and Indian militias that operated on St. Augustine's frontiers. Their role in the defense of the Spanish colony has not yet been appreciated. They were cavalry units that served in frontier reconnaissance and as guerrilla fighters. They had their own officers and patrolled independently, although Spanish infantry officers also commanded mixed groups of Spanish, free blacks, and Indians on scouting missions.[63] The Florida garrison was never able to maintain a full contingent, and these militias constituted an important asset for the short-handed governors.[64] Because England and Spain were so often at war during his administration, Governor Montiano probably depended on the black troops more than did subsequent Florida governors.

When the Spaniards mounted a major retaliatory offensive against Georgia in 1742, Governor Montiano once again employed his Mose militia. Montiano's war plans called for sending English-speaking blacks of the Mose militia to range the countryside gathering and arming slave recruits, which suggests that he placed great trust in their loyalty and ability, as well, perhaps, as in their desire to punish their former masters.[65] Bad weather, mishaps, and confusion plagued the operation, and several hundred of the Spanish forces were killed at Bloody Marsh on Saint Simon's island. By August, the Spaniards had returned to St. Augustine. Oglethorpe mounted two more attacks on St. Augustine in 1742 and 1743, but neither did major damage. An uneasy stalemate developed, punctuated occasionally by Indian and corsair raids.[66]

Corsairing was practiced by both the British and the Spanish during the 1740s and 1750s, and St. Augustine became a convenient base of operations for privateers commissioned by Spain. The capture and sale of prizes provided badly needed species and supplies for war-torn Florida, which had not received government subsidies in 1739, 1740, 1741, and 1745 and which struggled under the additional burden of maintaining the large number of Cuban reinforcements that had arrived in 1740.[67] Corsairing ships were manned by volunteers, some of whom were drawn from the free black community, for, as Governor Garcia noted, "without those of 'broken' color, blacks, and Indians, which abound in our towns in America, I do not know if we could arm a single corsair solely with Spaniards."[68] Unfortunately, when these men were captured, the British presupposed them by their color to be slaves and sold them for profit.

When the British ship *Revenge* captured a Spanish prize in July 1741, found aboard was a black named "Signior Capitano Francisco," who was "Capt. of a Comp'y of Indians, Mollattos, and Negroes that was att the Retaking of the Fort [Mose] at St. Augus'ne formerly taken Under the Command of that worthless G _____ O _____ pe who by his treachery suffered so many brave fellows to be mangled by those barbarians." His captors tied Francisco Menéndez to a gun and ordered the ship's doctor to pretend to castrate him (as Englishmen at Mose had been castrated), but while Menéndez "frankly owned" that he was Captain of the company that retook Mose, he denied ordering any atrocities, which he said the Florida Indians had committed. Menéndez stated that he had taken the commission as privateer in hopes of getting to Havana, and from there to Spain, to collect a reward for his bravery. Several other mulattoes on board were also interrogated and substantiated Menéndez's account, as did several of the whites, but "to make Sure and to make him remember that he bore such a Commission," the British gave him 200 lashes and then "pickled him and left him to the Doctor to take Care of his Sore A-se." The following month, the *Revenge* landed at New Providence, in the Bahamas, and her commander, Benjamin Norton, who was due the largest share of the prize, vehemently argued before the Admiralty Court that the blacks should be condemned as slaves. "Does not their Complexion and features tell all the world that they are of the blood of Negroes and have suckt Slavery and Cruelty from their Infancy?" He went on to describe Menéndez as "this Francisco that Cursed Seed of Cain, Curst from the foundation of the world, who has the Impudence to Come into this Court and plead that he is free. Slavery is too Good for such a Savage, nay all the Cruelty invented by man . . . the torments of the World to Come will not suffice." No record of Francisco's testimony appears in this account, but the Court ordered him sold as a slave, "according to the Laws of the plantation."[69] However, as we have seen, Menéndez was a man of unusual abilities. Whether he successfully appealed for his freedom in British courts as he had in the Spanish, was ransomed back by the Spanish in Florida, or escaped is unknown, but, by at least 1752, he was once again in command at Mose. This incident illustrates the extreme racial hatred some British felt for Spain's black allies, as well as the grave dangers the freedmen faced in taking up Spanish arms. Other blacks captured as privateers in the same period were never returned.[70]

Although unsuccessful, Governor Oglethorpe's invasion in 1740 had wreaked havoc in Spanish Florida. Mose and the other outlying forts had been destroyed, along with many of the crops and animals on which the community subsisted. For the next twelve years, the townspeople of Mose lived among the Spanish in St. Augustine. This interlude was critical to the integration of the Carolina group into the larger and more diverse society in the city. Wage lists in treasury accounts and military reports from this period show that they performed a variety of valuable functions for the community. Free blacks labored on government projects, were sailors and privateers, tracked escaped prisoners, and helped forage food for the city. In the spring, they rounded up wild cattle for slaughter and wild horses for cavalry mounts.[71] They probably led lives much like those of free blacks in other Spanish colonial ports and may have engaged in craft production, artisanry, and the provision of services.[72] Although certain racial restrictions existed, they were rarely enforced in a small frontier settlement such as St. Augustine, where more relaxed personal relations were the norm. Everyone knew everyone else, and this familiarity could be a source of assistance and protection for the free blacks of Mose, who had acquired at least a measure of acceptability.[73]

Parish registers reflect the great ethnic and racial diversity in Spanish Florida in these years. Because there were always fewer female runaways, the males of that group were forced to look to the local possibilities for marriage partners—either Indian women from the two outlying villages of Nuestra Señora de la Leche and Nuestra Señora de Tholomato, or free and slave women from St. Augustine. Interracial relationships were common, and families were restructured frequently when death struck and widowed men and women remarried. The core group of Carolina fugitives formed intricate ties among themselves for at least two generations. They married from within their group and served as witnesses at each other's weddings and as godparents for each other's children, sometimes many times over. They also entered into the same relationships with Indians, free blacks, and slaves from other locations. Some of these slaves eventually became free, which might suggest mutual assistance efforts by the black community. The people of Mose also formed ties of reciprocal obligation with important members of both the white and black communities through the mechanism of ritual brotherhood *(compadrazgo)*. A few examples should serve to illustrate the complex nature of these frontier relationships.

Francisco Garzía and his wife, Ana, fled together from Carolina and were among the original group freed by Governor Montiano. Francisco was black, and Ana, Indian. As slaves in St. Augustine, they had belonged to the royal treasurer, Don Salvador Garzía. Garzía observed the church requirement to have his slaves baptized and properly married, for the couple's children are listed as legitimate. Francisco and Ana's daughter, Francisca Xaviera, was born and baptized in St. Augustine in 1736, before her parents were freed by the governor. Her godfather was a free mulatto, Francisco Rexidor. This man also served as godfather for Francisco and Ana's son, Calisto, born free two years later. Garzía died sometime before 1759, for in that year his widow, Ana, married a black slave named Diego. Calisto disappeared from the record and presumably died, while Francisca Xaviera married Francisco Díaz, a free black from Carolina. Their two children, Miguel Francisco and María, were born at Mose, and Francisco Díaz served in the Mose militia.[74]

Juan Jacinto Rodríguez and his wife, Ana María Menéndez, were also among the first Carolina homesteaders at Mose. Shortly after the town was founded, their son Juan married Cecilia, a Mandingo from Carolina who was the slave of Juan's former owner, cavalry Captain Don Pedro Lamberto Horruytiner. Cecilia's sister-in-law, María Francisca, had served as godmother at Cecilia's baptism two years earlier. María Francisca married Marcos de Torres, a free and legitimate black from Cartagena, Colombia, during the time the Mose homesteaders lived in St. Augustine. Marcos de Torres and María Francisca had three children born while they lived in town, and María Francisca's brother, Juan, and his wife, Cecilia, served as the children's godparents. After Marcos de Torres died, María Francisca and her three orphaned children lived with her parents at Mose. In 1760, the widowed María Francisca married the widower, Thomas Chrisostomo.[75]

Thomas and his first wife were Congo slaves. Thomas belonged to Don Francisco Chrisostomo, and his wife, Ana María Ronquillo, to Juan Nicolás Ronquillo. The couple married in St. Augustine in 1745. Pedro Graxales, a Congo slave and his legitimate wife, María de la Concepción Hita, a Caravalí slave, were the godparents at the wedding. By 1759, Thomas was a free widower living alone at Mose. The next year, he and María Francisca were wed. By that time, Thomas's godfather, Pedro Graxales, was also living at Mose as a free man, but Pedro's wife and at least four children remained slaves in St. Augustine.[76]

A simple bicultural encounter model will not suffice to explain the extent of cultural adaptation at Mose and the formation of this African-Hispanic community.[77] Many of its members were born on the western coast of Africa and then spent at least some time in a British slave society before risking their lives to escape. Some had intimate contact for several years with the Yamassee Indians and fought other non-Christian Indian groups before reaching Spanish Florida. At least thirty-one became slaves of the Spanish prior to achieving free status. Once free, they associated closely with the remnants of the seven different Indian nations aggregated into the two outlying Indian towns. From 1740 until 1752, the Mose group lived within the city of St. Augustine; after that time, they were forcibly removed to a rebuilt settlement. Meanwhile, new infusions of Africans continued to be incorporated into the original Mose community through ties with godparents. Many historians now agree that, although the ex-slaves did not share a single culture, their common values and experiences in the Americas enabled them to form strong communities, as they did in Spanish Florida. Ira Berlin, Steven F. Miller, and Leslie S. Rowland have argued that British slaves understood their society "in the idiom of kinship" and that, for slaves, "familial and communal relations were one."[78] The Spaniards also viewed society as an extension of family structures. The institution of the extended kinship group *(parentela),* which included blood relations, fictive kin, and sometimes even household servants and slaves, and the institution of *clientela,* which bound powerful patrons and their personal dependents into a network of mutual obligations, were so deeply rooted in Spain that, according to one scholar, they might have been the "primary structure of Hispanic society." Thus African and Spanish views of family and society were highly compatible, and each group surely recognized the value that the other placed on kinship.[79]

Despite the relationships that developed between people of St. Augustine and the Mose settlers, there were objections to their presence in the Spanish city. Some complaints may have stemmed from racial prejudice or ethnocentrism. To some of the poorer Spanish, the free blacks represented competition in a ravaged economy. Indians allied to the British remained hostile to the Spaniards and raided the countryside with regularity. Plantations were neither safe nor productive. Havana could not provide its dependency with sufficient goods, and the few food shipments that reached St. Augustine were usually ruined. British goods were cheaper and better, and the governor was forced to depend on enemy suppliers for his needs. War and corsair raids on supplies shipped from Havana further strained the colony's ability to sustain its urban population. As new runaways continued to arrive, they only exacerbated the problem.[80] Finally, Melchor de Navarrete, who succeeded Montiano in 1749, decided to reestablish Mose. He reported his achievements in converting the newcomers, remarking that he withheld certificates of freedom until the supplicants had a satisfactory knowledge of doctrine. Navarrete also claimed to have resettled all the free blacks from Carolina at Mose.[81]

Governor Fulgencio García de Solís, who served from 1752 to 1755, refuted his predecessor's claims, stating that persistent illnesses among the blacks had prevented their relocation. When García attempted to remove the freedmen and women to Mose, he faced stubborn resistance. The governor complained that it was not fear of further Indian attacks but the "desire to live in complete liberty" that motivated the rebels. He "lightly" punished the two unnamed leaders of the resistance and threatened worse to those who continued to fight the resettlement. He fortified the town to allay their fears and finally effected the resettlement. In a familiar litany, he alluded to "bad customs," "spiritual backwardness," and "pernicious consequences" and condemned not only the original Mose settlers but also "those who have since fled the English colonies to join them." He was determined that they would have "no pretext which could excuse them" from living at Mose and sought to isolate them from "any dealings or communication with . . . the town within the walls."[82] The Spanish association of urbanization with the advance of civilization traditionally had as its corollary the idea that those living outside a city's boundaries were lacking in cultural and spiritual attainments. In his official papers, García evidenced a much lower opinion of the free blacks than had Governor Montiano, and by removing them "beyond the walls" he made a visible statement about their supposed inferiority.

García was no doubt angered by the rebellion he faced, and he was probably correct in contending that it actually arose from the free black desire to live in "complete liberty." The crown had many times reiterated its commitment to their freedom, and, after living in St. Augustine for thirteen years and repeatedly risking their lives in its defense, the free blacks surely recognized the eviction for the insult it represented. Possibly, after García's interim term ended, there was greater interaction between the peoples of St. Augustine and its satellite, as later governors did not display his antipathy toward the free blacks.[83] Governor García may also have been disturbed by the presence and influence of unacculturated Africans *(bozales)* among the latecomers. The "bad customs" that he alleged had so troubled his predecessors and himself might have been African cultural retentions. In 1744, Father Francisco Xavier Arturo baptized Domingo, a Caravalí slave, in extremis, with the comment that his "crudeness" prevented his understanding Christian doctrine.[84] Four years later, Miguel Domingo, a Congo slave, received a conditional baptism, because he told the priest that he had been baptized in his homeland, and continued to pray in his native language.[85]

Peter Wood's analysis of slave imports into South Carolina during the late 1730s determined that 70 percent of those arriving during this brief period came from the Congo-Angola region.[86] St. Augustine's church registers suggest a similar preponderance there but within a broader context of considerable ethnic diversity. The Spanish often recorded the nation of origin for the Africans among them, and, although these designations are troublesome and must be used with caution, they offer at least a general approximation of the origins of those recorded. One hundred and forty-seven black marriages were reported from 1735 to 1763, and fifty-two of those married were designated as Congos—twenty-six males and twenty-six females. The next largest group was the Caravalís, including nine males and nineteen females. The Mandingos constituted the third largest group and had nine males and four females. Also represented in the marriage registers were the Minas, Gambas, Lecumis, Sambas, Gangas, Araras, and Guineans.[87]

Governor García was required by royal policy to grant sanctuary to slave refugees, but he was not required to accommodate them in St. Augustine, and he did not. The chastened freedmen built new structures at Mose, including a church and a house for the Franciscan priest within the enclosed fort, as well as twenty-two shelters outside the fort for their own households. A diagram of the new fort, which had one side open on Mose Creek, shows the interior buildings described by Father Juan Joseph de Solana but not the houses of the villagers.[88] The only known census of Mose, from 1759, recorded twenty-two households with a population of sixty-seven individuals. Mose had almost twice as many male as female occupants, and almost a quarter of its population consisted of children under the age of fifteen. Thirteen of the twenty-two households belonged to nuclear or nuclear extended families, and fifty villagers, or 75 percent of the total population, lived with immediate members of their families. There were no female-headed households at this outpost, and nine households were composed solely of males. At the time of the census, four men lived alone, Francisco Roso, Antonio Caravallo, Thomas Chrisostomo, and Antonio Blanco, but at least two of those men, Roso and Chrisostomo, had family members among the slaves in St. Augustine. A third all-male household consisted of a father, Francisco de Torres, and his son, Juan de Arranzate. Francisco's wife and Juan's mother, Ana María, was a slave in St. Augustine. Pedro Graxales was also separated from his slave wife and their children but had a younger man, Manuel Rivera, attached to his household. Three other all-male households included a total of eleven men living together, at least three of whom had slave wives in St. Augustine.[89] Although spouses lived separately, parish registers record that children continued to be born of these unions and attest that family ties were maintained. Father Solana reported that some members of the Mose community were permitted to live in St. Augustine even though they continued to serve in the Mose militia. Several of those men appear on 1763 evacuation lists for Mose.[90]

The people of Mose were remarkably adaptable. They spoke several European and Indian languages, in addition to their own, and were exposed to a variety of subsistence techniques, craft and artistic traditions, labor patterns, and food ways. We know that the freedmen and women of Mose adopted certain elements of Spanish culture. For example, since their sanctuary was based on religious conversion, it was incumbent on them to exhibit their Catholicism. Their baptisms, marriages, and deaths were faithfully recorded in parish registers. But studies of other Hispanic colonies show that religious syncretism was widespread and tolerated by the church. Following centuries-old patterns set in Spain, Cuba's blacks organized religious brotherhoods by nations. They celebrated Catholic feast days dressed in traditional African costumes and with African music and instruments.[91] Because St. Augustine had such intimate contact with Cuba and blacks circulated between the two locations, it would not be surprising to find that Africans in Florida also observed some of their former religious practices.

Kathleen Deagan, of the Florida Museum of Natural History, currently directs an interdisciplinary team investigating Mose. In addition to locating and excavating the site, this group is exploring the process of cultural adaptation at Mose to determine what mixture of customs and material culture its residents adopted and what in their own traditions might have influenced Spanish culture.[92] One suggestive find is a handmade pewter medal that depicts St. Christopher on one side and a pattern resembling a Kongo star on the other.[93] Other recovered artifacts include military objects such as gunflints, a striker, and musket balls; and domestic articles such as metal buckles, a thimble, and pins, clay pipe bowls—of both local and European design—metal buttons, bone buttons—including one still in the process of manufacture—amber beads (perhaps from a rosary); and a variety of glass bottles and ceramic wares. Many of the latter are of English types, verifying documentary evidence of illicit, but necessary, trade with the enemy.

Preliminary analysis of faunal materials from the site indicates that the diet at Mose approximated that of indigenous villages and supports documentary evidence that the Indian and black villages resembled each other in many respects. Mose's villagers incorporated many estuarine resources and wild foods into their diet. The fish were net-caught, perhaps using African techniques. The people at Mose also caught and consumed deer, raccoon, opossum, and turtle to supplement the corn and beef occasionally provided them from government stores.[94]

Although noted for its poverty and the misery of its people, Mose survived as a free town and military outpost for St. Augustine until 1763, when, through the fortunes of war, Spain lost the province to the British. The Spanish evacuated St. Augustine and its dependent black and Indian towns, and the occupants were resettled in Cuba. The people of Mose left behind their meager homes and belongings and followed their hosts into exile to become homesteaders in Matanzas, Cuba—consigned once more to a rough frontier. The crown granted them new lands, a few tools, and a minimal subsidy, as well as an African slave to each of the leaders of the community; however, Spanish support was never sufficient, and the people from Mose suffered terrible privations at Matanzas. Some of them, including Francisco Menéndez, eventually relocated in Havana, which offered at least the possibility of a better life, and this last diaspora scattered the black community of Mose.[95]

Located on the periphery of St. Augustine, between the Spanish settlement and its aggressive neighbors, Mose's interstitial location paralleled the social position of its inhabitants—people who straddled cultures, pursued their own advantage, and in the process helped shape the colonial history of the Caribbean as well as an African-American culture. In 1784, Spain recovered Florida, and many Floridanos, or first-period colonists, returned from Cuba. It is possible that among these were some of the residents of Mose. During its second regime, however, the weakened Spanish government made no effort to reestablish either Indian missions or the free black town of Mose. Free blacks took pivotal roles on interethnic frontiers of Spanish America such as Florida, serving as interpreters, craftsmen, traders, scouts, cowboys, pilots, and militiamen. The towns they established made important contributions to Spanish settlement. They populated areas the Spaniards found too difficult or unpleasant, thereby extending or maintaining Spanish dominion. They buffered Spanish towns from the attacks of their enemies and provided them with effective military reserves.

Although there were other towns like Mose in Latin America, it was the only example of a free black town in the colonial South. It provides an important, and heretofore unstudied, variant in the experience of African-born peoples in what was to become the United States. Mose's inhabitants were able to parlay their initiative, determination, and military and economic skills into free status, an autonomy at least equivalent to that of Spain's Indian allies in Florida, and a town of their own. These gains were partially offset by the constant danger and deprivation to which the townspeople of Mose were subjected, but they remained in Mose, perhaps believing it their best possible option. Despite the adversities of slavery, flight, wars, and repeated displacements, the freedmen and women of Mose managed to maintain intricate family relationships over time and shape a viable community under extremely difficult conditions. They became an example and possibly a source of assistance to unfree blacks from neighboring British colonies, as well as those within Spanish Florida. The Spanish subsequently extended the religious sanctuary policy confirmed at Mose to other areas of the Caribbean and applied it to the disadvantage of Dutch and French slaveholders, as well as the British.[96] The lives and efforts of the people of Mose thus took on international significance. Moreover, their accomplishments outlived them. The second Spanish government recognized religious sanctuary from 1784 until it bowed to the pressures of the new U.S. government and its persuasive secretary of state, Thomas Jefferson, and abrogated the policy in 1790. Before that escape hatch closed, several hundred slaves belonging to British Loyalists followed the example of the people of Mose to achieve emancipation in Florida.[97] Thus the determined fugitives who struggled so hard to win their own freedom inadvertently furthered the cause of freedom for others whom they never knew.

Notes

This research was funded by the Spain/Florida Alliance, the Florida Legislature, the Program for Cultural Cooperation between Spain's Ministry of Culture and United States' Universities, and the Department of History of the University of Florida. An earlier version of this article was awarded the President's Prize by the Florida Historical Society. Dr. Kathleen Deagan was the principal investigator for the Ft. Mose archaeological project of the Florida Museum of Natural History, and Mr. Jack Williams permitted her team to excavate on his property. I would like to thank Jim Amelang, Bertram Wyatt-Brown, Cheryll Cody, David Colburn, Susan Kent, Helen Nader, J. TePaske, Eldon Turner, and Peter Wood for their comments, criticisms, and encouragement. I am also indebted to my anonymous readers and the *AHR* staff for their suggestions and editing.

1. An early classic that examined the triracial Southern frontier was Verner W. Crane, *The Southern Frontier, 1670–1732* (New York, 1981), but, as Peter Wood noted in his historiographic review, "'I Did the Best I Could for My Day': The Study of Early Black History during the Second Reconstruction, 1960–1976," *William and Mary Quarterly,* 3d ser., 35 (1978): 185–225, few scholars followed Crane's lead. The difficulty of the sources deterred some from crossing the cultural and linguistic frontier into Florida, but Latin Americanists have also neglected what were the northern boundaries of the Spanish empire. The "Borderlands" school pioneered by Herbert Bolton produced a number of important studies, but these focused primarily on the southwestern areas of the present-day United States. See Herbert E. Bolton, *The Spanish Borderlands, A Chronicle of Old Florida and the Southwest* (Toronto, 1921); and Herbert E. Bolton and Mary Ross, *The Debatable Land* (Berkeley, Calif., 1925). For a review of these borderland studies, see David Weber, "John Francis Bannon and the Historiography of the Spanish Borderlands," *Journal of the Southwest,* 29 (Winter 1987): 331–63.

2. Scholars who have attempted to explore the African experience in northern America through Spanish sources include John TePaske, "The Fugitive Slave: Intercolonial Rivalry and Spanish Slave Policy, 1687–1764," in Samuel Proctor, ed., *Eighteenth-Century Florida and Its Borderlands* (Gainesville, Fla., 1975), 1–12; Jack D. L. Holmes, "The Role of Blacks in Spanish Alabama: The Mobile District, 1780–1813," *Alabama Historical Quarterly,* 37 (Spring 1975): 5–18; Gilbert Din, "Cimarrones and the San Malo Band in Spanish Louisiana," *Louisiana History,* 21 (Summer 1980): 237–62; Jack D. Forbes, "Black Pioneers: The Spanish-Speaking Afroamericans of the Southwest," *Phylon,* 27 (1966): 233–46; Peter Stern, "Social Marginality and Acculturation on the Northern Frontier of New Spain" (Ph.D. dissertation, University of California, Berkeley, 1984); and Kimberly Hanger, "Free Blacks in Spanish New Orleans—The Transitional Decade, 1769–1779" (Masters thesis, University of Utah, 1985). Gwendolyn Midlo Hall has a detailed study of Africans in colonial Louisiana forthcoming that is drawn from Spanish as well as French sources.

3. Theodore G. Corbett, "Migration to a Spanish Imperial Frontier in the Seventeenth and Eighteenth Centuries: St. Augustine," *Hispanic American Historical Review,* 54 (August 1974): 419–20. Corbett noted that St. Augustine, the largest of the borderland settlements, also had the most blacks, slave and free, in the Spanish borderlands. As late as 1763, St. Augustine was larger than any other town in the southern colonies except Charleston. See Theodore G. Corbett, "Population Structure in Hispanic St. Augustine, 1629–1763," *Florida Historical Quarterly,* 54 (July 1975-April 1976): 268.

4. Peter Wood, *Black Majority; Negroes in Colonial South Carolina from 1670 through the Stono Rebellion* (New York, 1974), 239–68; Philip D. Morgan, "Colonial South Carolina

Runaways: Their Significance for Slave Culture," in *Slavery and Abolition,* 6 (December 1985): 57–78; Darrett Rutman and Anita Rutman, *A Place in Time: Middlesex County, Virginia, 1650–1750* (New York, 1984), 180–87.

5. The role of Africans as cultural agents is discussed in Wood, *Black Majority,* 35–63, 95–130. Also see Daniel Littlefield, *Rice and Slaves, Ethnicity and the Slave Trade in Colonial South Carolina* (Baton Rouge, La., 1981), 98–99. Wood also pointed out that "in literally every conflict in eighteenth-century South Carolina there were Negroes engaged on both sides"; Wood, *Black Majority,* 128–29.

6. Frank Tannenbaum, *Slave and Citizen* (New York, 1946). Tannenbaum's early view that institutional protections benefited slaves in Hispanic areas was challenged by scholars who found economic determinants of slave treatment more significant. See Eugene Genovese, "The Treatment of Slaves in Different Countries: Problems in the Application of the Comparative Method," in Laura Foner and Eugene Genovese, eds., *Slavery in the New World* (Englewood Cliffs, N.J., 1969), 202–10; Marvin Harris, *Patterns of Race in the Americas* (New York, 1964). Historians who have reviewed Spanish racial prejudice and discriminatory regulations include Lyle McAlister, "Social Structure and Social Change in New Spain," *Hispanic American Historical Review,* 43 (April 1963): 349–70; Magnus Mörner, *Race Mixture in the History of the Americas* (Boston, 1967); and Leslie B. Rout, Jr., *The African Experience in Spanish America, 1502 to the Present* (Cambridge, 1976). On the varieties of slave experiences, see Sidney M. Mintz and Richard Price, *An Anthropological Approach to the Afro-American Past: A Caribbean Perspective* (Philadelphia, 1976). On resistance in Latin America, see Richard Price, ed., *Maroon Societies, Rebel Slave Communities in the Americas* (Garden City, N.Y., 1973). On the formation of Creole cultures, see Charles Joyner, *Down by the Riverside, A South Carolina Slave Community* (Urbana, Ill., 1984). On black families, see Ira Berlin, "Time, Space and the Evolution of Afro-American Society on British Mainland North America," *AHR,* 85 (June 1980): 44–78. On black religion and African cultural retentions in the "New World," see Robert Farris Thompson, *Flash of the Spirit: African and Afro-American Art and Philosophy* (New York, 1984); and Margaret Washington Creel, *"A Peculiar People": Slave Religion and Community-Culture among the Gullahs* (New York, 1988). For an interesting comparison of African and British world views and attitudes, see Mechal Sobel, *The World They Made Together: Black and White Values in Eighteenth-Century Virginia* (Princeton, N.J., 1987).

7. Irene Wright, "Dispatches of Spanish Officials Bearing on the Free Negro Settlement of Gracia Real de Santa Teresa de Mose," *Journal of Negro History,* 9 (1924): 144–93; TePaske, "Fugitive Slaves"; Luis Arana, "The Mose Site," *El Escribano,* 10 (April 1973): 50–62; Kenneth Wiggins Porter, *The Negro on the American Frontier* (New York, 1971); Jane Landers, "Spanish Sanctuary; Fugitive Slaves in Florida, 1687–1790," *Florida Historical Quarterly,* 62 (September 1984): 296–313; Larry W. Kruger and Robert Hall, "Fort Mose: A Black Fort in Spanish Florida," *The Griot,* 6 (Spring 1987): 39–48.

8. Lyle N. McAlister, *Spain and Portugal in the New World, 1492–1700* (Minneapolis, Minn., 1984), 133–52.

9. On corporate privileges of the Spanish militias, see Lyle N. McAlister, *The "Fuero Militar" in New Spain, 1764–1800* (Gainesville, Fla., 1957); Herbert S. Klein, "The Colored Militia of Cuba: 1568–1868," *Caribbean Studies,* 6 (July 1966): 17–27; Allan J. Kuethe, "The Status of the Free Pardo in the Disciplined Militia of New Granada," *Journal of Negro History,* 56 (April 1971): 105–15; Roland C. McConnell, *Negro Troops of Antebellum Louisiana—A History of the Battalion of Free Men of Color* (Baton Rouge, La., 1968).

10. On the function and meaning of godparents, see George M. Foster, "Cofradia and Compadrazgo in Spain and Spanish America," *Southwestern Journal of Anthropology,* 9

(1953): 1–28; Sidney W. Mintz and Eric Wolf, "An Analysis of Ritual Co-Parenthood (Compadrazgo)," *Southwestern Journal of Anthropology,* 6 (1950): 341–67.

11. Tannenbaum, *Slave and Citizen.*

12. Genovese, "Treatment of Slaves"; Mörner, *Race Mixture;* Rout, *African Experience.* For a study of the law in practice, see Norman A. Meiklejohn, "The Observance of Negro Slave Legislation in Colonial Nueva Granada" (Masters thesis, Columbia University, 1968).

13. Hanger, "Free Blacks"; David W. Cohen and Jack P. Greene, eds., *Neither Slave nor Free, The Freedmen of African Descent in the Slave Societies of the New World* (Baltimore, Md., 1972); Landers, "Spanish Sanctuary"; Ira Berlin, *Slaves without Masters—The Free Negro in the Antebellum South* (New York, 1974), 108–32; Lyman L. Johnson, "Manumission in Colonial Buenos Aires," *Hispanic American Historical Review,* 59 (1979): 258–79; Frederick Bowser, "Free Persons of Color in Lima and Mexico City: Manumission and Opportunity, 1580–1650," in Stanley Engerman and Eugene D. Genovese, eds., *Slavery in the Western Hemisphere: Quantitative Studies* (Princeton, N.J., 1974), 331–68.

14. Richard Morse elegantly analyzed the concept of the *ciudad perfecta* and Spanish efforts to reproduce it in the New World in his chapter, "A Framework for Latin American Urban History" in Jorge Hardoy, ed., *Urbanization in Latin America: Approaches and Issues* (Garden City, N.Y., 1975), 57–107.

15. Richard Konetzke, "Estado y sociedad en las Indias," *Estudios Americanos,* 3 (1951): 33–58; Rolando Mellafe, *Negro Slavery in Latin America* (Berkeley, Calif., 1975), 109–17.

16. Meiklejohn, "Observance of Negro Slave Legislation," 103–14, 295–306; Carlos Federico Guillot, *Negros rebeldes y negro cimarrones: Perfil afroamericano en la historia del Nuevo Mundo durante el siglo XVI* (Buenos Aires, 1961); Miguel Acosta Saignes, *Vida de los esclavos negros en Venezuela* (Caracas, 1967), 249–84; R. K. Kent, "Palmares: An African State in Brazil," *Journal of African History,* 6 (1965): 161–75; Carlos Larrazábal Blanco, *Los negros y la esclavitud en Santo Domingo* (Santo Domingo, 1967).

17. Leon Campbell used this term in his article, "The Changing Racial and Administrative Structure of the Peruvian Military under the Later Bourbons," *The Americas,* 32 (July 1975): 117–33.

18. Colin Palmer, *Slaves of the White God-Blacks in Mexico, 1570–1650* (Cambridge, 1976); William Taylor, "The Foundation of Nuestra Señora de Guadalupe de los Morenos de Amapa," *The Americas,* 26 (April 1970): 442–46.

19. Richard Konetzke, *Colección de documentos para la historia de la formación social de Hispano-América, 1493–1810,* 3 vols. (Madrid, 1953–58), 2: 118–20.

20. For a later example of a buffer town, see John Hoyt Williams, "Trevegó on the Paraguayan Frontier: A Chapter in the Black History of the Americas," *Journal of Negro History,* 56 (October 1971): 272–83; and Germán de Granda, "Origen, función y estructura de un pueblo de negros y mulatos libres en el Paraguay del siglo XVIII (San Agustin de la Emboscada)," *Revista de Indias,* 43 (enero-junio 1983): 229–64.

21. Klein, "Colored Militia"; Kuethe, "Status of the Free Pardo."

22. Roster of Black and Mulatto Militia for St. Augustine, September 20, 1683, Santo Domingo (hereafter cited as SD), 266, Archivo General de Indias: Seville (hereafter cited as AGI).

23. Crane, *Southern Frontier,* 3–17; John Jay TePaske, *The Governorship of Spanish Florida, 1700–1763* (Durham, N.C., 1964), 3–6; Verne E. Chatelain, *The Defenses of Spanish Florida, 1565–1763* (Washington, D.C., 1941).

24. Letter from Mr. Randolph to the Board, June 28, 1699, in A.S. Salley, *Records of the British Public Records Office Relating to South Carolina, 1698–1700* (Columbia, S.C., 1946), 4: 89; Crane, *Southern Frontier,* 31–33.

25. "William Dunlop's Mission to St. Augustine in 1688," *South Carolina Historical and Genealogical Magazine,* 34 (January 1933): 1–30; Diego de Quiroga to the king. February 2, 1688, cited in Wright, "Dispatches," 150. Morton's stolen male slaves included Peter, Scipio, Doctor (whose name suggests a specialized function or skill), Cushi, Arro, Emo, Caesar, and Sambo. The women included Frank, Bess, and Mammy. Sambo was the Hausa name for a second son, while in Mende or Vai it meant "disgrace." Cushi may have been "Quashee," the Twi day-name for Sunday, which also came to signify "foolish" or "stupid." For a discussion of slave naming, see Wood, *Black Majority,* 181–86, among others. The men who stole the canoe were named Conano, Jesse, Jacque, Gran Domingo (Big Sunday), Cambo, Mingo, Dicque, and Robi. Wood suggests that forms of the name Jack derived from the African day-name for Wednesday, Quaco. Names of the two women and the little girl were not given. The owners of the fugitives who escaped in the canoe were: Samuel de Bordieu, Mingo, his wife and daughter; John Bird, two men; Joab Howe, one man; John Berresford, one woman; Christopher Smith, one man; Robert Cuthbert, three men. "William Dunlop's Mission," 4, 26, 28.

26. "William Dunlops' Mission," 25.

27. Royal officials to the king, March 3, 1689, cited in Wright, "Dispatches," 151–52.

28. Royal edict, November 7, 1693, SD 58–1–26 in the John B. Stetson Collection (hereafter cited as ST), P. K. Yonge Library of Florida History, University of Florida, Gainesville (hereafter cited as PKY). Also see "William Dunlop's Mission," 1–30.

29. The various petitions of Carolina fugitives gathered together by Governor Manuel de Montiano are found in SD 844, fols. 521–46, microfilm reel 15, PKY. They mention groups arriving in 1688, 1689, 1690, 1697, 1724, and 1725. Governor Joseph de Zuñiga reported that his predecessor, Governor Laureano de Torres y Ayala, on August 8, 1697, returned six blacks and an Indian who had escaped from Charlestown that year, "to avoid conflicts and ruptures between the two governments." Joseph de Zuñiga to the king, October 10, 1699, SD 844, microfilm reel 15, fol. 542, PKY.

30. Wood, *Black Majority,* 304–05. For a new overview of the broader demographic context, see Peter H. Wood, "The Changing Population of the Colonial South: An Overview by Race and Region, 1685–1790," in Peter H. Wood, Gregory A. Waselkov, and M. Thomas Hatley, eds., *Powhatan's Mantle: Indians in the Colonial Southeast* (Lincoln, Neb., 1989), 35–103.

31. Memorial of the Fugitives, 1724, SD 844, fol. 530, microfilm reel 15, PKY.

32. Governor Antonio de Benavides to the king, November 11, 1725, cited in Wright, "Dispatches," 164–66. The noted citizens who acquired the slaves filed various memorials to record their concerns about British threats to come take the slaves and the fact that British forces outnumbered Spanish. Memorial, August 26, 1729, SD 844, fols. 550–62. Governor Benavides then authorized their auction and gave the proceeds to a British envoy, Arthur Hauk. Accord, June 27, 1730, SD 844, fols. 564–66, microfilm reel 15, PKY.

33. Consulta by the Council of the Indies, April 12, 1731, cited in Wright, "Dispatches," 166–72.

34. Petition of Francisco Menéndez, November 21, 1740, SD 2658, AGI. On the role of the black militia in 1728, see TePaske, *Fugitive Slave,* 7.

35. Governor Arthur Middleton, June 6, 1728, British Public Record Office Transcripts, 13:61–67, cited in Wood, *Black Majority,* 305.

36. Royal edict, October 4, 1733, SD 58–1–24, ST; Royal edict, October 29, 1733, SD 58–1–24, ST.

37. Memorial of the Fugitives, SD 844, fols. 533–34, included in Manuel de Montiano to the king, March 3, 1738, SD 844, microfilm reel 15, PKY.

38. Memorial of Chief Jorge, SD 844, fols. 536–37, *ibid.* Jorge claimed to be the chief who had led the Yamassee uprising against the British. Jorge stated that he and the rest of the

Yamassee chiefs commonly made treaties with the slaves, and that he now wanted to help Menéndez and the three others who fought along with him become free. Mad Dog sold them into slavery for some casks of honey, corn, and liquor (*aguardiente*).

39. Decree of Manuel de Montiano, March 3, 1738, SD 844, fols. 566–75, microfilm reel 15, PKY. The eight slaves who were sold to Havana included "Antonio, an English slave from San Jorge [the Spanish name for Charlestown], another of the same name, Clemente, Andres, Bartholome Chino [the term for a mixed-blood], Juan Francisco Borne, Juan (English), Jose, who's other name is Mandingo, all of whom are from San Jorge."

40. Montiano to the king, February 16, 1739, SD 844, microfilm reel 15, PKY. The name is a composite of an existing Indian place name, Mose, the phrase that indicated that the new town was established by the king, Gracia Real, and the name of the town's patron saint, Teresa of Avilés, who was the patron saint of Spain.

41. *St. Augustine Expedition of 1740: A Report to the South Carolina General Assembly Reprinted from the Colonial Records of South Carolina with an introduction by John Tate Lanning* (Columbia, S.C., 1954), 25.

42. Report of Antonio de Benavides, SD 58–2–16/45, bundle 5725, ST.

43. Purchases and Payments for 1739, Cuba 446, AGI.

44. Manuel de Montiano to the king, February 16, 1739, SD 845, fol. 700, SD 845, microfilm reel 16, PKY. Fugitive Negroes of the English plantations to the king, June 10, 1738, SD 844, microfilm reel 15, PKY.

45. Council of the Indies, October 2, 1739, cited in Wright, "Dispatches," 178–80; Council of the Indies, September 28, 1740, SD 845, fol. 708, microfilm reel 16, PKY.

46. Manuel de Montiano to the king, February 16, 1739, SD 845, fol. 701, microfilm reel 16, PKY.

47. Manuel de Montiano to the king, September 16, 1740, SD 2658, AGI. Montiano's successor also stated that the townspeople of Mose were "under the dominion of their Captain and Lieutenant." Melchor de Navarrete to the Marqués de Ensenada, April 2, 1752, cited in Wright, "Dispatches," 185.

48. Evacuation report of Juan Joseph Eligio de la Puente, January 22, 1764, SD 2595, AGI; Price, *Maroon Societies,* 29–30.

49. Manuel de Montiano to the king, February 16, 1739, SD 845, fol. 700, microfilm reel 16, PKY; "Journal of William Stephens," cited in Wood, *Black Majority,* 307.

50. Claim of Captain Caleb Davis, September 17, 1751, SD 2584, AGI.

51. Manuel de Montiano to the king, March 13, 1739, Manuscript 19508, Biblioteca Nacional, Madrid.

52. Letter of Manuel de Montiano, August 19, 1739, "Letters of Montiano, Siege of St. Augustine," *Collections of the Georgia Historical Society* (Savannah, Ga., 1909), 7: 32.

53. "The Stono Rebellion and Its Consequences," in Wood, *Black Majority,* 308–26.

54. TePaske, *Governorship,* 140.

55. On January 8, 1740, Montiano sent Don Pedro Lamberto Horruytiner "with 25 horsemen from his company, 25 infantry and 30 Indians and free Negroes (of those who are fugitives from the English Colonies) to scout the country." Manuel de Montiano to the king, January 31, 1740, SD 2658, AGI. On January 27, 1740, Montiano sent Don Romualdo Ruiz del Moral out on a similar mission accompanied by "25 horsemen, 25 Indians, and 25 free Negroes." Montiano wrote, "The difficulty of getting information in our numerous thickets, lagoons and swamps, is so great as to make the thing almost impossible." Manuel de Montiano to the king, January 31, 1740, "Letters of Montiano," 7:36.

56. *St. Augustine Expedition,* 23. One was the escaped slave of Mrs. Parker, and the other claimed to have been carried away from Colonel Gibbs by the Indians.

57. Manuel de Montiano to the king, January 17, 1740, SD 2658, AGI. For Montiano's account of Oglethorpe's siege and the victory at Mose, see Manuel de Montiano to the king, August 9, 1740, SD 845, fols. 11–26, microfilm reel 16, PKY; and "Letters of Montiano," 7: 54–62.

58. Mills Lane, ed. *General Oglethorpe's Georgia: Colonial Letters, 1738–1743,* II (Savannah), 447. For more accounts of atrocities, see *St. Augustine Expedition of 1740,* 47; TePaske, *Governorship of Spanish Florida,* 143; Larry E. Ivers, *British Drums on the Southern Frontier, The Military Colonization of Georgia 1733–1749* (Chapel Hill, N.C., 1974). This account is written from British sources and therefore is inaccurate on many aspects of the Spanish history. Ivers seriously undercounts St. Augustine's population, glamorizes Oglethorpe's role, and fails to recognize the role of blacks at Mose and throughout the Anglo-Spanish conflict.

59. TePaske, *Governorship of Spanish Florida,* 144.

60. Manuel de Montiano to the king, January 31, 1740, SD 2658, AGI.

61. Memorial of Francisco Menéndez, November 21, 1740, SD 2658, AGI. Memorial of Francisco Menéndez, December 12, 1740, *ibid.*

62. The proprietary royal accountant for St. Augustine was Don Francisco Menéndez Márquez. The Menéndez Márquez family is the subject of several works by Amy Turner Bushnell. See "The Menéndez Márquez Cattle Barony at La Chua and the Determinants of Economic Expansion in Seventeenth-Century Florida," *Florida Historical Quarterly,* 56 (April 1978): 407–31; and *The King's Coffers, Proprietors of the Spanish Florida Treasury, 1565–1702* (Gainesville, Fla., 1981).

63. Manuel de Montiano to the king, January 22, 1740, "Letters of Montiano," 7: 32–42. Indian militias continued to serve Florida's governors, and in 1759 Cacique Bernardo Lachiche commanded a unit of twenty-eight men, by election of the other caciques. Report of Don Lucas de Palacio on the Spanish, Indian and Free Black Militias, April 30, 1759, SD 2604, AGI.

64. Although St. Augustine was allotted a troop complement of 350 men, Montiano had only 240 men fit for service in St. Augustine when the siege of 1740 ended. Manuel de Montiano to the king, August 9, 1740, SD 846, fol. 25 V, microfilm reel 16, PKY.

65. Manuel de Montiano to the captain general of Cuba, Don Juan Francisco de Güemes y Horcasitas, March 13, 1742, SD 2593, AGI; TePaske, *Governorship of Spanish Florida,* 146–52.

66. TePaske, *Governorship of Spanish Florida,* 152–55.

67. TePaske, *Governorship of Spanish Florida,* 100–05.

68. Fulgencio García de Solis to the king, August 25, 1752, SD 845, fols. 81–112, microfilm reel 17, PKY.

69. "Account of the Revenge," in John Franklin Jameson, ed., *Privateering and Piracy in the Colonial Period: Illustrative Documents* (New York, 1923), 402–11. My thanks to Charles Tingley for providing this source.

70. Report of Captain Fernando Laguna, October 7, 1752, SD 846, fols. 84–108, microfilm reel 17, PKY.

71. Michael C. Scardaville and Jesus Maria Belmonte, "Florida in the Late First Spanish Period: The Griñán Report," *El Escribano,* 16 (1979): 10.

72. Works that provide information on the life and labor of blacks in colonial Spanish America include: Jorge Juan and Antonio de Ulloa, "Eighteenth-Century Spanish American Towns—African and Afro-Hispanic Life and Labor in Cities and Suburbs," in Anne Pescatello, ed., *The African in Latin America* (New York, 1975): 106–11: Greene and Cohen, *Neither Slave nor Free;* and Louisa Schell Hoberman and Susan Migden Socolow, eds., *Cities and Society in Colonial America* (Albuquerque, N. Mex., 1986).

73. Michael P. Johnson and James L. Roark's work, *Black Masters: A Free Family of Color in the Old South* (New York, 1984), demonstrates how personalism might mediate race relations

even in a more rigid caste society, but free blacks always had to balance carefully their legal rights against the social limits accepted in their community. For other examples of upwardly mobile slaves from Spanish Florida, see Jane Landers, "Black Society in Spanish St. Augustine, 1784–1821" (Ph.D. dissertation, University of Florida, Gainesville, 1988).

74. In 1738, Francisco and Ana were the slaves of Don Salvador Garzía, SD 844, fols. 593–94, microfilm reel 15, PKY. Baptism of Francisca Xaviera, August 30, 1736, and baptism of Calisto, October 23, 1738, Black Baptisms, Cathedral Parish Records. Diocese of St. Augustine Catholic Center, Jacksonville (hereafter cited as CPR), microfilm reel 284 F, PKY. Marriage of the widowed Ana García Pedroso to Diego, the slave of Don Juan Joseph Eligio de la Puente, January 14, 1759, Black Marriages, CPR, microfilm reel 284 C, PKY. Baptism of Miguel Francisco, January 29, 1753, Black Baptisms, CPR, microfilm reel 284 F, PKY. Mose militia list, included in evacuation report of Juan Joseph Eligio de la Puente, January 22, 1764, SD 2595, AGI.

75. In 1738, Juan Jacinto Rodríguez and Ana María Menéndez were the slaves of Petronila Pérez, SD 844, fol. 594, PKY. They were married as slaves on October 9, 1735, CPR, 284 C, PKY. After Juan Jacinto died, Ana María married the free black, Antonio de Urisa, of the Lara nation on April 26, 1740, *ibid.* Juan Jacinto and Ana María's daughter, María Francisca, was baptized on October 11, 1736, while she was still the slave of Petronila Pérez, CPR, 284 F, PKY. Juan Lamberto Horruytiner married Cecilia Horruytiner on July 12, 1739, CPR, 284 C, PKY. Baptism of Cecilia, September 9, 1737, CPR, 284 F, PKY. Marriage of María Francisca to Marcos de Torres, August 20, 1742, CPR, 284 C, PKY. Baptism of their daughter, María, May 20, 1743, and their son Nicholás de la Concepción, January 10, 1746, CPR, 284 F, PKY. María Francisca and the children were living in her parents' home at the time of the 1759 census. Census of Father Gines Sánchez, February 12, 1759, SD 2604, AGI. Marriage of Thomas Chrisostomo and María Francisca, December 15, 1760, CPR, 284 C, PKY.

76. Marriage of Thomas Chrisostomo and Ana Maria Ronquillo, February 28, 1745, *ibid.* Baptism of Pedro Graxales, December 9, 1738, CPR, 284 F, PKY. Marriage of Pedro Graxales, Congo slave of Don Francisco Graxales, and María de la Concepción Hita, Caravalí slave of Don Pedro de Hita, January 19, 1744, CPR, 284 C, PKY. Baptisms of their children, María, November 4, 1744; Manuela de los Angeles, January 1, 1747; Ysidora de los Angeles, December 22, 1748; Joseph Ynisario, April 4, 1755; and Juana Feliciana, July 13, 1757, CPR, 284 F, PKY.

77. Mintz and Price, "Anthropological Approach."

78. Licenses for Slaves Imported into St. Augustine, 1762–1763, Cuba 472, AGI. Ira Berlin, Steven F. Miller, and Leslie S. Rowland, "Afro-American Families in the Transition from Slavery to Freedom," *Radical History Review,* 42 (1988): 89.

79. For a concise description of the importance of the extended family, *parentela,* and the system of personal dependency, *clientela,* in Spain, see McAlister, *Spain and Portugal,* 39–40.

80. TePaske, *Governorship,* 227–29. TePaske described the chronic financial shortages of Florida, saying that "poverty and want characterized life in Florida and pervaded all aspects of life." Father Juan Joseph de Solana also described Florida as a destitute colony, impoverished, despite its natural resources, by the continual attack of Indians loyal to the British. Father Juan Joseph de Solana to Bishop Pedro Agustin Morel de Sánchez, April 22, 1759, SD 516, microfilm reel 28 K, PKY.

81. Melchor de Navarrete to the Marqués de Ensenada, April 2, 1752, cited in Wright, "Dispatches," 184–86.

82. Fulgencio García de Solís to the king, November 29, 1752, SD, microfilm reel 17, PKY. Also, Fulgencio García de Solís to the king, December 7, 1752, cited in Wright, "Dispatches," 187–89.

83. Governors Alonso Fernández de Heredia and Lucas de Palacio both requested special financial assistance for the townspeople of Mose, citing their poverty. Alonso de Heredia to Julian de Arriaga, April 7, 1756, cited in Wright, "Dispatches," 193–94; the king to Lucas de Palacio, April 21, 1759, *ibid.*, 195.

84. Baptism of Miguel, 1744, CPR, 284 F, PKY.

85. Baptism of Miguel Domingo, January 26, 1748, CPR, 284 F, PKY.

86. Wood, *Black Majority,* 302.

87. Dr. Kathleen Deagan, Florida Museum of Natural History, University of Florida, Gainesville, provided these figures.

88. In a map drawn by Pablo Castello, 1763, 833 B, PKY.

89. Census of Gines Sánchez, February 12, 1759, SD 2604, AGI. Marriage of Francisco Roso, free Caravalí and María de la Cruz, Caravalí slave of Don Carlos Frison, January 8, 1743, CPR, 284 C, PKY; Baptism of Carlos Roso, November 4, 1743, CPR, 284 F, PKY. Marriage of Francisco Xavier de Torres, Mandingo, to Ana María, Mandinga slave of Josepha de Torres, February 1, 1752, CPR, 284 C, PKY. Others with slave wives in St. Augustine were Joseph de Peña, Caravalí, married to Ana María Ysquierdo, Conga slave of Don Juan Ysquierdo, January 29, 1743, *ibid.;* Juan Francisco de Torres, married to María Guillen slave of Joseph Guillen, January 21, 1743, *ibid.;* Joseph Fernández, Mandingo, married to Ana María, Caravalí slave, December 1, 1756, *ibid.;* Juan Baptista married to María de Jesus, August 17, 1757, *ibid.*

90. Report of Father Juan Joseph de Solana to Bishop Pedro Agustin Morel de Sánchez, April 22, 1759, SD 516, microfilm reel 28 K, PKY; Evacuation report of Juan Joseph Eligio de la Puente, January 22, 1764, SD 2595, AGI.

91. Fernando Ortiz, "La Fiesta Afro-Cubana del 'Dia de Reyes,'" *Revista Bimestre Cubana,* 15 (January-June 1920): 5–16.

92. Kathleen Deagan analyzes elements and patterns of cultural exchange and adaptation in several works. See *Artifacts of the Spanish Colonies of Florida and the Caribbean, 1500–1800* (Washington, D.C., 1987); *Spanish St. Augustine: The Archaeology of a Colonial Creole Community* (New York, 1983); *St. Augustine: First Urban Enclave in the United States* (Farmingdale, N.Y., 1982); and *Sex, Status and Role in the Mestizaje of Spanish Colonial Florida* (Gainesville, Fla., 1974). On African-American archaeology, see Theresa Singleton, *The Archaeology of Slavery and Plantation Life* (Orlando, Fla., 1985); and Leland Ferguson, "Looking for the 'Afro' in Colono-Indian Pottery," in Robert L. Schuyler, ed., *Archaeological Perspectives on Ethnicity in America: Afro-American and Asian American Culture History* (Farmingdale, N.Y., 1980), 14–28.

93. On Kongo-American connections, see Thompson, *Flash of the Spirit,* 112–15.

94. Personal communication from Kathleen Deagan, October 1989. On African fishing techniques in the colonial southeast, see Peter H. Wood, "'It Was a Negro Taught Them': A New Look at African Labor in Early South Carolina," *Journal of Asian and African Studies,* 9 (July and October 1974): 167–68.

95. Evacuation Report of Juan Joseph Eligio de la Puente, January 22, 1764, SD 2595, AGI. Accounts of the royal treasury of Matanzas, 1761–82, SD 1882, AGI. At least one family attempted to recover the losses of the evacuation, but they were denied on the basis of their color. Petition of María Gertrudis Roso, September 25, 1792, SD 2577, AGI.

96. Slaves escaped from Guadaloupe to Puerto Rico in 1752, and the case was still before the Council of the Indies twenty years later; Consulta, July 19, 1772. Slaves from the Danish colonies of Santa Cruz and Santo Thomas also fled to Puerto Rico in 1767, and eventually the governments signed a convention; Consulta, July 21, 1777. Slaves from the Dutch settlement at Esquibo fled to Guyana, October 22, 1802; Documents relating to fugitive slaves, Indiferente General 2787, AGI.

97. See Landers, "Spanish Sanctuary." Upon registering themselves and obtaining work contracts, slaves escaped from British colonists were freed by the second Spanish government; Census Returns, 1784–1814, East Florida Papers, PKY, microfilm reel 323 A; Royal decree, included in Captain General Luis de las Casas to Governor Manuel Vicente de Zéspedes, July 21, 1790, East Florida Papers, PKY, microfilm reel 1.

From Plantation to Campus: Progress, Community, and the Lay of the Land in Shaping the Early Tuskegee Campus
Kendrick Ian Grandison
Landscape architect

Kendrick Ian Grandison has done seminal work in the architecture of historically black Tuskegee University, previously Tuskegee Institute. He has also published "Landscapes of Terror: A Case Study of Tuskegee's Campus, 1881–1915," in Geography of Identity *edited by Patricia Yaeger (Vol. 5 of* Ratio *(1996) in a series published by the University of Michigan Institute for the Humanities). He also reviewed the* Southern Landscapes Past, Present, and Future *conference at the University of Mississippi's Center for the study of Southern Culture in Vol. 15, No. 2 of* Landscape Journal *(1996). He is currently assistant professor of landscape architecture at the University of Michigan School of Natural Resources and Environment.*

Whenthe Normal School for colored teachers at Tuskegee purchased an abandoned cotton plantation in Macon County Alabama in 1881, the seed was planted for principal Booker T. Washington's lofty vision of a center for uplifting the economically and socially impoverished Black Belt of Alabama.[1] "The Farm," as Mr. Washington referred to the site, consisted of 100 acres of spent farmland on which stood "a cabin, formally used as a dining room, an old kitchen, a stable, and an old hen-house" (Washington 1901, p. 130). The plantation mansion or "big house" had burned down during the war (Bontemps 1972, p. 188; Washington 1901, p. 128).

The future of the school seemed grim from the start. It was already $500 in debt, due to the purchase of the land, and had no funds for development. It faced a rapidly

Kendrick Ian Grandison, "From Plantation to Campus: Progress, Community, and the Lay of the Land in Shaping the Early Tuskegee Campus," Landscape Journal *15 (1), (1996): 6–22.*

growing number of students who, equally poor, were generally unable to finance their education. Furthermore, all of this took place in a post-Reconstruction setting hostile to its mission. Nonetheless, by 1900 the Farm was transformed into a campus so impressive that visitors would often refer to it as "Booker T. Washington's City." It had grown to include forty-six buildings on 2,300 acres of land valued at between $300,000 and $400,000 (Thrasher 1969, p. 39). Adding to this figure the school's endowment fund of $215,000 enabled Washington to proudly proclaim that "the value of the [institution's] total property is now nearly half a million dollars" (Washington 1901, p. 313).

The development of Tuskegee's campus is an inspiring story of the creativity and perseverance of African Americans as they struggled against and triumphed over formidable obstacles. While Tuskegee's story has been told many times and from many different points of view, it has never been studied and documented in relation to landscape architecture. Landscape architecture, the profession that is concerned with modifying outdoor spaces for human use and enjoyment, has generally failed to recognize the experiences and contributions of African Americans and other minorities in shaping the American landscape. Instead, landscape architectural history narrates the story of the American majority and its European predecessors.

Beyond the issue of race, landscape architectural history has focused, more strictly, on the experience of the wealthy and the powerful. From its study of the villas of the Medici in fifteenth century Italy to the palatial grounds of Louis XIV in seventeenth century France, from the romantic gardens of the titled elite of eighteenth century England, to the country place of the Vanderbilts in twentieth century America, landscape architecture has based its premises and procedures on the stories of those who fashioned environments with significant resources at their disposal and with powerful institutions under their control. The field has generally failed to grapple with the concept of "history from below" which has entered the scholarly discourse in other branches of history.

As a result, landscape architecture subscribes to an aesthetic standard which values capital-intensive design responses: those which are restricted only by the limitations of existing technology in their capacity to alter environments to meet human will. Thus, we cut and fill land, clear and redecorate it, push it this way and that, all in an effort to fulfill the desires of client and landscape architect alike to achieve particular notions of order and mastery. Furthermore, once our designs have been built, we must maintain them, often against natural forces, incurring significant environmental and financial cost. Power has blinded us to our vulnerability and our interdependence with natural systems. In this way, landscape architects, the mythic stewards of the land, have largely become complicit in an exploitative and unsustainable attitude toward environment.[2]

Beyond design product, this history has also influenced landscape architectural design process. Clients with access to financial resources, be they private developers or agencies of inner city revitalization, hire landscape architects to create their dreams. Construction documents are prepared and bid to contractors, and, as if by magic, shining new landscapes appear complete with accessories selected from catalogs and nursery guides, shipped to the site from remote heavens of mass production. This development fosters powerlessness: to the communities in which it occurs, it becomes an alien phenomenon under the control of the development gods whose swift actions command respect and awe. To the outside agents that own the process, community participation is often an encumbrance—an appendage to the process carried out because it may be mandated by law or because it could give the appearance of a genuine interest necessary to maintain "good community relations." Moreover, even in efforts to "revitalize" impoverished inner cities, these outside agencies rarely employ local personnel, who in this post-industrial economic setting are often in need of work and could benefit from retraining. While the process is most expedient according capitalism's prevailing wisdom, the choice forsakes a larger good: the well being of all the citizens of a sustainable community.

In this essay, I tell the story of a different development process and its physical results. Taking as my object of study the campus of Tuskegee University, I explore how the development of the campus responded to the circumstances that the fledging institution faced from 1881 to 1915, during Booker T. Washington's administration. First the economic, social, and political contexts of the school, as well as the physical and cultural features of its original site, will be established. The mechanism that evolved within this setting to develop the campus and to accomplish the other goals of the institution will be described. Finally, I will investigate the manner in which the layout of the campus itself responded to both its site and its broader context.

ECONOMIC, POLITICAL, AND
SOCIAL CONTEXT

Tuskegee University, located in Macon County, Alabama is in the heart of the Black Belt. This situation is at the root of the economic, political, and social circumstances faced by the fledging institution in 1881 (Figure 1). The legendary "Cotton Kingdom" was centered in the Black Belt because the region's fertile calcareous soils, which formed under the prairie that once dominated the area, and its mild climate met the exacting demands of cotton cultivation. The Black Belt rose to prominence before the Civil War as an important economic center in the United States. At its height, in 1860, when cotton accounted for about 60% of the United States' exports, Alabama accounted for 25% of this output, 50% of which came from the 10 Black Belt counties. Cotton, as is often said, was "King" of the Black Belt, its "Barons" being the planters who amassed fabulous personal wealth through its cultivation.

Enslaved Africans, the fuel of this prosperity, were brought to the area in increasing numbers as cotton production expanded during the 1850s, leading to the unusual demography of Tuskegee's region. Blacks outnumbered whites, by 1860 comprising between 60% and 90% of the total population in many of the Black Belt counties. In 1879, before Southern states had completely disenfranchised blacks, this majority possessed political power by virtue of its superior size. At the height of Reconstruction, virtually no representative to the Alabama legislature from a Black Belt county could be elected without the support of the black vote. Tuskegee, therefore, was located near the geographic and political center of the population it was established to serve.

FIGURE 1.

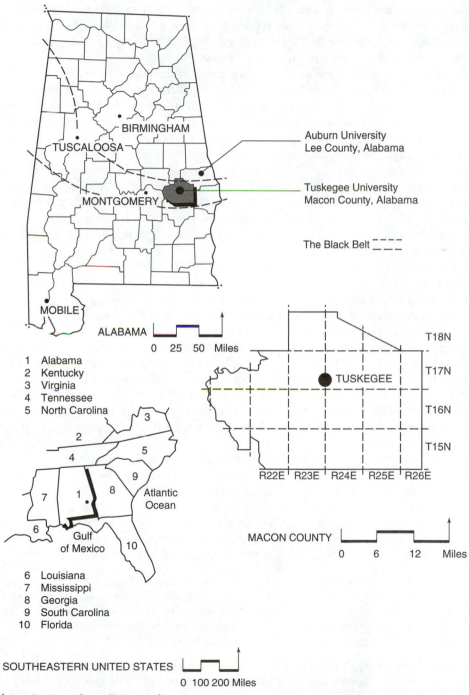

Auburn University
Lee County, Alabama

Tuskegee University
Macon County, Alabama

The Black Belt – – – –

ALABAMA
0 25 50 Miles

1   Alabama
2   Kentucky
3   Virginia
4   Tennessee
5   North Carolina

6   Louisiana
7   Mississippi
8   Georgia
9   South Carolina
10 Florida

MACON COUNTY
0   6   12   Miles

SOUTHEASTERN UNITED STATES
0 100 200 Miles

Tuskegee Institute (now University)

Because of these circumstances, the accounts say, Colonel W. F. Foster, a veteran of the Confederate Army who in 1879 was the democratic contender to the Alabama Senate, approached Louis Adams, a former slave and a highly regarded man in the Tuskegee community. Adams was an accomplished tinsmith and blacksmith during slavery. An industrious man, he learned to read and write even though he had no formal education. When the scarcity of tin during the Civil War curtailed his practice as a tinsmith, he successfully became an expert shoemaker and harnessmaker (Scipio 1987, p. 4; Bontemps 1972, p. 87; Washington 1901, p. 120). After the war, he established an informal trade school for blacks, passing on his skills to several apprentices at his workshop in town. He had become concerned that these trades, once practiced primarily by blacks, were not being carried on by the younger generation. The scale of his operation, however, was not sufficient to meet the need (Scipio 1987, p. 4; Washington 1915, p. 56). He therefore pledged the black vote to Foster with the understanding that Foster and A. L. Brooks, the Democratic contender to the State House, would support a proposal to establish a "Negro Normal School" at Tuskegee (Bontemps 1972, p. 88; Phelps-Stokes 1931, p. 7; Scott 1916, p. 3; Washington 1915, p. 56).

The spirit of public education pervaded the South. The first Morrill Act, passed in 1863, sought to provide practical education for the masses for the first time in America. With the end of the war in 1865, Southern states, now able to participate in this new program of higher education, moved swiftly to begin exploiting the provisions of the Act. Among the first schools to be endowed was Booker T. Washington's alma mater, the Hampton Normal and Agricultural Institute in Virginia; it subsequently became the state's "Negro land-grant college" from 1872 until 1920. The educational program, adopted by founder General Samuel Chapman Armstrong, emphasized agricultural and industrial education over the more traditional classical programs associated with other missionary schools for blacks. The Hampton approach stemmed from the belief that practical education would most immediately improve the plight of the impoverished rural black constituents the school served. This is the pragmatic philosophy that influenced the young Washington, influencing the educational approach he was to perfect at Tuskegee.

Hampton, however, as a black land-grant school was the exception rather than the rule: in 1881 blacks in Alabama and most of the South were largely locked out of the new "democratic" system of public education. Virginia was one of only four Southern states which, before the passage of the second Morrill Act in 1890, had directed funds to a black school, an accomplishment won only after prolonged debate in the state legislature. The former planter class of the Cotton Kingdom was fearful of and hostile toward black education, as Washington himself points out:

> There were not a few white people in the vicinity of Tuskegee who looked with some disfavor upon the project. They questioned its value to the coloured *(sic.)* people, and had a fear that it might result in bringing about trouble between the races. Some had the feeling that in proportion as the Negro received education, in the same proportion would his value decrease as an economic factor in the state. (1901, p. 119)

Blacks, however, took to education with fervor from the moment of emancipation (and before). They viewed it as the single greatest means of liberation from the land and the wretched manual labor associated with it, and from the indignities and proscriptions with which the South increasingly served them. W.E.B. Du Bois suggests that the "feeling of inferiority which slavery forced upon them fathered an intense desire to rise out of their condition by means of education." In his description of Savannah, Georgia in 1865, he dramatizes this, reporting that the bars which marked the old slave stalls of the Bryan Slave Mart had been knocked down to make room for seating to accommodate the "freed people of every age and shade," who "flocked" to this and other places "eager for that book learning which really seemed to them the key to their advance" (1962, pp. 638, 645).

By the end of Reconstruction, John Hope Franklin points out, the passion with which blacks sought education was fueled further by the fact that white Southerners, despite their opposition to black schools, seemed to tolerate them more than other agencies of black improvement. He documents, moreover, that additional stimulus was provided by the rise of philanthropy. Denominational boards such as the American Missionary Association expanded their support for institutions like Berea College in Kentucky, which advocated coeducation of the races before the turn of the century. Furthermore, when newly-rich industrialists from the North began to invest heavily in Southern textile and steel mills and in rail expansion, they created a demand for skilled labor; to educate the work force to meet that demand, they established educational foundations to support schools for the masses (1969, pp. 382–383). Between 1860 and 1900, some 260 such institutions of higher learning were financed across America. Though most were predominantly white institutions like Vanderbilt University (1873), Johns Hopkins University (1876), and the University of Chicago (1892), black education benefited tremendously as well. Several foundations, including the Peabody Education Fund, the Julius Rosenwald Fund, the Phelps-Stokes Fund, and the John F. Slater Fund, aimed specifically at "uplifting the lately emancipated masses" of the South. In 1881, therefore, despite Southern hostility toward black education, the political power of blacks in the Black Belt and their ardent desire for education now coincided with the demands of an emerging industrial economy creating a climate more hospitable to the birth of Tuskegee. When both Foster and Brooks were elected, they secured the passage of a bill to establish the school. On February 12, 1881, Alabama State Act No. 292 was approved, thus establishing the "Normal School for coloured teachers at Tuskegee."

Although the passage of the legislation was auspicious, its allowances for the proposed school were inauspicious at best. While the bill provided $2,000 per annum for teachers' salaries, no provisions were made for the procurement of physical plant and equipment; these were to be provided by "the people" who were to benefit from the venture. Of course the people were the African Americans of the Black Belt who, just 16 years out of slavery, had no money. A comparison with the funding directed to "public" land-grant schools of the time enables us to appreciate how small this appropriation for Tuskegee was. In the adjacent county, for instance, the Auburn Normal and Agricultural Institute (now Auburn University), on becoming Alabama's white land-grant college in 1872, began with an annual income of $20,529 generated by its land-grant endowment fund (Klien 1930, p. 10). Tuskegee's relatively negligible budget burdened its founder with a reasonable apprehension. Washington writes that during "the first days at Tuskegee I recall that night after night I would roll and toss on my bed, without sleep, because of the anxiety and uncertainty which we were in regarding money" (1901, p. 145).

Difficulty, however, when it does not exceed human will and capacity to survive, necessarily results in compromise and innovation as people adapt to their circumstances. Deficient funding, however, was simply more of the same to the African Americans who survived other physical and psychological adversities, and who still retained the remnants of the indomitable desire to succeed evoked by emancipation. The shortage of funds in the early days motivated a self-help approach toward accomplishing the school's goals of black education, campus development, and community building. The approach would evolve to integrate these three goals—originally General Armstrong's at Hampton—so efficiently that Tuskegee under Washington may well represent the fullest realization of the democratic tenants of the Morrill Acts among American institutions of higher learning.

In addition to the philosophy of self-help, the school's state-imposed poverty forced Washington into the position of fund-raiser, a skill he also borrowed from Armstrong but would eventually develop to the point that he became the undisputed wizard at exploiting the philanthropic sources of funds from the North. He gradually attracted the attention and then the financial resources of the North's most powerful industrialists, especially after Tuskegee's first decade, when its methods began to receive increasing national acclaim as the solution to the "Negro Problem." At first his contacts were through Armstrong, but he eventually established his own bonds with many wealthy donors, including Julius Rosenwald and Andrew Carnegie, as he wooed their support for his mission at Tuskegee. This support, of course, was not without its complications. For one thing, donors generally wished to have some control over the campuses they funded, imposing their aesthetic standards on them. For instance, buildings supported by the Phelps-Stokes Fund were generally designed by New York architect Issac Newton Stokes. Tuskegee's Phelps Hall, completed in 1892 with the financial backing of the organization, was most likely sited and designed by this architect (Dozier 1990, p. 116). This would have been at odds with Washington's desire for the campus to be created completely by blacks. Such compromises were required if Tuskegee was to attract and maintain financial friends, a vital supplement to the constraints on its access to power and privilege.

Of course, the school also grew up in a broader social context that shaped it no less than more immediate circumstances, especially regarding various aspects of black-white relations from emancipation on. In 1881, most blacks in the region were little better off than they had been before emancipation. During Reconstruction, Southern states devised various legal and extra-legal means to discourage efforts toward economic and social advancement in the black population, specifically seeking to ensure the population's continued exploitation as plantation laborers and so to benefit from the high price of cotton after the war. Franklin documents the frequent disregard for labor contracts between landowners and the new workers. Wages were often lower than those paid for hired slaves, or Freedmen during slavery, and were often paid at the end of the season in order to hold workers on the farm until harvesting was completed (1969, pp. 311, 398). Additionally, vagrancy laws, an important aspect of the so-called Black Codes, prevented blacks from refusing work (see Kennedy 1946, pp. 22–23). The convict lease system allowed convicts to serve out their sentences under private management. This, in conjunction with white control of the jury box, which disproportionately convicted and jailed blacks, enabled not only planters but also the new industrialists to take advantage of black labor (see Cable in Turner ed., pp. 69–70).

So successful was the continued exploitation of black labor that by 1881 the South was well on its way to economic recovery, producing more cotton than it did at the height of the Cotton Kingdom. African Americans contributed significantly to this rejuvenation, but, as during slavery, did not benefit from it. They were, instead, mired in a demoralizing cycle of poverty and dependence created by the various forms of sharecropping and land tenancy foisted on them. The situation is documented by Washington who, upon arriving at Tuskegee, spent a month touring the region in order to better understand the people he hoped to serve. He writes:

> In the plantation districts I found that, as a rule, the family slept in one room. . . . The common diet of the people was fat pork and corn bread . . . the meat, and the meal of which the bread was made, having been bought at a high price at a store in town, not withstanding the fact that the land all about the cabin homes could easily have been made to produce nearly every kind of garden vegetable that is raised any where in the country. Their one object seemed to be to plant nothing but cotton; and in many cases cotton was planted up to the door of the cabin. (1901, pp. 112–113)

McWhiney unwittingly shows how these conditions depended on the agricultural system:

> By 1876, the merchants of Eufaula—where the streets were clogged with cotton and the "stores bulged with bacon and flour" shipped in from the North—were supplied by Yankees with nearly everything, including "unlimited credit." . . . The merchants, in turn, encouraged the farmers who were dependent upon them for credit to plant only cotton and to buy everything else, including their meat and corn, at the store. . . . Landowners [therefore] . . . tended to discourage their croppers from raising anything eatable. It was simpler and more profitable for merchants and landowners to import barreled meat from the North and to sell it on credit at a smart mark-up to their customers and tenants. Any attention croppers gave to animal husbandry took time away from making the cotton crop they were expected to share with the landowners. One reason why cotton became so popular with postbellum landowners and merchants alike was that the tenants could not eat it. (quoted in Wiggins 1987, p. 128)

Blacks, forced to be dependent on landowners for provisions, were constantly in debt and, therefore, lacked the funds to improve their condition by purchasing land and becoming independent farmers. More than sixteen years after emancipation, they were still unable to control and benefit from their own labor. Thus, they resented the land and came to understand progress as liberation from the manual labor land represented. If Tuskegee was to achieve its goals, therefore, it would have had to be able to find ways of reversing this attitude. Since their labor was the only resource blacks had at their disposal and land was the resource with which they were familiar, Washington believed that a healthy attitude toward both had to be restored in order to begin the process of advancement.

Even when blacks could muster the capital, landowners resisted selling land to them for "they did not want [them] to enjoy the power that came with the ownership of land in the South" (Franklin 1969, p. 398). Terrorism by such secret organizations as the Ku Klux Klan augmented this resistance with violence against blacks who attempted to attain economic independence through property ownership or through new industrial jobs which paid better wages. W.E.B. Du Bois records the fate of blacks who were employed in building the railroad between Atlanta and Charlotte. Disguised men, he reports, "went there, took the Negroes and whipped them, and forced them back to the farms to work." He also describes the ultimate fate of a successful "coloured" independent farmer in Choctaw County, Alabama, where "masked men shot into his house and burned it. He and his neighbors were killed" (1962, p. 674).

The erosion of economic opportunity went hand-in-hand with the erosion of the political power blacks enjoyed in the Black Belt. Indeed, this was the primary target of the secret organizations of terror. Tuskegee's first two decades were marked, therefore, by increased violence in the region. By 1900, blacks were almost completely disenfranchised. A campus had to be built and classes taught in the midst of this reign of terror. Tuskegee's administration, on a subliminal if not a conscious level, had to take this situation into consideration as it planned its campus and developed its educational program.[3]

These then were the social, economic, and political conditions Tuskegee faced during its early days: an impoverished rural black population, demoralized by the failed promise of emancipation and Reconstruction, its intense desire for education matched by its resentment of manual labor; a Southern power structure as disapproving of the attempt to educate them as it was resolved to keep blacks a laboring class under its control. It was in this setting that Washington essayed his famous and controversial compromise with the South to trade black demands for immediate civil rights in return for a fair chance at economic opportunity. He believed, in accordance with the capitalistic spirit of his time and with the principles championed by his mentor, General Armstrong, that economic prosperity was the root of race improvement. Civil rights, he was convinced, would follow naturally as blacks became indispensable to the Southern economy. He advocated, as it were, a grass-roots approach to race improvement that began, hypothetically, with ordinary people acquiring property and training their minds and hands to reap the material profit dormant in it. Thus, in his famous address to an integrated audience at the Cotton States Exposition of 1895, he explained his philosophy in what has become known as "the great compromise":

> If there are efforts anywhere tending to curtail the fullest growth of the Negro, let these efforts be turned into stimulating, encouraging, and making him the most useful and intelligent citizen . . . The wisest among my race understand that the agitation of questions of social equality is the extremist folly, and that progress in the enjoyment of all privileges that will come to us must be the result of severe and constant struggle rather than artificial forcing. No race that has anything to contribute to the markets of the world is long in any degree ostracized.

And so, he implored his black audience:

> "Cast down your bucket where you are." . . . Cast it down in agriculture, mechanics in commerce, in domestic service, and in the professions. . . . Our greatest danger is that in

the great leap from slavery to freedom we may overlook the fact that the masses of us are to live by the production of our hands, and fail to keep in mind that we shall prosper in proportion as we learn to dignify and glorify the common labour *(sic.)* and put brains and skill into the common occupations of life. . . . No race can prosper till it learns that there is as much dignity in tilling a field as in writing a poem. (Washington 1901, pp. 218–225)

And to his white audience, after noting rather gingerly the chagrin of white Southerners in looking toward foreigners for "the prosperity of the South," he advised:

"Cast your bucket where you are." Cast it down among the eight millions of Negroes whose habits you know. . . . Casting down your bucket among my people, helping and encouraging them as you are doing on these grounds, and to the education of the head, hand, and heart, you will find that they will buy your surplus land, make blossom the waste places in your fields, and run your factories.

This is the philosophical underpinning of Tuskegee's famous program to uplift the black masses of the Black Belt. The basis of this program was the land on which the majority of Blacks in the region toiled, rather than in the cities of the West and North to which they were already fleeing at an "alarming" rate. Washington saw the path to the advancement of the race as beginning at the acquisition of the South's "surplus land," which would then "make blossom the waste places." Tuskegee was to become a means of demonstrating the efficacy of this philosophy, starting with the purchase of the abandoned Bowen cotton plantation.

THE SITE

What exactly were the natural and cultural features of this "waste place"? Its topography was shaped by the erosive force of running water, in a manner typical of the region. The heavy rainfall and clay-rich lateritic and podzolic soils prevalent in this part of Alabama result in high runoff. Streams dissected and broke a once level plain, the remnants of which remain as sinuous ridges with broad level tops. As can still be seen today, the main spine of the Tuskegee Ridge—the highest of these upland remnants in Macon County—flanks the southern edge of the property. Almost perpendicular to this extend a series of three broad spurs separated by two steep-sided valleys which collect and transfer runoff from the site to the Uphapee Creek (Figure 2).[4] The valleys must have been a distinctive feature of the site then as they are today. Rackham Holt (1943, p. 132) refers to one of these valleys when she tries to capture George Washington Carver's first view of the campus in 1898. The section of the campus referred to as the "Big Hungry," she notes, consisted of piney woods within which "roamed the Institute's thirty razorback hogs that looked as though they had been built for speed rather than the table." Her description suggests a landscape so rough that only the most rugged of animals could prosper on it. The site's natural features—its ridges and valleys—would have played an important role in dictating the initial layout of the campus, since limited funds would have restricted the potential for land sculpting. The buildings would have to accommodate the land rather than vice-versa.

FIGURE 2.

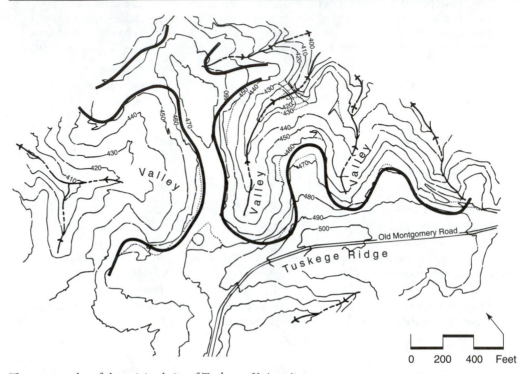

The topography of the original site of Tuskegee University.

What of the cultural features of the site? How would the new black owners of the property have related to its past, which they could only have viewed as sordid? A cotton plantation, the ultimate symbol of their bondage and desperation, the vehicle of their exploitation, was now to be reconceived as a symbol of freedom and as a means of progress. The irony is as gripping as that of holding the school for Blacks in the old Bryan Slave Mart in Savannah. A hen house, stable, and the other utility building which stood on the property became recitation rooms (Washington 1901, p. 130). These black people would have been aware that, in contrast, when the white college at Auburn opened its doors twenty-two years before, it was a fine, imposing, and spanking new four-story structure into which students stepped, built specifically for educational purposes. This contrast, as much as the resented land itself, would have been a sharp reminder of their marginal status.

Yet the circumstances would also have engendered a sense of hope. Sixteen years before, these people could not have owned that land. Instead, they would have been forced to labor on it without even owning the product of their sweat. Waste place though it might have been, it was still theirs. As much a reminder of a humble present, Tuskegee's plantation would have symbolized triumph and significant cause for optimism about the future. Indeed, the community demonstrated this in the outpouring of support it offered to aid the acquisition of the property: the institution had only $250 of the $500 cost of the property (Washington 1901, p. 128). When Washington and his "lady principal," Olivia Davidson, turned to the community to help raise the remaining funds, it responded with passion. Whether through local fund-raising festivals or through minimal individual contributions, the enthusiastic support for the purchase reflected the pride and the hope this spent place would have represented to the people of the region (see Harlan 1972, p. 172; Washington 1901, pp. 131–132, p. 141).

THE "TUSKEGEE MACHINE": AN ALTERNATIVE APPROACH TO DEVELOPMENT

In 1882 the fledging Tuskegee Normal School possessed 100 acres of abandoned farmland, but no funds to develop it. It faced a rapidly increasing student population anxious for education, but generally with limited finances. Northern philantrophy was financially supportive of the school's mission, but the South—Tuskegee's immediate context—was largely hostile. In response to these opportunities and constraints, Washington essayed a program of black self-help and conciliation with the South, which resulted in the famous "Tuskegee Machine." The concept which began at Hampton, as mentioned before, evolved with the expanding needs of the institution to become, by the turn of the century, a remarkable instrument of development for both campus and community (Figure 3). The process of development differed fundamentally from the conventional implementation of design in landscape architecture in that it was not an abstract linear mechanism bringing together discrete client, planner, and contractor entities to build the campus. Instead, it was a cyclical process that dissolved the boundaries between the three in the interest of integrating development with community uplift. By a necessary experiment—which exceeded the practical and democratic tenets of higher education championed by the Morrill Acts—Tuskegee's faculty became the primary planners of the campus, and its students became the contractors. In this way, the process yielded not just built environment, but also other benefits to both the institution and the community. These benefits, in turn, served as catalysts for the machine itself.

From the very beginning, therefore, the lack of development funds forced the school to look to the only other resource at its disposal: the muscle and minds of its student body and faculty. Hence, in 1882, Porter Hall, the school's first building, was designed by instructors and erected by students who worked after class hours to complete it (Washington 1901, p. 143). In recognizing and using the human resources at its disposal, the school addressed several of the constraints it faced. The physical development of the campus provided an opportunity for those students who could not afford their education to earn wages that paid for their schooling. Night school allowed them to work on the construction of the campus by day. Moreover, as they accomplished the task of building the campus, they also learned important lessons related to the

FIGURE 3.

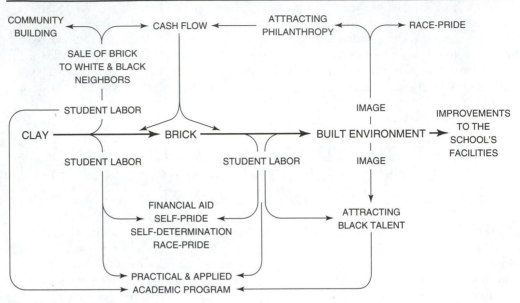

The "Tuskegee Machine."

utility of labor. The notion that one could improve the quality of one's condition by owning the products of one's labor was reinforced. Washington writes that, "after a little while, many students began to take great pride in telling their parents at the end of each month how much they had helped themselves through their work on the farm or in other industries" (1904, p. 42).

As students constructed the school's facilities, they learned the various trades which were required to accomplish this task—hence the industrial programs continued to expand as the needs of the institution grew. For example, since Porter Hall was a frame structure, saw-milling was established early in the history of the school to provide the lumber, followed by a practical program in frame-building construction. Later, the need for more permanent structures on the site led to the recognition of yet another unusual resource for campus development: the abundance of local clay. After many failed efforts, the school succeeded in manufacturing the bricks required to construct Alabama Hall in 1884 and the series of brick structures which followed it. Out of this came brick-making, brick-laying, and plastering as part of the school's industrial program (see Washington 1901, pp. 148–162; Washington 1904). With the development of buildings and farming operations, the need for a more substantial circulation system led to road layout and construction as an industrial program, which also ultimately discovered local chert as an attractive surfacing material (Edward Pryce 1987, personal conversation).

Eventually, Tuskegee was producing more brick than it needed to keep pace with its campus development. Capitalizing on the local demand for this product, the school began to sell excess stock to the community. This not only provided cash for continuing development and other financial needs, but also began to instill the principles of commerce in the minds of Tuskegee's students. Furthermore, white people began to patronize the school's sale of brick and other products and services, including brooms, mattresses, and blacksmithing services. At least locally, this exchange caused some rethinking of the original apprehension associated with the issue of black education and at first helped to ease hostilities.[5] Washington writes that "there came to be growing appreciation of the fact that industrial education of black people had a practical and vital bearing on the life of every white family in the South" (1904, p. 25). Tuskegee's industrial education came to be seen as a means of easing racial tensions in the South.

On a still broader practical level, the fact that the development of the campus was accomplished almost exclusively by former slaves served as an effective marketing tool for Tuskegee in terms of attracting both the money of philanthropists and new faculty. The exclamation "Booker T. Washington City," which impressed visitors would remark upon seeing the well-constructed public image of the campus, was accompanied by an increased confidence in the institution's educational philosophy and an increased willingness to support it financially. Funds for development previously absent began to flow—especially after Washington's address to the Atlanta Exposition—from foundations such as the Phelps-Stokes Fund and from individuals like Andrew Carnegie, who gave $600,000 in U.S. Steel bonds (Bennett 1964, p. 277). Tuskegee's self-made image also helped Washington attain his goal of an all-black institution, bringing to this remote section of Alabama some of the brightest black talent of the day. George Washington Carver, the most renowned among them, came to Tuskegee in 1898 from Iowa State University where he already had a promising career as a botanist. The architect R. R. Taylor, the first black graduate of the Massachusetts Institute of Technology, came to Tuskegee in 1892 to head the Mechanical Trades Department; he designed many of the campus buildings constructed during the Washington Administration. Considered the first black professional landscape architect, David Williston, after graduating from the landscape gardening program of Cornell University, arrived at Tuskegee in 1902. After 1910 he served as superintendent of buildings and grounds (Ehrenkrantz Group et al. 1987, p. 19).

Much has been made of Washington's "Tuskegee Machine" and its relegation of blacks to inferior practical education. Nonetheless, the system was not only a well-tuned response to the particular circumstances the school faced at the turn of the century, but may well represent—as I have already suggested—the fullest realization of the democratic goals of the Morrill Acts among American institutions of higher education. Furthermore, the building of Tuskegee's campus may be as close as we can come to a nineteenth-century model of what might be called socially sustainable development. Landscape practice today could do well to take as its model these achievements—the integration of physical development with community autonomy and empowerment, and the ability of the system to form the basis of positive cycles of improvement to both institution and community.

LAYOUT: A NECESSARY REFLECTION OF TOPOGRAPHY AND PHILOSOPHY

If the process by which Tuskegee's campus was developed accommodated the economic, social, and political realities of its region, then its layout accommodated both the opportunities and constraints that its site posed and reflected the philosophy that evolved in response to its regional context. Figure 4, adapted from an 1897 Sanborn Fire Insurance map of the campus, illustrates this.[6] Buildings were located on the

FIGURE 4.

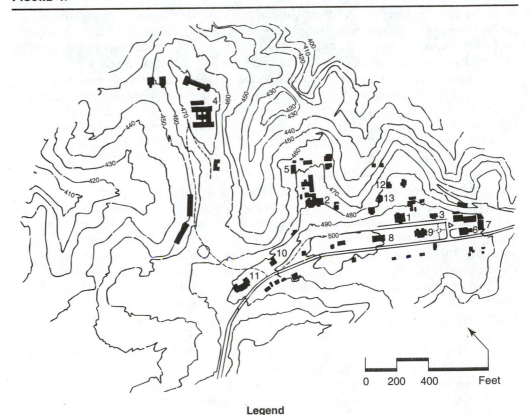

Legend

1. Porter Hall
2. Alabama Hall
3. Armstrong Hall
4. Horse and Cow Barn
5. Hamilton Cottage
6. Blacksmith Shop
7. Cassedy Hall

8. Phelps Hall
9. Thrasher Hall
10. Practice Cottage
11. Armstrong-Slater Memorial Agricultural Building
12. Parker Cottage
13. Scott Cottage

The campus layout of Tuskegee in 1897.

FIGURE 5.

Cattle grazing in low-lying areas near Tuskegee Institute in 1900.

high, level ground upon the ridges, while the low-lying valleys were almost without exception undeveloped; these wooded and grassy interior spaces of the campus served, in places, as pasture for the school's livestock (Figure 5). Thus, unlike the extensive formality we tend to associate with American college campuses, Tuskegee's overall layout pattern is primarily informal, its roadways and adjacent buildings turned this way and that in intimate response to the natural folds of the land. Any formal spaces, necessarily limited in extent, occur only in the areas that could readily accommodate them.

A walk through this original section of the campus today enables us to catch a glimpse of the visual ambiance created by the layout approach established over 100 years ago, as we explore possible reasons and principles that underlie this response. Standing on the main spine of Tuskegee ridge near what is today Carver Museum affords a viewer a sweeping view of the open space of the Big Valley as it rolls down from the ridge (Figure 6). On the ridge itself the campus assumes a limited formality, as it does in other places where sufficient level land was available. The scene is reminiscent of most American college campuses. Buildings directly flank both sides of the campus road with connecting courtyards, gardens, and access drives marking their entrances. Trees and pedestrian lights occur at regular intervals along the road, helping to unify the entire space much as they did 100 years ago. On the broad spurs that extend from the main spine of the ridge are quadrangles, the beginnings of which appear on

FIGURE 6.

A 1994 view of the valley below Tuskegee Ridge.

Figure 4, but which are more developed by 1909 (Figure 7). One, located where
Alabama Hall once sat, is formed by the former Carnegie Library to the south, White
and Douglas Halls to the west, Tompkins Hall to the east, and Huntington Hall to the
north. On the spur farthest to the east, another is defined by Rockefeller Hall to the
north and formal walkways as shown in the 1909 plan. Here manicured lawns, with
canopy trees and criss-crossing walks, resemble the quadrangles of many college campuses across America.

        These more formal sites were the public spaces where, especially on the main
spine of the ridge that faces Old Montgomery Road, Tuskegee's image could be propa-
gated and projected to outsiders. The "tasteful" spaces laid out and built by the black
students and staff of Tuskegee were probably a physical rebuttal to all who might
have doubted the capacity of former slaves to "build a civilization." Thus, it was here
that the military corps would hold its formal parades. Here, too, gala receptions would
welcome such distinguished guests as President McKinley in December 1898—and
photographs would document the reserved glamour of such occasions in order that it
might be generously shared with potential well-wishers and financial donors around
the world. This is where the school's ladies in wispy pastel dresses would sit on the
lawn in front of the rather spare facade of Alabama Hall to hear the school's band perform an afternoon concert (Figure 8): a picture of sober gentility that would have been
visible from Old Montgomery Road. While the scene thus served Washington's race-
lifting and fund-raising goals well, the frugal, even austere, facade of the building

FIGURE 7.

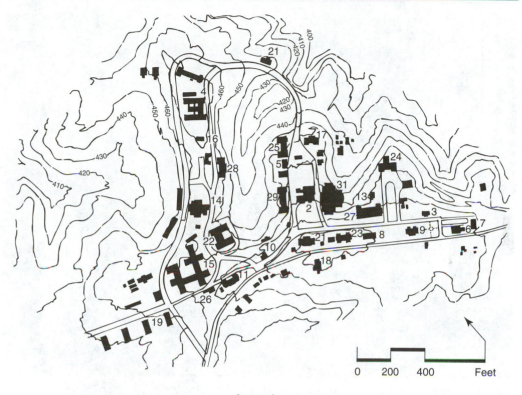

Legend

1. Porter Hall
2. Alabama Hall
3. Armstrong Hall
4. Horse and Cow Barn
5. Hamilton Cottage
6. Blacksmith Shop
7. Cassedy Hall
8. Phelps Hall
9. Thrasher Hall
10. Practice Cottage
11. Armstrong-Slater Memorial
    Agricultural Building
12. Parker Cottage
13. Scott Cottage
14. Chapel
15. Armstrong Memorial Boy's
    Trades Building
16. Dairy Barn
17. Huntington Hall
18. The Oaks
19. Emery Dormitories
20. Pinehurst Cottage
21. Carnegie Hall
22. Dorothy Hall
23. Administration Building
24. Rockefeller Hall
25. Douglass Hall
26. Byington Greenhouse
27. Collis P. Huntington Building
28. Tantum Hall
29. White Hall--being built
30. Milbank Agricultural Building
31. Tompkins Hall--being built

The campus layout of Tuskegee in 1909.

provided ample evidence to locals that there was no ambition for social equality with white Southerners. Alabama Hall, to be certain, was no Old Main—that elegant specimen of architecture that adorned the grounds of the then all-white, all-male Auburn University down the street. Washington conveyed a consciousness of this image when he rejected an alternative site for locating the proposed college chapel because in that

FIGURE 8.

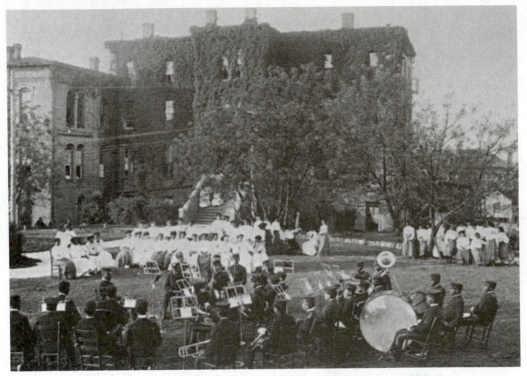

An afternoon performance in front of Alabama Hall, circa 1900.

location the structure would block the view of Alabama Hall from the road (Dozier 1990, p. 125).

The Big Valley below us, as we look from the ridge, offers a contrast to this public formality. It is a retreat from the show, a more private place that can be accessed only on foot. Compared to the tops of the ridges, its character seems unmanicured. Trees of such native species as Winged Elm, Sweetgum, and Live Oak stand here and there in undulating wild meadows and thickets so that, with the exception of lighting and campus walks recently paved in concrete, one can almost feel its pastoral past (Figure 5). As we amble down the slope to the bottom of the valley, we are immersed in the rustic quality of this low-lying inner space. Buildings perched along its edge look down on us, a reminder that we are still indeed on a college campus. It is in this space that the departure from more traditional campus aesthetics stimulates us to contemplate the underlying reasons for the layout.

The evidence suggests that, at least in the very early days of the campus, this informal layout response resulted from spontaneous development. Buildings were planned as need arose and sited in the most suitable locations without the guidance of a formal master plan. Alabama Hall, for example, the second major building to be constructed on the campus, was planned when "the problem of providing rooms for girls, as well as a larger boarding department for all students grew serious" (Washington 1901, p. 177). The building, as already indicated, was sited on the second of the three spurs which extended from the Tuskegee Ridge, where it would benefit from level ground, good views, and good drainage (this last was important given the area's heavy rainfall). Two years later, having solved the problem of housing for women, it became possible to address the pressing need to accommodate the men currently boarding outside the limits of the campus. Armstrong Hall, the third major building constructed on the campus, was planned to meet this need. Its location on the main spine of the Tuskegee Ridge affords similar advantages to Alabama's, as did the Blacksmith and Foundry Shop constructed in 1889 to house the school's evolving industrial program and a host of more minor structures.

Richard Dozier points out, however, that a formal plan for the campus was developed as early as 1903 with the planning of the chapel. He mentions a survey of the campus, which would have signaled the beginning of spatial planning through the use of maps. He also cites a note written by Taylor in 1904 to E. Scott, the school's financial manager:

> In making improvements or changes on the campus I should be very glad if you would consult either Mr. Williston or myself. The plan of the grounds has been made, and we are following these plans in making permanent improvements. (1990, p. 144)

Taylor apparently circulated copies of this note to all heads of departments in the hope of their compliance. But it is clear that, even after the formalization and centralization of the campus planning process, the principles established earlier continued to guide the choice of new building sites: the 1909 plan shows that lowlands were still avoided and that formal areas, which were even more pronounced, were still restricted to the level uplands (Figure 7). It becomes necessary, therefore, to look beyond spontaneity to explain the layout approach.

It is unlikely that the technology available to Tuskegee's planners and builders was the factor that limited their ability to utilize steep areas for building. In other aspects of campus development—such as designing and constructing some of the largest buildings in the region—they were mastering far more complicated technology than that required to push dirt around. A more reasonable explanation would be cost efficiency. The cost of extensive earth sculpting to accommodate a more formal campus might have been prohibitive, or at least such expenditure might have been considered too lavish, given both the financial constraints the school faced and the availability of other building sites. Statements in a March 1911 letter to Washington, probably from Seth Low, chairman of the trustees of the school, allude to this concern:

> Regarding consolidating Farming facilities by moving barns and other facilities to the vicinity of Milbanks Hall: I think it will be well to have a topographical map made of the land in the immediate vicinity of Milbank Hall, and also of the land that might be used if the barns were placed near the middle of the farm. With such a map, the question of the cost of grading could be easily studied. (Low to Washington 1911, p. 2)

It is also likely that even if Tuskegee's "trained" planners and designers desired a more conventional layout, the pragmatic and domineering Washington would have resisted

such misapplication of funds. So buildings continued to be placed on the
uplands, twisting and turning in response to the land, while the valleys remained
left-over inner space where topography made construction either too difficult or too
expensive.

   In some opposition to this explanation, however, stands Tantum Hall, a women's
dormitory that looks down upon the valley to the left (Figure 9). The monumentality
of its facade contrasts with the rolling, unmanicured ambiance of the valley in such an
unexpected manner that it teases one to explore the principles guiding the layout even
further. Taylor, who designed the structure, clearly intended this inner facade to be its
front as evidenced by one part of a March 1906 letter describing the building: "The
roof of the front porch is supported by six large ionic columns. Externally this porch
will be the main feature of the building" (quoted in Dozier 1990, p. 151). The less
grand facade to the back of the building faces the level top of the ridge upon which it
is built. This would have afforded easy vehicular, service, and pedestrian access from
the adjacent campus road on the crest of the ridge. The building itself separates the
public outer landscape on the ridge from the private, naturalistic, inner landscape of
the valley, which it fronts purposefully.

   The vivid contrast of the front of the building with its context is curious. Could it
have been merely an anomaly, a whimsical notion, and then a change of heart about
what should be the front and what should be the back of this section of the campus?
Probably not, because, though less dramatic, some of the other buildings in the vicinity
display a similar relationship to the valley. For example, the front and back facades of
James Hall, another women's dormitory, are at least equal in appearance. Like Tantum
Hall, this is a formal, symmetrical building with porches marking centrally located entrances at both its "front," facing a campus road, and its "back," facing the valley which
is accessible only by foot. While the view from the front porch is public, from the back
porch one affords a distinctly private and breathtaking view of the valley as it rolls quietly down and up again to the main campus road (Figure 10). From this vantage one
can see the monumental front of Tantum Hall, the clock tower of White Hall, and the facades of other campus buildings that sit on the edge of the space. It seems the perfect
spot for retreat and contemplation and so evokes another possible explanation for the
campus layout. It may have conveyed to the students residing in these buildings, Washington's philosophy regarding the bridge between property acquisition, agriculture, and
industry, and the improvement of the African-American people of the Black Belt. It is
reasonable to propose that the orientation of the residence halls manifests the desire to
convey these principles to Tuskegee's students. What better way to give physical form
to the philosophy than the classical porches and balconies of these residence halls ori-
enting purposefully to "unadorned" land upon which grazed the school's dairy herd?
Land, unembellished, proudly acquired, and productive as pasture, and as the source of
building materials would have been a worthy object of admiration and contemplation
particularly as a constant lesson of self-help and economic progress to those who would
have surveyed it from the porches of Tantum or James Halls, or from the large windows
of White or Douglas Halls.

   Students would have also learned to respect the authenticity of their locale. The
familiar rural Alabama environment, heretofore taken for granted and even despised,

FIGURE 9.

The facade of Tantum Hall facing Campus Road, 1994 (above) Tantum Hall overlooking the valley (below).

FIGURE 10.

The Big Valley from the back porch of James Hall.

was now related unabashedly to the classical architecture of high European culture.
The former slave plantation was now the object of sublime progress. The parity seems
to reinforce the belief that it was necessary for students to "Cast their buckets" where
they were by integrating their history in the South and their humble beginnings with
the highest aspirations for education and race progress. The physical concept, like the
philosophy of accommodation itself, seems to find opportunity in what could have
been a constraint. The section of campus that posed the most difficulty for building
became an opportunity to convey the most important lesson the school hoped to teach
its students. Rather than being dismissed as left-over space, the valley became the object of celebration and education. Whatever the reasons, the overall layout of the early
campus was remarkable for the manner in which it intimately fits its site. By not violating the constraints imposed by land, and by responding to the prevailing social conditions of the time, the campus reflected the spirit of its Alabama context.

The same cannot be said of at least one other campus in the area. The layout of
Auburn University, located in the adjacent county, is predominantly formal (Figure 11).
With its numerous axes, courtyards, and quadrangles, Auburn's campus takes the form
we tend to associate with American college campuses. To accommodate this pattern
on the dissected land of the area, extensive sections of the original site had to be cut
or filled to create terraces on which facilities could be formally arranged (Figure 12).
Remember that Auburn University, selected as Alabama's land-grant school in 1872,

FIGURE 11.

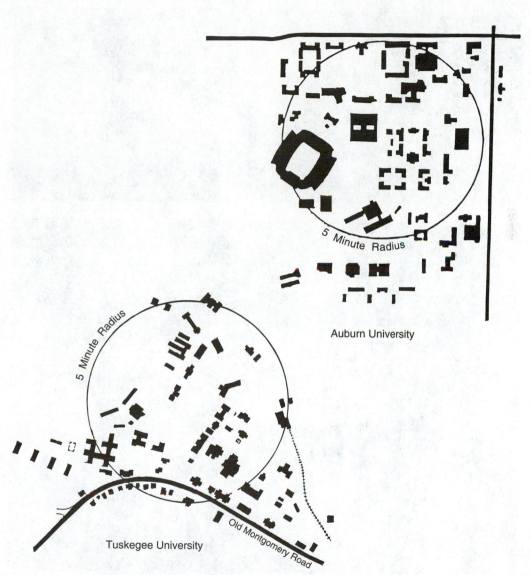

A comparison of the layouts of Auburn University and Tuskegee University.

received the annual yield of $20,529 from the state's land-grant endowment—as compared to the $2,000 per annum appropriated by Alabama for Tuskegee ten years later. The power of financial security produced an ethos of mastery, which in turn led to a physical product that contradicts not only the natural lay of the land, but also the spirit of the new democratic movement in American higher education. It is ironic that in its formality, Auburn's campus, like so many others, borrowed the aesthetic traditions of

FIGURE 12.

Benches in front of an Auburn University building (above). A terrace of an Auburn University building (below).

the very institutions of classical learning against which the land-grant college concept reacted. The predominant formality is an engineering accomplishment to be sure, but its essence does not speak to the freedom and inclusiveness inherent in the democratic ideals of the Morrill Acts.

CONCLUDING REMARKS:
CAMPUS AS HISTORICAL
ARTIFACT

The campus of Tuskegee University is significant to American history. It is an artifact not only of an important epoch in the experience of African Americans, but also of race relations in the South. In the midst of mounting repression and violence against Blacks, Washington essayed a program of conciliation and compromise with the Southern white power structure in the hope that his people would be allowed a fair chance at economic opportunity. So eloquent was his message to the ears of America's power-brokers that he was able to capture their attention and support. He rose to become the most powerful and influential African American of his time, hobnobbing with wealthy industrialists, and advising presidents, using the campus of Tuskegee University as both the symbol and the instrument of his quest.

In 1974, the section of the campus built during Washington's administration was designated a National Historic Site by the United States Congress. Since 1877, it has been managed as a national park by the University and the United States Department of the Interior, National Park Service. The twenty-six historic buildings that comprise the site are being renovated: their exteriors are being restored and their interiors retrofitted as the needs of a modern college campus are balanced with the requisites of historic preservation. Unfortunately, accompanying these renovations are site changes which compromise the historic integrity of the campus. Some of the relationships of the buildings to each other and to the topography, which I have described, seem not to have received adequate attention. For instance, the site improvements that accompanied the restoration of Tantum Hall have compromised the historic relationship between its front and its back and the once remarkable visual separation of vehicular and pedestrian traffic. Service areas, barrier-free access, and parking now occupy the facade facing the Big Valley, violating the visual integrity of both the monumental front of the building and the pastoral ambiance of the valley itself. Previously, the eastern valley within the historic district was extensively paved for surface parking lots. It would seem that the landscape—as distinct from buildings as isolated entities—has not been recognized as a historical artifact worthy of preservation.

This issue is by no means restricted to Tuskegee. Concerns regarding, for instance, preserving the landscapes of Civil War battlefields or the slave quarters of Monticello have also recently come up—so much so, the National Park Service in 1992 issued a special brochure to educate the public on the subject. Its message emphasizes the point that:

> Historic landscapes are cultural resources that are part of our national heritage. Like historic buildings and districts, these special places reveal aspects of our country's origins and development through their form and features and the ways they were used. They also reveal much about our evolving relationship to the natural world.

African Americans probably have an even greater stake in preserving their historic landscapes because so much of their history has been either misrepresented or left undocumented. Important stories of their experience are contained in "mute" forms like landscapes, rather than in texts self-consciously recording the past. Landscape is not a passive thing; it does not "just happen." Instead, it is shaped consciously and unconsciously by people to better meet their needs, and in the case of African Americans to meet their needs as they negotiate their place in a hostile environment. As such, landscape becomes an artifact in understanding not only the African-American past, but also the whole of American history.

Understanding Tuskegee's departures from norms of documented landscape architectural history can broaden our perspective on development to include the innovations of poor and marginalized people, heretofore ignored in favor of the contributions of the privileged few who could master and waste as they pleased. Albert Cowdrey, at the beginning of his environmental history of the South, reminds us appropriately of Roderick Nash's words: "The landscape . . . either developed or wild, is an historical document" (1983, p. v). Unwritten stories of black experience are there to be read in landscape. The fact that Tantum Hall fronts Tuskegee's Big Valley may be less an historical accident needing to be corrected according to our current standards of campus aesthetics than an opportunity to discern some dimension of black experience still to be rediscovered.

Notes

1. The Black Belt is that subdivision of Alabama's Coastal Plain which was the center of the legendary "Cotton Kingdom" of antebellum times. Washington (1901 p. 108), in explaining the origins of the name "Black Belt," alludes to its physical and social meanings:

   > So far as I can learn, the term was first used to designate a part of the country which was distinguished by the colour (sic.) of the soil. The part of the country possessing this thick, dark, and naturally rich soil was, of course, the part of the South where slaves were most profitable, and consequently were taken there in large numbers. Later, and especially since the war [Civil War], the term seems to be used in a wholly political sense—that it is to designate counties where black people outnumber whites.

2. For additional discussion on these issues see Bob Scarfo. 1987. "Stewardship: Exploring the Profession's Grand Delusion." *Landscape Architecture* 77(3): 46–51.

3. For an exploration of the impact of this terror on the landscape of the campus see forthcoming Grandison, Kenrick Ian. 1995. "Landscapes of Terror: A Case Study of Tuskegee's Campus, 1881–1915." In *Geography of Identity*. Edited by Patricia Yaeger. Volume 5 of *Ratio*, a series produced by the University of Michigan's Institute for Humanities. Ann Arbor: University of Michigan Press.

4. The topography of the original site depicted in Figure 2 is adapted from a modern topographic survey of the Tuskegee University campus compiled by Photogrammetric Engineers Inc. of Atlanta, Georgia. Solid contour lines were taken directly from the survey. Dotted contour lines were drawn by the author to suggest the most likely lay of the land where the location of buildings or other development interrupted the overall pattern formed by adjacent contours. Implicit in this approach is the assumption that the development caused little disturbance to the original lay of the land. In other words, the topography depicted by the survey approximates that of the site before buildings were placed on it. This was considered

a reasonable assumption for the following reasons: The general lay of the land conveyed by the survey, with the exception of relatively minor irregularities where buildings are located, is similar to that of adjacent undisturbed land. The siting of historic buildings corresponds closely with the undulating natural form of the land, creating an informal campus layout. For example, consider the orientation of the horse barn which was located to the north of the campus as indicated by a 1909 Sanborn Fire Insurance map of the campus (Figure 7). Rather than parallel or perpendicular to the WSW to ESE orientation of the adjacent cow barn, the horse barn was instead oriented from the NW to SE. The location at first glance appears to be irrational, careless, or at least odd until an examination of the topography indicates that it corresponded to the NW to SE orientation of the edge of the broad, elevated spur of the Tuskegee ridge upon which it was built. This approach to layout is evident throughout the campus, suggesting that the original form of the land was a critical factor influencing the form of the campus. Further discussion in support of this reading of the historic topography of the original site is included in the body of the article and hinges on evidence which indicates a concern for minimizing the cost of the grading required to fit buildings to site. A more comprehensive exploration of the accommodation of buildings to land at Tuskegee, including the issue of methodology, should be a worthy subject of a future paper.

5. When the sale of products of Tuskegee's campus came into direct competition with local merchants, tensions flared. At this point the resourceful Washington found new ways to keep the peace. For more on this issue see forthcoming Grandison 1995 referenced above.

6. Both Figures 4 and 7 were created using three sources of mapped information—the topographic survey of the campus mentioned before, 1897 and 1909 Sanborn Fire Insurance maps of the campus, and two figures included in Dozier (1990) based on these maps in collaboration with written sources. The three sources were synthesized. First, the topographic survey was used to locate those historic buildings constructed before 1915 which still exist on the campus. With these locations as reference points, the Sanborn Fire Insurance maps and Dozier's figures were used to "fill in the gaps"—to locate buildings which no longer exist on the campus and to locate historic paths, roads, and entrances. This was accomplished by bringing all the relevant mapped information to the same scale, overlaying, and tracing. Personal judgment was used to resolve conflicting information. In most such cases judgment was helped by corroborating written sources. The most important written sources used were Phelps-Stokes (1931) and Scipio (1987).

References

Bennett, Lerone, Jr. 1964. *Before the Mayflower: A History of the Negro in America 1619–1964.* Chicago: Johnson Publishing.

Bontemps, Arna. 1972. *Young Booker: Booker T. Washington's Early Days.* New York: Dodd, Mead & Company.

Cable, George W. *The Negro Question: A Selection of Writings on Civil Rights in the South,* edited by Arlin Turner. Garden City, New York: Doubleday Anchor Books, 1958.

Cowdrey, Albert. 1983. *This Land, This South an Environmental History.* Lexington, Kentucky: The University of Kentucky Press.

Dozier, Richard. 1990. "Tuskegee: Booker T. Washington's Contribution to the Education of Black Architects." Ph.D. diss., University of Michigan.

DuBois, W. E. B. 1962. *Black Reconstruction in America: An Essay Toward a History of the Part Which Black Folk Played in the Attempt to Reconstruct Democracy in America, 1860–1880.* New York: Russell & Russell.

The Ehrenkrantz Group et al. 1987. *Master Plan for Tuskegee Toward the Year 2000.* Nashville, TN.

Franklin, John Hope. 1969. *From Slavery to Freedom: A History of Negro Americans.* New York: Vintage Books.

Harlan, Louis. 1972. *Booker T. Washington: The Making of a Black Leader, 1856–1901.* London: Oxford University Press.

Holt, Rackham. 1943. *George Washington Carver: An American Biography.* Garden City, New York: Doubleday.

Kennedy, Stetson. 1946. *Southern Exposure.* Garden City, New York: Doubleday.

Klien, Arthur. 1930. *Survey of Land-Grant Colleges and Universities: Vol. I.* Washington: United States Government Printing Office.

Low, Seth to Booker T. Washington. 1911. Booker T. Washington Papers at the Tuskegee University Archives at the Hollis Burke Frissell Library. Box. 86 Misc. 1911, #470.

McWhiney, Grady. "The Revolution in Nineteenth-Century Alabama Agriculture." In *From Civil War to Civil Rights, Alabama 1860–1960: An Anthology from the Alabama Review,* edited by Sarah Woolfolk Wiggins. Tuscaloosa, Alabama: The University of Alabama Press, 1987.

Olmsted, Frederick Law. 1984. *The Cotton Kingdom: A Traveler's Observations on Cotton and Slavery in the American Slave States.* Edited by Arthur Schlesinger, Sr. New York: Random House.

Phelps-Stokes, Anson. 1931. *Tuskegee Institute, The First Fifty Years: Founder's Day Address. Fiftieth Anniversary Celebration.* Tuskegee: Tuskegee Institute Press.

Pryce, Edward. 1987. Personal Conversation.

Scipio, Albert. 1987. *Pre-War Days at Tuskegee: Historical Essay on Tuskegee Institute (1881–1943).* Silver Springs, Maryland: Roman Publications.

Scott, Emmett J. and Lyman Beecher Stowe. 1916. *Booker T. Washington, Builder of a Civilization.* Garden City, New York: Doubleday.

Thrasher, Max B. 1969. *Tuskegee: Its Story and Its Work.* New York: Negro Universities Press.

Turner, Arlin editor. 1958. *The Negro Question: A Selection of Writings on Civil Rights in the South.* Garden City, New York: Doubleday Anchor Books.

Washington, Booker. 1901. *Up From Slavery: An Autobiography.* Garden City, New York: Doubleday.

———. 1904. *Working with the Hand.* New York: Doubleday.

———. 1905. *Tuskegee & its People: Their Ideals and Achievements.* Freeport, New York: Books for Libraries Press.

———. 1915. *The Story of My Life and Work.* Washington D.C.: Austin-Jenkins.

Wiggins, Sarah Woolfolk ed. 1987. *From Civil War to Civil Rights, Alabama 1860–1960: An Anthology from the Alabama Review:* Tuscaloosa, Alabama: The University of Alabama Press.

United States Department of Agriculture and Alabama Department of Agriculture and Industries. 1944. Soil Survey: Macon County Alabama. Series 1937, No. 11, November.

Tradition and Innovation in African-American Yards

Grey Gundaker
Anthropologist

At the time of the publication of this article, Grey Gundaker was a Fellow in Landscape Architecture at Washington, D.C.'s Dumbarton Oaks. She recently published Signs of Diaspora/Diaspora of Signs: Literacies, Creolization, and Vernacular Practice in African America *(1998). Gundaker currently teaches in the American studies department at the College of William and Mary.*

Ruby Gilmore's home nests in layers of plywood, plastic, carpet, appliance parts, and other goods gathered for the resale and recycling business she began several years ago, after the death of her husband. The house itself is a bungalow, but only the up-per cornices of the porch and main structure show above draped white plastic sheets and slatted blinds that cascade down the facade. A red chain-link fence, also backed with white plastic, surrounds the property, with improvised mesh segments adding ex-tra height and elaborate sculptural patterns across the front. Several roots twine through the mesh.

At ground level, around the red pole supporting the mailbox, a gap in the opaque sheeting frames a small tableau. The objects are carefully arranged to show their important sides to the street: a white duck with a white dish framing its head in a ring of circular perforations (drainholes in a flower-pot dish), a white-chested statue of a collie dog, a tiny white Snoopy dog (a large Snoopy-like plush dog also stands guard on the garage roof) pushed into the branches of a magnificent cluster of white coral, sea shells, the head and large yellow eye of a plastic bird, rocks with a coat of white paint that has almost worn away, a weathered bouquet of red and white artificial hi-biscus, and a white plastic antlerless reindeer with one hoof raised—or perhaps the Holy Lamb rampant without a flag; regardless of its history this figure is salient for the piercing black eye that follows the gaze of the collie, Snoopy, and plastic bird out be-yond the fence to the street.

To the left of the front fence, a gate allows Mrs. Gilmore to drive her car into a carpeted space in the yard, the only area not filled with objects. The gate can be heard as well as seen. Brass doorbell chimes, cow bells, a horseshoe, and heavy iron bars rattle and ping at the slightest movement. Gauges, clock faces and dials, blue and red

Grey Gundaker, "Tradition and Innovation in African-American Yards," African Arts *(April 1993): 58–71, 94–96.*

plastic circles, a metal ring, a silver star bouncing on a spring and a circular brush with bristles forming sun-like rays are interspersed among the sounding devices.

When the gate is closed the dimensions of house and yard become unsettlingly ambiguous; silvery wire and white drapery seem to fold in on themselves endlessly, like a frozen waterfall. Sheets draped in a tentlike path to the front door obscure its exact location. The path is flanked by an artificial tree with drooping bunches of white fronds, a cross between a willow and a palm. Along the path hang several patches of bright color: green and yellow sheets, a life-size blue-and-white cardboard skeleton, two rainbow-striped windsocks with long dangling streamers, and a baseball cap perched over an indeterminate clump of objects, including two blue rectangular dust-pans hung where the shoulders should be. The clump is certainly a figure, and on either side the windsocks readily take on the character of masks covering an unseen and undulating persona. But these guardian identities are as ambiguous as the space they occupy. In the blink of an eye, closure between proximate objects dissolves, and identities subside into the mass of practical goods stacked in the yard for sale and personal use.

On the side of the house, a pinkly Caucasian Halloween mask with blotches on its face peeks over piles of building supplies. Printed signs repeat the visual warnings: Keep Out, Danger, No Parking in Driveway, Beware of Dog.

Across the United States, and especially in the South,[1] some African Americans decorate, dress, or work their yards using a flexible visual vocabulary[2] that creolizes and revitalizes American, European, and African traditions through everyday materials—tires, stones, twine, pinwheels, plumbing, planters, toys, and auto parts. Practitioners vary in age, affluence, and style of house. Many have owned homes for decades and retired from skilled trades; few have small children. Usually one person is the prime mover in the yard, but some sites have grown and changed with successive generations and owners.

The makers of these special yards work to please themselves and to instruct visitors in appropriate behavior, sometimes in the broadest spiritual sense. The work takes personal inventiveness, a cultural repertoire of signs that may be widely known or accessible only through special instruction,[3] and alertness to real-world political, historical, and economic conditions.

African-American dressed yards resonate with each other over great distances like elaborations of a code only partly visible. Ruby Gilmore's yard is not a "typical example" but a changeable yet cohesive expressive moment that exhibits visual parallels with numerous other examples. However, participants rarely express this wide-angle view. Most say they try to do "something different," and some echo casual observers who call their arrays of crafted and collected objects "junk" (interview, Mrs. A. J. Hammler, Chattanooga, Tennessee, Dec. 20, 1989).

For a maker to call his or her handsome yard junk may be modest, but it can also imply that the viewer is missing the obvious or asking inappropriate questions about what should be self-evident; for an observer to call the yard junk may point to a serious misunderstanding, since some yards comment on the maker's protection through divine power. Even more complex is the fact that in some yards the areas of so-called junk contain objects that refer both to past generations of a specific family (like iron pots or an old sewing machine) and to black traditions of grave decoration). This in turn suggests transatlantic parallels. For example, Wyatt MacGaffey states, "Throughout central Africa the rubbish heap is a metaphor for the grave, a point of contact with the world of the dead" (1977:148). Areas of "junk" also comprise miniature wildernesses that contrast with orderliness elsewhere in the yard; the distinction between wild and cultivated areas is significant in many areas of Africa. In general, the ambiguous term "junk" indexes both the insensitivity of some viewers to the yards and the parallel between indirection/multivalence in African-American speech and in meanings constructed by the yards' makers through recycled materials.[4]

Whatever terms and concepts eventually dominate scholarly discussion of African-American yards, they should originate with practitioners themselves.[5] Although we still know little about the vernacular language of yard work, clearly key terms exist, like "antique," implying that an object dates from the lifetime of one's ancestors, and "junk," with its overtones of marginality, invisibility, and the graveyard.

Most practitioners call their efforts "yard work" and "working in the yard."[6] Deceptively simple, these phrases call to mind richly nuanced African-American meanings for work, from food-on-the-table labor, to recreational puttering, to power-laden double talk that oscillates between spiritual and sexual connotations ("working in the spirit," "work me Lord," soul singer James Brown's "work me now," or the "mojo working" of the blues). Indeed, all the indigenous terms fit aspects of the practice. In addition to "work," I sometimes use "dress" because it accommodates private or borderline-invisible activities, like inserting bottles in the foundation of a house or sprinkling property boundaries with lime, as well as more public displays. I understand "dressing a yard" as transforming the functions and meanings of objects and the whole site, not mere surface decorating. The significance of this transformation shapes statements like Alabama sculptor Charlie Lucas's about his rural yard, where wire and old car parts rise into monumental dinosaurs and guardian figures: "It's just castoff stuff people throw away. Like people who've been cast off, and everybody thinks they're worth nothing. I've been there. Beat up, broken, down at the bottom. But I had this dream in my head, and that made me more than a piece of junk" (Lampell & Lampell 1989:220). Junk is the emergent stuff of rebirth.

The continuities and complexities of the yards raise many questions. How do practitioners view their yards? How do they relate to American, African, and European traditions? How do the yards fit into their communities? What do their makers have in common? What is the scope of the practice, and what kinds, styles, or genres—if any—are there? How do yard makers use everyday objects to construct meanings—and what meanings? How might yard work draw on other realms of expressive, religious, political, and economic activity?

Answering these questions will entail considerable research. In this article I approach the practice from several vantage points: first, sketching the historical background and explaining modes of communication; next, outlining recurring themes, organizing principles, and spatial relationships as well as variations on these relationships; and finally, following one theme across several yards: special seats and chairs that elaborate African-American values and give them physical shape.

FIGURE 1.

A recycled stove and rocking chair that form part of a memorial grouping created by Elijah Davenport.

HISTORICAL BACKGROUND

Until recently scholars have paid scant attention to how objects and special plantings are used to construct meaningful spaces in African-American yards.[7] Piecemeal references, however, suggest that the practice has considerable historical depth. Evidence also indicates variation linked to changes in American material culture and to African Americans' autonomy in designing living space, which has been greater than some might expect. Even under constraints of enslavement, African building expertise contributed to the types of housing erected in slave quarters and to several enduring architectural styles, including the shotgun house (Glassie 1968:221; Sobel 1987:111–26; Thompson 1989:117–23; Vlach 1975). The space around some buildings may also have benefited from more fugitive design initiatives that may even have flowed in the reverse direction, back to Africa: around houses built by former slaves who resettled in Liberia are pots, plantings, and borders of white stones arranged just as many black and white Southerners place them today (Belcher, Holsoe & Herman 1988:25, 75, 85, 89, 100, 114).

But themes that resurface in contemporary yards do not depend on specific objects; they reflect philosophical and practical means for shaping the significance of

FIGURE 2.

A Magnolia, Mississippi traditional African American grave surrounded by four trees.

whatever is at hand. Dell Upton points out that though they had few possessions, slaves in eighteenth-century Virginia showed a sense of personal territory by using locks on their doors and devoting free time to gardens, houses, and furnishings. "Slave landscapes," he notes, "went beyond the immediate vicinity of the quarters. They included the woods and the fields, where some measure of seclusion and secrecy was available," as well as neighboring plantations where friends, lovers, and relatives lived (Upton 1988:367).

Trees, fields, rocks, and other features of the landscape became invested with spiritual significance and interwoven with the life courses of individuals (see Sims 1981; Rawick 1972, vol. 19:8–9; Brewer 1958:7, 15–17; Day 1955:39, 43; Bass 1973). And again, as in architecture, African values reshaped parts of the New World landscape for the captives, their descendants, and some whites. The memoir of John Sale, son of a Mississippi planter, re-creates the scene when his nurse planted a tree bearing his name in her garden, timing the event at dawn to catch the strength of the rising sun (1929:15–17). Trees are commonly associated with individuals and the ancestors throughout much of West and Central Africa.[8] To this day, trees, especially cedars, at the head of black graves doubly testify to ancestral roots and to the soul's movement to heaven (Connor 1989:54; Thompson 1983:138–39).

Moreover, the association of the rising sun with youthful strength in Sale's name tree story parallels the "four moments of the sun" in Kongo cosmology (Thompson & Cornet 1981; MacGaffey 1986:42–56). This Kongo concept compounds the paths of the sun and human soul in one spatial-temporal equation, beginning at dawn with birth, progressing toward the apex of human strength at noon, and descending at sunset into an underwater spirit world that mirrors the world of the living—where the spiral of life begins again. The cosmogram—variously expressed as a circle enclosing a sun or cross, clock, spiral, or diamond with disks at the four points—recurs in the iconography of African-American churches, burials and yards. Complementing Christian notions of eternity, the cosmogram's merger of abstract principle with material expression is also characteristic of African religions. As Melville Herskovits says of the Dahomean *vodu,* the spirit is "localized" and, "while philosophically conceived as existing everywhere in space, must also have definite places to which it can be summoned, where it can be commanded . . . , and from which it can go forth to achieve those things desired of it" (1967, vol. 2:171).

Localization also involves mediating spiritual powers' access to home, yard, and human body. Interviewers for the book *Drums and Shadows*, searching out African survivals near Savannah, Georgia, during the Depression, found protective plantings (Georgia Writers' Project 1940:14–15) and charms with African antecedents (p. 7). A well-known passage describes George Boddison, known by the honorary title "The Second Mayor of Tin City," wearing what amounts to a portable bottle tree—a flashing crown of charms—upon his head (pp. 20–22; Thompson 1983:142–45; Thompson & Cornet 1981:178–81). Bottle trees, along with medicine-bottle containers and bottle borders in yards and graveyards, have been documented in the United States and West Indies for at least a century. During fieldwork I saw trees and bushes variously adorned with light bulbs, tin pans, glass jars, and empty medicine bottles. Consistent with the protective and healing associations of bottle trees, Bennie Lusane, a retired city worker in northeastern Georgia, decked a small cedar tree with empty prescription-pill bottles to commemorate surviving a serious illness. Inverted and broken vessels and a pipe at the base of the tree resemble grave decorations.

The *Drums and Shadows* interviewers also recorded suggestive details that they did not view as survivals or as visual expressions of folk religious beliefs: houses "closed away behind their fences" (p. 16) and built from automobile parts, pipes, sign boards, bed springs, and scrap iron (pp. 6–12).[9]

Memoirs and "local color" fiction also refer to relevant practices. Ronald Daise mentions an old Sea Island belief that a broom near the door would keep hags from entering the house (1986:98),[10] and Sara Brooks recalls sweeping her family yard in Alabama every Saturday (Simonsen 1986:69–70). Minnie Hite Moody's novel *Death is a Little Man* (1937) describes a yard with several recurring elements.

Even on Judith Street the women try to make the dooryards pretty. . . . Eenie Weaver has the fanciest dooryard, with a fine blue hydrangea in a tub . . . , and love-entangled trailing from old pots suspended from the ceiling. Her yard is swept clean and bare; the walking-path is set off from the yard itself by a double row of bright broken tiles salvaged from the dump, and outside the tiles is a spiky file of gladioli. . . .

(Moody 1937:241)

Some recent documentation has also appeared in exhibition catalogues and photograph collections devoted to "visionary," "self-taught," "outsider," and "folk" artists and architects.[11] The work varies greatly in quality, too often foregrounding artists' environments as deviant and exotic against an undifferentiated "mainstream" backdrop. This approach masks relationships between the featured sites and other sites with less dramatic displays of the same iconography. Still, these sources do yield valuable records of yards and works removed from sites for sale to collectors (e.g., see Perry 1989:52).

Finally, I am indebted to three scholars who have turned their attention directly to African-American yards: Robert Farris Thompson (1983, 1988, 1989, Thompson & Cornet 1981), Lizzetta LeFalle-Collins (1987), and Judith McWillie (1987, 1988, n.d.).

MODES OF COMMUNICATION

Communication in yards through objects and spatial arrangements is a broad topic. Most important, the African-American yards that concern me in this paper creolize multiple traditions from Old and New Worlds, so no monolithic cultural key can unlock what and how yards mean. Equally important, these yards are not the result of mere individual whim, nor do they resemble each other by accident.

Like the words "work" and "dress," yard communication is both multivalent and precise. Signifying visually, certain works, such as warnings to potential thieves, are made to be read in contrasting ways by people with malevolent or benevolent intentions. The self-knowledge of the viewer indexes appropriate interpretations, reinforced by signs like the figure of a dog, a common protective image in yards; or an all-seeing eye, which indicates that the home's owner and higher powers know the visitor's intentions.[12] The densely packed, sparkling wrapped yard of Ruby Gilmore wards off would-be robbers. But for welcome guests, the message of the yard echoes Mrs. Gilmore's spoken words: "All my protection comes from the Lord. He's all any of us has got to look after us and if you trust him he'll look after you good" (interview, Nov. 2, 1989).

In addition to visual signifying, yard communication involves (1) *redundancy,* when symbolic objects like the eye and the dog mutually reinforce a particular reading; (2) *allusion,* when objects suggest action (such as the soles of shoes nailed to a tree as if walking up the trunk) and speech (naming practices, puns like sole/soul, Bible verses, proverbs);[13] and (3) *proximity,* when objects are placed near or at the place or thing to be acted on: boundaries, thresholds, mailboxes, steps, walkways, trees, and flower beds. The characteristics of visual signifying, redundancy, allusion, and proximity, together with recurring objects and common organizing principles, sustain continuities across regional and individual variations.

RECURRING THEMES, ORGANIZING PRINCIPLES, AND USES OF SPACE

Robert Farris Thompson (1989) explores continuities among yards, showing that certain objects and principles share iconography and philosophy with traditions from the Central African kingdom of Kongo, the origin of approximately one-quarter to one-third of those enslaved in the antebellum South:[14]

> Yard-shows assimilate the artistic and philosophical values of classical Kongo culture. This lies manifest in the recurrence and assuredness of the major themes: (1) rock boundaries (2) mirrors on the porch . . . (3) jars or vessels, placed by the main door . . . (4) motion-emblems . . . (5) cosmograms, sometimes rendered as a diamond, sometimes as a circle (6) . . . herbs or flowers within the protective circle of a tire, sometimes white-washed, . . . [and made into a planter] (7) root sculptures, found images, dolls, plaster sculptures . . . stuffed animals (8) trees hung with shiny bottles, light bulbs, or tinfoil, shiny metal disks, . . . bones of animals (9) swept-earth yards . . . (10) graveyard-like decoration, including shells, pipes, rock piles, and sometimes even head-markers (11) plantings of protective herbs.
>
> (Thompson 1989:124)

Thompson has mentioned or pictured other themes, and my fieldwork also suggests additional ones:

(a) *Displays of skills* like topiary or masonry, sometimes related to a job held currently or prior to retirement.15
(b) *Iron bars and tools,* associated with the protective and curative powers of metal.[16]
(c) *Clothing*—frequently for the extremities: shoes, socks, gloves, hats.
(d) *Color* (in addition to white) on vessels, figures, and borders including combinations such as blue, red, and white; blue and yellow; black and white; black and red. Color symbolism in yards deserves more study in its own right and as a means of tracing relations between yard work and other expressive domains. The importance of red has been noted most often (Kemble 1863:77, 188; Ahlo 1976:216). Blue trims doors and windows because evil is said not to be able to cross the color of the sky (Crum 1940:40, 85; Cooley 1926:53; McTeer 1970:19; Thompson 1989:118, 140). In some African-American yards blue plays warning roles I have not found in European-American yards. According to Elaine Nichols (1989:12, 60), combining blue and yellow has ancestral and protective overtones in South Carolina grave decoration. The popularity of blue and yellow goes back to antebellum days.[17] This combination is common-place in Muslim charms (see illustrations in Koenig 1975; see Austin 1984 on African

Muslims in antebellum America), but in yards it also can indicate high-level Masonic membership.

(e) *Tying and wrapping* with strings, ribbons, wires, vines, and herbaceous borders at boundaries and thresholds as well as around objects. Tying and wrapping are traditional ways of enclosing charms and, more broadly, sealing intentions. They number among the features of African-American yard works and art works with clearest links to the African past. . . . Samuel Lawton describes pea vines planted around the edge of a grave to avenge murder (1939:219). Vines, blue ribbon, and strings of decodable or nondecodable script wrap some porches and yards. Beverly Robinson notes that food vines traditionally wrap the porches and fences of African-American homes throughout Los Angeles (1987:24–25).

(f) *Writing,* including name plaques initials, texts, behavioral instructions (e.g., "Welcome," "Beware of Dog"), personal emblems, and nondecodable script[18] (sometimes placed where tying and wrapping might otherwise be found).

(g) *Chairs, seats, and thrones.*

(h) *Filters against unwelcome influences, in the form of spirits and malevolent intentions,* including irregular paths, fans, sieves, and brooms, especially when hanging on the front door. A number of writers beginning in the nineteenth century have suggested that these filters protectively break up the straight paths followed by these spirits (Thompson 1983:222) or divert them into time-consuming activities (counting holes in the the sieve, broomstraws, rice grains, etc.) until danger passes at dawn (Jackson 1967:293).

(i) *Emblems of communication,* such as antennae, transmitters, receivers, electronic devices, grills/grids.[19]

(j) *Emblems of flight,* such as birds, rockets, airplanes, helicopters.[20]

(k) *Water hoses, imitation and real hand pumps and wells.*[21]

(l) *Tall posts, poles, towers.*

(m) *Clocks, timepieces, gauges.*[22] Like the next item, these are related to both the Kongo cosmogram and marks as prohibitive charms.

(n) *X or a Greek cross,* which protectively blocks a path, entrance, or exit (Steiner 1899:262; McTeer 1970:21). Probably the X reflects a confluence of African sources, especially Dahomean ground painting (into Haitian Vodou; K. Brown 1975) and the Kongo cosmogram.[23]

ORGANIZING PRINCIPLES

In addition to setting out the major themes of New World yards, Thompson outlines principles of organization that recall the Kongo *nkisi* (pl. *minkisi*) charm. In this tradition, medicinal materials (earth, bones, herbs) and material instructions to direct their energies are packaged together in bundles or sculpted forms. Some *minkisi* include a central mirror, echoed in mirrors found on the front exterior walls and doors of some African-American homes, indicating their role as a charm-container for spiritual energies—*minkisi* in toto:

There is a logic to the main visual principles of the yard-show: *motion* (wheels, tires, hub-caps, pinwheels); *containment* (jars, jugs, flasks, bottles, especially on trees and porches); *figuration* (plaster icons, dolls, root sculptures, metal images); and *medicine* (special plantings of healing herbs by the door or along the sides of the house).

(Thompson 1989:104)

To these I add several more principles: (a) *directional orientation,* both vertically and laterally, around the four cardinal directions (pointers, arrows, rockets, ladders, weather vanes, paths, whirligigs);[24] (b) *thresholds, transitional zones, conduits* (arches, pipes, wheels with open centers, bed frames);—gateways between this world and the next (Fenn 1985; Thompson & Cornet 1981:181–203);[25] (c) *self-description/self-definition* (groupings concerned with the persona of the yard's maker, using figurative elements, tools, clothing, texts, name plaques, crowns, shoes, chairs, icons of spiritual communication); (d) *instructions to visitors* (signs, texts, filtering mechanisms), which often complement self-descriptions; i.e., "This is who you are visiting and this is how you should behave when you do"; (e) *alternative spatial arrangements and special-purpose areas*.

This last "principle" is something of a catch-all of ways to fine-tune the yard as living and display space to the site as given. On the site-given side of the balance, elaborate yards with traditional and innovative ingredients occur mainly in three types of settings: least frequently, in garden-apartment-court complexes of public housing; more frequently, around farmhouses or newer homes (often ranch style) in rural areas; and most frequently, in established black residential neighborhoods with predominantly owner-occupied single-family dwellings, but sometimes duplexes. Of course, each type of setting constrains creative adaptation. The layout of public housing is rigid and tenants are hemmed in by rules like fire codes that prohibit objects near exits. Interpersonal constraints also apply, such as how residents get along, and whether it is wise to call attention to one's belongings.

SPATIAL RELATIONSHIPS

Rural homes are often clustered in small communities with yards of an acre or more. Some Southern families form compounds as new residences spring up on the lands of a home-place. Rural yards are relatively unconstrained, having generous flower and vegetable gardens and relaxation areas spread over the site. Marie Taylor has spent two decades perfecting her semi-rural yard in southwestern Delaware. Each tree has a circular enclosure that Mrs. Taylor says improves growth (interview, Feb. 27, 1990). Flowers accompany objects chosen for beauty, movement, and flash: pinwheels, windmills, a silver hubcap, red reflectors, a car headlight.

In urban or suburban black neighborhoods, lots usually occupy approximately one-tenth to one-fifth of an acre. Houses often sit toward the front and slightly to one side of the lot, leaving room for a driveway, or face the street symmetrically. Most have porches or stoops approached by cement walks. Overall, sites have a frontal and foursquare order that can be enhanced, undermined, or simply left intact.

FIGURE 3.

A memorial arrangement by Olivia Humphrey in Chattanooga, Tennessee, consisting of an antique iron pot suspended from a pipe-arch threshold.

In semi-urban yards the goal may be a showplace for public appreciation or private sanctuary. The "code" of yard work can generate deep and complex meanings, even in a compact space. Olivia Humphrey has made a small altar-like assemblage to family continuity in her side yard, partly hidden by a fence. It consists of white vessels and white lime powder, a substance that "bad things can't cross," encircling a container of water on a tree stump (Figure 3). Periodically Mrs. Humphrey repaints a black iron pot suspended from a pipe framework over the water so that it "stays nice" but "looks old" (interview, Nov. 19, 1990). A child's shoe placed on top of the porcelain vessels links a memento of childhood with signs of death, nurturance, and transition.

Several other adaptations figure prominently in reorganizing yards and forming links to other aspects of African-American life and values. One of these is the creation of intermediary living space, comparable to Washington, D.C., alleys (Borchert 1980), courtyards in Africa (Prussin 1982:56), and yards in the West Indian sense, which significantly were sometimes used for burials (Mintz 1974:246–47; Genovese 1976:537). Extensions of the porch or porch-like sitting areas, especially when the original porch has been enclosed, also fit into this category.

The maintenance of pointedly contrasting "wilderness" and "tame" areas is another adaptation. (A similar contrast may also be established in relation to space outside the yard.) The distinction between wilderness and cultivated areas is important in much of Africa and the New World (cf. Abrahams 1983:142), and in religions such as Santería (Cabrera 1954), Candomblé (Bastide 1978), and Shango (Simpson 1978). Sweeping the yard until no grass remains is a way to establish this contrast (Abrahams 1983:137). Borders, fences, and mowed lawns also create contrasting areas. In Kongo the wilderness is associated with the cemetery because traditionally burial grounds occupied the sites of villages abandoned by successive generations (MacGaffey 1986:56). In the yards I've visited, these little graveyard/wildernesses are also the areas called "junk."

Finally, yard makers may create special-purpose areas (for narrative tableaus or altars, but also for repairing cars or drying clothes). Adaptation coincides with virtually any yard work. Even adding planters by the front door subtly alters relations among elements: spatially, by emphasizing the importance of the threshold; temporally, by marking the place of the household in a historical stream.

STABILITY, VARIATION, AND IMPROVISATION

In African-American expressive culture, a dynamic relation between reiteration and improvisation is often a basic aesthetic and communicative pattern.[26] In yard work, improvisation establishes personal virtuosity—the "doing something different" that is an incentive for the work in the first place. The patterns of selection, placement, and spatial organization that I have discussed so far are stable enough that one can usually identify improvisations from or in relation to them. I do not mean to imply that particular yards are "tokens of a type"—some sort of concrete yard-parole to an abstract yard-langue. Rather, I am suggesting systematic variation along a spectrum of yard content and design. A few elements—including wheels, trees, white and reflective objects, cross and diamond shapes, and chairs—remain quite consistent over time and distance. Repetition of elements helps to cue interpretations and embody cultural and personal values such as rights in property, rights in personal decision making, and the importance of spiritual knowledge, to name only a few. Because yards articulate values, they resist classification based simply on content. The means for composing value statements are too complex, and visual aspects of yards almost always lap over into other sensory realms: the sound of chimes, the aroma of herbs, the richness of spoken or sung phrases.

Improvisation offers a way to overcome adverse circumstances. Through several years of scavenging, Ruby Gilmore filled her yard with wood, metal, and scrap accumulated for her recycling business. This paper opened with a description of how her yard looked in 1989. One morning in late October 1990, without warning (or adequate legal notice), city workers appeared with trucks and a bulldozer. When they finished three days later, Mrs. Gilmore's yard was stripped to bare dirt. Workers even uprooted her treasured climbing rose. The bulldozing set Mrs. Gilmore back financially, but did not break her spirit. Guided by prayer, she resolved to take on the mayor, learn her rights, and transform her ravaged property into a renewed source of income, protection and pride (interview, Nov. 2, 1990). Recalling yards of her youth, she swept the dirt into flowing patterns, retrieved her favorite china dog and white coral from a hiding place in a ditch, and created a compact group of object-admonitions by the front porch. Thanks to this play of repetition and improvisation Mrs. Gilmore's yard looks different than before the bulldozing, but it communicates similar messages.

Along with individual improvisations, yards in many communities have a recognizable style that conforms to contours of the practice elsewhere. Flexible clusters of resemblances come about through the use of locally made items or items used in local industry or agriculture, through flattering imitation of someone else's initiative, and probably many other ways. In Orangeburg, South Carolina, yards feature a cast concrete wheel surmounted by a pony whose legs follow the curve of the wheel. These wheels were produced in the area about twenty-five years ago. On the Virginia Eastern Shore, white abbreviated obelisks reminiscent of gravestones join tires, poles, and plants along the edges of many yards. And in Barbados, the red enamel wheels in a few yards originated in the sugar refineries.

Inconsequential in themselves, these repeating objects provide hubs from which improvisations spin off. Local styles also bring into focus how configurations stabilize elements as roughly "the same" in relation to values despite differences of locale and appearance. Even more variations result from innovations by individuals, never taking hold as a style, but remaining the special feature of one yard.

SPECIAL SEATS

Special seats and chairs are one of the recurring themes that give some yards recognizable presence. Though such seats occur in relatively few yards, they resemble each other across hundreds of miles. Rare compared with rock and tire boundaries, reflective and containing elements, and figuration, they can incorporate these and other themes. Special seats are not monolithic units but groupings whose parts retain separate identities with their own associations, at the same time that these parts are transformed through combination. Thus these seats defy simplistic tracking of discrete objects across yards. Doing so subverts their specialness, for most seats of themselves are just commonplace lawn, kitchen, or arm chairs brought outside.

Though usually nothing seems special about these seats at first glance, anomalies like the inhospitable angle of a chair, elevation off the ground, or the lack of a seat hint at their status. And because the human body orients to resting places and social spaces largely through habit, awareness that these seats are not quite ordinary, sometimes patently extraordinary, registers gradually, on some deeper level than mere recognition of surface cues. Further, in contrast to lawn furniture grouped for sociability, these seats usually stand apart from other chairs.

Yard seats cohere with a network of African-American religious, social, and expressive associations that interweaves chairs, stools, thrones, seats and allusions to sitting with visionary experience, powers of deities or spirits or persons, and the continuing influence in this world of deceased leaders and ancestors.[27] Thus special seats accrete meanings across settings: a chair on earth gains significance from chairs in visions of heaven; a memorial sent from the person who used it. Seats serve similar functions across the Afro-Atlantic diaspora, and in the United States, references to thrones, sitting, and special seats appear in African-American verbal art such as this nineteenth-century spiritual from coastal Georgia:

> *I have a mother in the promis'*
>   *land;*
> *I'm not so particular 'bout shakin'*
>   *her hand;*
> *But I heard an angel singin'.*
>
> *Oh, let her fly, let her fly,*
> *Lord, Lord, let her fly.*
> *Let her fly to Mt. Zion and sit*
>   *down.*
> *(Killion & Waller 1972:250)*

Seats also figure in accounts of religious experiences and visions. Charles Colcock Jones (1888:158–66) recorded in Gullah dialect the vision of Daddy Jupiter, an elderly and highly esteemed man who accompanied his master to the War of 1812. During the last year of his life, Daddy Jupiter saw the seat prepared for him in heaven.

> [D]e Lord, him call teh one angel, an eh tell um fuh bring one chair an set um down befo eh trone. Soon es dis bin done eh say: 'Jupiter, yuh you chair; set een um. Eh blants ter you.' . . . Eh hab gold rocker ter um. Eh hab welwet cushin een eh bottom. Eh hab high back, an arm stuff. . . . Me shame fuh sit in de chair, but de blessed Jesus, him courage me, an me tek me seat, an me so tankful dat me hab one chair in de mansion ee de sky.
>
> (Jones 1888:163)

George Wiley, a white Virginian, recounts a similar vision of an empty chair waiting in heaven for the enslaved "Uncle Phil" (Wiley 1905:29–34).

In earthly counterpoise to these heavenly chairs, a chair stands in for the deceased in the closing funeral scene of Zora Neale Hurston's novel *Jonah's Gourd Vine* (1990:201): "The high-backed, throne-like chair was decorated. Tight little sweaty bouquets from the woods and yards were crowded beside ornate floral pieces. . . . the flower-banked chair represented the body of Rev. Pearson . . ." This symbolism extends from church to cemetery through placing on graves real or styrofoam chairs covered in flowers (photos in M. R. Little 1989:131; Bunnen & Smith 1991:7).

The following quotation from A.R. Flowers's novel, *De Mojo Blues*, gives a vivid picture of how one special chair came to its owner.

> Something drew Tucept's attention and he looked up just as the chair was floating by in the water. A monster of a wood chair, with thick armrests and a high carved back. . . . It

had obviously been in the river for awhile and river artistry had carved it into flowing driftwood lines. The setting sun threw the grooves into deep relief and Tucept could almost see movement in the chair's fluid surface. . . . Carved into the back was an Xed circle. . . . He spent the next two years working on that chair. . . . He became obsessed with it, marveling over the twisted rivergrooved ridges. . . . He cleaned and regrooved the crossed sun in the high back. He found a rusty nail on the riverfront one day, drove it into the side of the chair and hung the little bag that he brought back from Nam on it.

(Flowers 1985:35)

Though fictional, this chair incorporated important yard themes: the cosmogram, iron implements, root sculpture and references to water, and a charm bag reminiscent of an *nkisi*. The chair in Flowers's novel bears an incised version of the "four moments of the sun" on its back (which, at least in the Memphis area where the novel is set, also goes by the name "the mojo sign"), and bears witness to the action of the river, which carried the chair to its owner and deepened the natural wood grain. These qualities prefigure powers that Tucept learns to direct as he becomes a conjurer in the course of the novel.

These brief passages indicate some of the main ideas that give seats special places in African-American yards, for they show them as sites of dignity, knowledge, and power, and also future status, pointed absence, and implied presence. Protective seats, positioned near thresholds, suggest a guardian for the property; thrones allude to judgment and authority, and construct an identity for the yard's maker (who is almost always male in the case of thrones); prayer seats set aside a place for spiritual communication; and memorial-ancestral seats honor deceased persons and family continuity. These roles can overlap in one seat. All types to varying degrees treat seats as points of intersection between material and spiritual worlds, between temporal and eternal channels of power. Seats therefore have much in common with altars.

One seat can serve several functions and one yard can have several seats. Bennie Lusane calls himself "the decorating man" in verses taped to the dashboard of his car (interview, May 16, 1990). He transformed a half-acre yard over the unusually short period of about a year, using handmade and found objects, including at least eight special seats—in addition to ordinary lawn chairs. One chair between paired golden "African" warrior figures guards the threshold to an alcove. The chair's guardian role is cued by its angle facing everyone who approaches the house, a red stop sign on the other side of the threshold, and two buttons like eyes in the back of the chair. Inside the alcove, tables display plastic flowers and stacked vessels reminiscent of burial mound "love offerings," while an assemblage on the wall celebrates the sensual side of loving women—their legs, breasts, and scent. Two single chairs and a *loveseat*—an aptly named couple's chair—line the walls. The chairs look commonplace, but long rusty nails stick up from their cushionless seats, making sitting down unthinkable. A blood-red substance half-fills a hypodermic vial on the back of the loveseat, along with "bloodline" plaques in the form of small coats of arms. Whiskey bottles mounted behind the backrest and bottle caps lining the arms simultaneously imply offerings and bottle-traps for negative influences, a double entendre characteristic of yard communication.

Outside the alcove in a grouping that also suggests spiritual-ancestral tribute, a white straight chair anchors one corner of a four-sided framework around a tree. A branching pole of bottles marks the opposite corner. Parallel arches on either side of the tree demarcate a threshold between worlds in a form also found on graves (Thompson & Cornet 1981:195). Clocks, whiteness, and silvery objects underscore reciprocity between graveyard and home-yard iconography.

Another chair in Mr. Lusane's yard combines thronelike scale with signs of spiritual insight. Like many special seats, it backs against a tall tree—in this case a pine that wears dark glasses tied to the trunk about ten feet above the ground. With one lens in and one out, the glasses create a lopsided stare that calls to mind a line in Arna Bontemps's novel *Black Thunder*. As he fills in the grave of a friend, a man says to the spirit of the deceased: "Anybody knows that dying ain't nothing. You got one eye shut and one eye open, old man" (1936:52). This imagery also has wider geographic scope: in Haitian Vodou, glasses missing one lens signify Gede, the lord of the dead and cemeteries, "because he sees into both the lands of the living and the dead" (K. Brown 1991:362). In Mr. Lusane's yard, bottles and pipes join other signs of endurance, enthronement, flight, and sight around his chair.

Bennie Lusane's seats are solidly personal, built with local materials like bottles from his wife's Avon business and clock faces discarded by a nearby factory. They also include some of the characteristics that recur from yard to yard. In general, a special seat stands apart from other chairs and near an imposing tree or tall pipes or poles. Nearby one will usually find iron (in the form of stakes, tools, chains, horseshoes, pipes, etc.), vessels or containers, and emblems of directional orientation and motion, which may coincide with the cosmogram. Quite a few configurations also include horned animal skulls, arches or thresholds, poles or white cylinders, and sending-receiving devices including grills that resemble television antennas.

Like other aspects of yards, seats can gain and lose specific content while retaining general identity. Johnson Smith changes his seat whenever he has practical need for part of the grouping or simply feels the urge for yard work. His yard holds out an ever pending promise of dissolution into ordinary mess. Faces seem to congeal from piles of scrap. The broken crockery and pipes of miniature graveyards in the corners of the yard fade into the scratchy excavations of Mrs. Smith's chickens. For a while, the special seat was a wheelchair filled with shiny aluminum pans, beside clay vessels and a white propane cylinder. A year later, a white chair replaced the wheelchair, which then became a holder for herbs. Through these changes, the arrangement has retained a long pipe leaning against the tree, an iron cowbell and chain, and dangling strands of yellow beads and blue water hose. Also suspended from the tree are a red metal insecticide sprayer, a rectangular wire grill, and a plaque shaped like a stained glass apple at the fork of the tree: a communication receiver and a reminder of Adam's choice in Eden at the branches' parting of ways.

The yard of Elijah Davenport in rural Clarke County, Georgia, contains two kinds of special seats. One is part of a configuration that seems to suggest that the yard's owner is a recipient of spiritual communication. It consists of a tree standing within a diamond laid out in white quartz. Holes in the seat of the chair repeat this shape: the cosmogram doubling with the "four eyes" sign of spiritual sight (Wahlman 1986:72; Thompson 1978:29; Gundaker 1992:136–55). In place of the chair's original back, a barred metal circle—a barbecue grill resembling an antenna—has been bound to two iron rods perpendicular to the seat.

The other special seat in Mr. Davenport's yard forms a memorial tableau that includes a white pillar bearing a tray of small figures and broken vessels, a bentwood rocking chair, and other mementos of a woman's life: a woodburning range with the words "Home Comfort" on the oven, and a heart-shaped metal dish. These join objects evoking traditional African-American burial—pipes, white quartz, yellow and blue colored objects, a stone slab, an iron disk—and objects evoking both domesticity and burial—a lamp, a clock, white porcelain plates, glass jars, a blue agateware washbasin. The fact that the woodstove lies on its side interweaves domesticity with death, for inversion points to the other side of the mirror, the spirit world. Reference to an unseen occupant of the rocking chair is underlined by the angle of the chair—tilted forward as if someone were bracing her body on the arms in order to stand up.[28]

Sometimes in an arrangement a chair merges with parts of a physical body. It took some months for me to realize that the old kitchen chair, detergent bottles, bucket, pipe, and hose that Gyp Packnett incorporated into his backyard fence were in fact the figures of a man and a woman, with the chair seat forming the woman's lap. "That's right," he said, "I don't know who they are or where they come from, but I do know they where they suppose to be" (interview, June 14, 1991).

Special seats such as these embody the ways yard work speaks to and reconstitutes important personal experiences and cultural values in material form. Several seats stress multidirectional movement and communication: chairs that mobilize an implicit body in the midst of a spiritually charged space. In memorial seats, icons of family continuity combine with signs of burial: tributes, but perhaps also requests in the African tradition that personal attributes of the deceased remain behind to benefit the living (Thompson & Cornet 1981:145). The ones like those of Bennie Lusane and Tucept, the character in Flowers's novel, mark off spaces in which imbalances of power are redressed through the assertion of strong identities for their owners.

More broadly, a typology of seats and their functions, such as the one that is emerging here, can help contextualize other African-American seats and thrones in museums and private art collections that up to now have been treated as largely disconnected from specific genres or relatively widely known cues to interpretation. The most striking is surely that of the African-American artist and visionary James Hampton. His masterpiece, *The Throne of the Third Heaven of the Nations Millennium General Assembly,* elaborates issues of spiritual power and insight on a massive scale. Other important examples are the *Blue Throne* made by Leroy Person, now part of the Lynch Collection of Outsider Art at North Carolina Wesleyan College, and a throne linked to a Presbyterian church in Texas carved from a single block of wood by an unknown artist (Vlach 1978:38–39). All three of these thrones include iconography and allusions that also arise in African-American yards, such as the wheel, use of personal script, and references to moral judgment, authority, and mediation through images of creatures like birds, butterflies, and amphibians.

It seems apparent, then, that yard work draws on and contributes to other spheres of African-American expression. However, many questions remain about the nature of order across these yards, the lives of their makers, the myriad elaborations spread over the country, and their significance. In this article I have tried to show that yards vary owing to the wide assortment of commercial and found objects and plants, constraints and possibilities for adaptation offered by particular sites, and the makers' aesthetic predilections. Yet, many commonalities also exist. These result in part from parallels in the histories of makers (including aspects of the African past), in local styles, in the selection of objects and the principles that organize them, and in intersections of yard work with other areas of expression such as dressing the body in life and burial in death; and from a stable set of values.

Thus these yards are not isolated or autonomous: if a fence sets a piece of property apart, it nonetheless addresses the world outside the fence as well as the world within. Far from being either mere enactments of decorative routine ("yard art") or eccentric gestures toward some ever receding horizon outside culture ("outsider art"), dressed yards contribute to and are shaped by the ongoing cultural processes that make sense of everyday works and lives.

Notes

1. My focus on the South is largely a matter of convenience. African Americans have created striking yards in black neighborhoods across the country. Research elsewhere includes New Haven (Thompson 1989:141) and Los Angeles, where the California Afro-American Museum presented the pioneering exhibition "Home and Yard: Black Folk Life Expressions in Los Angeles." Migration from the West Indies has also enriched the visual scene in urban areas (see Perry 1989:44–45).
2. Wyatt MacGaffey (1988) uses this concept to elucidate Kongo *nkisi* charms.
3. For example, initiation into the Masons or thorough knowledge of the Bible, especially the Book of Revelation.
4. Herskovits links New World indirection with African patterns of behavior (1958:154–58).
5. Certainly, identity and self-definition lie at the heart of cultural politics, but there are research stakes as well. For example, some yards communicate through puns and allusions to speech (also see Thompson 1989; cf. MacGaffey 1988; Dalby 1968:168; Leiris 1960). Imposed terms mask these forms of communication and ignore the African-American gift for inventing new words, transforming the "standard" lexicon (Banks 1975, Johnson 1972), and using loan translations (Abrahams & Szwed 1982:36–37) or intact words from African languages (Vass 1979, Dalby 1972, Turner 1949).
6. Practitioners and researchers also use more specific terms. Based on his interviews, Robert Farris Thompson (1988, 1989) has referred to "spirit gardens," mainly for burials and burial-like areas, and "yard-shows," for yard displays in general. "Decorate" occurs in general conversation and occasionally in connection with "hoodoo" (Hyatt 1970:935). "Dress" crops up in spiritually activating or neutralizing procedures such as medicating houses against intrusion (Hyatt 1970:935, 1161), gardens and fruit trees to promote fertility and ward off thieves (Bell 1893:1–3), and adding substances to altars (Hurston 1978:59), and the Sea Island custom of "dressing the house" with fresh newspapers on the interior walls and fresh paint outside at Christmas (Cooley 1926:143).
7. Studies by cultural geographers and landscape designers are Westmacott (1992), Lemaistre (1988), Wilhelm (1975). Though focused primarily on vernacular architecture Jopling includes important comparative material (1988:135, 150, 171, 205, 255).
8. For example, see Partridge (1905:271–73) for ancestral trees in the Cross River area, MacGaffey (1977:149) for hollow trees as ancestral abode and origin of mankind in Kongo belief, Little (1967:219–20) for prayers and offerings to ancestors at special trees among the Mende.

9. The interviewers' omission is not surprising since at the time there was little precedent for white outsiders to see these details in this way; even Herskovits (1958:136–37) and Puckett (1926:10–12) assumed a paucity of visual and material cultural survivals in the U.S. "Poverty" crops up often as an explanation for the use of found materials in yards (but see Greenfield 1986). Patently, residents of many sites visited in the Depression and after were poor. And bed springs do make functional fences. However, this does not explain why bed springs and headboards recur today in yards of settled property-owners in comfortable middle- and lower-middle-class neighborhoods. A possible explanation is that the spiral springs serve as filters, catching negative influences in their coils.

10. Puckett (1926:218) cites N.W. Thomas's report that among the Timne people of Sierra Leone "a broom will be hung on the door that the house may be 'clean' and no bad sickness come in." Robert Farris Thompson suggests brooms relate to flight, as in the plantation-era practice of jumping the broom on the occasion of marriage to signify a bond that transcends the divide between matter and spirit (pers. com., Aug. 1989).

11. For a few of these catalogues and collections see Walker Art Center (1974), Livingston and Beardsley (1982), Stanley, Kelley and Manley (1981), University of Southwestern Louisiana (1987), Adele (1989), and Manley (1989).

   These euphemistic descriptions of artists seem more accurately to reflect art market and institutional relations than the nature of the artist's training or motives.

12. The all-seeing, disembodied eye is found in many visual traditions around the world (Koenig 1975). Important uses of this sign in African America include the drawing of an eye surrounded by sacred writing in the prayer room of Sister Gertrude Morgan in New Orleans (Livingston & Beardsley 1982:46; Horowitz 1975:26). James Hampton centered a concentric circular image with characteristics of both the eye and the sun on the blackboard found after his death near his *Throne* (photo in Gould 1987:57). The eye also appears on African-American grave markers, usually at top center where it sometimes means membership in the Odd Fellows fraternity.

13. John Szwed (pers. com., Sept. 1988) points out a similar pun in a laminated pine relief by Daniel Pressley depicting two people crushed beneath a foot and titled "The Souls Beneath Defeats" (item number 94 in Hemphill 1976).

14. Thompson bases this approximation (1988:57) on Philip Curtin's 1977 lecture at Yale University and Rawley's *The Trans-Atlantic Slave Trade* (1981:335). Far from obliterating their cultures, slavery forced captives (and also free African Americans) to emphasize similarities in their heritages and to achieve adaptations that interleaved diverse traditions without necessarily obscuring all traces of their origins. Case studies include Sterling Stuckey (1987) on the ring shout, and Walter Pitts (1989) on reinterpretation in contemporary Afro-Baptist ritual, following Herskovits (1958). My paper assumes that African retentions exist, and draws on African sources as well as folktales and New World black religions with recognized African linkages. However, my present purpose is to describe the yards, not to recapitulate the argument for retentions.

15. This point has been made about "outsider" artists in North Carolina by Roger Manley (1989) and by Bronner (1986, 1989) concerning "cultural praxis" in yard environments in Harrisburg, Pennsylvania.

16. Phil Peek reviews uses of metal for protective and curative purposes in Africa and the U.S. (1978:111). Also relevant: the burial custom of inserting metal pipes into graves, the association of metal objects like locks and chains with enslavement, and the BaKongo use of iron pegs to indicate commitment (Laman 1957:113).

17. Belle Kierney, a slaveholder's daughter who made dresses for black women after the Civil War, recalled that the color combination ordered most was "bright yellow calico trimmed with blue" (1900:55). See Wahlman (1987) for a summary of Africanisms associated with various colors.

18. The African legacy in New World black scripts is discussed by Thompson (1983, 1988, 1989), Wahlman (1987), and Gundaker (1992). McWillie (1987, 1991) examines the use of nondecodable script by visionary artists such as Minnie Evans and J.B. Murray, and reports fieldwork on "writing in the unknown tongue" in healing and divination.

19. The theme of transmitters and receivers appears in the work of J.B. Murray (reproduced on the back cover of INTAR 1988) and Lonnie Holley, who uses TV sets to fence part of his property in Birmingham, Alabama.

20. The airborne imagery that informs these emblems probably draws on both the Judeo-Christian iconography of ascent and transcendence, such as climbing Jacob's ladder, and such African derived lore of flight as Porter (1945) summarizes in "The Flying Africans."

21. Johnson Smith speaks of looped hoses that tie a tree with water (interview, Lumberton, Mississippi; Dec. 2, 1990). Victor Melancon relates the miniature pump in his front yard with the cool, deep spring water of the countryside and the way people got water in the old days (interview, Hammond, Louisiana; June 15, 1991).

22. Timepieces also concern contemporary African-American artists Z.B. Armstrong (McWillie 1987, n.d) and Frank Albert Jones (Adele 1989:40–51).

23. See Gundaker 1992:136–216 for an extended discussion. These signs are distributed across the South and the West Indies, protecting vacant houses in Dominica, an electric generator on New Providence, Bahamas, and cradles of infants in Trinidad. Hyatt's interviews (1970–1978) mention the cross mark countless times, linking it to the crossroads, site of offerings, pacts, and the parting of the ways. On homes and thresholds in thresholds in the U.S. the X is often accompanied by O (see illustration in Yolles 1989 of a wall painted by Tyree Guyton of Detroit). This O has several connotations: full coverage of a situation (each "I" dotted and "T" crossed), an all-seeing eye, and a conduit like the open end of a pipe.

24. Objects orient through placement and behavior (weather vane), or as tools for moving through space (ladder), or both (helicopter). Verticality and four-directional movement may combine. Ishmael Reed notes, "Crossroads figures in Vodoun are associated with elevators because going from time to time is like riding an elevator. The time elevator is such a smooth ride that you feel as if you are standing still" (1988:126). Whirligigs have been associated with spiritual powers by some African Americans at least since early this century, and probably much earlier. In a composite tale pieced together from nine informants, John Bennett tells of "Domingo, the black constable, . . . the greatest conjurer and necromancer that ever lived in the lowlands of Carolina since the days of Gullah Jack" (1946:109). "He had a curious whirligig on top of his house by which to control the wind" and sold fair winds to sailors (1946:114). Compare this with a whirligig in the collection of the Museum of American Folk Art (Livingston & Beardsley 1982:64) Louisiana artist David Butler made for his yard. He painted it with a Greek cross containing a circle in each quadrant (see Thompson 1989:113) and applied cut out fish and birds that imply mastery of heights and depths.

25. See Lawton 1939:196 on the grave as a threshold through which objects are poured. Bed frames serve as fences and gates to the "memory garden" areas of the yards of Mrs. A.J. Hamler and Gyp Packnett. Robert Farris Thompson suggests that the holes in wheels put in trees as warnings are gates to the world of the dead, reminding intruders where property owners plan to send them (pers. com., Aug. 1989).

26. It has been suggested that improvisation is an African and African-American *tradition,* in contrast with the European notion of improvisation as a break with tradition (Stearns & Stearns 1964:15; Leon 1987).

27. Also see David Brown (1989:459–77) on thrones in Afro-Cuban religion, and Mikelle Smith Omari (1989:56) on thrones in Afro-Brazilian Egun Society rituals. Though seats serve several functions in the U.S., I find an Egun-like ancestral focus to be the most important single impulse in creation of these works. I hope to discuss this further in the future.

28. Compare with the folk belief that chairs rocking on their own are moved by ghosts, and a chair in a story by Ernest Gaines (1968:27) that is inseparable from the woman who used it.

References Cited

Abrahams, Roger D. 1983. *The Man of Words in the West Indies Performance and the Emergence of Creole Culture*. Baltimore Johns Hopkins University Press.

Abrahams, Roger D. and John F. Szwed (eds.). 1982. *After Africa: Extracts from British Travel Accounts and Journals of the Seventeenth, Eighteenth, and Nineteenth Centuries Concerning the Slaves, Their Manners, and Customs in the British West Indies*. New Haven: Yale University Press.

Adele, Lynn. 1989. *Black History/Black Vision: The Visionary Image in Texas*. M. Huntington Art Gallery, The University of Texas. Austin: University of Texas Press.

Ahlo, Olli. 1976. *The Religion of the Slaves: A Study of the Religious Tradition and Behaviour of Plantation Slaves in the United States, 1830–1865*. Helsinki: FF Communications no 217.

Austin, Allan D. 1984. *African Muslims in Antebellum America A Sourcebook*. New York: Garland Publishing.

Banks, Carl J., Jr. 1975. *Banks Dictionary of the Black Ghetto Language*. Los Angeles: Saidi Publications.

Bass, Ruth. 1973. "The Little Man," in Alan Dundes, ed. *Mother Wit from the Laughing Barrel: Readings in the Interpretation of Afro-American Folklore*, pp. 388–96. Englewood Cliffs, NJ Prentice Hall.

Bastide, Roger. 1978. *The African Religions of Brazil: Toward a Sociology of the Interpenetration of Civilizations*. Baltimore: Johns Hopkins University Press.

Belcher, Max, Svend E. Holsoe and Bernard L. Herman. 1988. *A Land and Life Remembered: Americo-Liberian Folk Architecture*. Athens: University of Georgia Press.

Bell, Hesketh J. 1893. *Obeah: Witchcraft in the West Indies*. 2nd ed. London: Sampson Low, Marston.

Bennett, John. 1946. *The Doctor to the Dead: Grotesque Legends and Folk Tales of Old Charleston*. New York: Rinehart.

Bolton, H. Carrington. 1891. "Decoration of Graves of Negroes in South Carolina," *Journal of American Folklore* 4, 14:214.

Bontemps, Arna. 1936. *Black Thunder*. Reprint, Boston: Beacon Press, 1968.

Borchert, James. 1980. *Alley Life in Washington: Family, Community, Religion and Folklife in the City, 1850–1970*. Urbana: University of Illinois Press.

Borgatti, Jean M. 1990. "Portraiture in Africa," *African Arts* 23, 3:35–39, 101.

Brewer, John Mason. 1958. *Dog Ghosts and Other Texas Negro Folk Tales*. Austin: University of Texas Press.

Bronner, Simon J. 1989. "Two Home-Built Environments: A Comparison in Praxis." Paper presented at the Annual Meeting of the American Folklore Society, Oct. 18–22, 1989, Philadelphia, PA.

Bronner, Simon J. 1986. "The House on Penn Street: Creativity and Conflict in Folk Art," in *Folk Art and Art Worlds,* eds. John Michael Vlach and Simon J. Bronner, pp. 123–49. Ann Arbor, MI: UMI Research Press.

Brown, David Hilary. 1989. "The Garden in the Machine: Afro- Cuban Sacred Art and Performance in Urban New Jersey and New York." Ph.D. dissertation, Yale University.

Brown, Karen McCarthy. 1991. *Mama Lola*. Berkeley: University of California Press.

Brown, Karen McCarthy. 1975. "The *VeVe* of Haitian Vodou: A Structural Analysis of Visual Imagery." Ph.D. dissertation, Temple University.

Bunnen, Lucinda and Virginia Warren Smith. 1991. *Scoring in Heaven: Gravestones and Cemetery Art of the American Sunbelt States*. New York: Aperture Books.

Cabrera, Lydia. 1954. *El Monte*. Havana: Ediciones CR.

Chatelain, Heli. 1894. *Folk-Tales of Angola*. Memoirs of the American Folklore Society, vol. 1. Boston: Houghton, Mifflin.

Connor, Cynthia. 1989. "Archeological Analysis of African- American Mortuary Behavior," in *The Last Miles of the Way: African-American Homegoing Traditions,* ed. Elaine Nichols, pp. 51–55. Columbia: South Carolina State Museum.

Cooley, Rossa Belle. 1926. *Homes of the Freed*. New York: New Republic.

Crum, Mason. 1940. *Gullah: Negro Life in the Carolina Sea Islands*. Durham, NC: Duke University Press.

Daise, Ronald. 1986. *Reminiscences of Sea Island Heritage*. Orangeburg, SC: Sandlapper Publishing.

Dalby, David. 1972. "The African Element in American English," in *Rappin' and Stylin' Out,* ed. Thomas Kochman, pp. 170–86. Urbana: University of Illinois Press.

Dalby, David. 1968. "The Indigenous Scripts of West Africa and Surinam: Their Inspiration and Design," *African Language Studies* 9:156–97.

Day, Beth. 1955. The *Little Professor of Piney Woods: The Story of Professor Laurence Jones*. New York: Julian Messner.

Drewal, Margaret Thompson. 1990. "Portraiture and the Construction of Reality in Yorubaland and Beyond," *African Arts* 23, 3:40–49, 101.

Flowers A.R., 1985. *De Mojo Blues*. New York: Ballantine.

Gaines, Ernest J. 1968. "Just Like a Tree," reprinted in *Memory of Kin,* ed. Mary Helen Washington, pp. 13–38. New York: Anchor, 1991.

Genovese, Eugene D. 1976. *Roll, Jordan, Roll: The World the Slaves Made*. New York: Vintage.

Georgia Writers' Project. 1940. *Drums and Shadows: Survival Studies among the Georgia Coastal Negroes*. Reprinted, Athens: University of Georgia Press, 1986.

Glassie, Henry. 1968. *Pattern in the Material Folk Culture of the Eastern United States*. Philadelphia: University of Pennsylvania.

Gould, Stephen Jay. 1987. "James Hampton's Throne and the Dual Nature of Time," *Smithsonian Studies in American Art* 1, 1:46–57.

Gundaker, Grey. 1992. "'Without Parse of Script': The Interaction of Conventional Literacy and Vernacular Practice in African American Expressive Culture." Ph.D. dissertation, Yale University.

Hartigan, Lynda. 1977. *The Throne of the Third Heaven of the Nations Millennium General Assembly*. Montgomery: Montgomery Museum of Art.

Hemphill, Herbert W., Jr. (ed.). 1976. *Folk Sculpture USA*. Brooklyn: Brooklyn Museum.

Herskovits, Melville J. 1967. *Dahomey: An Ancient West African Kingdom,* vol. 2. Evanston, IL: Northwestern University Press.

Herskovits, Melville J. 1958. *The Myth of the Negro Past*. Boston: Beacon Press.

Horowitz, Elinor Lander. 1975. *Contemporary American Folk Artists*. Philadelphia: J. B. Lippincott.

Hurston, Zora Neale. 1978. *Mules and Men*. Bloomington: University of Indiana Press. Reprint of 1935 ed., Philadelphia: Lippicott.

Hurston, Zora Neale. 1934. *Jonah's Gourd Vine*. Philadelphia: J. B. Lippincott. Reprinted, New York: Perennial Library, Harper & Row, 1990.

Hyatt, Harry Middleton. 1970–1978. *Hoodoo—Conjuration—Witchcraft—Rootwork,* 5 vols. Cambridge, MD: Western Publishing.

INTAR Latin American Gallery. 1988. *Another Face of the Diamond: Pathways through the Black Atlantic South*. New York: INTAR.

Jackson, Bruce. 1967. *The Negro and His Folklore in Nineteenth Century Periodicals*. Austin: University of Texas Press.

Johnson, Ken. 1972. "The Vocabulary of Race," in *Rappin' and Stylin' Out,* ed. T. Kochman. Urbana: University of Illinois Press.

Jones, Charles Colcock. 1888. *Negro Myths from the Georgia Coast, Told in the Vernacular*. Boston, New York: Houghton, Mifflin.

Jopling, Carol. 1988. *Puerto Rican Houses in Sociohistorical Perspective*. Knoxville: University of Tennessee Press.

Kierney, Belle. 1900. *A Slaveholder's Daughter*. New York: The Abbey Press.

Kemble, Frances Ann. 1863. *Journal of Residence on a Georgia Plantation in 1838–1839*. London: Longmans.

Killion, Ronald G. and Charles T. Waller. 1972. *A Treasury of Georgia Folklore*. Atlanta: Cherokee Publishing.

Koenig, Otto. 1975. *Unnotiv Auge*. Munich: R. Piper & Co. Verlag.

Laman, Karl. 1962. *The Kongo,* vol. 3. Uppsala: Studia Ethnographia Upsaliensia, XII.

Lampell, Ramona and Millard Lampell with David Larkin. 1989. *O, Appalachia: Artists of the Southern Mountains,* pp. 89– 99, 218–235. New York: Stewart, Tabori & Chang.

Lawton, Samuel Miller. 1939. "The Religious Life of South Carolina Coastal and Sea Island Negroes." Ph.D. dissertation, George Peabody College for Teachers.

LeFalle-Collins, Lizzetta. 1987. *Home and Yard: Black Folk Life Expressions in Los Angeles*. Los Angeles: California Afro-American Museum.

Leiris, Michel. 1960. "On the Use of Catholic Religious Prints by the Practitioners of Voodoo in Haiti," *Evergreen Review* 4, 13:84–94.

Lemaistre, Elise Eugenia. 1988. "In Search of a Garden: African Americans and the Land in Piedmont Georgia from 1850 to the Present, with Proto-types for Reconstruction and Interpretation." M.A. thesis, University of Georgia.

Leon, Eli. 1987. *Who'd a Thought It: Improvisation in African -American Quilt Making*. San Francisco: San Francisco Craft and Folk Art Museum.

Little, Kenneth. 1967. *The Mende of Sierra Leone*. London: Routledge & Kegan Paul.

Little, M. Ruth. 1989. "Afro-American Grave Markers in North Carolina," in *Markers VI: The Journal of the Association for Gravestone Studies,* pp. 103–34. Boston: University Press of America.

Livingston, Jane and John Beardsley. 1982. *Black Folk Art in America, 1930–1980*. Jackson: University Press of Mississippi.

MacGaffey, Wyatt. 1988. "Complexity, Astonishment and Power: The Visual Vocabulary of Kongo Minkisi," *Journal of Southern African Studies* 14, 2:189–203.

MacGaffey, Wyatt. 1986. *Religion and Society in Africa: The BaKongo of Lower Zaire*. Chicago: University of Chicago Press.

MacGaffey, Wyatt. 1977. "The Black Loincloth and the Son of Nzambi Mpungu," in *Forms of Folklore in Africa: Narrative, Poetic, Gnomic, Dramatic,* ed. Bernth Lindfors., pp. 144–51. Austin: University of Texas Press.

Manley, Roger. 1989. *Signs and Wonders: Outsider Art Inside North Carolina*. Chapel Hill: University of North Carolina Press.

McTeer, J. E. 1970. *High Sheriff of the Low Country*. Beaufort, SC: Beaufort Book Company.

McWillie, Judith. 1991. "Writing in an Unknown Tongue," in *Cultural Perspectives on the American South,* ed. Charles Reagan Wilson, pp. 103–17. New York: Gordon & Breach.

McWillie, Judith. 1988. "Introduction," in *Another Face of the Diamond: Pathways through the Black Atlantic South*. New York: INTAR Latin American Gallery.

McWillie, Judith. 1987. "Another Face of the Diamond: Afro-American Traditional Art from the Deep South," *The Clarion* 12, 4:42–53.

McWillie, Judith. n.d. "An African Legacy in the Yard-Shows of the Georgia Piedmont." Photocopy. Athens: Dept. of Art, University of Georgia.

Michael, Dorothy Jean. 1943. "Grave Decoration," *Publications of the Texas Folklore Society* 18:129–36.

Mintz, Sidney W. 1974. "Houses and Yards among Caribbean Peasantries," in *Caribbean Transformations,* ed. Sidney Mintz, pp. 225–50. New York: Columbia University Press.

Moody, Minnie Hite. 1937. "Prologue from Death is a Little Man," in *Readings in Georgia Literature,* ed. William T. Wynn, pp. 239–42. Atlanta: Turner E. Smith.

Nichols, Elaine (ed.). 1989. *The Last Miles of the Way: African-American Homegoing Traditions, 1890-Present.* Columbia: South Carolina State Museum.

Partridge, Charles. 1905. *Cross River Natives: Being Some Notes on the Primitive Pagans of Obubura Hill District, Southern Nigeria.* London: Hutchinson.

Peek, Phil. 1978. "Afro-American Material Culture and the Afro-American Craftsman," *Southern Folklore Quarterly* 42:109–34.

Perry, Regenia A. 1989. "African Art and African-American Folk Art: A Stylistic and Spiritual Kinship," in *Black Art: Ancestral Legacy,* pp. 35–52. Dallas: Dallas Museum of Art.

Pitts, Walter. 1989. "'If You Caint Get the Boat, Take a Log': Cultural Reinterpretation in the Afro-Baptist Ritual," *American Ethnologist* 16, 2:279–92.

Porter, Kenneth. 1945. "The Flying Africans," in *Primer for White Folks,* ed. Bucklin Moon, pp. 171–75. Garden City, NY: Doubleday, Doran.

Prussin, Labelle. 1982. "Islamic Architecture in West Africa: The Foulbe and Manding Models," *VIA 5: Determinants of Form.* Cambridge, MA: MIT Press.

Puckett, Newbell Niles. 1926. *Folk Beliefs of the Southern Negro.* Chapel Hill: University of North Carolina Press.

Rawick, George (ed.). 1972. *God Struck Me Dead* (Fisk University). Vol. 19, *The American Slave: A Composite Autobiography.* Westport, CT: Greenwood Press.

Rawley, James A. 1981. *The Trans-Atlantic Slave Trade.* New York: W.W. Norton.

Reed, Ishmael. 1988. *The Terrible Twos.* New York: Atheneum.

Robinson, Beverly J. 1987. "Vernacular Spaces and Folklife Studies within Los Angeles' African American Community," in *Home and Yard: Black Folk Life Expressions in Los Angeles,* ed. Lizzetta LeFalle-Collins, pp. 20–27. Los Angeles: California Afro-American Museum.

Sale, John B. 1929. *The Tree Named John.* Chapel Hill: University of North Carolina Press.

Simonsen, Thordis (ed.). 1986. *You May Plow Here: The Narrative of Sara Brooks.* New York: Simon & Schuster.

Simpson, George Eaton. 1978. *Black Religions of the New World.* New York: Columbia University Press.

Sims, Barbara. 1981. "Facts in the Life of a Black Mississippi-Louisiana Healer," *Mississippi Folklore Register* 15, 2:63–69.

Smith Omari, Mikelle. 1989. "The Role of the Gods in Afro-Brazilian Ancestral Ritual," *African Arts,* 23, 1:54–61, 103–4.

Sobel, Mechal. 1979. *Trablin' On: The Slave Journey to an Afro-Baptist Faith.* Westport, CT: Greenwood Press.

Stanley, Tom, John Kelley and Roger Manley. 1981. *Worth Keeping: Found Artists of the Carolinas.* Columbia: Columbia Museums of Art and Science.

Stearns, Marshall and Jean Stearns. 1964. *Jazz Dance: The Story of American Vernacular Dance.* New York: Schirmer Books.

Steiner, Roland. 1899. "Superstitions and Beliefs from Central Georgia," *Journal of American Folk-Lore* 12, 47:261–71.

Stuckey, Sterling. 1987. *Slave Culture: Nationalist Theory and the Foundations of Black America.* New York: Oxford University Press.

Thompson, Robert Farris. 1989. "The Song That Named the Land: The Visionary Presence of African-American Art," in *Black Art: Ancestral Legacy.* Dallas: Dallas Museum of Art.

Thompson, Robert Farris. 1988. "The Circle and the Branded Renascent Kongo-American Art," in *Another Face of the Diamond: Pathways through the Black Atlantic South.* pp. 23–59. New York: INTAR Latin American Gallery.

Thompson, Robert Farris. 1983. *Flash of the Spirit: African and Afro-American Art and Philosophy.* New York: Random House.

Thompson, Robert Farris. 1978. "Black Ideographic Writing Calabar to Cuba," *Yale Alumnae Magazine* 42, 2:29–33.

Thompson, Robert Farris and Joseph Cornet. 1981. *The Four Moments of the Sun: Kongo Art in Two Worlds.* Washington DC: National Gallery of Art.

Turner, Lorenzo Dow. 1949. *Africanisms in the Gullah Dialect* Chicago: University of Chicago Press.

University of Southwestern Louisiana. 1987. *Baking in the Sun: Visionary Images from the South.* Lafayette: University Art Museum, University of Southwestern Louisiana.

Upton, Dell. 1988. "White and Black Landscapes in Eighteenth Century Virginia," in *Material Life in America,* ed. Robert Blair, St. George, pp. 357–69. Boston: Northeastern University Press.

Vass, Winifred Kellersberger. 1979. *The Bantu-Speaking Heritage of the United States.* Los Angeles: Center for Afro-American Studies, UCLA.

Vlach, John Michael. 1978. *The Afro-American Tradition in the Decorative Arts.* Cleveland: Cleveland Museum of Art.

Vlach, John Michael. 1975. "Sources for the Shotgun House: African and Caribbean Antecedents for Afro-American Architecture." Ph.D. dissertation, Indiana University.

Wahlman, Maude Southwell. 1987. "Africanisms in Afro-American Visionary Arts," in *Baking in the Sun Visionary Images from the South.* Lafayette: University Art Museum, University of Southwestern Louisiana.

Wahlman, Maude Southwell. 1986. "African Symbolism in Afro-American Quilts," *African Arts* 20, 1:68–76, 99.

Walker Art Center. 1974. *Naives and Visionaries.* New York: E.P. Dutton.

Westmacott, Richard. 1992. *African-American Gardens and Yards in the Rural South.* Knoxville: University of Tennessee Press.

Westmacott, Richard. n.d. "Pattern and Practice in Traditional Black Gardens in Rural Georgia." Photocopy, School of Environmental Design. Athens: University of Georgia.

Wiley, George. 1905. *Southern Plantation Stories and Sketches.* Reprinted, Freeport, NY: Books for Libraries, 1971.

Wilhelm, Gene, Jr. 1975. "Dooryard Gardens and Gardening in the Black Community of Brushy, Texas," *Geographical Review.* 65:73–92.

Yolles, Sandra. 1989. "Vasari Diary: Junk Magic," *ArtNews.* Oct. 27.

Suggested Reading

Battle, Marcia. *Harlem Photographs, 1932–1940 by Aaron Siskind.* New Haven, Conn.: Eastern Press and The Smithsonian Institution Press, 1990.

Bethal, Elizabeth R. *Promiseland: A Century of Life in a Negro Community.* Philadelphia: Temple University Press, 1981.

Bremer, Sidney H. "The Urban Home of The Harlem Renaissance." In *Urban Intersections: Meetings of Life and Literature in United States Cities,* pp. 132–164. Urbana: University of Illinois Press, 1992.

Brochert, James. *Alley Life in Washington: Family, Community, Religion, and Folklore in the City, 1850–1970,* pp. 132–164. Urbana: University of Illinois Press, 1980.

Cheek, Charles D., and Amy Friedlander. "Pottery and Pig's Feet: Space, Ethnicity, and Neighborhood in Washington, D.C., 1880–1940." *Historical Archaelogy* 24 (1) (1990): 34–60.

Christian, Marcus. *Negro Ironworks of Louisiana, 1718–1900.* Gretna, La.: Pelican Publishing, 1972.

Combes, John D. "Ethnography, Archaeology, and Burial Practices Among Coastal South Carolina Blacks." *Conference on Historical Site Archaeology Papers* 7. Columbia, S.C.: Institute of Archaeology and Anthropology, 1972.

Crader, Diana. "Faunal Remains from the Slave Quarter at Monticello, Charlottesville, Virginia." *Archaeozoologia* 3 (1/2) (1989): 229–236.

———. *Black Heritage Sites. The North.* New York: The New Press, 1996.

Curtis, Nancy C. *Black Heritage Sites. The South.* New York: The New Press, 1996.

Dabbs, Edith M. *Face of an Island: Leigh Richmond Miner's Photographs of Saint Helena Island.* New York: Grossman, 1971.

Henri, Florette. *Black Migration: Movement North, 1900–1920.* Garden City, N.Y.: Anchor Press, 1975.

Hill, Mozell C. "The All-Negro Communities of Oklahoma: The Natural History of a Social Movement." *Journal of Negro History,* 31 (3) (1946): 254–268.

Hurston, Zora Neale. "Appendix B. Views of Eatonville," in *The Florida Negro. A Federal Writers' Project Legacy,* edited by Gary W. McDonogh, pp. 144–161. Jackson: University Press of Mississippi, 1993.

Ingersoll, Ernest. "The Decoration of Negro Graves." *Journal of American Folklore,* 4 (1892): 68–69.

Joyner, Charles. The Creolization of Slave Folklore: All Saints Parish, South Carolina, as a Test Case." *Historical Reflections* 6 (2) (1979): 435–453.

Kimball, Gregg D. "African-Virginians and the Vernacular Building Tradition in Richmond City, 1790–1860." *Perspectives in Vernacular Architecture* 4 (1991): 121–129.

'Let This Be Your Home': The African American Migration to Philadelphia, 1900–1940. Philadelphia: Afro-American Historical and Cultural Museum, 1990.

Morris, Ann, and Henrietta Ambrose, compilers. *North Webster: A Photographic History of a Black Community.* Bloomington: Indiana University Press, 1993.

Moutoussamy-Ashe, Jeanne. *Daufuskie Island. A Photographic Essay.* Columbia: University of South Carolina Press, 1982.

Otey, Frank M., and Alice M. Grant. *Eatonville, Florida: A Brief History of One of America's First Freedmen's Towns.* Winter Park, Fla.: 4-G Publishers, 1989.

Painter, Nell Irvin. *Exodusters: Black Migration to Kansas After Reconstruction* [1976]. Reprint, Lawrence: University of Kansas Press, 1986.

Quinn, Edythe Ann. "'The Hills' in the Mid-Nineteenth Century: The History of a Rural Afro-American Community in Westchester County, New York." *Afro-Americans in New York Life and History* 14 (2) (1990): 35–50.

Ramphele, Mamphela. *A Bed Called Home. Life in the Migrant Labour Hostels of Cape Town.* Athens: Ohio University Press, 1993.

Trotter, Joe William, Jr. *The Great Migration in Historical Perspective. New Dimensions of Race, Class, and Gender.* Bloomington: Indiana University Press, 1991.

Vlach, John Michael. "The Craftsman and the Communal Image: Philip Simmons, Charleston Blacksmith." *Family Heritage* 2 (February 1979): 14–19.

Westacott, Richard. *African-American Gardens and Yards in the Rural South*. Knoxville: University of Tennessee Press, 1992.

Wiese, Andrew. "Places of Our Own: Suburban Black Towns Before 1960." *Journal of Urban History* (May 1993): 30–54.

Wilhelm, Gene, Jr. "Dooryard Gardens and Gardening in the Black Community of Brushy, Texas." *Geographical Review* 65 (1975): 73–92.

Williams, Lee. "Concentrated Residences: The Case of Black Toledo, 1890–1930." *Phylon* (June 1982).

Willis, Deborah, and Jane Lusaka, eds. *Visual Journal. Harlem and D.C. in the Thirties and Forties*. Washington, D.C.: The Center for African American History and Culture and the Smithsonian Institution Press, 1996.

Wright, Roberta Hughes and Wilbur B. Hughes III. *Lay Down Body. Living History in African American Cemeteries*. Detroit: Visible Ink, 1996.

Selected Videos, Films, CD-ROMs, and Slides

California Newsreel

Family Across the Sea. Tim Carrier, director. Produced by South Carolina Educational TV, 1991. 56 minutes.

Goin' To Chicago. George King, producer/director. University of Mississippi, 1994. 38 minutes. Video.

Miles of Smiles. Years of Struggle [The Brotherhood of Sleeping Car Porters]. Paul Wagner and Jack Santino, producers. 1983. 58 minutes. 16mm.

Cinema Guild

Gandy Dancers [African American railroad track laborers]. Barry Domfield and Maggie Holtzberg-Call, directors, 1994. VHS Video.

Films for the Humanities & Sciences

Digging for Slaves; The Excavation of American Slave Sites. 50 minutes. Color. Video and Videodisc Program.

PBS Video

Roots of Resistance—A Story of the Underground Railroad. Orlando Bagwell, producer. AMEX 216-CR94, 1989. 60 minutes.

Chapter 4

PLASTIC AND OTHER
VISUAL ARTS

Robert Farris Thompson's interview in *African Arts*[1] provides a good dividing point between concepts of African American culture (Chapters 1–3 in this volume) and what comes from these concepts: their realization in the tactile world. This chapter, "Plastic and Other Visual Arts," riffs on commentaries of cosmology, movement—the dance—, and space and place. It looks at traditional art forms, that originated in the American South, which have influenced African American art throughout the United States. These art forms are firmly based on Herskovits's survivalisms from Africa and the Caribbean, and their transformations. As with African and African American cosmology, movement (or dance), and space and place, plastic and other visual arts are concrete representations of African American spirit and life. Once again, through the utilitarian and ritualistic potentialities of these art forms, the material and spiritual meet. What we see is representative black *Atlantic* art.

The writers of these essays on plastic and visual arts are versed in folk culture and arts in their various manifestations, which include textile arts, basket making, wood carving, and sculpture (particularly pottery). These discussions contribute to an understanding of the visionary and spiritual qualities of people we call "folk" artists—those talented if not genius members of the community who are without benefit of formal training. Their work, in many cases, is for their own spiritual development, for domestic and church rituals, and for the adulation, praise, and worship of God. Artists may be otherwise "employed," but their vocation, like that of members of religious communities, is their life's work—God's work. What is also significant is that these art forms are part of the renewal principle in the African-descended community: it is about the retrieval of discarded things, about their reutilization, about rebirth and revitalization—the recycling of used, but still valuable, artifacts recording human existence. As Judy McWillie writes in "Another Face of the Diamond," this community of artists is linked neither by artists' associations nor by artist newsletters. It is linked rather by "certain [and shared] iconography"

---

1 Donald J. Cosentino, "Interview with Robert Farris Thompson," *African Arts* 25 (4) (1992): 53–63.

which include "water imagery and mirrors, embellishments in star and diamond shapes, color signatures, and specific processes and techniques . . ."[2] McWillie reminds us that the visual plastic arts also mimic the African American and African musical forms, specifically blues-jazz, "imparting meaning and *harmony* [emphasis mine] to an otherwise disconnected . . . experience" (remarks she cites from historian Eugene Metcalf) and are a founding tradition of "Afro-Atlantic" or creole culture.[3] In this essay, also, McWillie invokes the Bakongo diamond that we have previously seen in the spirit yards, in burial grounds and burial objects, and as the primary symbol of African cosmology—the link between the sphere of the living, and through the instrument of water, the sphere of the ancestors.[4]

Included in this repertoire of visionary art are representations of what has been called, in this volume, "nonalphabetic" writing. These are the pictographs of storytelling quilts and the ideographs in other quilt designs. There are also writings "in the spirit" that may parallel the oral form of speaking in tongues, and the "signing" works of other folk artists. This is *art,* also, that exemplifies life in the black community: art created by talented persons who are, more importantly, ordinary if unrecognized members of those communities. Many folk artists create art that is not only personal, but that is shown to very few persons. Such an artist was James Hampton whose *Throne* and altar were only discovered after his death (although a few persons had seen them while he was alive). This art often reflects the most secret cosmological and metaphysical feelings and beliefs of their creators. These are the works of (folk) artists whose primary aesthetic purpose is secondarily, if at all, commercial in the sense in which the Western world usually shows appreciation for art: buy it, display it, don't touch (it). Author Gregory Day has explained it eloquently in one of his essays, where he writes of Carolinian traditional arts. He says these traditional arts are intertwined in the "collective labor activities" of the community, that is, hunting and gathering, fishing, gardening, harvesting, house building, and crafts making.[5] This then is traditional art meant to be *used,* not only for the mundane, but for the sacred. The vehicles may be pottery, sculpture, or even basketry, which, as Day has written, were on one hand an integral part of the plantation economy used in winnowing, harvesting, and the transporting of the products of slave labor, but on the other a foundation of black rural and urban community life when used as the collection plate during Sunday church services.[6]

Maude Southwell Wahlman's essay, "African Symbolism in Afro-American Quilts," shows the association between music and the oral tradition and quilt making, especially within the context of the improvisatory in blues-jazz. And in quilting, although an art historically practiced by both men and women, we see women's *power.* In this traditional art, early American quilts were considered to be protective and "medicines of God," in

[2] Judy McWillie, "Another Face of the Diamond," *The Clarion* 12 (4) (1987): 42–53.

[3] Ibid., p. 46.

[4] See Chapter 1 on cosmology.

5. Gregory Day, "Afro-Carolinian Art. Towards the History of a Southern Expressive Tradition," *Contemporary Art/Southwest* 1 (January-February 1978): 10–21.

[6] Ibid.

counteracting negative influences of the unseen spirit world—by those who used them and those who created them. Those who created them were often considered spirit workers. Wahlman's essay illustrates, once again, the continuity between Africa and the African diaspora and in a tactile way indicates movement and storytelling text in terms of the rhythm, weaving, lines, and color in the cloth or fabric.[7] Her comment that the contributions of these artists "suggests that the unique way in which any culture *encodes* [emphasis mine] beauty in the seen world is an indispensible tool for coping with an indifferent or hostile reality"[8] evokes Robert Farris Thompson's "cool" or that which is "good" and balanced. This raises the point again of a connection between textiles and the process of weaving, the matter of "text," including written text. In *Cloth as Metaphor: Nigerian Textiles from The Museum of Cultural History,* published by The Museum of Cultural History, UCLA, and The Regents of the University of California,[9] cloth or textiles are discussed as representing the "fabric of life," a symbol and a metaphor. In speaking of a festival masquerade, it states, "The word acts as a charm, just as the cloth itself is a charm added to the masquerades. Embodying power, the cloth has become a symbol of power and its name a metaphor for power."[10]

This musical tradition is manifested also in the sculpture of folk artist James Thomas. William Ferris's "Vision in Afro-American Folk Art: The Sculpture of James Thomas" discusses Thomas's work as derivative of the traditional African art of wood carving, reflected in a wood sculpture or a walking stick—created pieces of the sculptor that are representations of a vision that is "plucked" from his "dreams," and are "signs." The essay connects black folk art with black life and the role and place of the creator-artist within the community. "To create a man's image is to have power and control over him. . . . The folk artist thus becomes a powerful and at times frightening force within the black community, somewhat similar to the Griot of West Africa"[11]—in other words, the folk artist is a person of strong medicine.

Finally, Lynda Roscoe Hartigan writes, once again, about James Hampton and "The Throne of the Third Heaven of the Nations Millenium General Assembly." What comes to mind, in terms of visionary art and artists, especially in the case of Hampton's *Throne,*

---

7 In *African Islam* (Washington, D.C.: The Smithsonian Institution and London: Ethnographica Ltd., 1983), Rene A. Bravmann writes, "A man may drape himself in a cloth covered with colourful squares and endless repetitions of Allah, swathing his body in God's name. . . . Brillant and sparkling squares of colour (magenta, blue, orange and yellow) applied with a brush establish a vibrant grid for the cloth, but what is most remarkable is the name "Allah" written in the interstices between the squares and elsewhere. This textile is full of God's presence, like the sounds in a community of his believers . . ." (pp. 26–27). See also the chapter, "God's Secrets—Shaped in Silence" about charms as written words and pictures (pp. 32–45).

8 Maude Southwell Wahlman, "African Symbolism in Afro-American Quilts," *African Arts* 20 (1)(1986):68–76, 99.

9 Regents of the University of California. *Cloth as Metaphor: Nigerian Textiles from the Museum of Cultural History.* Los Angeles: The Museum of Cultural History, UCLA, 1983.

10 Ibid., p. 33. See footnote 7 on *African Islam.* Also note *I Am Not Myself: The Art of African Masquerade* edited by Herbert M. Cole. Los Angeles: Museum of Cultural History, UCLA, 1985.

11 William Ferris, "Vision in Afro-American Folk Art: The Sculpture of James Thomas," *Journal of American Folklore,* 88 (348) (1975): 127.

are chapter headings in *African Islam,*[12]: "A Passion for the Words of God," and most especially "God's Secrets—Shaped in Silence." Of course, Hampton was a fundamentalist Christian, not a Muslim, but he created in silence. Only after his death, did his *Throne* see the light of day. James Hampton worked as a janitor for the federal government and learned the value of refuse: gold and alumumum foil wrappings, bottles, cigarette boxes, used light bulbs, cardboard and insulation board, desk blotters, plastic, jelly glasses, pieces of newspaper, coffee can metal, tacks, nails, sewing pins. His tools and instruments were the discards of everyday life, refashioned to create a sacred, holy work. His work was in the recycling of garbage and of (it was his hope) religious belief—in a sense of born-again efforts—in anticipation of the millenium. His writing in the spirit, in his indiscipherable journal, indicates a passion for the word of God coming not only out of dreams and visions but from actual visitations. His "studio" was a small space in a garage where he worked, at night, after his day job. There are indications that the *Throne* was, at his death, a work in progress.

Hampton's *Throne* reflects the Old and New Testaments and, as with any prophet, deals with the millenium and with the Book of Revelations. In his own way, Hampton was an educator (teacher), trying to warn God's people about the future. As Hartigan suggests, the image of his vision, which is awesome, may not reveal its real reason for being. It was not an end in itself but a means to an end. She writes, "As one concentrates on the radiance, symmetry, decorative patterns, and eccentric improvisation of *The Throne,* Hampton's primary intention, to create a vehicle for religious renewal and teaching may be overlooked."[13] It is that latter intention, which, I believe, actually makes Hampton's *Throne* an "African American" idea.

---

[12] Rene A. Bravmann, *African Islam.* Washington, D.C.: The Smithsonian Institution and London: Ethnographica Ltd., 1983.

[13] Lynda Roscoe Hartigan, "James Hampton: *The Throne of the Third Heaven of the Nations Millenium General Assembly,"* 1977, p. 5. See also Hartigan's exhibition guide for the Walker Art Center in Minneapolis, *Naives and Visionaries* (Minneapolis: Walker Art Center, 1974, pp. 13–19), on Hampton's *Throne.*

Another Face of the Diamond
Judy McWillie
Artist

*At the time of the publication of this article, Judy McWillie was professor
of painting and drawing at the University of Georgia. Since 1969, she has
been researching and documenting the work of African American
visionary (folk) artists.*

For more than a century, Afro-American traditional art from the deep South has functioned as an agent of spiritual vitality and social renewal in a region shaped by the oldest co-existence of Western and non-Western influence on the North American continent. Today, professional artists based in the South, along with collectors and museum curators, are bringing attention to the remarkable continuity of black Atlantic art. Moreover, they are proving that a significant visual tradition, while only recently recognized, has been operating for centuries on the mainland. In celebrating the range and duration of the Afro-Atlantic tradition, these southerners are exploring a long-neglected contribution to American history.

By the time Harriet Powers completed her *Bible Quilt* in Athens, Georgia, around 1895, the direct importation of new slaves within the continental United States had been illegal for nearly ninety years. In spite of the congressional ban of 1808. Africans continued to arrive along the South's Atlantic coast. Rather than being brought through the West Indies, where they would normally have been indoctrinated for several years, they were smuggled directly from Africa. Most of these new slaves were from the Angolan region of West Central Africa in the vicinity of the Congo River,[1] an area, called *Kongo* territory in today's literature, that encompasses modern Angola and Zaire.[2] The presence of these newly arrived Africans in the decades preceding the Civil War is thought to account for the Gullah dialect ("Ngola") still spoken today among the coastal black population of South Carolina and Georgia.[3] During the period of direct importation, African languages, particularly Bantu, along with religion and philosophy entered American life.[4] American slave communities, often several generations removed from their origins in West Africa, inherited a new consciousness of their origins through the newcomers.[5]

Records indicate that some emancipated Africans of Harriet Powers' generation would have remembered life on both sides of the Atlantic, adapting the traditional values of the Old World to circumstances in America.[6] As a result, black Southern society, which Lerone Bennett called "the veil within the veil,"[7] developed its own unique

Judy McWillie, "Another Face of the Diamond," Clarion, *12 (4) (1987): 42–53.*

orientation, assimilating every appropriate spiritual and aesthetic resource in the environment. In religion, black Americans fused aspects of African spirituality with European Christianity and Native American belief. They extended this attitude of inclusiveness to other dimensions of American cultural life, as well. In music, dance, and literature, along with cuisine, agriculture, architecture, and art, a new creolized tradition was born.

This Afro-Atlantic tradition encouraged distinct creative values which, from the beginning, were rooted in religion and spirituality. Western distinctions that differentiate between the spiritual and the aesthetic did not, and still do not, apply. One need only encounter such famous monuments of black vernacular art as the quilt of Harriet Powers or the *Throne* of James Hampton to recognize this fundamental orientation. Praise of God and celebration of his authority remain the most consistent themes in black folk art, and account, in part, for its cultural continuities.

In travels through the Mississippi Delta to New Orleans, across Alabama to the Georgia and South Carolina low country, collectors, scholars and professional artists are documenting the religious lives of black folk artists, identifying common iconography and recurring themes. They encounter attitudes and perceptions among folk artists that situate them outside the aesthetic orientation of contemporary Western art. When the professional sculptor John Geldersma met David Butler twelve years ago near New Orleans, he soon gained first-hand experience of these distinctions. "Two years after our meeting," said Geldersma, "we traded works. My work was a carved wooden boat on rockers; his was a fanciful boat cut from a piece of flattened-out corrugated roofing metal painted black, white, and red. His boat hangs on the wall in my living room. My boat is hidden behind his bed."[8] Butler later told Geldersma that his cut-outs, called "spirit shields," had been made in order to overcome "a period of acute nervousness following the death of his wife."[9] In titling his work according to its spiritual function and detaching himself from his own objects as well as Geldersma's, Butler instinctively rejected the Western notion of art as an enterprise within the worldly order.

Similar attitudes prevailed among other black folk artists. Many denied that they were making "art" at all. A widely revered "Spiritual Doctor" affirmed his mission passionately and succinctly one evening in refusing to allow photographs of his masterful sculptures. "This has nothing to do with art," he said. "It is more than one could contain, and nobody can do it on their own. This is God's work."[10] He insisted on anonymity and refused any association with the removal or documentation of his work.

Those who entered public life, like David Butler, were reluctant to establish prices for their works, leaving such decisions to others. Sister Gertrude Morgan, in fact, gave away her paintings to the congregation of her small church in New Orleans. She alerted collectors to their spiritual function by supplementing the paintings with copies of her poems and songs, composed as a means of "witnessing the Word."[11]

Sister Morgan, Bessie Harvey, James Hampton, Minnie Evans, William Edmondson, Jesse Aaron, and many other artists, began their work after experiencing initiatory religious visions. The evidence of these visionaries increases with practically each new discovery of a black folk artist, making researchers realize that personal religious visions are in keeping with tradition in certain communities.

The folk artists' accounts are consistent with the Fisk University oral history, *God Struck Me Dead*, published in 1941, in which one hundred former slaves from Tennessee detailed their own visions in rich, evocative language. Although spiritual initiation through visionary experience is a tradition, all of these accounts were unique to the individual involved.[12]

Almost as frequent as visions, an incident of healing has occurred, either as a formative event in the life of an artist or a self-expressed goal of their work. Clarence Burse, of Memphis, Tennessee, explained that he recovered from a stroke after God instructed him to create his yard assemblage of mirrors and brightly colored objects. Bessie Harvey confirmed that God "touched" her, regardless of the gloomy prognosis of her doctors, and that she too subsequently regained her health and became a prolific worker, as she describes it, "in the Spirit."[13]

Most of these artists exhibit what art historian and collector Regenia Perry calls "a fantastic ingenuity for turning cast off objects into art works."[14] For example, Charlie Lucas, an Alabama artist, redeemed the waste and refuse of vacant lots and landfills to create *Let My Spirit Flow Free* and *Hidden Faces*. James Hampton too used found materials such as light bulbs and furniture fragments in building the armature of his resplendent *Throne of the Third Heaven of the Nation's Millenium General Assembly*, now on permanent display at the National Museum of American Art at the Smithsonian.

By the same token, certain iconography, such as water imagery and mirrors, embellishments in star and diamond shapes, color signatures, and specific processes and techniques also recur among different artists, regardless of their isolation from one another. Similar imagery surfaces repeatedly in the material culture of their communities.

• • •

These models of expression are perpetuating themselves even among younger artists, despite comments in the catalogue *Black Folk Art in America: 1930–1980*[15] that, "If we believe at all in the promise of our society, we shall soon see the end of much that generates this art." While the "Black Folk Art" exhibition, organized by the Corcoran Gallery of Art in 1982, established Afro-American folk art as a popular commodity, it left the impression that the rich affirmations characterizing the inner lives of the represented artists were but a poignant reminder of a time when black people in the South were still dominated by a quasi-colonial political system. If, as the catalogue essay went on to say, we were witnessing "the sudden maturation of a material culture even as the conditions essential to its existence seem to be disappearing," then black folk art would flourish only in a fundamentally hostile social milieu.

On the contrary, evidence proves that the strength of black folk art results, not from the social or economic plight of Americans recovering from slavery, but from the individual initiative of artists discovered to be working within the founding traditions of Afro-Atlantic culture. Lonnie Holley, 36, an Alabama artist, has updated classic African themes such as paying homage to one's ancestors by creating shrines, altars, and power objects that combine modern materials with ancient motifs. Holley makes sculptures, like *The Old King*, in order to express his perception that an artist creates both from the resources of his own life and the energies accumulated in previous generations. His authority arises through this system which anoints him as a priest and enhances his spiritual powers.

The noted historian of black religion. Albert Raboteau, has observed: "African influences remained vital on this side of the Atlantic, not because they were preserved as 'pure' orthodoxy but because they were transformed."[16] He understood, first-hand, the black American penchant for gracing the environment with a synthesis of spiritual and aesthetic influences, and would have agreed with social historian Eugene Metcalf's comment that Afro-American folk art behaves similarly to black musical forms such as jazz and blues, "imparting meaning and harmony to an otherwise disconnected . . . experience."[17] Improvisation and creolization distinguish the creative process of these artists, situating them within a whole spectrum of Afro/Christian spirituality longstanding in the Americas. Though Protestantism in the South de-emphasized the use of worship vessels and elaborate ritual, it nevertheless had social values in common with Kongo religion, including a strong transpersonal emphasis and the "born again" commitment to God and community.[18] "Forms of ritual, systems of belief, and fundamental perspectives" have not died out; they are widespread, both visibly and subliminally.[19]

The legacy of compounded significance, inclusiveness, and inherited authority applies to those who have been initiated by powerful "Spiritual Doctors." Such attitudes extend, even today, from the deep South into Brooklyn and Harlem, where southern blacks congregated in their own neighborhoods following the migrations of the 1920s and 1930s. B. Robinson, formerly of Beaufort, South Carolina, established a "candle store" in Harlem after he moved north forty years ago. There, he sells potions, mojos, spiritual oils, and icons, and participates in divination and counseling. In Beaufort, he had been acquainted with the legendary "root workers," Dr. Eagle and Dr. Buzzard.

Today, Robinson, whose card introduces him as "one who has turned many tears into joy," also creates complex assemblages in his store-front window. Ordinary consumer objects are constellated with icons from every available religious tradition, recalling Kongo funerary customs in which every-day objects are presented as holy offerings that maintain a physical relationship between the living and the dead. Each object's history is taken into account and its earthly function remains intact, even if the circumstances are extrasensory. Some objects are those last used by a loved one before death, such as a medicine flask or a cup. Others provide the spirit with light and encouragement throughout its journey into the next world. A genre of commemorative funerary urns evolved within this tradition. Ceramic or glass pots are decorated with family paraphernalia such as lodge pins, buttons, mirrors, and other momentos, along with items that appear to be repeatedly used: shells, small flasks of earth, teeth, chains, and dog figurines. John Vlach remarked that the found object tradition confused some whites, who overlooked the ritual significance of clocks, oil lamps, and automobile headlights in cemeteries, dismissing them as "late period garbage."[20]

There was no mistaking the ritual intent of Reverend Cyrus Bowens' famous wooden markers at Sunbury, Georgia, however. Renowned for his ability to discover fragments from nature that had strong spiritual associations,[21] Bowens had an initiatory vision that instructed him to "make images in wood in honor of the family dead."[22] He used found pieces of pine that had anthropomorphic qualities to create two serpents and a human figure for the grave enclosure he and his family built during the 1930's, near the Baptist church where he was the minister. It is significant that in his technique for creating these works he preserved the integrity of the uncommon natural formations and only smoothed, conditioned, and arranged them to release a new identity. Venturing too far with adornment or fabrication would have obscured the found object's double nature.

• • •

J. B. Murry's house in rural southern Georgia is physically distant from the door of his Kongo ancestors, but he is, nevertheless, a witness to their traditional concept that an artist is a spiritual mediator, charged with responsibilities that extend beyond the physical world. Sometime during the late 1970's, Murry, who had been a life-long farmer, accepted the call of a vision that compelled him to "act religion" and "write in the Spirit." Murry explained, "After that, the eagle crossed my eye; and that is why I can see things some more folks can't see."[23] Today, at 76, he creates complex abstract paintings that function as visual chants and aids for deep meditation. These paintings begin with improvised, rhythmic marks that spill over onto surfaces as diverse as wall board, enameled stove tops, and the glass screens of discarded television sets. Similar works on paper are the focus of a divination ceremony in which the artist and a visitor "read" a painting through a bottle of clear water, held over it like a lens. The ceremony begins with the Lord's Prayer recited "through the water" and continues with the petition, "Lord, give me a mind of what the water says, give me a louder word up." In the profound silence of the environment, the reflection of the painting in the water acts as a centering device, allowing Murry time to respond to his visitors with an insightful meditation on their expressed needs. A period of prayer follows, during which visitors offer personal intentions and Murry affirms them with gratitude to God. The motion of the water discerns whether a prayer was spiritually acceptable.[24]

Tracking the path of Kongo/Christian spirituality across the deep South frequently leads to individuals like Murry, whose teachings are introduced through visual, rather than verbal, means. Often they function as neighborhood counselors. Dilmus Hall of Athens, Georgia, fashioned visual allegories out of concrete and wood that were illustrations for his ethical teachings. Like an Old World African *griot*, he rewarded visitors with folk tales, scriptural narratives, and dialogues on history and current events. "Remember," he often warned them, with characteristic high-pitched laughter, "you can't catch a frog with a snake!" Hall's taste for fun established a warm and casual atmosphere while he delivered the serious lessons derived from the subject matter of his sculptures. To express the nature of temptation, for instance, he created *The Devil and the Drunk Man,* a life-sized concrete tableau. He explained: "The devil is roaring in the drunk man's ear, saying that he will stop the noise if the man will take a drink. When the man takes it, the devil roars louder and knocks him out." The most popular of Hall's sculptures, the crucifixes, show Christ with a toothpick threaded horizontally through the mouth. This invention was a visual representation of one of his bible stories, which always contained apocryphal episodes: "When Christ was on the cross and he spoke to the Good Thief, the Bible says he stopped dying and held death between his teeth."[25] Andy Nasisse, a collector and ceramics professor at the University of Georgia, introduced Hall's work to the public in the early 1980s, assuring the artist a steady stream of visitors before his death earlier this year.

Louanne La Roche of Hilton Head. South Carolina, responded with enthusiasm when she met Z. B. Armstrong in 1985 and began collecting his mailboxes, urns, and vending machines. The artist had found these objects, and then transformed them by painting them white and "signing" their exposed surfaces, inside and out, with a gridded network of black and red lines. Armstrong's initiatory vision arrived in the form of an angel who told him to make art "about what time is like." This obsession led him to paint on old calendars and, later, to draw his grids on every accessible surface of reclaimed objects, declaring that each square represented a "past or future day." Later he invented the calendar wheel, his own mystical device for measuring the temporal nature of things. When asked to interpret one of these constructions, he answered, "They explain themselves. God will forget the bad and remember the good."

A careful review of the collecting activity surrounding these artists reveals as much about our culture as the artists themselves, who, after all, do not live in a remote environment distanced by time and anonymity. They are Americans, aware of mass media, as well as the race relations in the twentieth century, and their interaction with collectors brings them into mainstream contemporary society, with all its pluralistic complexities. In an early New York exhibition of J. B. Murry's work, his paintings were shown in conjunction with European "art brut," an association that probably developed because of his earlier commitment to a state hospital for "acting religion." During that hospitalization, he tried to heal patients through the laying on of hands. When two guards disagreed over whether he should be allowed to do his "spiritual work," a physician settled the controversy by securing Murry's release. After several interviews, he saw no pathology in the man whose situation reminded him of a previous encounter with a "root doctor" in a small Georgia town who applied for staff privileges at the local health clinic.[26] . . . In fact, all of his experiences are well within tradition. The hospitalization, it was later discovered, was an economic matter.

Murry's technique of "writing in the Spirit" is surprisingly common. The North Carolina artist, Minnie Evans, used "signing" as a decorative invention in her exotic drawings. Lonnie Holley, of Alabama, paints the ceiling of his house with abstract ciphers. Leroy Person, also of North Carolina, carved wooden panels in a cryptic script reminiscent of the "alphabet" of James Hampton, whose only surviving notebook. *St. James Revelation,* has been the subject of mystery and controversy since its discovery after the artist's death in 1964. Joe Light, of Memphis. Tennessee, copied what he called "Abraham's writing" on wooden plaques and placed them in his yard for all to see. During a personal interview in Spring 1987, however, J. B. Murry gave a forthright explanation of the practice: "If I wrote in A's and B's, it would be me doing the writing. But, this way God is doing it. People who are pure at heart can tell what the writing says, through the water. They can't read it unless they are spiritual people." A contemporary poet from Zaire, Fu-Kiau Bunseki, gives an almost identical account of the function of visual glossolalia on Kongo ceremonial mannequins: "These are messages that come to our world from other realms . . . Because the message is rising from another world into our own, it should be used someday, there should be someone here to discover and de-code it."[27] The Spiritual Baptists of Trinidad, too, engage in the practice of ecstatic "signing" (writing in an unknown tongue) and other Afro/Christian rituals, that evolved after Protestant Christianity was brought to Trinidad in 1787 by an ex-slave from Georgia, George Liele.[28] They also institutionalize their desire for spiritual rebirth by entering a three-day "mourning" period in which the supplicant prays for an instructive apparition or dream,[29] the same method recommended in some black churches in the South when a member is enduring a personal crisis.

Writers such as Robert Farris Thompson, Albert Raboteau, and Stephen Jay Gould are beginning to rescue artists like J. B. Murry from their imposed role as eccentrics. In a remarkable essay for the *Smithsonian Studies in American Art,* "James Hampton's Throne and the Dual Nature of Time,"[30] . . . Gould reconciles James Hampton's vision with Western religious tradition in such a way that the *Throne of the Third Heaven* becomes a universal icon. . . . The point here is that Afro-American vernacular art is as American as it is African, and some of it, like Hampton's *Throne,* is as sophisticated in its intentions and solutions as most noble monuments of world culture.

Meanwhile, collectors are exploring ways to develop means of supporting black folk artists while being sensitive to the traditional integrity of their work. Such issues have been of special concern to William Arnett, of Atlanta, Georgia, who spent twenty years developing a collection of African Art and biblical antiquities before turning to black vernacular art. . . . "Each black artist I have dealt with makes work for personal use, never to be sold to the public and often not even to be shown; that is, private pieces that embody his or her own philosophical and spiritual concepts. Each has also, at times, found it necessary to create 'tourist' pieces that are aesthetically pleasing to a collector's taste, but barely even hint at the artist's real vision. Several have told me of requests they've had over the years to 'bring down,' 'tone down,' or 'calm down' their work to make it acceptable to the buyer. All express sadness at being asked to do this."

Most collections of Afro-American traditional art have been modeled after collections of contemporary art in which objects are de-contextualized, associated with the European categories of painting and sculpture, and then prized for their aesthetic qualities. But Arnett's emphasis grew out of his background in ancient art. He explains, "I find that I use the same set of criteria in collecting this art as I have always used in collecting the art of ancient and traditional civilizations. The object must first be authentic, made by the artist for usually spiritual purposes within the traditions of his culture. Content and context are crucial: What does the object mean? How is the object used? Of course, aesthetic beauty is important, but it is essential to understand *their* aesthetic and never to judge the works of other cultures by our own presumptions."

Regenia Perry continues to remind collectors, however, that while black Atlantic art evolved from traditional principles, these artists structure their work according to the organizing powers of their own particular mind.[31] Arnett agrees, and adds that the deeply personal nature of this art is inevitable, since the artists must reconcile several traditions in their environment along with the demands of their inner lives. He explains: "I am thinking now of an artist such as Archie Byron, of Atlanta, whose ancestors were black, European, and Native American. His life is a synthesis of more than one tradition, and this synthesis would not have happened in terms of his art work unless he initiated it. Artists like Byron are living examples of the *creole* experience, which is certainly one of the strengths of black vernacular art."

Archie Byron's openness to the world around him is exemplified by his monumental bas relief *Anatomy,* which is a timeless reminder of life's fundamentals. Beginning with male and female fertility, *Anatomy* depicts life as it extends itself to the next generation, creating a new individual. The continuous flow of spiritual authority from one generation to the next is a basic theme in Afro-Atlantic art. At times it addresses the passage between life and death, at others it celebrates the instant of spontaneous contact between the latent and the conscious, which is birth. The special emphasis on this continuum owes its origins, again, to Africa where the integrity of the family remains essential for the well-being of the individual. Here, society includes those who have passed on, as well as those yet to come.

Though African artists usually resist literal imitation of the human form, black American artists freely combine representation and abstraction. Byron's *Anatomy* introduces a new sophistication to this process in both its iconography and its form. The ancestors, situated on either side of the parents, are abstracted by memory, though they still cooperate in life's renewal and are reflected in the features of subsequent generations. Their eyes dominated the foreground, while the small, inexperienced eyes of the newly born have been projected spacially into the background. This planar composition reverses time's normal behavior. If we read this progression vertically, the eyes of the past are the foundation of the tree of life, while the child's eyes surmount those of the other generations, signaling the hope of the future. The processes essential to life's renewal are activated through the senses, which Byron sees as channels of communication.

The complexity of these concepts never interferes with the unity of *Anatomy*. A centralized face, generated from the interaction of all of these forces, stares out at the world with its own reverent eyes. The gaze shifts continually between the old and the new. At once, the whole continuum reacts with the gesture of praise and ascent, welcoming both the presence of God and the embrace of the community. Archie Byron, the owner of an Atlanta bait and tackle shop, has created a magnificent visual praise poem, ringing with compassion and authority. It is a tribute to the social continuity and spiritual vision of black Americans.

Those desiring an in-depth introduction to the cross-over of traditional Kongo belief from Africa to the deep South can begin with a basic text. *The Four Moments of the Sun: Kongo Art in Two Worlds,* a catalogue for the 1980 National Gallery of Art exhibition, organized by Robert Farris Thompson and Joseph Cornet. The title refers to a cosmogram that has become the signatory emblem of black southern traditional culture: a diamond shape, sometimes extended with a sphere at each point. The sign represents the same life cycle Archie Byron celebrated in *Anatomy*. It "emphasizes that man, as such, moves in God's time, not his own, while one portion of it takes the name of God, *Kalunga*."[32] The diamond bisected by a horizontal line is interpreted as two mountains opposed at the base, one reflecting the other in the ocean, with the Kalunga line connoting the spiritual water that divides heaven and earth.[33]

The thread of emblematic diamonds across the Afro-American South winds its way through quiet middle class neighborhoods in Mobile, Alabama, to neon colored decorations on the facades of Honky Tonks in Memphis. James Hampton attached it to the front of the mighty *Throne* in his original installation in a small, rented garage in Washington, D.C.[34] Harriet Powers' famous *Quilt* in the Museum of Fine Arts in Boston displays it in the panel devoted to Job praying for his enemies, with a clearly articulated sun at each point. A singular white diamond on a window shutter distinguishes Bessie Harvey's home near Knoxville, Tennessee. Dilmus Hall covered the exterior facade of his house with bright blue diamonds and painted an unmistakable rendition of the cosmogram on his living room ceiling sometime during the 1950's. The sign surfaces again as storefront graffiti in Atlanta and continues to less than a mile from the Atlantic coast in the Georgia tidewater region. There on the grave of a Baptist minister at Sunbury, is a homemade concrete slab with a large diamond shape cut into the surface and a strong horizontal incision dividing it in half. Offshore, in the "Behavior" cemetery on Sapelo Island, it emerges again in the center of a clearing, on the oldest grave recorded there.

The social dilemmas associated with collecting and nurturing black folk art remain complex and challenging. However, the rapidly growing body of new information about the religious orientation and traditional continuities of this art forecasts a greater understanding of still another dimension of the American experience, promising deeper insights and confirming that the rewards of meaning outweigh the threats of illusion.

Notes

1. Winifred Kellersberger Vass, *The Bantu Speaking Heritage of the United States* (Los Angeles, CA: Center for Afro American Studies, University of California, 1979), pp. 17–19.
2. The spelling of Kongo, with a "K," refers to the culture of the Bakongo people and other Bantu speaking nations of West Africa, as distinct from the political entities, the Belgian Congo and the Peoples' Republic of Congo-Brazzaville. See Robert Farris Thompson, *Flash of the Spirit,* p. 103.
3. Vass, *The Bantu Speaking Heritage of the United States,* p. 19.
4. Ibid., p. 3.
5. Ira Berlin, "The Making of Americans," *American Visions.* February, 1987, pp. 26–30.
6. *Drums and Shadows.* The Georgia Writers' Project of the Works Progress Administration, Savannah Unit, (Athens, GA and London, U.K.: The University of Georgia Press, 1940).
7. Lerone Bennett, Jr., *Before the Mayflower: A History of Black America* (New York: Penguin Books, 1984), p. 107.
8. *Shared Visions/Separate Realities.* (Catalogue: Orlando, Fla., Valencia Community College, 1985), p. 2.
9. Ibid., p. 4.
10. Interview, December, 1985.
11. Thanks to Regenia Perry, Professor of Art History. Virginia Commonwealth University, Richmond, Virginia, for her insights in personal interviews.
12. *God Struck Me Dead: Religious Conversion Experiences and Autobiographies of Negro Ex-Slaves.* Social Science Institute of Fisk University, (Nashville, TN, 1941).
13. Interview with Bessie Harvey, June, 1987.
14. Interview with Regenia Perry, May, 1987.
15. John Beardsley, "Spiritual Epics," *Black Folk Art in America 1930–1980.* (Jackson, MS: The University of Mississippi and the Center for the Study of Southern Culture, 1982), p. 50.
16. Albert J. Raboteau, *Slave Religion: The "Invisible Institution" in the Antebellum South.* (New York: Oxford University Press, 1978), p. 4.
17. Eugene W. Metcalf, "Black Art, Folk Art, and Social Control." *Winterthur Portfolio.* 1983, p. 282.
18. Mircea Eliade, *The Sacred and the Profane: The Nature of Religion.* (New York: Harcourt Brace Jovanovich, 1959, translated from the French by Willard R. Trask), p. 191.

19. Raboteau, *Slave Religion: The "Invisible Institution" in the Antebellum South,* pp. 4–42.

20. John Michael Vlach, *The Afro American Tradition in the Decorative Arts.* (Cleveland, OH: The Cleveland Museum of Art, 1978), p. 139.

21. Robert Farris Thompson, "Siras Bowens of Sunbury, Georgia: A Tidewater Artist in the Afro American Visual Tradition," *Chant of Saints,* (Chicago, IL: University of Chicago Press, 1979), pp. 230–240.

22. Ibid.

23. Interview with J. B. Murry, May 1985.

24. Ibid.

25. Interview with Dilmus Hall, February, 1981.

26. Interview with Dr. William Rawlings, Sandersville, GA, May, 1985.

27. Robert Farris Thompson and Joseph Cornet. *The Four Moments of the Sun: Kongo Art in Two Worlds.* (Washington, DC. The National Gallery of Art, 1981) p. 69.

28. Raboreau, *Slave Religion,* p. 28.

29. Ibid., p. 29.

30. Stephen Jay Gould, "James Hampton's Throne and the Dual Nature of Time." *Smithsonian Studies in American Art,* Spring, 1987, pp. 47–58.

31. Paul Radin, "Status, Phantasy, and Christian Dogma," an introduction to *God Struck Me Dead,* (Westport, CT: Greenwood Publishing Co., 1972), pp. iv–xi.

32. Thompson and Cornet, *The Four Moments of the Sun,* p. 44.

33. Thompson, *Flash of the Spirit,* p. 106.

34. Lynda Hartigan, *The Throne of the Third Heaven of the Nations Millenium General Assembly.* (Montgomery, AL: The Montgomery Museum of Fine Arts, 1977).

African Symbolism in Afro-American Quilts

Maude Southwell Wahlman
Art historian

Maude Southwell Wahlman is also the author of Signs and Symbols. African Images in African-American Quilts *(1993), "Religious Symbolism in African American Quits,"* The Clarion, *(vol. 14, no. 2, Spring 1989), "Continuities between African Textiles and Afro-American Quilts," in* Traditions in Cloth *(1985), "Gifts of the Spirit: Religious Symbols in Afro-American Folk Arts," in* Gifts of The Spirit *(1984), and an article on quiltmaking in* The Encyclopedia of Southern Culture *(1990). Wahlman is chair of the department of art at the University of Central Florida at Orlando.*

Maude Southwell Wahlman, "African Symbolism in Afro-American Quilts," African Arts *20 (1) (1986): 68–76, 99.*

FIGURE 1.

An Afro-Suriname strip cape from the collection of Christopher Healy.

The influence of African slaves on music, dance, and speech in the Caribbean and the Americas, where they were sent between 1650 and 1850, has long been documented.[1] Their impact on folk arts like quiltmaking is less well known (Thompson 1969, Vlach 1978, Wahlman & Scully 1982). Yet it is possible to trace African textile techniques, aesthetic preferences, and religious symbols that were adapted by black quiltmakers in the New World. There they mixed and sorted their own traditions, then combined them with Euro-American and American Indian[2] idioms to create unique creolized arts.

   Probably invented by Mande peoples, strip-weaving technology spread via Mande Dyula traders throughout West Africa (Thompson 1983:209–10). For centuries in that part of the continent, most cloth has been constructed from strips woven on small portable men's looms and sewn together. The African preference for strip textiles continued in the New World in the Afro-Brazilian garment called *pano de costa* (Thompson 1983:213). A nineteenth-century illustration (Denis 1823:pl. 136) shows a Mandelike loincloth in Suriname made from three strips of cotton, two patterned and the center one plain, as in nineteenth-century Asante cloth from Ghana. At that time black women on Suriname coastal plantations also made patchwork textiles (*mamio*) and festive costumes for special hostesses (*a meki sani*) from patterned and striped handkerchiefs (Thompson 1983:296–97). Maroon peoples, composed of slaves who escaped to the Suriname rainforest, continued the African tradition: both Djula and Saramaka women fashioned strip textiles (Figure 1).

• • •

Strip clothing was also made in the United States as seen in a 1930s photograph (Welty 1971:106). In addition strips dominate many Afro-American quilt patterns (Figs. 2,3), including the oldest style of pieced quilt, sometimes called "Lazy Gal"; an old strip pattern made from "strings" of cloth, comparable to weft bands of color, called "Spider Leg" and its blocked version, a creolization of African and Anglo-American elements called "Twin Sisters" or "Spider Web." One quilt made between 1825 and 1850 by Afro-Americans living in Jackson Hill, Georgia, was done in the "Wild Goose Chase" pattern, with rows of triangles separated by wide strips (Reynolds 1978:6–7). This pattern remains popular all over the United States especially among Afro-American women. While strips may also be used in Anglo-American quilts, they appear as only one of many geometric patterns. Whether consisting of a single piece or many small scraps of cloth, strips are a dominant design element as well as a chief construction technique in both West African textiles and Afro-American quilts.

When woven strips of various patterns are sewn together in West Africa the resulting cloth is asymmetrical, unpredictable in design. The aesthetic of these "off beat" patterns, as Thompson (1974:11) calls them, is preferred. African wide-loom women's textiles were also sewn together to create asymmetrical designs. Wide-loom weaving was once done by black women in the United States, the same women who made quilts, and it was they who probably preserved certain African cloth traditions. One of them, Luiza Combs, was born in Guinea (ca. 1853), but at about age 10 she arrived in Tennessee. One example of her wide-loom weaving survives. Made in 1890, it comprises two panels of brightly colored horizontal stripes that when stitched together created an asymmetrical effect similar to West African woven cloth. Judith Chase (1980:135–58) noted that ". . . most old [Afro-American] coverlets were woven in two strips seamed down the center to make them wide enough to cover a bed. Interestingly enough there sometimes appears to be no attempt to match the pattern where the seam is made. Considering the obvious dexterity of the weaver, this may be an Africanism." A contemporary Afro-American quilt from Maryland, described by Peter Holmes (1977), also features horizontal strips that were offset when the two panels were joined.

Multiple patterning is another characteristic shared by African and Caribbean textiles and Afro-American quilts. In Africa the number and complexity of patterns in a fabric increase in accordance with the owner's prestige, power, and wealth (Cole & Ross 1977:24, pl. IV). Cloth woven for kings or priests may feature a variety of patterns

FIGURE 2.

An Afro-American strip quilt by Martha Jane Pettaway, Alabama.

within as well as between strips (see Sieber 1972:192). Contemporary Afro-American quilts retain this aesthetic: lines, designs, and colors vary with a persistence that cannot be explained by a lack of cloth in the right color or pattern. Thompson (1983:221) has suggested that asymmetrical and multiple-patterned strip cloths in West Africa have more than an aesthetic function: they also serve to keep evil spirits away, as "evil travels in straight lines."

Afro-American quiltmakers went one step further by introducing improvisation, establishing a pattern in one square—often one of traditional Euro-American origin—and varying it in size, arrangement, and color in successive squares. Through

FIGURE 3.

An Afro-American strip quilt by Sarah Mary Taylor, Mississippi.

improvisation, they maintain African principles of multiple patterning, asymmetry, and unpredictable rhythms and tensions similar to those found in other Afro-American arts such as blues, jazz, and dance.

Besides piecing, in which strip patterns may dominate, the other basic quilt construction technique known in Europe, Africa, and the United States is appliqué. While Euro-American appliquéd quilts are primarily decorative, Afro-American counterparts often relate stories and ideas in the same manner as African appliquéd textiles.

• • •

Haitian flags, featuring painted and appliquéd scenes embellished with sequins and beads, have numerous possible roots: European flags, Fon banners of the Republic of Benin, Fante flags of Ghana, Ejagham cloth and Ibibio funerary hangings of Nigeria, and Kongo flags of Zaire and Angola. *Mpeeve,* Kikongo for "flag," refers to both fluttering and the presence of unseen spirits. Honoring Vodun gods, Haitian flags announce the coming of a particular spirit to a shrine at a ceremony. After independence in 1804, many Haitians migrated to New Orleans where African textile influences in these flags combined with Euro-American images. Thompson (1981:191) has noted that the Kongo idea of agitating cloth or a flag to open the door to the other world with honor continues in New Orleans with the use of Afro-American jazz funeral-march umbrellas, appliquéd in bright colors and adorned with bells, feathers, flowers, and ribbons.

Afro-American quilts mirror the diverse influences that shape the lives of black women in the United States. Appliquéd examples may incorporate iconography drawn from imagination, Southern rural black culture, and popular American culture shaped by television, magazines, and advertising. Their secular imagery is countered in appliquéd Bible textiles, a tradition probably connected to two 1775 Bible cloths from New Orleans. Although it cannot be proven that these were made by a black woman, certain features indicate strong continuities with African techniques and ideographic symbols. Florence Peto (1939:56–57) wrote: "Although there is no available history to help identify the origin of the items . . . they are among the most interesting and unique patchwork creations that I have encountered. Two panels (9´9˝ long; 6´6˝ wide), consist each of thirty six appliqued picture blocks which tell the story of the Testaments, Old and New respectively. They have a Latin, an old world appearance, although they are said to derive from New Orleans, where they quite possibly adorned the walls of a convent or private chapel. The technique employed in applying the patches differs markedly from that used generally by American colonial and pioneer needleworkers; they suggest the fingers of a creole woman. No edges have been turned under; patches have been applied and then outlined with a thin, round, black and white cord held in place with couching stitches . . . The episode blocks, seven inches square, are separated by three inch wide bands of gold cloth to which have been appliqued the Greek fret border in white—all edges outlined with cord. The upper inscription, Dictus Anno Sancto, may be translated, 'dedicated to the Holy Year.' The lower inscription, '1775.'"

The raw edges of the appliquéd figures on these two Bible cloths, a characteristic shared by many Afro-American quilts, are like those of the leather cut-outs found on Nigerian Yoruba Egungun costumes and bags, used by priests for the god Shango. These bags *(laba shango)* feature square frames with appliquéd human figures posed in the sign for lightning (one arm up, one arm down) which also signifies motion in the Ejagham writing system *(nsibidi)*. The ideographic designs surrounding the 1775 textiles are similar to Ejagham signs for speech and motion.

Two Afro-American appliquéd quilts made by Harriet Powers in 1886 and 1898, illustrate scenes from the Bible as well as local historical events.[3] Both quilts are made in three rows of scenes, each scene placed within a square outlined with narrow strips. Marie-Jeanne Adams (1980:12–38) notes, ". . . the details of the stitching show that the squares were put together in vertical columns, which is evidence that on some level of her thought, Mrs. Powers grouped the scenes in vertical order." This vertical arrangement may be a reflection of the West African strip-weaving tradition.

Adams speculates on possible African influences on Powers, who was born in Georgia in 1837 (1980:12–28): "By the time her parents' generation would have come to the South, most slaves were being imported from the Congo and Angola. Even if they came from West Africa and from Dahomey, they would not necessarily be knowledgeable in the appliqué techniques. [Fon] appliquéd cloths were made . . . in the capital city of Abomey by family guilds of tailors, all retainers of the monarch, and the guilds included only men and young boys. It seems most likely that she could have acquired a knowledge of [this] African style by hearsay only from other, older house slaves of her 'old miss' or from her parents or other older persons."

Afro-American quilt designs may also have been inspired by African writing traditions, which often use cloth as a medium for ideographs. Writing is considered sacred and protective, associated with knowledge, power, and intelligence. In Mali, Bamana women paint esoteric designs on cloth called *bokolanfini,* woven by men on a narrow loom. The fabric is used for women's wrappers and protective clothing for hunters. Also in West Africa, Mande peoples encase pieces of religious writing, indigenous and Islamic, in protective leather charms that are worn around the neck or sewn to gowns. Numerous bundles containing script were sewn onto quilted war shirts and horse blankets as a further defensive measure. In the Republic of Benin, the Fon paint religious signs on the ground. In Nigeria, *nsibidi* appears on Ejagham secret-society buildings, metal fans, and calabashes, as well as woven costumes and resist-dyed and appliquéd cloths. In Central Africa, priests use symbolic art forms related to the Kongo cosmogram, a circle with four points representing birth, life, death, and rebirth in the world of the ancestors, under the sea (Thompson 1983; Janzen & MacGaffey 1974; Bunseki 1969).

• • •

These ideographs may appear in Afro-American quilts as well. Checks are a popular old pattern remembered from early childhood. It is a salvage design that can be made from the smallest scraps and that allows for maximum contrast between scraps without elaborate preplanning. Checks are also transformed into the popular "Nine Patch" block design borrowed from Anglo-American quiltmaking tradition. One can speculate that Afro-Americans adopted "Nine Patch" and other checked and triangle patterns like "Wild Goose Chase" because they resembled the leopard society cloths of their heritage.[4]

Cross-like patterns also occur frequently in Afro-American quilts. Although now interpreted as Christian crosses, they could once have been adopted because of a resemblance to the Kongo symbol for the four points of the sun. Mary Twining (1977:188) comments on the design of a quilt made by Mrs. Robert Johnson of John's Island, South Carolina: "It was not a Christian cross, according to residents. . . . It represented danger, evil and bad feelings."

The "Broken Stove" or "Love Knot" pattern is another Afro-American quilting favorite. It features a circle divided into quadrants, usually in contrasting materials. Pecolia Warner calls this circle the "eyes" of the stove and of the quilt. The four eyes may allude to the Ejagham belief in two sets of eyes, the second set being for spiritual vision. . . .

In Harriet Power's Bible quilts, the most elaborate shapes are the suns. Afro-American quiltmakers could have preferred sun-like designs because they remembered Ejagham, Kongo, Haitian, or Cuban signs, or because they were similar to established Afro-American patterns. I postulate that sun-like motifs were originally adopted and creolized as religious symbols deriving from the Kongo cosmogram, and then their meanings were forgotten. Considering the fact that one-third of the blacks in the United States can trace their ancestry to Zaire and Angola, this is not improbable.

Writing continued to have protective symbolism in Afro-American culture, even when the writing was in English. Newsprint placed on the walls of Southern homes, and into shoes as well, protected against the elements or evil enslaving spirits, who, it was believed "would have to stop and read the words of each chopped up column" before they could do any harm (Bass 1973:393).[5] Vestiges of these protective writing traditions also occur in the folk arts. Quilts with hard-to-read asymmetrical designs and multiple patterns have the same function as newspapered walls (e.g., Vlach 1978:74, 139). While contemporary quilters do not talk about confusing strangers or warding off evil spirits with their quilts, their aesthetic choices are simply traditions that once had protective significance and that may well have been a continuation of protective African texts.

Another African concept that reappeared in the New World, and eventually in Afro-American quilts, is the healing or protective charm, of which there are two types. The first, from West Africa, has already been mentioned: the small square packet, often of red leather, enclosing script; these are worn around the neck and on hunting and religious costumes as protection against evil.[6] The second type, from Central Africa, the Kongo *nkisi* (pl. *minkisi*), or "medicines of God," appears in numerous forms. Janzen and MacGaffey (1974:37) note that the earliest Kongo charms were ceramic vessels with liquid medicines; later versions contained symbolic medicines that referred to the watery ancestral world and to things whose names were puns for verbs of action. The enclosed objects fall into two classes: those significant for their visual form (e.g., shells, graveyard earth, clay) and objects considered important because the terms for them are similar to verbs of action. . . . One type in cloth, usually red, was tied at the neck, with feathers at the top (Thompson 1983: pl. 72).

• • •

In Haiti, the Kongo cloth charm is still very much alive in the form of *pacquet kongo,* small tightly wound charms enclosed in cloth, now with arms, beads around the neck, ribbons, and sequins (Thompson 1983:31–36). Some have earrings or lace ruffles and are meant to represent female spirits. Maya Deren (1953:275) noted that "Pacquets Congo . . . are bound as magical safeguards . . . whose efficiency depends on the technique of careful wrapping (the idea being to enclose the soul well, so as to keep it from evil). . . ."

In Haiti and Cuba, one also finds allusions to the Kongo *mbaka,* little red men thought to be messengers from the dead (Herskovits 1971:239–44); called *baka,* they look like miniature Kongo mummies. . . .

In the United States, these red human forms—*mbaka,* the Kongo mummy, and *pacquet congo*—have evolved into Vodun dolls. Often they are made with pins to activate them, just as Kongo wooden charms are activated by nails. The painters Nellie Mae Rowe and Lizzie Wilkerson both made dolls with red arms and legs, but neither woman would explain why she used that color:[7] although the symbolism of Vodun dolls may have been forgotten, their form continued. Two quiltmakers' appliqué designs feature red men and "Dolly Dimple Dolls," reminiscent of Vodun dolls.

The Afro-American *mojo,* also known as a "hand," is a cloth charm that fuses West and Central African concepts. Charms contain a soul, a spiritual spark or force, called *mooyo* in Kikongo (Thompson 1984).[8] *Mojo* refers to a hex or spell, healing medicine, and the charm or amulet used to lift a spell or protect one from evil forces. Zora Neal Hurston (1931:414) wrote about a "hand": "Take a piece of the fig leaf, sycamore bark, John de Conquer root, John de Conquer vine, three paradise seeds. Take a piece of paper and draw a square and let the party write his wishes. Begin, 'I want to be successful in all my undertakings.' Then cut the paper from around the square and let him tear it up fine and throw it in front of the business place or house or wherever he wants. Put the square in the 'hand' and sew it all up in red flannel. Sew with a strong thread and when seams are closed, pass the thread back and forth through the bag 'til all the thread is used up. To pour on 'hand:' oil of anise, oil of rose geranium, violet perfume, oil of lavender, verbena, bay rum. 'Hand' must be re-newed every six months."

To get rid of bad spirits, a person could put foot scrapings in a silk bag and toss it into a river, uttering "Go yo Devil, yogo" (Hyatt 1974, 2895). Likewise, pieces of silky cloth were gathered into pockets and sewn onto large cloths, often quilted. Such coverlets, called Yoyo quilts, retain the aesthetic form—if not the meaning— of *mojo*.

The Afro-American "Pineapple" quilt pattern may represent another vestige of cloth charms. It is made from squares of cloth folded twice into smaller squares and then sewn together so that only the points show as triangular shapes. These tips over-lap each other to create a three-dimensional, sculptural surface, not unlike a soft ver-sion of a Kongo nail-embellished *nkisi*. In one quilt all the tips are arranged into nine circles, each with a pocket in the center that can be opened by prying up a few of the triangles. This technique is widespread from Mississippi and Alabama to Connecticut.

Today Afro-American quiltmakers incorporate images derived from their daily lives. Their appliqués reproduce illustrations from books and magazines and record dreamed designs. Some, however, continue using traditional images such as human or doll forms as well as hands. Sarah Mary Taylor of Mississippi produced a quilt she calls "Mermaid" (formerly known as "Rabbit") because of the large figures appliquéd onto white squares. Numerous small red squares like the *mojo* or "hand" also occur, and one such red square has a blue hand appliquéd adjacent to it. This quiltmaker has made numerous quilts that play on the symbolic connotations and aesthetic qualities of the hand image.

The epitome of the Afro-American charm-like quilt is an example by Arester Earl. It has pleated and stuffed shell shapes in materials (mostly silky) of many colors and pat-terns, sewn onto red cloth. The quilt is significant because it illustrates three important Kongo religious references: "medicines of God," enclosed in cloth; the shell, emblem of the world of Kongo ancestors; and the cross, or the Kongo cosmogram. That a quilt could have naively combined these potent Kongo symbols seems unlikely.

Protective Afro-American quilts may also borrow Anglo-American patterns that imply action in their names (e.g., "Flying Geese," "Rocky Road to California," "Drunkards Path"), or forms (e.g., in "Bear's Paw"). They recall the objects contained as medicines in Kongo charms, objects whose names are puns for verbs of action.

The bold colors and large designs of Afro-American textiles originate in the com-municative function of African textiles, used to indicate status, wealth, occupation, and history. The strong color contrasts in the latter insure a cloth's readability at a distance and in strong sunlight. Similar brilliant colors are found in Afro-American quilts although the function has become strictly aesthetic.[9]

Afro-American quilt colors can be traced to African protective traditions as well, Bunseki (1969) notes that when a person is painted with red, white, and black spots during a Kongo healing ceremony, it signifies that he has the power to defend himself against "annihilating powers." These colors are used to fight disturbing influences in the world of the living. The addition of yellow indicates a contest with forces from the dead.

Thompson (1977–80) says that among the Yoruba, white, identified with the god Obatala, represents character, pure intentions, and the source of knowledge. Red is associated with Shango, the god of thunder, and is also a symbol of *ashe,* the power to make things happen and to make things multiply, possessed by kings as well as Shango. The god's red and white beads symbolize the balance of character and power. Blue symbolizes coolness, composure, calculated thought, control, and generosity.

In Haiti, Yoruba-Fon and Central African Bantu color symbolism seem to have melded together in the red-and-white striped shirts, called *mayo,* which are worn as protection against evil by Vodun followers (Stebich 1978:113). And for the United States, Thompson (1983:221) notes: "Nellie Brag, an old Black woman of the Canton, Ohio, area in the first half of the 20th century was asked why she often went about wearing one red sock with a deliberately mismatched white one. Years later, after trust and friendship had been established between her and her interlocutor, she told the reason why: 'to keep spirits away.'" Even today, black coeds at the University of Mississippi can be seen wearing tights with one red and one black leg.

Among the quiltmakers of Sea Island, Georgia, colors are warm or cold, emphasizing reds, blues, or whites. Red signifies danger, fire, conflict, and passion; blue is a good color used on doors to keep away bad spirits; white is a color that makes one good—a color used at weddings, funerals, and parties. Mary Twining (1977:189) wrote: "Red, blue, black, and white are four important colors whose significance [to Sea Islanders] is linked to a deeper set of values and beliefs in culture. These have meanings beyond an exciting combination of colors which work well together. . . . The quilts are often made in striking chromatic contrasts such as red/blue or red/white—color combinations which suggest the binary opposites hot/cool, good/bad, safe/dangerous which are some of the dichotomous predicates that make up the dynamics of human societies."

Although color may have symbolic significance to many Afro-American quilt-makers,[10] most simply explain that color choices are determined by maximum contrast. Sometimes colors are symmetrically or consistently arranged. More often scraps are pieced together as they come out of a bag or box, with aesthetic decisions made at the last minute. Because quiltmakers usually work with salvage materials of many patterns and colors, this piecing technique encourages asymmetrical designs and multiple patterns.

In 1980 Pecolia Warner made a red, white, and blue striped quilt based on the American flag. She said that she dreamed of the quilt after seeing a flag at the post office. In her hands it has become an Afro-American version of the protective Haitian *mayo,* featuring strips, bright contrasting colors, large designs, asymmetry, at least two patterns, and stars resembling the Ejagham symbol for speech.

We have seen that Afro-American quilt patterns derive from rich cultural traditions. If only one or two African forms were evident, one could suspect coincidence, but the numerous similarities strongly suggest a link to Central African Kongo and various West African cultures. Indeed, more than one third of Afro-Americans are descended from the Kongo and Kongo-influenced peoples, and an equally impressive number from West African peoples.

Like many other Afro-American folk artists, quiltmakers are inspired by dreams that recall the imagery of their childhood in which they were exposed to folk religious concepts and visual symbols. That so much of their art has ties to African and Afro-Latin American religious forms, whose meaning could not always be verbalized, may indicate an unconscious revival of these cultural systems. Paul Bohannan (1973) wrote: "Culture is coded in memory, in behavior, in materials, in language, in art, in writing, and computers . . . the most important thing about culture is that it is always encoded twice—once within the human being, in electrical and chemical form, and once outside the human being in some other form." I would submit that for Afro-Americans their most highly valued ideas, such as African protective religious concepts, are encoded in many forms: the visual arts, song, dance, and even speech.

Ideas encoded in objects sometimes last longer than those retained in the mind or in words. George Kubler (1976:50–51) wrote: "The artist is not a free agent obeying only his own will. His situation is rigidly bound by a chain of prior events. The chain is invisible to him and it limits his motion. He is not aware of it as a chain but only as a *vis a tergo,* as the force of events behind him." These comments are particularly insightful when applied to Afro-American folk artists, who have so often been labeled idiosyncratic because they could not articulate the African traditions that shaped their visions, dreams, and arts. We can only guess whether their use of African symbolic forms is unconscious, or if they know the meanings behind the symbols but refuse to disclose them.[11]

Afro-American artists maintaining this creolized aesthetic demonstrate the power and vision of African cultural traditions in contemporary American society, affirming the extraordinary tenacity of African religious ideas over hundreds of years in the face of major obstacles. Their contribution suggests that the unique way in which any culture encodes beauty in the seen world is an indispensable tool for coping with an indifferent or hostile reality.

Notes

1. See Herskovits (1941, 1955), Courlander (1960). Szwed and Abraham (1979), and Wood (1974).
2. American Indian traditions appear mostly in Afro-Latin American textiles and Mardi Gras costumes. African ideas also occur in Seminole Indian patchwork textiles. . . .
3. The earlier quilt was exhibited at the Cotton Fair in Athens, Georgia, in 1886. Purchased in 1891 by Jennie Smith, it was eventually given to the Smithsonian Institution. Its display at

the 1896 Cotton States Exposition in Atlanta resulted in the commissioning of the second Bible quilt as a gift for the Reverend Charles Culber Hall. This quilt was given to the Boston Museum of Fine Arts in 1964.

4. Retention of leopard society traditions makes sense in terrns of slave trading history, for Old Calabar, at the mouth of the Cross River, was a major slave port. Check symbolism is retained in secret society costumes in Cuba, where an equally great number of Cross River peoples were sent.

5. Trudier Harris (pers. com., March 1984) tells me this concept derives from the Afro-American practice of leaving a Bible open at night; the power of religious words would protect a family against evil. And Roger Abrahams (pers. com., 1985) related that in many literate cultures, one put a Bible under a pillow to have a wish fulfilled or to protect a child; the practice of enclosing magical holy words to increase their power is found widely in early literate cultures. He noted that the Bible is used not only as an amulet but as a divining tool as well; a person looking for guidance would open the Bible and read the first verse he encountered, and it would contain a sign indicating what action to take.

6. In Brazil, Thompson (1981:18) found variations on this theme; one example has writing on the red plastic film covering styrofoam.

7. Jean Ellen Jones, personal communication, 1984.

8. The *y* in *mooyo* lightly changes to a *j* (Robert Farris Thompson pers. com., 1984).

9. This work is best seen from a distance in contrast to pastel New England quilts meant to be inspected in intimate settings.

10. Zora Neal Hurston (1931:385) documented the following color symbolism: red for victory; pink for love; green for driving off evil spirits; blue for success and protection and for causing death; yellow for money; brown for drawing money and people; lavender for causing harm; and black for death or evil. For Pecolia Warner (pers. com., 1980) the colors in her quilts also had meanings beyond their aesthetic function. She said, "Red represents blood. But I like to put it in quilts—makes it brighter and show up. Blue is for truth. White is for peace . . . When a person dies you see the family wear all black. In a quilt that doesn't represent mourning. That makes it show up. They say that gold is for love. Silver is for peace. Brass is for trouble . . . Yellow is like gold; it means love."

11. For example, their reluctance may stem from the incompatibility of Vodun symbols with Christianity.

Bibliography

Adams, Marie-Jeanne. 1980. "The Harriet Powers Pictorial Quilts," *Black Art* 3, 4.

Bass, Ruth. 1973. "Mojo and The Little Man." in *Mother Wit and the Laughing Barrel,* ed. Alan Dundes, New York: Prentice Hall.

Bohannan, Paul. 1973. "Rethinking Culture: A Project for Current Anthropologists," *Current Anthropology* 14, 4:357–72.

Bunseki, Fu-Kiau. 1969. *Nza Kengo,* Kinshasa.

Chase, Judith. 1980. "Afro-American Heritage from Ante-Bellum Black Craftsmen," in Afro-American Folk Arts and Crafts. *Southern Folklore Quarterly,* ed. William Ferris.

Cole, Herbert and Doran Ross. 1977. *The Arts of Ghana.* Los Angeles: Museum of Cultural History, UCLA.

Courlander, Harold. 1960. *The Drum and the Hoe. The Life and Love of Haitian People.* Berkeley: University of California Press.

Deren, Maya. 1953. *Divine Horsemen: The Living Gods of Haiti.* New York: Thames & Hudson.

Herskovits, Melville. 1941. *Myth of the Negro Past*. Boston: Beacon Press.

Herskovits, Melville. 1955. *Cultural Anthropology*. New York: Knopf.

Herskovits, Melville. 1971. *Life in a Haitian Valley*. Garden City, N.Y.: Anchor Books.

Holmes, Peter. 1977. "Alice Bolling and the Quilt Fence." Yale College.

Hurston, Zora Neal. 1931. "Voodoo in America." *Journal of American Folklore* 44.

Janzen, John and Wyatt McGaffey. 1974. *An Anthology of Kongo Religion*. Lawrence: The University of Kansas Press.

Kubler, George. 1976. *The Shape of Time*. Yale University Press.

Peto, Florence. 1939. *Historic Quilts*. New York: American Historical Company.

Rodman, Selden. 1973. *The Miracle of Haitian Art*. New York: Doubleday & Co.

Stebich, Ute. 1978. *Haitian Art*. New York: Brooklyn Museum.

Szwed, John and Roger Abraham. 1979. *An Annotated Bibliography of Afro-American Folk Culture*. Philadelphia: The American Folklore Society Bibliographic and Special Series.

Talbot, P.A. 1912. *In The Shadow of the Bush*. London: William Heinemann.

Thompson, Robert Farris. 1974. *African Art in Motion*. Los Angeles: University of California Press.

Thompson, Robert Farris. 1981. *Four Moments of the Sun: Kongo Art in Two Worlds* (with Joseph Cornet). Washington, D.C.: The National Gallery.

Thompson, Robert Farris. 1983. *Flash of the Spirit: African and Afro-American Art and Philosophy*. New York: Random House.

Turner, Victor. 1967. *The Forest of Symbols*. New York: Cornell University Press.

Vlach, John Michael. 1978. *The Afro-American Tradition in the Decorative Arts*. Cleveland: The Cleveland Museum of Art.

Wahlman, Maude Southwell and John Scully. 1982. "Aesthetic Principles in Afro-American Quilts," in *Folk Arts and Crafts*, ed. William Ferris, Boston: G. K. Hall.

Welty, Eudora. 1971. *One Time, One Place* New York: Random House.

Wood, Peter. 1974. *The Black Majority*. New York: W. W. Norton.

Vision in Afro-American Folk Art

William Ferris
Anthropologist and folklorist

William Ferris is author of Blues from the Delta *(1978), editor of* Folk Arts and Crafts *(1982), and author of "If You Ain't Got It in Your Head, You Can't Do It in Your Hand: James Thomas, Mississippi Delta Folk Sculptor," in* Studies in the Literary Imagination *(vol. 3, 1970). Since mid-1998 Ferris, who is on the faculty of the University of Mississippi, has been the chairman of the National Endowment for the Humanities.*

William Ferris "Vision in Afro-American Folk Art: The Sculpture of James Thomas," Journal of American Folklore *88 (348) (1975): 115–131.*

James Thomas is a gifted blues musician, tale teller, and clay sculptor in Leland, Mississippi, the heart of the Mississippi Delta. I have followed the evolution of his sculpture over the past six years. Already, in four years, my earlier study of his work is dated, reflecting Thomas' speed and creativity in developing new sculptural forms.[1]

Research on Thomas' art has raised questions about the study of Afro-American folk art within western intellectual frames. Anthropologists and folklorists generally define folk culture as a spectrum of songs, tales, and material culture passed on from generation to generation within a community. This approach to Afro-American culture is linear and is classically illustrated in Melville Herskovits *The Myth of the Negro Past* where folk traditions are traced from African forms to New World survivals.[2] Scholars thus assume that master musicians, narrators, and craftsmen train younger blacks, thus assuring the survival of Afro-American folk culture.

James Thomas, however, states that his sculpture is largely self-taught rather than developed from other artists. His statement seems reasonable considering the frequency of appearance of new forms and color patterns in his repertoire. Thomas acquires new images, or "futures" as he terms them, for sculpture in his dreams. He molds them in clay while they are fresh in his mind, for "if you can't hold it in your head, you can't shape it." He says, "The dreams just come to me. If I'm working with clay, you have that on your mind when you lay down. You dream some. Then you get up and try."[3]

A striking parallel to Thomas' artistic images and their source in dreams is seen in other Afro-American folk artists such as Harmon Young, a wood sculptor in Georgia Both use the term "futures" to describe fresh sculptural forms found in dreams, and both Thomas and Young have the hope of sculpting an entire human form in their respective mediums of clay and wood.[4]

Dreams are a major force in the imagination of both artists, and images which emerge from their dreams follow patterns consistent with each other and with traditional Afro-American styles.[5] There seems to be a spiritual or subconscious level in Afro-American folk art through which the artist recreates images of his past, and this dimension of Afro-American experience helps explain how artists hundreds of miles apart can create similar images and even use the same language to describe their "futures."[6]

Thomas clearly recalls significant dreams which have affected his art and life. These dreams were "signs" which presented new artistic images and sometimes warned him of imminent danger. One striking example occurred in 1954, the year of the Supreme Court decision to desegregate public schools.

> I dreamed once in nineteen and fifty-four that I was laying down by a pond of water and seemed some men was shooting at me. Two or three of them shooting at me, and every time they shot, the bullet would hit out in the water. Never would hit close by me. And that Saturday night was when those two or three white men got killed in Holmes County by a colored man named Ed Noll. He was selling whiskey and they tried to break in on him. He killed the white men and shot the tires on the ambulance when they come to pick up the dead. They said he would shoot combs out of his wife's head with a rifle and

wouldn't even touch her head. He could lay down in a wagon and kill hawks flying in the air. They called him sharp-shooting Ed Noll. I can't see why you have never heard of him. In nineteen fifty-four how old were you?

[Ferris] I was fourteen.

You were probably too young then to check on the news. Had your mind on playing ball or playing with girls.

AESTHETIC OF THE UGLY

Both Thomas and Young show a preference for what might be termed an "aesthetic of the ugly." Both create grotesque human images, and both feel these images are of greater interest to the viewer than more conventional shapes would be. Thomas' skulls are good examples of the "ugly," and he is conscious of it:

> A skull has got to be ugly cause it's nothing but bones and teeth. People are more likely to be interested in something like that than they would be in a bird [which he often makes]. They'd rather see a skull. Then too, a lot of people have never seen a real skull and they're probably wondering how it will be when they die. They say "Will I be in the same shape that skull there is in?"

This preference for ugliness is an aesthetic choice which reverses traditional white concepts of beauty somewhat like the black use of "bad" to mean good. The "bad" man (pronounced "baaadd") in the context of the toast and blues is a black out-law who affirms himself against white society. Thus both "bad" and "ugly" assume positive value within the Afro-American folk aesthetic in a significant reversal of white usage of the terms.[7]

Ugliness is a theme in black oral tradition as well as in sculpture, and it usually assumes a humorous tone. Bo Diddley, for example, often engaged his maracas player, Jerome Green, in a series of ugly boasts similar to the dozens. Each would comment on the other's ugliness in phrases such as:

> I took your girl home for a drink but that chick look so ugly she had to sneak up on a glass to get a drink of water.

> You got nerve to call somebody ugly. Why you so ugly that the stork that brought you in the world oughta be arrested.

> That's all right. My momma didn't have to put a sheet over my head so sleep could slip up on me.

> You should be ashamed of yourself calling people ugly.

> I didn't call you ugly. I said you was ruined. That's all.

> You know something. You look like you been whipped with a ugly stick.[8]

I recorded a similar session near Thomas' home in Leland in which one speaker responded with the following boast: "Speaking of ugliness, I got a friend up a Tunica named Joe Dillard. He's so ugly that you could sue God for making him and get all of Hell and half of Heaven. That cat knows he's ugly. He's so ugly 'till when he was born they had to slap him and make him cry so they could tell where his mouth was." Ugliness is clearly an important theme in Afro-American folk culture and is developed in both oral and material forms. Implicit in the ugly or grotesque sculpture of Thomas is an inversion of conventional white taste, a reinterpretation of aesthetics within Afro-American folk culture.

THOMAS AND HERSKOVITS

In viewing the life and art of James Thomas, the approach of Herskovits must be qualified in two points. First, contrary to Herskovits' belief that only oral lore survived in the United States,[9] there is an Afro-American tradition of folk sculpture which is alive and well. Thomas' work is complemented by that of his wife and son, who both make faces and animals for their friends in Leland. Interestingly, the white owner of a furniture store where Thomas works part-time has also begun making faces and skulls which he displays in his store.

A second qualification of Herskovits is that the individual artist and his tradition must be studied with equal care. There is often a tendency in folklore to document "traditions" through recordings (music and tales) and photographs (art and crafts) without considering the artists who produce them.[10] Black folk art reflects the creator's personal life as well as culturally determined forms and aesthetics. Thomas' art, for example, cannot be fully understood without knowledge of his life as a black man in Mississippi:

> If you'd worked as hard as I did, if you'd known a dream you couldn't tell it. You couldn't hardly hold up at the work I did. I have pulled five hundred foot cables up and down those Mississippi hills all day long and not have nothing but a box of crackers for dinner and some water. And I have worked all day long trying to get some money to buy food for my children.

Today Thomas works as a gravedigger, an occupation which reflects itself in the theme of death which permeates his folktales, blues, and sculpture. Images of skulls often "roll across" his mind; Thomas' friends associate him with death and jokingly greet him with phrases like "Don't come after me. I'm not ready to die yet." Death and burial rites are major themes in Afro-American culture, and Thomas' life serves to define and focus these themes in forms of folk art.[11]

The Delta region, Thomas' occupation, and his artistic sensitivity are major influences on his sculpture, which is a part of a larger "Afro-American tradition." We must never forget that this tradition is borne within the life of an artist who is constantly reshaping and redefining his own art in variations of this broader folk tradition. Without an appreciation of Thomas' life we have at best half of the rich picture of his sculpture and its role in Afro American folklore.

THE ARTIST'S CHILDHOOD

James "Son Ford" Thomas was born October 14, 1926, near Eden in Yazoo County, Mississippi, in the red clay hills which surround the Mississippi Delta. As a child he began making clay imitations of animals, patterning his first work after similar figures made by his uncle. He later made clay models of Ford tractors and was nicknamed "Son Ford."

> I used to make little tractors. I haven't made them in a long time. I used to make them and put me some sticks through there [as axles] and made me some wheels and let it dry and then I'd have something to roll across the floor. I would make them Ford tractors and they started to call me 'Son Ford' from then on.

The clay which Thomas worked is called "gumbo clay" and is found in a very pliable form in the hills of Yazoo County. As a child, he made his figures more durable by baking them in a stove or fireplace until they became red with heat. This firing made the clay figures as hard as bricks, and afterward he used them as toys or sold them to local whites. He described how he heated the figures:

> I would just let 'em dry and that hill clay, you could put it in the stove and bake it or if you had a fireplace put it there. In the wintertime I'd make me a dog or something, and I'd throw it in the fire and let it cook and let it turn red. Sometime my grandaddy would go to put a stick of wood in there, and I'd jerk it out quick, and he'd tell me. "Keep that mess outta that fireplace. I can't keep no wood in it."
> It would git just like a brick and it would rattle.

Other than with his uncle, Thomas has had no continuing contact with artists who work with clay. His work has been highly personal, and perhaps the most unusual figures in his repertoire are heads and skulls which often have openings in their tops that serve as containers or ashtrays. Asked when he first began his work, he replied:

> It was a long time ago, I wouldn't know just how old I was. When I was going to school, that's how I got my money to buy my paper and pencils, because my momma and grand-momma waddn't able to buy none of that stuff for me. I would make different things that looked good enough for me to sell, you know. The white people around there, they'd help me out and buy some. The highest I ever sold when I was small, one day, I sold some horses, and I got three dollars for them. A fellow from Vicksburg was over at Eden, and I had them in a box. He said, "Where you git them little horses?"
>
> I say, "I made them."
>
> He say, "I give you three dollars for them."
>
> Well that sounded big then, and I just handed him the whole box. It waddn't too hard for me to catch on. My uncle, he first made something looked like a mule. After he quit, well I taken that trade up. If he had kept on, he probably could do as good as me. But now I doubt whether he could make anything.
>
> [Ferris] Where'd you get the idea for the skull?
>
> Well, the first time I made a skull I was living with my grandpoppa in Yazoo County. The first one I made, I brought it in the house and set it up on the shelf. So my grandaddy

come. He looked up there and he jumped. He say, "Boy, you git this thing outta my house and don't bring another in here. I already can't rest for spooks now."

[Ferris] What made you make that, Son?

Well, whatever come to my mind, that's what I'd do. Most of the time when I was young, I never did fool with no boys or nothing. If I waddn't fishing, I was hunting, and I hardly ever would play with anybody. Just anything would cross my mind. I'd do that.

From this explanation, Thomas' decision to mold faces and skulls from clay seems to have been spontaneous and not to have arisen from having ever witnessed similar art forms. Though it is possible Thomas' uncle or others in the area made clay skulls as well as animals, Thomas never mentions it. These highly individual creations are used within the black folk community of Leland and function as important examples of Afro-American folk art. Local blacks value them highly, and their meaning for both the artist and those who possess the art is relevant to our understanding of their community.

SCULPTURAL REPERTOIRE

During my visits with Thomas, I attempted to collect his "total repertoire" of sculpture and found that as I worked with him and encouraged him to make clay figures, he expanded his repertoire and began to make figures he had never made previously. During my study he made a deer, a rabbit, a red bird, quail, fish, human skulls, human heads, a crane, a bullfrog, an alligator, a man in a coffin, a crawfish, a black man with sunglasses, a Chinaman, miniature busts, heads of George Washington and Abraham Lincoln, and a rattlesnake. These figures were made as gifts for friends, who frequently exhibit them as decoration in windows facing the street.

Thomas's ability to expand his repertoire at will through his imagination made the concept of collecting a "total repertoire" invalid. I felt the most fruitful approach would be to analyze the aesthetic values active in his creation of both new and old art forms. His work was clearly in flux, and no two figures, whether animals, faces, or skulls, were shaped or painted alike. Most of the animals were painted with whatever paints happened to be at hand, and eyes were often made from matchheads pressed into the clay so that only the colored tip showed.

Thomas's work on the folk level utilizes aesthetic theory and innovation in a way comparable to that of artists working on other, more formal levels. As a self-taught artist, he learns quickly from those professionally trained. During visits in my folklore classes at Jackson State College in 1970 and 1971, he worked several hours with Marcus Douyon, a Haitian ceramist on the art faculty. Mr. Douyon suggested that Thomas build his clay skulls around tightly packed newspaper to reduce their weight and the possibility of explosion when fired. Though he has no facilities for firing in Leland, Thomas now makes most of his skulls in this manner to reduce their weight and to save clay. During this period he also began inscribing faces and skulls with phrases such as "Made by James Thomas 1971" and "Made in Leland by James Thomas."

Thomas' statement, quoted earlier, that he rarely played with other children reflects a sensitivity which I feel is an important part of his character. He is consciously aware of himself as an artist and has laid plans in his own mind for more ambitious work with sculpture should he ever have the opportunity to develop his art. He told me that he often dreams of molding an entire man from clay if he can find enough materials for his work.

> If I could go to a mountain where they have this clay like I uses, I believe I could put a whole statue of a man in the mountain standing up. I believe I could do that. If the clay works right I could start at the head and come down to the feets. I believe I could work a state! [statue]

> [Ferris] How big would he be?

> As big as a man. I haven't ever did it, but I believe I could do it.

Since moving to Leland, Mississippi, Thomas has worked in a funeral home where he "digs and covers" graves for fifteen dollars a grave and where he also helps with the embalming. His art reflects these experiences; one of the clay figures he made during my visits was a dead man in a coffin. Thomas told me he was in the process of defining his ideal form for this subject and was unsatisfied with the results of his efforts. I asked him:

> Where did you get the idea for a man in a casket, Son?

> Well I do that kind of work and that rolled across my mind. I didn't git that casket shaped just like I wanta. But whatever funeral home I be at next. I'm gonner pick up me a casket book and I'm gonner make a better casket than that. If you ain't got it in your head, you can't do it in your hand. You got to have it in your head what to do.

> [Ferris] How would you make a better casket than that one?

> I would look at the picture and git the future of it better. If you can't hold it in your head, you can't shape it. Just like a person's writing, if you can't make a A, you can't make nar'n.

Thomas' statement emphasizes the necessity of conceptualizing a subject before it can be articulated in clay. During the above conversation he had still not determined a satisfactory shape and color for his clay casket.

Similar aesthetic considerations were involved in successive attempts to improve each of his animals. In many cases these ideas were frustrated by lack of materials, like the brightly colored paints he uses on most of his work. Usually his colors are faithful to the actual color of animals—frog-green, quail-brown, rattlesnake-brown, and crane-white. Although these clay animals are intended to reproduce accurately the shape and size of actual animals, their coloring always varies so that each version of an animal is distinct. Such variation is apparently by design: Thomas made no attempt at exactly reproducing animals according to patterns used previously. Creative variation of color is characteristic of his work and indicates an aesthetic versatility which is present in all of his figures.

General discussions of folk art have stressed the tension between function and decoration and argue that functional considerations are always foremost.[12] Decoration of a quilt or basket, for example, will never be allowed to interfere with their basic function within the folk culture. Thomas' sculpture, however, shows an evolution from function to decoration. His early skulls, for example, were designed for use as ashtrays or containers for papers, while more recent skulls have not been hollowed in the top.

Thomas also frequently uses paint on his faces rather than simply displaying the natural clay surface. Wherever possible, other material is incorporated into his clay sculpture. Marbles and match tips are used as eyes, cotton and a doll's hair for hair, and tin foil as reflectors in the eye sockets. His most recent innovation is a pair of flashing red Christmas lights which serve as eyes in a black cat. The black cat plays a major role in voodoo practice, and Thomas consciously chose red as the flashing color.

Red is a dominant theme in black folk culture and recurs in clothing, quilts, lawn decorations (such as painted tires), folk paintings, and in voodoo.[13] Robert Thompson stresses the importance of red as a "hot" color which has important symbolic associations in both Africa and the New World.[14] Thomas plans to make a skull with eye sockets that will hold flashing red lights. "I was thinking about making a skull and want to put me some red lights that would be showing in the eyes and teeth. Where the teeth are at, let that hollow [behind the eyes] come all the way down to where them teeth are and when you turn the light on, well that sure would be a picture. You could see the teeth and eyes at night."

SKULLS

Artistic versatility is best expressed in the skulls Thomas makes; in spite of their frightening appearance, they are used by his adult friends as ashtrays and as holders for pencils and letters. These skulls, like his animals, are formed from gumbo clay and their Negroid features may account in part for their popularity among his friends. Interestingly, Thomas has none of his clay objects in his own home, though they are displayed on mantels and in windows of many homes around his neighborhood. I asked him which object of all his repertoire he would prefer to keep in his home and he replied:

> If I had to choose something in my house? Well, I wouldn't mind having the skull in my house, because I make it for a ashtray or for my friends when they come around for a show. It's a lot of pleasure in it.
>
> [Ferris] What kind of pleasure?
>
> Well, just like if Sonny Boy [a local friend] would come over there, it would be a pleasure for me to let him see something I made, something everybody can't do.

Thomas thus considers his work a form of art and is proud of it because it represents an accomplishment which is uniquely his own. He is proud that his work has been recognized and conspicuously displayed by other blacks in Leland.

The actual process by which his skulls are molded begins with the shaping of a large lump of clay into a form roughly resembling a face. Thomas first rubs vaseline on his hands so that clay will not stick on them. He works in a squatting position. At intervals he moves back from the clay to get a better perspective. Once the clay face is formed with eyes, a nose, and a mouth, a large piece of clay is scooped out of the top if the skull is to be used as an ashtray.

At this point he smears vaseline over the entire clay face, which is worked by hand until all of the surface is smooth and surface blemishes have been reduced. A knife is then used to cut out eyes so that the interior space is visible through these holes. He slices the nose off with the knife and uses a stick to form openings for the nostrils. The mouth is split and spread open with the knife, and kernels of corn are set on both its top and bottom to represent teeth. These kernels of corn have their bases cut off to prevent germination and growth in the moist clay.[15]

Finally, he cuts circular holes on each side of the skull to represent ear openings and spreads putty over all of the clay surface to give it added strength. This use of putty is important since the clay which Thomas uses is not very strong, and he is unable to fire it. Unless this putty is added, the clay is likely to split after a few weeks. Sometimes he paints details such as eyebrows over the putty to give it added effect. During my interviews with Thomas he explained how he views each stage in the molding of his skulls.

> You first shape it up like a regular man's head. Then you cuts it down to a skellepin head because you couldn't make a skellepin head straight out without cutting it down. You have to cut it down to a skellepin head.
>
> That's the onlest way you can git a shape. When you hold your finger that way, making the eyes, that's the face of a man there. You takes both thumbs at the same time and notice I squeeze it in. Then I come down like that. Well that makes the shape there. There and down. Then you go back and where you done mashed up there with your eyes, that's automatic your nose. Then you build up on that. Then you notice when I cut that nose off, that was for to git the holes in the direct place.
>
> Now if I were gonner make a solid man, it would of been like that other one I had at the house there. I wouldn't have cut that nose out and I wouldn't of cut that eyes out. That would of been just a solid man like that man's head there. It wouldn't have been a skull.
>
> The cause of me taking that top out of his head, that's for a ash tray. That's bout the best ash tray you can have, cause you can make it big enough you know.
>
> You know the reason I cut that corn off? The first one I made over here I noticed the teethes come out. They would move. I checked on it and I seed where it was sprouting at. The first one I made a long time ago, I never did pay it no 'tention. I was through with it and gone.
>
> I checked that one up at Shelby's and it had that corn sprouting in there. That's where I decided the next one I would make, I would cut that off of there where it wouldn't sprout too quick.

Then I got another idea if it keeps on sprouting, I decided I'd try painting the teeth there. Paint them white and git me some clear varnish so it'll shine.

[Ferris] You thought of that yourself?

That come to me not too long ago, I hadn't never give it a trial yet. But I believe I can take something and cut some teeth in there and it might do a better job.

This final statement indicates how Thomas is consciously developing and improving techniques of his work. Past designs of both animals and skulls are modified with each creation in an effort to improve form and colors.

The skulls which he had made were all given to adults, whereas many of his animals were given to children, suggesting that the former are considered more important for the artist and are given only to his contemporaries. Animals are less serious expressions and are appropriate gifts for neighborhood children.[16]

One notable exception is a clay rattlesnake which Thomas gave to his close friend Gussie Tobe who "decorated his car with it" by placing the snake in the back window. Gussie Tobe chose the snake as decoration and significantly one of his favorite folktales is that of the "revived serpent."[17] Snakes recur as a theme in Afro-American tales, blues, and sculpture and may reflect influences of Damballah, the chief voodoo god who is also a snake. Thomas first saw a rattlesnake while cutting timber in the hills near Eden. "I kept it in my mind and when I had time I made one in clay to show my momma how they look." His mother lived at Itta Bena in the Delta where rattlesnakes are never seen.

BLACK FACES

Sculpture of faces and heads is widespread in African art, and often statues of complete human figures accentuate the head by enlarging it in proportion to the rest of the body.[18] As a sculptor of heads, both his medium and his subject are firmly rooted in Afro-American art. In both Africa and America the head has significance as the most vital and sensitive part of the body. Hoodoo spells focus on the head through devices such as conjured hats which produce severe headaches, loss of memory, and eventual death. The power of voodoo doctors also emanates from their heads, and "to be strong in de haid" or have "strength of haid"[19] is the key element in conjuration. The symbolic importance of the head in Afro-American lore thus underscores the significance of Thomas' sculpture. Thomas' faces are colored with dark paint, making Negroid characteristics much more apparent than in the skulls. Of two such faces he made in my presence, he scooped out one for an ashtray and glued cotton hair painted black on the top of the other. These examples indicate how he uses his own race as a model to create human faces which suggest racial pride through identification with black features.

Thomas' faces reflect his relationship with the black community in Leland, and at times the resemblance between a clay figure and a particular local black is so unmistakable that his friends comment on it. Once they called the person sculpted in to see his clay image and asked him if he had ever seen anyone who looked like the figure. He was very nervous and refused to admit any resemblance between himself and the clay figure. After he left, the group joked about his nervousness and the connection between the man and his clay imitation.

Implicit in this incident is a sense of the awe with which local blacks regard Thomas and his sculpture. To create a man's image is to have power and control over him; clay faces stand as an extension of the person and in part define his image in the black community. This vital relation between the black artist and his community is also present in Thomas' blues when he introduces names, occupations, and physical traits of individuals in his audience in verses created during performances in local jook points. In both his sculpture and his blues he is defining reality through artistic images which communicate on a fundamental emotional level in the black folk community. The folk artist thus becomes a powerful and at times frightening force within the black community, somewhat similar to the *Griot* of West Africa.[20]

Thomas' clay faces are also responses to the white community in that they present an image of the black man as poised and proud. In traditional racial "etiquette" the black man was expected to look at the ground when facing a white. These wide-eyed faces stare directly ahead with pride and are similar to the frozen faces rural blacks assume when photographed. Here is no image of the smiling, happy black eating watermelon or standing on the lawn—hand extended—ready to hold the master's horse. Each clay face stands firmly in a tradition of African and Afro-American sculpture which Robert Thompson has termed "cool."[21]

Thomas is sensitive to white stereotypes and commented on the statues of blacks common on the lawns of wealthy whites:

> Tell me why if you see a statue of a man in a white person's yard it will be a black man. They make him black all over and have his lips red and his eyes white. Most of the time you see him, if he ain't got a fishing pole, he got a hoe. I reckon it's an invitation to work. Trying to make the colored folks work. When you see one with a hoe it's to let us know it's all we can do. Well Old John did more than hoe—right around the house.

"Old John" refers to the black trickster figure in folktales set during slavery. John works around the house of "Ol' Marster" and "Ol' Miss," the white plantation owner and his wife.[22] One of Thomas' favorite tales describes how John is tricked into sticking his hand up Ol' Miss's dress. The theme of John, the yard boy, and his sexual relations with the white woman inside the house is widespread in Delta folktales, and, like Thomas' clay faces, it counters the stereotyped white impression of blacks as depicted in their lawn statues.

Thomas also explains his making of clay quail in terms of white and black relations in rural Mississippi. He says that, traditionally, blacks were not allowed to kill quail, fat game birds which are a delicacy and are hunted with bird dogs. Blackbirds were considered appropriate for blacks, quail for whites. Several of his black friends prominently display sculptures of fat quail on their mantles in Leland.

One new facial theme appeared in 1973 during a visit at Yale University when Thomas molded a Chinese face in clay. I asked him why he made it and he replied: "When I was shaping the clay up a Chinaman was the first shape I got. That ball of clay was shaped like a Chinaman's head and so I completed it out with the nose and mouth of a Chinaman. I'm gonna try another Chinaman when I get back to Leland." When he returned tŏ Leland he made a second Chinese face and placed wire-rimmed glasses on it. A Chinese merchant runs the grocery store in Thomas' neighborhood and Thomas once remarked to his son, "It looks like ever nickel I give you, the Chinaman gets." Chinese also appear in Thomas' folktales in the role of shrewd merchants and reflect the numerous Chinese-owned grocery stores in towns throughout the Delta.[23]

EYES

The physical relationship of eyes to the rest of the face is important for Thomas in judging the success or failure of his overall sculpture and is the key axis around which the rest of the face—nose, mouth, and ears—is organized. As mentioned earlier, eye contact or the lack of it defines racial relationships in the rural South. Traditionally, blacks were expected when encountering a white to remove their hats and look at the ground as part of a complex racial etiquette which defined the roles of whites and blacks.[24] One man in Clarksdale recalled how blacks addressed whites in the past: "Like you have your hat on and walk up to a white man, you'd pull that hat off. Then you'd take the itch you was so scared of that white man, scratch under your arm and in your head. That's the scratch and don't never look him in the eye."

Eyes are also very important in black voodoo and sanctified religion. A Mississippi hoodoo doctor, for example, is called a "two face," implying he has eyes in both directions and can see both past and future. Hoodoo doctors and sanctified faith healers rely on the power of their eyes in their respective work of spells and healing. Puckett points out that the hoodoo doctor "is always in a deep study, looking at some distant object."[25] Thomas also uses the phrase "deep study" to describe the vision embodied in his clay faces.

The eyes of each face are a critical part of its composition, and Thomas feels he has still not mastered them. In looking at the folk art of another black artist, Lester Willis, his first comment was on the eyes of faces and how Willis either succeeded or failed in rendering them. Speaking of his own sculpture he said:

> There is one thing I'd like to improve on and that's the eyes. You have to draw your eyes in there before you can get em lined up. Your eyes are on a level with your ears. They can't be a bit higher than your ears and they can't be no lower. They got to be the same level your ears is and that's why you don't have no trouble making glasses. If some people's eyes was down below their nose, they couldn't get no glasses to fit 'em.

Recently, a sanctified faith healer stressed the importance of "power eyes" which give one the strength to cure disease, and both hoodoo doctors and faith healers believe that supernatural powers are reflected through their eyes. Thomas is said by some to have similar power in his own eyes, and his sculpture's link with dreams suggests that important parallels exist between his work as an artist and that of the hoodoo doctor and faith healer. The role of eyes as symbols of power is fundamental in both.

COMMON THEMES IN
SCULPTURE AND ORAL LORE

James Thomas' life embodies the rich spectrum of black folklore, and during my work with him I collected extensive repertoires of prose narrative and blues. His sculpture and oral lore are both primarily male traditions and strongly reflect the sex of their creator. To my knowledge, Thomas has never played or sung with female blues performers in Leland. Vocal and instrumental accompaniment is supplied by men of his age, and tale-telling or "lying" sessions are also performed exclusively by males, with women sometimes in the audience.[26] Occasionally, young boys are allowed to participate in these sessions, performing solo dances, accompanying the music with percussion on drums or paper boxes, or listening to jokes, but young girls are never present. Thomas' blues and tales both develop a male perspective; the blues tend either to lament the loss of or to plea for the favors of a woman's love. In his tales the chief protagonists, such as "Old John" and "Graveyard John," are male, and women appear only in minor roles. And in his sculpture, Thomas has never molded the face or bust of a woman, limiting his repertoire exclusively to male images.

All the animals in his repertoire are indigenous to Mississippi, and all have been seen by Thomas during his lifetime. As Kenneth Goldstein noted in his study of Willie Robbie's art, the folk artist deals with the familiar; Thomas' work focuses on subjects which are a part of his environment.[27] In this sense the sculpture contrasts with the verbal lore of Delta blacks, with which Thomas is familiar, which describes animals, such as monkeys and elephants, that are not found in the region. Thomas' clay figures thus seem less versatile in subject matter than their verbal equivalents. Perhaps because the sculpture is primarily centered in one individual, it cannot be transmitted with the speed and flexibility of oral lore.

Water is a major theme of Afro-American folklore, and Thomas' sculpture selectively focuses on Delta animals which live in ponds and rivers.[28] These animals include fish (bream, catfish, and alligator gar), crawfish, frogs, and alligators. Both water and the specific animals he selects have symbolic power in voodoo.

Water is also a fundamental part of baptismal ceremonies, and one of Thomas's folktales describes a woman summoned into the river to be baptized by her preacher. When she looks in terror beyond the preacher, he calls, "Come on into the water, Sister. Don't be afraid of the Devil." She replies, "But I don't like that thing behind you." The preacher looks over his shoulder, sees an alligator, and cries, "I don't either," as they both run out of the water. The alligator appears repeatedly as a theme in folk sculpture, hoodoo, tales, and dance.[29]

Thomas' blues also stress the theme of water in lines such as "I been drifting, drifting, like a ship out on the sea." In our last conversation I asked Thomas his thoughts on water and he replied: "You couldn't make it without no water, couldn't live without it. I don't care what kind of soda water you drink you gonner want some water later." Water is basic to life, and its importance is symbolically reflected in Thomas' sculpture and oral lore.

Throughout his lore (sculpture, blues, and tales), death is also a recurrent theme. Clay skulls and a dead man in a coffin reflect his interest in the process of death and its effect on human flesh. He is keenly aware of the color of bones and tries to paint his skulls so that they accurately resemble dry bones: "I paint it dull-looking white. The duller it is the more it favors the skull. A skull is not real white and not real dark, just kind of dirty-looking white. Got yellow places all in it. That's the way a dead person's bones is."

Bones also appear as a theme in one of Thomas' tales about a preacher and a friend who agree to spend the night in a haunted house in return for two hundred and fifty dollars. As the preacher is sitting in the house he hears the words, "Flicktem, Flucktem who down the dillem, whoa ho!" three times. Then,

> Down come a bone right on the floor. Next another bone come down. All the little bones began to connect up and so after a while the head fell on and was sitting there looking at them.
>
> Preacher said, "There's a whole man now."
>
> The other man said, "Yeah, and I'm gonna get out of here too."
>
> The preacher outran the other man and the ghost tapped the other man on the shoulder and said. "You ain't running is you?"
>
> "Yes I is, I'm doing all I can."

Thomas openly acknowledges belief in ghosts, and the story of "Flicktem" is in part a comment on those who tamper with death and the supernatural. A similar theme appears in the tale of Graveyard John, a gravedigger who digs up a grave at night to steal jewels and a watch from a woman he had buried earlier in the day. The woman was mistakenly buried when she "went off in a trance," and as John struggles to pull off her ring she wraps her arms and legs around his body and rides him out of the grave and across sage fields to her house. In the latter tale the correspondences between Thomas' life and his lore are clear. The story of Graveyard John is one of his favorites, and I recorded less complete versions from Thomas' children, who shared it with their contemporaries.

Thomas is an accomplished blues guitarist who plays regularly for local blacks in the home of his friend, Shelby "Poppa Jazz" Brown. During blues sessions, I collected thirty-four blues songs which Thomas sang, accompanying himself with his own guitar. Their verses point to death as the inevitable end lovers face. One of his favorite verses is:

> *You may be beautiful but you sure got to die some day.*
> *You may be beautiful but you sure got to die some day.*
> *I want a little of your loving before you fade away.*

While the *carpe diem* theme is not unique to the blues, it assumes a special significance in the context of Thomas's life.

All these genres—sculpture, tales, and blues—present their audience with fundamental reality, or, in Thomas' terms, "a deep study." Man must die, and recognition of death defines and focuses one's view of life. Death levels all flesh, black and white, rich and poor, and presents a clear vision of life for Thomas, a vision which defines his art and philosophy of life: "White folks and black folks got to learn to live together. You may not need me today but you'll need me one day. I may not need you today, but I'll need you one day. We all going the same place, and that's down in the clay."

James Thomas' skulls and faces emerge from Mississippi Delta clay and embody an ultimate statement of life and death as they stare in testament to the vision of one black man creating and responding to his community and history. James Thomas' art is a major affirmation of Afro-American culture and of dreams which endure.

Notes

1. William Ferris, "If You Ain't Got It in Your Head, You Can't Do It in Your Hand: James Thomas, Mississippi Delta Folk Sculptor." *Studies in the Literary Imagination,* 3 (1970), 89, 107. Field research for this study was supported by grants from the National Science Foundation, the Wenner-Gren Foundation, and the National Institute of Mental Health.
2. Melville Herskovits, *The Myth of the Negro Past* (Boston, 1967), 1–33.
3. This quote and all by him that follow are transcribed from tapes I recorded with James Thomas.
4. Rhonda S. Johnson. "Imaginations," unpublished research paper written at Georgia State University in 1970.
5. Dreams as a theme in Afro-American folk culture are discussed in Newbell Niles Puckett *The Magic and Folk Beliefs of the Southern Negro* (New York, 1969), 469, 109, 220, 188, and 328, and in *Drums and Shadows* (New York, 1972), 5, 72, 78, and 92. In a recent unpublished interview with Simon Bronner, Sam Chapman described how his blues verses come to him through dreams.
6. Johnson 3.
7. The earliest discussion of black "badness" is H. C. Brearley's "Ba-ad Nigger," *The South Atlantic Quarterly,* 38 (1939), 74–81. Herskovits objected to the study in a reply, "A Letter to the Editors: Some Comments by Professor Herskovits," *The South Atlantic Quarterly,* 39 (1940), 350–351. An important discussion by Alan Dundes of the literature on the subject is in his *Mother Wit from the Laughing Barrel* (Englewood Cliffs, New Jersey, 1973), 578–581.
8. Bo Diddley, "Say Man," *Bo Diddley's 16 All-time Greatest Hits,* Checker Record 2989. Side 1 Selection 3, 1968. Another exchange between Bo Diddley and Jerome Green includes the phrase "I heard you had a new job standing in front of a doctor's office making people sick." Bo Diddley, "Signifying Blues," *Bo Diddley/In the Spotlight,* Checker Record 2976. Side 1, Selection 4. Zora Neale Hurston describes a similar verbal session on ugliness in *Mules and Men* (New York, 1970), 94.
9. Herskovits, *The Myth of the Negro Past,* 136–137.
10. Ibid., 207 ff.
11. Ibid., 197ff and 200ff.

12. Henry Glassie, "Folk Art," in *Folklore and Folklife,* ed. Richard Dorson (Chicago, 1972), 253–254.

13. Puckett, *Magic and Folk Beliefs of the Southern Negro,* 220–310.

14. Robert Thompson, *African Art in Motion* (Berkeley, 1974), 162. In a recent conversation Thompson suggested that the color red and its associations are often in polarity with the cool colors he discussed in "An Aesthetic of the Cool." *African Arts,* 7 (1973), 41–43, 64–67, 89. Victor Turner discussed red as a major theme in Ndembu culture in *The Forest of Symbols* (Ithaca, 1970), 57–90. Turner mentions that the color is linked to red clay (p. 70). Harold Conklin reviews the study of color symbolism in "Color Categorization," *American Anthropologist,* 75 (1973).

15. Corn is also used in Haitian voodoo ritual in Vévé, ritual drawings which are made with corn meal. Harold Courlander, *The Drum and the Hoe* (Berkeley, 1960), 124.

16. Similar clay figures—roosters, dogs, cows, and people—are made in Haiti, and Coutlander suggests their purpose "is obscure, but it is likely that they are intended for use in Vodun ritual." (*The Drum and the Hoe,* 124).

17. A transcription and discussion of this tale appear in William Ferris, "The Collection of Racial Lore," *New York Folklore Quarterly,* 27 (1974), 273–275.

18. For examples see Paul Radin and James Johnson Sweeney, eds., *African Folktales and Sculpture* (New York, 1952), and Robert Thompson, *African Art and Black Gods and Kings* (Los Angeles, 1971).

19. Puckett, *The Magic and Folk Beliefs of the Southern Negro,* 189. Herskovits describes how among the Ashanti the water spirit enters the head of the devotee, "causing him to fling himself, possessed, into the water." (*The Myth of the Negro Past,* 233). During summer months Delta blacks often line their hats with fig leaves to keep their heads cool.

20. G. Gorer, *African Dances* (London, 1935), 55. Yvonne Lange's "The Griot of Senegambia: A Preliminary Survey" (unpublished paper written at University of Pennsylvania, 1967) is a valuable survey of *Griot* traditions.

21. "An Aesthetic of the Cool," 41, 43, 64-67, 89.

22. A number of "John" tales are included in Richard Dorson, *American Negro Folktales* (New York, 1967), 124, 170.

23. A thorough sociological study of Chinese in the Delta is James W. Loewen's *The Mississipi Chinese* (Cambridge, 1971).

24. This aspect of southern culture is developed in Bertram Doyle. *The Etiquette of Race Relations* (New York, 1967), 124-170.

25. *The Magic and Folk Beliefs of the Southern Negro,* 202.

26. Thomas' blues are transcribed and discussed in William Ferris, *Blues from the Delta* (London, 1970). Both his blues and sculpture are presented in a film, *James Thomas, Delta Artist,* which is distributed by the Center for Southern Folklore, 3756 Mimosa, Memphis, Tennessee.

27. Kenneth Goldstein, "Willie Robbie: Folk Artist of the Buchan District Aberdeenshire," in *Folklore in Action: Essays in Honor of MacEdward Leach* (Philadelphia, 1962), 101–111.

28. Herskovits, *The Myth of the Negro Past,* 233.

29. To "do the alligator" the male dancer gets on all fours and moves his body to the rhythm of the music over his partner lying on her back, or, in a solo dance, over the floor. Puckett lists numerous references to alligators in voodoo tradition (*The Magic and Folk Beliefs of the Southern Negro,* 39, 165, 186, 346, and 507). The alligator recurs as a theme in Afro-American folk sculpture, and Georgia examples are recorded in *Drums and Shadows,* 65, 121, 145. David Evans discusses a recent example in an unpublished article, "Afro-American Folk Sculpture from Parchman Penitentiary." Another recent example from Louisville, Kentucky, was photographed by Robert Thompson.

James Hampton: *The Throne of the Third Heaven of the Nations Millenium General Assembly*

Lynda Roscoe Hartigan
Museum curator

Lynda Roscoe Hartigan has contributed to the exhibition volume Unsigned, Unsung—Whereabouts Unknown: Make-Do Art of the American Outlands *(1993) and to* Made with Passion *(1990). She is the author of* Sharing Traditions: Five Black Artists in Nineteenth-Century America: From the Collections of the National Museum of American Art *(1985). Hartigan has written an earlier article on the Hampton Throne in the Minneapolis Walker Art Center exhibition catalogue* Naives and Visionaries *(1974).*

Around 1950 James Hampton approached a merchant in Washington, D.C., about renting an unheated, poorly lit garage in a deteriorating residential neighborhood. Hampton explained that he was "working on something" and he needed a larger space than that available in his room in a nearby boarding house. By November 4, 1964, when he died of cancer, he had built one hundred eighty glittering objects in the garage. That "something" had become *The Throne of the Third Heaven of the Nations Millenium General Assembly* (see Figure 1).

The little that is known about James Hampton has been gleaned from his employment and army records, a surviving elderly relative in South Carolina, and a handful of people in Washington who visited the garage. Hampton was born on April 8, 1909, in Elloree, South Carolina, a small rural community. His father, after whom James was named, was a black gospel singer and preacher of sorts who abandoned his wife and four children for his itinerant calling. At the age of nineteen Hampton left South Carolina and joined the family of one of his older brothers in Washington, D.C. In an application for government employment, he claimed to have received a tenth-grade education from an elite black high school in the district, but no trace of Hampton's attendance has been found in the school's records. From 1939 to 1942 he was a short order cook in several local cafes until he joined the federal labor force. Shortly thereafter, he was inducted into the army and served with the 385th Aviation Squadron in Texas, Seattle, Hawaii, and the jungles of Saipan and Guam. The duties of his noncombatant unit included carpentry and maintenance of air strips. Hampton returned to

Lynda Roscoe Hartigan, James Hampton. The Throne of The Third Heaven of The Nations Millenium General Assembly *(Washington, D.C.: National Collection of Fine Arts, Smithsonian Institution, 1977).*

FIGURE 1.

James Hampton with his "Throne of the Third Heaven of the Nation's Millennium" in its early stages.

Washington with an honorable discharge in 1945. A year later he was hired by the General Services Administration as a janitor, a job he retained until his death.

Hampton's acquaintances have described him as a small, bespectacled, soft-spoken man. Although he talked about finding a holy woman to help him with his project, Hampton never married and had few, if any, friends. Occasionally he returned to South Carolina to visit his sister and oldest brother for the summer. By ordinary standards, Hampton's life was uneventful; however, at some point he began to believe that God and his angels had visited him, not in a dream but in physical form, and had spoken directly to him. The date and circumstances of this first mystical experience are unknown. Nevertheless, Hampton claimed that such visions persisted throughout his life. The earliest vision that he recorded on paper occurred when he was twenty-two: "This is true that the great Moses the giver of the tenth commandment appeared in Washington, D.C. April 11, 1931." Of his last dated vision he stated: "This design is proof of the Virgin Mary descending into Heaven, November 1950. It is also spoken of by Pope Pius XII." The Pope had proclaimed the Assumption of the Virgin as church dogma on that day.

Inspired by such visions, Hampton dedicated himself to building *The Throne of the Third Heaven of the Nations Millenium General Assembly*. He probably had initiated the project before renting the garage in 1950, but an exact date cannot be established. Although one small unit in the assemblage is labeled "Made on Guam, April 14, 1945," no substantial proof exists to confirm that Hampton made the object while he was overseas.

After finishing his janitorial duties around midnight, Hampton would return to the garage every night to work for five or six hours. He believed that God visited him there regularly to direct him in *The Throne's* fabrication.

A woman who worked with Hampton since the 1950s remembers that he was diligent and seemed religious, yet he seldom mentioned religion at work, and did not press his convictions on her when she visited the garage. Hampton told her that he wanted to be a minister when he retired; one can only speculate that he planned a ministry in a storefront church similar to those found in many of Washington's black residential areas.

• • •

When Hampton died in 1964, his sister (who saw *The Throne* for the first time when she came north to claim her brother's body) had neither the resources nor the inclination to transport or preserve the work. Fortunately, the garage owner, hoping to rent the garage without destroying his tenant's project, sought to bring it to public attention. He contacted a reporter who wrote an article for a local newspaper. Also, he advertised the garage for rent, and, coincidentally, a Washington photographer responded. Eventually, news of *The Throne's* existence spread to staff members of the National Collection of Fine Arts, and the work was acquired.

Hampton had once remarked to his landlord: "That's my life. I'll finish it before I die." Nevertheless, *The Throne* is probably incomplete. When examined by the museum's personnel, the work in the garage, though symmetrically organized, was found with several units haphazardly located, as if intended to be included at a later time. Cartons of small incomplete parts were also found, as well as odds and ends of furniture, which were probably destined for future pieces.

An ingenious selection and use of materials and an innate feeling for design characterize Hampton's radiant work. A poor man, he applied his imagination to the transformation of discarded materials. Merchants in the used furniture district near the garage remember that Hampton would browse, inquire about prices, and sometimes return with a child's wagon to carry away his purchases. All of the objects are covered with different grades of gold and aluminum foils removed from store displays, bottles, cigarette boxes, and rolls of kitchen foil. Hampton paid neighborhood bums for the foil on their wine bottles and he himself walked the streets with a croker sack in which to carry his finds. Also gathered were used light bulbs, cardboard, insulation board, kraft paper, desk blotters, and sheets of transparent plastic, probably from the trash of the government buildings where he worked.

It was at first believed that the foil covered a substructure of wooden furniture only. Restoration of the objects, however, has revealed that Hampton often relied on layers of insulation board to construct the armature of each piece. The framework of several units consists of hollow cardboard cylinders removed from rolls of carpeting. In other cases, the original furniture is easily identified. The throne chair, for example, is essentially an old armchair, complete with faded red cloth cushion, while two semicircular pieces are a large round table sawed in half.

Many of the larger objects rise from square or rectangular bases equipped with rusty metal casters to facilitate moving them. Small stands are formed by drawers turned upside-down and mounted on cheap glass vases. Jelly glasses and light bulbs covered with foil often complete tops and corners of objects, while kraft paper and cardboard are the foundations for decorative forms such as stars and wings. The edges of tables are sometimes trimmed with slender tubes of electrical cable camouflaged with gold foil. Rows of small knobs are made of balls of crumpled foil or newspaper covered with foil. Glittering gold and silver dominate the color scheme. Touches of green are provided by desk blotters used to cover table tops and other areas. Tan cardboard and kraft paper (faded from a deep purple) lend a more subdued note to the ensemble. Other variations, unnoticed until the objects are examined closely, are small areas of manila paper covered with intricate designs drawn with blue and brown ink.

Hampton's unusual application of materials provides delightful surprises and makes one curious about his construction methods. The artist glued or nailed strips of cardboard or metal (cut from coffee cans) to connect the major vertical elements with horizontal bases. Upholstery tacks, small nails, and simple sewing pins were used to attach most of the structural and decorative elements. The foil was either wrapped or glued; in many instances wrapped foil was the only means of keeping all of the parts together, as the nails and pins were not long enough to pierce every layer of material. This naive, additive method accounts for the fragility of most of the objects.

A makeshift wooden platform set against the wall at the far end of the building was Hampton's only major structural addition to the garage. Most of the objects on the platform were arranged in three roughly parallel rows, with the remaining pieces on the floor immediately in front and along the side walls. There is no evidence that Hampton had any assistance in constructing this "stage" or in moving the large objects (many of which must be lifted by two people to ensure safe handling). Detailed plans were not found in the garage or boarding house after his death, yet, because Hampton was severely limited in space he must have carefully visualized the organization at the outset. Pieces intended for the upper level were probably constructed on the platform itself and rolled into position on casters. The size and number of objects concentrated at one end of the garage with little space between them created an effect of overwhelming density. A generally frontal, horizontal orientation and the unifying brightness of the foil give *The Throne,* despite the fragility of its parts, a sturdy and solid appearance.

The throne chair at the rear center of the platform is the heart of the assemblage. Pairs of objects, matching almost exactly in all details, including dimensions, were placed in corresponding locations, radiating out from each side. In addition, each object is, in itself, symmetrical along several axes. Labels on the objects indicate that to the viewer's left, the pieces refer to the New Testament, Jesus, and Grace. To the right, the system is based on the Old Testament, Moses, and Law. While many of these forms—throne or mercy seat, altar table, pulpits, offertory tables, and chairs—suggest

FIGURE 2.

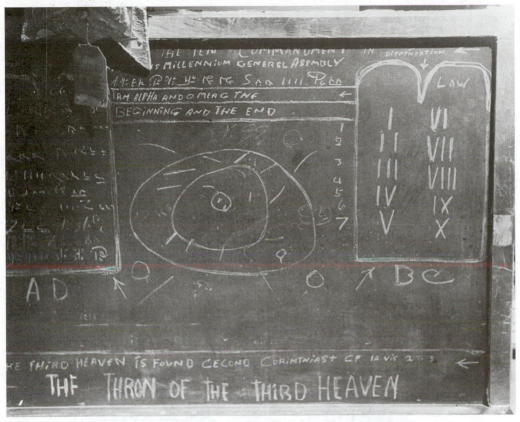

A detail of James Hampton's blackboard.

traditional church appointments, the purpose of others is obscure. Reinforcing the distinction between the Old and New Testaments are wooden plaques decorated with foil and ink designs and hung on the side walls of the garage (see Figures 2 and 3). Those on the left bear the names of the Apostles; to the right are listed the Prophets.

The visual impact of these curious, coherently organized objects prompts questions about their meaning. Hampton did not record an explanation of the underlying religious impulse, but from scattered clues found on the pieces themselves, it is possible to suggest some aspects of his intention and message. Attached to many of the objects are labels with references to the Millennium and Revelation chapters 20 and 21, which describe the first Resurrection, the judgment of the dead before God, and the new heaven and earth. On one of the pieces Hampton wrote: "the word millenium means 'the return of Christ and a part of the Kingdom of God on earth.'" Deeply affected by the Book of Revelation, Hampton must have believed in the inevitability of the Second Coming; he, in fact, told one friend that we are living in the last millennium. *The Throne* may have been built to ensure his personal salvation as well as to warn and instruct others. An adage found on his bulletin board is telling: "Where

FIGURE 3.

A plaque with James Hampton's cryptic script.

There Is No Vision The People Perish." Visionary experiences and the expectation of a literal Second Coming are not uncommon among the fundamentalist members of the black community, and Hampton's Baptist background is likely to have shaped his subsequent religious orientation.

Intriguing parallels exist between certain details of the Book of Revelation and *The Throne.* When God showed Saint John the events of the Second Coming in a vision, he instructed John to record them in a little book in a cryptic language. It is possible that Hampton believed that he had received a similarly portentous vision, for, in addition to building *The Throne,* he developed an indecipherable script that he said God had given to him. Hampton filled a small notebook with this script and on the bottom of each page wrote "Revelation." Named as author of the book is Saint James, Hampton's chosen eponym, suggesting that although a humble man, he may, nonetheless, have fancied himself a holy figure or prophet like Saint John. The book may contain Hampton's translation of John's revelations, or, possibly, an entirely original religion based on his own vision. The script also appears on labels attached to each object, usually following an English word or phrase, suggesting a translation into his mysterious language (see Figure 3). Composed of graceful characters resembling those of semitic or oriental languages, the script is the product of an uneducated man who printed his misspelled English words in childlike capital letters. It may indeed be inspired writing or it may be an artistic creation devoid of any meaning.

The Throne parallels the Book of Revelation in other respects. John saw God on a throne of shining silver and gold surrounded by a multitude of angels, and Hampton obviously strove to capture that splendor. The birdlike wing forms, Hampton's dominant decorative motif, may have been his interpretation of the angels described by John. However, whether or not Hampton expected his throne chair to be occupied at the Second Coming is not known.

Despite Hampton's Baptist background, he was not a member of a congregation in Washington. He believed that there is only one God and therefore no need for different religions. An important encounter with the Reverend A. J. Tyler, a popular black minister who died in 1936, may have occurred in one of the neighborhood churches he occasionally visited. The Mount Airy Baptist Church, where Tyler served, was not far from Hampton's boarding house, and it is possible that the Reverend inspired Hampton during a revival meeting or Sunday sermon. Tyler was noted for having said that in Washington, the city of monuments, there were no monuments to Jesus. Still hanging over the door of the Mount Airy Baptist Church is an electric sign. "Monument to Jesus," which Tyler had installed. Hampton may have been intrigued by the minister's idea for a monument to Jesus; the word "monument" is entered in one of his notebooks, and numerous references to A. J. Tyler appear in the assemblage. Many pieces bear labels reading "Tyler Baptist Church," although Tyler never preached in a church of that name. Hampton indicated in his notebooks that Saint James was the pastor of "The Tyler Baptist Church." Tyler may have been a model for Hampton, and this element of commemoration seems to have mingled freely with his belief in the Second Coming.

As one concentrates on the radiance, symmetry, decorative patterns, and eccentric improvisation of *The Throne*, Hampton's primary intention, to create a vehicle for religious renewal and teaching may be overlooked. Preserved and admired as a work of art, however, it enjoys exposure more far-reaching than Hampton could ever have hoped for. *The Throne* stands as remarkable testimony to his devotion, patience, faith, and imagination.

Suggested Reading

Another Face in the Diamond: Pathways Through the Black Atlantic South [Exhibition Catalog]. New York: INTAR Latin American Gallery, 1989.

Barfield, Rodney. "North Carolina Black Material Culture: A Research Opportunity." *North Carolina Folklore Journal* 27 (November 1979): 61–66.

Benberry, Cuesta. *Always There: The African-American Presence in American Quilts*. Louisville: The Kentucky Quilt Project, 1992.

Broken Star: Post Civil War Quilts Made by Black Women. Dallas: Museum of African-American Life and Culture, 1986.

Burrison, John A. "Afro-American Folk Pottery in the South." *Southern Folklore Quarterly* 42 (1978): 175–199.

Castleman, Craig. *Getting Up: Subway Graffiti in New York*. Cambridge: MIT Press, 1982.

Chase, Judith Wragg. *Afro-American Art and Craft*. New York: Van Nostrand Reinhold, 1971.

Constable, Leslie. "Amazing Grace: The Life and Times of Elijah Pierce." *Dialogue: An Art Journal* (May-June 1990): 28–29.

Davis, Gerald L. "Afro-American Coil Basketry in Charleston County, South Carolina: Affective Characteristics of an Artist Craft in a Social Context." In *American Folklore*, edited by Don Yoder, pp. 151–184. Austin: University of Texas Press, 1976.

Dodson, Angela. "Secrets of The Quilts [An elderly woman's recitation of the code passed down through her family sheds new light on how quilts helped slaves escape to freedom]." *Essence*, vol. 29, no. 10, February 1999: 146–148.

Dorsey, Frances. *For John Cox's Daughter: African-American Quilts from the Southeastern United States* [Exhibition Catalog]. Ann Arbor: University of Michigan, 1991.

———, ed. *Afro-American Folk Art and Crafts*. Jackson: University Press of Mississippi, 1983.

Ferris, William. "Black Folk Art and Crafts: A Mississippi Sample" [Photo Essay]. *Southern Folklore Quarterly* 42 (1978): 209–241.

Folk Art Finder. "Elijah Pierce, Wood Carver." Vol. 13 (January-March 1992): 4–7.

Fry, Gladys-Marie. "Harriet Powers: Portrait of a Black Quilter." *Missing Pieces: Georgia Folk Art, 1770–1976*, edited by Anna Wadsworth, pp. 16–23. Atlanta: Georgia Council for the Arts and Humanities, 1976.

———. *Stitched from the Soul. Slave Quilts from the Ante-Bellum South*. New York: Dutton Studio Books, 1990.

Fuller, Edmund L. *Visions in Stone: The Sculpture of William Edmondson*. Pittsburgh: University of Pittsburgh Press, 1973.

Galassi, Peter. *Roy DeCarava: A Retrospective*. New York: The Museum of Modern Art, 1996.

Glass, Barbara, ed. *Uncommon Beauty in Common Objects. The Legacy of African American Craft Art*. Wilberforce, Ohio: National Afro-American Museum and Cultural Center, 1993.

Grundin, Eva Ungar. *Stitching Memories: African-American Story Quilts*. Williamstown, Mass.: Williams College Museum of Art, 1990.

Gumbo Ya Ya: Anthology of Contemporary African-American Women Artists. New York: Midmarch Arts Press, 1995.

Henkes, Robert. *The Art of Black American Women. Works of Twenty-Four Artists of The Twentieth Century*. Jefferson, North Carolina: McFarland & Company, Inc., Publishers, 1993.

Historic Photographs of Addison N. Scurlock, The. Exhibition catalog. Washington, D.C.: Corcoran Gallery of Art, 1976.

Hoster, Jay. "Elijah Pierce: An American Original. He Preaches Sermons in Wood." *Cleveland Plain Dealer Magazine*, Nov. 11, 1979, pp. 22–23, 29, 31, 33, 39–40.

Igoe, Lynn Moody, and James Igoe. *250 Years of Afro-American Art: An Annotated Bibliography*. New York: R.R. Bowker, 1981.

Johnson, Thomas L., and Philip C. Dunn. *A True Likeness. The Black South of Richard Samuel Roberts 1920–1936* [Photography]. Columbia, S.C.: Brucooli Clark, 1986.

Lornell, Kip. "Black Material Culture." *South Folklore Quarterly* 42(1978): 287–294.

Marty, Kathy. "Impressions of a Folk Artist: An Afternoon with Elijah Pierce." *Journal of the Ohio Folklore Society* (Spring 1972): 29–33.

Memory and Metaphor. The Art of Romare Bearden, 1940–1987. Introduction by Kinshasha Holman Conwill. Essays by Mary Schmidt Campbell and Sharon F. Patton. New York: The Studio Museum in Harlem and Oxford University Press, 1991.

Morris, Ann, and Henrietta Ambrose, compilers. *North Webster: A Photographic History of a Black Community.* Bloomington: Indiana University Press, 1993.

Moutoussamy-Ashe, Jeanne. *Daufuskie Island. A Photographic Essay.* Columbia: University of South Carolina Press, 1982.

Myers, Betty. "Gullah Basketry." *Craft Horizons* 36(3) (1976): 30–31, 81.

Natanson, Nicholas. *The Black Image in the New Deal: The Politics of FSA Photography.* Knoxville: University of Tennessee Press, 1992.

———. "Robert McNeill and Black Government Photographers." *History of Photography* 19(1) (1995): 26–30.

North Carolina Museum of History. *Thomas Day, Cabinetmaker. An Exhibition* [Catalog]. Raleigh: Hall Printing Company, 1975.

Orbach, Barbara, and Nicholas Natanson. "The Mirror Image: Black Washington in World War II Era Federal Photographs." *Washington History* 4(1) (1992): 5–25.

Ramsey, Bets. "The Land of Cotton: Quiltmaking by African-American Women in Three Southern States." *Uncoverings,* Vol. 9 of The Research of the American Quilt Study Group, edited by Laurel Horton, pp. 9–28.

Sink, Susan. *Traditional Crafts and Craftsmanship in America: A Selected Bibliography.* Publication of The American Folklore Center, No. 11, Library of Congress, 1983. [Reprinted with *Additions from Traditional Craftsmanship in America: A Diagnostic Report.* Washington, D.C.: National Council for the Traditional Arts, 1983.]

Thompson, Robert Farris. *Flash of the Spirit: African and Afro-American Art and Philosophy.* New York: Random House, 1983.

Tobin, Jacqueline, and Raymond Dobard. *Hidden in Plain View: The Secret Story of Quilts and The Underground Railroad.* New York: Doubleday, 1999.

Treadwell, David. "Sermons in Wood." *Ebony Magazine* (July 1974): 67–74.

University of South Carolina Press. *Gullah Images. The Art of Jonathon Green,* 1996.

Wahlman, Maude Southwell. "Gifts of the Spirit: Religious Symbolism in Afro-American Arts." In *Gifts of the Spirit* [Exhibition Catalog]. Asheville, N.C.: Southern Highland Handicraft Guild, 1984.

———. "Continuities Between African Textiles and Afro-American Quilts." In *Traditions in Cloth.* Los Angeles: California African-American Museum, 1985.

———. *Signs and Symbols. African Images in African-American Quilts.* New York: Studio Books in association with the Museum of American Folk Art, 1993.

Wheat, Ellen Harkins, with contributions by Patricia Hills. *Jacob Lawrence: American Painter.* Seattle: University of Washington, 1986.

Wheat, Ellen Harkins. *Jacob Lawrence: The 'Frederick Douglass' and 'Harriet Tubman' Series of 1938–1940.* Hampton, Va.: Hampton University Museum, 1991.

Wiggins, William H. "The Wooden Chains That Bind: A Look at a Shared Creation of Two Diaspora Woodcarvers." In *Black People and Their Culture,* edited by Linn Shapiro. Washington, D.C.: Smithsonian Institution, 1976: 29–32.

Willis, Deborah, ed. *Picturing Us. African American Identity in Photography*. New York: The New Press, 1994.

Willis, Deborah, and Jane Lusaka, eds. *Visual Journal. Harlem and D.C. in the Thirties and Forties*. Washington, D.C.: The Center for African American History and Culture and The Smithsonian Institution Press, 1996.

Willis-Braithwaite, Deborah. *Van Der Zee, Photographer 1886–1983*. New York: Harry N. Abrams, Inc., Publisher. In association with The National Portrait Gallery, Smithsonian Institution, 1993.

Wilson, Judith. "Black Folk Art: A Vision Endures." *Museum* (March-April 1982): 39–41.

Selected Videos, Films, CD-ROMS, and Slides

Art in America [(4) Black Artists of the USA]. Syracuse University Classroom Film/Video Rental Center. Handel, 1977. 25 minutes.

Black Art: Ancestral Legacy. The African Impulse in African-American Art. Universal Color Slide Company. Book and set of 25 slides.

Elijah Pierce, Woodcarver. Mary Ann Williams, producer. Department of Black Studies, Ohio State University (Columbus), 1976. 29 minutes.

Faith Ringgold: The Last Story Quilt. Library Video Company. DO546. 30 minutes.

Harlem Renaissance. Art of Black America. Universal Color Slide Company. Book and set of 20 slides.

James Thomas, Delta Artist. Center for the Study of Southern Culture. [University of Mississippi]

Kindred Spirits: Contemporary African-American Artists. PBS Videos. Produced by KERA, 1992. KISP-000-SC95. 30 minutes.

Lasting Impressions [Profile of lithograph artist Robert Blackburn], Gail Jansen, director. Cinema Guild.

Chapter 5

RITUALS, CEREMONY, AND MUSIC

"Rituals, Ceremony, and Music" further elaborates on spiritual issues discussed previously. As we examine the sacred and the secular, the chapter particularly focuses on the Afro-Baptist and Afro-Methodist denominations of Protestantism. African survivalisms revealed in these rituals, ceremonies, and music are also investigated. This chapter is not only a discussion about religion per se, but about family and community and the survival mechanisms, with spiritual contexts, that have sustained black people for over three centuries in the United States.

Beginning with the sacred, "Rituals, Ceremony, and Music" flows into what might be considered (and in some cases is) the secular. These distinctions are arguably artificial, and as we will see, the traditional lines between sacred and secular are thin. The process, and passages, of living are a kind of theater. The preacher-warrior, whom we first saw in Vincent Harding's *There Is a River,* is the intellectual leader of the community—and also a director with a script, who historically has been involved in all aspects of community existence from the obvious (the religious), to the human (civil) rights and black convention movements, to influencing African American language and communications techniques. And in fact, rituals, ceremony, and music do constitute a mode of speaking and articulation that indicates what is important to African American life—both individually as well as communally. The readings in Chapter 5 also focus on the issues of leadership, influence, position and advancement, self-realization, and the instruction and guidance needed for meeting life passages. These are areas where cosmology, space and place, plastic and other visual arts, and "dynamics of language" converge. Whereas other chapters in *How Sweet the Sound* provide a basic vocabulary and conceptual system for understanding African American history, this chapter discusses the dynamics and combinations of elements that distinguish the African American from, for example, the Anglo-American and Irish American, and from America's Native peoples. "Rituals, Ceremonies, and Music" also shows, most clearly, the adaptive and syncretic nature of African America. The essays and articles in this pivotal chapter illustrate how fundamental this triad is to culture, survival, and to the attainment and maintenance of black freedom in the Americas. The chapter supports the proactive voice maintained in the anthology, a voice that also portrays the substantial, and traditional, roles of African American women who have been arbiters between black and white peoples and within the black community and the black family.

Ruby Terrill Lomax accompanied folklorist husband and folk song collector John A. Lomax on his field trips, and in "Negro Baptizings" she describes a baptism they witnessed in 1940. Here she illustrates the connection between the water rituals of Africa and African America and shows the water line as a natural connection between ancestors, the living who are part of the Afro-Baptist ritual of total immersion, and the concepts of rebirth and resurrection. We visualize baptism candidates dressed from head to toe in white garments, being led to the water. We hear their processional chant, "Let's Go Down to Jurdan." Through the symbolic "death of sin" and their subsequent possession by the Holy Spirit, baptism is the occasion of the candidate's rebirth.

With Lewis V. Baldwin's "Festivity and Celebration in a Black Methodist Tradition, 1813–1981," we move to the festival called the "Big August Quarterly." This annual observance in African Methodism, specifically African *Union* Methodism, celebrates the black denomination that was founded by freedman Peter Spencer in 1805. Wilmington, Delaware, in August, became a mecca for commemorating African Union Methodism. Its location within Protestantism became a place for black expressions of freedom and, unofficially, for the articulation and planning for either the abolition of slavery or escape from enslavement. Following Peter Spencer's passing, the festival also became a celebration of his life. His tomb became "the shrine of every lover of freedom,"[1] and annual pilgrimages were made there. Since 1979, the Big August Quarterly has been transformed into the annual Founder's Day of the African Union Theological Protestant Conference.

● ● ●

Audrey L. Brown and Josephine A. Beoku-Betts, in their respective essays "Women and Ritual Authority in Afro-American Baptist Churches of Rural Florida" and "We Got Our Way of Cooking Things: Women, Food and Preservation of Cultural Identity Among the Gullah," discuss the traditional role of women within the ritual worlds of Africa and the African diaspora. Brown creates an ethos for the Afro-Baptist rural Florida community, church family, and nuclear family. It is an ethos with symbols and the coda of black Christian behavior based on the social organization/relationships and dynamics of significant church women whose role and position is derivative from the men in church leadership roles—especially husbands but also fathers. Although this discussion is specifically about church women, it is also about being a role model to the whole community. The role model, in this instance, is a traditional woman touting the "procreative, life-affirming qualities of the female and thereby transmit[ting] these qualities from one generation to another."[2] Not only is this a leadership position but an educative one besides. The essay ends with a phenomenal praise poem to the Afro-Baptist woman taken from one year's Women's Day Address.

Beoku-Betts's essay continues the discussion of rituals practiced in a ceremonial way by women and girls as well as a discussion of Sea Island culture that has been an

---

[1] Lewis V. Baldwin, "Festival and Celebration in a Black Methodist Tradition, 1813–1981," *Methodist History* 20 (July 1982): 183–191.

[2] Audrey L. Brown, "Women and Ritual Authority in Afro-American Baptist Churches of Rural Florida," *Anthology and Humanism Quarterly* 13 (1988): 7.

important thread in this volume. She identifies the extraordinary in the seemingly ordinary and has thus found, in food choice or dietary practices, food preparation and meal sharing, important insights into community efforts for Gullah cultural preservation and transmission, especially in an era of real estate development assaults on the Sea Islands and the subsequent emigration of island young people.

In her telling of how she acquired the narratives that inform her research and article, Beoku-Betts, a sociologist, provides a fine example of a womanist scholar's perspective and how she employed it in her data collection and analysis. It serves her well in her interpretation of her respondents' narratives. By becoming a part of the community, as a guest and active participant, she earns the trust of her hosts. All this is put within the context not only of Gullah ritual but also Gullah social organization and socialization. She writes, "although food preparation, under pressure of dominant cultural practices, may be viewed as a measure of gender inequality and of women's subordination in the household, it also can promote resistance and strengthen cultural identity in marginalized cultural groups."[3]

Central to this discussion of Gullah traditions is rice culture, which these islands in the United States share with some West African societies from which many of their ancestors came. Beoku-Betts, from Sierra Leone, shows how this staple food is the glue that holds the community together and also "locates" it. Rice is not only the staple of Gullah life but also a bridge between African Americans and their African heritage. As a ceremonial food, rice creates a "meal" and supports a community within the community—which Beoku-Betts reveals here—the circle of girls and women.

• • •

Alan Lomax, son of John A. Lomax, is also a folklorist and folk song collector. In "I Got the Blues," he engaged, in "dialogue," several bluesmen who are involved as much in subterfuge and masquerading as in educating him (and us) in the language and dynamics of the blues song, the truest original *African* American form of sung language in the United States.[4] "I Got the Blues" reads like an excerpt from an epic, part of the heroic poem marking the travail and passages of black people through the American wilderness. It is part of the language that scholar and blues historian Albert Murray has called a "heroic dialogue," which has humor, wit, intelligence, common sense, and caution. Lomax writes, [we were] ". . . three blues musicians [Sib, Leroy, and Natchez] and myself [Alan Lomax] 'where nobody gonna bother us,' they said. 'No laws or nothin'"[5] It is a journey through secular music that was born out of the spiritual, taking the road not followed by gospel music. Lomax learned his lessons well: "I Got the Blues" is a wonderful example of storytelling in black vernacular tradition by a white man! And he has understanding too as he writes woefully and truly:

---

[3] Josephine Beoku-Betts, "We Got Our Way of Cooking Things: Women, Food and Preservation of Cultural Identity," *Gender & Society* 9 (5) (1995): 536.

[4] The spiritual also has an European counterpart. The blues, as part of blues and jazz, *springs* from the experience alone of black people in the United States.

[5] Alan Lomax, "I Got the Blues," *Common Ground* 8 (4) (1948): 38.

Now for an instant we understand each other. Now in this moment of laughter, the thongs and the chains, the harsh customs of dominance, the stupefying and brutalizing lies of race had lost their fallacious dignity, but only for an instant. The magic night had gone. Back in Memphis our night's friendship and understanding would vanish like this morning's mist under the pitiless southern sun. The blues would begin again their eternal rhythm, their eternal ironic comment . . .[6]

Negro Baptizings

Ruby Terrill Lomax
University administrator and
collector of American folk songs

Ruby Terrill Lomax was the second wife of the late folklorist John A. Lomax (father of Alan Lomax—one of the authors included in this anthology). Terrill Lomax was Dean of Women at the University of Texas at Austin prior to her marriage. This essay was written after she accompanied and assisted her husband in collecting American folk songs during a 1940 trip to Mississippi.

Let's go down to Jurdan,
Let's go down to Jurdan,
Let's go down to Jurdan,
Religion's so sweet.

So runs the processional hymn of rural Negro baptizings all over the South. The River "Jurdan" marks the dividing line between physical life in this world and heavenly life beyond:

On Jordan's stormy banks I stand—(they line it off)
And cast a wishful eye
To Can(y)aan's fair and happy land
Where my possessions lie.

Just so immersion in the river's waters symbolizes death to the sins of this world and resurrection to life in Christ. I don't have the statistics, but there is no doubt that most Southern Negroes "belong" to either the Methodist or the Baptist church, with the

---

[6] Ibid., p. 52.

Ruby Terrill Lomax, "Negro Baptizings" Publications of the Texas Folk-Lore Society, *19 (1944): 1–8.*

majority leaning to the Baptist, perhaps because of the very symbolism and drama of its ritual of baptism. And Negro preachers of Baptist faith can cite you scholarly proof of the correctness of their adopted form of baptism.

One Sunday evening Colonel Richard Kimball heard a group of Negroes gathering on the river bank, at the base of Lookout Mountain, just below his Chattanooga home. All sounds indicated a baptismal service in preparation. As Colonel Kimball's daughter had never seen a Negro baptizing, father and daughter joined the group on the river bank. White friends are always welcome guests at any Negro service. When the Kimballs arrived, the deacons had already escorted the line of candidates to their places in the water and the preacher was beginning his prayer:

> Dear Heavenly Father, we have gathered here this evenin' to give the holy service of baptism to these friends who have repented of their sins. By being baptized they wish to tell the world that they have buried their lives of sin and will rise up from this watery grave in newness of life with all their sins washed away.
>
> And, oh, our Heavenly Father, we thank Thee that us Baptists know the true way of baptism; because, Oh Lord, we know that the word baptize comes from the Greek word *bapto*, which means "Stick 'em under."

So simple and sincere was the preacher's explanation to the Lord, and through the Lord to his congregation, that only after the Kimballs had turned away from the service a half hour later did the vivid, if incongruous, phrase, "Stick 'em under" strike them with full force and send them into peals of laughter.

Sometimes the Negro himself, with no tinge of irreverence, finds a bit of comedy in this most solemn ceremony of baptism:

> *Methodists, Methodists, (he chants), you is dead*
> *'Caze you pour water on de baby's head;*
> *Babtists, Babtists, you is right,*
> *Caze you puts dem candidates out-a sight.*

Who of us when he was a child hasn't had his risibles roused almost to the point of exploding at some most solemn moment in a church service? The following verse may easily have had its inspiration in a real and perhaps fatal accident during a solemn baptizing:

> *Went to de river to be baptized,*
> *Stepped on a root and got capsized;*
> *De river was deep an' de preacher was weak,*
> *So de nigger went to Heaven from de bottom of de creek.*

The principal baptizing of the year in most Negro communities is held the last Sunday of the annual "protracted meetin'", which lasts ten days or two weeks in the summer or in the early fall after crops are put by. And the baptizing is a solemn and impressive service.

In the summer of 1940 I was traveling with my husband, John A. Lomax, as he searched for folk songs in Mississippi. We were told in Natchez that Clara Musique had between three and four hundred Negro families living on her plantation and we should probably find preaching services, that being the third Sunday, where we could hear some good spirituals and perhaps locate singers of work songs. Clara Musique is the widow of a well known and wealthy Negro physician, from whom she inherited the plantation. When we stopped about ten miles out from Natchez to get explicit directions, we learned that the crowds of Negroes we saw on foot, in wagons, buggies, automobiles and trucks were bound for a baptizing. We followed the trail of dust through the fields as far as we thought safe to take our car. (Unluckily we parked our car in a baggasse bog, but Negro men, even at risk of soiling their Sunday best, cheerfully pushed us out to solid ground.) After introducing ourselves to the preacher we joined the crowd for a half mile walk to the banks of the river where the baptizing pool had been staked out earlier in the day. About three hundred Negro witnesses assembled. As we went along we gathered that there were nine candidates for baptism. (St. Peter's had had a baptizing that morning two hours before, but "St. Peter's is 'Piscopal and don't 'quire immersion like us Baptists." But this one candidate, it seems, asked to be "put clean under like Jesus," and so for her they had a "real baptizing" this time.) And now the Baptists were coming with their nine new converts.

There was plenty of time for "howdys" and exchange of news before we heard the chanted song that called our attention to the procession in white. First came the preacher, followed by the deacons and other assistants, and then came the nine candidates, one or two more women than men, as I recall. All were dressed in white, at least from the waist up, and all had white head coverings. The preacher had on a white silk long coat and cap, but the deacons and the candidates, not frequently having need of such equipment, had used great ingenuity in assembling their costumes of white. For the head there were maid's caps, bakers' and chefs' caps, boudoir caps and painters', with somewhat less variety in jackets and robes.

"Let's go down to the Jurdan" was the burden of the processional chant. On the sandy beach of the river the group halted and the throng of witnesses crowded around them. The preacher read sentences from a little book; some were scripture quotations, some were long involved doctrinal declarations whose big words he found difficult to master. Now and then a word in a quotation would give him a new text for a fresh ten minutes' discourse. As if to allow the preacher opportunity to catch his breath, a brother would interrupt with a prayer or a hymn; one lined off the hymn, "Heaven Is My Home," another raised "I'm On My Way to the City," with similar "turnings" to "I Started for the Kingdom and I Can't Turn Back"; another brother interrupted with "When I Gets on my Dying Bed" and "His Name is on my Tongue." Perhaps these hymns and prayers and ejaculations (one sister kept insisting, "Take yo' time and TELL hit!") were rather interweavings than interruptions, for, without design, they were timed perfectly to build the crowd up to the desired state of exaltation.

> I can remember only disconnected fragments of the hour's sermon at the river's side:
> "Too many preachers got de clo'se on but de man ain't in 'em."
> "Heap of us waits to pray 'till we's swoll wid de asthmy ["Right here!" cried a sister] or whupped down by de fever." ["Dat's me," claimed another.]
> "When de court sets, ev'ybody gits pitiful."
> "God has no respectable person."

The preacher used the not unusual pronunciation "mi-cles" for miracles. His most surprising phrase he repeated several times during the services: "Borned of de Holy Speariment."

At last the preacher moved forward into the water and took his position between the two upright stakes.

Wade in de water—[one sister raised the tune]
Wade in de water, chillun,
Wade in de water,
God goin' trouble de water.

The deacons formed a lane from the preacher to the beach, and the candidates came forward. Each candidate was assisted to his position beside the preacher. In most cases the ceremony for the men and boys was simple enough; a statement by the preacher, a simple yes or a nod from the candidate, the immersing, and then the candidate was guided back to the dry beach where a friend threw a coat about him. When the women candidates came to the water's edge, I noticed that they all had cords wrapped around from the knees down. At first I thought that this was contrived to keep the dress from floating, to save embarrassment. But I learned that it served another purpose; for every woman came up out of the water either writhing or helplessly inert, and the wrapping of her limbs made her body easier to carry and to control. To members of the female candidate's family, especially to mothers and sisters, "holders" were assigned to prevent them from falling or doing harm to themselves when they became overjoyed at sight of their kin "being resurrected from the death of sin." All of this took place with the accompaniment of crescendos of moanings and singing, punctuated by shouts of rejoicing from the sympathizing throng of witnesses.

The preacher delayed long over three candidates—one who "had wandered far," another whose "father died in his sins and is already in Hell," the third, an elderly woman, over whom the church members evidently had prayed long; her case merited a fifteen minute talk. All that time she stood in water so cold that it must have chilled her through and through. Holders assigned to the family and special friends of this hard-won new child of God, were clearing space and otherwise preparing for a great demonstration.

We left the crowd at this point. As we walked away the preacher was immersing this last candidate "two feet under: we digs de mortal grave six feet deep; four feet for de box and two feet to kivver. So I buries de candidates two feet under de water to show dey is dead to sin."

Later from Clara Musique's front porch we saw the crowd walking singly and in groups along the path to the church house two miles away, where the deacons would start the services with singing and the first money offering, while the preacher and the newly baptized members found dry clothes in nearby homes. Two women had ridden with us to the crossroad. It was past noontime and they had nothing with them to eat that we could see, but Clara Musique said there would be plenty of food for all. The afternoon services would close in time for members to get home and do their evening chores before dark. The inspiration and exaltation from the day's baptismal and devotional services would buoy them up for the mundane tasks of the week ahead.

John B. Jones, a former Texas A. and M. student from Houston, who was very helpful to John Lomax in the early days of his folk song hunting, has described a Negro baptizing which he came upon one day in Alabama:

The scene was set in a rocky gorge, the banks of which were festooned with overhanging cedars; the sparkling pool of clear water was surrounded by a shelving bank, so that the place formed a natural amphitheatre. In this spot was assembled a large group of Negroes, the women and children dressed in bright colors. The gorge rang with their merry laughter and light-hearted chatter until the minister, a solemn-faced, deep-voiced, white-haired old man, lifted his hand for silence. Then the crowd sang, as only Negroes can sing, a spiritual in which the terrors of death and hell are described in a way to startle the imagination. Next, a visiting preacher prayed, the audience joining in with vocal approval, from time to time repeating the words that impressed them most. As the candidates for baptism, ten or twelve in number, approached the water-side, they were led out, one by one, by two deacons to the preacher standing in the middle of the pool, while the crowd sang:

> *Let's go down to Jurdan, let's go down to Jurdan,*
> *De clear river Jurdan is mighty deep;*
> *Let's go down to Jurdan,*
> *De old river Jurdan is mighty deep,*
> *But 'ligion is so sweet.*

Then, beginning with the smallest girl, each candidate was baptized. Just before one was immersed the congregation would sing:

> *Missionary Baptist is my name, Missionary Baptist is my name,*
> *Missionary Baptist is my name, 'ligion is so sweet.*
> *De Lord said baptism it must be, for 'ligion is so sweet;*
> *De Lord said baptism it must be, we are goin' to 'bey His will.*
> *De Lord said baptism it must be, for 'ligion is so sweet.*
> *What kind o' man is He? All things they obey His will.*
> *What kind o' man is He? He spoke to de sea and de sea was still.*
> *De Lord said baptism it must be, de li'l' Babe in de manger,*
> *What kind o' manner o' man is He? He walk on de land an' He walk on de sea*
> *An' all things here obey His will; He speaks to de sea an' de sea is still,*
> *An' 'ligion is so sweet.*

Each candidate as he came up out of the water was seized with a queer sort of physical convulsion, which my yardman, Sam, afterwards explained to me as "the working of the Holy Spirit." The final outbreak of the candidate when he was on terra firma was to stretch out his arms and wave them in a vain effort to fly. A large, fleshy woman was "seized with the Spirit" just before her baptism and had to be taken out of the water until she became calm. She was then baptized and again underwent a weird seizure. The last man baptized was a muscular ditch-digger who required four strong men to get him out of the pool. I heard the minister, who was being pushed out towards the deep water, mutter to his helpers: "Get him out-a here before he drowns us all." As each candidate was led out of the water the congregation sang with splendid effect:

> *New bawn, new b-a-w-n,*
> *New-bawn child, new-bawn child;*
> *Like a li'l' Babe in a manger,*
> *De ole River Jurdan was mighty deep.*
> *But 'ligion was so sweet.*

By the time the service was over the sun's rays no longer reached the bottom of the gorge. The quiet of evening fell, a breeze came up and stirred the branches of the fragrant cedars. The crowd seemed awed by the influence of a most sacred and solemn ceremony, the effect of which had been intensified, now and then, by the shrill voices of the women in shouts of religious ecstasy. The baptized persons stood around with the crowd grouped about them, as the old minister with hands outstretched to heaven invoked a benediction. And then again they sang, in a minor key, wonderfully sweet and touching:

> *De old River Jurdan was so deep,*
> *An' now our brother in Christ we greet;*
> *De old River Jurdan was so deep,*
> *But 'ligion was so sweet.*
> *He said baptism it must be*
> *If He from sin'll set us free,*
> *An' all things here obey His will,*
> *Spoke to de sea an' de sea was still,*
> *For 'ligion was so sweet.*

Slowly the shadows darkened while with occasional shouts of joy the crowd trooped away, and the baptizing was over. Yet not quite, for from down the gorge came floating back to me the song:

> *When my blood runs chilly an' cold, I'se got to go,*
> *'Way beyond the Sun.*
> *Ef you can't bear no crosses, you can't wear no crown,*
> *'Way beyond the Sun.*
> *I'se got a mother in the Beulah Land, she's callin' me,*
> *'Way beyond the Sun.*
> *Do, Lord, do, Lord, do remember me,*
> *Oh, do, Lord, do, Lord, do remember me,*
> *Oh, do, Lord, do, Lord, do remember me,*
> *Oh, do, Lord, remember me.*

Festivity and Celebration in a Black Methodist Tradition, 1813–1981

Lewis V. Baldwin

Lewis V. Baldwin is the author of Toward the Beloved Community. Martin Luther King, Jr. and South Africa *(1995),* To Make the Wounded Whole: The

Lewis V. Baldwin, "Festivity and Celebration in a Black Methodist Tradition, 1813–1981," Methodist History 20 (July 1982): 183–191.

Cultural Legacy of Martin Luther King, Jr. *(1992),* There Is a Balm in Gilead:
The Cultural Roots of Martin Luther King, Jr. *(1991),* The Mark of a Man:
Peter Spencer and the African Union Methodist Tradition: The Man, The
Movement, The Message, and The Legacy *(1987), and* "Invisible" Strands in
African Methodism: A History of the African Union Methodist Protestant and
Union American Methodist Episcopal Churches, 1805–1980 *(1983).*
Currently, Lewis Baldwin is associate professor in Religious Studies
at Vanderbilt University.

It was widely held in the nineteenth century that black Americans were incorrigibly religious. Given certain considerations, this was by no means an exaggerated assumption. Many blacks of that period had come out of West African backgrounds where they had been born into religions, where religion for them was a daily preoccupation, and where there was no sharp dichotomy drawn between religion and other departments of life.[1] That firm attraction toward religion was clearly reinforced in the experience of slavery, because in religion blacks found not only salvation, but freedom—freedom to be themselves, and freedom to be celebrative, festive, and responsive. They also found a profound sense of community which was invariably strengthened by the exigencies of slave life. Nowhere is this more evident than in the worship tradition forged by black slaves. That tradition—characterized largely by prayer, sermon, song, and the frenzy—has survived to this day in some measure, prompting Harvey Cox, the eminent Harvard scholar, to contend that blacks have "a more festive and feeling-oriented approach to life."[2]

The historic relevance and significance of Cox's contention, when viewed within the context of the black religious experience, becomes remarkably clear when the history of Wilmington, Delaware's Big August Quarterly is considered. This annual observance has the distinction of being Wilmington's oldest folk festival, black America's first major religious festival, and African Methodism's only denominational festival.[3] It was started in 1814 by Peter Spencer, a Maryland ex-slave, who, after breaking with the predominantly white Methodist Episcopal structure, had organized the Union Church of African Members in 1813.[4] Spencer chose the last Sunday in August as the most appropriate time for the festival because the end of the harvest season was in sight. Most of the grain and hay had been harvested, fruits were ripening, subsistence was cheaper, and black Methodists, slave and free, could take the weekend off to congregate at the Mother Union Church of Africans on French Street for a day of social intercourse and religious celebration.[5]

Many of the black people who established Big Quarterly were slaves, some of whom were not far removed from Africa. In the pre-Civil War days scores of Africa's dark children, bearing identification papers and orders from their masters for articles of clothing, walked from lower Delaware, Maryland, and Virginia, arriving in Wilmington foot sore and dusty.[6] Others came aboard steamboats, in hay wagons, in ox-carts, and on mule-back. The strong slave-retrieving efforts exercised in parts of Maryland, Delaware, and Pennsylvania gave masters the necessary confidence to allow their slaves the freedom to attend Big Quarterly.[7] *The Delaware State Journal,* an early Wilmington newspaper, gave this descriptive account of those who appeared at the festival in 1845:

> Colored folks—Our town, on Sunday last was pretty well filled by "colored folks," who came to attend a religious meeting, called, generally, "the Big Quarterly." All sizes, of both sexes, and all ages, and we might say all colors, for there was a sample from the jetty African to the almost white-faced mulatto, were present. The aged came with their gray heads and bowed forms, and little infant children were carried in the arms—some chuckling forth their pleasure, others squalling out their dissatisfaction. Some were clad in plain habiliments, others, both male and female, reached at the bon ton, and moustaches and imperials, bowed and smiled complacently at the side of full skirts and flounces. Many of these people came from a great distance, and it is believed that Philadelphia furnished about 1,000. The whole company were well dressed, and with a few exceptions, as far as we can learn, conducted themselves in an orderly manner. The services at the "Union" Church were performed with proper decorum and gravity.[8]

Once in Wilmington, slaves and free blacks mingled with some degree of freedom despite the almost ubiquitous presence of overseers, slave catchers, sheriffs, and U.S. Marshals. Some spoke of the daily hardships inflicted by the system of unpaid labor, and plotted their escape into Philadelphia and other free territories. Others rejoiced in the promise of freedom which they felt was somehow ingrained in the religion of Jesus Christ. Still others engaged in storytelling as they partook of the large quantities of chitterlings, collard greens, roasted ears, spare-ribs, watermelons, and other so-called "soul" foods.[9]

From the beginning, the Big August Quarterly was primarily a religious festival held in commemoration of the founding of African Union Methodism. It was comparable in many ways to the enthusiastic revivals and camp meeting services of the white Methodists. This was obvious in the decorum of the celebrants who engaged in "the old-time religion."[10] The order of services always followed a set pattern, beginning with the early Sunday morning love feast celebrated in traditional Methodist fashion. Prayer, testimony, and song were commonly a part of this ceremony. Emotions often reached fever pitch as the celebrants, breaking bread and drinking water, tightly embraced each other while singing songs inspired by the slave experience:

> *One more time, Lord;*
> *One more time,*
> *Lord I'm glad to be in the Service,*
> *One more time.*

and:

> *And are we yet alive,*
> *To see each other's face.*[11]

In the typical Big Quarterly worship experience, love feast was followed by a period of informal fellowship. Dark faces would beam with happiness and eyes would fill with tears as the worshippers shared their common joy in God's acceptance of their personhood. Oftentimes as they engaged in informal chat their emotional cup would run over, and uncontrollable shouting would result. This was all in accord with their manner as a spiritual and emotional people.

The remainder of Big Quarterly Sunday was commonly given to preaching, singing, and shouting. Services were generally held at Ezion M.E. Church, which was organized by Spencer in 1805, and at the Mother Union Church of Africans. Tents were constructed at times to accommodate the throngs of worshippers. Spencer, William Anderson, and Isaac Barney—the most powerful leaders of African Union Methodism in the antebellum period—almost always conducted the services. One can imagine that the sermons they preached, and the consoling words they spoke, were always of immense importance to a bruised and battered people who were confronted daily with the question of the meaning of their existence. Undoubtedly, the spirits of many were lifted into a transcendent moment, and some were thus prepared to endure another year of hardship, toil, and struggle.[12]

A new twist was sometimes added to the services by those who injected ceremonies and practices which obviously came from Africa. One such ceremony, which took place at Big August Quarterly celebrations throughout the nineteenth century, bore a striking similarity to the "ring shout" which has been practiced for centuries among Gullah blacks of the Georgia-South Carolina Sea Coast areas. A nineteenth century Wilmington newspaper reporter gave a brief description of the ceremony, which usually drew a crowd of curious white observers:

> Several circles were formed, consisting of about a dozen persons each. They sang words of their own composition, but they, however, had the effect of making the participants happy. Their feelings were expressed by clapping of hands in chorus. A recognized leader was placed in the circle who made the desired gestures and he was promptly imitated. Large and curious crowds gathered around the circles.[13]

After 1843, the year of Peter Spencer's death, the festival became a lasting tribute to his memory. Spencer's tomb became "the shrine of every lover of freedom," and throngs of African Methodists went to great lengths to "make this annual pilgrimage to the cradle of African Union Methodism, and to help the memory of Father Spencer to live on and on."[14] Each year thousands marched up the hill on French Street to the rear of the Mother Union Church of Africans and stood at the grave which "was covered by old-fashioned marble slabs lying on brick piers."[15] The deep silence of the occasion was often broken as the pilgrims lifted their voices:

> *Father Spencer's body lies molding in the clay,*
> *Father Spencer's body lies molding in the clay,*
> *His Church is marching on.*

And there were these lines:

> *Oh, where is Father Spencer?*
> *I wonder where he's gone?*
> *The Church is all in mourning,*
> *And he cannot be found.*[16]

The pilgrimage to Spencer's grave was of such significance that Wilmington soon earned an enduring reputation as "the Mecca of people of African descent." A nineteenth century Wilmington newspaper editor observed:

For nearly a century this city has been the Mecca of the African race in the United States. A pilgrimage to the Church and to the grave of Peter Spencer was to them as sacred a duty as is the visit to the prophet's tomb, to the pious Mohammedan.[17]

The Big August Quarterly remained an unbroken tradition through most of the pre-Civil War years. Between 1851–56, the spirit of the festival waned as a result of serious internal bickering among the leaders of the Union Church of African Members. The dispute, which focused on the right of one Ellis Saunders to discharge duties as a presiding officer of the church, led to a schism. Thirty-one of the forty congregations broke away under Saunders and Isaac Barney and formed the Union American Methodist Episcopal Church. The remaining nine continued as the African Union Church. In 1866, this small body merged with the First Colored Methodist Protestant Church. The resulting body became the African Union First Colored Methodist Protestant Church, commonly known as the African Union Methodist Protestant Church. Interestingly enough, both the U.A.M.E. and A.U.M.P. Churches continued to support Big Quarterly after the split.[18]

The festival was abandoned for a brief time during the Civil War for obvious reasons. Blacks as well as whites were caught up in civil conflict, and had little time to engage in the kind of festivity and celebration traditionally associated with Big Quarterly. After the war, the festival was revived as "a day of reunion, feasting, and jubilee."[19]

Late nineteenth century Wilmington newspapers—such as *Every Evening, The Evening Journal, The Morning News,* and *The Sunday Morning Star*—consistently contended that Big Quarterly declined in attendance and enthusiasm after plantation slavery was abolished. Alice Dunbar-Nelson, writing about the festival in the early 1930s, challenged this contention and showed how Big Quarterly "was re-established with even more fervor and brilliancy immediately after emancipation."[20] The great attendance and excitement associated with the festival reached higher levels, despite a growing number of blacks and whites who attacked it as a relic of slavery times, and who urged black Methodist leaders to work toward abolishing it.[21] The 1865 celebration, the first held after emancipation, was not only very spirited and animated, but drew a very large crowd. Five thousand visitors were present for the festival in 1867.[22] A record crowd of 20,000 appeared at Big Quarterly in 1879. Ten thousand participated in the festivities in 1892. The overwhelming majority of those who supported the festival during these years were black, but whites also appeared in considerable numbers.[23]

The religious dimension of Big Quarterly remained its most noticeable feature. The churches with roots in the Spencer tradition—Ezion M.E. Church, Mother U.A.M.E. Church, and Mother A.U.M.P. Church—were frequently filled to their capacities with worshippers.[24] These churches stood in close proximity to each other in the vicinity of French Street in Wilmington, and this made them the centers of Big Quarterly religious services. Of these churches, the Mother A.U.M.P. Church remained the principal point of attraction because the graves of Peter Spencer, William Anderson, and the other saints of the church were on its property. Each year tents had to be constructed to accommodate the vast crowds who appeared. The day always began with the early morning love feast, followed by services that would continue well into the night.[25]

Many of the rituals and ceremonies that characterized the festival in the nineteenth century were vividly described in Wilmington newspapers. The songs heard at the 1889 celebration left an indelible mark on the memory of one of the reporters for

The Morning News. He wrote the following: "One voice began in a low tremulous tone while others joined in with voices hardly louder than whispers":

> *Jesus has not shut the gate,*
> *Somebody dying every day.*
> *I know that I am not too late,*
> *Somebody dying every day.*[26]

The editor continued:

> As the volume increased, the sound rose to an exuberant shout. The singers bodies swayed up and down and back and forth, like the levers of a mighty engine. The stamp of their feet was like the thud of steam against a piston, and the clapping of their hands was like the clatter of the rackets and springs of machinery. In themselves the sounds were harsh and thumping, but somehow it was all in harmony with the scene and music. . . . Streams of perspiration ran down their faces, their voices grew husky and the music became mere gutteral sounds, not words. It seemed human endurance would fail, but they held on until with a shout, a scream, and a face that shone with joy, a woman came leaping from the midst of the crowd, made her way easily where others had been blocked, and reached the street still shouting.[27]

His impression of the prayer that followed was equally striking:

> The prayer which follows is a passionate appeal for aid. It is fervent. It may be ungrammatical in its construction, but it is eloquent. The supplicant tries to bring Divine Power to the earth and tries to lift the penitent to the skies. He implores aid, confesses sin and exhorts to the exercise of faith. His brethren around him aid with responses. Shouts of "No!" "Yes!" "Amen!" and "Do Lord!" coach him and augment his effort until it often seems as if the man's heart would leap from his throat in excess of emotion. There are comical sides and shades to such a scene and such activities, but no one laughs, no one scoffs. Everyone looks with intense interest at the actors, fearing that some great thing will happen and they not see it.[28]

The pivotal point of the services was always the preaching. Simple Bible-based sermons, which were typical of the Methodist tradition generally, were the rule. Certain preachers were noted for their oratorical and homiletical skills, and were almost always designated to deliver the keynote sermons. One such preacher was Abram George of the A.U.M.P. Conference, whose sermons frequently electrified the celebrants. One reporter of Wilmington's *The Evening Journal* was literally captivated by George's powerful sermon at the 1880 Big August Quarterly:

> His style was very graphic and exceedingly dramatic. He referred to the "Kingdential throne" in glowing terms, and eulogized Moses in his original way. After telling of the wonderful crossing of the Red Sea, he said "It was not Moses' Rod what did it, but the power of God." The colored brethren would urge him on by crying out, "preach it!" "preach Jesus!" One old fellow in a white linen coat stood up in the aisle in front of him and by his exclamations and antics made himself almost as conspicuous as the preacher.[29]

Another such preacher was Daniel Russell, Sr., who was known as "a pulpit actor and genius." His keynote sermon at the 1883 festival attracted the attention of an editor of *The Delaware State Journal:*

He took a running text on "True Belief," and delivered his address without notes. His manner was earnest and enthusiastic, and the points of his sermon were emphasized by grotesque gestures. He divided his attention between the audience and brother ministers sitting in the pulpit, frequently turning to them for signs of approval.[30]

The most interesting part of the services was always the "ring ceremonies," which obviously reflected a strong African influence. *The Delaware Gazette and State Journal* offered an extensive description of these ceremonies as they occurred at the 1889 Big August Quarterly:

> In the basement of the church a hundred or more men formed a circle and swayed to and fro, sometimes fast and sometimes slow, according to the metre of the hymn sung. . . . Those who formed the inner line of the human ring were the most violent in their movements and most of the time perspired so freely that they could not have been more wet if a hose had been turned upon them. Frantically they urged one another to more violent feats of gymnastic devotion, clapping their hands, jumping and shouting, and occasionally groaning. When they grew weary they dropped upon their knees and prayers were offered. The women were modest and did not help form rings. Instead they sang and watched the proceedings with interest.[31]

Some of the ceremonies and practices associated with the Big August Quarterly in the nineteenth century were discontinued in the twentieth century. The "ring ceremonies," and other practices linked to the African background, were largely abandoned at the turn of the century. Early morning love feasts were no longer held annually after 1955. Beginning in the late 1950's, Gospel songs slowly displaced the slave spirituals as the most popular type of black sacred music heard at the festivals.[32]

The Big August Quarterly also changed in other ways. The invention of cars and other modern and more convenient means of transportation brought larger crowds from distant states like Virginia, South Carolina, and North Carolina. Wilmington newspapers provided fairly accurate estimates of the increases in attendance. Some 15,000 visitors were present for the festival in 1925; 14,000 attended in 1940.[33] Such figures render absurd the claim, made by some Wilmington newspapers, that the Big August Quarterly dropped significantly in attendance in the twentieth century.[34] However, this was the case in the 1960's. The 100 or so who appeared for the festival in 1969 were an all-time low. This dismal showing was due primarily to the fact that this was to be the last Big August Quarterly held on French Street. The Mother A.U.M.P. Church at 819 French Street, which had been the main focal point for the festival since 1814, was relocated to Franklin Street in Wilmington in accordance with urban renewal plans.[35]

Between 1969 and 1979, the festival amounted largely to an annual founder's day, attended by the few blacks who made up the A.U.M.P. Conference. Early in 1980 this writer completed the first extensive work on the history and cultural significance of the Big August Quarterly, and this gave rise to a movement to return the festival to French Street.[36] The 1980 and 1981 celebrations were held on French Street, where an average of 3,000 celebrants gathered in what has recently become known as "The Peter Spencer Plaza." Interestingly enough, attempts to revive the festival have received the support of some of Delaware's most prominent white public officials, such as

Wilmington's mayor William T. McLaughlin, and Delaware's State Senator Joseph Biden.[37]

A most disturbing development in recent years has been the lack of strong support given Big Quarterly by Ezion United Methodist Church and Mother U.A.M.E. Church. This signals a radical departure from their actions in the past with respect to the festival. In the nineteenth century these churches worked closely with the Mother A.U.M.P. Church in supporting the festival as a lasting tribute to Peter Spencer and African Union Methodism. One can only hope that in the future these churches will once again unite in making Big Quarterly an exciting day of festivity and celebration. Otherwise, African Union Methodism could lose a vital part of its rich tradition.

Notes

1. Leroi Jones, *Blues People: Negro Music in White America* (New York: William Morrow & Company, 1963), p. 34.
2. Harvey Cox, *The Feast of Fools: A Theological Essay on Festivity and Fantasy* (Cambridge: The Harvard University Press, 1969), pp. 17, 25, and 51.
3. "Wilmington's Oldest Folk Festival." *The Big Quarterly Program Booklet* (August 27, 1978), pp. 1–4; and Alice Dunbar-Nelson, *Big Quarterly in Wilmington* (Wilmington: published by the author, 1932), pp. 1–5.
4. *The Morning News,* Wilmington, Delaware (August 26, 1889), p. 1.
5. *Ibid.*
6. *Ibid.*
7. *The Delaware Gazette and Peninsula Advertiser,* Wilmington, Delaware (September 26, 1816) pp. 1–2; *The Delaware Gazette,* Wilmington, Delaware (September 1, 1857), p. 2; and *The Evening Journal,* Wilmington, Delaware (August 30, 1967), p. 29.
8. *The Delaware State Journal,* Wilmington, Delaware (September 2, 1845) p. 3.
9. *The Morning News* (August 26, 1889), p. 1.
10. *The Sunday Morning Star,* Wilmington, Delaware (August 27, 1933), p. 10.
11. *The Morning News* (August 26, 1889), p. 1.
12. *Ibid.*
13. *The Morning News* (September 1, 1884), p. 1; and *The Morning News* (August 31, 1885), p. 1.
14. *The Tomb of Peter Spencer: A Pamphlet* (Wilmington: T. E. Bolden, Printer, n.d.), pp. 1–2.
15. *The Morning News* (August 26, 1889), p. 1.
16. Lewis V. Baldwin, "Invisible Strands in African Methodism: A History of the African Union Methodist Protestant and Union American Methodist Episcopal Churches, 1805–1980" (Ph.D. dissertation, Northwestern University, 1980), Chapters IV and VI.
17. *The Morning News* (August 26, 1889), p. 1.
18. Baldwin, "Invisible Strands in African Methodism," Chapters VI and VII.
19. Anna T. Lincoln, *Wilmington, Delaware: Three Centuries Under Four Flags, 1609–1937* (Rutland, Vermont: The Tuttle Publishing Company, 1937), p. 167.
20. Nelson, *Big Quarterly in Wilmington,* p. 2.

21. Baldwin, "Invisible Strands in African Methodism," Chapter VI.
22. *The Morning News* (August 27, 1888), p. 1; and *The Evening Journal* (August 26, 1895), p. 1.
23. Baldwin, "Invisible Strands in African Methodism," Chapter VI.
24. *Ibid.*
25. *Ibid.*
26. *The Morning News* (August 26, 1889), p. 1.
27. *Ibid.*
28. *Ibid.*
29. *Every Evening,* Wilmington, Delaware (August 30, 1880), p. 1.
30. *The Delaware State Journal* (August 30, 1883), p. 1.
31. *The Delaware Gazette and State Journal,* Wilmington, Delaware (August 29, 1889), p. 3.
32. Baldwin, "Invisible Strands in African Methodism," Chapters VI-VIII.
33. *The Evening Journal* (August 31, 1925), p. 9; and *The Morning News* (August 26, 1940) p. 1.
34. Baldwin, "Invisible Strands in African Methodism," Chapter VII.
35. *Ibid.,* Chapter VIII.
36. Baldwin, "Invisible Strands in African Methodism," Chapters IV and VI-VIII.
37. Mayor William T. McLaughlin to the Mother A.U.F.C.M.P. Church, Wilmington, Delaware (January 12, 1981); and *The Delaware Valley Star,* Wilmington, Delaware (August 26, 1981), pp. 2–3.

Women and Ritual Authority in Afro-American Baptist Churches of Rural Florida

Audrey L. Brown
Anthropologist

Audrey L. Brown, who has a doctorate in education, is currently completing another in anthropology. Her research for the following article was conducted from 1980 to 1985 in rural Florida where she employed oral history techniques and personal observations in assessing the ritualistic roles of Afro-Baptist church women. She also studied church women, from 1988 to 1989, in Jamaica with a Fulbright fellowship.

Audrey L. Brown, Women and Ritual Authority in Afro-American Baptist Churches of Rural Florida," Anthropology and Humanism Quarterly *13 (1988): 2–10.*

God created woman to be helpmate for man . . . and throughout history, Women of God
have been getting the job done.

—Sister Lillie Mae McIntire,
Woman's Day Address

SUMMARY

Religious systems, according to Clifford Geertz, incorporate significant symbols that
both express and order society and in so doing make theory fact and religion work.
This article, which describes women's roles of ritual authority in North Central Florida
rural Afro-American Baptist churches, argues that these roles symbolically provide
models *of* and models *for* womanhood that have infused the Afro-American family
with the creative energy to transcend the constraints placed upon its continuity and
development.

INTRODUCTION

Although women are nominally equals in the socio-political organization of rural Afro-
Baptist church communities in Florida, in fact they are subordinated to males in formal
and informal ritual authority roles. Even though women are often better educated than
males and frequently economically independent, it is their nurturing and sustaining
qualities that are glorified in church life. Female assertive behavior or aggressive leadership is discouraged and censored. The subordination of women to men is achieved
through the active complicity by women. Older women assist in developing voluntary
submission in young females through precept and by example.

An older woman of the church, who, despite being 72, refers to herself[1] as the
pastor's daughter, explained.

"The important thing is she [the Pastor's wife] should be ready at any time, when
any problem or work is slack in the church she is in a position to correct it . . . give
instruction about . . ."

"To men and women?" I asked.

She hesitated. "To women," and with a laugh, added, "Because when she goes to
the men she's steppin' ahead ah da deacons."

The adaptive interrelationship between religion and the Afro-American Family as
a social institution is examined here through ethnographic description. Supported in
turn by ethnohistorical reconstruction, and historical accounts, and oral traditions of
the church women as interpreted by myself, an Afro-American anthropologist. This description is illuminated with Geertz's (1966) insight that religious patterns provide models *of* and models *for* social reality in that they both explain and shape day-to-day human existence (pp. 69). During the course of human evolution, there has of necessity
been "the increasing reliance [by us] upon 'systems of significant symbols' (language,
art, myth, ritual) for orientation, communication, and self-control" (Geertz 1973,
345–46). In *Local Knowledge* (1983), Geertz again emphasizes the importance of

"significant symbols" in the constitution of culture and suggests that ritual dramas shape experience, which in turn orders society. "Reiterated form, staged and acted by its own audience makes . . . theory fact" (pp. 20–30).

The manner in which Afro-Baptist theory is made fact and how it acts both as a model of black family life and a model for women's role in that life is presented in three roles of women in the Afro-Baptist church of rural Florida. These are a generalized social role, an informal ritual specialist role, and a more formal ritual specialist role.

GENERALIZED SOCIAL ROLE

Afro-Baptist church women are organized, and organize themselves, into "missionary circles." Each local church Home Mission Society may have circles that represent different age sets from schoolaged children through elder church women. The oldest women are those usually referred to as "missionaries" or "church mothers." Not every church has a mission society that includes all age sets. The congregation may be too small or members may have moved from the rural area where the church is located and are unable to attend church meetings held during the week.

The meetings of the Home Mission Society are settings in which women communicate the ethos of the church in regard to expected female behaviors. Missionaries help the sick, elderly, or needy. The local missionary society is part of women's auxiliaries at the tri-county, state, and national levels within the organizational structure of the Afro-Baptist church. The Home Mission Society is usually led by the current pastor's wife, a deaconess, or an informal ritual specialist who may simply be called "Sister Teacher." Although the missionary society is a female organization, at every level, from local to national, their annual meetings always include male church leaders who conduct devotionals and preach sermons. Young, prepubertal boys may participate in the school age circle of the Home Mission Society. These males are frequently assigned specialized functions that set them apart in quasi-leadership roles, e.g., pianists, secretaries, or ushers.

The Home Mission Society as a social organization of women has been part of the Afro-Baptist church as far back as the earliest written records found, i.e., 1859, which describe local, state, regional, or national Afro-Baptist Church organization (A Concise History of Canaan Baptist Church [1945] 1966; Baptist General State Convention of Florida 1939–40; Dwelle [n.d., ca. 1913]; Journal of the Thirty-Second Annual Session of the National Baptist Convention 1912, 1913; Cook 1890; Report of the Nineteenth Anniversary of the American Baptist Missionary Convention 1859 [Jordan 1930]).

Another setting in which women communicate the ethos expected of them is Sunday School. As teachers of other women or of prepubertal children, women are integrated into the educational arm of the church. Although women may occasionally serve as Sunday School superintendent, a deacon usually holds this office, often the same one for twenty, thirty, or forty years. Women who become Sunday School teachers are frequently pastors' wives or daughters, deaconesses, women with a lot of "spirit" and knowledge of the "book," i.e., the Bible, or they may be women with higher education.

Still another setting that includes women is the Church Conference or monthly business meeting. In these meetings, women have an equal vote in issues that arise, and in some churches they are frequently elected as church clerks or financial secretaries or even may hold secular church offices such as trustee. In other churches women are not elected to any offices. Observation and oral history suggest that although women may vote and hold offices in the church they are not decision-makers. They may keep up with the "finance" or "have their say," but they vote in favor of what the elder males support or else abstain from voting. Often when "discord" is expected, women stay home. "Uncle Joe told me to stay away from that meeting, before he have to go up side somebody's head." This meant that if another male were rude to the speaker, her uncle would be very angry, a circumstance to be avoided, if "being of one accord," the objective of the Conference, was to be met.

In general, then, women act in church social roles that are oriented toward the nurturing and sustaining qualities of women: participation in religious education of young children, adolescent and adult females of all ages; care of the sick, elderly, and needy, and follow male leadership in maintaining accord in the church family. They serve as role models of social, moral, and ethical behaviors expected of Christian women within the context of the Afro-Baptist religion. Although all women are expected to be role models, the pastor's wife and deaconesses have an absolute obligation to so behave both within the church and in the secular community.

Pastors' Wives and Deaconesses

Symbolic of the prototypical relationship of males and females in the rural Afro-Baptist church communities, pastors' wives and deaconesses acquire their status only through marriage to a man of God. Regardless of a woman's Christian virtue, she cannot become a deaconess unless she is married to a deacon. In the church I came to know the best, Ol' Ship of Zion Missionary Baptist Church [a pseudonym], all the deaconesses were either daughters in the founding families in the church or wives of the sons of these founding families.[2] Pastors and their wives, on the other hand, in all of the observed churches, were from different church communities other than the one in which they served. Zion has had only two pastors called from its own church family in more than 100 years, although a number of males of the church had been called to the ministry.

A pastor's wife serves as *the* social role model for the women of the church. She represents the church women in various intra- and inter-community activities, associations, and conventions. Traditionally, the pastor's wife was better educated than other church women, and she, or the pastor's daughter, was frequently the community school teacher. Today pastors' wives are school teachers, civil servants, or nurses. As more women complete college and graduate studies this tradition has begun to extend to deaconesses. Many are professional or practical nurses, accountants, and if not teachers, teachers' aides. They work in public programs for the aged, food stamp programs, and the like, and belong to sororities and other philanthropic community clubs. Thus, pastors' wives and deaconesses are exemplars of academic and economic achievement for church women and for women in the secular community.

In the churches studied, only one pastor's wife had fewer than three children. In accordance with the Afro-Baptist concept of motherhood as sacred, most of the older wives of pastors had eight or more children, while the younger ones had from three to five. With some exceptions, deaconesses followed the same pattern. Once a pastor's wife, unless divorced, always a pastor's wife. After the death of a pastor his wife becomes one of a group of women with special status in the church: pastors' widows. The Afro-Baptist church has provided for pastors' widows economically and recognized them as having a special social status since at least 1840 (Jordan 1930, 67–68 and chapter 12; Burrough Manuscripts and Papers 1901–61). Although it was understood that some pastors were divorced, I never had a former wife of a pastor pointed out to me. At Zion, however, there were three pastors' widows. These women continue to have the social status afforded to a pastor's wife, and, in the social organization of the church women, they are ranked hierarchically, according to their age and longevity of service, immediately below the present pastor's wife, who is known as "The First Lady of the church."

The First Lady of the church is not only a social role model for academic achievement, employment, community activities, and motherhood, she is also a role model for appropriate dress and interpersonal relationships. If the First Lady is not singing in the choir or playing the piano, which she usually is, she is seated in a special seat in the front of the church. She dresses stylishly and always wear a hat.

Elizabeth Bostick, at age 72, recalls her mother's obligations.

"In the role, of . . . arah . . . pastor's wife, the Christians expect his wife to be an outstanding woman because she's the First Lady of the Church . . . and she is very important among women . . . so therefore she needs to have a attitude that is very pleasing . . . wear a smile . . . not a grin . . . and uh . . . she should be courteous at all times. She should be interested in people such as knowing how to counsel them if she should see something wrong. Knowing how to approach them. Knowing how to turn them off. You know its very important that we know how to meet people . . . entertain them . . . and turn them off."

"Turn them off?"

"Like you know . . . like we're gonna leave . . . 'well have a good day' . . . 'I enjoyed talkin' to you.'"

"What kind of works are expected of a minister's wife?"

"A minister's wife, I think, should be involved in all parts of the church, no specific, because it takes on missionary, teachin', and everything. She should be qualified."

"Did your mother do all these things?"

"Yes."

"Spiritually, what is a minister's wife supposed to be?"

"She shouldn't be cold, she should be full of spirit, because First Timothy tells us that. She should be full of the Holy Spirit" (Bostick 1984).

The one area in which the First Lady never participates during her husband's lifetime is the Church Conference. But after a pastor's death, his widow may be highly active in the business affairs of the church, which is usually the last one her husband pastored. (However, pastor's widows are highly active in Church Conferences.)

Deaconesses, like pastors' wives, also acquire their position by virtue of marriage. Unlike the pastor's wife, they serve for life even if they divorce or are divorced by their husbands. The difference between a pastor's wife and a deaconess in this regard symbolically suggests that the desired marriage of enduring relationships that extend throughout life is projected by the union of the pastor and his wife and is a model *for* marriage. On the other hand, the deaconesses project the model *of* marriage, one that is symbolically representative of social reality, that is, marriage does not always work and the woman may or may not be at fault.

As female ritual elders of the church, deaconesses are expected to not only demonstrate symbolically, but also to teach implicitly, the ethos of the community as it concerns appropriate female behavior. The teaching is done formally in adult female Sunday School classes by using the lesson to point out an individual's shortcomings without "calling no names." Informally, the teaching is carried out in private admonishments or tales of a deaconess' experiences as a wife or young unmarried woman. This usually occurs between relatives. Example is as important as precept. The oldest deaconess at Zion was severely reprimanded by a new, young pastor in front of the Church Conference. He questioned why she had not "called a meeting of the Deaconess Board." Although the woman was old enough to be his grandmother and in great pain from a life-threatening illness, of which he was unaware, and facing major surgery, she submitted to his reprimand without excuse. Pulling herself to her feet, she apologized for not carrying out her duty. Her submission was total.

Deaconesses give asked for, and unasked for, advice to younger women when their behavior is inappropriate. In reference to my husband, one deaconess told me, "He ain't suppose to cook no meals. What he gonna cook fo' when he got a great big ol' woman to cook fo' him?" This type of admonition may even extend to guidance about proper sexual behavior, although outright discussion of sexual matters is rare among the women of the church. If it is known that a woman is experiencing stress because of "trouble in the home," or if she is suspected of "gettin' outta line" herself, comments are "dropped" in conversation. "I don' go befo' my husband," which means that the husband has the final word; or "If we keep busy with the Lord's work, we don' have time fo' idle spirits," that is, jealousy, envy, and hate are "idle spirits."

Deaconesses may be Sister Teachers in Sunday School, be elected to the offices of trustee, treasurer, church clerk, and financial secretary, or sing in the choir.[3] The oldest deaconess may act in the role of informal ritual specialist.

INFORMAL RITUAL
SPECIALIST ROLE

As informal ritual specialists women may participate in prayer bands, which are small groups, mostly women, led by a deacon or pastor. The bands meet regularly to pray together and may be called upon to go into homes where there is a special need for prayer. Prayer is usually offered for the purpose of directing the power of the Holy Spirit toward healing the sick and "helpin' peoples with personals," that is, problems of one type or another. Prayer bands may be called upon to raise the Holy Spirit before special religious ceremonies, such as revivals or Women's Day services. The bands do so by praying, testifying, and singing old, often unwritten songs.

Church Mothers are the foremost among the informal ritual specialists in any church. These women are seventy or older and are known to have lived a Christian life throughout their adult years. In church, they are seated in the front, on the right-hand side, to the pastor's left. The pastor's wife and pastors' widows, regardless of their ages, and elderly pastors' daughters, sit with them. These women face the elder males and deacons seated on the opposite side of the church to the pastor's right. During religious ceremonies, the Church Mothers are the most vocal in the antiphonal call and response between the pastor or deacons and the church congregation.

The most highly specialized among the informal ritual leaders are those whom the Holy Spirit possesses. Although I have observed younger women and even males possessed by the Holy Spirit elsewhere, in the rural Afro-Baptist churches in Florida only post-menopausal women were regular informal specialists in "raisin' the Holy Spirit." This is similar to a popular belief in the Caribbean that the onset and end of a woman's child-bearing years are marked by an upsurge of mysticism and religious manifestations. "God calls the would-be diviner in her adolescence," says McKenzie (1977, xii). Two elder women of Zion who said they could "foretell and heal" also said they first knew they were "peculiar" when they were adolescents.

In our church, the Ol' Ship of Zion, Miss Mary, age 92 in 1986 and no longer able to attend church, was between 1980 and 1984 one of the two women the Holy Spirit often possessed. Miss Mary was also a specialist in "raisin'" the Holy Spirit. Every Sunday morning service she "raised a song" in counterpoint with the praying of the deacon conducting the Deacon's Devotional at the beginning of the service. As the Deacon's prayer began to entreat the Lord, "Holy Father you done brought us from a mighty long ways, and fo' that caus' we gonna ask yo' to hav' Mercy," Miss Mary began to sing, first alone and then joined by the other women, some singing and some crying out for the Lord's mercy. The Deacon's prayer, Miss Mary's song, and the women's cries combined to form a polyrhythmic entreaty for the Holy Spirit to come to the church.

DEACON: . . . and fo' that caus' we gonna ask yo' to hav' Mercy . . .

MISS MARY: . . . Lord, ha . . . a . . . av' Mercy . . .

WOMEN: Mercy . . . Lord . . . Mercy . . .

MISS MARY: Send yo' Sp . . . ir . . . rit . . .

WOMEN: Oh yes Lord . . . Please Lord, Yes . . . Mercy, Mercy

DEACON: Yo brought us from a mighty long way Lord, over highways and the byways, up until present time

MISS MARY AND WOMEN: O . . . oh . . . Ho . . . ly Sp . . . ir . . . rit . . . Let Yo Spi . . . ir . . . rit . . . Come down . . .

After Miss Mary stopped coming to church, for a few Sundays no one raised "her" song, then one Sunday morning another elderly woman started the call for the Holy Spirit to come down.[4]

FORMAL RITUAL SPECIALIST

Oh Lord . . . Oh Lord . . . I want ya to take care of me. . . . I want ya to *teach* me Jesus
. . . *How* . . . to be . . . a Mother. . . . Have Mercy dear Lord. . . . I know now my children is all grown . . . I'm just now beginnin' . . . to be . . . a Mother.

—Woman's Devotional Prayer
Women's Day Service
Union Baptist Church
Dunellon, Florida, 1984

These words of prayer rendered fervently during devotional service on the occasion of Women's Day were offered by a woman who, upon entering the maturity of
her life, pleads for knowledge that she, too, may be like the archetype of women, the
Mother of the Church. The Mother of the Church is the only formal role of ritual authority that a woman may hold in the rural Afro-Baptist communities I studied. The
role of the Mother has been dated back as early as 1866, when in Flemington, Florida
"Mother Jennie Behn" was one of the three founders of Canaan Baptist Church (A
Concise History of Canaan Baptist Church 1966 [1944]). The most sacred values of
Afro-Baptist rural society are embodied in the Mother of the Church: The sanctity of
life; the creative energy of the Holy Spirit renewed through birth and spiritual rebirth;
integration of religion, family, and kinship bonds; all are expressed in the ritual symbolism associated with the Mother of the Church as well as in the social characteristics
of the women who are elected to the position.

A Life-Time Obligation

Upon the death of her predecessor, The Mother of the Church is elected by the Church
Conference. Each Mother serves for life, although terms may overlap as the probable
successor begins to assume the present Mother's functions when age or infirmity prevents her from carrying them out. Such is the case at Zion today. The Mother who was
elected "when I was about seventy" is at age 92 no longer able to carry the basket.
Her probable successor, who, like the present Mother, is the granddaughter of an earlier Mother, performs the duties.[5] The office of Mother of the Church is theoretically
open to any church mother, who has "never left the church." At Zion, however, the office has historically rotated among the oldest females of the founding families. In the
past when a Mother died and there was no eligible candidate by age or spirituality in
the "next" family, the role rotated from mother to daughter and then sister of a single
family. Serving the Church Family for life symbolically reflects the social expectations
of a woman's life-long obligation to serve her family of birth and her family of
marriage.

Birthin' the Church and the Church Family

After the Civil War and well into the twentieth century, the Mother of the Church was
quite literally just that. Mothers are named as one of the church founders in history

after history. At Zion and Canaan the first Mothers were also community midwives. They knew the mysteries of "birthin' and healin' herbs" for the treatment of infant and female problems. During the tenure of the first three Mothers of Zion, about 1880 to 1937, oral history and census data indicate not a single neonatal, and only one maternal death, occurred in childbirth. In Jamaica, among the Revivalists, a religious group that evolved from eighteenth-century African and Afro-American Baptist preachers who immigrated there from Georgia, the Mothers or Mammies of the early bands were also "Nanas," that is, midwives in their religious community (Beckwith 1923, Hogg 1964). This suggests that the ritual status and role functions of the Mother of the Church are old traditions in the folk religions that evolved from the Baptist model among people of African descent in the New World.

In the past Mothers of the Church also recruited women to be "soldiers for the Lord." The Mothers gave instruction to females about to enter marriage on moral, social, and physical requirements of being a married woman. "Mammy Austin would take us girls aside jus fo' us got married an' tell us' how to act to us husbands" (Cousin Rosabelle, age 82). In times past the Mother also examined the female baptism candidates to determine if they were spiritually "ready fo' baptism." On the other hand, oral history and photographs of baptisms in the early twentieth century support the argument that women did not participate in the actual baptism, and Simpson (1956) reports that Mothers of Jamaica Revivalist Bands might carry out all leadership functions except baptism.[6] Today, in rural Florida the Mother assists females before and after baptism but never enters the baptismal pool.

"Carryin' the Basket," Feeding the Church Family

Symbolically providing a model *for* the absolute obligation of women in the church communities studied, the Mothers provide actual food and spiritual nourishment for their families as long as they are physically able. "Carryin' the basket" means preparation of the Lord's Supper; care of the ritual implements used in serving the Supper; transportation of the sacrament and ritual implements to the church, and "settin' the Table" for the Supper. In the past, the Mother would actually bake the bread for the Supper, pressing it thin, dry, and wafer-like with a flat iron until it "cracked." The bread, wine, table linens, "pitcha," and "tumbla" from which all members of the Church Family would "drink the blood of Jesus," were carried to the church in the basket. The importance of this symbolic act is highlighted when elders are asked about past Mothers of the Church. They respond by saying, "you mean who carried the basket?" or, "lets see now, I think Mammy Austin was carryin' the basket abouts in them days." The symbolic significance of carrying the basket is so great at Zion that the same basket that has been used as long as the elders can remember is still carried by the current Mother of the Church. At other churches, however, carrying the basket, is a figure of speech. At many churches, both rural and urban, the deacons have taken over the act of "settin' the Table." This suggests a model *of* a changing social reality where men are responsible for providing food for the family.

The role of the Mother of the Church is changing at Zion. Earlier, Mothers had a greater role than at present in the "callin' of a pastor," and today they no longer as a matter of course offer religiously oriented advice to girls on how to enter the world of women. They continue to participate in the ritual symbolism of the ceremonies marking a pastor's installation or the anniversary of it, and they continue to symbolically carry the basket. As birthing and healing functions are relinquished, the Mothers are taking on economic roles in the sociopolitical organization of the church.

Despite changing, the role of the Mother of the church remains central to rural Afro-Baptist cosmology. Its significance is highlighted by the morning worship service on Mother's Day. This ceremony is second only to funerals in attendance. Family members, affines, and fictive kin who do not attend any other ceremony will travel hundreds of miles to return to the "church home" for Mother's Day services.

Intra-Cultural and Cross-Cultural Parallels

The Mother of the Church plays a principal role in every rural Floridian Afro-Baptist church I studied except one. The one exception is a church that was formed after the Civil War by a split of a white church between former slave masters and their former slaves. All of the other churches were founded independently by slaves before Emancipation or former slaves and their descendants during the Reconstruction or PostReconstruction period. Interestingly, two churches formed by splinter groups of the church without a Mother have had a Mother of the Church since their inception.

The Mother of the Church has been identified in other southern churches, both rural and urban, and to date the role has also been identified in three northern urban churches. A similar role is found among the Jamaica Revivalists (Reynolds 1988; Barrett 1977; Hogg 1964; Simpson 1956; Beckwith 1929, 1923). Mothers have also been identified in video documentation of contemporary Spiritual Baptists in Tobago, another group with ethnohistorical linkages to antebellum Afro-Americans (Trinidad and Tobago Television 1983). A similar title is given to the wife of Simon Kimbangu (Martin 1975). The Kimbanguist is an African Christian church based in Zaire that has linkages to American Baptist missionaries, including many Afro-Americans and Afro-Jamaicans who were there from 1840 to 1916 (Brown 1986b). The symbolism inherent in the role of Mother of the Church seems to call to people of African origins who come in contact with the Baptist denomination.

ONTOLOGICAL IMPLICATIONS

By providing models *of* and models *for* ideal womanhood, the roles of ritual authority among women in Afro-Baptist churches in rural Florida reinforce the procreative, life-affirming qualities of the female and thereby transmit these qualities from one generation to another. These positive models are reaffirmed by inclusion into the church's oral traditions. Indeed, I never heard a sermon in Florida emphasizing negative Biblical models of women, such as Jezebel or Delilah.

It has been suggested that the religious symbolism found in the Afro-Baptist churches depict "images of women *reduced* . . . to their sexual function . . . arising from mythical beliefs that . . . female sexuality is polluting . . . and a conceptualization of the female image as evil" ([emphasis added] Hoch-Smith and Spring 1978). On the contrary, it is argued here that the metaphoric grounding of the ritual and symbolic representation of women in Motherhood, as found in the Afro-Baptist church, is related to the creative energy of human reproductive capacities. The positive force of this energy and the nurturing and the sustaining qualities of women have enabled peoples of African descent to transcend historical and contemporary societal constraints imposed upon their sociocultural survival and growth. The qualities of ideal womanhood and the symbolism implicit in the Mother of the Church "family" represent the integration of a moral philosophy and cultural praxes grounded in traditional African values. Moreover, it is argued that women's roles of ritual authority serve ontological purposes of providing models *of* and models *for* the Afro-American family, models that have been a major factor in contributing to its survival and evolution.

The symbolic reaffirmation of the roles of women in Afro-American society as found in the rural Floridian Afro-Baptist churches is articulated once a year at Women's Day. As part of a tradition that dates to the late nineteenth and early twentieth century (A. S. Jacobs 1985; Burroughs 1901–61), a woman, usually of higher education, describes the qualities that women should possess in an address delivered in rhythmic meter, which is poetry.

Praise Poem to the Afro-Baptist Woman: Excerpts of a Women's Day Address

A virtuous *woman is a perfect gift* . . .
A spirit-filled *woman*
Is truly a wonder . . .
Surrounded by trouble
She will not *go* under.
She calls on the Living God *for strength*
She is indeed a gift.

The righteous *woman is up by dawn.*
To put the Holy Armor of God on
For she knows she must fight
In order to win
The escalating war against Satan *and* Sin . . .

Let us be grateful for this gift . . .

When God made the Universe . . .

and all that we see . . .
He knew man's life would not always be a bed
of roses . . .
So He prepared *for it.*

In my mind I can imagine
The Almighty God in his heavenly worship
Preparing women *to be* present . . .
At the right time
At the right place
At history's unfolding.

Back in Genesis, God considered Abraham
That in order to make him
Father *of the* Faithful
He needed a Mother *of* Nations

So God took a lump of clay
He rolled it around in his hand
And shaped it in his own image
And in his own likeness . . .

He put in some Faith
A pinch of Courage
A length of Longevity
Blew into it the breadth of life
and gave it to Abraham . . .
The Mother of Nations *. . . her name was Sara*

and history kept on rolling along.

After God arranged for Moses
To go down into Egypt
To bring the children out . . .
And Pharaoh's Army was drowning . . .
He needed someone else to lead the Children of
Israel
In A Song *of* Victory *and* Thanksgiving *. . .*

So God reached down
And scooped up some clay
He fashioned it in His own image
He put in Love
He put in Hope
He put in a Song
And presented the Children of Israel
With Miriam, the Sister of Moses

And she Sa . . . ang
. . . I will sing unto the Lord
For He has triumphed gloriously . . .
The Lord is my Strength
And thy psalm
He has become my Salvation
My Faith
And I will Exalt *Him . . .*

As history kept unfolding
God kept preparing women
to meet the needs *of* His *people*
When Naomi felt empty
And bitter about the tragedies in her life . . .
God foresaw her condition
And He reached down

And took a lump of clay
Rounded it in His own hand
Until He made it in His own image . . .

He put in some Compassion
Put in some Loyalty
Put in Friendship
Blew into it the breath of life
And there was Ruth
Daughter-in-law to Naomi
Saying . . . "Treat me not
to leave thee
Nor return from following after thee
For your people shall be my people
And your God my God . . ."

I thank God for this great gift
of Virtuous Woman
And you ought to thank God
For the Gift of BEING a Woman . . .

When the Jews needed courage
God gave them the gift of Esther

God has been taking care of his own for a long
time
Then in his foresight God thought and thought
The world got so wicked
And sin was so widespread
That the use of offering and sacrifice
Was not enough *to pay for the* Sins *of* Mankind

So God thought and thought and thought
He said . . .
I know *what the world needs*
The world needs a Savior
Perfect, Blameless, Faultless, Pure . . .

He looked over the vast wilderness of Glory . . .

And He found nothing
And no one worthy
So he said . . .
I will give my only . . .
My ONLY . . .
Begotten Son . . .
a body . . .
Let him be Born of a *WOMAN*

You know the story . . .

So God reached out . . .
He gathered up some clay . . .
He rounded it in his hand . . .

He shaped it . . .
He put in Faith
He put in Purity
He put in Holiness
He put in Long Suffering
He put in a Song of Praise
. . . and handed the world the gift
. . . of Virgin Mary *. . .*

and she said . . .
    "My soul doth magnify the Lord
    My spirit has rejoiced in God
    my Savior
    For He has reconsidered
    His lowly handmaiden
    All generations shall call me . . . What? . . .
    BLESSED.

"Blessed . . . Blessed . . . Blessed," the other women rejoice.

—Sister Lillie Mae McIntyre
Women's Day Address
Union Baptist Church
Dunellon, Florida, 1984
(Brown 1983–84)

Notes

1. Sister Bostick had been raised by her older brother, who was a pastor, and his wife. Her grandfather was the founding deacon of Ol' Ship of Zion Missionary Baptist Church. Both her maternal and paternal grandmothers had been Mother's of the Church. She referred to herself as a pastor's daughter although in reality she was not. However she was a key informant whose knowledge of the church social forms was extremely valuable.

2. I found through oral history and observation that the husbands of women who were descendants of the church founding families were in most cases elected to the Deaconate, making it possible for their wives to become deaconesses. Although there were "incomer" married couples in the church, i.e., persons not descendants of the founding families, who might have been eligible to become deacons or deaconesses, the only "incomer" males elected were persons who had married into the community.

3. The choir is also a group of informal ritual specialists. They are not discussed here because they include members of all ages and both sexes.

4. Miss Mary died in her sleep at age 93 in April 1987.

5. In February 1988 the Lord called Aunt Sista, Harriet Lewis, Acting Mother of the Church, home a few weeks short of her 85th birthday, while the Mother of the Church, Cousin Reason, lives on at age 94 in June 1988.

6. During a recent access site visit to Jamaica in preparation for activating a Fulbright Senior Research Scholar award which I have received for the 1988–89 cycle, "Kapo," the Patriarch of St. Michael's Revival Tabernacle told me that today women "bishops" were allowed to baptize. He stated that "they knew when they shouldn't go in the water because of their nature," alluding to women's menses. However, the women "bishops" and "evangelists, two of each, whom I observed during the Pentacostal services at St. Michael's all appeared to be

around fifty or older, apparently past their child-bearing years. The Patriarch said his bands had been studied in the fifties by "Eaton George Simpson" and in the sixties by Dr. Edward Seaga.

References Cited

Barrett, Leonard. 1977. African religion in the Americas: The islands in between. In *African religions: A symposium,* ed. Newell S. Booth, pp. 183–216. New York: NOK Publishers Ltd.

Beckwith, Maria. 1923. Some religious cults in Jamaica. *American Journal of Psychology* 34:32–34.

Beckwith, Maria. 1929. *Black roadways: A study of Jamaica folklife.* Chapel Hill, NC: University of North Carolina Press.

Bostick, Elizabeth, age 72 in 1984. Oral history interview with Audrey L. Brown (transcription and audiotape) for Oral History Project, Center for Florida Studies, Florida State Museum, University of Florida, Gainesville, directed by Dr. Samuel Proctor.

Brown, Audrey L. Manuscript a. Gimme that ol' time religion: African continuities in ritual authority of folk Afro-Baptist church communities: Cross-cultural comparative analysis, Jamaica Revivalists and Kimbanguists of Zaire. (unpublished manuscript.)

Brown, Audrey L. Manuscript b. To Africa with love: Contributions of Afro-American Missionaries to the Kongo Motherland. (unpublished manuscript.)

Burroughs, Nannie. 1910–1961. Papers of Nannie Burroughs. Division of Manuscripts, Library of Congress.

A concise history of Canaan Baptist Church. 1966 [1945]. Ocala, FL: Florida Watchman Press.

Cook, Mary V. 1890. The work for Baptist women. In *The Negro Baptist pulpit,* ed. E. M. Brawley, pp. 271–86. Philadelphia, PA: American Baptist Publication Society.

Dwelle, J. H. [ca. 1913]. *A brief history of black Baptists in North America.* Pittsburgh, PA: Pioneer Printing Press.

Geertz, Clifford. 1966. Religion as a cultural system. In *Anthropological approaches to the study of religion,* ed. Michael Banton, pp. 1–46. London: Tavistock Publications.

Geertz, Clifford. 1973. Thick description. In *The Interpretation of Culture: Selected essays,* ed. Clifford Geertz, pp. 3–30. New York: Basic Books.

Geertz, Clifford. 1983. Blurred genre: The refiguration of social thought. In *Local knowledge: Further essays in interpretive anthropology,* ed. Clifford Geertz, pp. 19–35. New York: Basic Books.

Hoch-Smith, Judith, and Anita Spring. 1978. *Women in ritual and symbolic roles.* New York: Plenum Press.

Hogg, Donald W. 1964. Jamaican religions: A study in variations. Ph.D diss., Yale University.

Jacobs, Annie Reason Staggers. 1984–1986. Personal communication with cousin Ree, Mother of the Church and a pastor's daughter, age 92 in 1986.

Jordan, Lewis G. 1930. *Negro Baptist history 1750–1930.* Nashville, TN: The Sunday School Publishing Board, National Baptist Convention.

Journal of the thirty-second annual session of the National Baptist Convention. 1913. Nashville, TN: National Baptist Publishing Board.

Martin, Marie L. 1975 [1971]. *Kimbangu, an African prophet and his church,* trans. D. M. Moore. Grand Rapids, MI: William B. Erdman.

McKenzie, Hermione. 1977. Caribbean women: Yesterday, today, tomorrow. *Savacou* 13(June):viii–xv.

Reynolds, "Kapo" Mallica. 1988. Personal communication with the patriarch of St. Michaels Revival Tabernacle and its "bands" in other parishes, Kingston, Jamaica. "Kapo" was 77 in 1988.

Simpson, George E. 1956. Jamaica revival cults. *Social and Economic Studies* 5(4):1434.

The Baptist General State Convention of Florida. 1939–1940. *Guide for senior missionary workers of the Women's Missionary and Educational Convention.* (Prepared by Mrs. H. D. Parker [a pastor's wife].) Ocala, Florida: Florida Watchman Press.

Trinidad and Tobago Television. *The African presence in Trinidad and Tobago,* Parts I, II, III (120 minute videotape) Joy Gouldner, Producer, ca. 1983.

We Got Our Way of Cooking Things: Women, Food, and Preservation of Cultural Identity among the Gullah

Josephine A. Beoku-Betts
Sociologist

Josephine A. Beoku-Betts's research focuses on the significance of the historical and cultural roles of women in preserving the culture of African American Sea Island communities in Georgia and South Carolina. She also researches Third World development issues especially as they relate to the gender implications of science and technology policies in Africa, in training and employment. She is currently teaching at Florida Atlantic University in the Women's Studies department.

Food preparation and dietary practices have rarely been studied by sociologists, although they hold great potential for an understanding of gendered social relations, knowledge construction, and cultural identity in communities. Because this area of work and cultural activity traditionally has been viewed as a "natural role" for women,

Josephine A. Beoku-Betts, "We Got Our Way of Cooking Things: Women, Food, and Preservation of Cultural Identity among the Gullah," Gender & Society 9 (5) (1995): 535–555.

AUTHOR'S NOTE: This article is a revised version of presentations given at the annual meetings of the American Folklore Society, Jacksonville, Florida, October, 1992, and the South East Women's Studies Association, Nashville, Tennessee, April, 1993. The data were gathered under grants received from the University of Georgia Research Foundation and the University of Wisconsin-Madison, Summer Faculty Mini-Grant. I wish to thank Linda Grant, Jude Preissle, Doris Slesinger, Edward Wellin, the editor, and the two anonymous reviewers for their challenging comments and helpful advice on earlier versions of the article. My special thanks also go to the Gullah families who welcomed me so warmly into their homes and the many women who shared their experiences with me.

its value has not been acknowledged seriously or appreciated in the production of cultural knowledge systems (Smith 1987, 18–9). Analysis of the relationship between women and food preparation practices, however, can broaden our understanding of the construction and maintenance of tradition in culturally defined systems, a neglected aspect of the study of social organization within the discipline of sociology. Feminist studies show that examination of this aspect of women's work clarifies the character and significance of women's household activities (DeVault 1991; Oakley 1974). Even though food preparation perpetuates relations of gender inequality in the household, under given circumstances it can provide a valued identity, a source of empowerment for women, and a means to perpetuate group survival (DeVault 1991, 232).

This article illuminates how women, as primary actors responsible for managing and preparing food in the household and the community, contribute to our understanding of the formation and continuance of food-related cultural practices in Gullah communities . . . although food preparation, under pressure of dominant cultural practices, may be viewed as a measure of gender inequality and of women's subordination in the household, it also can promote resistance and strengthen cultural identity in marginalized cultural groups.

By drawing on the analytical constructs of an Afrocentric value system (self-reliance, women-centered networks, the use of dialogue and connectedness with community, spirituality, and extended family), Black feminist studies provide a framework for conceptualizing knowledge construction and cultural identity from the perspective of Black women's lives (Gilkes 1988; Gray White 1985; Collins 1990; Reagon 1986; Steady 1981; Terborg-Penn 1987). These studies show that cultural beliefs, values, and traditions are transmitted largely in women-dominated contexts such as the home, the church, and other community settings.

• • •

Historically in Gullah communities, both men and women have played a vital role in procuring and preparing the food necessary for their families' survival. Studies, however, reveal very few examples of men's activities in domestic food preparation. Food preparation in Gullah households tends to be gender-specific and organized around particular tasks; each successive task is more highly gender-stratified. Although men are more likely to engage in activities such as hunting, fishing, gardening, and preparing meat and seafood for cooking and barbecues, women also participate in these activities when they choose to do so. Although most men are knowledgeable about cooking, and most mothers seem to teach both their sons and daughters how to cook, men rarely cook regularly in the household. Women more often take responsibility for cooking and feeding, and they appear to be the custodians of food rituals and practices that perpetuate the group's survival.

DATA SOURCES
AND ANALYSIS

This study uses ethnographic data based on my field observations and semistructured interviews with 22 Gullah women in the Sea Islands and neighboring mainland communities in South Carolina (Wadmalow, St. Helena, John's, Edisto, and Coosaw Islands) and Georgia (Sapelo and St. Simon's Islands, and Harris Neck community) over several visits made between 1989 and 1992. My research interest in this region stems from my background as an African scholar who was raised in a West African rice-cultivating society; later I conducted research on rural households and rice cultivation in that society. As a result, I felt that I was uniquely prepared to examine historical and cultural connections in the food practices of West African and Gullah rice cultures. To collect naturalistic observational data on the significance of Gullah food practices, I arranged to stay with selected families in two of the communities I studied. I also kept a journal of my daily experiences and observations while living with my host families.

Women participating in the study were drawn from each of the communities mentioned above. The criteria for selection were that they were descendants of formerly enslaved African Americans from these islands and that they had been raised there. I found participants through key individuals and community organizations. Through snowballing and by a process of proving my credibility as an African woman researcher interested in making cultural connections between the rice culture of West Africa and the rice culture of the Gullah, I selected a number of women willing to work with me as study participants.

• • •

The strategies I used to gain access and establish trust among the participants varied according to the situation of each community. In communities where local residents seemed to be better informed about their African heritage, I worked under the auspices of key individuals and community groups. Sometimes they sent a representative to accompany me to interviews and extended invitations to social events to which I might not have had access otherwise. In other communities, where local residents seemed more reluctant to talk to outside researchers because of negative experiences in the past, it worked to my advantage to distance myself from my university affiliation and to engage myself in the life of these communities. In one community, regular attendance at church services and midday meals at a local community center helped me develop a kinlike relationship with two respected senior women. They taught me the importance of being associated as the guest, relative, or friend of a respected person to gain acceptance among community residents.

Study participants range in age from 35 to 75. They include nine widows living alone or with their children or grandchildren, two single parents, and eleven married women living with their families. Most of the younger women are employed in service or public-sector jobs; the older women are more likely to be homemakers or retired from wage employment. Although the youngest respondent has two years of college education and the oldest has no formal schooling, education for the majority ranges from completion of the third to the twelfth grade. All names used in the study are pseudonyms.

Eight other women whom I asked to interview declined to participate in the study. Most of these women came from one particular community and were the daughters of older women who were participating. They were more ambivalent about my presence than were their mothers because they felt that past experiences with university researchers or journalists had proved to be exploitative. Time constraints from family responsibilities and wage employment also contributed to these women's reluctance to participate.

In analyzing the interviews with study participants, I regarded their narratives both as individual accounts of daily experiences in managing food practices and as a form of custodianship and conveyance of oral traditions about the significance of the Gullah food system. I took this approach because many of the interviews contained an element of reflection about the past as a backdrop for commentary on the present. Although some of this reflection was deliberate because of my interest in establishing historical and cultural connections, the participants and the other community members to whom I spoke also tended to organize their talk so as to provide a background to contextualize their meaning.

• • •

The data were transcribed almost verbatim, although I did some light editing (such as inserting explanatory or connecting words in a bracket) or excluded small sections of an interview when the material seemed somewhat peripheral to the issue under discussion. After transcribing the taped data, I searched for themes repeated in both taped and untaped interviews, focusing on the rituals and management of food preparation over several stages of the process. My aim was to develop a detailed understanding of these ritual practices in the Gullah household. By looking for detailed, perhaps even mundane, information about each stage of food preparation, styles of cooking, flavors of food, eating practices, and (if possible) the meanings attached to these practices, I hoped to show any variety occurring among households and to establish connections for historical and sociological analysis. I also used my daily journal entries to provide context when analyzing the data.

THE SIGNIFICANCE OF THE GULLAH

Gullah communities in the Sea Islands and neighboring mainland regions in Georgia and South Carolina provide a unique opportunity to study some of the distinctive elements of African cultural influences on African American culture in the United States. Despite variations in the demographic structures and economic practices of communities on or near these islands, strong similarities exist in proximity of location and in historical and cultural background. One significant characteristic of these communities, for example, is that most residents are descendants of enslaved Africans who worked on these islands as early as the seventeenth century. Beginning in that period, Africans were captured and transported as slaves from various regions in Africa, extending from Angola to the Upper Guinea Coast region of West Africa. Between 1670 and 1800, however, Africans from rice-cultivating regions in West Africa, such as Liberia, Sierra Leone, Senegal, Gambia, and Guinea, were sought because of their knowledge of cultivation of rice, which was then a lucrative crop in Georgia and South Carolina

(Holloway 1990, 4; Littlefield 1981; Wood 1974). Rice planters were particularly interested in enslaving Africans from the "Rice Coast" of West Africa because the planters themselves lacked knowledge about rice cultivation in tropical conditions. The system of rice cultivation adopted in these coastal regions of Georgia and South Carolina drew on the labor patterns and technical knowledge of the enslaved West Africans (Littlefield 1981; Opala 1987; Wood 1974).

Because of the geographical isolation of these islands, cohesive communities evolved and preserved African cultural traditions more fully than in any other group of African Americans in the United States. These traditions are represented in the Gullah language spoken among Sea Islanders, in birth and naming practices, in folktales, in handicrafts such as grass-basket weaving, carved walking sticks, and fishing nets, in religious beliefs and practices, and in a food culture based on rice (Creel 1990; Georgia Writers' Project [1940] 1986; Jones-Jackson 1987; Opala 1987; Turner 1949).

Today the sources of livelihood in these Sea Island communities vary according to available economic opportunities. In communities such as John's, Wadmalow, Edisto, St. Helena, Ladies, and Hilton Head Islands, many inhabitants are engaged in the vegetable truck industry; others are involved in fishing, crabbing, and marketing of crafts. Most of the young and the old in these communities garden, fish, hunt, and sell crafts and other services to supplement their incomes (Jones-Jackson 1987, 17). As a result of development of the tourist industry, such as on Hilton Head and St. Simon's Islands, many inhabitants (particularly women) work in minimum wage service positions. Limited employment opportunities on islands still inaccessible by bridge, such as Sapelo Island in Georgia and Daufuskie Island in South Carolina, have led many of the younger or more highly educated community members to seek work elsewhere, causing an imbalance in the age structure of their populations. Sapelo Island, for example, has a population of just 67 people; a disproportionate number are in the economically dependent years, over 60 and under 18.

CONNECTIONS BETWEEN THE NATURAL ENVIRONMENT AND GULLAH FOOD PRACTICES

The value of self-sufficiency in food supply is an integral aspect of the Gullah food system. Men and women of all ages are conversant with hunting, fishing, and gardening as ways to provide food. From an early age, both men and women are socialized into the concept and the practice of self-sufficiency as a primary goal of the food system and are encouraged to participate in the outdoor food-procuring activities of parents and other kin or community members. Velma Moore, a woman in her mid-40s and a key participant in my study, became sensitive to environmental causes when, as a child, she accompanied both parents on daily walks in the woods. This experience taught her a variety of survival skills involving the use of the island's natural resources for subsistence and medicine. She learned how and where to collect medicinal herbs, and when and for what purpose they should be used. She also learned various folk remedies that had been passed down in her family for generations, such as life ever-lasting tea for colds or leaves of the mullien plant for fever. Velma recollected that when she was a child, her mother kept these herbs on hand in the kitchen and stood over a reluctant patient to make sure every sip of the tea was consumed. Now married and the mother of five children, Velma pointed out that she encourages the practice of these traditions among her sons and daughters. She even performs regionally as a storyteller and writes local newspaper articles about the significance of these traditions in her culture.

Grandparents also play an important role in developing children's skills in food self-sufficiency. A typical example was Maisie Gables, a lively and active woman about 70 years of age. When I interviewed Miss Maisie, as she was called, I did not know that our scheduled appointments conflicted with her plans to go fishing with her five-year-old granddaughter, whom she was teaching to fish. Miss Maisie explained later that her granddaughter liked fishing from an early age, so she had decided to cultivate this interest by teaching her the necessary skills, as she had once been taught by her mother. By transmitting these skills, which are part of collective memory, the senior generation of Gullah women fosters and sustains cultural identity intergenerationally, thus broadening the base of cultural knowledge in the community.

While the Gullah depend on their natural surroundings as a reliable source of food, they also have a deep understanding of their coexistence with other living things and believe that the use of these resources should be moderate and nonexploitative. This sense of shared membership in the natural environment stems from Gullah belief systems, which emphasize harmony and social exchange between the human and the natural world. Such a view is influenced by African spiritual beliefs, which are community centered and involve a set of relationships involving God, the ancestors, other human beings (including those yet unborn), and other living and nonliving things. In this complex system of relationships, the well-being of the whole is paramount; individual existence is woven into the whole.[1]

Some aspects of this worldview are reflected in my interview with Velma Moore. She describes herself as a self-taught woman, although "self-taught" does not adequately describe her intelligence, strong will, and vast knowledge of Gullah history and culture. During one interview, she revealed that she, like many Gullah women, had been taught to hunt and would do so if necessary. Even so, she considered herself a keen environmentalist, with concern for the protection of nature, and would not engage in such activities for recreation because "it is not sporting to go up and kill animals that can't shoot you back." In other words, although she would rely on these resources for survival, anything beyond that purpose would threaten the harmony with nature.

Velma also expressed concern about the threat of environmental destruction in the region, a result of increasing tourism and economic development. She conceptualized this problem in connection with the struggle to preserve her own endangered cultural heritage:

> I always felt that if you don't deal with one and the other, if you just strictly deal with one, then you're losing the rest of it. Because you cannot have stabilization in a minority

community in this area here unless you recognize the culture and the environment. And if you mess up the environment, and you move the people away because the environment is not right, then you are taking away their culture at the same time. So if you take away their land, you are also taking away the culture when you move the people, and so forth. (Velma Moore, 1991)

In making this connection between the threat of environmental destruction and the survival of her own cultural heritage, Velma reveals an awareness of her relationship, represented by culture, with other living beings, both human and nonhuman. She does not distinguish between the two because she perceives them as natural allies in a struggle to protect tradition from the intrusion of dominant cultural practices. Because both are woven into her existence, the survival of one depends on that of the other and must be defined and challenged from this standpoint.

Interviews with Gullah women suggest that engagement in fishing, gardening, hunting, and other outdoor activities is not based strictly on gender role divisions. Although many of the outdoor activities related to food procurement are men's domain, women are more likely to be associated with these activities than men are with activities regarded as women's domain. In other words, it seems that at each successive stage of food preparation (which can overlap somewhat), work activities become more gender-specific. This is true, for example, of role expectations in some fishing activities, such as men's use of the cast-net method and women's use of the reel and rod method.

• • •

Women make judgments about what is appropriate for them, which give them some flexibility in choosing activities they wish to pursue. In the Moore family, for instance, Velma's husband and son were responsible for planting vegetable crops for their garden, while Velma took responsibility for weeding and maintaining the garden. Velma, however, also expected their help in weeding because she did not want to be burdened with an activity that is monotonous and unpopular among men. Similar attitudes were revealed in my discussions with these women:

INTERVIEWER: Do you both do the same type of fishing?

VELMA MOORE: Well, yes and no. We both fish with the reel rod and he fishes with the cast net more than I do, although occasionally I go fishing with the cast net, too. But he basically does that.

INTERVIEWER: But you do cast-net fishing, too?

VELMA: Oh yeah. Most of us women here can. Most—I retract that—most of the older womens here can.

INTERVIEWER: You mean you still go hunting?

WILLIETTA DAVIES: Um hum. Like we [self and husband] go hunting for coon and thing in the night. We goes with the truck. We usually go at night anywhere around the island. I use an A-22 gun and a flashlight. I like to take the light and blind their eyes. I catch the eyes of that raccoon, and I stop and shoot.

INTERVIEWER: What do you catch?

WILLIETTA: Raccoon, possum.

INTERVIEWER: I can't believe that (laugh).

WILLIETTA: That's the only two sport I like now. I don't go dancing and I don't drink. I like to go [hunting] and fishing, and that's the truth. I love it.

THE CENTRALITY OF RICE
IN GULLAH CULTURE

Dependence on rice as a staple food is the most significant way the Gullah express cultural identity through food practices. Rice is the main food that links Gullah dietary traditions with the food traditions of West African rice cultures; women play a primary role in fostering the continuance of these practices. In such cultures a person is not considered to have eaten a full meal unless rice is included.

Although most Gullah families no longer cultivate rice regularly, people are still conscious of its significance. Rice was described as the central part of the main family meal by at least 90 percent of the women I interviewed. Typical were responses like

It's the one that makes us fat because we go to sleep on it. . . . My father used to say, "Eat something that sticks to your rib." (Velma Moore, 1991)

Many people feel if rice isn't cooked, they haven't eaten. Take my grandson, for instance. No matter what you cook, whether it's potatoes or macaroni, you have to prepare a separate portion of rice for him. Otherwise he'll feel like he hasn't eaten. (Carla Bates, 1989)

Rice is security. If you have some rice, you'll never starve. It is a bellyful. You should never find a cupboard without it. (Precious Edwards, 1992)

Well, they have to have that rice 'cause, see, they be working hard at the farm and they have to have something to give them strength. They don't hardly bother with too much grits. They eat that grits in the morning now. But when dinnertime come they have to have that rice. They always say that Black people like too much rice. They don't eat like the white people. I don't know why they always say so. (Wilma Davies, 1991)

Because of Gullah women's daily involvement in food preparation in the home, they are very conversant with the stories and traditions passed down in their families about the significance of rice to their culture. On the occasions when I stayed as a guest in study participants' homes and helped prepare evening meals, women often shared stories and folktales with me, as well as songs and dances connected with their rice culture. On Sapelo Island I learned about formerly enslaved women who prepared special rice cakes made with honey for their families on particular days and months of the year, in observance of Muslim religious festivals.[2] Women also told me about folk traditions such as a song called "Blow Tony Blow." This accompanied a traditional dance still performed by Gullah women at cultural festivals to demonstrate how rice grain was removed from its husk with a flat, round, woven grass-basket called a fanner.

Several elderly women also recalled a time when rice held such a special place in their communities that children were not permitted to eat it except on Sundays or special occasions:

They have folklore on rice down here. One of the things we grew up with, for instance, after the birth of a child you wasn't given rice—no rice. Because rice is supposed to been too starchy for the newborn baby to digest through the mother's milk, and so you wasn't given rice to eat at all. (Velma Moore, 1991)

Some of the old folks believe that rice was also a cure for sick chickens, believe it or not. If your chicken were looking like they were kind of sick, you was to feed them raw rice, and it supposed to make them feel better. So they will take raw rice and toss them in the chicken yard. (Velma Moore, 1991)

I've known people to parch rice and make their coffee. Put it in the frying pan or something, and you toss it lightly and keep shaking it lightly until it brown—you mix it and you can drink it, and you put water and you make [it] like coffee. (Velma Moore, 1991)

• • •

Although pressure from a dominant culture may weaken their ability to reproduce their knowledge and perceptions of themselves and of their world, the ability to remember and to create a communion of memory in the group provides the foundation for establishing membership and continuity of that group. A parallel can be drawn in the role of Gullah women in maintaining a sense of shared tradition through food practices. Through their recollections of stories and songs and in their performance of dances and enactments of past traditions, they create a frame of reference alternative to those promoted in the dominant culture, while at the same time transmitting collective memory to the next generation.

One way of promoting an alternative frame of value reference through food practices is in the daily observance of strict rituals of rice preparation. In Gullah and West African rice cultures, for example, it is typical to commence the preparation of rice by picking out any dirt or dark looking grains from the rice before washing it. Then the rice is washed vigorously between the hands a number of times before it is considered clean enough for cooking. As a girl growing up in Sierra Leone, I was taught to cook rice in this way. I still follow this practice faithfully, even though most of the rice available for sale today in the United States is labeled as prewashed.

Whenever Gullah women speak of cooking rice, they distinguish between the various types of grains before explaining which cooking method will be most appropriate for a particular grain. They also take pride in describing the proper texture and consistency of a well-cooked pot of rice, although the suggestion that food must have a particular appearance to be satisfying is as culturally specific to the Gullah as to other ethnic groups.[3] Indeed, the belief that well-cooked rice must be heavy to be filling to the stomach is a cultural trait that the Gullah share with many African societies that eat heavy staple foods (Bascom 1977, 83; Friedman 1990, 83).

Gullah women also control the interaction of their food practices with those of the dominant culture by emphasizing the preferred place of rice in the main meal. For example, even though foods associated with other ethnic groups are generally eaten in Gullah families (e.g., lasagna, pizza, hamburgers), the women I interviewed tend to categorize such foods as snacks, not meals. To illustrate this point, the following discussion took place between me and one participant.

BETTY: Well, occasionally there is, you know, maybe lasagna. That is an occasional thing. Um, pizza is something that the kids love. And we have that like—that is never a meal. That's like if you have a bunch of guys dropping over and you are going to have pizza and pop, or tea, and a salad, you know, something like that. But it is never a meal, never.

INTERVIEWER: For you it is like a snack.

BETTY: Yeah, it is more like a snack. Yeah, definitely. It's like a snack. . . . You need to have some type of rice. (Betty Smith, 1992)

In the following accounts of how various women cook a pot of white rice, we see how Gullah women establish cultural boundaries by situating rice at the center of their food system:

INTERVIEWER: How do you like to prepare your rice?

MAISIE: Well, I scrub it real good with water. With my hands scrub all that dirt off it.

INTERVIEWER: Yes, that's how we do it too back home.

MAISIE: I know, I'd say most Black people [do that]. Some Black people don't wash it you know, they try to take the vitamins from it. How can you eat all them germs? [If] I can't wash it [then] I don't want it. Then I put [the rice] in my pot and just put enough water, you know, to steam it without draining it off. I don't drain my rice. That's it. (Maisie Gables, 1991)

Two others commented

Well, I don't like it real dry and I don't like it real soft. Just medium. Some people, they cook their rice so that all the grain just fall apart, but I don't like it real dry. I wash all that stuff off. Pick those strings and things out of it 'cause you have to take all that out. So we wash it good. Now the one that you plant and beat yourself has more starch on it than the one you buy at the store. And you have to wash it real good. [Then] I average the water, put a little soda in it. I don't use so much salt now. And if it have too much water on it, I pour it off. Then I let it boil according to what kind of heat—now that you have electric or gas stove, now you see you turn it down medium until it soak down. I don't wait until it get real moist. Even up [turn the heat] on it to steam it down. (Willietta Davies, 1991)

and

Gosh, some of that depends on the rice too because you got short grain rice, you got long grain rice. And sometime you tend to fix one a little different from the other. I basically starts mine in cold water, I wash it in the same pot. I will just pour it in the pot. We don't measure it. So I just pour it in the pot what I think the amount I need. I go to the sink and I'll wash it . . . twice to clean it off. Pour the necessary water back on it and salt it and put it on the fire, and let it come to a full boil. The heat is usually reduced about three times, 'cause it's high until it starts boiling, then the middle, you let it cook a little normally for a while, then once all the water has evaporated or boiled into the rice, then you turn it real low so that it stay back there and soak and get just right. (Velma Moore, 1991)

Each of these examples reflects a sense of continuity of tradition as each stage of the process is described. For example, measurements are not discussed. This means that such recipes have been handed down by word of mouth and depend to some extent on one's particular taste. Also, each person emphasizes that the rice has to be washed well and that it must be cooked in just enough water to allow it to steam on its own, without the interference of draining or stirring. All of these descriptions might be said to follow a common tradition handed down from the period of slavery and still practiced in present-day West African rice cultures.

These examples also reveal that the task of cooking rice is laborious and time consuming. The Gullah, however, are fairly conservative in accepting innovations that might alter some of their existing practices. For example, labor-saving devices such as rice cookers, now in common use, do not seem to be used in the Gullah households I visited. One possible example of this cultural conservatism can be demonstrated in the story of a rice cooker I gave to a family with whom I often stay and with whom I had shared the joys of a rice cooker when they visited my home. Although they appreciated the gift and showed it off to neighbors and family members, on two subsequent visits I noticed that it was still in its box and that rice was cooked in the familiar way. The family's reluctance to use the cooker more regularly might imply a lack of respect for custom, as well as fear of jeopardizing the survival of a tradition that is already endangered.

• • •

RITUALS AND NORMS OF MEAL PREPARATION

Gullah culture is influenced strongly by rules and norms of West African food preparation. Many women who cook perpetuate these practices daily. One of these practices involves the selection, the amounts, and the combination of seasonings for food. These elements differentiate Gullah cooking practices from those of other cultures, according to many women I interviewed. Although the Gullah identify certain foods as their own, such as Hoppin' John (rice cooked with peas and smoked meat), red rice, rice served with a plate of shrimp and okra stew, and collard greens and cornbread, the interaction between European American, Native American, and African American food systems in the South has carried these popular southern dishes across ethnic lines. One way in which Gullah women try to control cultural boundaries in their way of cooking these foods, as distinct from other southern practices, is to assert that although similar foods are eaten by others in the South, their style of preparation and the type of seasonings they use are different. Just as most African cooking is characteristically well seasoned with salt, pepper, onions, garlic, and smoked meat and fish, Gullah food is flavored with a combination of seasonings such as onions, salt, and pepper, as well as fresh and smoked meats such as bacon, pigs' feet, salt pork, and (increasingly) smoked turkey wings (to reduce fat content). The Gullah women's views are expressed clearly in the following statements:

> **INTERVIEWER:** As an African American living in this area, what do you think makes the food you eat different?

Culture and what's available to you. I call it a "make do" society on Sapelo because you can't run to the supermarket to get things. We are plain cooking. We use salt, pepper, and onion as basic additives. Our flavoring comes from the type of meat we put in it. Bacon is white folks' food, pig tails, neck bones, and ham hock is what we use. Soul food is what other Americans call it, but we consider these to be foods we always ate. We never label ourselves or our food. (Velma Moore, 1991)

On Sapelo you got things like red peas and rice. You know, they cook the same things on that side over there too, but we assume that we have the monopoly on it, that nobody cooks it the way we cook it . . . although they call it the same thing, the ingredients may be a little different than they use, or the taste is definitely different. So it's considered Sapelo food. I mean very few places you go [where] they cook oysters and rice or they cook clam and gravy the way we do, and stuff like that. So we got our way of cooking things. So we pretty proud of calling it Sapelo food. Yes. (Vanessa Buck, 1989)

By claiming these features of the food system as their own through daily cooking practices, and by situating this knowledge in the community through the use of such words as "we" and "strictly ours," the Gullah women maintain the credibility and validity of a familiar and recognizable tradition in resistance to pressure to conform to dominant cultural practices.

A strong preference for food produced and prepared from natural ingredients is another norm of Gullah food practice. In many of my interviews, women stated that much of the food they prepare for their families is grown locally and naturally. When asked to comment on what makes Gullah food distinctive, Betty Smith, who is married, in her mid-40s, and an active community and church member, explains:

A lot of what we eat is locally grown. Not the rice, but everything else. We dabble in other things that are imported, but . . . I guess the type of food we eat is indigenous to this area. It's what we have kind of grown up on. Most of my food is still prepared traditionally. My rice is usually boiled. I don't buy parboiled rice. I don't buy too many processed foods.

Annie Willis, who is in her 70s and also is active in church and community activities, lamented the demise of locally grown foods and expressed concern about the quality, taste, and health implications of store-bought foods:

When I was a child coming up, we never used to put fertilizer in our crop to rush up the food. Food used to taste much better then than now. The old folks didn't have as many health problem as we are having and they ate all those forbidden foods. I think it's the fertilizers and chemicals they put in the food now. Seem to me that children were more healthy in those days than they are now. (Annie Willis, 1989)

The suggestion that the younger generation of Gullah may no longer prepare food strictly from naturally produced sources implies that the Gullah way of producing and preparing food is symbolically significant and a mark of their difference from other cultures. These statements also reflect a concern for the customs and traditions threatened by the influence of urban development in the region. By recalling a past that their foremothers and forefathers created, these women set a context in which the values of their community can be understood and reclaimed for future generations of Gullah.

The women's statements also reveal concern about the expectations of custom and tradition and how these can be accommodated to the demands of present-day family life and employment. Certainly many of the traditional foods eaten by the Gullah must be time-consuming to prepare, and one cannot always prepare them regularly if one has a full-time job or other commitments. How do women cope in these circumstances? Several women employed outside the home admitted that they had made some adjustments. Pat Forest, a 43-year-old woman who is employed full time as a nursing aide in a local health clinic, lives with her husband and four children, who range from 10 to 22 years of age. Because of the demands of her job and her role as primary caregiver in the family, I was not surprised to learn that she prepares red rice by using a precooked tomato-based sauce rather than cooking from scratch. Traditionalists in the community would frown on this type of cooking, however. Some women told me that they often save time by preparing part of the meal the night before serving it or that they might prepare traditional meals only on specific days of the week such as Saturday and Sunday. Some women even said that they simply do not set a time for the main evening meal until it is prepared to their satisfaction. Several also mentioned that they had taught their sons and daughters to take on some of the basic responsibilities of cooking, especially the daily pot of rice.

The ways in which these women manipulate time constraints to accommodate the customary demands of their food practices suggest efforts to uphold the central role of these food practices in the home, but also to exercise the flexibility needed for modern living. Although the women show respect for the culture and even express some guilt about failure to conform fully, their actions suggest that they are walking a fine line (albeit rationalized by time pressures): They are maintaining tradition while adjusting to modern influences that potentially might endanger that tradition.

In common with West African cultures, the Gullah tend to prepare excess amounts of food for a meal in case someone should pay a visit. In West Africa, in fact, it would be embarrassing for a host to prepare or send out for food for unexpected guests (Bascom 1951, 52; Finnegan 1965, 67). Even under the economic constraints facing many West African societies today, such a tradition is upheld as strongly as possible because it is still viewed as a mark of prestige for both the head of the household and the cook. Although the Gullah do not necessarily view this tradition as a symbol of prestige, some of its elements are common in many of the homes I visited while conducting this study. As Velma Moore explained to me:

> I'm always able to feed another person in my home. People [here] will automatically cook something more just in case a stranger drops in.

· · ·

EFFORTS TO TRANSMIT TRADITIONAL FOOD PRACTICES

Much effort is being made to keep these traditions alive through oral tradition and everyday practice. Observers are pessimistic about what the future holds for a people who now consider themselves an endangered species (Singleton 1982, 38). One of the leading concerns expressed by residents of these communities is that the survival of this coastal culture is threatened by the rapid economic growth and development of tourist centers in the region. According to Emory Campbell, director of the Penn Center on St. Helena Island, South Carolina:

> The Black native population of these islands is now endangered, and we don't have too much time to protect oysters, fish, and crab. Developers just come in and roll over who-ever is there, move them out or roll over them and change their culture, change their way of life, destroy the environment, and therefore the culture has to be changed. (Singleton, 1982, 38)

The lack of stable employment opportunities on these islands is also cause for con-cern, because it has created an imbalance in the age structure; a high percentage of young adults leave for employment elsewhere. Also, it is felt that the drive toward a more materialistic way of life in the region will lead, in the long term, to an array of social problems such as alcoholism, marital conflicts, and youth delinquency (Singleton 1982, 38). The task of transmitting cultural traditions to a rapidly declining younger generation of Gullah poses a challenge to those committed to preserving this way of life. Such transmission will be difficult unless the living context of the culture can be preserved according to Charles Joyner, a folklorist and scholar of Gullah history and culture (Nixon 1993, 56). The women I interviewed also expressed this attitude:

> You've got to have culture in order to make your community stable and stay in one place. And so how else can white people come in and say, "Oh, these people down here speak Gullah or Geechee," and want to learn more about your culture, but at the same time they want to buy your land and push you out. How can you come down and visit me in my area, but I'm hanging on by a thread because you want my area. What do you sup-pose they'll show their friends and talk about? You know, they'll say, "This used to be a Gullah community, a Geechee community, but now they all live there in the heart of Atlanta or someplace else." It's not going to work. You can't move papa from [here], sit him in the middle of Atlanta, and say, "Make your cast net." Who's he going to sell cast net to in the middle of Atlanta? . . . all of a sudden he'll die. So you can't move the cul-ture and tradition from one area and just plant it in another area. . . . You've got to nurture it here, pass it down, teach children, and so forth. It's a slow process. You've got to know how to do it and you can teach other people how to do it. (Velma Moore, 1991)

In view of these concerns, how does the analysis of women's role as carriers of food preparation practices inform us about cultural survival strategies among the Gullah? How do women transmit knowledge of these practices to the younger genera-tion? How do their strategies relate to emerging themes in the study of Black women?

Perhaps the most relevant context for understanding knowledge transmission among Gullah women may be African-derived cultural practices that stress mother-hood, self-reliance and autonomy, extended family, and community-centered networks (Collins 1990; Steady 1981). Each practice is centered in either the home or the com-munity, and the two spheres of activity are mutually reinforcing. Within these domains an alternative framework of identity is constructed and women serve as transmitters of cultural knowledge.

The concept of motherhood illustrates how women use their spheres of activity to transmit cultural traditions. Motherhood among the Gullah is not limited to a biological relationship, but also can embrace other relationships with women termed "other-mothers" (women who assist bloodmothers by sharing mothering responsibilities) (Collins 1990, 119). Othermothers may include grandmothers, sisters, aunts, or cousins who take on child care, emotional support, and even long-term responsibilities for rearing each other's children. According to Jones-Jackson (1987), "It is not unusual for a child [in the Sea Islands] to reach adulthood living not more than a block from the natural parent but residing with another relative who is perhaps childless or more financially secure" (p. 24). It is also common to see a neighbor helping to prepare a meal next door or being offered a meal without concern that parental permission would be required.

The concept of family extends beyond the nuclear family to include extended and even fictive family ties. Responsibilities and obligations within the family are defined in this context; they facilitate the development of family communities where relatives live close to each other, and promote cooperative values through shared roles and socialization practices. Women of all generations, as mothers and as extended- family members, play a critical role in fostering self-reliance and a sense of collective memory in their children of both genders. They do so through the daily preparation and eating of traditional foods and by using informal conversation to teach family history and cultural traditions.

I learned about the use of informal conversation when I attended a funeral at the home of a Gullah family. In the evening, after the funeral ceremonies were finished and most people had left, all the women of the family sat together in the living room with their children at their feet, eating and telling each other family stories. Someone asked about the people in a family photograph. My hostess described the context in which the photo was taken (which happened to be a family meal) and recalled each family member present, including the wife and mother, who was in the kitchen cooking when the photo was taken. Because children are expected to eventually manage their own lives, both sons and daughters are taught the skills of self-reliance through cooking. Parents believe that their children must know these things to survive in the wider culture.

Much of this socialization takes place around the mother or in the family, but much is also learned from trial and error. Velma Moore recalls:

> I learned to cook by trial and error and mama. Nobody teaches you how to cook, not over here. They allow you to play cook in the kitchen and watch them. Tradition always learned towards girls cooking, but that boy, if he was hungry, he was expected to go in there and fix something for himself. Not that he had to sit there and starve all week until somebody's sister come home. So he learned how to cook, just like his sisters did. If a parent was home and he was home, they'd come up and ask him, "Hey, you was home all day. How come you didn't put on the rice?" or "How come you didn't boil the beans or something?" And so they would ask him the question that they would ask girls. At least I know mama did (laugh).

Strong bonds between women are also established through women-centered networks, which promote cooperative values in child care and informal economic activities (such as grass-basket weaving and quilting), in the opportunity to share experiences and ideas and in fostering the development of positive self-images, self-affirming roles, and self-reliance as women (Bush 1986, 120; Collins 1990, 119; Steady 1981, 6). The social exchange of goods and services and the flow of information and ideas that emanate from this type of networking encourage the development of positive self-images and community awareness in the children in these communities. While staying with Gullah families, I often observed exchanging and giving of food and other goods and services among women and their families, although many people commented that this practice was declining. Often when people went fishing or gathered vegetables and pecans, the women sent these foods to neighbors and friends, especially elderly individuals or couples who could no longer move around easily.

Finally, as Jones (1986) points out, preparation and serving of food by Black women in a secular communion of fellowship "symbolize[s] the spiritual component of collective survival" (p. 230). Women who prepare food for church activities play a vital role in helping these community-centered institutions to become sites of cultural preservation and spiritual fellowship, because food is an integral part of the ritual activities associated with spiritual fellowship. During the planning of church functions such as church anniversaries, weddings, and funerals, women who are known for their skills in preparing particular dishes are usually asked to prepare foods such as collard greens, red rice, peas and rice, cornbread, and chicken.

> When we go on a church picnic, we have a little cook-out like hot dogs and hamburgers, stuff like that. When we have the anniversary of the church, we cook soul food. And we have collard greens, and string beans, butter beans, fried chicken, some kind of roasts, macaroni and cheese, cornbread, and red rice. (Bernice Brown, 1989)

> We eat our food every day on St. Helena Island, and we also eat it at church anniversaries, weddings, and funerals. When we raise money to help the church, like women's day, the pastor's anniversary, the choir anniversary, we cook our food. (Queenie Moore, 1989)

Some women, including a study participant from Wadmalow Island, also raise funds for their church by preparing meals for sale in their homes.[5] Organizing such a party often involved considerable work in preparing traditional dishes such as red rice, fried fish, barbecued pigs' feet, collard greens, and shrimps and okra served with rice. Usually, my informant's friends and relatives helped her to prepare the food. Members of the church congregation and other community members then were expected to show their support by attending the party and paying for the food as they would in a restaurant.

By extending food preparation to embrace the church family, the actions of women, who usually do this work, promote a sense of shared tradition and spiritual identity among church members, especially among youths and those who lack the time or talent to practice these traditions. This activity also reinforces community-centered networks by providing a context for dialogue, mutual mentoring, and spiritual development, especially among women in the community (Young 1992, 16).[6]

• • •

Notes

1. See Margaret Washington Creel (1990) and Patricia Jones-Jackson (1987, especially 24–28). A good background to African spiritual philosophy is John Mbiti (1969).
2. Former slaves Katie Brown and Shad Hall from Sapelo Island, Georgia, when interviewed by the Federal Writers' Project in the 1930s, vividly described a special rice cake made with honey that their African Muslim grandmother prepared for the family on particular Muslim fast days (Georgia Writers' Project [1940] 1986, 162, 167). Thomas Winterbottom ([1803] 1969), a British physician who worked in Sierra Leone at the end of the eighteenth century, also reported that the Muslims he encountered liked to make cakes of rice and honey.
3. One may find that even when a meal displays the qualities they claim it must have to be satisfying or filling, it still might not be acceptable to a given people if that food is not their preferred staple.
4. See Charles Joyner (1984, 96) for a description of how rice was cooked on some slave plantations in South Carolina, given by Goliah, who was enslaved on the plantation of Robert F. W. Allston.
5. Interview with May Taylor, Wadmalow Island, 1989.
6. Although I recognize the important contributions of Gullah women in the development of the Black church and in its spiritual leadership and community development activities, they have made this contribution at the expense of holding leadership positions. In the formal authority structure of African American churches, men generally control these positions. Women lack due recognition and status, and they continue to fight to attain a measure of power and influence in many Black churches. At the same time, they have shown different patterns of leadership within the church community by fostering a sense of collective autonomy and "woman consciousness" (Gilkes 1988, 228). Like the activities of women who organize voluntary missionary societies, teach Sunday school, raise funds, and become prayer band leaders and church mothers, the activities of women who prepare food for church functions show that women use this sphere of influence in the church to foster a sense of shared tradition and spiritual identity in their communities.

References

Bascom, W. 1951. Yoruba food. *Africa* 21:41–53.

———. 1977. Some Yoruba ways with yams. In *The anthropologist's cookbook,* edited by J. Kuper, New York: Universe Books.

Bush, B. 1986. "The family tree is not cut": Women and cultural resistance in slave family life in the British Caribbean. In *In resistance: Studies in African, Caribbean, and Afro-American history,* edited by G. Y. Okihiro. Amherst: University of Massachusetts Press.

Chodorow, N. 1978. *The reproduction of mothering.* Berkeley: University of California Press.

Collins, P. Hill. 1990. *Black feminist thought: Knowledge, consciousness, and the politics of empowerment.* Boston: Unwin Hyman.

Creel, M. Washington. 1990. Gullah attitudes toward life and death. *Africanisms in African-American culture,* edited by Joseph E. Holloway. Bloomington: Indiana University Press.

Davis, A. 1971. Reflections on the Black woman's role in the community of slaves. *Black Scholar* (December):3–15.

DeVault, M. L. 1991. *Feeding the family: The social organization of caring as gendered work.* Chicago: University of Chicago Press.

Finnegan, R. S. 1965. *Survey of the Limba people of northern Sierra Leone*. London: Her Majesty's Stationery Office.

Friedman, C. G. 1990. Africans and African-Americans: An ethnohistorical view and symbolic analysis of food habits. In *Encounters with American ethnic cultures,* edited by P. Kilbride, J. C. Goodale, and E. R. Ameisen. Tuscaloosa: University of Alabama Press.

Georgia Writers' Project. [1940] 1986. *Drums and shadows: Survival studies among the Georgia coastal Negroes*. Athens: University of Georgia Press.

Gilkes, C. 1988. "Together and in harness": Women's traditions in the Sanctified Church. In *Black women in America: Social science perspectives,* edited by M. R. Malson, E. Mudimbe-Boyi, Jean F. O'Barr, and M. Wyer. Chicago: University of Chicago Press.

Gray White, D. 1985. *Ar'n't I a woman? Female slaves in the plantation South*. New York: W. W. Norton.

Hill Collins, P. 1990. *Black feminist thought: Knowledge, consciousness, and the politics of empowerment*. Boston and London: Unwin Hyman.

Hochschild, A. R., and A. Machung. 1989. *The second shift: Working parents and the revolution at home*. New York: Viking.

Holloway, J. 1990. *Africanisms in American culture*. Bloomington: Indiana University Press.

Jones, J. 1986. *Labor of love, labor of sorrow: Black women, work, and the family from slavery to the present*. New York: Vintage Books.

Jones-Jackson, P. 1987. *When roots die: Endangered traditions on the Sea Islands*. Athens: University of Georgia Press.

Joyner, C. 1984. *Down by the riverside: A South Carolina slave community*. Urbana: University of Illinois Press.

Littlefield, D. 1981. *Rice and slaves: Ethnicity and the slave trade in colonial South Carolina*. Baton Rouge: Louisiana State University Press.

Mbiti, J. 1969. *African religions and philosophy*. New York: Praeger.

Minon, R. 1993. Cultures in conflict: Sea Island communities are fighting for their survival, stirring new hopes along the coast of South Carolina. *Southern Exposure* (Fall): 53–56.

Oakley, A. 1974. *The sociology of housework*. New York: Pantheon.

Opala, J. 1987. *The Sierra Leone–Gullah connection*. Freetown: USIS.

Oral, R. A. 1985. *The Madonna of 115th street: Faith and community in Italian Harlem, 1880–1950*. New Haven, Conn: Yale University Press.

Reagon, B. Johnson. 1986. African diaspora women: The making of cultural workers. *Feminist Studies* 12:77–90.

Singleton, V. 1982. We are an endangered species: An interview with Emory Campbell. *Southern Exposure* 10:37–39.

Smith, D. E . 1987. *The everyday world as problematic: A feminist sociology*. Boston: Northeastern University Press.

Steady, F. 1981. *The Black woman cross-culturally*. Cambridge, Mass: Schenkman.

Strauss, A. L. 1990. *Qualitative analysis for social scientists*. Cambridge: Cambridge University Press.

Tarborg-Penn, R. 1987. *Women in Africa and the African diaspora*. Washington, D.C.: Howard University Press.

Turner, L. 1949. *Africanisms in the Gullah dialect*. Chicago: University of Chicago Press.

Williams, B. 1985. Why migrant women feed their husbands tamales: Foodways as a basis for a revisionist view of Tejano family life. In *Ethnic and regional foodways in the United States: The performance of group identity,* edited by L. Keller Brown and K. Mussell. Knoxville: University of Tennessee Press.

Winterbottom, T. [1803] 1969. *An account of the Native Africans in the neighbourhood of Sierra Leone*. London: Frank Cass.

Wood, P. 1974. *Black majority: Negroes in colonial South Carolina from 1670 through the Stono Rebellion*. New York: Alfred A. Knopf.

Young, K. Porter. 1992. *Notes on sisterhood, kinship, and marriage in an African-American South Carolina Sea Island community*. Memphis, Tenn.: Memphis State University, Center for Research on Women.

I Got the Blues

Alan Lomax
Folklorist/Musicologist

Alan Lomax worked with his father, folklorist John A. Lomax, at the Library of Congress's Archives of American Folksong, and from 1946 to 1949 he was director of folk music at Decca Records. Alan Lomax has produced educational radio programs on folk music and was director of the Cantometrics Project (the international study of folk song within its cultural matrix) at Columbia University. He is the author of numerous books and articles including The Land Where the Blues Began *(1993),* Mister Jelly Roll *(1973 [1950]),* The Rainbow Sign *(1959),* Folk Song Style and Culture *(1968) and with his father as coauthor* American Ballads and Folksongs *(1934),* Negro Folk Songs as Sung by Leadbelly *(1936),* Folk Song: U.S.A. *(1954 [1947]), and* Hard Hitting Songs for Hard-Hit People *(1967).*

I got the blues,
But I'm too damn mean to cry . . .

The last chord sounded on Leroy's guitar, the last blues of the evening.

"Well," Natchez told me, "I reckon now you got an idea about the blues around Memphis."

"I reckon I have," I said.

"Yeah, that police in Memphis had you singin' the blues," he chuckled. About that time the hard-faced man who ran the honkey-tonk blew out the lamp. Old Natchez picked up the nearly empty gin bottle, Leroy and Sib grabbed the guitars, and the four of us walked out into the two o'clock dark. It was black out there. You could

Alan Lomax, "I Got the Blues," Common Ground *8 (4) (1948): 38–52.*

feel the Delta night rubbing itself against your cheek.

We sat down on the front step and smoked. The stars hung just above our heads, like fireflies caught in the dark tangle of the night. I felt good. Sib, Leroy, and Natchez had been singing for several hours, and every blues had been like another drink of raw gin. The brights and shadows of their blues reflected the wonderful and hateful land of the South that had produced all of us. We were warmed with the undeniable vitality and humanity that the blues carry beneath their melancholy.

I wasn't sure exactly where I was and I didn't much care. The man who owned the little country tonk was named Hamp, they told me. This was Hamp's place, somewhere out in the Arkansas blackland across the river from Memphis. It was a one-room shanty store that doubled as a country bar room at night, a place where the people who made the cotton in this fat land came to dance and gamble and commit a bit of friendly mayhem. Tonight it had been a refuge for the three blues musicians and myself—"where nobody gonna bother us," they said. "No laws or nothin'."

We had needed a hole to hide in. When we had come racing across the river bridge from Memphis into this dark plain, we had had the feeling that we were pursued, that we would like to keep on going right out of this world. We were running away from the Memphis police and their attitudes about human relations. Not that we had committed a crime; we had just forgotten, temporarily, that we were in the South.

I had hit Beale Street in Memphis about the first cool of the evening, and, as usual, had begun to poke around for folk singers. A Negro bartender told me I wasn't allowed in any of the Beale Street joints because of a new segregation ordinance. So I paraded Beale Street until I heard the music I wanted coming from a barber shop. Natchez and Leroy were playing their boxes to Sib's harmonica-blowing. When they had collected their tips, we sat down together in a vacant lot to talk blues, but a dribble-chinned Memphis cop interrupted our libations and harshly ordered us to move on. "We don't want no Washington Yankee foolin' around niggertown," he said. "If you like this nigger music, take it back North with you. We don't like it down here in the South."

With the cop pacing behind us, our feet dragged in a chain-gang walk up Beale Street. We piled into my car and headed out of town, and, by what was said, I knew that the Memphis cop had made these blues singers my friends. They tried to make a joke of the whole incident, but in the pauses between laughs Leroy kept saying, "Man, just as soon as I can rake and scrape money together, I'm gonna leave this country and they ain't never gonna see me down here again."

At Hamp's place we solaced ourselves with gin and with hours of the blues. Child of this fertile Delta land, voice of the voiceless black masses, the blues crept into the back windows of America maybe forty years ago and since then has colored the whole of American popular music. Hill-billy singers, hot jazz blowers, crooners like Crosby, cowboy yodelers—all these have learned from the native folk blues. Now the blues is a big, lonesome wind blowing around the world. Now the whole world can feel, uncoiling in its ear, this somber music of the Mississippi. And yet no one had ever thought to ask the makers of these songs—these ragged meister-singers—why they sang.

Now we sat together in the Delta night, smoking and saying little. Here was Natchez, who had helped to birth the blues forty years ago in this same Delta country.

Here was young Leroy, making the blues for his own time. Finally here was Sib, the buffoon of the blues, who, like all fools, expressed in apish gestures the sorrows of life.

I turned to Natchez. You couldn't tell how old he was by looking at him. You just knew that he was old and strong, like the big live-oaks in these bottoms. "Natchez," I said, "tell me why you sing the blues."

There was a pause in which the insects and little animals of the night joined together in the sound that is the earth breathing in its sleep. Then Natchez began in his grave and hesitant way.

"Some people say that the blues is—a cow wantin' to see her calf, but I don't say it like that. I say it's a man that's got a good woman that turns him down. Like when you sing—

If you see my milk cow, tell her to hurry home,
'Cause I ain't had no lovin' since she been gone . . .

Things like that happen, you know. You want to see your lovin' babe, you want to see her bad, and she be gone. That gives you the blues:

I woke up this mornin' just about an hour before day,
Reached and grabbed the pillow where my baby used to lay. . . ."

Natchez paused and looked at Sib, the stutterer—Sib, the slightly addled one. On Sib's dark brow a frown was eternally in conflict with the clownish grin that twitched the corners of his mouth. No one could sing Sib's blues because they were a complete expression of Sib—his stammering speech, his wild and idiot humors, his untrammelled fancy. Natchez, who treated him like a child, would yet sit back and play for an hour while Sib indulged in rhymes and stanzas which no other singer could ever invent. "So what do you think about it, Sib?" said Natchez softly. "You must have some reason why you have the blues."

Sib began to speak in his plaintive way, the words tumbling out of him in a rush as if he were afraid someone might interrupt him at any moment. "I'll tell you, Natchez, it really worries me to think I had a sweet little girl named Annie Belle. You know, we used to go to school together and grew along up together. So I wanted to love her and I axed her mother for her and she turnt me down. That cause me to sing the blues:

Good mornin', little school girl,
Good mornin', little school girl,
May I go home wid you?
May I go home wid you?
You can tell your mama and your papa
That Sib's a little school boy, too. . . .

"Her parents thought I wasn't the right boy for Annie Belle. They turnt me down, and then I just got to thinkin' and that started me to drinkin' and from that I got the blues."

Truly, they have sung ten thousand blues verses about lack of love. Open the big book of the blues and you will find all the bitterness, all the frustration, all the anger, and all the heartbreak that accompany love when people live precariously in the slums.

Sib went on spurting words, but Natchez interrupted him by directing the question to Leroy. "Now what do you think about the blues situation, old Leroy?"

"Tell you, Natchez, the blues have hope me a lot. Yes, sir, the blues will help a man. When I has trouble, when I'm feelin' low down and disgusted and can't be satisfied, you know how it is sometimes—

I woke up this mornin' with the blues all round my bed,
Went to eat my breakfast, had blues all in my bread. . . .

Then singin' a blues like that is the onliest thing to ease my situation."

But Natchez wasn't satisfied. "Yeah, you feel better. The blues helps a man to explain his feelin's, but why do he feel blue in the first place?"

"Here's my thought on it," Sib came busting in. "We er-uh colored people have had so much trouble, but we's a people that tries to be happy anyway, you ever notice that? Because we never had so much, we tries to make the best of life. We don't have nothin', but we try to be jolly anyway; we don't let nothin' worry us too much. You take them old-fashioned country suppers." (As Sib talked, you could see him smacking his lips over the barbecued ribs and the field-ripe watermelons he had eaten.) "I thought I was a rich man when I'd go there with a dollar in my pocket. I never was used to much anyway, you understand? Always had to work."

He paused, and the puzzled and angry frown triumphed over the happy-go-lucky grin that twitched at his lips. "One year we cleaned up a whole big bottom where the willows was thick. The mud was so heavy I many times stalled four mules to a wagon down there. We'd work and clean up a bottom in the winter so we could plant it next summer. And I think this. You work hard all the year and you expectin' your money once a year, and, when that year wind up, you don't get nothin'; then you get the idea that 'I ain't doin' no good no way an' what's the use of livin'?' You know? You'll have all them funny thoughts like that."

Natchez, softly, "Sho, sho."

"And that gives you the blues, the po' man's heart disease. I remember I used to sing the blues down in that old black bottom—

I could hear my name,
My black name, a-ringin'
All up an' down the line.
I could hear my name,
My black name, a-ringin'
All up an' down the line.
Now I don't believe I'm doin' nothin'
But gradually throwin' away my time. . . ."

Sib put his harmonica to his lips and began to play. It was hardly music. It was a compound of shrieks and squeals and moans, like a farm in a tornado, where the cries of terror from the animals and the human beings are mixed with the noise of splitting planks and cracking timbers, and all are swallowed up in the howl of the storm. The words and phrases burst out in spasms through the harmonica as if Sib had learned to sing through the metal reeds because he was unable to express his feelings adequately in his own throat. Presently Natchez and Leroy joined Sib, underscoring his harmonica with their two guitars, until the song had run out in him. In the silence that followed, they chuckled quietly together. "That's the blues, man. That's purely it."

"You see what I mean about the blues expressin' a man's feelin', Natchez?" said Leroy.

"Yeah," Natchez replied. "It looks like the blues gits started thataway—when a man is goin' down some country road, whistlin' and singin' to himself somethin' or another like—

> *Hey, I feel like hollerin' and I feel like cryin',*
> *Hey, I feel like hollerin' and I feel like cryin',*
> *I'm here today, Lawd, but tomorrow I'll be gone,*
> *I'm here today, Lawd, but tomorrow I'll be gone.*

He don't play no instrument or nothin'. He just hollers about what's worryin' him."

"They the jump-up blues," added Leroy. "They just jump up in your mind when you be down in trouble. Like those little numbers like they have over in Tennessee." And Leroy began to sing in his rich baritone—

> *"Well, have you ever been to Nashville,*
> *Well, have you ever been to Nashville,*
> *Have you ever been to Nashville,*
> *O Lawdy, to the Nashville pen?*
> *Boys, if you don't stop stealin',*
> *Boys, if you don't stop stealin',*
> *Boys, if you don't stop stealin',*
> *O buddy, you'll go back again. . . .*

That's what I mean about the heart part. You singin' the way you feel from the heart."

"That's right, man," from Sib.

"Nobody could play behind them jumped-up blues," said Natchez, "because they ain't got no music to 'em. They ain't never been wrote down and won't never be, and I reckon all blues originated from just such stuff as that."

Out of the lonesome field hollers, out of the chain-gang chants, out of the full-throated choruses of the road builders, the clearers of swamps, the lifters and the toters—out of the biting irony, the power and savage strength and anger of work-songs—sprang the blues. Here was music with its tap root in African singing—Africa, the continent of communal work, the preeminent continent of the work-song. The work-song flowered under slavery and put forth its thorns after reconstruction. Forty-odd years ago singers like Natchez began to set these old cadences "to music," making their banjos, their guitars, and their pianos sound the work-gang chorus. Thus the old work-songs, given a regular harmonic form, became dance music in the unstable and uncertain world of the southern Negro worker. Here, from the experience of Leroy and Natchez, had come confirmation for my own notions about the origin of the blues.

"You sing about things you want to do or things you want to know or—" Leroy continued—"things that really have happened to you."

"And," Natchez added, "some people that haven't had no hardship, they don't know how it is with the poor man that has had hardships and still has them."

"Yeah, classics and stuff like that," said Leroy, lumping musicians who played written music with all the secure and wealthy and privileged people in the world. "People like that don't know what the blues is."

"Naw, they couldn't play the blues if they wanted to," Sib said with great scorn.

"What I mean," explained Leroy, "it takes a man who *had* the blues to really *play* the blues. Yeah, you got to be *blue* to sing the blues, and that's the truth:

> I was down in the bottom with the mud up to my knees,
> I was workin' for my baby, she was so hard to please.
> I worked all the summer, Lord, and all the fall,
> Went home to take my Christmas, good pardner, in my overalls. . . ."

Natchez scrooched up on the step and spat far into the night. He could spit like a muleskinner. His voice rang now with authority.

"Let's come to a showdown now. Just where did the blues originate from? I'm thinkin' they didn't start in the North—in Chicago or New York or Pennsylvania."

"Naw, man, they started in the South," from Sib.

"From slavery, I'm thinkin'," Leroy muttered, half to himself.

"All right, then what we really want to know is why and how come a man in the South *have* the blues. Now I've worked on levee camps, in road camps, and in extra gangs on the railroad and everywhere. I've heard guys singin'—'Mm-mp' this and 'Mm-mp' that—and they was really expressin' their feelings from their heart the only way they knowed how.

"I've knowed guys that wanted to cuss out the boss and was afraid to go up to his face and tell him what they wanted to tell him. And I've heered a guy sing those things to the boss when he were out behind a wagon, hookin' up the horses. He'd make out like a horse stepped on his foot and he'd say, 'Get off my foot, goddamit!'— saying just what he wanted to say to his boss, only talkin' to the horse—'You got no business doin' me like that! Get offa my foot!'"

"That's just my idea, Natchez," Leroy broke in. "The blues is mostly revenge. You want to say something (and you know how we was situated so we couldn't say or do a lot of things we wanted to), and so you sing it. Like a friend of mine. He was workin' down on a railroad section gang a long time ago. I don't remember when it was. Anyhow, this friend of mine looked at the boss lyin' up in the shade sleepin' while him an' his buddies was out there shakin' those ties. He wanted to say something about it, but he couldn't you know. So that give him the blues and he sung a little number about—

> Ratty, ratty section,
> Ratty, ratty crew,
> The captain's gettin' ratty, boys,
> I b'lieve I'm gonna rat some, too.

Meanin' that he was signifying and getting his revenge through songs."

"And he didn't quit because he didn't know where he gonna find his next job," Natchez added.

"Yeah, and maybe he had one of those jobs you *couldn't* quit." Leroy chuckled.

"What you mean? Sumpin' like a chain gang?" Sib asked.

"Naw, I mean one of the jobs only way you could quit was to run off," said Leroy.

"Man, how they gonna hold you?" from Sib, querulously.

"They hold you just like this, Sib, boy. You didn't have no payday on them jobs. They give you an allowance in the commissary store for you an' yo' woman. You draw on that allowance, so much a week, and after it was up, that's all you git. Most boys didn't know how to read and write and figger and so they charge them what they wants, like twenty-five dollars for a side of side meat. And you gonna stay there till you paid for that meat, Sib, maybe gettin' twenty-five cents a day wages. When you take a notion to leave, they tell you, 'Well, you owe us four hundred dollars.'"

"Four hundred dollars! Aw, be quiet, man." Sib started to laugh his mad and infectious laugh.

"I said four hundred dollars," Leroy cut in. "Just for eatin' and sleepin'."

Natchez took up the story. "Suppose you be workin' a team of mules and one git his leg broke and have to be killed? That's your mule, then! Yessir, that dead mule is one you bought and you gonna work right on that job till you pay for him or slip off some way."

"Whyn't you say somethin' about it?" Sib inquired plaintively.

"Say something about it and you might go just like that mule," Natchez said seriously. "All odds are against you, even your own people."

"That's right," agreed Leroy. "The white man don't all the time do those things. It's some of your own people at times will do those dirty deeds because they're told to do them, and they do what they're told."

Treat a group of people as if they had no right to dignity, allow these people no security, make them bend their knees and bow their heads, and some of them will conform to slavery in their souls. Perhaps these so-called "Uncle Toms" are the most grievous result of the slavery system.

Natchez interrupted my reflections. "Looky here, Leroy. Did you ever work for the Loran brothers?"

"You mean those guys that built all these levees up and down the river from Memphis? Sho, man, I've worked for the bigges' part of the Loran family—Mister Isum Loran, Mister Bill Loran, Mister Charley Loran—all them. I think them Lorans are something like the Rockefeller family. When a kid is born, *he* Loran junior. They got Loran the second, Loran the third, Loran the fourth. They always been and they is now— Loran brothers—some of them big business mens in towns, some of them running extry gangs and levee camps and road camps. And *they* were peoples wouldn't allow a man to quit unless they got tired of him and drove him away."

"That's right," Leroy chuckled. "And you remember how the boys used to sing—

I axed Mister Charley—
What time of day:
He looked at me,
Threw his watch away.

I axed Mister Charley
Just to give me one dime.
'Go on, old nigger,
You a dime behind!'

I axed Mister Charley
Just to give me my time,
'Go on, old nigger,
You're time behind!'. . ."

I had heard this levee camp blues from one end of the South to the other. It was the epic of the muleskinner, the man who did the dirt-moving jobs before the bulldozer was developed, the Negro who, working his big mule-drawn scoop, piled up the levees, graded the roads, and dug the canals of the South. This muleskinning blues has thousands of verses, attached to the mournfulest wailing tune in the world, a tune I never was able to sing myself until they put me on K.P. in the Army, and the mess sergeant began to look like a levee camp boss looks to a muleskinner.

All the way from the Brazos bottoms of Texas to the tidewater country of Virginia I had heard Negro muleskinners chant their complaint against Mister Charley but, although I had asked a score of singers, I had never found one who could identify him. I grinned with excitement. Maybe here, under the knee of one of the Loran brothers' levees, I had at last discovered the identity of my elusive Mister Charley.

I asked my second question of the evening. "Who is this 'Mister Charley'?"

"Mister Charley Loran," Natchez immediately responded.

"What sort of a man is he?" I asked.

"Well," Leroy drawled, "now I couldn't hardly describe him to you. You know, it's hard for a colored man to talk like a white man anyhow." (Leroy was talking for my benefit now. He had been reminded there was a white man listening there in the dark. He began to rib me gently.) "Mister Charley was one of them *real* Southerners; had a voice that would scare you to death whenever he'd come out with all that crap of his. Always in his shirt sleeves, I don't care how early in the mornin' and how cold it was."

"Night or day." Natchez began to chuckle with him. "Didn't make no difference to Mister Charley what time it was."

"Don't care how early he'd get up, you gonna get up, too. He'd holler—

Big bell call you, little bell warn you,
If you don't come now, I'm gonna break in on you. . . .

And he *meant* it."

"Sho he did," laughed Natchez. "He the man originated the old-time eight-hour shift down here. Know what I mean? Eight hours in the morning and eight more in the afternoon."

Sib kept adding eight to eight and getting sixteen and going off into peal after peal of high whinnying laughter. In this shared laughter I felt the three had again accepted me. I asked another question.

"I'd always heard of this Mister Charley in the song as 'the mercy man.' Is *he* the same as Charley Loran?"

"Naw, man, that's Mister Charley *Hulen*, the best friend we had down in this part of the country, really a friend to our people. He was the man we all run to when somebody mistreated us," Natchez told me.

"Otherwise known as 'the mercy man,'" Leroy added. "Now I remember an incident about Charley Hulen happen in Hughes, Arkansas. It's hard to believe it, but I know it for a fact. They had a Negro there name Bolden, run a honkey-tonk and had a lot of property. In fact the sheriff of the county lived in one of Bolden's houses. But he wouldn't pay Bolden no rent, just stayed there and gave Bolden a 'whuppin' every time Bolden asked him for his money."

"That's what he did," said Natchez, listening, seeing it, feeling it in his guts.

"So this Bolden happen to be, as they say, one of Charley Hulen's niggers. He finally got up nerve to go tell Mister Charley what was goin' on. So Charley Hulen tells the police, say, 'Saturday evenin' at one o'clock, meet me. I'm killin' you or you kill me.' And that's what happen. He met that sheriff that Saturday and told him, 'I come to kill you. You been messin' with one of my niggers.'

"The police started after his gun and Charley Hulen shot him through the heart. So they pulled that police over out the street, and let the honkey-tonk roll on." Softly, seeing it, wondering about it, he repeated, "Yeah, man, let the old honkey-tonk roll *right* on."

"Toughest places I ever seen," said Natchez, "were some of them honkey-tonks, call them barrel-houses, in Charley Loran's camps. Negroes all be in there gamblin', you know, and some of them short guys couldn't quite reach up to the crap table—and I've seed them pull a dead man up there and stand on him."

"Yeah, stand on 'em. I've seed that," Leroy said.

But Natchez had more to tell. "Down in them barrel-houses in Loran's levee camps I've seen them stand on a dead man and shoot craps all night long; and I've heard Loran come around and say, 'If you boys keep out the grave, I'll keep you out the jail.' Yeah, and I've heard him say, 'Kill a nigger, hire another. But kill a mule and I'll have to buy another.'"

"That's just what he believed, Natchez," Leroy said, in anger and at the same time with curious pride. "Peoples like him had another word, too. On those camps, when the fellows were wore down from carrying logs or doing some kind of heavy work, the bosses used to say, '*Burn out, burn up. Fall out, fall dead!*' That was the best you could do. You had to work yourself to death or you proved that you were a good man, that's all."

"Main thing about it is that some of those people down there didn't think a Negro ever get *tired!*' Natchez' ordinarily quiet voice broke with a sound that was half sob, half growl. "'They'd work him—work him till he couldn't work, see! You couldn't *tell* 'em you was tired."

"Why couldn't you?" I asked.

"They'd crack you 'cross the head with a stick or maybe kill you. One of those things. You just had to keep on workin' whether you was tired or not. From what they call 'can to can't.' That mean you start to work when you just can see—early in the mornin'—and work right on till you can't see no more at night."

"Only man ever helped us about our work was Charley Hulen, the mercy man," said Leroy. "He used to come out and say, "Those fellows are tired; give 'em some rest.' Ain't he the man, Natchez, cut them sixteen hours a day down to eight?"

"Right in this section he was," Natchez replied.

"How did he do it?" I asked.

"Why, he and his son, Little Charley, just didn't like the way things was going on, so they just come in and taken over, that's all. Otherwise they was the baddest men down through this part of the country. Both of them was ex-cowboys from Texas and sharpshooters. Could shoot like nobody's business. So after they taken over, that made it a lot better. And it's still better today."

"You mean the people were just scared of old man Hulen and his boy?" I asked.

"That's right," Leroy said. "I'll tell you how bad they was scared. You know they put up a law in Arkansas—no *hitchhikin'*. It made it kinda tough on a fellow to move around and change jobs if he wanted to. So, one afternoon I were hitchhikin' a ride to Little Rock and a fellow by the name of Mister Gotch stopped in his car. He were one of the baddest mens down in this country."

"He was so bad he was scared of hisself," Natchez chuckled.

"So Mister Gotch say to me. 'What you doin' hitchhikin', boy?' Called me 'boy.'

"I say, 'I'm tryin' to get home to work.'

"He say, 'Well, who do you work for?'

"I tell him"—Leroy imitated the mild and insinuating way he made his reply—'I work for Mister Charley Hulen.' You know what that man told me? He say, 'Come on, I'll take you there!'"

Sib, Natchez, and Leroy threw back their heads and laughed, laughed quietly and long, as if they shared some old joke, burdened with irony, but bearable out of long acquaintance. "Any other time. . . . Or if you'd worked for another man. . . . Or if you hadn't been workin'. . . . You'd got a whuppin'. . . . Or went to jail or the farm and worked for no pay. . . . That's it, worked for no pay!" came bursting out between chuckles. "But, since I worked for Mister Charley Hulen, Mister Gotch taken me to his place. Scared to bother me, because I was one of Mister Charley's mens," Leroy went on.

"One of his niggers!"

"Yeah. So Mister Gotch took me in his car. Even gave me a drink!"

Natchez, shaking his head in wonder, chuckled. "They'll do that, too."

"You know, Leroy," Natchez said, "you and I worked in all kind of camps—levee camps, road camps, rock quarries and all—but what I want to get at is—how we lived in those places? I mean in tents and eatin' scrap food other people had refused, such as old bags of beans and stuff they couldn't sell."

Leroy, beginning to howl with laughter over the old and painful joke he recalled, interrupted, "And they had a name for it in the camp I was in—

La-la-loo!
If you don't like it,
He do!"

Natchez, chuckling with him, "Yeah, but you'll *like* it!"

"Unh-hunh, you might not like it when you first get there, but you'll like it before you leave." Leroy was still laughing.

Natchez went on, forcing us to savor the dirt, see the hoggish way the men had to live. "They'd just go out in those big truck gardens and pull up greens by the sackful, take 'em down to some lake or creek, sort of shake 'em off in the water, and cook 'em, roots, stalk, and all, in one of them big fifty-two gallon pots."

Leroy, beginning to laugh his big laugh again, broke in. "And if you found a worm in your greens and say, 'Captain, I found a worm here,' he'd say, 'What the hell you expect for nothing?'"

Natchez and Sib burst out in great yells of laughter, as Leroy hurried on to top his own story: "And then some fellow over 'long the table would holler, 'Gimme that piece of meat!'"

"Yeah, I've heard that—'Gimme that piece of meat! Don't throw it away!'" Natchez gasped out between the gusts of laughter that were shaking his whole body. Sib couldn't sit still any longer; his laughter was riding him too hard. He went staggering off down the dark path, beating his arms in the air, squealing and guffawing like a wild animal.

When we had recovered from this healing' laughter, Leroy added thoughtfully, "Those guys seemed to get a kick out of the whole thing."

"Well, in them times what did you know? What did you know?" Natchez asked the night and the stars.

> *"Ham and eggs, pork and beans,*
> *I would-a ate more, but the cook wasn't clean."*

"Did you ever see those guys they called 'table-walkers'?" Natchez went on.
"Yeah, many times," said Leroy.

"I mean one of these guys had made up his mind he didn't care whether he died or no; was just tired of the way he'd been living and the kind of food he'd been eating. He'd snatch out his .45 revolver, get up on one end of the mess table and walk it, what I mean, walk right down the whole length, tromping his big dirty feets in everybody's plates, grabbin' up your food."

"Those guys were what you might call 'tough peoples,'" Leroy said respectfully.

"Yeah, 'cause they know they gonna get a whuppin' from the boss," Natchez agreed.

"He may have that .45, that so-called tough guy," Leroy went on, "but, when the white man come, *he'll* whup him with that .45 right on his hip. White man won't have no gun or nothin'. Just come in and say, 'Lay down there, fellow; I'm gonna whup you.'" Leroy spoke quietly, with bitter, weary irony. "So this tough guy gonna lay right down and the white man would kick the gun out of his scabbard and give him a whuppin'." There was a pause. We could all see the big, black figure cowering on the earth and the white man standing over him with a stick, beating him as he might a chicken-killing hound. After a moment, almost in a whisper, Leroy continued, "After this table-walker get his whuppin', he'd pick up that big pistol he toted and go on back to work.

> *Well, you kicked and stomped and beat me,*
> *And you called that fun, and you called that fun.*
> *If I catch you in my home town,*
> *Gonna make you run, gonna make you run. . . ."*

"Yeah," Natchez said. "Then maybe this guy that took the beating would come out there on the job and kill one of his buddies. I've seen that many times."

"If you were a good worker, you could kill anybody down there," Leroy added.

"What you mean is—" Natchez rapped this out—"you could kill anybody down there as long as you kill a *Negro!*"

"Any *Negro.*" Leroy's voice was flat and painstakingly logical, as if he were reading the rules out of a book. "If you could work better than him and you were sorry! But don't go killin' a good worker!"

"That's right," said Natchez. "You could kill anybody you want in those days, if you could work better than him.

> *Stagolee, he went a-walkin' in that red-hot broilin' sun;*
> *He said, 'Bring me my big pistol, I wants my forty one.'*
> *Stagolee, he went a-walkin' with his .40 gun in his hand;*
> *He said, 'I feel mistreated this mornin', I could kill most any man.'"*

The small hot breeze of midnight had died away and the dawn wind had not yet begun to stir. The night wrapped around us a choking black blanket of stillness and quiet. The quiet voices of Natchez and Leroy moved on with the sureness and strength of the great river that had given them birth.

They were both entertainers. They had made their way safely and even pleasantly through their violent world, their guitars slung around their necks—like talismans. Wearing these talismans, they had entered into all the secret places of this land, had moved safely through its most dangerous jungles, past all its killers, who, seeing their talismans, had smiled upon them. They lived the magic life of fools. (Remember the hard drawling voice—"I got a nigger on my place that can keep you laughin' all day. I don't know where he gets all the stories he tells and them songs of his. Reckon he makes them up, nigger-like. And sing! Sing like a mockin' bird. You ought to hear him. You'd split your sides.") Now these buffoons with their clear artist's vision were making a picture of their world, a terrifying picture of which they were not at all afraid. They were at home with it.

"You know, Natchez," said Leroy, "we had a *few* Negroes around here that wasn't *afraid* of white people. They actually talked back to them. People like that they called 'crazy'—'crazy niggers.' I wonder why do they call them crazy and bad because they speak up for their rights?"

"They afraid they might *ruin* the other Negroes, make *them* crazy enough to talk back," said Natchez. "I had a crazy uncle and they hung him. My uncle was a man that, if he worked, he wanted his pay. And he could figger as good as a white man. Fact of the matter, he had a better education than some of them and they would go to him for advice."

Leroy chuckled. "Um-hum, a lot of the white peoples down here are about as dumb as we are."

"Anyhow," Natchez went on, "this is how they found out my uncle was really a crazy nigger. One day his white boss come to his house and told him, say, 'Sam, I want you to git that woman of yours out of the house and put her to work.' Say,

'It's no woman on this plantation sits up in the shade and don't work but Mizz Anne.'

"An' my uncle say, 'Well, who is Mizz Anne?'

"The white man tell him, 'Mizz Anne is my wife.'

"My uncle say, 'Well, I'm sorry, Mister Crowther, but my wife is named Anne, too, and *she* sets up in the shade and *she* don't come out in the field and work!'

"The man say, 'She *got* to come out there.'

"My uncle look at him. 'There's one Mizz Anne that's a *Negro* and *she* ain't gonna work in the field.'

"The white man jumps off his horse and my uncle whipped him and run him and his horse off his place." Natchez went on in a flat and weary voice to finish his story. "So the white man rode to town and he got him a gang and come back after my uncle. My uncle shot four or five of them, but they finally caught him and hung him. So that's the story of *him!* Yeah, that's the story of my *crazy* uncle."

"Lynched him," Sib muttered.

"Fifty or sixty of them come out there and killed him." Natchez began to speak with mounting rage. "That was on account of him trying to protect his own *wife*. Because he didn't want his own *wife* to work out on the farm when she had a new baby there at the house an' was expecting another one pretty soon!

"I've seed this happen, too. One boy I know was likin' the same girl a white man was likin'. The white man told the colored boy not to marry the colored girl, because *he* wanted her for hisself. The boy told him he loved the girl and was going to marry her, so the white guy say, 'You can't git no license here!'

"Well, the boy and girl ran off to another town and they got married and then come back home. The white fellow asked if they was really married and they told him they were. Now this girl figger if she showed him the license he would leave her go. She showed him the license, so they went and got her husband and killed him. Then they come back and got her—she was in a fam'ly way—and they killed her. Then they went and killed the boy's daddy and they killed his mother, and then, one of the brothers, *he* tried to fight and they killed *him*. So they killed twelve in that one family. That family was named Belcher, and all this happened at a place they call Longdale, Arkansas, way out in the woods from Goulds, Arkansas."

Without any more feeling than one would recall a storm or a flood or any other past disaster, Leroy commented, "Yeah, I heard of that, heard all about it."

"It was no protection at all that the poor peoples got in places like that back in those days," Natchez went on with calm anger. "You try to fight back, then it's not just you they gonna get. It's anybody in your family. Like if I have three brothers and do something and they can't catch me, they'll catch the brothers."

"It don't matter to them—just anybody in the family," Leroy said.

"You might do things and get away. But why do something or another and get your whole family kilt? You know what I mean?"

"I know it!"

"That's what they got on you, see?"

"Yeah, that's what they got on you," observed Natchez. "And if your family have a girl *they* like, you might's well's to let them *have* her, because if you don't, they liable to do something outrageous. When they see a Negro woman they like, they gonna have her, if they want her, especially down here.

> *If I feel tomorrow, like I feel today,*
> *If I feel tomorrow, like I feel today,*
> *Stand right here and look a thousand miles away.*
>
> *I'm goin' to the river, set down on the ground;*
> *I'm goin' to the river, set down on the ground;*
> *When the blues overtake me, I'll jump overboard and drown.*
>
> *I feel my hell a-risin', a-risin' every day;*
> *I feel my hell a-risin', a-risin' every day;*
> *Someday it'll bust this levee and wash the whole wide world away. . . ."*

"You know, they's another kind of Negro the white man call bad," Natchez went on. "A bad seed, a seed that ruins the rest of the Negroes, by opening their eyes and telling them things they don't know."

"Otherwise he is a smart Negro," Leroy chuckled.

"Yeah," said Natchez. "He would git the Chicago Defender, for an instance, and bring it down here and read it to the Negroes."

"Speakin' of the Chicago Defender," Leroy interrupted, "I were in a place once they called Marigold, Mississippi. They had a restaurant there and in the back they had a room with a peephole in the door. I thought it was a crap game goin' on back there and I went back to see. Fact of the business, I were kind of stranded and I wanted to shoot some craps and make me a stake, if I could.

"And you know what they were doin' back there? They were readin' the Chicago Defender and had a lookout man on the door. If a white man had come in the restaurant, they'd stick the Defender in the stove. Burn it up. And start playin' checkers." Leroy laughed. "That's the way they had to smuggle the Defender down there. Now if they'd caught this fellow that brought the Defender, they'd have called him a bad nigger."

"Might-a killed him."

"Yeah. He was the kind they call a *really* bad Negro—a man that has the nerve to smuggle the Defender into Mississippi where they don't even allow the paper to be put off the train."

The Chicago Defender has more than a hundred thousand circulation among Negro readers. It is far from radical. It prints news about Negro life, much that does not appear in the non-Negro press.

"That's what makes the Negro so *tetchious* till today," Natchez said. "He have been denied in so many places until if a gang of guys is, for an instance, standing in some certain place and they say to them *all*, 'You fellas, git back and don't stand there,' the Negroes in the crowd figger they're pointin' straight to them. A lot of times they don't mean that. They really mean they don't want *nobody* standin' there, but the Negro thinks, straight off, they referrin' to him because he's black."

Sib had been listening to his two older friends for a long time. He had had no experience of the deeps of the South—the work camps, the prison farms, the wild life of the river that they had known. He was a boy right off the farm, whose half-mad genius on his Woolworth harmonica was gradually leading him out into the world.

But Sib knew how it was to feel "black and tetchious."

"Well, boys, I'll tell you what happen to me. My mother, she bought a mule from er-uh Captain Jack, who was the boss of the county farm at my home. It was a nice mule. But, by me bein' young—you know how young boys are?—I rode this mule down, run him, you understand. After all, Captain Jack didn't have nothin' to say. He'd done sold the mule to my mother. And this mule finally got mired up in the bottom."

"You say married? Is that the mule you married?"

"Naw, naw, mired, mired up in the mud."

"That *must* be the mule you bought the hat for," Leroy cracked, and all three men burst into guffaws of country laughter, while Sib kept stuttering his story.

"Naw, it ain't! Now listen! Just this old mule got mired up and *died* down there in the bottom."

"I understand."

"Yeah. So er-uh Captain Jack, he told my mother that he was just crazy to git his hands on that stuttering fool of hers. Which was me. Said he was gonna do me just like I did the mule. Get me out there on the gang and—"

"I understand," said Natchez, now grave.

"And my mother had to just scuffle to keep me offa that gang. Ever' little move I'd make, he was watchin' me. And, after all, he done *sold* the mule and she done *paid* him. But he say I killed the mule and—"

Natchez interrupted sharply. "You see the main point is that word they have down here—'Kill a nigger, hire another one. Kill a mule, buy another one.' All these things, everything we've talked about, all these blues and everything, come under that one word. Fact of the business, back not long ago, a Negro didn't mean no more to a white man than a mule."

"Didn't mean as much," said Leroy.

"A black man," Natchez went on, "to what they looked at, was just a *black face*. I knew a man (they call him Mister White) had a plantation about fifty or sixty miles square and he didn't even want a Negro to come *through* his place. The government highway ran through his land, you know? What they call a pike, a main highway where everybody had to go, but he built a special road, ran all around his place, and when you got there it was a sign said 'NEGRO TURN.' You had to turn off the highway and go all around his plantation."

"I knew him, knew him well," Leroy muttered.

"And this Mister White had all white fences around his place. The trees, he painted them white as high as he could reach. All his cattle, his sheeps, goats, hogs, cows, mules, hosses, and everything on his place was white. Anytime one of his animals have a black calf or a black goat—whatsonever it was—Mister White give it to the niggers. Even down to the chickens. He had all white chickens, too. And when a chicken would hatch off some black chickens, he'd say, "Take those chickens out and find a nigger and give 'em to him. Get rid of 'em. I won't have no nigger chickens on this plantation!'"

"I've seed all that, too," said Leroy. "And you know the time a Negro and a white man was standin' by a railroad crossin'? They was talkin', you know. The white man was tellin' the Negro what he wanted him to do. So along come another Negro drivin' a wagon with a white mule hitched to it. Well, the railin' was kinda high at this crossin' and the wheels got caught and the wagon stopped. This Negro who was drivin' begin to holler at that mule. 'Get up!' he says. 'Get along there.'

"So the white man holler up there and asked him, say, 'Hey you, don't you know that's a white mule you talkin' to?'

"'Yassuh, boss,' the Negro tell him. 'Get up, *Mister* Mule!'"

Natchez and Leroy began to guffaw, and, after a moment, when he got the point of the joke, Sib's laughter burst over him in torrents. Again he went staggering down the path, howling with glee and beating his arms helplessly in the air. So we all laughed together in the early morning breeze, blowing the blues out of our lungs and hearts in gusts of wild laughter.

"And how about that Prince Albert tobacco?" gasped Natchez, when he could speak again.

"I've heard of that," said Leroy.

"You know you couldn't go into one of these here little country stores and say, 'Gimme a can of Prince Albert'? Not with that white man on the can."

"What would you say?"

"Gimme a can of *Mister* Prince Albert!"

We were caught up in the gales of squalling laughter that racked Sib, until we must have looked like a party of madmen capering there in the dawn under the lee of the levee. We were howling down the absurdity, the perversity, and the madness that grips the land on which we stood, a beautiful and fecund land, rich in food and genius and good living and song, yet turned into a sort of purgatory by fear.

Now for an instant we understood each other. Now in this moment of laughter, the thongs and the chains, the harsh customs of dominance, the stupefying and brutalizing lies of race had lost their fallacious dignity, but only for an instant. The magic night had gone. Back in Memphis our night's friendship and understanding would vanish like this morning's mist under the pitiless southern sun. The blues would begin again their eternal rhythm, their eternal ironic comment:

> *The blues jumped a rabbit, run him a solid mile,*
> *When the blues overtaken him, he hollered like a baby child. . . .*

"Yeah," said Natchez, his face showing somberly now in the hard light of the July morning, "that's the way things go down around these little southern places—enough to give anybody the blues."

Suggested Reading

Abrahams, Roger D. "Afro-American Worksongs on Land and Sea." In *By Land and Sea: Studies in the Folklore of Work and Leisure Honoring Horace P. Beck on His Sixty-Fifth Birthday,* edited by Roger D. Abrahams, Kenneth S. Goldstein and Wayland Hand, pp. 1–9. Hatboro, Pa.: 1985.

———*Deep Down in the Jungle: Negro Narrative Folklore from the Streets on Philadelphia.* Chicago: Aldine, 1970.

Adler, Bill. *Rap: Portraits and Lyrics of a Generation of Black Rockers.* New York: St. Martin's Press, 1991.

African Methodist Pocket Hymn Book, The. Philadelphia: AME Book Concern, 1816.

Allen, Richard, compiler. *A Collection of Spiritual Songs and Hymns, Selected from Various Authors.* Philadelphia: Printed by John Ormrod, 1801.

Ames, Russell. "Protest and Irony in Negro Folksong." *Science and Society,* 14 (3) No 3, (1950): 193–213.

Banks, Frank D. "Plantation Courtship." *The Journal of American Folk-Lore* 7 (1894): 147–149.

Barlow, William. *"Looking Up at Down": The Emergence of Blues Culture.* Philadelphia: Temple University Press, 1989.

Barrett, Leonard E. *Soul-Force: African Heritage in Afro-American Religion.* Garden City, N.Y.: Anchor Books, 1974.

Black Music in Our Culture. Curricular Ideas on the Subjects, Materials and Problems [1970]. Dominque-Rene de Lerma et al., contributors. Reprint, Kent, Ohio: Kent State University Press, 1972.

Bordelon, Pamela, editor. *Writings By Zora Neale Hurston from The Federal Writers' Project: Go Gator and Muddy The Water.* New York: W.W. Norton & Company, 1999.

Brown Sterling. "The Blues." *Phylon* 12 (4) (1952): 286–292.

Cable, George Washington. "Creole Slave Songs." *Century Magazine* 31 (6) (1886): 807–828.

Carawan, Guy. "Spiritual Singing in the South Carolina Sea Islands." *Caravan* 19–20 (June-July 1960): 20–25.

———, compiler. *We Shall Overcome! Songs of the Southern Freedom Movement.* New York: Oak Publications, 1963.

Carter, Harold. *The Prayer Tradition of Black People.* Valley Forge, Pa.: Judson, 1976.

Castleman, Craig. *Getting Up: Subway Graffiti in New York.* Cambridge: MIT Press, 1982.

Chernoff, John Miller. *African Rhythm and African Sensibility: Aesthetics and Social Action in African Musical Idioms.* Chicago: University of Chicago Press, 1979.

Costello, Mark. *Signifying Rappers.* Boston: Ecco Press, 1989.

Dance, Daryl Cumber. *Shuckin' and Jivin'.* Bloomington: Indiana University Press, 1978.

Davis, Angela Y. "Black Women and Music: A Historical Legacy of Struggle." In *Wild Women in the Whirlwind: Afro-American Culture and the Contemporary Literary Renaissance,* edited by Joanne M. Braxton and Andree Nicola McLaughlin, pp. 3–21. New Brunswick, N.J.: Rutgers University Press, 1990.

Davis, Angela. *Blues Legacies and Black Feminism: Gertrude "Ma" Rainey, Bessie Smith, and Billie Holiday.* New York: Pantheon Books, 1998.

de Albuquerque, Klaus. "Folk Medicine in the South Carolina Sea Islands." *Review of Afro-American Issues and Culture* 2 (2) (1981): 44–74.

Dett, Robert Nathaniel. *The Development of the Negro Spiritual.* Minneapolis: Schitt, Hall & McCreary, 1936.

Dill, Bonnie Thornton. "The Dialectics of Black Womanhood." *Signs* 4 (3) (1979): 543–555.

Dundes, Alan. *Mother Wit. From The Laughing Barrel. Readings in the Interpretation of Afro-American Folklore* [1973]. Reprint, Jackson: University Press of Mississippi, 1990.

Eisen, Jonathon, compiler. *The Age of Rock. Sound of the American Cultural Revolution: A Reader.* New York: Random House, 1969.

Ellison, Mary. *Lyrical Protest. Black Music's Struggle Against Discrimination.* New York: Praeger, 1989.

Epstein, Dena J. "Slave Music in the United States Before 1860." *Notes* 20 (2) (1963): 195–212 and 20 (3) (1963): 377–390.

Escott, Paul D. *Slavery Remembered: A Record of Twentieth-Century Slave Narratives.* Chapel Hill: University of North Carolina Press, 1979.

Eurie, Joseph D., and James G. Spady. *Nation Conscious Rap: The Hip Hop Version.* New York PC International, 1991.

Ferris, William R., Jr. "Black Prose Narrative in the Mississippi Delta." *Journal of American Folk Lore* 85 (336) (1972): 140–151.

Gavins, Raymond. "North Carolina Black Folklore and Song in the Age of Segregation: Toward Another Meaning of Survival." *The North Carolina Historical Review* 66 (4) (1989): 412–442.

Gorn, Elliott J. "Black Spirits: The Ghostlore of Afro-American Slaves." *American Quarterly,* 36 (4) (1985): 141–156.

Hazzard-Gordon, Katrina. *Jookin'.* Philadelphia: Temple University Press, 1991.

Herskovits, Melville Jean. "Drums and Drummers in Afro-Brazilian Cult Life." *Musical Quarterly* 30 (4) (1944): 447–492.

Hubbard, Dolan. *The Sermon and the African American Literary Imagination.* Columbia: University of Missouri Press, 1994.

Hyatt, Henry. *Hoodo-Conjuration-Witchcraft-Rootwork* (No. 4). Hannibal, Mo.: Western Publications, 1974.

Jackson, Bruce. "The Other Kind of Doctor: Conjure and Magic in Black American Folk Medicine." In *American Folk Medicine,* edited by Wayland D. Hand, pp. 259–272. Berkeley: University of California Press, 1976.

Johnson, Guy B. "Double Meaning in the Popular Negro Blues." *Journal of Abnormal and Social Psychology* 22 (1927–1928): 12–20.

Keyes, Cherly. "Verbal Art Performance in Rap Music: The Conversation of the 80s." *Folklore Forum* 17 (Fall 1984): 143–152.

Kuna, Ralph. "Hoodo: The Indigenous Medicine and Psychiatry of the Black American." *Mankind Quarterly* 18 (1977): 137–151.

Leiding, Harriette Kershaw. *Street Cries of an Old Southern City.* Charleston: 1910.

Levine, Lawrence. *Black Culture and Black Consciousness.* New York: Oxford University Press, 1977.

Lomax, Alan. *Folk Song Style and Culture.* Washington, D.C.: American Association for The Advancement of Science Publication, No. 88, 1968.

Longini, Muriel Davis. "Folk Songs of Chicago Negroes." *Journal of American FolkLore* 52 (203) (1939): 96–111.

Lornell, Christopher. "Pre-Blues Black Music in Piedmont North Carolina." *North Carolina Folklore* 23 (February 1975)

Lott, Eric. "Double-V, Double-Time: Behop's Politics of Style." *Callaloo* 2 (3) (1988): 146–150.

Mapson J. Wendell, Jr. *The Ministry of Music in the Black Church.* Valley Forge, Pa.: Judson Press, 1984.

McDonald, Morris J. "The Management of Grief: A Study of Black Funeral Practices." *Omega* 4 (2) (1973): 139–148.

McKinney, Don S. "Brer Rabbit and Brother Martin Luther King, Jr.: The Folktale Background of the Birmingham Protest." *The Journal of Religious Thought* 46 (2) (1989–1990): 42–52.

McRobbie, Angela, ed. *Zoot Suits and Second-Hand Dresses: An Anthology of Fashion and Music.* Boston: Unwin Hyman, 1988.

Mercer, Kobena. "Black Hair/Style Politics." *New Formations,* vol. 3: pp. 33–54. Cambridge: MIT Press, 1990.

Murray, Albert. *Stomping the Blues* [1976]. Reprint, New York: Vintage Books, 1982.

Nelson, George. *Hip Hop America.* New York: Viking Press, 1998.

Nicholas, Elaine, ed. *The Last Miles of the Way: African-American Homecoming Traditions, 1890-Present*. Columbia: South Carolina State Museum, 1989.

Niles, Lyndrey A. "Rhetorical Characteristics of Traditional Black Preaching." *Journal of Black Studies* (September 1984): 41–52.

Odum, Howard W. "Folk Song and Folk Poetry as Found in the Secular Songs of the Southern Negroes." *Journal of American Folklore* 24 (1911): 255–294.

Ogren, Kathy J. *The Jazz Revolution: Twenties America and the Meaning of Jazz*. New York: Oxford University Press, 1989.

Oseloka, O. "African Ritual Drama: An Institution for Moral Instruction." Unpublished manuscript, School of Speech, Northwestern University, n.d.

Oster, Harry. "Negro Humor: John and Old Marster." *Journal of the Folklore Institute,* 5 (1968): 42–57.

Phylon. "The Sacred/Profane Dialectic in Delta Blues: The Life and Lyrics of Sonny Boy Williamson." Vol. 67, No. 4 (1987): 317–326.

Pitts, Walter. "Like a Tree Planted by the Water. The Musical Cycle in the African American Baptist Ritual." *Journal of American Folklore* 104 (413) (1991): 318–340.

Reagon, Bernice Johnson and Sweet Honey in The Rock. *We Who Believe in Freedom. Sweet Honey in The Rock . . . Still on The Journey*. New York: Anchor Books, 1993.

Rooks, Noliwe M. *Hair Raising. Beauty, Culture, and African American Women*. New Brunswick, N.J.: Rutgers University Press, 1996.

Smiley, Portia. "Foot Wash in Alabama and North Carolina." *Southern Workman* 25 (April 1896): 101–102.

Some, Malidoma Patrice. *Of Water and the Spirit. Ritual, Magic, and Initiation in the Life of an African Shaman*. New York: Penguin Books, 1994.

Spencer, Jon Michael. *Black Hymnody: A Hymnological History of the African-American Church*. Knoxville: University of Tennessee Press, 1992.

———. *Protest and Praise: Sacred Music of Black Religion*. Minneapolis: Fortress Press, 1990.

———. *Sacred Symphony. The Chanted Sermon of the Black Preacher*. Westport, Conn.: Greenwood Press, 1987.

———. *Sing a New Song. Liberating Black Hymnody*. Minneapolis: Fortress Press, 1995.

———, ed. *The Emergence of Rap in Black Sacred Music* 5 (1) (1991). Special Issue.

Starks, George, Jr. "Black Music in the Sea Islands of South Carolina: Its Cultural Context, Continuity and Change." Ph.D. dissertation, Wesleyan University, 1972.

Thrower, Sarah. "The Spirituals of the Gullah Negro in South Carolina." Master's thesis in music. Cincinnati: B.M. College of Music, 1954.

Thurman, Howard. *Deep River. Reflections on the Religious Insight of Certain Negro Spirituals* [1955]. Port Washington, N.Y.: Kennikat Press, 1969.

Tracey, Hugh. "Tina's Lullaby." *Journal of the African Music Society* 2 (1961): 99–101.

Wahlman, Maude Southwell. "Gifts of the Spirit: Religious Symbolism in Afro-American Arts." In *Gifts of The Spirit*. Asheville, N.C.: Southern Highlands Handicraft Guild, 1984.

Watson, A. P., and Clifton H. Johnson, eds. *God Struck Me Dead: Religious Conversion Experiences and Autobiographies of Negro Ex-Slaves*. Philadelphia: Pilgrim, 1969.

Wepman, Dennis, Ronald Newman, and Murray Binderman. *The Life: The Lore and Folk Poetry of the Black Hustler*. Philadelphia: University of Pennsylvania Press, 1976.

White, Deborah Gray. "The Lives of Slave Women." *Southern Exposure* 12 (6) (1984): 32–39.

Wiggins, William H., Jr. *O Freedom: Afro-American Freedom Celebrations*. Knoxville: University of Tennessee Press, 1987.

Willis, Andre Craddock. "Rap Music and the Black Musical Tradition: A Critical Assessment." *Radical America* 23 (4) (1991): 29–38.

Work, John Welsey, Jr. *Folk Song of the American Negro* [1915]. Reprint, New York: Negro Universities Press, 1969.

Selected Discography:
Albums, Cassettes, and CDs

Spirituals and Gospel

Afro-American Spirituals, Work Songs and Ballads, edited by Alan Lomax. Album 3/Five 78 RPM Records (AAFS 11–15) and AAFS L3/LP 33 1/3 RPM.

The Church of God and Saints of Christ. *In Him I Live; Choral Songs and Solos*. (LYRCD-7423) (CD).

Elder Charles Beck and Congregation. *Urban Holiness Service*. Recorded and edited by William H. Tallmadge. Folkways FR 8901.

Daise, Ron, and Natalie Daise. *We'll Stand the Storm (and other spirituals)*. G.O.G. Enterprises, 1989 (c).

Fathers and Sons: Male Gospel Groups. (SPIRIT- 1001) (CD).

The Gospel at Colonus. Warner Brother Records 1–25182, 1985.

Gospel Warrior. (SPIRIT-1003) (CD).

The Great Gospel Women. (SH-6004) (CD).

The Great Gospel Men. (SH-6005) (CD).

Roland Hayes Sings the Life of Christ. As Told Through Afro-American Folksong. With Reginald Boardman, Piano. Vanguard Everyman Classics, 1976. SRV 35250.

Mahalia Jackson. Columbia CL 644.

Negro Religious Songs and Services, edited by B. A. Botkin. Album 10/Five 78 RPM Records (AAFS 46–50) and AAFS L10/LP 33 1/3 RPM.

Dock Reed and Vera Hall Ward. Spirituals. Recorded and edited by Harold Courlander. Folkways FA 2038.

Paul Robeson. *Songs of Free Men/Spirituals*. Columbia, 1945.

Paul Robeson. *Songs of My People*. RCA 1972. Reissue of *Paul Robeson. Black Spirituals and Work Songs (1925–1929)*.

Paul Robeson. *Swing Low Sweet Chariot*. Columbia Records, 1949.

Sweet Honey in the Rock. *Feel Something Drawing Me On*. Flying Fish Records, 1985. FF-90375.

Ten Years of Black Country Religion. Yazoo 1022.

Wade in the Water, Vols. 1–4, 4 CD Set, SF-40072–75 [Vol. 1 *African American Spirituals: The Concert Tradition* (SF-40072), Vol. II *African American Congregational Singing: 19th Century Roots* (SF-40073), Vol. III *African American Gospel: The Pioneering Composers* (SF-40074), Vol. IV *African American Community Gospel* (SF-40075)].

Clara Ward. *Gospel Concert*. Dot 3138.

Freedom Songs

Sing for Freedom: The Story of the Civil Rights Movement Through Its Songs. Book/CD Set SO-105. Compiled by Guy and Candie Carawan.
Sweet Honey in the Rock: All for Freedom. MFPD-2230 (CD).

Ragtime, Blues/Jazz

Afro-American Blues and Game Songs, edited by Alan Lomax. Album 4/Five 78 RPM Records (AAFS 16–20) and AAFS L4/LP 33 1/3 RPM.
Anderson, T. J., Conductor. *Classic Rags and Ragtime Songs. The Smithsonian Collection.* N001.1975.
Atlantic Jazz Piano. Atlantic Recording Corporation, 1986. 81707–1 Stereo.
Lil Hardin Armstrong. *Satchmo and Me.* [Oral history by Lil Hardin Armstrong] Riverside RLP 12–120.
Young Louis: "The Side Man." [Lil's Hot Shots and Louis Armstrong's Hot Five]. MCA 1301.
Big Bills. "Unemployment Stomp." Vocalion 04378.
T. Bones Blues. Atlantic [Canada] 8258 (c).
Blind Blake: Ragtime Guitar's Foremost Fingerpicker. Yazoo 1068.
Blues in the Mississippi Night. Collected and edited by A. Lomax. United Artists UAL 4027.
Betty Carter. *Round Midnight.* Roulette ROU (S) 5005.
Sam Charters, Compiler. *Ragtime 1. The City, Brass Bands, and Nickel Pianos.* [c. 1904–1931]. Folkways. RBF 17. 1971.
Ida Cox. *Blue Ain't Nothing Else But Milestones.* MFP 2015.
Ida Cox. *Wild Women Don't Have the Blues. Foremothers, Vol. 1.* Rosetta RR 1304.
Reverend Gary Davis—1935–1949. Yazoo 1023.
Basic Miles. The Classic Performances of Miles Davis. Columbia Records/CBS, Inc. 1973. PC32025.
Birth of the Cool, Miles Davis. Capitol DT-1974.
Fats Domino. *The Fabulous "Mr. D".* Imperial LP 9055.
Dorothy Donegan. *The Many Faces of Dorothy Donegan.* Mahogany 558.101.
Duke Ellington Recollections of the Big Band Era. Atlantic Recording Corporation, 1982 [1974]. 90043–4.
Duke Ellington. *Sophisticated Lady.* BMG Music, 1992. [1972] Bluebird 07863–61071–4.
The Entertainer: Music of Scott Joplin. (SH-98015) (CD).
Essays in Ragtime. Folkways FG 3563.
Buster "Buzz" Ezell. "Roosevelt and Hitler," Fort Valley Blues, Matchbox SDM 260.
The Best of Ella Fitzerald, Vol. 1. MCA (2)—4047.
The Best of Ella Fitzerald, Vol. 2. MCA (2)—4016.
Forty Years of Women in Jazz. Stash STB 001.
Dexter Gordon. *American Classic.* Elecktra/Asylum Records, 1982. El-60126.
Dexter Gordon. *Daddy Plays the Horn.* Affinity Records, 1983. AFF 103.
Dexter Gordon. *One Flight Up.* Blue Note, 1985. BST 84176.
W. C. Handy. "Aunt Hager's Blues," Okeh 4789.
Coleman Hawkins. *Body and Soul.* Bluebird, 1939.
History of Jazz, edited by Frederic Ramsey, Jr. Folkways FJ 2801, 2811, 11 vols.
Billie Holiday. *God Bless the Child.* CBS M66273.
Billie Holiday. The Golden Years. Columbia Records, 1962. C3L21, Volumes I, II, III.
Billie Holiday. *The Voice of Jazz.* Verve 2304104, Volume I.
A Date with Lena Horne. 1944. With Fletcher Henderson. Sunbeam 212.

Jazz Women: A Feminist Retrospective. Stash ST 109.

Blind Lemon Johnson. "Lonesome House Blues," Yazoo 1069.

Blind Willie Johnson. *Praise God I'm Satisfied*. Yazoo 1058.

James P. Johnson. *Snowy Morning Blues*. Columbia Records, 1927.

J. J. Johnson. *Eight Ball*. King 4400.

J. J. Johnson. *Groovin'*. Blue Note 1506.

J. J. Johnson. *Neckbones*. Warner Brothers 1272.

Robert Johnson. The Complete Recordings. Columbia C346222 (c,d).

Tommie Johnson. *Cool Drink of Water Blues*. Wolf WSE 104.

Bessie Jones. *So Glad I'm Here*. Rounder 2015 (c).

Scott Joplin, King of Ragtime: His Life and Music. Written and directed by Ward Botsford;
    narrated by Gordon Gould (Sine Qua Non). Meet the Classics MC 331, 1977.

Scott Joplin. *Treemonisha*. Selections. Audiophile AP-71/2 and Riverside RLP 126.

Andy Kirk and His Clouds of Joy: Instrumentally Speaking, 1936–1942. MCA Jazz Heritage
    Series 1308.

Leadbelly [Huddie Ledbetter]. *Leadbelly Sings Folk Songs*. Smithsonian/Folkways 40010 (c,d)

John Lewis. *The Bridge Game. Based on J. S. Bach's "The Well-Tempered Clavier" Book I, Vol. 2*.
    Philips, 1986. 826698–1.

John Lewis. *Morpheus*. Prestige 7025.

John Lewis. Rouge. *Capitol* T-762.

Carmen/Billie. Carmen McRae Sings "Lover Man" and Other Billie Holiday Classics. Columbia PC
    37002.

Blind Willie McTell, The Library of Congress Session. Melodeon 7323 [1940 Recordings].

Ellis Marsalis and Eddie Harris. *Homecoming*. Spindletop Records, 1985. STP-105.

Mean Mothers: Independent Women's Blues, Vol. 1. Rosetta RR 1300.

Charles Mingus. *Epitaph*. CBS Records Inc., 1990. C2T45428. C2T46081 & 46082, 2 vols. (CD).

Thelonious Monk. Live at the Jazz Workshop. Columbia Records/CBS Inc., 1982. C238269 C38270
    Stereo.

Thelonious Monk. *Underground*. Columbia Records/CBS Inc. CJT 40785, 1968.

Jelly Roll Morton. [Morton talks, plays, and sings] Recorded by Alan Lomax. Riverside 9001–9012.

Charlie Parker. *The Complete Savoy Studio Sessions*. Arista Records, Inc. S5J5500, 1978.

The Charlie Parker Sides. Norman Granz Jam Session. Verve. 833564–1, 1976.

Charley Patton—Founder of the Delta Blues. Yazoo 1020, 2-LP set.

Little Esther Philips. The Complete Savoy Recordings. Savoy SJL 2258 (c,d).

Esther Phillips. *Confessin' the Blues*. Atlantic Recording Corp., SD 1680, 1976.

Esther Phillips with Beck. *For All We Know*. KUDU Records. KU 28-Stereo. 1976.

*Ragtime: "Cake-Walks, Military Bands. Ragtime Orchestras, Coon Concerts, Blues and Jass,"
    Vol. 2 (1900–1921)*. RCA [France] PM 42402. Black and White Series, Vol. 190.

Ragtime. Piano Roll Classics by S. Joplin, S. Turpin, et al. Riverside RLP 12–126.

Ragtime: A Recorded Documentary (1899–1929). Piedmont PLP 13158 [Out of Print].

Ma Rainey's Black Bottom. Yazoo 671.

Red, White & Blues: Women Sing of America. Rosetta RR 1302.

Roots of Rock. YAZ-1063 (CD).

St. Louis Blues—The Depression. Yazoo 1030.

Nina Simone. *The Best of Nina Simone*. RCA Victor LSP 4374.

Bessie Smith. Great Original Performances, 1925–33. BBC REB 602 (c,d).

Bessie Smith. "Nobody Knows You When You're Down and Out," Columbia 14853—D.

Bessie Smith. *"Tain't Nobody's Business If I Do," The World's Greatest Blues Singer*. CBS 66258.

Bessie Smith. *Nobody's Blues But Mine*. Columbia G31093.

Mamie Smith. Complete Recorded Works in Chronological Order, Vol. 1-Vol. 5. Document 551–555.

Songs We Taught Your Mother. Prestige/Bluesville 1052.

Victoria Spivey. *The Recorded Legacy of the Blues*. Spivey Reissues LP 2001.

Stepping on The Gas: Rags to Jazz—1913–1927. New World Records NW 269.

Willard "Rambling" Thomas. *Ramblin' Thomas: Chicago Blues*. Biograph BLP 12004, 1928.

"The Divine Sarah." Sarah Vaughn/The Early Years. With Tadd Dameron and Bud Powell. Musicraft MSV 504.

The Voice of the Blues—Bottleneck Guitar Masterpieces. Yazoo 1046.

The Best of Dinah Washington. Roulette ROU (s) 42014.

Jazzin' Babies' Blues. Ethel Waters, 1921–27, Vol. 2. Biograph BLP 12026.

The Best of Muddy Waters. Chess 9255 (c).

Muddy Waters. Rollin' Stone. (1948–59). Chess [UK] (d Red1).

Muddy Waters. *Trouble No More*. Chess CH 9291 (c,d).

Peetie Wheatstraw and Kokomo Arnold. Classic Blues BC-4.

The Best of Mary Lou Williams. Pablo (S) 2310 856.

Mary Lou Williams. *Mary Lou's Mass*. Mary 102.

Mary Lou Williams. Folkways 2843.

Mary Lou Williams and Cecil Taylor: Embraced. Pablo Live 2620–108.

Mary Lou Williams, The Asch Recordings, 1944–47. Folkways FA 2966.

Mary Lou Williams. *First Lady of the Piano*. Inner City IC 7006.

Mary Lou Williams. *Zodiac Suite*. Folkways 32844.

Women's Railroad Blues: Sorry But I Can't Take You. Rosetta RR 1301.

Rhythm and Blues

A Tribute to Curtis Mayfield. Warner Brothers Records, Inc. 9362–45500–2, 1994.

Rap

Big Daddy Kane. *It's a Big Daddy Thing*. Cold Chillin', 1989.

Boogie Down Productions. *Ghetto Music: The Blueprint of Hip Hop*. Jive/Zomba, 1989.

Ice Cube. *Amerikkka's Most Wanted*. Profile, 1990.

Kid Frost. *Hispanic Causin' Panic*. Virgin, 1990.

L. L. Cool J. *Bad*. Def Jam, 1987.

Marley Marl. *In Control: Volume I*. Cold Chillin/Warner Bros., 1992.

NWA. *Niggaz4life*. Priority, 1991.

NWA. *Straight Outta Compton*. Priority, 1989.

Public Enemy. *Fear of a Black Planet*. Def Jam, 1990.

Gil Scott-Heron. *The Revolution Will Not Be Televised*. Fly and Dutchman, 1969.

Work and Prison Songs and Hollers

The McIntosh County Shouters: Slave Shout Songs from the Coast of Georgia. Recorded by Art Rosenbuam. Album No. FE 4344. New York: Folkways Records, 1984.

Negro Prison Camp Songs. Ethnic Folkways Library FE 4475.
Negro Work Songs and Calls, edited by B. A. Botkin. Album 8/5–78 RPM Records (AAFS 36–40)
    and AAFS L8/LP 33 1/3 RPM. The Archives of Folk Song. Library of Congress.
Harry Oster, collector and editor. *Angola Prisoner's Blues,* Folk Lyric LSS A-3; *Prison Work Songs
    [LA Prison],* Folk Lyric LSS A-5; *Angola Prison Spirituals,* Folk Lyric LSS A-6; *Rev. Pearly
    Brown-Georgia Street Singer,* Folk Lyric FL-108; *Those Prison Blues* [Sung by Robert Pete
    Williams, LA Prison Singer], Folk Lyric FL-109.
Wake Up Deadman: Black Convict Worksongs. RDR-2013 (CD).

Storytelling

Animal Tales Told in the Gullah Dialect. By Albert H. Stoddard of Savannah, Ga. AAFS L44–462
    LP 33 1/3 RPM.
Emmanuel Dunn. "John and the Stones." [John and Old Marster Cycle stories] Recorded by Harry
    Oster. Motif 1971.
Maum Chrish' Chaa'stun. A Gullah Story. By Virginia M. Gerty. Track Eight Records.
    TE007, 1979.
Josh White. "The Story of John Henry." Elektra Records 123-A.

Toasts and Boasts

Speckled Red. *Speckled Red: The Dirty Dozens.* Delmark DL 601.
Sunnyland Slim. "Shake It." Prestige/Bluesville 1016.
Bessie Smith. "Gimme a Pigfoot." Okeh 8945 (78 RPM).
Joe Turner. "Watch That Jive." Savoy MG 14016.
Muddy Waters. "Hoochie Coochie." Chess 1427.
Muddy Waters. "Long Distance Call." Chess LP 1427.

Various

Afro-American Blues and Game Songs. Edited by Alan Lomax. Library of Congress Recording
    AAFS 14.
Pink Anderson and Gary Davis. *American Street Songs.* [Sacred and Secular Negro Street Singing
    from South Carolina and Harlem]. Riverside RLP 12–611.
Been in the Storm So Long. From Johns Island, South Carolina. Folkways FS 3842.
Big Bill Brownzy Interviewed by Studs Terkel. Folkways FG 3586.
William Levi Dawson. *Negro Folk Symphony.* Decca DL-10077.
One Two Three and a Zing Zing Zing, edited by Tony Schwartz. Folkways FC 7003.
Paul Robeson: Ballad for Americans and Carnegie Hall Concert, Vol. 2. Vanguard, 1965.
Play and Dance Songs and Tunes, edited by B. A. Botkin. Library of Congress recording
    AAFS L9.
Skip Rope. Folkways FC 7029.
Sweet Honey in the Rock: Still on the Journey. EBD2525 (CD).
Sweet Honey in the Rock: I Got Shoes. MLPD-9–42534-2 (CD).

Traveling Through the Jungle: Negro Fife and Drum Band. Music from the Deep South. Testament T-2223.
Words from the Frontlines: Excerpts from the Great Speeches of Malcolm X. RCA Records. 66132–2/4.

Selected Videos, Films, CD-ROMs and Slides

Audio-Visual Center of Indiana University

American Music: From Folk to Jazz and Pop. ABC; McGraw-Hill, 46 minutes. 2 reels. RS-689.
Begone Dull Care. [Animation of jazz composition performed by Oscar Peterson Trio.] McLaren Film Series; NFBC, 8 minutes. RSC-197 (color).
Dance: Echoes of Jazz. NET; Indiana University A-V Center, 30 minutes. RS-660.
Helen Tamiris and Her Negro Spirituals. Nagtam; McGraw-Hill, 16 minutes. RS 593.

California Newsreel

Bird. [Charlie Parker] David Valdes, executive producer. Warner Home Video, Inc., 1989. 161 minutes.
Round Midnight. [American jazz expatriates in Paris] Irwin Winkler, producer, 1987. Warner Home Video, Inc. 132 minutes.
Saturday Night. Sunday Morning: The Travels of Gatemouth Moore. [Blues musician turned evangelical preacher]. Louis Guido, producer/director, 1992. 70 Minutes.
We Shall Overcome. Jim Brown, director, 1989. 58 minutes.
Wild Women Don't Have the Blues. Carole van Valkenburgh and Christine Dall, 1989. 58 minutes.

Center for Southern Folklore

Gravel Springs Fife and Drum. Produced by William Ferris, Judy Peiser, and David Evans, 1991. 10 minutes.

Center for the Study of Southern Culture

Beale Street. Produced by Alexis Krasilovsky, Ann Rickey, and Walter Baldwin, 1989. 29 minutes.
Mississippi Delta Blues. Produced by Anthony Herrera. 29 minutes.
Shoutin' the Blues. Produced by Agrinsky Films. 16 minutes.

Film-Maker's Cooperative

Bessie Smith. Produced by Charles Levine, 1968. 13.5 minutes.

Jane Balfour Films, Ltd.

The Land Where the Blues Began. Produced by Alan Lomax, 1981. 60 minutes.

Kino on Video

Art Blakey: The Jazz Messenger. 78 minutes.
Big City Blues: Son Seals. 28 minutes.
Chicago Blues. Featuring Muddy Waters. 1972. 50 minutes.
Jazz in Exile. Featuring Dexter Gordon and Phil Woods. 58 minutes.
Jazz Shorts. Featuring Charlie Parker, Duke Ellington, Gil Scott-Heron et al. 30 minutes.
Last of the Blue Devils. Featuring Count Basie, Big Joe Turner et al. 1979. 90 minutes.
The Leaders: Jazz in Paris. 54 minutes.
Mystery, Mr. Ra [Sun Ra]. 51 minutes.
Mingus: Charles Mingus, 1968. 58 minutes.
The Ornette Coleman Trio. 26 minutes.
Percy Mayfield [Poet laureate of the blues]. 30 minutes.
Sun Ra: A Joyful Noise. 60 minutes.
The Universal Mind of Bill Evans, 1966. 45 minutes.

Library Video Company

Masters of American Music Series. Five-volume set. A1005-B. 60 minutes each. [*Count Basie: Swinging the Blues*, A1006-B; *John Coltrane: The World According to John*, A1007-B; *Thelonious Monk: American Composer*, A1008-B; *Sarah Vaughan: The Divine One*, A1009-B; *The Story of Jazz: The First Authoritative Program on the History of Jazz*, A1010-B]
Roots of Gospel Series. Two-volume set. A5100-B. 40–60 minutes each.
We Shall Overcome. Harry Belafonte narrates story of civil rights anthem. D6005. 58 minutes.

Multicultural Media

Blues Houseparty: Masters of the Piedmont Blues. BH-001. 60 minutes.
Bluesland: A Portrait in American Music. BMG-80087–3. 85 minutes.
Chicago Blues: Muddy Waters. RHAP-9012. 50 minutes.
The Ladies Sing the Blues. VIEW-1313. 60 minutes.
Lighnin' Hopkins: Rare Performances 1960–1979. VI-13022. 52 minutes.
Mance Lipscomb in Concert. V-13011. With accompanying book. 58 minutes.
Elizabeth Cotten. [Ragtime, blues performer] V-13019. With accompanying booklet. 59 minutes.

The Story of Jazz. BMG-80088–3. 97 minutes.
Tryin' to Get Home: A History of African American Song. HJ-001. 55 minutes.

Public Broadcasting Service (PBS) Videos

Amazing Grace with Bill Moyers. Produced by Public Affairs Television, 1990. AMAG-000C–CR94. 90 minutes.
The Dancing Man—Peg Leg Bates. Produced by Dave Davidson and Amber Edwards in association with Hudson West Productions and South Carolina ETC, 1992. DANM-000-CR94. 60 minutes.
From Jumpstreet. [Thirteen-part Series on the black musical heritage: *Black Influence in the Recording Industry,* 30 minutes; *Black Music in Theater and Film,* 30 minutes; *Blues: Country to City,* 30 minutes; *Dance to the Music,* 30 minutes; *Early Jazz,* 30 minutes; *Gospel and Spirituals,* 30 minutes; *Jazz Gets Blue,* 30 minutes; *Jazz People,* 30 minutes; *Jazz Vocalists,* 30 minutes; *Rhythm and Blues,* 30 minutes; *Soul,* 30 minutes; *The Source of Soul,* 30 minutes; *West African Heritage,* 30 minutes] Produced by WETA, Washington, D.C., 1980. FJSG-000-CR94.
That Rhythm, Those Blues. From *The American Experience.* George T. Nierenberg, producer. AMEX-110-CR94, 1988. 60 minutes.

Syracuse University Classroom Film/Video Rental Center

Scott Joplin [King of Ragtime]. Narrated by Eartha Kitt. Pyramid, 1977. 15 minutes.

Time Life Video and Television

Good Rockin' Tonight. Produced and directed by Bud Friedgen. J 592–02.

Universal Color Slide Company

Alberta Hunter. V23129. Color and stereo. 60 minutes.
Mabel Mercer: Cabaret Artist "Forever and Always." V23135. Hi-Fi Stereo. 58 minutes.

Updata

History of the Blues. CD 2320 DOS MAC. (CD-ROM)

Chapter 6

DYNAMICS OF LANGUAGE

In this chapter, we once again hear the community, the expressions of unity, among African Americans with soundings that began in the era of enslavement continuing to the present time. "Dynamics of Language" supports Melville Herskovits's thesis of continuity between African and African American history and culture. This is seen most clearly in the Sea Islands off the coasts of the Carolinas, Georgia, and Florida. Because language is the mother of culture and subsequently of history, we glimpse African-derived American society in the Gullah tongue. This Africanism, Gullah, also known as Geechee, is the object of much controversy. Even some younger members of the contemporary Gullah community have viewed the language of their forebears, even of their own parents, as a form of "substandard" English. They have perceived the traditional arts of basketry and wood carving as unsophisticated and unworthy of passing on to their own children. However, in Charles Joyner's essay, "Gullah: A Creole Language," we hear another and more powerful estimation of the language and how it contributed to survival during the slavocracy and can help illustrate the nature of masking and masquerade in Africa-informed America. "Dynamics of Language" indicates the "how" of language, and the motivations and usage to which language is put by those using it for particular reasons.

Gullah language and culture are the last vestiges of African traditions that were brought to the United States by the first African captives. It is derived from a Caribbean Afro-pidgin, which, by merging African speech rhythms with African and English words, created the creole that Joyner discusses. Gullah is an oral language, created in and for the present time and thus, at the moment of its articulation, is a living language with its own accompanying gestures and intonations. These gestures and intonations add to an African American oral tradition based on indirection and double textuality that is used, as Joyner says so eloquently, not only to reveal but to conceal. Gullah protects and allows its users to "mask" and isolate themselves from the influences of the dominant society, just as being islanders isolates them geographically from the mainland. The language is noted for its uniqueness of verbal pronounal, and nominal systems of pluralization, its nongender distinctions, and its present active voice. Thus, in a sense, it too is a place located in black consciousness and cosmology. The importance Gullah speakers attach to naming traditions and to secrecy about one's true name once again shows the power *nommo* has for African peoples. The association of day, weather, and season (which also place a person), and the circumstances of one's birth attach a cosmological aura around the individual being named and possess great spiritual content.

Closing the chapter is a sermon recorded by anthropologist Gerald L. Davis in *"I Got the Word in Me and I Can Sing It, You Know." A Study of the Performed African-American Sermon*. Included in this work are five recorded sermons with an accompanying analysis of each. For "Dynamics of Language," I selected one of two sermons by the Rev. Carl J. Anderson entitled, "Ezekiel and the Vision of Dry Bones." This jeremiad, an example of a prophetic warning, contains what Davis describes as the "African-American performed word":

> Certainly no one event is more compelling for me than the performance of the Word—God's codebook for secular living and sacred example—and the masterful, electric interpretation of that codebook, through the use of expressive language systems for the accomplished African-American preacher.[1]

Davis writes in his preface, also, about the connectedness between the crafted sermon and the "structured complexities of language invention and expressive language forms in African America."[2] Not only does Rev. Anderson's sermon illustrate sacred performance, but it also suggests the call-and-response aspect of the black church and the movements and gestures of the preacher (as well as, in this case, the lack of movement by some members of the congregation, whom Rev. Anderson admonishes because they have not brought their Bibles and are not "studying" the word, along with him, as he speaks). This sermon is another "sounding" that the black and white signals of written words can not contain.

---

1 Gerald L. Davis, *"I Got the Word in Me and I Can Sing It, You Know." A Study of the Performed African-American Sermon* (Philadelphia: University of Pennsylvania Press, 1985), p. xiv. Davis's comments on the American South as the source of African American culture and on the style of the African American "preacher" being "southern" are worth noting (see pp. 9–10). He also notes the antithesis to the Herskovits/Du Bois/Dunham theory of African survivalism: E. Franklin Frazier's, *The Negro Church in America* (New York: Schocken, 1964).

2 Ibid.

Gullah: A Creole Language

Charles Joyner
Folklorist/Historian

Charles W. Joyner is the author of Folk Song in South Carolina *(1971) and
"Oral History as Communicative Event: A Folkloristic Perspective" in* Oral
History Review *(1979: 47–52). He is widely published in many aspects of
Southern culture. Currently, Joyner is the Burroughs Distinguished Professor
of history at Coastal Carolina University.*

1

• • •

As a moving force in the creation of Afro-American culture in the crucible of slavery,
the development of Gullah was comparable to the development of English, German,
or French in the creation of these respective national cultures.

2

It is now impossible to say with any certainty what Gullah sounded like as spoken
by the slaves. The Gullah speech of present-day All Saints Parish [Editor's note: All
Saints Parish, located in the South Carolina lowcountry, is also known as "Waccamaw
Neck" because it is between the Waccamaw River and the Atlantic Ocean. The parish
is on what is called the "rice coast" where the richest rice plantations were. This volume concentrates on the Lower All Saints Parish, which is in Georgetown District.] is
probably no more than a pale reflection of antebellum slave speech. Such sources as
Genevieve Willcox Chandler's interviews with ex-slaves who had learned to speak the
language in the mid-nineteenth century offer tantalizing glimpses of its vocabulary and
its pronunciation and an opportunity to discover its grammatical rules.

   As a language Gullah did not behave like English; it formed plurals and indicated
possession and negation differently; it used a somewhat simpler system of pronouns
and a somewhat more complex system of verbs than did English. Certain of the most

Charles Joyner, "Gullah: A Creole Language," in Down by the Riverside. A South Carolina Slave Community
(Urbana: University of Illinois Press, 1984), pp. 196–224.

distinctive features of the language merit brief consideration here. To concentrate on Gullah as spoken by the last generation of slaves in All Saints Parish, in the context of slave folklife, is not to imply that their speech was unrelated to black speech elsewhere and at other times—any more than studies of contemporary black speech in comparative linguistics imply that speech exists in isolation from other aspects of culture.

Gullah pronouns in All Saints Parish made no distinction between men and women. In this behavior Gullah retained a structure common to a number of African languages, such as Ibo, Ga, and Yoruba. The initial all-purpose Gullah pronoun was *e,* as in "After de war *'e* come back and took into big drinking and was' 'em till *'e* fall tru" (After the war he came back and took into big drinking and wasted it [his money] until it fell through [i.e., he lost it]). *E* served as the masculine, feminine, and neuter pronoun. Later, under the influence of English, *he* became the all-purpose Gullah pronoun, although *e* was not completely replaced during slavery, when the last generation of slaves was learning to speak the language. The Gullah pronoun *he* was not the same, however, as the English pronoun *he,* but served for masculine, feminine, and neuter gender. Interchangeable with *e, he* could serve as a subject or to indicate possession, as in "*He* broke *he* whiskey jug" (He broke his whiskey jug), or "Sam *he* husband name" (Sam was her husband's name).[1] The Gullah pronoun for objects in All Saints Parish was *em,* which served for masculine, feminine, and neuter gender, whether singular or plural, as in "See *'em* the one time" ([I] saw him once); "Grandfather took old Miss Sally on he back to hid *'em* in the wood where Maussa" (Grandfather took old Miss Sally on his back to hide her in the woods where the master [was hiding]); "He couldn't believe *'em*" (He couldn't believe it); and "Flat *'em* all up to Marlboro" ([They] took them all on flatboats up to Marlboro [District]).[2]

Gullah pronouns of the slavery period were more complex than English pronouns in one respect, however: Gullah included a form for second person plural, which English lacks. Standard English pronouns cannot distinguish between singular and plural in second person. Writers variously represent the Gullah pronoun for second person plural as *yinnah* or *unna.* Like other Gullah pronouns, the same form was used as a subject or to indicate possession, as in "*Yinnah* talk big storm hang people up on tree?" (Are you [all] talking about the big storm that hung people up in the trees?) or "if *unna* kyant behave *unna* self, I'll tek yu straight home!" (If you can't behave yourselves, I'll take you straight home).[3]

Two other features of the Gullah nominal system that distinguished it from English should be mentioned. One was that Gullah speakers marked possession by juxtaposition rather than by word forms, as in "*He* people wuz always free" (His people were always free) or "Joshuaway been *Cindy* pa" (Joshua was Cindy's father). The other distinctive feature of the Gullah nominal system was the practice of non-redundant plurals. If pluralization were otherwise indicated in a Gullah sentence, it was not also indicated by the noun, as in "Dan'l and Summer two both my *uncle*" (Both Daniel and Summer were my uncles).[4] This practice was in sharp contrast to English, which required agreement in number between determiners and the nouns they modify.

The prepositions of slave speech in All Saints Parish, unlike English prepositions, did not use different forms to indicate whether one was approaching some location or one was already there. The same form was used for approach prepositions—

"Old people used to go *to* Richmond Hill, Laurel Hill, and Wachesaw and have those prayer-meeting"—or for static-locative prepositions—"One stop *to* Sandy Island, Montarena landing" (One [Yankee gun boat] stopped at Sandy Island, Mt. Arena landing).[5]

The verbal system of Gullah was considerably more complex than that of English. First, equating verbs occurred in past tense, as in "When my mother *been* young woman, work in rice" (When my mother was a young woman, she worked in rice); but they were usually omitted in present tense, as in "Dem Yankee wicked kind a people, drive me from me home" (Those Yankees are a wicked kind of people to drive me from my home). The omission of an equating verb is called zero copula. Gullah sentences used zero copula for verbal adjectives, as in "I *glad* for freedom till I *fool*" (I was so glad for freedom that I appeared foolish). In this regard, Gullah retains the verbal adjective construction of several West African languages, including Ewe, Fante, Kikongo, and Yoruba, but contrasts strongly with English.[6]

Another All Saints Gullah construction that retained West African linguistic forms was the combination of verbs both to take an object and to serve as a connective. The most common verbs used in this construction were *say* and *go* (usually in the form *gone*). The following are examples: "One gentman at de gate *tell me say* he Messus broder, is Messus dare in?" (A gentleman at the gate told me he is the Mistress's brother; is the Mistress therein?) and "They didn't do a God thing but *gone and put* a beating on you, darling" (They didn't do a God's thing but put a beating on you, darling). In this usage the slaves retained both the form and the function of the same construction in Ibo and Twi.[7]

Perhaps the most unique feature of the Gullah verbal system was its distinction between continuing and momentary actions (aspect) rather than specifying the relative time of the action (tense). In their emphasis on aspect over time, Gullah speakers in All Saints Parish retained the grammatical rules of such West African languages as Ewe, Kimbundu, Mandinka, and Yoruba.[8] Unlike English, Gullah rarely distinguished between present and past tenses in the verbal system. When the slaves did mark past tense in Gullah, they used the verb form *been:* "When the Yankee come I *been* on the loom" (When the Yankees came I was on the loom). In the preceding sentence, ex-slave Ellen Godfrey used both marked and unmarked verb forms for simple past tense (*been* and *come,* respectively). If the slaves only occasionally marked past tense, they often marked aspect, whether ongoing, completed, or habitual. They indicated continuing actions by using the old creole form *duh* preceding the verb or the newer form *-ing* following the verb: "Yuh can't rest, bubber, w'en hag *duh* ride yuh" (You can't rest, brother, when a hag is riding you [i.e., when you have nightmares]), or "You *getting* this beating not for you task—for you flesh!" (You are getting this beating not for [failing to finish] your task—[but] for your flesh!). *Duh* and *-ing* were interchangeable but were not used together. Waccamaw slaves marked continuing actions in the past with *been* plus the action verb, as in "Aunt Ellen *been looking* for you all day" (Aunt Ellen has been looking for you all day). The slaves indicated habitual actions, past or present, by using *be* plus the action verb, as for example, "You orter *be* carry money with you" (You should [habitually] carry money with you).[9]

Similarly, Gullah speakers on the Waccamaw rice plantations distinguished between ongoing and momentary negation in their speech. Momentary negation was indicated by *ain't,* as in "I *ain't* want him" (I did not want him). The slaves marked ongoing negation by *didn't*—as in "Maussa *didn't* low you to marry till you twenty-two" (The master did not allow you to marry until you were twenty-two)—for past on-going negation, and by *don't*—as in "They *don't* eat much"—for present ongoing negation. It is perhaps more appropriate to regard *didn't* and *don't* as full negators in their own right, rather than as contractions of *do* or *did* plus a negator. Multiple negation was often used in Gullah for additional emphasis, as in "She say she *never couldn't* refuse when the old people ask for a drink" (She said she could never refuse when the old people asked for a drink).[10]

Furthermore, when Hagar Brown exclaimed, "I *too* glad my chillun ain't born then!" (I am very glad my children had not been born then!), or when one of the slaves at Hagley told Emily Weston, "See, ma'am, young duck *bery* lobe run bout, and your pen broke!" (See, ma'am, young ducks very much love to run about, and your pen broke [and your hog ate two of my ducks]), they exemplified a continuity with African ways of modifying adjectives and adverbs.[11]

Three final distinctive features of slave speech should be discussed. One is that certain verbs that normally take complements in English did not necessarily take complements in Gullah. Margaret Bryant's lament, "Missus, I *ain't wuth.* I *ain't wuth!*" (I am not worth [anything, i.e., I am not feeling very good]), requires a complement in English, but not in Gullah. Second, Gullah speakers expressed passive voice in a construction that would indicate active voice in English, as, for example, "How come you *wanter bury* Watsaw?" (Why do you want to be buried at Wachesaw?) or "A crow *kin eat*" (A crow can be eaten [i.e., is edible]). A similar construction is prominent in Afro-American speech in Jamaica. Third, the slaves transformed declarations into yes/no questions by adding the word *enty* at the end of statements, as in "Chillun, ain't find duh plum, enty?" (Children, you didn't find the plums [did you]?). *Enty* has been variously translated as *n'est ce pas* and *ain't it.*[12]

The last generation of slaves in All Saints Parish thus spoke a language that differed from English in several fundamental features. The slaves did not distinguish between location and approach in their prepositions, nor among genders in their pronouns. They indicated pluralization only once in a sentence, but they used distinctive forms of the second person pronoun to distinguish between singular and plural. They designated possession by juxtaposition. In their verbal system the use of equating verbs was varied, but other verbs were combined in distinctive ways. Both verbs and negators distinguished between ongoing and momentary actions rather than when those actions might have taken place. Negation could be intensified by using multiple negators. Verbal complements could be omitted. The same form was used for active or passive voice; declarative sentences could be made into questions by the use of the interrogative tag *enty.* While house servants may have spoken nearly standard English, many Gullah speakers in the Waccamaw rice fields were quite consistent in their use of these features. Whatever else might be said of the relationships between black and white speech in America, Gullah—as spoken by the last generation of slaves—followed a different set of grammatical rules than did English. Those white commentators who considered Gullah an imperfect result of "a savage and primitive people's endeavor to acquire for themselves the highly organized language of a very highly civilized race" were not only racist, but linguistically ignorant.[13] However much Gullah and English may have shared the same vocabulary, Gullah and English were not the same language.

3

Gullah did not, of course, spring forth full-grown in the mid-nineteenth century. Its roots, however, remain wrapped in linguistic controversy. Linguistic pronouncements are notoriously hazardous, and historians have generally been reluctant to make them. An acceptable explanation is likely to be complex, for the making of a language is not a simple process. If historical and linguistic evidence are put together, however, some of the answers seem neither elusive nor ambiguous. In retrospect it seems clear that the speech of the slaves on Waccamaw rice plantations resulted from the convergence of a number of African languages with English. The resulting speech, Gullah, exemplified a creole language, which in turn developed from an earlier pidgin. The terms *pidgin* and *creole,* although frequently misunderstood, are technical linguistic terms and imply no value judgments, derogatory or otherwise. A pidgin is by definition a second language: it has no native speakers. Pidgins are developed as a means of communication among speakers of various languages. The linguistic elements in a pidgin are simplified within a context of restricted use—usually for trade. Pidgins are neither broken languages nor distortions of the grammatical structure of the source languages. On the contrary, pidgins are quite regular in grammatical structure as the result of the simplification process, although their specific grammatical patterns may not be the same as those of any single source language. Whenever a pidgin is passed on to succeeding generations as a native tongue, it is said to be a creole language. Since creole languages must serve all the functions of a language, not just the limited linguistic interactions for which pidgins are devised, creole languages expand rapidly in complexity in succeeding generations. This intricate process in which a language based upon the convergence of other languages undergoes expansion in both use and form is called creolization.[14]

To gain some perspective on the creolization process in Gullah, it may be helpful to move back in time from All Saints Parish in the mid-nineteenth century to West Africa in the age of the slave trade, simply to note the varieties and structural similarities of West African languages. West Africa was a region of several hundred mutually unintelligible languages. With a constant need for communication with neighboring peoples who spoke diverse tongues, linguistic skills became highly developed among West Africans. Many in the Senegal-Gambia region, for instance, were bilingual, fluent in both Wolof and Mandingo, the two most widespread languages of the region. Bilingualism at some level was a necessity in polyglot West Africa. Despite their mutual unintelligibility, however, there were several similar linguistic patterns that African languages shared and that set them apart from other languages of the world. In particular, the two great West African language families, Bantu and Sudanese, shared strong structural similarities.[15]

Thus the process of pidginization began in Africa out of the need for speakers of disparate languages to communicate with one another, and the process was helped along by structural similarities among otherwise different tongues. Perhaps the most unusual catalyst for pidginization, and certainly the most ironic, was the slave trade. In the slave baracoons of the West African coast and in the wretched shipholds of the Middle Passage, enslaved Africans from various regions, speakers of distinct tongues with centuries of tradition behind them, were forced to seek similarities in their languages and to develop whatever means of communication they could. Wolof speakers from Senegambia may have served as interpreters among the enslaved Africans and between the slaves and their captors, lending a strong Wolof cast to the emerging pidgin.[16]

Pidginization became widespread among Africans in the New World. Those linguistic patterns among the mutually unintelligible languages most familiar to the largest number of Africans had the best chance of surviving in the new pidgin. Much of the vocabulary was supplied by the alien languages of the masters. Thus there developed an Afro-Dutch pidgin in the Virgin Islands; Afro-Portuguese pidgins in Brazil and Curaçao; Afro-Spanish pidgins in Cuba, Puerto Rico, and Colombia; Afro-French pidgins in Louisiana, French Guiana (influenced by Portuguese), Haiti, Guadeloupe, Grenada, and other Antilles. There were both Afro-French and Afro-English pidgins in Trinidad and Tobago. Afro-English pidgins developed in Barbados, Antigua, Guyana, Jamaica, and South Carolina. The Dutch colony of Surinam was a special case. It developed an Afro-English pidgin as well as an Afro-Portuguese pidgin with strong English lexical influences, rather than an Afro-Dutch pidgin. Many of these pidgins were adopted by succeeding generations and became creoles.[17]

The first generation of slaves in South Carolina came mostly from the Caribbean, where they had already learned an Afro-English pidgin. Because they constituted only a small proportion of Carolina's small population, and because in their generation contacts between enslaved Africans and their English-speaking masters were of necessity close and personal, their speech may have been nearer to standard English than that of later generations who came directly from Africa. But the great expansion of rice culture in the early eighteenth century brought about an enormous increase in the young colony's slave trade. The expansion in both rice and slaves was caused in part by the opening up of the rich rice lands north of the Santee, including those along the Waccamaw. The importation of thousands of slaves annually from West Africa fostered intercultural contact on a scale unprecedented in South Carolina, not only between Africans and Europeans, but among diverse groups of Africans. With a higher ratio of Africans to Europeans than anywhere else on the North American mainland, Georgetown District became the mainland equivalent of a Caribbean colony in the eighteenth and nineteenth centuries. The rice planters, when they purchased slaves, preferred Africans from the Senegal-Gambia region, from the rice-growing regions of the Windward Coast, and from the Congo-Angola region. Nearly 40 percent of the Africans enslaved and brought to South Carolina between 1730 and the end of the legal slave trade came from Angola. Another 20 percent came from Senegambia, and the other 40 percent variously from the Windward and Gold coasts, Sierra Leone, and elsewhere. The growing Waccamaw plantations shared fully in these human imports.[18]

But the dominant linguistic features of the emerging pidgin were not necessarily the same as the dominant regional origins of the enslaved Africans. The linguistic features capable of being comprehended by the largest number of slaves, whatever their native tongues, were most likely to survive; those least comprehensible were least likely to survive. Some languages, such as Wolof, had been even more widespread as second languages in Africa than as native tongues. The chances that features of such languages would survive were far greater than those of a language that functioned only as a native tongue. Furthermore, if English and any given African language or languages shared some feature, it had a better chance of surviving than features that strongly differed. Certainly not all African features were retained, nor were all English features acquired.[19]

But most Africans coming into the Waccamaw region in the eighteenth century spoke little if any English. When confronted with the harsh dilemmas of their new environment—as slaves of alien, white-skinned people whose shouted commands they could not understand—their response must have been to lapse into silence, struggling to find meaning in the words yelled at them, straining to isolate some familiar sound in the stream of gibberish. Where once they had lived among family and friends whose languages and folkways they shared, now they found themselves among strangers who had also fallen victim to the slave trade, strangers who could understand neither one another nor their white masters. Two overwhelming needs—to comprehend the masters and to comprehend one another—had profound and complex, and sometimes contradictory, effects on the linguistic response of the Africans to their enslavement. If there were forces at work on the plantations to discourage retention of their native languages, there were also circumstances that had an opposite effect. While the social dominance of the masters served as a strong incentive to learn English, the numerical dominance of the blacks facilitated their retention of African patterns of speech. While they lacked a common linguistic heritage, through trial and error in their efforts to communicate with one another Africans increasingly became aware of common elements in their diverse tongues. More and more they found other speakers of their own or similar African languages. Out of these opposing tendencies—to learn English and to retain African speech patterns—they created a new language: Gullah.[20]

This new language took root to such an extent among enslaved Africans that it was passed on to succeeding generations on the Waccamaw and elsewhere in the lowcountry. To African-born slaves Gullah would have remained a pidgin, a second language, but to the American-born generations it was a creole, a native tongue. Once Gullah acquired native speakers and assumed all the functions of a language, it expanded rapidly in complexity. From then on, incoming Africans learned Gullah neither through trial-and-error nor from the plantation whites, but from American-born blacks.[21]

Gullah had not one but many African sources. Perhaps the most conspicuous was Wolof, but elements from Sierra Leone were especially important in the new language; and there were also influences from Fante, Ga, Kikongo, Kimbundu, Mandinka, Twi, Ewe, Ibo, and Yoruba. But African languages were not, of course, the only influences on the development of Gullah. As Gullah passed from the pidgin to the creole stage in the early eighteenth century, the Carolina lowcountry was one of the most linguistically diversified areas on the North American mainland. The sources of the All Saints population included not only slaves from various parts of West Africa but also the French Huguenot Belins, LaBruces, and Mazyks; the Allstons and Westons from England; the Frasers, Heriots, Nesbits, and Wards from Scotland; the Tuckers from the Bahamas; and the Middletons from Barbados. In Charleston were also heard Quakers with their distinctive use of English as well as other British settlers with regional accents from such places as Warwickshire, Lancashire, Ulster, and Jamaica. There were also speakers of German, Spanish, and Portuguese, and even of Creek and Cherokee. While the ultimate influence of these linguistic strains varied with their social and political valuation, a discernible lowcountry English—which was both influenced by, and influential upon, Gullah—emerged in this complex linguistic environment.[22]

If there was a European influence on the speech of the slaves, there was a corresponding African influence on the speech of the masters. In the lopsided demographic circumstances of the lowcountry nearly all whites necessarily had much contact with blacks, but many blacks had only limited contact with whites. The Waccamaw planters by and large learned to talk like their slaves rather than expecting their slaves to talk like them. Creolization on the Waccamaw was not limited to one race. It left its mark on the posterity of both transplanted Africans and transplanted Europeans and influenced their speech patterns in ways still apparent. It is not surprising, given the demographic dominance of Africans, that whites were affected by the linguistic patterns of the blacks. Northern and English visitors rarely failed to note the extent to which the planters, outnumbered nine to one by their slaves, absorbed elements of Gullah. An English traveler referred to the speech of the planters as "that peculiar accent derived from almost exclusive association with negroes." A northern correspondent wrote that "the children of the planters, brought up on the plantations, and allowed to run in the woods with the little negroes, acquired the same dialect; and to-day many a gentleman's son regrets that it is apparent in his speech." Many of the white plantation children perhaps learned their first language from a Gullah-speaking nurse, thus becoming native speakers of Gullah, and learned English as a second language. Some apparently never really mastered English. It was said of Benjamin Allston, Sr., of Turkey Hill, the father of Martha Allston Pyatt, that "his language was like a negro's, not only in pronunciation, but even in tone." Many of the Waccamaw rice planters remained fluently bilingual in Gullah and English from their childhood throughout their lives. Others would have been at least passively bilingual, able to comprehend the Gullah of their slaves but not to speak it.[23]

Those slaves who came into the greatest contact with whites also became actively or passively bilingual in Gullah and English. Creolization did not cause slave speech to develop in a completely uniform way; as early as the eighteenth century slaves were observed along a speech continuum ranging from the pidgin of the newly arrived Africans to fully standard and even elegant English, depending upon access to education. House servants played an important role in dual creolization. They helped to bring Gullah into the Big House and standard English—that is, the regional standard—to the cabins on the street.[24]

Thus Gullah developed in a situation of language contact on the Waccamaw, with reciprocal influences of African and English features upon both the creole language and the regional standard. The English of the whites and the Gullah of the blacks were similar enough in vocabulary to permit relatively easy communication, despite some occasional difficulties, but different enough for some whites to regard Gullah as a corrupted form of English and thus evidence of the mental indolence or incapacity of the slaves. Doubtless even the Waccamaw rice planters had occasional difficulties in understanding the slaves. Any number of factors might work to foster difficulties in master-slave communication. The masters' problems in comprehending the slaves' speech, however, did not always result from inherent difficulties in the interaction of languages that were similar but not identical. Thriving on ambiguity and paralinguistics, Gullah speakers proved their language to be as adept in impeding communication as in facilitating it. Gullah could reveal, but it could also conceal; and slaves had a stake in concealing information from the masters. By cloaking African words with their African meanings behind English words with similar sounds, slaves may have constructed a code through which they could communicate with one another while keeping the masters uninformed.[25]

4

The African penchant for using indirect and highly ambiguous speech, for speaking in parables, was adapted by slaves on the Waccamaw rice plantations to a new natural, social, and linguistic environment. This aspect of creolization was strikingly illustrated in their proverbs. African-born slaves undoubtedly brought with them numerous African proverbs, although none survived on the Waccamaw in its original African form. This loss is not surprising, for proverbs depend upon the skillful use of metaphor, and the translation of metaphor from one language to another is always difficult and sometimes impossible. Even today attempts to make literal translations of proverbs from one language to another are often meaningless to readers not conversant with the original tongue. Since the enslaved Africans came from many different linguistic stocks, and since their emerging pidgin language did not (in its pidgin stage) offer a sufficiently large metaphoric repertory from which to choose even roughly equivalent metaphors, poetic translations were even more difficult than literal ones. To say that African proverbs themselves did not survive on the Waccamaw is not to say, however, that the grammar of African proverb usage—both as a means of aesthetic variation upon drab everyday speech and as a means of avoiding the painful effects and insults of direct commentary—did not persist in the proverbs of the new language.[26]

By employing the grammar of African proverb performance and the largely English vocabulary of the new creole language, All Saints slaves were able to transform older African proverbs into metaphors of their collective experience on the Waccamaw rice plantations. Some African proverbs were retained virtually unchanged in Gullah. The Hausa proverb "Chattering doesn't cook the rice" continued in All Saints Parish as "Promisin' talk don' cook rice." Another Hausa proverb—"Does dog eat dog?"—retained even its rhetorical question format in the Gullah "Dat's dog eat dog, enty?" The Gullah proverb "Empty sack can't stand upright alone" was a Waccamaw version of the Mandingo "It is hard for an empty sack to stand upright." And the Dahomey distinction between rhetoric and reality, "The mouth talks plenty that the heart does not say," reappeared on the Waccamaw as "Heart don't mean ever thing mouth say."[27] Other African proverbs, however, underwent minor changes. The Fante proverb "One bird in the hand is worth ten in the sky" became the Gullah "Most kill bird don't make stew" (An almost killed bird does not make a stew). The Dahomey

"Crooked wood makes crooked ashes" became "Onpossible [impossible] to get straight wood from crooked timber." And the Bantu proverb "Every beast roars in its own den" became the Gullah "Every frog praise its own pond if it dry."[28] The wording of proverbs was relatively fixed, but, like all forms of folklore, proverbs were subject to variation. Usually the variation was minor, but more radical changes in the imagery were not infrequent as African proverbs were adapted to a new environment. The difficulty of translating meaning and rhetoric at the same time made some African proverbs resistant to direct translation. In such cases, the slaves retained the meaning of the African proverbs but completely transmuted the rhetoric into metaphors more meaningful to their new environment. Thus the Gullah proverb "Most hook fish don't help dry hominy" (An almost hooked fish [one not quite caught] does not improve the taste of dry hominy) is related in meaning to the Yoruba proverb "'Nearly' is an individual we invariably meet on the way"; but it is related in rhetoric to another Gullah proverb "Most kill bird don't make stew." Similarly, the Gullah proverb "Chip don't fall far from block" is related semantically, but not rhetorically, to the Fante proverb "No one needs to teach the leopard's child how to spring."[29]

The proverbs of the slaves were more fixed in their structural patterns than in their wording. Among the common structural patterns were the *If A then B* formula, as in "Ef you hol' you Mad e would kill eby Glad" (If you hold your anger, it will kill all your happiness), and the rhetorical question pattern—so common in Africa—as in "Don' hol' nuttin down deep een you heart. Ain' God gi' you mout fo talk' em?" (Do not hold anything deep down in your heart. Did God not give you a mouth with which to talk about it?).[30] Perhaps the most common structural forms were simple positive or negative propositions ("Change gwine come" [is inevitable] or "One clean sheet can' soil another" [cannot soil another]); double propositions ("It takes a thief to catch a thief. Nightwalkers meet nightwalkers"); or even triple propositions ("So I totes mah powder en sulphur en I carries mah stick in mah han en I puts mah truss in Gawd" (So I carry my powder and sulfur and I carry my stick in my hand and I put my trust in God).[31] Multiple propositions in a proverb proved an apt structure for the slaves to use in making invidious distinctions, as in "Man p'int, but God disapp'int." Perhaps the most striking use of this structural form by the slaves was in their proverbs contrasting blacks and whites. "Black people rule sickness with magic," one such proverb contends, "but white people get sick and die." "People ain' got no business tryin' to be Gawd," another advises. "Not black people anyways. Let de white people go on. Dey is gwine to hell anyhow!"[32]

The slaves used their proverbs as metaphors of social relations, that is, to indicate relationships among the elements of the proverb, between the proverb and the real world, and, by extension, among the elements of the real world. Through their proverbs the slaves made distinctions by comparison and contrast and commented upon how things happened, affirming or denying equivalence ("Det wan ditch you ain fuh jump" [Death is one ditch you cannot jump] or "Hell ain' no hole. A hole 'ud git full")[33] and causation ("Likker'll make you not know you mama" [Liquor will make you not know your mother] or "The master didn't make all the world in a day"). A variation on negative equivalence was the proverb in which one element was greater than the other, such as "There are more ways to kill a dog than to choke him with butter."[34]

The slaves' use of proverbs in All Saints Parish cannot be completely understood without reference to the proverb's strategy, that is, to its plan for relating the situation described within the proverb to the real-life social relations to which the proverb was being applied. Perhaps the most frequent use of proverbs was to offer advice. A proverb might present either of two mutually exclusive strategies—it might recommend an action or it might suggest that the situation was normal and could not be changed, thereby promoting acceptance or resignation. These recommendations were, of course, given indirectly, metaphorically. "Work while it is day" and "Put yuh bess foot fo moss" (Put your best foot foremost [forward]) are examples of the *action* strategy. Hagar Brown's "Don't let 'em put dey hand in your eye! Some people gouge 'em" counseled defensive action. Gullah speakers on the Waccamaw had an interesting inversion of the widespread proverb "Still waters run deep," which reversed the strategy from a counsel of taciturnity and reticence to one of action, advice made more powerful by coupling the reversal of strategy with a metaphorical relationship between water and the ritual purification of baptism: "Still water gits stale an' scummy too quick. It can' wash away sin."[35] The practical experience of rice field and swamp found poetic expression in slave proverbs.

That trouble is a natural condition of the world was suggested by the Gullah proverb "Trouble goin' fall!" Here was an example of the *acceptance* strategy. "Trouble made for man," the proverb warned. "Ain't goin fall on the ground! Goin fall on somebody!" There was no way to anticipate trouble, another proverb cautioned, all one could do was "just take it like I takes it!" When asked, "How you take it?" the speaker replied, "As it come! As it come!" Still another proverb counseled patience, for troubles come and troubles go: "A march that comes in like a lion will go out as quiet as a new-born lamb."[36] Some proverbs suggested that the hearer was responsible for his or her own misfortunes and that nothing was to be done except to accept the consequences: "You's made a hard bed for you sef, now you got to lie in it." Other proverbs advised treating misfortune as a necessary learning experience, for example, "Sad we got to be burn 'fore we learn" and "Burn child dread fire, you know." Still others suggested that, however hard the misfortunes might be, they could be borne. According to one proverb, "Eby back is fitted to de bu'den" (Every back is fitted to the burden). According to Sabe Rutledge, "What God got lot out for a man he'll get it."[37]

Two important elements of Gullah proverbs were their sense of authority—a result of their detachment and generalization—and their ambiguous and allusive poetic nature, which made it possible for them to be used in a variety of ways. The proverbs of the slaves were set off from ordinary speech by such poetic devices as alliteration ("Sin is easier to stand dan shame"), rhyme ("Tit fuh tat, butter fuh fat, ef yuh kill my dawg, I kill yuh cat"), repetition ("Heavy hearts make heavy steps"), personification ("Every frog praise its own pond if it dry!"), meter ("Rob Peter to pay Paul"), and parallelism ("Mo rain, mo ress, but fair wedder bin bess").[38] Because of such poetic qualities and their allusiveness and ambiguity, metaphoric proverbs were broadly applicable. They could be cited with equal authority in a wide range of situations. Indeed, it was possible for a slave in All Saints Parish to advise either action or inaction in any situation by means of an appropriate proverb. This flexibility has sometimes made proverbs seem contradictory to modern readers, but, just as a language gives its speakers words for saying either yes or no, the Gullah proverb repertory enabled the slaves to offer whatever advice seemed appropriate to the situation, and to do so in heightened poetic language. The Gullah proverb repertory contained proverbs touting boldness ("Cards an' dice is like all in life; dey ever falls well for bold players") or caution ("Er good run bettuh dan uh bad stan" [A good run is better than a bad stand]) with equal art and with equal authority.[39]

The full meaning of any given proverb was only clear in the context of its use. As a Fante proverb has it, "There is no proverb without the situation." There were no specialized occasions for reciting proverbs on the rice plantations of the Waccamaw. Some forms of folk expression, such as the telling of folk tales, were set apart for the evening after the rice field tasks were accomplished; but proverbs were recited on any occasion that language could be used. Proverbs could be used for the artistic ornamentation of everyday discourse, or they could be used in informal litigation—that is, in the settling of conflicts, tensions, and arguments among the slaves. Although the Gullah proverbs were rather straightforward in their application of metaphor, they were one of the most complex folklore genres in their extreme sensitivity to context.[40] Unfortunately, there are no known descriptions of the contexts of proverb usage in All Saints Parish during slavery. In this regard, as in other linguistic matters, one must be more tentative and less precise than one would wish.

5

Inevitably, personal accounts of language interaction among the slaves were rare. Like the languages of Africa, Gullah expressed a high degree of ambiguity and double entendre in face-to-face speech. Since Gullah was an oral rather than a written language, slaves on the Waccamaw rice plantations must have developed a heightened sensitivity to vocal intonation, gestures, and kinesics. The intonations of slave speech must be considered within the context of the tonal languages of some of the Africans who were brought to South Carolina as slaves—Bini, Ewe, Fante, Ga, Ibo, Mandingo, and others. Gullah speakers did not regularly use tone to distinguish meaning, as many African languages do. In slave parlance, however, words did sometimes carry different—or even opposite—meanings depending upon intonation. For example, the adjective *bad,* when intoned by a slave on a slow, falling tone (like *baaad*), could be an expression of admiration for another slave who successfully flouted Ole Maussa's rules. More common, however, was the retention of African intonation patterns in Gullah sentences without their African meanings. These included such practices as high or mid-level tones at the end of declarative sentences, rising tones at the end of declarative sentences, level tones throughout a statement, use of tones that fell from high to mid, use of tones that rose from low or mid to high, and the use of level tones at the end of questions. These intonation patterns did not occur under similar conditions in English. The typical expectations of English were that sentences would use generally level tones, with a falling tone at the end of statements and a rising tone at the end of questions. Not only did Gullah differ strongly from English in intonation but also in patterns of loudness or softness, of syllable and breath dynamics, and in the use of pitch and stress.[41]

The transition from an oral to a written language gave rise to increasing English influences upon Gullah—direct influences upon some slaves, indirect influences upon others. Despite legal prohibitions against teaching slaves to read and write in South Carolina, many masters and more mistresses, including Emily Weston of Hagley and Mary Vereen Magill of Richmond Hill, taught at least some of their slaves to read the Bible. Emily Weston gave Testaments to the graduates of her literacy classes. Surviving letters from such slaves as Mulatto Joe to Robert F. W. Allston, Samuel Taylor to Elizabeth Blyth, Mary Ann (surname unknown) to Emily Jordan, and George Simons to Francis Weston testify to the ability of some slaves to write as well as to read. Some slaves, such as Prince, the Westons' coachman, were even considered to be bookish. But while slave literacy seems to have been relatively widespread on the Waccamaw, it was not intensive. Only a small proportion of the slaves on any plantation ever learned to read or write.[42]

Literate slaves had a more intensive encounter with the language of highest prestige, English, than did other Gullah speakers. Their continuous contact with English was not only influential on their own speech but also on that of other slaves with whom they were in daily communication. Gullah gradually shed more and more of its creole characteristics and acquired a greater resemblance to English. This process was an example of decreolization, and during the nineteenth century it fostered an increasing degree of local variation in slave speech.[43] One of the most important changes in Gullah during decreolization was the tendency for it to lose more and more of its surviving African words and to replace them with words from English. Gullah also shifted grammatically in the direction of the regional standard, although it retained a number of structural differences that stemmed from differences in the histories of the two languages. Underlying these changes in vocabulary and grammar were such factors as the relative prestige of speakers, contact across social strata, and value orientations among each group.[44]

Decreolization is a more rapid form of linguistic change than the usual internal language change. What has all too often been considered an imperfect process of deletion from the regional standard can now be seen as an ongoing addition to a creole language. In decreolization, unlike other forms of linguistic change, grammar tends to change before sound. Decreolization tends to create a continuum among speakers from the creole toward the regional standard. The process of decreolization began in slavery, mainly affecting house servants, but the rapid linguistic change that is usually associated with decreolization had to wait until the breakdown of rigid social stratification, which was partially accomplished by emancipation.[45]

6

Another way in which the slaves preserved their African linguistic heritage was exemplified in their naming practices. For the slaves of All Saints Parish, as for their African ancestors, naming was socially significant, almost mystical, and illustrated personal and historical experiences, attitudes toward life, and human values. In many African societies the power to name was perceived as the power to control, to order reality. Thus the slaves and the masters vied with one another for the right to name the children. Probably most slave names on the vast Waccamaw rice plantations were chosen by the slaves themselves. Certainly with the high annual birth rate among the slaves many masters found it easier to leave such matters to the slaves. But other masters, perhaps in recognition of the power inherent in naming, insisted on their right to name the slave children. As a result, many slaves were given two names: one an outer or public name, given by the master, the other an inner or basket name, given by the parents and used only among kin and friends. Sabe Rutledge, for instance, although known by his African name *Sabe* among the other slaves, was called *Newman* by his master. His grandfather, the driver at The Ark plantation, was also known by different names in the Big House and on the slave street: "They called him Rodrick Rutledge for shortness," Sabe Rutledge later recalled. "My grandpa *real* name Jim."[46]

The use of basket names did not stem exclusively from master/slave competition over the right to name, but followed traditional African double-naming customs. Basket names, even as late as the mid-nineteenth century, were often words of African origins. In All Saints Parish, as in the Caribbean, one general pattern was to name children one of the African day names, after the day of the week on which they were born. All seven African day names appear to have been still in use on the Waccamaw as late as the Civil War.[47] See the table on the following page for a comparison of the day names and African derivatives.

Day names were not the only African names common among the slaves of All Saints Parish. The following list, although by no means exhaustive, does at least demonstrate an extraordinary perpetuation of African names among Waccamaw slaves after several generations in the New World.[48]

ENGLISH	AFRICAN	ENGLISH	AFRICAN
Affa	Affy	Rina	Rhina
Binah	Binah	Saby	Sabe
Binyky	Binky	Sambo	Sambo
Cotta	Cotta	Sango	Sancho
Congo	Kongy	Satirah	Satira
Fante	Fany	Sawny	Sawney, Sawne
Mingo	Mingo	Sena	Cinda
Minto	Minta, Minda	Sibbey	Sibby
Monda	Munder	Yono	Yanie

But African continuities were not manifested solely in the static retention of easily recognized African names. On the contrary, behind many of the apparently English names in the plantation records were African naming practices. The transition from the sound spoken by the slaves to the script written by the masters was not always accomplished without a certain cultural transformation. What the master thought a given spoken name to be and what a slave thought a given spoken name to be were not always

Distribution of African Day Names in Antebellum All Saints Parish

DAY OF WEEK	GHANA	GUYANA	JAMAICA	ALL SAINTS
		Masculine Names		
Sunday	Kouassi	Couachi	Quashee	Quashey, Quash
Monday	Kodio	Codio	Cudjo	Cudjo
Tuesday	Kouamina	Couamina	Cubbenah	Ben ?
Wednesday	Kouakau	Couacou	Quaco	Quacco
Thursday	Yao	Yao	Quao	Quauo
Friday	Kofi	Cofi	Cuffee	Cuffee
Saturday	Kouami	Couami	Quamin	Tommy ?
		Feminine Names		
Sunday	Akouassiba	Corrachiba	Quashiba	Quasheba
Monday	Adioula	Adioula	Juba	Juba
Tuesday	Aminaba	Amba	Beneba	Bina, Bhina, Venus, Venice
Wednesday	Akouba	Acouba	Cuba	Cupid
Thursday	Ayaba	Yaba	Abba	Abby
Friday	Afouba	Affiba	Phibba	Phoebe, Phebe, Pheby
Saturday	Amoriba	Abiniba	Mimba	Minda, Pemba

the same. In many cases the masters wrote into their records whatever English name sounded most like the name spoken by the slave. If a slave couple informed their master that they had named their son *Keta,* a common name among the Yoruba, Hausa, and Bambara, the master might have understood the child's name to be *Cato.* Similarly, if a slave couple told a planter that they had named their daughter *Haga,* a Mandingo name, he might have written *Hagar* into his records. The Mandingo name *Heke,* meaning a powerful animal, may have survived behind the English name *Hercules,* often spelled Hackless in the slave lists (and still pronounced that way) in All Saints Parish. The following is a sampling of English names from Waccamaw plantation records that may have been homonyms of African names:[49]

ENGLISH	AFRICAN	ENGLISH	AFRICAN
Abby	Abanna	Jemmy	Jeminah
Abraham	Abra	Joe	Cudjo
Billy	Bilah	Lizzie	Liceta
Ben	Bungoh	Moses	Moosa
Dunkin	Dunke	Pat	Pattoe
Esther	Esher	Sam	Samba
Jack	Jaeceo	Quinny	Quenchy
		Trim	Tremba

In other cases the African meaning was retained behind a direct translation of the name into English. Day names were frequently translated from their African names into their English equivalents. Such day names as *Monday* and *Friday* were quite common among All Saints slaves, as were such other seasonal basket names as *March, April, August, Summer,* and *Winter.* An ex-slave, Monday Holmes, described how he came to be named: "My RIGHT name been Samson but I never been call dat YET. Name Samson outer the Bible. Calls me MONDAY 'cause I born that day."[50]

The creolization process, by which African ways of using language were applied to a new tongue, produced such new seasonal basket names as *Christmas.* All Saints slaves continued other African approaches to naming as well, although the specific names produced were not African. The African tradition of naming children after conditions at the time of their birth—the weather, the appearance or temperament of the child, or the attitude of the parents toward the birth—was reflected on the Waccamaw in such names as *Snow, Brass, Boney, Lazy, Handful, Grace, Welcome, Fortune,* and *Hardtimes.* Similarly, slave names on the Waccamaw revealed the adaptation to English of African patterns of naming after localities (*London, Paris, Dublin,* and *Scotland*) and after titles (*King Agrippa, Prince, Doctor,* and *Gentry*). On the other hand, the masters' influence was clear in the abundance of classical (*Caesar, Brutus, Nero, Cato, Juno,* and *Pompey*), literary (*Hamlet*), and historical (*Washington* and *Napoleon*) names. Biblical names seem to have been popular with both masters and slave parents (*Abraham, Amos, Dan'l, Esau, Esther, Isaac, Israel, Lazrus, Peter, Paul,* and *Mary*). Secondary names were often necessary to distinguish among slaves who shared the same name. Occasionally occupational names (*Driver Sam, Cooper Sam, Driver Primus,* or *Carpenter Tom*) were used to make such distinctions, but more commonly they were made on the basis of age (*Big Joe, Little Joe, Old Nancy, New Rachel,* or *Grandma Kit*), physical appearance (*Long Scipio*), or genealogy (*Cato's Mary, Bob's Rachel,* or *Minder's Joe*).[51]

Sometimes genealogical relationships were reflected in slave naming practices in other ways. At least some All Saints slaves continued to follow the African pattern of having children named by their grandparents. Hagar Brown's mother, for instance, insisted on naming her grandchild. As Hagar Brown recalled many years later, "Had me gang of chillun when ma die. I had Samuel, I had Elias, I had Arthur, I had Beck. Oh, my God! Man, go way! I had Sally! I had Sally again. I didn't want to give the name 'Sally' again. Say, 'First Sally come carry girl.' Ma say, 'Gin 'em name "Sally"' I faid (afraid) that other one come back for him. Had to do what Ma say. Had to please 'em. Ma name Sally."[52]

Plantation records fail to reveal the extent to which slaves on the Waccamaw, with or without their masters' permission, used surnames among themselves; but there are tantalizing glimpses in the memories of aged ex-slaves and the observations of perceptive visitors, such as Wyndham Malet. Malet noted, "The negroes have family names, but you never hear them used except among themselves, they call them 'titles,' e.g. Mrs. W's second footman is Gabriel, his family name Knox; Mary, the housemaid's title, is Green." Some slaves took their titles from their masters. According to ex-slave Mariah Heywood, "Grandma Harriet, (Harriet Mortor wuz her title but that time they always gone by they Master title). Joe Heywood was Joe Belin—he was Parson Belin man—he take the Heywood title after mancipation. Poinsette (Uncle Fred) ALWAYS carry that title. That day, all the right hand servant always take they Massa title." After emancipation some slaves—like Joe Heywood—refused to keep their master's surname and chose another. Others—like Fred Poinsette—retained the titles they had used in slavery, even if it had been the surname of their former masters. It should be remembered that the use of titles was not between master and slave, but among the slaves themselves. If some adopted their master's surname as a title, others chose their titles on the basis of personal characteristics. Margaret Bryant described how her husband had chosen his title on the basis of his pre-eminence as a carpenter. "Husband title, husband nichel (initial) been 'One.' Number one carpenter—give 'em that name Michael One—and he give 'em that name." Few slaves appear to have adopted their owners' surnames as titles; fewer still adopted new titles at emancipation. Elizabeth Collins, a young English woman who served as house-keeper at Hagley plantation from 1859 to 1864, wrote, "It must be remembered the ne-groes have their *titles* as well as the white man. I have often noticed they used them among themselves, and have no doubt if slavery is abolished that they will claim the recognition of their *titles*." Apparently they did so. Certainly there was little correlation in the manuscript census records for All Saints Parish in 1870 between the surnames of the freedmen and the surnames of the largest slaveholders in 1860, such as Ward and Weston (although there were numerous black Allstons, Alstons, and Pyatts). It seems likely that some slaves adopted their owners' names as titles in bondage, but most did not. Many of those who did abandoned them upon emancipation.[53]

Through their insistence upon their right to name their own children, Waccamaw slaves successfully (for the most part) asserted control over a critical area of their lives. Through their adoption of titles, no less than through their perpetuation of African tra-ditions of naming, the slaves of All Saints Parish proclaimed their sense of identity and community, and of continuities with their individual and communal pasts. In the cre-olization process they retained some African names outright, and they adopted some English names outright. More commonly, if less obviously, they adapted African gram-mars of naming to the needs of a new linguistic and social environment. Since one's name is his most basic label of identity, it was no trivial accomplishment.

7

Thus, by every device of sound and syntax, semantics and lexicon, gesture and intona-tion, the slaves combined elements of their various African heritages to create a new creole language. There were, of course, British contributions to Gullah, particularly in matters of vocabulary and to some extent in pronunciation. The sources of most, al-though not all, of the word forms in the creole were to be found in British regional di-alects. There were no British parallels, however, for many of the grammatical patterns of Gullah, which shared many structural features with West African languages and with the creole languages of the Caribbean. The culture contact of transplanted Africans and transplanted Europeans in All Saints Parish fostered processes of creolization by which African pronunciations, meanings, and grammatical patterns converged with English vocabulary and some English pronunciations and meanings. Gullah, originating as a pidgin, became the native tongue of the black speech community. In the course of creolization Gullah passed from pidgin to creole to the beginnings of decreolization in the direction of the regional standard.[54]

Not the least of the ironies of Afro-American history is that aspects of black speech related to Gullah are now stigmatized by many blacks as well as whites as illiterate or associated with field hands, in contrast to the high prestige of "proper" English. In retrospect one should be more impressed with the success of the slaves, a people of diverse linguistic backgrounds and limited opportunities, in creating a creole language and culture than appalled at their "failure" to adopt *in toto* the language and culture of their masters. The continuing—and sometimes acrimonious—debate on the relationship among Gullah, other manifestations of black speech, and the speech of whites is beyond the scope of this study. Whatever its significance to present-day controversies, Gullah was critically important to the slaves, creating a special bond among them. The continuation of numerous features of Gullah into contemporary black English, indeed the continuation of Gullah itself, surely points to its importance as a potent symbol of cultural unity among the slaves who developed it and passed it on to posterity. The potent symbol stood for a potent reality. Speech communities, to an even greater extent than political communities, imply a shared culture and world view. Since Gullah was susceptible to individual manipulation, it was the shared property of everyone in the speech community, packed with the symbols of that community's culture and its values. Slaves could not communicate with one another, could not offer proverbial advice, and could not name their children without using the symbols held in common by the community and embodied in its language. Thus Gullah became perhaps the principal means by which the slave community molded the individual into its culture.[55] To create a living language would seem a greater accomplishment than to preserve one, and the slaves of All Saints Parish shared fully in that accomplishment. After the creolization of Gullah by the slaves, who could remain unaware of their linguistic achievement or doubt its central position in slave folklife?

Notes

1. A speech community is defined linguistically as "a community sharing knowledge of rules for the conduct and interpretation of speech. Such sharing comprises knowledge of at least one form of speech, and knowledge also of its patterns of use. Both conditions are necessary." See Dell Hymes, *Foundations in Sociolinguistics: An Ethnographic Approach* (Philadelphia, 1974), 51; John Gumperz, "The Speech Community," in Pier Paolo Giglioli, ed., *Language and Social Context* (Harmondsworth, England, 1972), 219–31. For a discussion of the relationships between language and community, see Roger D. Abrahams, "Talking My Talk: Black English and Social Segmentation in Black Communities," *Florida FL Reporter,* 10 (1972), 29–58. On relationships between culture and identity, see A. Irving Hallowell, *Culture and Experience* (Philadelphia, 1955), 75–100. On the role of language in the pressure of groups upon individuals, see Lucien Febvre, "History and Psychology," in Peter Burke, ed., *A New Kind of History: From the Writings of Lucien Febvre,* trans. K. Folka (New York, 1973), 4.
2. Ben Horry, in Slave Narratives: A Folk History of Slavery in the United States from Interviews with Former Slaves. Typewritten records prepared by the Federal Writers' Project,

1936–38 (microfilm), 14, part ii, 323, 325; Welcome Bees, Slave Narratives, 14, part i, 49; Patricia Causey Nichols, "Linguistic Change in Gullah: Sex, Age, and Mobility" (Ph.D. diss., Stanford University, 1976), 86–111, esp. 104-7. Nichols's dissertation was based on fieldwork in All Saints Parish in the 1970s. See also Irma Cunningham, "A Syntactic Analysis of Sea Island Creole ('Gullah')" (Ph.D. diss., University of Michigan, 1970), 21–22, 200–201; William A. Stewart, "Continuity and Change in American Negro Dialects," *Florida FL Reporter,* 6 (1968), 3; Loreto Todd, *Pidgins and Creoles* (London, 1974), 17. Cf. Dennis R. Craig, "Education and Creole English in the West Indies: Some Sociolinguistic Factors," in Dell Hymes, ed., *Pidginization and Creolization of Languages* (Cambridge, 1971), 382.

3. Welcome Bees, Slave Narratives, 14, part i, 50; Gabe Lance, Slave Narratives, 14, part iii, 91; Ben Horry, Slave Narratives, 14, part ii, 320; Ellen Godfrey, Slave Narratives, 14, part ii, 154.

4. Louisa Brown, Slave Narratives, 14, part i, 115; Pringle, *Chronicles of Chicora Wood,* 168.

5. Mariah Heywood, Slave Narratives, 14, part ii, 284; Ben Horry, Slave Narratives, 14, part ii, 322, 309.

6. Mariah Heywood, Slave Narratives, 14, part ii, 285; Ben Horry, Slave Narratives, 14, part ii, 310; Patricia C. Nichols, "*To* and *From* in Gullah: An Evolutionary View," paper presented at annual meeting of Linguistic Society of America, San Diego, Calif., Dec. 1973; Nichols, "Linguistic Change in Gullah," 65–82.

7. Welcome Bees, Slave Narratives, 14, part i, 49; Elizabeth Collins, *Memories of the Southern States* (Taunton, England, 1865), 17; Charles A. Ferguson, "Aspects of Copula and the Notion of Simplicity: A Study of Normal Speech, Baby Talk, and Pidgins," in Hymes, ed., *Pidginization and Creolization of Languages,* 141–50; Ralph W. Fasold, "One Hundred Years from Syntax to Phonology," in Sanford Steever et al., eds., *Diachronic Syntax* (Chicago, 1976), 79–87; J. L. Dillard, *Black English: Its History and Usage in the United States* (New York, 1972), 49; Stewart, "Continuity and Change in American Negro Dialects," 3.

8. Hagar Brown, Slave Narratives, 14, part i, 110; Ellen Godfrey, Slave Narratives, 14, part ii, 156; Lorenzo Dow Turner, *Africanisms in the Gullah Dialect* (Chicago, 1949), 216.

9. Collins, *Memories of the Southern States,* 19; Hagar Brown, Slave Narratives, 14, part i, 109; Turner, *Africanisms in the Gullah Dialect,* 209–13.

10. Turner, *Africanisms in the Gullah Dialect,* 225–27; Todd, *Pidgins and Creoles,* 67; Joseph H. Greenberg, "Africa as a Linguistic Area," in William R. Bascom and Melville J. Herskovits, eds., *Continuity and Change in African Cultures* (Chicago, 1959), 23; William A. Stewart, "Foreign Language Teaching Methods in Quasi-Foreign Language Situations," in William A. Stewart, ed., *Non-Standard Speech and the Teaching of English* (Washington, D.C., 1964), 18; B. Comrie, *Aspect* (Cambridge, 1976); Ralph W. Fasold, *Tense Marking in Black English: A Linguistic and Social Analysis* (Arlington, Va., 1972).

11. Ellen Godfrey, Slave Narratives, 14, part ii, 154, 159, 162; *South Carolina Folk Tales,* compiled by Workers of the Writers' Program of the Work Projects Administration in the State of South Carolina (Columbia, 1941), 93 (collected by Genevieve Willcox Chandler in All Saints Parish); Ben Horry, Slave Narratives, 14, part ii, 312, 300. Cf. John Rickford, "The Insights of the Mesolect," in David DeCamp and Ian F. Hancock, eds., *Pidgins and Creoles: Current Trends and Prospects* (Washington, D.C., 1974).

12. Ellen Godfrey, Slave Narratives, 14, part ii, 165; Welcome Bees, Slave Narratives, 14, part i, 50; Ben Horry, Slave Narratives, 14, part ii, 299; Cunningham, "Syntactic Analysis of Sea Island Creole," 84; "Grandma Kit and Aunt Mariah Heywood," WPA Mss., SCL.

13. Hagar Brown, Slave Narratives, 14, part i, 283; Collins, *Memories of the Southern States,* 80. This continuity was also manifested in Afro-American speech communities elsewhere in the slave South and in the Caribbean as well. See Melville J. Herskovits, *The Myth of the Negro Past* (New York, 1941; rpt. Boston, 1958), 283; Todd, *Pidgins and Creoles,* 283.

14. Margaret Bryant, Slave Narratives, 14, part i, 145; Hagar Brown, Slave Narratives, 14, part i, 110; Hagar Brown, WPA Mss.; David DeCamp, "Toward a Generative Analysis of a Post-Creole Speech Continuum," in Hymes, ed., *Pidginization and Creolization of Languages,* 363; Ben Horry, Slave Narratives, 14, part ii, 316; William A. Stewart, "Patterns of Grammatical Change in Gullah," paper read in symposium Society and Culture in South Carolina, Charleston, Mar. 27, 1976; Turner, *Africanisms in the Gullah Dialect,* 247. Patricia C. Nichols analyzes *enty* as *ain't ee,* personal communication, Oct. 19, 1981.

15. John Bennett, "Gullah: A Negro Patois," *South Atlantic Quarterly,* 7 (1908), 340. For similar sentiments see Reed Smith, *Gullah* (Columbia, 1926), 22–23; Ambrose Gonzales, *The Black Border: Gullah Stories of the Carolina Coast* (Columbia, 1922), 10–17.

16. Systematic study of pidgin and creole languages is a relatively recent phenomenon. Hugo Schuchardt, who published an article on Lingua Franca early in this century ("Die Lingua Franca," *Zietschrift fur Romanische Philologie,* 33 [1909], 441–61), is generally considered the father of pidgin scholarship. Creole scholarship did not commence until the 1930s with the work of John Reinecke on Hawaiian Creole (*Language and Dialect in Hawaii: A Sociolinguistic History to 1835* [Honolulu, 1969]) and that of Turner on Gullah (*Africanisms in the Gullah Dialect*). Since the 1960s creole scholarship has expanded rapidly. On Gullah as a creole language, see Robert A. Hall, *Pidgin and Creole Languages* (Ithaca, 1965), 15; William A. Stewart, "Sociolinguistic Factors in the History of American Negro Dialects," *Florida FL Reporter,* 5 (1967), 12–13; Todd, *Pidgins and Creoles,* 5–6, 54, 67; Dillard, *Black English,* 76. On the definition of creolization, see Hymes, introduction to part iii of Hymes, ed., *Pidginization and Creolization of Languages,* 84. On the complexity of interrelationships in the creolization process, see the following essays in Hymes, ed., *Pidginization and Creolization of Languages:* Sidney Mintz, "The Socio-historical Background of Pidginization and Creolization" (153-68); Mervyn C. Alleyne, "Acculturation and the Cultural Matrix of Creolization" (169–86); David DeCamp, "Introduction: The Study of Pidgin and Creole Languages" (13–39).

17. Basil Davidson, *Black Mother: The Years of the African Slave Trade* (Boston, 1961), 218; Greenberg, "Africa as a Linguistic Area," 15–27; Herskovits, *Myth of the Negro Past,* 50; Ivan Vansertima, "African Linguistic and Mythological Structures in the World," in Rhoda Goldstein, ed., *Black Life and Culture in the United States* (New York, 1971), 12–35. On the one hand, African languages tended to feature simple vowel and consonant systems with implosive consonant sounds and few consonant blends. On the other hand, African languages tended to have rather complex morphologies with complicated nominal taxonomies and intricate verbal derivatives that expressed causative, reflexive, passive, and motional action or being.

18. Todd, *Pidgins and Creoles,* 67; Hall, *Pidgin and Creole Languages,* 9, 25; Peter H. Wood, *Black Majority: Negroes in Colonial South Carolina from 1670 through the Stono Rebellion* (New York, 1974), 173–74; David Dalby, "Americanisms That May Once have Been Africanisms," *The Times* (London), June 19, 1969, 9. There are still numerous pidgin and creole languages in West Africa, including a pidginized Kikongo in the Congo-Angolan area and a pidginized Hausa in Nigeria, Arabic-based pidgins in Nigeria, French-based pidgins on the Ivory Coast, Portuguese-based pidgins and creoles in Guinea and Senegal, and English-based pidgins and creoles in the Cameroons, Liberia, Sierra Leone, and Gambia. See Ian F. Hancock, "A Survey of the Pidgins and Creoles of the World," in Hymes, ed., *Pidginization and Creolizaiton of Languages,* 516–19.

19. William A. Stewart, "Nonstandard Speech Patterns," *Baltimore Bulletin of Education,* 43 (1967), 52–65; J. L. Dillard, "Non-standard Negro Dialects: Convergence or Divergence?" *Florida FL Reporter,* 6 (1968), 9–12, rpt. In Norman E. Whitten, Jr., and John F. Szwed, eds., *Afro-American Anthropology: Contemporary Perspectives* (New York, 1970), 119–26; Ralph

W. Fasold, "Decreolization and Autonomous Language Change," *Florida FL Reporter,* 10 (1972), 9; Hancock, "Survey of the Pidgins and Creoles of the World," 512–15. On the development of an Afro-English creole in Dutch Surinam, see Charles R. Boxer, *The Dutch Seaborne Empire, 1600–1800* (New York, 1965), 241.

20. Wood, *Black Majority,* 174–75, 179, 340; George C. Rogers, Jr., *The History of Georgetown County, South Carolina* (Columbia, 1970), 29, 53–54, 342–43; Converse D. Clowse, *Economic Beginnings in Colonial South Carolina, 1670–1730* (Columbia, 1971), 122–32, 230–34; Philip D. Curtin, *The Atlantic Slave Trade: A Census* (Madison, 1969), 145, 156–58; Elizabeth Donnan, "The Slave Trade into South Carolina before the Revolution," *AHR,* 33 (1927-28), 816–17; Daniel C. Littlefield, *Rice and Slaves: Ethnicity and the Slave Trade in Colonial South Carolina* (Baton Rouge, 1981), 33–55.

21. Wood, *Black Majority,* 185; Dalby, "Americanisms That May Once Have Been Africanisms," 9; Stewart, "Nonstandard Speech Patterns," 52–65; Dillard, "Non-standard Negro Dialects," 119–26; Fasold, "Decreolization," 9. Cf. Frederic G. Cassidy, *Jamaica Talk: Three Hundred Years of the English Language in Jamaica* (London, 1961), 49–50.

22. Nichols, "Linguistic Change in Gullah," 1–2; Todd, *Pidgins and Creoles,* 7, 9–10, 15, 25–27, 50–51; Stewart, "Sociolinguistic Factors in the History of American Negro Dialects," 11–29; Vansertima, "African Linguistic and Mythological Structures," 12–35; Wood, *Black Majority,* 175–80. Cf. Cassidy, *Jamaica Talk,* 15–19; Littlefield, *Rice and Slaves,* 156–60.

23. Stewart, "Sociolinguistic Factors in the History of American Negro Dialects," 12; Wood, *Black Majority,* 186-87; Todd, *Pidgins and Creoles,* 5-6, 54, 67; Dillard, *Black English,* 76.

24. Dalby, "Americanisms That May Once Have Been Africanisms," 9; Greenberg, "Africa as a Linguistic Area," 23; P. E. H. Hair, "Sierra Leone Items in the Gullah Dialect of American English," *Sierra Leone Language Review,* 4 (1965), 79–84; Turner, *Africanisms in the Gullah Dialect,* 209–16, 225–27, 278–91; Nichols, "Linguistic Change in Gullah," 104–7; Todd, *Pidgins and Creoles,* 17, 67; Stewart, "Continuity and Change in American Negro Dialects," 3, and his "Foreign Language Teaching Methods in Quasi-Foreign Language Situations," 18; Dillard, *Black English,* 56–57; Wood, *Black Majority,* 169–70; George C. Rogers, Jr., *Charleston in the Age of the Pinckneys* (Norman, 1969), 76–77.

25. "An Englishman in South Carolina," 693; King, *Great South,* 429; G.M., "South Carolina," *New England Magazine,* 1 (Sept.–Oct. 1831), 249–50; William A. Stewart, "More on Black-White Speech Relationships," *Florida FL Reporter,* II (1973), 35–40; Bennett, "Gullah," 339; Samuel Gaillard Stoney, ed., "The Memoirs of Frederick Adolphus Porcher," *SCHM,* 47 (1946), 92–93; Rogers, *Charleston,* 79; Raven I. McDavid, Jr., and Virginia Glenn McDavid, "The Relationship of the Speech of American Negroes to the Speech of the Whites," *American Speech,* 26 (1951), 3–17. A similar linguistic situation prevailed in the Caribbean. In Jamaica, for example, Lady Nugent complained that "the Creole language is not confined to the negroes. Many of the ladies who have not been educated in England, speak a sort of Broken English, with an indolent drawling out of their words, that is tiresome if not disgusting." See Henry Preston Vaughan Nunn, *Lady Nugent's Journal of Her Residence in Jamaica from 1801 to 1805,* ed. P. Wright (Oxford, 1966), 98. Cf. Cassidy, *Jamaica Talk,* 21–23.

26. Allen W. Read, "The Speech of Negroes in Colonial America," *JNH,* 24 (1939), 247–58; Stewart, "Sociolinguistic Factors in the History of American Negro Dialects," 29; Duncan Clinch Heyward, *Seed from Madagascar* (Chapel Hill, 1937), 188–89. Cf. Allen W. Read, "Bilingualism in the Middle Colonies," *American Speech,* 12 (1937), 93–99. What I am describing as bilingualism would be considered *diglossia* by those who consider Gullah to be a dialect of English rather than a creole language. Diglossia is the use of two or more varieties of the same language under different conditions. See Charles A. Ferguson, "Diglossia," in Giglioli, ed., *Language and Social Context,* 232–51.

27. Elizabeth C. Traugott, "Principles in the History of American English—A Reply," *Florida FL Reporter,* 10 (1972), 5–6, 56; Stewart, "Socio-linguistic Factors in the History of American Negro Dialects," 11, 13, 29; Dalby, "Americanisms That May Once Have Been Africanisms," 9; Gilbert Osofsky, ed., *Puttin' On Ole Massa* (New York, 1969), 26. Apparently some planters regarded Gullah and other creoles to be a kind of baby-talk. See Edgar T. Thompson, *Plantation Societies, Race Relations, and the South: The Regimentation of Populations* (Durham, N.C., 1975), 133–34. Linguists who have espoused the baby-talk thesis included Leonard Bloomfield, *Language* (New York, 1933), 472–75, and Hall, *Pidgin and Creole Languages,* 5, 86. DeCamp convincingly challenges the baby-talk thesis in his "Introduction: The Study of Pidgin and Creole Languages," 18–23. A sophisticated restatement, emphasizing that all languages tend to simplify in similar ways for those who are regarded as unable to comprehend the community's "normal" speech, is Ferguson, "Aspects of Copula," 141–50. On the dynamics of linguistic contact, see Uriel Weinreich, *Languages in Contact* (New York, 1953). A recent overview of the literature is Ralph W. Fasold, "The Relation between Black and White Speech in the South," *American Speech,* 56 (1981), 168–89. On Afro-American uses of language to conceal, cf. M. G. Smith, "Some Aspects of Social Structure in the British Caribbean about 1820," *Social and Economic Studies,* 1 (1953), 70; Grace Sims Holt, " 'Inversion' in Black Communication," in Thomas Kochman, ed., *Rappin' and Stylin' Out; Communication in Urban Black America* (Urbana, 1972), 152–59. Such interpretations may be taken to injudicious and unreliable extremes, and have been by Miles Mark Fisher in his *Negro Slave Songs of the United States* (New York, 1953). It should be noted in fairness that planters often perceived that they were being "put on," but played the game out of a sense of *noblesse oblige.*

28. Cf. Lawrence W. Levine, *Black Culture and Black Consciousness: Afro-American Folk Thought from Slavery to Freedom* (New York, 1977), 6, 444; Alan Dundes, *Mother Wit from the Laughing Barrel: Readings in the Interpretation of Afro-American Folklore* (Englewood Cliffs, N.J., 1973), 246–47. On the functions of proverbs and indirect speech in Africa, see Ethel M. Albert, " 'Rhetoric,' 'Logic,' and 'Poetics' in Burundi," *AA,* 66 (1964), 35–54; John C. Messenger, "The Role of Proverbs in a Nigerian Judicial System," *Southwestern Journal of Anthropology,* 15 (1959), 64-73; Ruth Finnegan, *Oral Literature in Africa* (Oxford, 1970), 393–408; Peter Seitel, "Proverbs: A Social Use of Metaphor," *Genre,* 2 (1969), 146-60; David Dwyer, *An Introduction to West African Pidgin English* (East Lansing, 1967), 98.

29. Selwyn Gurney Champion, *Racial Proverbs: A Selection of the World's Proverbs, Arranged Linguistically.* . . . (London, 1938), 515, 524, 533, 599; Julia Peterkin, *Scarlet Sister Mary* (Indianapolis, 1928), 215, and her *Black April* (Indianapolis, 1927), 43; Lillie Knox, in WPA Mss. On the importance of the oral rhetorical question format in Africa see Finnegan, *Oral Literature,* 401. While ethnographic writings (even reports in travel accounts by undiscerning amateurs) are readily accepted by scholars as primary sources, an explanation is required for attempting to use fiction as a source of factual information. This is all the more necessary if one wishes to use fiction written by a southern white woman in the age of Jim Crow as a source for facts on Afro-American culture. Peterkin spent part of her early life on the Waccamaw Neck and remained a part-time resident for most of her adult life. Her novels are recognizably set in the area—*Scarlet Sister Mary* on "Blue Brook" (Brookgreen) plantation, *Black April* on Sandy Island. Many environmental and cultural features of her novels are still verifiable on the Waccamaw Neck. Other cultural features have been reported by folklorists and linguists in other Gullah-speaking communities (see Richard M. Dorson, *American Folklore* [Chicago, 1959], 7; Ann Sullivan Haskell, "The Representation of Gullah-Influenced Dialects in Twentieth Century South Carolina Prose" [Ph.D. diss., University of Pennsylvania, 1968]; and Stewart, "More on Black-White Speech Relationships," 38). Thus by

the tests of exposure to the culture and verification of specific cultural details within the community and of general cultural details in other Gullah-speaking communities, one is ready to credit Peterkin's primary knowledge of Gullah proverbs on the Waccamaw. See also Francis W. Bradley, "South Carolina Proverbs," *SFQ,* 1 (1937), 57–101.

30. Lillie Knox, in WPA Mss.; James Boyd Christensen, "The Role of Proverbs in Fante Culture," in Elliott P. Skinner, ed., *Peoples and Cultures of Africa* (Garden City, N.Y., 1973), 523 (cf. Bradley, "South Carolina Proverbs," 78); Champion, *Racial Proverbs,* 509, 525.

31. Lillie Knox, in WPA Mss.; Champion, *Racial Proverbs,* 606 (cf. Finnegan, *Oral Literature,* 401–2); Christensen, "The Role of Proverbs in Fante Culture," 523.

32. Julia Peterkin, in *Poetry: A Magazine of Verse,* 27 (1923), 60.

33. Ella Small, in WPA Mss.; Peterkin, *Black April,* 56, 131; cf. Bradley, "South Carolina Proverbs," 69, 77.

34. Patience Pennington [Elizabeth Allston Pringle], *A Woman Rice Planter* (New York, 1914), 37; Peterkin, *Black April,* 125, 247.

35. Informant unknown, WPA Mss.; Julia Peterkin, in *Poetry: A Magazine of Verse,* 25 (1925), 240–43 (cf. Her *Scarlet Sister Mary,* 173).

36. Hagar Brown and Lillie Knox, both in WPA Mss. (cf. Bradley, "South Carolina Proverbs," 70, and the African novelist Chinua Achebe, *Arrow of God* [Garden City, N.Y., 1965], 213).

37. On strategy, see Kenneth Burke, *The Philosophy of Literary Form* (New York, 1957), 3–4; Seitel, "Proverbs," 150–51; Lillie Knox and Hagar Brown, both in WPA Mss.; Peterkin, *Black April,* 68 (cf. Bradley, "South Carolina Proverbs," 96).

38. Informant unknown, WPA Mss.; Peterkin, *Black April,* 68 (cf. Bradley, "South Carolina Proverbs," 84, 99).

39. Peterkin, *Scarlet Sister Mary,* 132; Lillie Knox, in WPA Mss.; Julia Peterkin, "Teaching Jim," in Frank Durham, ed., *The Collected Short Stories of Julia Peterkin* (Columbia, 1970), 218–23 (cf. Bradley, "South Carolina Proverbs," 65); Julia Peterkin, *Green Thursday* (New York, 1924), 130; Sabe Rutledge, Slave Narratives, 14, part iv, 63.

40. Peterkin, *Black April,* 146 (cf. The Hausa proverb "Doing mischief is pleasanter than repairing it" in Champion, *Racial Proverbs,* 534); WPA Mss. (cf. Bradley, "South Carolina Proverbs," 95); Peterkin, *Green Thursday,* 129; Lillie Knox, in WPA Mss.; (cf. Bradley, "South Carolina Proverbs," 90).

41. Peterkin, *Bright Skin* (Indianapolis, 1932), 39; WPA Mss. Cf. Elsie Clews Parsons, "Folk-Lore from St. Helena Island, South Carolina," *JAF,* 38 (1925), 228.

42. Christensen, "The Roll of Proverbs in Fante Culture," 510. Cf. Finnegan, *Oral Literature,* 394–418; E. Ojo Arewa and Alan Dundes, "Proverbs and the Ethnography of Speaking Folklore," *AA,* 66, pt. 2 (1964), 70–85; Charles Bird, "Heroic Songs of the Mande Hunters," in Richard M. Dorson, ed., *African Folklore* (Garden City, N.Y., 1972), 275-93; Roger D. Abrahams, "A Rhetoric of Everyday Life: Conversational Genres," *SFQ,* 32 (1968), 44–59, and his "Introductory Remarks to a Rhetorical Theory of Folklore," *JAF,* 81 (1968), 143–57; Dan Ben-Amos, "Folklore in African Society," in Bernth Lindfors, ed., *Forms of Folklore in Africa: Narrative, Poetic, Gnomic, Dramatic* (Austin, 1977), 22.

43. On the importance of speech interaction in culture, see Bertram Wyatt-Brown, "The Ideal Typology and Ante-Bellum Southern History: A Testing of a New Approach," *Societas,* 5 (1975), 4; Richard Bauman, "Verbal Art as Performance," *AA,* 77 (1975), 293; Erving Goffman's: "The Neglected Situation," *ibid.,* 66 (1964), 133–36, *Encounters: Two Studies in the Sociology of Interaction* (Indianapolis, 1961), and *Behavior in Public Places* (New York, 1963); Kenneth R. Johnson, "Black Kinesics—Some Non-Verbal Communication Patterns in the Black Culture," *Florida FL Reporter,* 9 (1971), 17–20, 57; Dell Hymes, "Competence and Performance in Linguistic Theory," in R. Huxley and E. Ingram, eds., *Language Acquisition:*

Models and Methods (New York, 1971), 3–23; Beryl L. Bailey, "Towards a New Perspective in Negro English Dialectology," *American Speech,* 40 (1965), 171–77. On the distinction between *bad* and *baaad* in Afro-American culture, see H. C. Brearley, "Ba-ad Nigger," *South Atlantic Quarterly,* 38 (1939), 75–81; William H. Wiggins, Jr., "Jack Johnson as Bad Nigger: The Folklore of His Life," *Black Scholar,* 2 (1971), 39. On ambiguity and intonation in African languages, see Dwyer, *Introduction to West African Pidgin English,* 98; Greenberg, "Africa as a Linguistic Area," 23; Lorenzo Dow Turner, "Problems Confronting the Investigator of Gullah," *Publications of the American Dialect Society,* 9 (1947), 74–84. On Gullah's distinctive uses of syllable and breath dynamics, pitch, volume, and stress, see William A. Stewart, "Observations on the Problems of Defining Negro Dialect," *Florida FL Reporter,* 9 (1971), 48–49.

44. David J. McCord, ed., *Statutes at Large of South Carolina* (Columbia, 1840), 7:468; Mss. Diary of Emily Esdaile Weston for 1859, in private possession, Jan. 30, Feb. 13, 26–27, Mar. 6, 13, Dec. 4, 1859 (hereafter cited as Emily Weston diary); Malet, *Errand to the South,* 50, 57, 68, 204–5; Emily R. Reynolds and Joan Reynolds Faunt, *Biographical Directory of the Senate of the State of South Carolina, 1776–1964* (Columbia, 1964), 334; Lawrence C. Bryant, "Negro Legislators in South Carolina, 1868-1902" (mimeograph), SCA (Bruce Williams, one of the Richmond Hill slaves taught to read and write by Mary Vereen Magill, served as state senator from 1876 to 1902); Mulatto Joe to Robert F. W. Allston, Sept. 23, 1823, and Samuel Taylor to Elizabeth Blyth, Sept. 2, 1838, both in Robert F. W. Allston Papers, SCHS; Mary Ann (surname unknown) to Emily Jordan, Feb. 23, 1861, in Daniel W. Jordan Papers, DUL; George Simons to Francis Weston, June 5, 1864, in Weston Family Papers, SCL. The low proportion of black literacy is strikingly evident in the mss. federal census population schedules for 1870, SCA. Even allowing for the possibility that the most literate slaves left the parish after emancipation, the estimate of W. E. B. Du Bois that about 5 percent of the slaves were literate by 1860 seems about right for All Saints Parish. See his *Black Reconstruction: An Essay toward a History for the Part which Black Folk Played in the Attempt to Reconstruct Democracy in America* (New York, 1935), 638.

45. Fasold, "Decreolization and Autonomous Language Change," 9; Stewart, "Sociolinguistic Factors in the History of American Negro Dialects," 12-13, and his "Patterns of Grammatical Change in Gullah"; Hall, *Pidgin and Creole Languages,* 15; Bennett, "Gullah," 336*n.*

46. Stewart, "Continuity and Change in American Negro Dialects," 3. Linguists call the replacement of words while maintaining the structure relexification. One theory claims that creoles originated as Portuguese trade pidgins and were relexified with English words on the West African coast. See Todd, *Pidgins and Creoles,* 33–42.

47. Nichols, "Linguistic Change in Gullah," 3–4; J. L. Dillard, "The Historian's History and the Reconstructionist's History in the Tracing of Linguistic Variants," *Florida FL Reporter,* 11 (1973), 41, and his *Black English,* 102; William A. Stewart, "Historical and Structural Bases for the Recognition of Negro Dialect," *Monograph Series on Languages and Linguistics,* 22 (Washington, D.C., 1969), 239–47, and his "Sociolinguistic Factors in the History of American Negro Dialects," 13, 29; John J. Gumperz, "Linguistic Anthropology in Society," *AA,* 76 (1974), 791; DeCamp, "Toward a Generative Analysis of a Post-Creole Speech Continuum," 349-70.

48. Sabe Rutledge, Slave Narratives, 14, part iv, 59, and in WPA Mss. On the importance given to naming in African societies, see H. A. Wieschoff, "The Social Significance of Names among the Ibo of Nigeria," *AA,* 43 (1941), 212–22. Orlando Patterson offers an incisive discussion of the importance of naming cross-culturally in his *Slavery and Social Death: A Comparative Study* (Cambridge, Mass., 1982), 54–55. See also William F. Murphy, "A Note on the Significance of Names," *Psychoanalytic Quarterly,* 26 (1957), 91–106. On the planters' contribution

to slave naming, see Newbell Niles Puckett, "Names of American Negro Slaves," in George Peter Murdock, ed., *Studies in the Science of Society Presented to Albert Galloway Keller* (New Haven, 1937), 471–94. Cf. Hennig Cohen, "Slave Names in Colonial South Carolina," *American Speech,* 28 (1952), 102–7; Naomi C. Chappell, "Negro Names," *American Speech,* 4 (1929), 272–75; Urban T. Holmes, "A Study in Negro Onomastics," *American Speech,* 5 (1930), 462–67; Arthur Palmer Hudson, "Some Curious Negro Names," *Southern Folklore Quarterly,* 2 (1938), 179–93; Ruby Terrill Lomax, "Negro Nicknames," *Publications of the Texas Folklore Society,* 18 (1943), 163-71.

49. Slave lists, estate of Francis Marion Weston, 1855, slave lists, estate of Plowden C. J. Weston, 1864, and slave lists, estate of John D. Magill, 1864, all in Office of Probate Judge, Georgetown County Court House; Emily Weston to William St. J. Mazyck, conveyance of real and personal estate, Aug. 14, 1864, Temporary Deeds, Book A, Register of Deeds, Georgetown County Court House; "Book of Things Given Out March 27, 1809," Charlotte Ann Allston Mss., 1804–20, in private possession. On African day names, see John Mbiti, *African Religions and Philosophy* (Garden City, N.Y., 1969), ch. 3; Roger Bastide, *African Civilisations in the New World,* trans. Peter Green (New York, 1971), 100; Edward Long, *The History of Jamaica* (London, 1774), 3:417; David DeCamp, "African Day Names in Jamaica," *Language,* 43 (1967), 139–49; Orlando Patterson, *The Sociology of Slavery* (London, 1967), 174; M. Delafosse, "De quelques persistances d'ordre ethnographique chez les descendants des Nègres transplantés aux Antilles et a la Guyane," *Revue d'Ethnologie et de Sociologie,* 3 (1912), 234–37; Turner, *Africanisms in the Gullah Dialect,* 31–43; Dillard, *Black English,* 123–35; Wood, *Black Majority,* 181.

50. The slave names in the list above and in the discussions that follow are from a master sample of more than 700 separate names, many of them occurring ten times or more, which I compiled from the above inventories; the Slave Narratives of All Saints Parish; the Emily Weston diary; the Daniel W. Jordan papers; and the Robert F. W. Allston Papers. For the African names see Puckett, "Names of American Negro Slaves," 471–94; H. L. Mencken, *The American Language,* 4th ed. (New York, 1936), 524; Wood, *Black Majority,* 181–82. On New World continuities with African naming practices, see Herskovits, *Myth of the Negro Past,* 190–94; Turner, *Africanisms in the Gullah Dialect,* 31–43, and his "Problems Confronting the Investigator of Gullah," 74–84; Daniel E. Huger Smith, "A Plantation Boyhood," in Alice R. Huger Smith and Herbert Ravenel Sass, eds., *A Carolina Rice Plantation of the Fifties* (New York, 1930), 71; Duncan Clinch Heyward, *Seed from Madagascar* (Chapel Hill, 1937), 97; Willie Lee Rose, *Rehearsal for Reconstruction: The Port Royal Experiment* (Indianapolis, 1964), 97; Richard and Sally Price, "Sarameka Onomastics: An Afro-American Naming System," *Ethnology,* 11(1972), 341–67.

51. These names are found *passim* in the Slave Narratives from All Saints Parish and the Emily Weston diary, as well as in slave lists in Francis Marion Weston estate; Plowden C. J. Weston estate; John D. Magill estate; Charlotte Ann Allston Mss.; Robert F. W. Allston Papers; Daniel W. Jordan Papers. For the African names, see Puckett, "Names of American Negro Slaves," 471–94; Mencken, *American Language,* 524; Wood, *Black Majority,* 181–85. Cf. Turner, *Africanisms in the Gullah Dialect,* 92–109; Dillard, *Black English,* 129–32.

52. Robert F. W. Allston Papers; Francis Marion Weston inventory; Plowden Weston inventory; Emily Weston diary; Monday Samson Holmes, Free Woods, S.C., WPA Mss. Cf. Cohen, "Slave Names in Colonial South Carolina," 104.

53. These names are found *passim* in the Slave Narratives and WPA Mss. from All Saints Parish; Robert F. W. Allston Papers; Emily Weston diary.

54. Hagar Brown, Slave Narratives, 14, part i, 112. On the African tradition of children's being named by grandparents, see Meyer Fortes, "Kinship and Marriage among the Ashanti," in

A. R. Radcliffe-Brown and Daryll Forde, eds., *African Systems of Kinship and Marriage* (London, 1950), 276.

55. Malet, *Errand to the South,* 6; Mariah Heywood, Slave Narratives, 14, part ii, 284; Margaret Bryant, Slave Narratives, 14, part i, 146; Collins, *Memories of the Southern States,* 5. Cf. Heyward, *Seed from Madagascar,* 98. For a discussion of surnames cross-culturally, see Patterson, *Slavery and Social Death,* 56–58.

56. Stewart, "Sociolinguistic Factors in the History of American Negro Dialects," 29, and his "Continuity and Change," 3–14; Cassidy, *Jamaica Talk,* 17–20; Melville J. and Frances S. Herskovits, *Suriname Folk-Lore* (New York, 1936), 78–81, 116–18; David Dalby, *Black through White: Patterns of Communication* (Bloomington, Ind., 1970), 6; Hymes, "Introduction," 84; Elizabeth C. Traugott, "Pidgins, Creoles, and the Origins of Vernacular Black English," in D. S. Harrison and T. Trabasso, *Black English: A Seminar* (Hillsdale, N.J., 1976), 84–85.

57. On the stigma of non-standard English, see Claudia Mitchell-Kernan, *Language Behavior in a Black Urban Community* (Berkeley, 1969), 42-48, 60–66; William Labov, *The Social Stratification of English in New York City* (Washington, D.C., 1966), 495–96. On language as a symbol of shared culture, see David G. Mandelbaum, ed., *Selected Writings of Edward Sapir in Culture, Language, and Personality* (Berkeley, 1949), 15; William C. Spengemann and L. R. Lundquist, "Autobiography and the American Myth," in Hennig Cohen, ed., *The American Culture: Approaches to the Study of the United States* (Boston, 1968), 495–96; C. Wright Mills, "Language, Logic, and Culture," *American Sociological Review,* 4 (1939), 677. On the impact of language on culture (rather than language as a reflector of culture), see Michael Silverstein, "Language as a Part of Culture," in Sol Tax and Leslie G. Freeman, eds., *Horizons of Anthropology,* 2d ed. (Chicago, 1977), 130. This interpretation has been taken to deterministic extremes by Benjamin Lee Whorf ("Science and Linguistics," in Eleanor Maccoby, ed., *Readings in Social Psychology* [New York, 1958], 5) and Basil L. Bernstein ("Social Class and Linguistic Development: A Theory of Social Learning," in A. H. Halsey et al., eds., *Education, Economy, and Society* [New York, 1961]). See also the critique by Gary J. Miller, "Linguistic Constructions of Reality," in Howard Shapiro, ed., *Human Perspectives* (New York, 1972), 84–93.

Ezekiel and the Vision of Dry Bones
Reverend Carl J. Anderson
Baptist minister

At the time several of his sermons were published in Gerald Davis's I Got the
Word in Me and I Can Sing It, You Know: A Study of the Performed
African-American Sermon *(1985), Rev. Anderson was pastor of Saint John's
Missionary Baptist Church in Oakland, California. Davis wrote of him that
"In many ways, he is the prototypical contemporary urban African
American preacher blending the sophistication and savvy of the successful
urban politician and businessman with the earthiness and mother wit of the
Black Southern rural church tradition."*

If you have your Bibles ready
You may turn with me
To the thirty-seventh chapters of the book of Ezekiel
And we're going to read
The first, second and third verse
"The hand of the Lord
Was upon me
And carried me out in the Spirit of the Lord
And set me down
In the midst of the valley which was full of bones"
You understand that
"And cause me to pass by them round about
And behold there was very many in the open valley
And lo, they were very dry"
You understand me
I want to use as my theme tonight
Ezekiel and the Vision of Dry Bones
You understand
Not dry bones in the valley
But Ezekiel and the Vision of Dry Bones
And this is one message from the Lord that you cannot run away
from it
Yes sir
He that is led by the Spirit

"Ezekiel and the Vision of Dry Bones" [a sermon by Rev. Carl J. Anderson], in I Got the Word in Me and I Can
Sing It, You Know. A Study of the Performed African-American Sermon, *by Gerald L. Davis,
pp. 136–142 (Philadelphia: University of Pennsylvania Press, 1985).*

They are the sons of God
And I feel sorry for that individual
That only loves sin
And runs from the Gospel
For it will take the Gospel to save your soul
Now this new Ezekiel signifies God's way of thinking
Ezekiel is known as one of the most mysterious Hebrew prophets
Yes sir
And he began, well, as a boy
He grew up under the influence of Jeremiah
And he began to prophesy at the age of thirty
And for twenty-two years preached by the River of Shafar
At Talabinth
And history says he died at the age of fifty-two
Now this man Ezekiel styles himself
The son of man
Several times he uses this expression
"Thus sayeth the Lord"
You understand me
And you'll find one hundred and seventeen times
Yes sir
The times of his prophesy was stormy and traditional
Ezekiel had two audiences
One real and present, the exiled about him
And the other the whole house of Israel
You understand me
Yes sir
And you'll find many dry Christians in church
As I oftentimes say
I wouldn't have a religion I can't feel
Ezekiel used allegories or parables such as those of Israel as a
founding child
Representing one with a sound body but unable to walk
Do you understand me
And second as a lioness
Third a stately figure
And fourth a vine doomed
Yes sir
He employed symbolic actions depicting the siege of Jerusalem
By dividing his hair into three parts
Do you understand me
First part to be burned
Second part to be smitten
And the third part to be scattered representing
Do you understand me

Israel and Jerusalem when one-third of the city was smitten
With the sword and the gates were set on fire
Help me Lord
Another third representing the scattered Jews all over the world
today
Now by way of parenthesis
I sometimes wonder why
The Lord chose that the hair from Ezekiel's head would be divided
three times
Yes sir
And then as I began to search
I find that one is Heaven's unity number
And seven is Heaven's sacred number
You understand me
But three is Heaven's complete number
Whatever God does He does completely
Am I right about it
I want the world to know
That there are three Heavenly bodies
Yes sir
The sun
Moon
And the planets
Guide me Lord
The earth is constituted of three great elements
They are land, water and air
And these have three different forms
You understand me
And they are solid, liquid and vapor
Help me Holy Spirit
Yes sir
Three kinds of animal life
Animals that inhabit the earth
Fish inhabit the waters
And fowls the air
Am I right about it?
Well, I turn to the Bible
And I read where Noah had three sons
Sham, Ham and Jephtha
Yes sir
You know it's difficult
To preach to people who do not read their Bible
Yes sir
And I read where Moses was hidden for three months
Can I get a witness?

Yeah, his life was divided into three periods
Forty years in Pharaoh's house
Forty years in the wilderness
And forty years in leadership
You understand me
And the workmen of Solomon's temple
Were divided into three classes
Seventy thousand entered apprentices
Eighty thousand fellow craftsmen
And three thousand six hundred master masons
Help me Holy Spirit
And not only that, Daniel prayed three times a day
Yes sir
So you see three is important
The Hebrew children
Shadrack, Meshack and Abednego
Composed Heaven's fireproof unit
Yes sir
And when Jesus was born
Three wise men came from the East
And presented three kinds of gifts
Am I right about it?
When the Master wanted to confirm his divine nature
And mission in the minds of disciples
He took three of them
Peter, James and John
Am I right about it
Yeah, and He took them into a high mountain
Apart and was transfigured before them
And Peter got happy there
And said
Let us build three tabernacles
Am I right about it?
Yes sir
One for Thee
One for Moses
And one for Elijah
So the Lord told Ezekiel to divide his hair
After having shaved his head with a barber's razor
In three parts
Ezekiel used other symbols
He stood out on the street and ate bread with feminine hands
Representing the failing of the stall of life
He set his furniture out of his house
In the broad daylight

Representing the holy vessels and the furniture of the temple
Would be moved out before their eyes
Not only did he speak by parables and symbols
But he saw, he saw visions of the glory of God
Am I right about it?
Yes sir
Of the restored sanctuary and of our discourse this evening
Of the valley of dry bones
My brothers and sisters
In the Lord there are many valleys
Am I right about it?
Now the children of Israel were pictured as in bondage
While in Babylon, Ezekiel was with them in servitude
He heard their cry as is recorded in the one hundred thirty-seventh number of
        the Psalms
Judah had lost her political existence as a nation
And their temple was destroyed
And the beautiful service of Jehovah was abolished
I'll hook this train up in a minute
And the walls of Jerusalem was torn down
And the gates had been set on fire
All because the nations had been unfaithful to God
And prepared that their very name was going to be wiped out
From the remembrance of God
In their sorrow they cried
Our bones are dry
You understand me
Our hopes is lost
And we are cut off from our parts
They looked upon themselves, children
As dead in the sight of God
You know it's a bad thing to walk around with the name Christian and do not
        have no spirit
Am I right about it?
They would find that they resemble the body in the grave
Which nothing remains
And I see Ezekiel he was true to his calling
Yes sir
And he was wearied over the plight of Judah
And the Lord set him down in the valley that was full of bones
Yeah, he saw
You understand me
He saw the flesh
Had been devoured
So to speak

By animals and vultures
He saw bones had been bleached by the chilly winds and
parching sun
Yeah, he saw bones scattered by the rolling chariots and the
clattering of the horses
And these bones were dry
Do you understand me
They were so dry no footsteps could be heard anywhere
Yeah, it's a sad thing
Yeah, to go to church and find Christians all dry
Yeah, and when the Lord said
Yes sir, when the Lord said make a joyful noise
Am I right about it?
Make it unto the Lord all ye lambs
And right now the world is making their noise
The nightclubs are dancing by the tune of the band
Yeah, and the blues and rock and roll singers
Yeah, those who set around are clapping their hands and they're
saying to their favorite singer "Come on!"
You understand me
And I think that you shouldn't mind me crying about Jesus
Yeah, I want to make a noise about the Lord Jesus Christ
I'm so glad
That I'm able to make a noise
And He's been so good to me
Yeah, has He been good to you
Somebody said that the Lord was so good to them
But they never make any noise about what the Lord has said
A woman met Jesus down at the well
You understand me
And He told her everything that she had done
She dropped the water pot and ran downtown saying
"Come and see a man that told me all that I did!"
Oh Lord
Yeah, now this woman can tell what Jesus done for her
Yeah, I think the church ought to witness what the Lord has done
for you
Yeah, early one morning
Yeah, I found the Lord
Yes I did
I was in the valley of dry bones
Yeah, I had no God on my side
Yeah, I didn't have no spirit
To make me shout

But when I found the Lord
I found joy
Yeah, joy
Yeah, joy was found
I found joy
Peace to my dying soul

Suggested Reading

Abrahams, Roger D. "Playing the Dozens." *Journal of American Folklore* 75 (July-September 1962): 209–220.

———. *Deep Down in the Jungle: Negro Narrative Folklore from the Streets of Philadelphia* (1st rev. ed.). Chicago: Aldine, 1970.

Boadu, Samuel Osei. "African Oral Artistry and the New Social Order." In *African Culture. The Rhythms of Unity,* edited by Molefi Kete Asante and Kariamu Welsh Asante, pp. 83–90. Trenton, N.J.: African World Press, 1990.

Brewer, J. Mason. *The Word on the Brazos: Negro Preacher Tales from the Brazos Bottoms of Texas.* Austin: University of Texas Press, 1953.

Brown, Sterling A. "Negro Folk Expression." *Phylon,* 14 (Spring 1953): 50–60.

Calloway, Thomas, Carolyn and John Louis Lucaites, eds. *Martin Luther King, Jr., and the Sermonic Power of Public Discourse.* Tuscaloosa: University of Alabama Press, 1993.

Cole, Herbert M., ed. *"I Am Not Myself." The Art of African Masquerade.* Los Angeles: Museum of Cultural History, 1985, by Regents of the University of California.

Costello, Mark. *Signifying Rappers.* Boston: Ecco Press, 1989.

Dance, Daryl Cumber. *Shuckin' and Jivin'.* Bloomington: Indiana University Press, 1978.

Dundes, Alan. *Mother Wit. From The Laughing Barrel. Readings in The Interpretation of Afro-American Folklore* [1973]. Reprint, Jackson: University Press of Mississippi, 1990.

Ellison, Mary. *Lyrical Protest. Black Music's Struggle against Discrimination.* New York: Praeger, 1989.

Eurie, Joseph D., and James G. Spady. *Nation Conscious Rap: The Hip Hop Version.* New York: PC International, 1991.

Faulk, John Henry. "Ten Negro Sermons," Master's thesis, University of Texas, 1940.

Harrison, Paul Carter. *The Drama of Nommo: Black Theatre in the African Continuum.* New York: Grove Press, 1972.

Hazzard-Gordon, Katrina. *Jookin'.* Philadelphia: Temple University Press, 1991.

Henderson, Stephen E. *Understanding the New Black Poetry: Black Speech and Black Music as Poetic References.* New York: Morrow, 1973.

Holt, Grace Sims. "Inversion' in Black Communication." *Florida FL Reporter* (Spring/Fall 1971): 41–43, 55.

Hood, James Walker. *The Negro in the Christian Pulpit; or, The Two Characters and Two Destinies Delineated in Twenty-One Practical Sermons.* Raleigh: Edwards Broughton, 1884.

James, Willis Laurence. "The Romance of the Negro Folk Cry in America." *Phylon* 16(Spring 1955): 15–30.

Johnson, Guy B. "Double Meaning in the Popular Negro Blues." *Journal of Abnormal and Social Psychology* 22(1927–28): 12–20.

Johnson, James Weldon. *God's Trombones: Seven Negro Sermons in Verse*. New York: Viking Press, 1964.

Jones, Gayl. *Liberating Voices. Oral Tradition in African American Literature*. New York: Penguin Books, 1991.

Joyner, Charles W. "The Unusual Task of the Gospel Preacher: Afro-American Folk Preaching on Sandy Island, South Carolina." Typescript, n.d.

Keyes, Charyl. "Verbal Art Performance in Rap Music: The Conversation of the 80s." *Folklore Forum* 17(Fall 1984): 143–152.

Leiding, Harriette Kershaw. *Street Cries of an Old Southern City*. Charleston: 1910.

Mitchell, Henry. *Black Preaching*. Philadelphia: J.B. Lippincott, 1970.

Murray, Albert. *Stomping the Blues* [1976]. Reprint, New York: Vintage Books, 1982.

Nelson, Havelock, and Michael A. Gonzales. *Bring the Noise: A Guide to Rap Music and Hip Hop Culture*. New York: Crown, 1991.

Niles, Lyndrey A. "Rhetorical Characteristics of Traditional Black Preaching." *Journal of Black Studies* (September 1984): 41–52.

Oster, Harry. "Negro Humor: John and Old Marster." *Journal of the Folklore Institute,* 5 (1968): 42–57.

Philpot, William M., ed. *Best Black Sermons*. Valley Forge, Pa.: Judson Press, 1972.

Phylon. "The Sacred/Profane Dialectic in Delta Blues: The Life and Lyrics of Sonny Boy Williamson," Vol. 48, No. 4(1987): 317–326.

Pipes, William H. *Say Amen, Brother! Old-time Negro Preaching: A Study in American Frustration*. New York: William-Frederick Press, 1951.

Rhame, John. "Flaming Youth: A Story in Gullah Dialect." *American Speech,* 8 (1933): 39–43.

Roberts, John W. "Joning: An Afro-American Verbal Form in St. Louis." *Journal of the Folklore Institute* 19(1) (1982): 61–70.

Rose, Tricia. *Black Noise. Rap Music and Black Culture in Contemporary America*. Hanover, N.H.: University Press of New England, 1994.

Scott, Manuel Lee. *The Gospel from the Ghetto: Sermons from a Black Pulpit*. Nashville: Broadman Press, 1973.

"Sermon of an Ante-Bellum Negro Preacher." *Southern Workman* 30: 655–658.

Sidran, Ben. *Black Talk*. New York: Holt, Rinehart and Winston, 1971.

Simmons, Donald C. "Possible West African Sources for the American Negro 'Dozens.'" *Journal of American Folklore* 76(October/December 1963): 339–340.

Smith, Donald H. *Martin Luther King, Jr.: Rhetorician of Revolt*. Ph.D. dissertation, Department of Speech, University of Wisconsin, August 1964.

Smitherman, Geneva. *Talkin' and Testifyin': The Language of Black America*. Boston: Houghton Mifflin, 1977.

Spillers, Hortense J. "Martin Luther King and the Style of the Black Sermon." *Black Scholar* 3(September 1971): 14–27.

Vass, Winifred Kellersberger. *The Bantu-Speaking Heritage of the United States*. Los Angeles: University of California, Center for Afro-American Studies, 1979.

Vaughn-Cooke, Anna Fay. "The Black Preaching Style: Historical Development and Characteristics." *Languages and Linguistics: Working Papers,* No. 5: 28–39.

Walker, Wyatt Tee. "Song, Sermon and the Spoken Word: A Symposium on the Folk Base of Black American Literature." *SAGALA. A Journal of Arts and Ideas* (Summer 1980): 12–20.

Selected Videos, Films,
CD-ROMs and Slides

The Performed Word. Produced by Gerald L. Davis. Red Taurus Films. Ethnodocumentary
available in videotape and distributed by the Center for Southern Folklore, Memphis, TN,
and the Anthropology Film Center, Santa Fe, NM, 1981.

Juba. WETA, Washington, D.C. 1978. JUBA-000-CR94 [Four-part series: *The Legend of Harriet
Tubman,* 15 minutes; *Why Stories,* 15 minutes; *Brer Rabbit Stories,* 15 minutes; *How Stories
Came to Be,* 15 minutes]. PBS Videos.

Story of English. [No. 5, Black on White] Films, Inc. Syracuse University Classroom Film/Video
Rental Center. 58 mins. 1987.

The Gospel at Colonus. Peter Weinberg and Theodore Salata, executive producers. 90 minutes.
Updata.

Chapter 7

AFRICAN AMERICAN SPEECHMAKING

How Sweet the Sound is an anthology about *nommo,*[1] about the spoken word and the oral and vernacular traditions. This last chapter discusses African American oratory in the United States in the nineteenth and twentieth centuries. The oratory shows the persistent struggle of this community to achieve liberty and justice for itself and others. We can recognize the voice of Rev. Jesse Jackson and the now silent voices of Dr. Martin Luther King, Jr., U.S. Representative Barbara Jordan (D-Tex.), and Fannie Lou Hamer because they are so distinctive and have been impressed on our minds. Selecting speeches to accommodate the themes of the anthology, therefore, was a daunting task. Many may not recognize other voices: Vincent Harding's or even that of Mary McLeod Bethune and certainly not that of Frederick Douglass, which we can only imagine because it was not recorded electronically. But the message of them all, coming out of some phase and time of the struggle for human rights, is loud, clear, and continuous. Themes of struggle, community initiative, self-help, justice, government intervention, racism, and discrimination did not end with the passage of the Thirteenth, Fourteenth, and Fifteenth Amendments to the Constitution. They are with this country today, on the cusp of the twenty-first century.

Along the way, *nommo* in the United States has taken the form of the story, of the jeremiad (the warning of the prophetic voice), the sermon, the commencement address . . . and it has been about "soul," about that which is "spiritual"; about values—about American history since the appearance of the European and the African and about the legacy of that history which we live with still. In combination, the following speeches are part history lesson, part sermon and very powerful in their affect because they are about truth telling and calls for action. There is also, for example in the words of abolitionist Frederick Douglass, some of the trickster and double textuality. The audiences have been the black community(ies) and people of other ethnic groups, and the message has essentially been the same: America has not yet become the America it can be.

---

1 Molefi Kete Asante has a very informative discussion of *nommo.* See "African Foundations of Nommo" in the chapter "The Idea of a Metatheory," in *The Afrocentric Idea* (Philadelphia: Temple University Press, 1987), pp. 59–80.

What W. E. B. Du Bois wrote in 1903 is still true today: "the problem of the Twentieth Century is the problem of the color line."[2]

Almost a century later, President William Jefferson Clinton, in what the White House noted would be a significant address of his presidency, told the graduates of the University of California at San Diego that race was their "greatest challenge." He continued, "Of all the questions of discrimination and prejudice that still exist in our society, the most perplexing one is the oldest, and in some ways today the newest, the problem of race."[3]

It would seem that the president himself heard, if not the words of the orators, their spirit, especially that of Dr. King who defines America's moral oratory for this century. The president spoke of the necessity for racial unity and racial inclusion, but the racial text, although it now must also include Latinos, Asians, Africans, and other ethnic groups, is still basically the dialectic between black and white.[4] He reiterated, in similar words, what African Americans have been saying since the Revolutionary era in their response to Thomas Jefferson's Declaration of Independence, which declared all men to be equal: that there is "the possibility of really living up to our primary allegiance to the values America stands for."[5]

It has been, from the very beginning, the black response that democracy and slavocracy are not possible in the same space. In their very persons, enslaved people were living, breathing evidence of dichotomies within the founding documents about what freedom really means. In fact, freedom was the opposite of the physical toil of African peoples. Their lives and travail made it possible for other people not only to be free but to craft the modern concept of democracy. Democracy in America meant, for the Founders, not wanting to walk in the shoes of those they enslaved. It meant personal freedom and equal opportunities at the cost of those of other persons. When the country's president makes the statement, 221 years after the Declaration of Independence started this revolution in political thought, that "Our founders sought to form a more perfect union. The humility and hope of that phrase is the story of America, and it is our mission today . . . ," he indicates the improvisational and ameliorative aspects of Revolutionary era American statescraft. What the Founders sought was something *more* perfect and it was—*more* perfect than the aristocratic and feudal systems of Old World Europe, but it was and is not "perfect" yet. That "something" still needs to be defined and then made, finally, to work.

Freedom, responsibility for self, family, and community, full citizenship, dignity, pride, and finally to be an American, with all that suggests after centuries of travail, were

---

[2] W. E. B. Du Bois, *The Souls of Black Folk* [1903]. (Reprint, New York: A Signet Classic, 1969), p. xi.

[3] *New York Times*, June 15, 1997, p. 16.

[4] For example, the correspondence between Thomas Jefferson and African American astronomer Benjamin Banneker. See *The Portable Thomas Jefferson*, edited by Merrill D. Peterson, p. 454 (New York: Penguin Books, 1985); and "Copy of a Letter from Benjamin Banneker, to the Secretary of State, with His Answer, 1792," in *Early Negro Writing, 1760–1837. Selected and Introduced by Dorothy Porter*, edited by Porter (Baltimore: Black Classic Press. 1995), pp. 324–329. Also see the public correspondence between Ralph Ellison and the critic Irving Howe in Ellison's *Shadow and Act* (New York: Vintage Books, 1972), pp. 107–143; and Howe's "Black Boys and Native Sons," in *Dissent* (Autumn 1963): 353–368.

[5] *New York Times*, June 15, 1997, p. 16.

the goals of the African Americans who remained in the United States after the American Revolution and through the Civil War and Reconstruction. Most African Americans saw the "promise" of America, the "promissory note" of which Dr. King spoke; saw the "dream," still deferred for too many. President Clinton acknowledged that laws have broken down racial barriers but there is still more to be done. Just as Dr. King and Malcolm X before him understood, the discussion is no longer about law because the Constitution amended should be enough. It is about the spirit of the law: issues of soul and heart, and discourse with one's fellow citizens.[6] In announcing a national commission on race, to be headed by the eminent historian John Hope Franklin, whose seminal work *From Slavery to Freedom*[7] as a history text made its own history when it was first published in 1947, the president said he wanted the country to start a national "conversation" with town meetings and other venues where black and white people in particular would talk to one another and maybe even listen to one another. But black people, as the readings in this chapter show, have always talked to the country, in servitude and citizenship, of the "promises" of the great experiment in American democracy—and of the contribution they were willing to make to realize the promise.

The speeches in this chapter were given by Frederick Douglass, abolitionist; Mary McLeod Bethune, black clubwoman, educator, and adviser to President Franklin D. Roosevelt; and Vincent Harding, with whom this anthology opened. These fighters for racial justice did so, and do so, in the spirit as well as in the rough-and-tumble world. They span 120 years and share a common belief in the words of the Declaration of Independence and in the Constitution, as amended, that made black people legally free. The constant refrain, or riff, in the orators' words comes from the Founders themselves. The critical assessment is that we, fellow citizens, still must measure ourselves by those words and if we do must find ourselves wanting. They all ask this question: How can there be limits on the freedom of anyone on such arbitrary criteria as race, a human-made concept? How can there be such limits placed, especially, against a people who have proven time and again how much they want to be part of this society as it was bought with the "blood, sweat, and tears" of their forebears? These are serious and often critical orations, yet there is evidence in them of an understanding of human nature, a willingness to forgive, the potential of redemption for the past, and calls for reconciliation in the future. They are part of the traditional and rooted hope that has brought black people this far in their human rights efforts—and also women, the disabled, the elderly, the poor, the young—"all God's children." The struggle for freedom, that *How Sweet the Sound* is revealing, has been evolutionary, and not just for African Americans but for all Americans and those around the world who love freedom and still seek it.

Frederick Douglass's "Oration in Memory of Abraham Lincoln" does not have the punch of the better known "What to the American Slave Is Your Fourth of July?" but in its subtlety, I would suggest, it is even more powerful. It was given in 1876 on the eleventh anniversary of the assassination of the former president and on the occasion of

---

6 Malcolm X, in a speech, said, "All they [the United States government] have to do is go by that thing they call the Constitution. It needs no more bills, it needs no more amendments, it needs no more anything. All it needs is a little sincere application." Malcolm X, The Leverett House Forum of March 18, 1964, in *Malcolm X: Speeches at Harvard,* edited by Archie Epps, p. 139 (New York: Paragon Books, 1991).

7 John Hope Franklin, *From Slavery to Freedom.* (New York: Knopf, 1947).

the unveiling of the Freedman's Monument dedicated to him: a monument that was commissioned and paid for by persons free little more than a decade. The "Oration in Memory of Abraham Lincoln" has several layers, and Douglass saw the occasion as a signal event in the history of black people in the United States. This was a community, or "black," monument and also a national one. The now-free African American community was acknowledging the role President Lincoln played in its final attainment of constitutional freedom, the granting of citizenship, and the vote for black men.

Douglass notes that this social and political transformation of the African American even includes the fact that finally they can assemble together in the nation's capital, without fear of reprisal, for what previously would have been an "unlawful" coming together. He says, for Africans in America, this is "the first time in the history of our people . . . [that they] march conspiciously in the line of this time-honored custom"—of remembering a great "public man."[8] There are repetitions of language, riffs like "we are here," about the "sentiment" that created the gathering. Douglass is telling a story, if not also a cautionary one. It is an effective speech, although not a particularly emotional one. For Douglass, it does not matter *why* Lincoln freed those still in servitude, it is not necessary that the assassinated president had affection for them or thought of them as equal to himself. It is important that as president, Lincoln did his job, which *also* resulted in Civil War amendments to the Constitution. It was the right thing to do and at the same time the only way to save the Union.

It is also a speech with a double text. What is it that Douglass is suggesting the African American community is showing appreciation for? Lincoln, he says on this occasion, was a white man with the interests of white men paramount in his mind, not the interests of the slave or even free blacks of prominence. He was the leader of white America, *their* president with all the predispositions and prejudices that might imply. Douglass has negotiated and reconciled the notion of commemoration with critical assessment:

> Our faith in him was often taxed and strained to the uttermost, but it never failed. When he tarried long in the mountain; when he strangely told us that we were the cause of the war; when he still more strangely told us that we were to leave the land in which we were born; when he refused to employ our arms in defense of the Union . . . when we saw all this, and more, we were at times grieved, stunned, and greatly bewildered; but our hearts believed while they ached and bled. . . . Despite the mist and haze that surrounded him; despite the tumult, the hurry, and confusion of the hour, we were able to take a comprehensive view of Abraham Lincoln, and to make reasonable allowance for the circumstances of his position. We saw him, measured him, and estimated him . . .[9]

And they found him human.

Frederick Douglass put this commemoration for the author of the Emancipation Proclamation in historical and political context, and he made an important distinction between having hatred for slavery and feelings of shared manhood [sic] with enslaved persons, or free and freed blacks. He critiqued the Civil War presidency and the country and said, "We are here" now and there is no going back.

---

8 Philip S. Foner, ed., *The Life and Writings of Frederick Douglass. Reconstruction and After Vol. IV* (New York: International Publishers, 1975), p. 311.

9 Ibid., p. 313.

Mary McLeod Bethune's life is replete with achievements. She is especially well known as a member of President Franklin D. Roosevelt's "black cabinet." This group of African Americans, some of the "best and brightest," what W. E. B. Du Bois called the "talented tenth," signified the most influential and educated black Americans of the time. They surrounded the president of the United States and advised him on concerns and issues in their community and the nation. Bethune would eventually become the head of the Division of Negro Affairs in the National Youth Administration, which was part of the so-called alphabet agencies, established during the Depression years to aid America's poorest citizens who included African Americans. In addition, she was an officer of the NAACP, founder and president of the National Council of Negro Women, and cofounder of the historically black college, Bethune-Cookman College.

In 1949 Bethune presented the keynote address at the annual conference of the Association for the Study of Afro-American Life and History, which was founded by historian Carter G. Woodson. In her address, "The Negro in Retrospect and Prospect," she discusses the unity of the black community and its need to organize—"pulling ourselves together." She says that efforts at organization would advance the struggle against "timorous people afraid of their future; afraid of their own form of government [democracy]; afraid of their fellowmen!"[10] Just as journalist Ida B. Wells-Barnett before her, Bethune was also a clubwoman. She organized black women, and her organization, The National Council of Negro Women, has been and continues to be in the forefront of community service and lobbying on behalf of the African American community and people of African descent around the world. Her commitment to global racial peace was acknowledged in 1945 when she was named adviser to the U.S. delegation to the San Francisco founding conference of the United Nations.

The 1949 address was given on the verge of a new decade and in the context of the sankofa: the African mythical forward- and backward-looking bird. Bethune took this occasion to look backward and also forward to a future that would, in great part, be built on that foundation of foremothers and forefathers, an historical Hall of Fame of significant and millenial leaders of the race. And she was clear that at times these leaders did not speak with one voice but they all had one objective in mind, just different means of achieving it. "Power," however, rather than the "Negro" as "problem," or race relations in terms of Du Bois's twentieth-century "color line," were the context in which most Americans should talk about African Americans, she believed. "Power" (empowerment) was the cornerstone of her remarks. Bethune juxtaposed the idea of power within the African American community, with what she calls the "world's controlling minority [and what it] must do about us!" She rejects as inappropriate "back-to-Africa" movements and "separate-as-the-fingers" ideologies of Marcus Garvey and Booker T. Washington and suggests that the African American community can empower itself as it learns more about the world and the world learns more about it.

For her, for example, the involvement of African people in the United States with world affairs like the two world wars and the participation of black servicemen and women, was also a response to their centuries of struggle for freedom and justice

---

[10] Mary McLeod Bethune, "The Negro in Retrospect and Prospect," *Journal of Negro History* 35 (1950): 10.

that they were fighting to extend to parts of the world that did not have democratic institutions.

This is a hopeful speech and credibly so; Bethune has every reason to expect that the future will be good to black people, especially in what she calls the "Atomic Age." The threat of a nuclear holocaust, with the potential to destroy the world, she believed would unify the world. That as a result, "Many people . . . [will] regard their neighbors—across the street and across the world—with a more friendly eye, and . . . [stimulate] fresh interest in the application of the Golden Rule."[11] Bethune, in "The Negro in Retrospect and Prospect," is speaking about an historic circle of black people within a larger global circle of the self-interest of the human race.

Vincent Harding, historian-theologian/human rights activist, gave his speech, "For the Best and the Brightest," at the Fifth Annual Memorial Lecture of The Society for Values in Higher Education. The phrase "best and brightest" was coined by David Halberstam in his book about the young movers and shakers in the Kennedy Administration of the 1960s who created a Camelot on the Potomac as they ran the federal government.[12] In this speech, Harding is discussing those *other* "best and brightest"—young African American girls and boys whom his nephew Charles, a librarian in Chicago, said "are dying here," spiritually and physically, especially in the inner cities of America.

Vincent Harding opened *How Sweet the Sound,* placing the 1999 student of history on the coast of Africa with ancestors about to embark on a life-transforming journey, not only for themselves but also for the descendants of those who will survive the Middle Passage. For this memorial lecture, Harding is being introduced as part of the freedom movement of the 1960s and as a prophet; as founder of the Institute of the Black World and the first director of the Martin Luther King, Jr. Center; and as a person who was also in the vanguard of the black studies movement on American college campuses.

As a witness, Vincent Harding places himself in the tradition of such African American theologians as the late Dr. Benjamin Mays, teacher and mentor to Dr. King and former president of Morehouse College, and the late theologian Howard Thurman. Harding, also, starts with what he calls the "grand and basic purpose of our nation: to form a more perfect union."[13] In none of the speeches in this chapter have we gotten far away from that basic text—nor very far from "community," which increasingly goes beyond that of African Americans. In phrases from the founding documents, Harding seems to say, this was *your* experiment in democracy, and a good one, on paper. It is time to take it further and give it flesh and life. In a poignant moment, he juxtaposes the Constitution with Harlem Renaissance poet Langston Hughes's "O Let America Be America," which speaks of redemption, change, and hope, and with his nephew's "Some of our best and brightest children are dying here."[14] Harding and other contemporary commentators are concerned also that "the community" has been split by class. There are persons still "enslaved" due to the lack of educational and economic opportunities. His speech talks about the need to negotiate initiatives between the community itself,

---

[11] Ibid., p. 19.

[12] David Halberstam, *The Best and the Brightest* (New York: Random House, 1972).

[13] Speech, "For the Best and the Brightest," p. 2.

[14] Ibid. [Charles Freeney], p. 3.

that is, self-help, and the responsibilities of government. He reminds his audience of African America's history of fighting for freedom, of taking care of its own and others. He revives the legacy of the ringshout—of community—and of spirituality. Capsulizing the spirit of African American people, we hear him say this:

> Always, it seems to me, always when we have been at our best, black people have known that it was absolutely necessary to maintain a creative tension between the need to improve ourselves and the need to improve the nation. As the old song says, "You can't have one without the other." Black people understood that—self-improvement, national improvement. . . . Self-help and the transformation of civilization itself—that has been the heart of the historic movements among black people for freedom and justice in this country, and it seems to me that the argument that is going on [between the need for self-help and the responsibilities of governmental intervention] misses the history of that kind of constant creative tension, misses our need to establish the tension again.[15]

Harding uses this occasion to critique not only America but the African American community and particularly its middle class. He says this is "a fundamental critique of the culture of the mainstream, a culture that is essentially acquisitive in its materialism . . . a culture in which violence has been enthroned as the norm—as normal as white supremacy once was and to some degree still is."[16] Harding critiques American society in terms of its "values" and says there must be a revolution there too.

In this speech, Vincent Harding uses the prefix "re." He speaks of the black community "*re*-visioning," "*re*-creating," having "*re*newal," "*re*discovery," "*re*construction," and being "*re*-defined," and "*re*-projected." Out of the "junkyards"/"spirit yards" of African and African American cosmology, aesthetics, and philosophy has come the stuff of the *re*-creation of African America with its ancient values and also the *re*-creation, the Reconstruction, of America. Out of the African American community, as so often in the past, will come the leadership to guide the country in right directions as we approach the new millenium. America has seen, in this community, historically, "our connectedness to each other, our oneness, our interdependence, across the essentially superficial lines of race and class."[17] And Harding also talks about the spirit and soul. For the tasks ahead, African Americans must be people "whose souls are rested." He says,

> Have you not known? Have you not heard? The Lord is the everlasting God, the creator of the ends of the earth. He does not, She does not grow faint or grow weary. Her understanding is unsearchable. He gives power to the faint . . . and young people shall fall exhausted, but they who wait for the Lord shall renew their strength. They shall mount up with wings like eagles. They shall run and not be weary. They shall walk and not faint.[18]

---

[15] Ibid., p. 6.

[16] Ibid., p. 8.

[17] Ibid., p. 7.

[18] Ibid., p. 17.

Oration in Memory of Abraham Lincoln
Frederick Douglass
Abolitionist/Journalist/Orator/
Social reformer/Fugitive slave

*Frederick Douglass (1817–1895) was born enslaved and became one of the
most influential and best known abolitionists of the nineteenth century,
especially with the publication of his* Narrative of the Life of Frederick
Douglass, an American Slave as Written by Himself *(1845). He published
four volumes of autobiography and edited the* North Star *(1847–1851),*
Frederick Douglass's Paper *(1851–1860),* Douglass's Monthly *(1859–1863),
and* New National Era *(1870–1874). Douglass was a confidant and adviser
to President Abraham Lincoln. From 1877 to 1881, he served as U.S.
marshal for the District of Columbia (D.C.) and was recorder of deeds for
D.C. from 1881 to 1886. He was Chargé d'Affaires for Santo Domingo and
minister to Haiti from 1889 to 1891.*

ORATION IN MEMORY OF ABRAHAM LINCOLN, delivered at the Unveiling of
the Freedmen's Monument in Memory of Abraham Lincoln, in Lincoln Park,
Washington, D.C., April 14, 1876

Friends and Fellow-citizens:

I warmly congratulate you upon the highly interesting object which has caused
you to assemble in such numbers and spirit as you have today. This occasion is in some
respects remarkable. Wise and thoughtful men of our race, who shall come after us, and
study the lesson of our history in the United States; who shall survey the long and
dreary spaces over which we have traveled; who shall count the links in the great chain
of events by which we have reached our present position, will make a note of this occasion; they will think of it and speak of it with a sense of manly pride and complacency.

I congratulate you, also, upon the very favorable circumstances in which we
meet today. They are high, inspiring, and uncommon. They lend grace, glory, and significance to the object for which we have met. Nowhere else in this great country,
with its uncounted towns and cities, unlimited wealth, and immeasurable territory
extending from sea to sea, could conditions be found more favorable to the success of
this occasion than here.

Frederick Douglass's "Oration in Memory of Abraham Lincoln" in **The Life and Writings of Frederick Douglass.**
Reconstruction and After *(Vol. 4), edited by Philip S. Foner (New York: International Publishers, 1975), pp.
309–319.*

We stand today at the national center to perform something like a national act—an act which is to go into history; and we are here where every pulsation of the national heart can be heard, felt, and reciprocated. A thousand wires, fed with thought and winged with lightning, put us in instantaneous communication with the loyal and true men all over this country.

Few facts could better illustrate the vast and wonderful change which has taken place in our condition as a people than the fact of our assembling here for the purpose we have today. Harmless, beautiful, proper, and praiseworthy as this demonstration is, I cannot forget that no such demonstration would have been tolerated here twenty years ago. The spirit of slavery and barbarism, which still lingers to blight and destroy in some dark and distant parts of our country, would have made our assembling here the signal and excuse for opening upon us all the flood-gates of wrath and violence. That we are here in peace today is a compliment and a credit to American civilization, and a prophecy of still greater national enlightenment and progress in the future. I refer to the past not in malice, for this is no day for malice; but simply to place more distinctly in front the gratifying and glorious change which has come both to our white fellow-citizens and ourselves, and to congratulate all upon the contrast between now and then; the new dispensation of freedom with its thousand blessings to both races, and the old dispensation of slavery with its ten thousand evils to both races—white and black. In view, then, of the past, the present, and the future, with the long and dark history of our bondage behind us, and with liberty, progress, and enlightenment before us, I again congratulate you upon this auspicious day and hour.

Friends and fellow-citizens, the story of our presence here is soon and easily told. We are here in the District of Columbia, here in the city of Washington, the most luminous point of American territory; a city recently transformed and made beautiful in its body and in its spirit; we are here in the place where the ablest and best men of the country are sent to devise the policy, enact the laws, and shape the destiny of the Republic; we are here, with the stately pillars and majestic dome of the Capitol of the nation looking down upon us; we are here, with the broad earth freshly adorned with the foliage and flowers of spring for our church, and all races, colors, and conditions of men for our congregation—in a word, we are here to express, as best we may, by appropriate forms and ceremonies, our grateful sense of the vast, high, and preëminent services rendered to ourselves, to our race, to our country, and to the whole world by Abraham Lincoln.

The sentiment that brings us here to-day is one of the noblest that can stir and thrill the human heart. It has crowned and made glorious the high places of all civilized nations with the grandest and most enduring works of art, designed to illustrate the characters and perpetuate the memories of great public men. It is the sentiment which from year to year adorns with fragrant and beautiful flowers the graves of our loyal, brave, and patriotic soldiers who fell in defence of the Union and liberty. It is the sentiment of gratitude and appreciation, which often, in the presence of many who hear me, has filled yonder heights of Arlington with the eloquence of eulogy and the sublime enthusiasm of poetry and song; a sentiment which can never die while the Republic lives.

For the first time in the history of our people, and in the history of the whole American people, we join in this high worship, and march conspicuously in the line of this time-honored custom. First things are always interesting, and this is one of our first things. It is the first time that, in this form and manner, we have sought to do honor to an American great man, however deserving and illustrious. I commend the fact to notice; let it be told in every part of the Republic; let men of all parties and opinions hear it; let those who despise us, not less than those who respect us, know that now and here, in the spirit of liberty, loyalty, and gratitude, let it be known everywhere, and by everybody who takes an interest in human progress and in the amelioration of the condition of mankind, that, in the presence and with the approval of the members of the American House of Representatives, reflecting the general sentiment of the country; that in the presence of that august body, the American Senate, representing the highest intelligence and the calmest judgment of the country; in the presence of the Supreme Court and Chief-Justice of the United States, to whose decisions we all patriotically bow; in the presence and under the steady eye of the honored and trusted President of the United States, with the members of his wise and patriotic Cabinet, we, the colored people, newly emancipated and rejoicing in our blood-bought freedom, near the close of the first century in the life of this Republic, have now and here unveiled, set apart, and dedicated a monument of enduring granite and bronze, in every line, feature, and figure of which the men of this generation may read, and those of after-coming generations may read, something of the exalted character and great works of Abraham Lincoln, the first martyr President of the United States.

Fellow-citizens, in what we have said and done today, and in what we may say and do hereafter, we disclaim everything like arrogance and assumption. We claim for ourselves no superior devotion to the character, history, and memory of the illustrious name whose monument we have here dedicated today. We fully comprehend the relation of Abraham Lincoln both to ourselves and to the white people of the United States. Truth is proper and beautiful at all times and in all places, and it is never more proper and beautiful in any case than when speaking of a great public man whose example is likely to be commended for honor and imitation long after his departure to the solemn shades, the silent continents of eternity. It must be admitted, truth compels me to admit, even here in the presence of the monument we have erected to his memory, Abraham Lincoln was not, in the fullest sense of the word, either our man or our model. In his interests, in his associations, in his habits of thought, and in his prejudices, he was a white man.

He was preëminently the white man's President, entirely devoted to the welfare of white men. He was ready and willing at any time during the first years of his administration to deny, postpone, and sacrifice the rights of humanity in the colored people to promote the welfare of the white people of this country. In all his education and feeling he was an American of the Americans. He came into the Presidential chair upon one principle alone, namely, opposition to the extension of slavery. His arguments in furtherance of this policy had their motive and mainspring in his patriotic devotion to the interests of his own race. To protect, defend, and perpetuate slavery in the states where it existed Abraham Lincoln was not less ready than any other President to draw the sword of the nation. He was ready to execute all the supposed guarantees of the United States Constitution in favor of the slave system anywhere inside the slave states. He was willing to pursue, recapture, and send back the fugitive slave to his master, and to suppress a slave rising for liberty, though his guilty master were already in arms against the Government. The race to which we belong were not the special objects of his consideration. Knowing this, I concede to you, my white fellow-citizens, a preëminence in this worship at once full and supreme. First, midst, and last, you and yours were the objects of his deepest affection and his most earnest solicitude. You are the children of Abraham Lincoln. We are at best only his step-children; children by adoption, children by forces of circumstances and necessity. To you it especially belongs to sound his praises, to preserve and perpetuate his memory, to multiply his statues, to hang his pictures high upon your walls, and commend his example, for to you he was a great and glorious friend and benefactor. Instead of supplanting you at his altar, we would exhort you to build high his monuments; let them be of the most costly material, of the most cunning workmanship; let their forms be symmetrical, beautiful, and perfect; let their bases be upon solid rocks, and their summits lean against the unchanging blue, overhanging sky, and let them endure forever! But while in the abundance of your wealth, and in the fullness of your just and patriotic devotion, you do all this, we entreat you to despise not the humble offering we this day unveil to view; for while Abraham Lincoln saved for you a country, he delivered us from a bondage, according to Jefferson, one hour of which was worse than ages of the oppression your fathers rose in rebellion to oppose.

Fellow-citizens, ours is no new-born zeal and devotion—merely a thing of this moment. The name of Abraham Lincoln was near and dear to our hearts in the darkest and most perilous hours of the Republic. We were no more ashamed of him when shrouded in clouds of darkness, of doubt, and defeat than when we saw him crowned with victory, honor, and glory. Our faith in him was often taxed and strained to the uttermost, but it never failed. When he tarried long in the mountain; when he strangely told us that we were the cause of the war; when he still more strangely told us that we were to leave the land in which we were born; when he refused to employ our arms in defence of the Union; when, after accepting our services as colored soldiers, he refused to retaliate our murder and torture as colored prisoners; when he told us he would save the Union if he could with slavery; when he revoked the Proclamation of Emancipation of General Fremont; when he refused to remove the popular commander of the Army of the Potomac, in the days of its inaction and defeat, who was more zealous in his efforts to protect slavery than to suppress rebellion; when we saw all this, and more, we were at times grieved, stunned, and greatly bewildered; but our hearts believed while they ached and bled. Nor was this, even at that time, a blind and unreasoning superstition. Despite the mist and haze that surrounded him; despite the tumult, the hurry, and confusion of the hour, we were able to take a comprehensive view of Abraham Lincoln, and to make reasonable allowance for the circumstances of his position. We saw him, measured him, and estimated him; not by stray utterances to injudicious and tedious delegations, who often tried his patience; not by isolated facts torn from their connection; not by any partial and imperfect glimpses, caught at inopportune moments; but by a broad survey, in the light of the stern logic of great events, and in view of that divinity which shapes our ends, rough hew them how we will, we came to the conclusion that the hour and the man of our redemption had somehow met in the person of Abraham Lincoln. It mattered little to us what language he might employ on special occasions; it mattered little to us, when we fully knew him, whether he was swift or slow in his movements; it was enough for us that Abraham Lincoln was at the head of a great movement, and was in living and earnest sympathy with that movement, which, in the nature of things, must go on until slavery should be utterly and forever abolished in the United States.

When, therefore, it shall be asked what we have to do with the memory of Abraham Lincoln, or what Abraham Lincoln had to do with us, the answer is ready, full, and complete. Though he loved Cæsar less than Rome, though the Union was more to him than our freedom or our future, under his wise and beneficent rule we saw ourselves gradually lifted from the depths of slavery to the heights of liberty and manhood; under his wise and beneficent rule, and by measures approved and vigorously pressed by him, we saw that the handwriting of ages, in the form of prejudice and proscription, was rapidly fading away from the face of our whole country; under his rule, and in due time, about as soon after all as the country could tolerate the strange spectacle, we saw our brave sons and brothers laying off the rags of bondage, and being clothed all over in the blue uniforms of the soldiers of the United States; under his rule we saw two hundred thousand of our dark and dusky people responding to the call of Abraham Lincoln, and with muskets on their shoulders, and eagles on their buttons, timing their high footsteps to liberty and union under the national flag; under his rule we saw the independence of the black republic of Haiti, the special object of slaveholding aversion and horror, fully recognized, and her minister, a colored gentleman, duly received here in the city of Washington; under his rule we saw the internal slave-trade, which so long disgraced the nation, abolished, and slavery abolished in the District of Columbia; under his rule we saw for the first time the law enforced against the foreign slave trade, and the first slave-trader hanged like any other pirate or murderer; under his rule, assisted by the greatest captain of our age, and his inspiration, we saw the Confederate States, based upon the idea that our race must be slaves, and slaves forever, battered to pieces and scattered to the four winds; under his rule, and in the fullness of time, we saw Abraham Lincoln, after giving the slaveholders three months' grace in which to save their hateful slave system, penning the immortal paper, which, though special in its language, was general in its principles and effect, making slavery forever impossible in the United States. Though we waited long, we saw all this and more.

Can any colored man, or any white man friendly to the freedom of all men, ever forget the night which followed the first day of January, 1863, when the world was to see if Abraham Lincoln would prove to be as good as his word? I shall never forget that memorable night, when in a distant city I waited and watched at a public meeting, with three thousand others not less anxious than myself, for the word of deliverance which we have heard read today. Nor shall I ever forget the outburst of joy and thanksgiving that rent the air when the lightning brought to us the emancipation proclamation. In that happy hour we forgot all delay, and forgot all tardiness, forgot that the President had bribed the rebels to lay down their arms by a promise to withhold the bolt which would smite the slave-system with destruction; and we were thenceforward willing to allow the President all the latitude of time, phraseology, and every honorable device that statesmanship might require for the achievement of a great and beneficent measure of liberty and progress.

Fellow-citizens, there is little necessity on this occasion to speak at length and critically of this great and good man, and of his high mission in the world. That ground has been fully occupied and completely covered both here and elsewhere. The whole field of fact and fancy has been gleaned and garnered. Any man can say things that are true of Abraham Lincoln, but no man can say anything that is new of Abraham Lincoln. His personal traits and public acts are better known to the American people than are those of any other man of his age. He was a mystery to no man who saw him and heard him. Though high in position, the humblest could approach him and feel at home in his presence. Though deep, he was transparent; though strong, he was gentle; though decided and pronounced in his convictions, he was tolerant towards those who differed from him, and patient under reproaches. Even those who only knew him through his public utterance obtained a tolerably clear idea of his character and personality. The image of the man went out with his words, and those who read them knew him.

I have said that President Lincoln was a white man, and shared the prejudices common to his countrymen towards the colored race. Looking back to his times and to the condition of his country, we are compelled to admit that this unfriendly feeling on his part may be safely set down as one element of his wonderful success in organizing the loyal American people for the tremendous conflict before them, and bringing them safely through that conflict. His great mission was to accomplish two things: first, to save his country from dismemberment and ruin; and, second, to free his country from the great crime of slavery. To do one or the other, or both, he must have the earnest sympathy and the powerful coöperation of his loyal fellow-countrymen. Without this primary and essential condition to success his efforts must have been vain and utterly fruitless. Had he put the abolition of slavery before the salvation of the Union, he would have inevitably driven from him a powerful class of the American people and rendered resistance to rebellion impossible. Viewed from the genuine abolition ground, Mr. Lincoln seemed tardy, cold, dull, and indifferent; but measuring him by the sentiment of his country, a sentiment he was bound as a statesman to consult, he was swift, zealous, radical, and determined.

Though Mr. Lincoln shared the prejudices of his white fellow-countrymen against the Negro, it is hardly necessary to say that in his heart of hearts he loathed and hated slavery. . . .* The man who could say, "Fondly do we hope, fervently do we pray, that this mighty scourge of war shall soon pass away, yet if God wills it continue till all the wealth piled by two hundred years of bondage shall have been wasted, and each drop of blood drawn by the lash shall have been paid for by one drawn by the sword, the judgments of the Lord are true and righteous altogether," gives all needed proof of his feeling on the subject of slavery. He was willing, while the South was loyal, that it

---

*"I am naturally anti-slavery. If slavery is not wrong, nothing is wrong. I cannot remember when I did not so think and feel."—*Letter of Mr. Lincoln to Mr. Hodges, of Kentucky,* April 4, 1864.

should have its pound of flesh, because he thought that it was so nominated in the bond; but farther than this no earthly power could make him go.

Fellow-citizens, whatever else in this world may be partial, unjust, and uncertain, time, time! is impartial, just, and certain in its action. In the realm of mind, as well as in the realm of matter, it is a great worker, and often works wonders. The honest and comprehensive statesman, clearly discerning the needs of his country, and earnestly endeavoring to do his whole duty, though covered and blistered with reproaches, may safely leave his course to the silent judgment of time. Few great public men have ever been the victims of fiercer denunciation than Abraham Lincoln was during his administration. He was often wounded in the house of his friends. Reproaches came thick and fast upon him from within and from without, and from opposite quarters. He was assailed by Abolitionists; he was assailed by slaveholders; he was assailed by the men who were for peace at any price; he was assailed by those who were for a more vigorous prosecution of the war; he was assailed for not making the war an abolition war; and he was bitterly assailed for making the war an abolition war.

But now behold the change: the judgment of the present hour is, that taking him for all in all, measuring the tremendous magnitude of the work before him, considering the necessary means to ends, and surveying the end from the beginning, infinite wisdom has seldom sent any man into the world better fitted for his mission than Abraham Lincoln. His birth, his training, and his natural endowments, both mental and physical, were strongly in his favor. Born and reared among the lowly, a stranger to wealth and luxury, compelled to grapple single-handed with the flintiest hardships of life, from tender youth to sturdy manhood, he grew strong in the manly and heroic qualities demanded by the great mission to which he was called by the votes of his countrymen. The hard condition of his early life, which would have depressed and broken down weaker men, only gave greater life, vigor, and buoyancy to the heroic spirit of Abraham Lincoln. He was ready for any kind and any quality of work. What other young men dreaded in the shape of toil, he took hold of with the utmost cheerfulness.

> *"A spade, a rake, a hoe,*
> *A pick-axe, or a bill;*
> *A hook to reap, a scythe to mow,*
> *A flail, or what you will."*

All day long he could split heavy rails in the woods, and half the night long he could study his English Grammar by the uncertain flare and glare of the light made by a pine-knot. He was at home on the land with his axe, with his maul, with gluts, and his wedges; and he was equally at home on water, with his oars, with his poles, with his planks, and with his boat-hooks. And whether in his flat-boat on the Mississippi River, or at the fireside of his frontier cabin, he was a man of work. A son of toil himself, he was linked in brotherly sympathy with the sons of toil in every loyal part of the Republic. This very fact gave him tremendous power with the American people, and materially contributed not only to selecting him to the Presidency, but in sustaining his administration of the Government.

Upon his inauguration as President of the United States, an office, even when assumed under the most favorable conditions, fitted to tax and strain the largest abilities,

Abraham Lincoln was met by a tremendous crisis. He was called upon not merely to administer the Government, but to decide, in the face of terrible odds, the fate of the Republic.

A formidable rebellion rose in his path before him; the Union was already practically dissolved; his country was torn and rent asunder at the center. Hostile armies were already organized against the Republic, armed with the munitions of war which the Republic had provided for its own defence. The tremendous question for him to decide was whether his country should survive the crisis and flourish, or be dismembered and perish. His predecessor in office had already decided the question in favor of national dismemberment, by denying to it the right of self-defence and self-preservation—a right which belongs to the meanest insect.

Happily for the country, happily for you and for me, the judgment of James Buchanan, the patrician, was not the judgment of Abraham Lincoln, the plebeian. He brought his strong common sense, sharpened in the school of adversity, to bear upon the question. He did not hesitate, he did not doubt, he did not falter; but at once resolved that at whatever peril, at whatever cost, the union of the States should be preserved. A patriot himself, his faith was strong and unwavering in the patriotism of his countrymen. Timid men said before Mr. Lincoln's inauguration, that we had seen the last President of the United States. A voice in influential quarters said, "Let the Union slide." Some said that a Union maintained by the sword was worthless. Others said a rebellion of 8,000,000 cannot be suppressed; but in the midst of all this tumult and timidity, and against all this, Abraham Lincoln was clear in his duty, and had an oath in heaven. He calmly and bravely heard the voice of doubt and fear all around him; but he had an oath in heaven, and there was not power enough on earth to make this honest boatman, backwoodsman, and broad-handed splitter of rails evade or violate that sacred oath. He had not been schooled in the ethics of slavery; his plain life had favored his love of truth. He had not been taught that treason and perjury were the proof of honor and honesty. His moral training was against his saying one thing when he meant another. The trust that Abraham Lincoln had in himself and in the people was surprising and grand, but it was also enlightened and well founded. He knew the American people better than they knew themselves, and his truth was based upon this knowledge.

Fellow-citizens, the fourteenth day of April, 1865, of which this is the eleventh anniversary, is now and will ever remain a memorable day in the annals of this Republic. It was on the evening of this day, while a fierce and sanguinary rebellion was in the last stages of its desolating power; while its armies were broken and scattered before the invincible armies of Grant and Sherman; while a great nation, torn and rent by war, was already beginning to raise to the skies loud anthems of joy at the dawn of peace, it was startled, amazed, and overwhelmed by the crowning crime of slavery—the assassination of Abraham Lincoln. It was a new crime, a pure act of malice. No purpose of the rebellion was to be served by it. It was the simple gratification of a hell-black spirit of revenge. But it has done good after all. It has filled the country with a deeper abhorrence of slavery and a deeper love for the great liberator.

Had Abraham Lincoln died from any of the numerous ills to which flesh is heir; had he reached that good old age of which his vigorous constitution and his temperate habits gave promise; had he been permitted to see the end of his great work; had the solemn curtain of death come down but gradually—we should still have been smitten with a heavy grief, and treasured his name lovingly. But dying as he did die, by the red hand of violence, killed, assassinated, taken off without warning, not because of personal hate—for no man who knew Abraham Lincoln could hate him—but because of his fidelity to union and liberty, he is doubly dear to us, and his memory will be precious forever.

Fellow-citizens, I end, as I began, with congratulations. We have done a good work for our race today. In doing honor to the memory of our friend and liberator, we have been doing highest honors to ourselves and those who come after us; we have been fastening ourselves to a name and fame imperishable and immortal; we have also been defending ourselves from a blighting scandal. When now it shall be said that the colored man is soulless, that he has no appreciation of benefits or benefactors; when the foul reproach of ingratitude is hurled at us, and it is attempted to scourge us beyond the range of human brotherhood, we may calmly point to the monument we have this day erected to the memory of Abraham Lincoln.

The Negro in Retrospect and Prospect
Mary McLeod Bethune
Clubwoman/Presidential adviser/
Government official/College founder
and administrator

Mary McLeod Bethune (1875–1955) was cofounder and president of Bethune-Cookman College, a coeducational historically black college in Florida. She served as vice president of the NAACP and was founder and president of the National Council of Negro Women. During Franklin D. Roosevelt's tenure as president, Bethune was his special adviser on minority affairs and director of Division of Negro Affairs of the National Youth Administration. During World War II, she served as special assistant to the secretary of war for selection of slots at the first officer candidate schools for WACS. Mrs. Bethune was also an adviser to the U.S. delegation to the 1945 founding conference of the United Nations in San Francisco. In 1974 a bronze statue of her was placed in a public park in the District of Columbia not far from the Capitol. It was the first statute in the federal city portraying either a woman or an African American.

Mary McLeod Bethune, "The Negro in Retrospect and Prospect," an address delivered at the 1949 annual meeting of the Association for the Study of Negro Life and History (New York), Journal of Negro History *35 (1950): 9–19.*

A decade ago, or even five years ago, few would have predicted that the position of the Negro in world affairs would have attained its present significance. The world has been moving rapidly. Well might we pause, then, today to view the Negro in retrospect and prospect.

My splendid audience, here, will join with me in paying tribute to the builders of earlier days, who laid the foundation for today's advance. But we shall not stop overlong to praise our warriors, Louverture and Peter Salem; our churchmen, Allen, Bryan and Garnett; our statesmen, Frederick Douglass and Grimké; or our educators, Booker T. Washington and Lucy Laney, for their greatest tribute, their greatest monument—the greatest monument to all our black heroes since the Negro first set foot in the New World—is the influence which you and I, my friends, are wielding in the world today.

Those of us who are a little older will recall that as we arrived at maturity and took our places as participants in the immediate world about us we quickly learned that we were regarded as a "problem." We spent our early years as adults with the term "Negro problem" dragging at our feet—slowing our steps.

Always we heard discussed the question of what the world's *controlling minority must do about us.* Always—in religion, in education, in employment, there it was— what must be done with the "Negro element?" The pattern of our education, for better or for worse, was worked out *for* us. Someone else decided what we should study, and, outside of the Negro denominations, where we should pray.

We oldsters must take off our hats to ourselves, that through those trying years we did not lose sight of our objectives under the tremendous pressures exerted to induce us to accommodate ourselves to the acceptance of what was clearly illogical and untenable in human relations.

Out of the many fine developments of that period, that one fact stands out sharply—it was a period of pulling ourselves together; of girding our minds and our spirits for an aggressive struggle against the forces of reaction—of timorous people afraid of their future; afraid of their own form of government; afraid of their fellowmen!

We recently went through a revival of the colonization projects and of panicky back-to-Africa proposals, with the Marcus Garvey movement gathering considerable strength among the frustrated of darker hue before it finally collapsed. We had already gone through the separate-as-the-fingers period in which paradoxically the growth of a great educational philosophy. [Industrial education as exemplified by Tuskegee Institute] paralleled, in its initiation and development, that of a less-far-sighted social philosophy of appeasement to separatists. [Editor's note: Booker T. Washington's so-called "accommodationist" approach versus W. E. B. Du Bois's "integrationist" approach.]

All this represented the thinking of those not yet grown up to the implications of a practicing democracy—to the implications of spiritual and social progress at a time when our country was assuming its place as a world power—was fast moving into position as *the greatest* of world powers!

This represented the days when we were outgrowing our twenties and thirties and forties—and some of us our fifties—when we began in larger numbers to pull to pieces this "Negro problem," this "color problem," to analyze its parts, to determine what manner of phenomenon was dogging our footsteps. We were determined to find out how much of this "problem," if any, was basic difference, and how much of it was suppression and inhibition and fear—and WHOSE!

These were the days when Negro leadership concluded at long last that what the Negro had to deal with, first and foremost, was not so much his own thinking as the stereo-typed, nervous thinking of the world's non-colored minority! And with that conclusion the so-called "Negro problem" ceased to drag at our feet.

We took the pieces of that "problem" and spread them out on the conference table of the world. We looked at them dispassionately and objectively and said to the world:

"See here! Here is the difficulty! The difficulty is the hard, democratic way of life that you are unwilling to face; the way of life that is not for the self-satisfied or the indolent, or for the smug, or for the fearful who have faith only in themselves—but the only way that leads to peace, among neighbors or among nations."

And there came a period of transition in the world's thinking. The world began to worry about us—about what we "wanted"—which was a sign of progress. And we began to know more surely just what we wanted. It has been only five years since fourteen of us produced, on request, a volume of essays called, "WHAT THE NEGRO WANTS," edited by our friend, Rayford W. Logan, and published by the University of North Carolina Press. In 344 pages of comment and analysis, eleven of which were mine, we succeeded in saying that we want precisely what everybody else wants, and find no good reason for being apologetic about it.

We were supposed to represent all shades of thought. What shade I was supposed to represent I do not know. But when we were all through itemizing our "wants" and laid them on the table, the only person remotely apologizing for that list was the publisher, and I doubt if his dissent convinced even himself of the value of further hedging!

How has "the Negro," as the term is used, arrived this close to unity? The answer might well be summarized in the reply of a leader who has retained his poise and objectivity, when asked for his opinion of a fellow-Negro who had thrown his controls to the wind. It was simply a difference of reactions, he replied. We all want the same things. We all intend to get them. We've all been hurt, and the hurt affects us in different ways. That was a sensible, factual answer—a statement to which all citizens of the world must sooner or later face up. It reflects a healthy trend away from denunciation of those who have difficulty in functioning in the midst of racial pressures, and a growing will and desire to find a common denominator on which to base constructive, concerted action.

These hurts are sometimes very useful, and serve us better than we sometimes realize. They have drawn us together. They have drawn friends to us. They have made us organization-minded. They have solidified us and our organizations with the organizations of others, on an intelligently aggressive front.

The movement of the Negro worker from the farms of the South to industry, especially Northern industry, has increased his consciousness of the power of organization. He has been forced to observe the operation of unions—those which have excluded him as well as those which have welcomed him. He has watched his fellow-workers bargaining for himself—on all fronts. He has learned that he, too, has resources of value. He has learned that when he offers his wares as an individual, he is a *peddler.* When he offers them as an organization, he is a *power!*

So, as the eyes of the Negro have opened to his own significance as a power, and the burden of his morale-destroying label as a "problem" has begun to fall away from him, his fellow-Americans, his fellow-citizens of the world, have begun to see the futility of attempting to keep him forever in bondage, in any kind of bondage, however polite the name by which it may be called—parallel culture, separate but equal, or racial integrity. And of the last mentioned it might be said that it is a theory practiced least by those who proclaim it most, with results in hybrid population which preclude argument!

We know that the franchise has not been extended solely from altruistic motives. But in an era of government by pressures, we have constantly improved our techniques in the application of pressures, and so have pushed back, steadily, the areas of unrepresentative government.

We may agree or disagree with any given cause or opinion, but the fact of growing unity of effort remains. Conscientious objectors picket the French Embassy to protest the imprisonment, in France, of another conscientious objector. There is a Negro among them. The steel workers bargain for increased benefits. There are many Negroes among them. The president of a great steel company comes out and talks with these workers, to get their views at first hand. Veterans, teachers, domestic workers, farm workers, university women, men and women of many interests, are united for service to humanity on many fronts. Negroes are a part of organizations representing all of these without racial distinction. And while there will be need for special effort by and with Negroes, to enable them to move fully and freely in the normal life of this country, which is *their* country, so long as any obstructions remain—the concept is rapidly gaining ground that their needs as first-class citizens are indistinguishable from the needs of any other first-class citizens, and that the objectives of all are identical.

All racial barriers, as such, may not fall, today or tomorrow, but they will not be able to stand long, before the determined advance of citizens of all races, shedding their cumbersome, outgrown racial complexes, in their march toward democratic living.

There have been some very interesting developments in this stretching out process. One of the most interesting has been the gradual disappearance of the one-spokesman concept. Negroes now listen with great respect, not to just one or two people who can "speak for" them, but to many people who speak with authority, not from pinnacles, but from vantage points gained by mingling, observing and working with the masses.

Consequently, their fellow-citizens who are public servants, from the highest post in the land to the most obscure, also listen with respect, to a growing body of Negro leadership, which does not necessarily "think alike," on ways and means, but which holds with remarkable consistency to a common objective.

Trends in world affairs have broadened our vision of the world, and the world's vision of us, and have forced a larger measure of thinking upon the masses.

The terrible lessons of world conflict have educated all of us. The youth from our firesides, for whom we have worked and prayed and sacrificed, have gone to the ends of the earth to battle with other youth. *Where* did they go? For what *reason* did they go? Will they have to go again? What influences are abroad in the world that keep the peoples of the world at one another's throats—that have made compulsory military service a normal expectancy for the youth of this generation? What can we do about these influences? What controls can we use?

And then the boys who lived to return to us—what were their observations and reactions to other parts of the world—to other peoples, some of whom we called "friends," some of whom we called "allies," some of whom we called "neutrals," and some of whom we called "enemies"—but all human beings, like ourselves, with special problems, about which, heretofore, we had not known too much, nor had been too much concerned?

It did something to us! It took us out of ourselves! We saw something bigger than we had before envisioned. Our thinking expanded and became less subjective. Our sphere of action broadened. We did not forget that we were Negroes, but the fact became less important, to us and to others.

The advent of the Atomic Age flattened out a great deal of race consciousness among all peoples. It eliminated at one sweep, the zones of "safe living"—the places where it was possible for one part of the world placidly to ignore any other part. Ideologies became more important than race. Mankind began regrouping itself around ideologies rather than around color. The mass of Negroes found in the democratic ideal, freedom to work out progress in an imperfect world.

The Negro press immediately recognized the scope of this enlarged interest, and met it by sending sage and seasoned writers to every corner of the globe to report their findings on social, economic and political functioning, in other world areas with heavily mixed populations.

Acceptance of our more cosmopolitan interests and growing economic strength is reflected in the advertising seen in publications slanted to Negro readers, and not infrequently in national publications slanted to all of Main Street. Negro mothers, Negro babies, Negro scientists, Negro skilled workers, Negro glamour girls, Negro athletes and entertainers greet one from advertisements promoting everything from baby food to automobiles—bidding for the dollars earned and spent by the darker brother.

This concession to our buying power did not just *happen*. It is the result of the skillful, persistent assembling and presentation of authentic data on the Negro by Negro advertising folk, to whom we may well take off our hats.

The concession to Negro buying power has been followed, and we say this advisedly, by concession to Negro thinking, power and influence through organizations in which Negroes have interest. In the academic world, administrators, teachers have found that intellect, like disease, knows no barriers of race. Either it is there or it is not. If it is there, it should be available to all. To make it available to all, educational institutions in increasing numbers are seeking the best brains available in sciences, in the humanities, in the arts, to impart knowledge to those who seek it, regardless of the race of the scholar who possesses it.

In the academic world, the student, young or old—the serious seeker of truth and wisdom with which to live more adequately—is determinedly pushing aside the specious arguments of separation. He is saying that if he is to live successfully in a world of people whose origins are as varied as their complexions, he must know these people. In order to know them, he is seeking them out—seeking to enter schools known as "Negro schools." As many of us know, this is true in very many places even in the Deep South; and, contrary to superficial opinion, those who are apply-ing are not "transplanted Yankees." For the most part they are sons and daughters of the South, girding themselves, understandingly for life in a changing world. At Howard University, in Washington, white students have registered this year from as far south as Houston, Texas, and as far north as Massachusetts—to learn and to learn to live.

Hardly any cause of consequence essays to go before the public, these days, without recognition of the influence of the Negro minority by acquisition of one or more Negro members on its staff to serve as liaison officers in contacts with special organizations.

A professional organization which has pointedly avoided Negroes in its member-ship, in spite of noteworthy achievements of Negroes in its field, suddenly becomes "Negro conscious" in the midst of a fight on social legislation of which it disapproves and hastily appoints a Negro to its directing body. It was an attempt to replace like color with like interests. And while the action will probably change few minds, its im-plications are food for thought—we are no longer PEDDLERS!

In the fight for civil rights led by the President of the United States, government has bowed to the inevitable. In some areas, it has bowed graciously; in other areas, grudgingly. But the few outposts that have undertaken to ignore or evade official di-rectives, are clinging to another lost cause. "The Army," to quote one leading daily publication, "will continue to manufacture a Negro problem for itself, so long as it em-ploys criteria of race rather than ability, anywhere along the line." And the same holds true for every branch of government and every phase of civilian life.

Without indulging in self-applause, we can very well turn for a brief moment at this point in our march forward and view, with a feeling of so-far-so-good, the gains we have made and held. As mature people we shall waste no time in over-admiration. Long stretches of the road to the full life we shall achieve still lie ahead. But we are traveling with our eyes open and our wits about us, and in traversing the unseen stretches ahead we shall have the benefit of techniques developed and proved in con-quering the rough terrain behind.

As the Negro moves out in his newly-recognized capacity as a power to be reckoned with, it will be well to remember that not only courage but caution has a place in progress. The caution of which I speak does not mean fearfulness of new ideas, or of putting them into action. It means avoidance of the not-too-good American tendency of those too impatient, too emotion-swayed, or just too lazy-minded to weigh men and measures objectively, to brand, denounce and attack. We shall live more harmoniously if we learn to do without the clichés and shibboleths and catch-words which clutter and confuse our thinking.

I would caution that when the opportunity to advance a step presents itself, we should take that step and thank God for it, whether we consider the motive behind it to be dictated by love, by justice, or by expediency, provided only *that there is no booby-trap behind it!*

The caution of which I speak would call for a more general facing of facts calmly and courageously. This great organization with which we are meeting, today, has pioneered, under the leadership of Carter Godwin Woodson, in providing us with many of the facts necessary to progress. My kind of caution would call for acceptance of the responsibility of being informed; for strengthening of moral character; for an increase in formal and informal education at the expense of personal sacrifice . . . It would call for an increase in religion, not to "drown our sorrows," but to inspire our souls; not as an "opiate," but as a balance-wheel—as a recognition that mankind does not know all and will never know all, and does have and can rely upon a spiritual objective.

I firmly believe that the world is on its way toward greater unity, that this country is on its way to a fuller realization of democracy, and that the part of the Negro in both movements is one of increased strength and significance.

The one world toward which we are rapidly moving will not, I think, be a world of one race, or a world of one thought, but a world of mutual understanding, respect and tolerance, based on knowledge of ourselves and knowledge of our neighbors. In such a world as this we are entering, not race, but racial barriers will disappear, because in spite of D.A.R.'s, Gray Ladies, and other groups who avoid their fellowmen, there will be too much work in the world to do for any group to waste time in building futile fences around the fears of economic or intellectual competition, or challenge to their self-assumed controls, which lead to their rigidity and keep them perpetually out of step with progress.

The progress of the world will call for the best that all of us have to give. And in giving it we shall continue to move on in the directions indicated by individual aptitudes and abilities, knowing that the world is gradually recovering from the long sickness of mind—the unbalance—which has heretofore kept its peoples living in little camps of isolation, intolerance and suspicion.

Whether or not possession of the atom bomb by this country or many countries will mean the end of civilization, only God knows. But I feel that we should daily rejoice in the certainty that it has caused many people to regard their neighbors—across the street and across the world—with a more friendly eye, and has marvelously stimulated fresh interest in the application of the Golden Rule.

I see no cause for discouragement, in viewing the years ahead. Democracy in this country is neither dead nor dying. As every mother knows, the pangs of childbirth are keenest just before the child is born. If our hurts are great, now; if our country is torn with controversy over the expansion of social responsibility, over the acceptance of civil rights, it is because a new and more powerful democracy is being born, to serve more greatly the people of all races, of this country, and of the world.

For the Best and the Brightest
Vincent Harding
Historian/Theologian

See Vincent Harding's biographical sketch in Chapter 1.

I consider it a great privilege to be called tonight into the company of this magnificent cloud of witnesses that we have honored. The ones that I knew best across the years were Benjamin Mays, Howard Thurman, and Charles Lawrence. And the one thing that I want to say especially about my uncle, father, advisor, confessor, Howard Thurman, and about Charles Lawrence, was that they were both great laughers. Young Chuck Lawrence, in the magnificent eulogy that he did on the occasion of his father's memorial service, recalled from his childhood that whenever they were in crowds like this and the children were down below people's waist-levels and had to find their father, all they did was stand still for a moment and listen for his laugh, then they would know where Charles was. So I thank God for those whose lives are marked by their laughter.

Honoring these witnesses, this evening I'd like to explore with you some concerns that are of great moment to me and to many other people at this point in history. I want to try to find some way to enter into the rising discussion and debate now taking place concerning the status of the Black poor in America—a debate, a discussion, that is constantly laid out before us on television screens and in major print media, presenting all of the disturbing stories and statistics of teen-age pregnancies, of unemployment, of black-on-black crime, poor school performance, welfare dependency and the terrors of the drug trade. And always the question, "Who is to blame?" rises to the surface. For me the more important part of the debate and discussion must focus upon the question of "What shall we do?" By "we," I mean all compassionate human beings, but especially those who are citizens of this nation. As some of you know, in response to that question, "What shall we do?" there are two major positions being staked out in the discussion and debate—one that is called in a condensed way, "self-help," the other, "civil rights strategies," or self-help versus massive federal intervention.

What I'd like to do tonight is to try to make a modest, very tentative, contribution in the arena of the debate. Before anything else, though, I want to acknowledge the fact that my daughter, Rachel Elizabeth Harding (who is present here), has been of great assistance to me in shaping what it is that I'm trying to get at, because she has

Vincent Harding, "For the Best and the Brightest," The Fifth Annual Memorial Lecture of The Society for Values in Higher Education, *1993: 1–17.*

come at it not only through her own reading and wisdom, but through her own intu-ition and experiences. The fact that her perspective often seems to hook up with my own sense of things, gives me great assurance. At the outset, I should also warn you of how very close this subject is to me and I refuse to pretend to anything called scholarly objectivity here. For the fact is that not only did I grow up in Harlem and the South Bronx, but Rosemarie and I have raised—now just beyond their teenage life—two magnificent and beautiful children who have taught us many things, and one of them has to do with the need for tremendous sensitivity to the pains of the young. So I want you to know that I am coming from the heart of this affair and not from any of its outer edges.

Tonight I am using three texts. The first text is something that has been on my mind a great deal recently. I'm not sure why. Perhaps it's because I've been recently living so close to Philadelphia. But whatever the reason the words have been growing in me as I search for a way to define the purpose and direction of our nation and its people at this sometimes frightening point in our history. As I look at our country and try to see what its future might be in the midst of all of its destructive problems—as well as in the midst of all of its great creative gifts and possibilities—the words of the preamble to the constitution of the United States keep coming back to me as words that I think need to be taken seriously again. "We the people of the United States, in order to form a more perfect union, establish justice, ensure domestic tranquility, pro-vide for the common defense, promote the general welfare, and secure the blessings of liberty to ourselves and our posterity, do ordain and establish this Constitution for the United States of America." In other words, at its best, as it has been nurtured by every generation's most deeply committed men and women, this has been the grand and basic purpose of our nation: to form a more perfect union.

The second text is a poem that arises from the hearts of those who have insisted on maintaining the vision of a more perfect union at the center of the painful realities of their own lives. The poem is one that I love, Langston Hughes' "O Let America Be America." Towards the end Hughes says, "Oh, yes,/ I say it plain,/ America never was America to me,/ And yet I swear this oath,/ America will be,/ An ever-living seed/its dream/ lies deep in the heart of me. /We, the people, must redeem/ Our land, the mines, the plants, the rivers, the mountains and the endless plains./ All, all the stretch of these great green states/ And make America again."

The third text comes from a telephone conversation that I had earlier today. It was with one of my favorite people, my wife's oldest nephew who lives in Chicago and who has been through many trials and terrors with us in the South and elsewhere. He is a man of exemplary courage and compassion and he's a librarian in the Chicago Public Library system. His library is right in the middle of what is considered to be one of the most difficult communities, neighborhoods, non-communities, of the black experience in the North—North Lawndale on the West side of Chicago. Charles went into North Lawndale about five years ago to give leadership to the Frederick Douglass Library and he made it into something filled with beauty, unexpected possibilities and hope for the young men and women who came there. But not long ago he felt that he had to leave, that the struggle he was carrying on was a battle of tremendous stress, tremendous cost, and he simply was not able to continue it any longer in the midst of a situation that had so much anguish built into it. As we talked this afternoon about some of the debate that's been going on and his own feelings about it, he spoke about the young people who have come through that library and whom he sees on the streets (he spends a lot of his time on the streets). Even in the midst of his decision to leave and to go to another library, he said to me, "Vincent, we've got to do something. Some of our best and brightest children are dying here." That's not quite the same thing as "the underclass." "Some of our best and brightest children are dying here."

Those are my texts. The Preamble, Langston and Charles. Now let me go on.

In a way, the situation is outlined for us in a quotation that *Time* magazine carried late last year from one of our mutual friends, Bill Wilson, the justly influential sociologist at the University of Chicago. Wilson was being questioned concerning his views about the black victims of urban poverty and about other related issues. He said that, as he understood it, the plight of the black poor is unquestionably the result of historical racial prejudice and discrimination that created a large disadvantaged population that is now especially vulnerable to current social and economic changes. Then he added, "It is as though racism, having put the black underclass in its place, stepped aside to watch technological change finish the job." In the light of that reflection, it was hard to avoid the challenge presented to me and many people like me when Nicholas Lemann published his two fascinating articles on "The Origins of the Underclass," in the *Atlantic Monthly* for June and July of 1986. Without placing blame, simply reporting, Lemann said that it was not only racism that had stepped aside from this deserted set of black communities, but that crucial elements of the black middle class had also stepped aside, moved away, leaving many inner-city black communities bereft of the role models, the encouragement and the affirmation that they so badly need, that all peoples need. The comments by Professor Wilson remind us that part of the current debate is over the question of how much of a role does both current and historical racism play in the creation of the problem. But Lemann comes closer to my central concern. In the light of the situation that wrings cries from the heart of people like Charles Freeney, the more crucial issue for me is, what can we do? What shall we do? As I said, there are now two basic positions that have been staked out. One is condensed under the rubric of black self-help. Black people, according to this approach, have major, if not exclusive, responsibility for changing the situation. Those who put it forward do not always provide extensive lists of what they mean by self-help, but much of it focuses on such steps as providing middle-class role models, perhaps creating some black businesses in the devastated communities, raising questions of moral values in the black community and providing educational assistance. Much of this emphasis is clearly geared toward moving as many young people as possible toward what is loosely referred to as "the American mainstream." For many of its adherents, this is the fundamental purpose of the self-help strategies. At the same moment, self-help proponents often claim that what they call "the old civil rights strategies" that led to massive federal intervention to solve problems are neither appropriate nor wise in these neo-conservative times.

The other position, briefly stated, is that the federal government, representing the larger society, must still take major responsibility for addressing the structural settings which contribute so much to social disorganization. Jobs, education, day-care centers, improved housing, these are among the items usually mentioned. These spokespersons, usually considered more traditionally liberal and anti-Reagan in their views, often say that the needs for change in the black urban situation are much too large to be left to private responses and, indeed, that that is not a responsible choice for a major democratic society. Those are the arguments in the situation. Now I'd like to put forward some of my own initial responses.

First, without focusing on the names of the persons usually associated with the debate (because that is not at all important to me), I want to offer a critique of the terms of the debate. I want to suggest what I see as some of its limitations and misconceptions. I want to propose some ways of deepening the discussion in order to move forward to a level that will actually speak to the cries of those who are in need. Eventually, I want to look at some ways in which the historic black struggle for freedom, especially that of the 1950's and 1960's, may still offer some greater light than we think on the possibilities for change in our society, beginning on the hardest grounds of the deserted, black, lower-class communities.

Now, in terms of the critique, let me try to identify several important problems that I see in the current debate. First, I find that most of the debate tends to be a-historical, especially on the self-help side. Most of the debate forgets, ignores, or is unaware of the fact that the black struggle for justice in the United States of America has always involved both/and, both self-help *and* the demand for larger societal action. At every phase it has never been one or the other. During the time of slavery there was self-help all over the black community, starting from the self-help that broke the fugitives out of slavery to the self-help that received them in the North, that hid them, that carried them on the way to freedom (or semi-freedom) in the northern states and Canada. Nor can we forget such self-help as was built into the various black Women's Aid Societies, the self-help that was represented by the Lyceum societies and their creative attempts to raise the cultural level of our community. And at the same moment there was an unrelenting struggle to challenge the federal government, the national community, to take on its responsibilities as well.

During Reconstruction after the Civil War, black people, if they were not doing anything else, were organizing among themselves in many ways, creating institutions, newspapers, churches, a variety of self-help organizations, as well as black-led political organizations. And at the same time they were demanding federal protection, federal aid, federal redistribution of land in the cause of justice, federal laws to make possible their fullest participation in the political process. Always the two things were going on at the same time. All through the terrible period of American democratic schizophrenia called "separate-but-equal"—throughout that period when blacks were constantly under physical, economic and psychological attack—there was much self-help going on. When we hear the name Garvey, or Father Divine, or the Nation of Islam, it is important to recognize these as examples, sometimes at deep and expensive levels, of self-help. Then, at the same moment, there was an outspoken black insistence on

federal action against lynching, on federal action to establish protection of their citizenship rights, a demand for federal relief in economically hard times.

Always, it seems to me, always when we have been at our best, black people
have known that it was absolutely necessary to maintain a creative tension between
the need to improve ourselves and the need to improve the nation. As the old song
says, "You can't have one without the other." Black people understood that—self-
improvement, national improvement. Don't you hear it in the name of the new organization established in Montgomery, Alabama in December, 1955, The Montgomery
Improvement Association? What better self-help can you have than that? But at the
first meeting, we also hear the primary spokesman making it very clear that self-
improvement, even to the level of getting the right to sit on buses, was not the limit of
the vision. He says to the people gathered in tremendous hope around him at Holt
Street Baptist Church, "If you will protest courageously and yet with dignity and
Christian love, when the history books are written in future generations the historians
will have to pause and say, 'There lived a great people—a black people—who injected new meaning and dignity into the veins of civilization.' This is our challenge
and our overwhelming responsibility." Self-help and the transformation of civilization
itself—that has been the heart of the historic movements among black people for freedom and justice in this country, and it seems to me that the argument that is going on
misses the history of that kind of constant creative tension, misses our need to establish the tension again.

Another thing that I want to say about the current debate is that it places the issue of poverty in America too exclusively in the black community. Now I understand
why that's done. In many ways black poverty is—if I may be forgiven the pun—more
colorful than white poverty. It is probably also more publishable than white poverty.
Of course, in addition, the black people in the debate often feel a particular sense of
responsibility to keep zeroing in on the issues of what they call "the black underclass." All this is understandable, but there are obviously problems in doing this. There
are psychological problems. There are political problems. There are factual problems.
Tonight, I will also focus on the black poor as those who seem most trapped by the
combination of race, economics and culture. Nevertheless, always remember, please,
that harsh poverty is a reality for millions of white *and* black people in America, especially women and children. The majority of the poor are not black. Many of us need to
be thinking long and serious thoughts about these folks as well.

The third thing I want to suggest about the debate is that not only do the choices
between self-help and federal intervention miss the truth of black history and the truth
of our current society, but put in those terms, they tend to deny some of the nation's
most essential values, values which are vital among us when we are best as a nation,
and values which we absolutely need to nurture if we are going to continue as a nation. For instance, both of these debate formulations diminish the importance of "We
the people of the United States." They narrow down an understanding of "the general
welfare." They do not understand the possibilities of our need for a new definition of
"the common defense" or for "domestic tranquility." They fail to grasp the fact that neither the concept of black self-help, especially as defined and mediated by an absentee
middle-class, nor the image of some impersonal "federal government" will serve our

need for "a more perfect union." Neither of these sides takes into itself the great empowering vision that we need, of a people organized to work for their good and for the good of the nation as a whole. These narrow arguments either miss or dangerously narrow the central democratic project, or what it seems to me ought to be the central democratic project, that is, the ongoing task of re-creating, constantly re-creating the American nation. "America, you've never been America to me/ And yet I swear you will be."

Black people have always given leadership to this task of re-visioning, re-creating. The terms of the debate ignore that historic role, deny that role in many ways to black young people who need a creative challenge for their lives. Indeed, by ignoring that and playing it down there is a self-defeatism about the idea of self-help, because what is missed in the debate is the possibility that one of the grandest forms of self-help is the development of the capacity to become politically responsible citizens who do not wait or plead or preach for "federal intervention" but who organize and move their own lives in such a way that inventive new forms of governmental response are absolutely necessary. Federal intervention has never come primarily by people pleading for it. It has come by people organizing in such a way that they make a new engagement necessary. This is missed in the debate. There are no democratic organizers there.

The other part of the best values of our society that I think is missed is the power of our deepest spiritual roots, roots that have always insisted on our connectedness to each other, our oneness, our interdependence, across the essentially superficial lines of race and class. Neither a narrowly defined self-help, nor impersonal federal intervention opens up access to those deep spiritual sources, sources which I believe will surely be needed by all persons who are serious about the need for more than cosmetic changes in the United States of America—more than toe-dipping in the main stream.

Located here is still another element of the critique that I'd like to put forward. It appears to me that the current debate is primarily directed toward what seems—especially on the self-help side—to be a severely limited and uncritical appraisal of the mainstream of America. There is simply no serious critique of the mainstream toward which it is trying to push and pull the poor. Several problems are involved there. One is that even though some of the discussants are economists, they speak very rarely about the fact that the life of mainstream middle class America is built on structural unemployment of the poor, that the mainstream as it presently exists depends upon that out-class. Unemployment and underemployment are essential elements of the mainstream as we know it today.

In addition, serious observers have reminded us that to look carefully at the mainstream, one would have to raise the question of what are the effects of American middle-class, mainstream life on the poor people of the world and their habitats. For it is clear that just as the mainstream in America is built on our outcasts here, so mainstream America is built on the poverty of people elsewhere. How do you pull the poor into that, and when will we start to tell them that major parts of the earth's resources are non-renewable, and that the earth, itself, cannot afford a vast explosion of America's middle-class, mainstream style of life? In other words, it seems to me that somewhere in the discussion there has to be a fundamental critique of the culture of the mainstream, a culture that is essentially acquisitive in its materialism, pleasure-seeking in its groping toward meaning, a culture in which violence has been enthroned as the norm—as normal as white supremacy once was and to some degree still is. It was this culture that Martin Luther King faced and challenged when, near the close of his life, he said repeatedly that we need "a revolution in the values" of American society. No such word comes out of the current debate at all, simply a beckoning into the mainstream.

Finally, especially with *these* young people, someone needs to explain what mainstream America does with young people for whom it has no use. We need to ask them to think second thoughts about the military as a place "to be all that you can be." Someone needs to speak this word in the midst of the present discussion, and because we don't speak it, from my perspective we are breaking with a long black tradition. We are losing a tradition that has always been double-edged, moved by a vision that seeks to open the mainstream and at the same moment determines to transform the mainstream, never one without the other. "I swear you will be."

The last aspect of the critique that I want to bring to the debate is that it appears that there is a great tendency to misinterpret the movement of the 1950's and 1960's. When the debate participants refer to "civil rights strategies" they seem to equate "civil rights strategies" with some kind of abject plea for government intervention, or with passive, politely marching people who are waiting for help. The fact is that the central strategies of the civil rights movement—or as it was called by those who were participating, the "freedom movement"—need to be re-visited. The central strategies of that movement were strategies of organizing, mobilizing and inspiring deeply committed persons and communities to re-vision themselves, to focus their eyes on the prize, to move together with a sense of power, to re-vision the nation and to *insist* with the gathered power of their lives that the nation be faithful to its best self. Those were the central strategies of the movement, not passive pleas for federal intervention.

As a result, at the height of the movement, the fundamental reality was the renewal of a people who were determined to transform their country. They were "We the people," becoming more and more, in everything, "We the people," constantly recognizing their we-ness and their people-ness in creatively insistent ways. That was at the heart of the civil rights/freedom movement, and I think there are powerful contemporary implications in understanding that this was a movement in which people rediscovered, re-defined and re-projected themselves. For example, I think that it is very important that wherever we went in the South—Montgomery, Albany, Birmingham, St. Augustine, Jackson, Greenwood, Selma—wherever there was an active movement going on, the local black crime rate dropped substantially, sometimes to almost nothing. What does that mean for today?

Now, I want to make it very clear as I complete the critiques that I mean these critiques to be gentle and friendly, partly because we are all rank amateurs at our tasks at this historical juncture. It's very important to remember this. We are trying to create a society that is unlike anything that has ever existed or anything that exists now. We, at our best, are being called to be creators of a new society. Not long before his assassination Martin King said, "The movement for black rights has become far more than that. It has opened up to us problems that are systemic in American society and, therefore, what is required now is radical reconstruction of the systems themselves." When we are most serious about the challenge of what shall we do with, for and about the poor we recognize that we are involved in a new creation, at least "a radical reconstruction."

That is why we must be gentle, because we don't know yet how to get there, and we must go forward together, recognizing that we need all of our wisdom, all of our skills to overcome a centuries-long legacy of slavery, white supremacy and legalized segregation, brutality, and discrimination. We are also dealing with the effects that this legacy has on the minds and hearts of white and black people, and all kinds of other people who come here from abroad and imbibe the legacy very quickly. We are trying to create a society in which we are overcoming that. We are trying to create a society in which we are developing a multi-racial order that honors all of our heritages, where we will never again see textbooks teaching our children that there is only one "great" American heritage, the one that begins in England. We are trying to develop a multi-racial society in which not only all of our heritages are honored but in which they are creatively nurtured in a variety of ways and continuously poured into our constantly evolving larger society. We don't know how to do that yet, but if we are determined, we can learn.

We are also creating a society in which economic justice can be developed, where women, men and children can find ways to meet their basic material needs without overburdening the fragile eco-systems of our globe and without exploiting our sisters and brothers in other parts of the earth. That is a grand enterprise. We are trying to create a society in which democracy is taken seriously and is not just a periodic two-or four-year trip to a ballot box. That's nothing. That can be done any place under almost any circumstances. What we are trying to do is to create a society in which we encourage the fullest possible human development of all of our peoples, constantly finding new ways to engage ourselves in the great task of creating a more just and perfect union for ourselves and for posterity. That is what democracy is about.

Then, of course, we are trying to create a pluralistic society in which some of the best spiritual resources of humankind are now available to us. We are trying to open ourselves to these old-new resources so that they can strengthen us for the tasks of recreating ourselves, recreating our nation, so that they can encourage us to participate with others in the defense of the earth itself. We are trying to create a society with such spiritual values that we will remember always that our security cannot be real when it threatens the security of our sisters and brothers elsewhere; that our security is illusionary when it is built on the threat to destroy the earth. We are trying to create that kind of society and, as the old folks used to say, that's more than a notion.

Now I want to close off with some of the ways in which it seems to me that the call from the heart of the submerged black communities may open us up toward the kind of re-creating that we have before us. I want to consider some of the ways in which, through deepening our sense of the most recent past and keeping ourselves painfully sensitive to Charles Freeney's cry from North Lawndale, we may look in new directions or renew older pathways and open ourselves to crucial questions all along the way.

If we're going to move beyond the present level of debate to try to find some ways in which we can, indeed, create a more just and perfect union in this country, in which all of us will be involved, and not just some cadre of experts, then I think it is necessary for us to take with absolute seriousness Mr. Lemann's observations on the loss of the black middleclass to the daily life of the black underclass community, and vice versa. Especially is this important if we look at it in the light of the Southern movement experience and re-collect the tremendously important role of organizers in that situation. If we look at it that way, then we have to face the strong possibility that there can be very little serious help for the situation that we face among the urban black poor without some of us who have left deciding to find ways to return and re-group. It may be partially, temporarily, semi-permanently, but I don't think there's any way of getting around that.

That can be a frightening thought. And if black folks are scared, I know how the rest of you are likely feeling. What we need are organized teachers, encouragers, seek-ers, artists, singers, all seeking to rediscover and re-make that common ground, which some of our traditions claim to be the ground where we find the divine—among the poorest and the most outcast. Some of us have to deal with that. Some of us have to recognize the possibilities that we are called to share the experiences and the dangers and in that process to help build the outposts of hope.

When Charles Freeney was letting people know that he was going to leave the li-brary, one of the young men came up to him and said, do you think you'll ever come back here? Charles thought his young friend was talking about the library and he said, "Well you know, I'm sure that some times I'll come back, maybe not to work, but cer-tainly to visit the library." And the guy said, "No, I'm not talking about the library. I'm talking about now that you're not working here, will you ever come back to our neighborhood?" If we hear that question, if we hear the question under it, then we be-gin to struggle with what it means and how it feels to be young and black and a pariah, a social leper. Somebody has to embrace those young men and women, and their communities, in order to change them. Somebody has to say, "I'm here with you to carry on the struggle." As I see it, such folks were central to the transformation of the South. They are probably also crucial to the transformation of the North. By the way, who will live with the white poor?

It seems to me that only in the context of these kinds of questions can we talk seriously about self-help or the role of the national government, because when we hear some of the things that are being said, we realize that they cannot be addressed from a distance. The president of the Urban League recently made a major statement about black family problems. He then concluded by saying, "Individual black people must accept responsibility for themselves and for preserving the family values that have helped us to survive." But then you stop and say, preserve black family values in North Lawndale? How do you do that? In West Philly, how do you do that? What are the black family values on which black people have built such strong and surviv-ing families? One of the great values is the value of work. That is one of the great differences between the South and poverty and the North and poverty. In the past, Black people in the South who were in poverty were always working. Black people in the North in poverty very often were not working. Being poor and not working is a tough one, just like being rich and not working is a tough one. That's one of the great bases of the black family, work.

Another of the great bases is hope, hope that your children are going to be able to make it beyond where you are. In earlier times, people were able to see signs of that all around them and to know that they could do it. Hope is built on community, a sense of assurance that there are other people around who care about your children, for instance. Rosemarie and I reflect on the fact that we grew up in Harlem and Chicago and knew that if we got out of line a block away from our house there would be somebody who would be saying, "I'm gonna tell your Momma. I know where you live." Those were a part of the values on which the black family was built. And, of course, the black family was built on that founding value of religion, the belief, as Martin used to put it, that we are dealing with a God who can "make a way out of no way." Now, if we ever needed a way out of no way, we certainly need it now. But where is that now, that time of faith, that spark of hope, that ground of spirituality on which self-esteem is deeply based?

I wanted to mention those as simply matters for our reflection and now I want to say some very specific things about self-help and federal intervention in this larger context. As I understand it and as I've tried to make clear, self-help—however it's defined—is going to have to come primarily from the inside, not from the black or the white suburbs but from the inside. If I were courageous enough to be at some of those spots at this moment, spots where we have been in the past, here are some of the things that I would want to be doing with those young people. The self-help that would seem crucial to me would have to include the development of a sense of history—a sense of where they are, where they came from. A sense of both the terrors and the beauties of their past. I am still convinced that human beings—white, black, or green—cannot be fully themselves without a sense of their past. So I would think that it would be absolutely necessary for a sense of context, a sense of beauty, a sense of struggle. So, if I were in North Lawndale I would be sharing the new "Eyes on the Prize" freedom movement documentary with the young people there.

I think self-help, for me, would also include helping our young people to break out of the trap of that little world of North Lawndale. You know some of them consider it a major occasion to travel five miles to the South side. Some of them have never been there. The same city, the same so-called black community, but they've never been there. Some of them have never been downtown in Chicago. If I were there I would be trying to introduce them, I think, to some of the world, the marvelous world that is theirs and some of the critical issues for the future of the world. I would assume that as young people they, like young people all over the world, have a great responsibility for the world's future. So, as part of self-help I would insist that they know something about the peace and justice movements of our time and what this has to do with them, something about the ways other youth in other times and places have worked for change. They would need to learn about the ecological crises that are so important for their children and their children's children. They would know about world poverty.

They would be studying and talking about new roles for women and men. I would hope that self-help would certainly include the bringing in and the developing of creative arts, a variety of new music, dance, graphic arts, poetry, sharing with one another, learning from one another, writing for one another. I would show them the film that I just saw again the other night, "Soldier Girl," about what happens to a group of black and white young women who come from poor backgrounds primarily and who see the military as the only way out for themselves. I would show it to them again and again and then work with them to struggle with this whole question of whether or not that really is all they can be. I would talk to them out of my own experience with the military, to ask them to think about the ways in which an increasingly militarized culture encourages us to deny our connectedness to our brothers and sisters elsewhere, like Russia and Nicaragua and Grenada.

Of course, as I see it, there is no way that one could help young people unless some steps were taken to point some path beyond American individualism and false patriotism, so that they might become really lovers of the earth. I would want them to see some other parts of the world. It would cost money, but we would find a way to travel. I would want them to learn, to find alternatives to the American mainstream as they know it. Indeed, I would be working with them to create alternatives, because what we're clearly talking about now is the need for new values, new spirit—not just jobs, but new values, new spirit, new creativities.

My nephew, Charles Freeney, said, "I was walking among some of those young men the other day and as I looked at them I felt, oh, my God, how brittle this life has made them, how touchy and how dangerous." I would want somehow to find some way to be hugging those young men until the brittleness seeped out of them, letting them know that touching is all right in contexts other than creating babies.

It seems to me that self-help for the young women would have to mean finding new ways to value themselves, finding ways to affirm themselves, other than having a man maul over them or take them on the path of single motherhood. For both young men and women I know that Charles is right when he says, "Vincent, you can't imagine how many new drugs have come into this community. They're cheaper than many of the other ones, and they are terribly dangerous." Self-help must speak to that or it speaks no truth.

Now the last word is on the matter of what I call not federal intervention but social and societal responsibility. As I have noted earlier, I am convinced that self-help and societal responsibility must be joined together. As I understand it, from what little I know about those communities, and communities like them, there must be work. There must be work for which people are paid. There must be work which is led and taught by serious, skilled, compassionate older workers. There must be work that is guided by people who have learned the discipline of work, so that they can help those who do not know the experience of ordered work to enter into that valuable discipline. There must be jobs of community rehabilitation in their own communities, and jobs that will take them to work with others in the common communities of the downtowns and the forests and the parks. There must be jobs with others not only from their own community, but jobs with unknown others. Remember there are always others. There are others, for instance, who are also best and bright and white and dying, some because of poverty, some because of wealth, all because of uselessness, and there must be a way to bring those young sisters and brothers together to work for the general welfare, for the common defense. That's central, it seems to me—work, serious work, paid work for all who can work and will work. Of course, what happens is that this must constantly take place against the background of a nation that is redefining the nature of work for everybody, redefining what we really need as a gross national product. Do we really need seventy-two kinds of toilet paper? Is that central to the democrat project? We must be constantly re-learning how to focus ourselves to create what is really needed, not simply what is profitable in our society.

Let me mention a few other things and then I'm really finished, and I guess you are, too, at this hour. It's clear that if you're going to have work for everybody including women and men who have children, we're going to have to have creative day care. That's what we mean by social responsibility. We can't expect the corner churches to take care of that. If we're going to have work for everybody, some of that work should also be tied to a whole re-thinking of the educational system and a transformation of that system from pre-school on up, and it has to be available to anybody who really wants it, as far as he or she can go. And somehow one of my visions of this new North Lawndale is that in this place the teenagers will be reconnected with the children and with the older folks and will become caretakers in a way for those who are less able than themselves. I want to help train them for that. I want to help change the whole atmosphere of the society so that can regularly happen—former gang members walking around with three-year-old boys and girls and taking them to the park which will then be in existence, even if it is not now.

Yes, now the word for those of us who are here on this special night. My sense is that this kind of thing cannot be without serious work on the part of intellectuals and educators, without serious thought about some of our own career priorities. I think that just as it happened in the fifties and sixties some of us are going to have to focus in anew, to search anew, to commit major energies as professionals and as citizens to respond to the cry from the black and white North Lawndales. We're going to have to find ways of creating new programs, new departments, new institutes, all involving engaged, non-abstract explorations of the central questions of our society, encouraging students to experiment in a variety of wild ways that we got frightened off from in the sixties, but which have to come again in many ways in the nineties. We need generations now of black, white, brown, green women and men who will give this enterprise the same unstinting creative attention that we gave to breaking the bonds of slavery, that we gave to knocking down the walls of legal segregation, that we gave to breaking some of the chains of injustice to women. We've got to focus, because "some of our best and brightest children are dying here."

And I come back to Martin King because what I think he knew, what SNCC knew, what CORE knew—what they and many others knew in the freedom movement was that people themselves must be empowered to re-vision themselves and to re-vision their possibilities. That's what King was trying to do in 1967 and '68. That's what the Poor Peoples' Campaign as he originally envisioned it was—dealing with racism, dealing with poverty, dealing with militarism. He was calling not only on blacks but on Appalachian whites, on Native Americans, on Hispanics, on the allies of the poor, whatever their state; he was challenging them to change themselves and their nation. As I see it, those critical paths are still before us, and the so-called black underclass are simply opening them up again for us to decide what are we going to do with them, about them. As I see it, King's call to revolutionary, structural transformation based on compassionate, non-violent self-esteem, and esteem for all life, is still the call. As it was for King, it is a dangerous call. There are great risks in working with people who have not really believed in themselves, ever. There are great risks in challenging a nation to become its best self. There are serious dangers, but there are also magnificent surprises, I suspect, in store for us all.

You know, here's the way I would sum it up. I have a feeling that the message that Martin King got from the black woman in Montgomery is still the message for us. She was in her late sixties, early seventies in 1956, walking every day in the bus boycott, walking several miles back and forth every day from work. He asked her why she was walking when she could get a ride. She just said, well, it felt better to her to walk, because she was walking for her children and for her grandchildren, trying to establish something for them. So she could say to King, "Oh, Dr. King, my feets is tired but my soul is rested."

What I am suggesting is simply that, through a combination of serious mutual aid on personal levels and a series of audacious, costly, risky experiments on a societal level, we need to begin creating everywhere some people whose souls are rested. Young men who are no longer brittle, touchy or dangerous but whose souls are rested. Young women who are no longer anxious about being loved but whose souls are rested. Not just because they've learned meditation or because they gave their lives to Allah, Jesus or the Great Life—all of which I think are very important—but whose souls are rested because they have engaged themselves in taking ever-increasing responsibility for their future and for the future of others, for creating a more perfect union. Remember the Roman Catholic Bishops. Not long ago they had a Public Interest commercial that said, "If you want peace, work for justice." If you want peace, work for justice. Maybe that peace is both internal and external. If you want internal peace then work for the justice that'll get your soul rested. And maybe the other side applies. If you want real justice in a society, then let people who have come to be at peace with themselves work with you.

Well, there it is. Sometimes I don't know what to do with such realities, I confess to you. But when I don't know what to do I keep hearing Charles, "Vincent, we've got to do something. The best and brightest children are dying here." So, not knowing what else to do, I often move to the grounds that have been occupied long before me and I listen to the questions and to the answers that have been raised throughout my life and the lives of others, and I share them with you, my sisters and brothers, who I assume also don't know what to do right now. "Have you not known? Have you not heard? The Lord is the everlasting God, the creator of the ends of the earth. He does not, She does not grow faint or grow weary. Her understanding is unsearchable. He gives power to the faint and to those who have no might. She increases strength. Even youths shall faint and be weary and young people shall fall exhausted, but they who wait for the Lord shall renew their strength. They shall mount up with wings like eagles. They shall run and not be weary. They shall walk and not faint." That's all I can do. Peace be with you.

Suggested Reading

Blassingame, John W., ed. et al. *The Frederick Douglass Papers*. New Haven: Yale University Press, 1979.

Breitman, George, ed. *Malcolm X Speaks: Selected Speeches and Statements*. New York: Pathfinder, 1989.

Clark, Steve, ed. *February 1965: The Final Speeches. Malcolm X*. New York: Pathfinder, 1992.

Epps, Archie, ed. *Malcolm X: Speeches at Harvard*. New York: Paragon House, 1991.

Foner, Philip S., ed. *The Life and Writings of Frederick Douglass: Reconstruction and After* (Vol. 4) New York: International Publishers, 1975.

———, ed., with tribute by Dr. Martin Luther King, Jr. *W. E. B. Du Bois Speaks. Speeches and Addresses, 1890–1919* (Vol. 1) [1970]. Reprint, New York: Pathfinder, 1991.

———, ed. *W. E. B. Du Bois Speaks. Speeches and Addresses, 1910–1963* (Vol. 2) [1970]. Reprint, New York: Pathfinder, 1991.

———, and Robert James Branham, eds. *Lift Every Voice. African American Oratory, 1787–1900*. Tuscaloosa: University of Alabama Press, 1998.

Halliburton, Warren J., ed. *Historic Speeches of African Americans*. New York: Franklin Watts, 1993.

Henry, Charles P., ed. *Ralph J. Bunche. Selected Speeches and Writings*. Ann Arbor: University of Michigan Press, 1995.

Loewenberg, Bert James, and Ruth Bogin, eds. *Black Women in Nineteenth-Century American Life. Their Words, Their Thoughts, Their Feelings* [1976]. Reprint, University Park: Pennsylvania State University Press, 1993.

Logan, Shirley Wilson, ed. *With Pen and Voice. A Critical Anthology of Nineteenth-Century African-American Women*. Carbondale and Edwardsville: Southern Illinois University Press, 1995.

Nelson, Alice Ruth Moore Dunbar, ed. *Masterpieces of Negro Eloquence: The Best Speeches Delivered by the Negro from the Days of Slavery to the Present Time* [New York: Bookery Publishers, 1914]. New York: Johnson Reprint, 1970.

Royster, Jacqueline Jones, ed. *Southern Horrors and Other Writings: The Anti-Lynching Campaign of Ida B. Wells, 1892–1900*. Boston: Bedford Books, 1997.

Smith, Arthur Lee (Molefi Kete Asante), and Stephen Robb, eds. *The Voice of Black Rhetoric: Selections*. Boston: Allyn & Bacon, 1971.

Straub, Deborah Gillan. *Voices of Multicultural America: Notable Speeches Delivered by African, Asian, Hispanic, and Native Americans, 1790–1995*. New York: Gale Research, 1996.

Vital Issues: The Journal of African American Speeches, 1990-Present.

Walker, Robbie Jean, ed. *The Rhetoric of Struggle: Public Address by African American Women*. New York Garland, 1992.

Woodson, Carter Godwin. *Negro Orators and Their Orations*. Washington, D.C.: Associated Publishers, 1925.

Selected Videos, Films, CD-ROM, and Slides

Cinema Guild

Ida B. Wells. Rex Barnett, director. Cinema Guild. Color. VHS Video. 27 mins. 1993.
Mary McLeod Bethune: The Spirit of A Champion. Rex Barnett, director. Cinema Guild. Color. VHS Video. 30 mins. 1996.

Films for the Humanities & Sciences

Presenting Mr. Frederick Douglass: "The Lesson of the Hour" [Performance by Fred Morsell]. Films for the Humanities & Sciences. Color. Video. 60 mins.

MLK Jr. Center for Nonviolent Change, Inc.

The "I Have A Dream" Speech as delivered by Dr. M.L.K., Aug. 1963. Michael S. R. Johnson, producer and editor. B&W. Videocassette. 18 mins. 1985.

Selected Bibliography

Bibliographies

Barfield, Rodney. "North Carolina Black Material Culture: A Research Opportunity." *North Carolina Folklore Journal* 27 (November 1979): 61–66.

Delaunay, Charles. *New Hot Discography: The Standard Directory of Recorded Jazz,* edited by Walter E. Schaap and George Avakian. New York: 1948.

Igoe, Lynn Moody, and James Igoe. *250 Years of Afro-American Art: An Annotated Bibliography.* New York: R.R. Bowker, 1981.

Lornell, Kip. "Black Material Culture." *South Folklore Quarterly* 42 (1978): 287–294.

Merriam, Alan P., with the assistance of Robert J. Benford. *A Bibliography of Jazz.* Philadelphia: American Folklore Society, 1954.

Reisner, Robert George. *The Literature of Jazz: A Preliminary Bibliography.* New York: New York Public Library, 1954.

Salwen, Bert, and Geoffrey M. Gyrisco. "An Annotated Bibliography. Archaeology of Black American Culture *11593",* Vol. 3, No. 1, February/March 1978 [U.S. Department of the Interior, Heritage Conservation and Recreation Service].

Sink, Susan. *Traditional Crafts and Craftsmanship in America: A Selected Bibliography.* Publication of the American Folklore Center, No. 11, Library of Congress, 1983. [Reprinted with additions from Traditional Craftsmanship in America: A Diagnostic Report, Washington, D.C.: National Council for the Traditional Arts, 1983.]

Smith, Charles Edward, Jr., with Frederic Ramsey Jr., Charlies Payne Rogers, and William Russell. *The Jazz Record Book.* New York: 1942.

Thieme, Darius L. "Negro Folksong Scholarship in the United States." *African Music Society Journal* (3) (1960): 67–72.

Upton, Dell. "Ordinary Buildings: A Bibliographical Essay on American Vernacular Architecture." *American Studies International* 19 (2) (1981): 57–75.

Articles, Chapters, Books, and Monographs

Adams, Marie-Jeanne. "The Harriet Powers Pictorial Quilts." *Black Art Magazine* (4) (1977): 12–28.

Adler, Bill. *Rap: Portraits and Lyrics of a Generation of Black Rockers*. New York: St. Martin's Press, 1991.

African Methodist Pocket Hymn Book, The. Philadelphia: AME Book Concern, 1816.

Allen, William Francis, compiler and collector, with Charles Pickard Ware, and Lucy McKim Garrison, with new piano arrangements and guitar chords by Irving Schlein. *Slave Songs of the United States; The Complete Original Collection (136 Songs)*. New York: Oak Publications, 1965 [1867].

Ballard, Allen R. *One More Day's Journey: The Making of Black Philadelphia*. Philadelphia: Institute for the Study of Human Issues, 1984.

Banes, Sally. *The Evolution of Breaking: Dancing from the Street to the Stage*. Paper, Fifth International Conference on Culture and Communication, Philadelphia, March 24–26, 1983.

Brewer, J. Mason. *Worser Days and Better Times: The Folklore of the North Carolina Negro*. Chicago: Quadrangle Books, 1965.

Campbell, Edward D. C., Jr., with Kym S. Rice, eds. *Before Freedom Came. African-American Life in the Antebellum South*. Richmond: The Museum of the Confederacy, and Charlottesville: University Press of Virginia, 1991.

Carawan, Guy, and Candie Carawan. *Freedom Is a Constant Struggle; Songs of the Freedom Movement with Documentary Photographs*. New York: Oak Publications, 1968.

Chilkovsky, Nadia. "Analysis and Notations of Basic Afro-American Movements." In *Jazz Dance. The Story of American Vernacular Dance* [1964], edited by Marshall and Jean Stearnes, pp. 421–422+. New York: Schirmer Books, 1979.

Come Sunday. Photographs by Thomas Roma. New York: The Museum of Modern Art.

Conway, Cecelia. *The Afro-American Tradition of the Folk Banjo*. Ph.D. dissertation, University of North Carolina at Chapel Hill, 1980.

Craft, David. *The Negro Leagues: 40 Years of Black Professional Baseball in Words and Pictures*. Avenel, N.J.: Crescent Books, 1993.

Cusack, Thomas. *Jelly Roll Morton; An Essay in Discography*. London: Cassell, 1952.

Dash, Julie. *Daughters of the Dust. The Making of an African American Woman's Film*. New York: the New Press, 1992.

Davis, Stephen. *Reggae Bloodlines*. New York: De Capo Press, 1977.

Demeusy, Bertrand, compiler. *Discography of Lionel Hampton, 1954–1958*. Basel: Jazz-Publications, 1962.

Dett, Robert Nathaniel. *Religious Folk-Songs of the Negro as Sung at Hampton Institute*. Hampton, Va.: Hampton Institute Press, 1927.

Dorsey, Frances. *For John Cox's Daughter: African-American Quilts from the Southeastern United States* (Exhibition Catalog). Ann Arbor: University of Michigan, 1991.

Drake, St. Clair, and Horace R. Cayton. *Black Metropolis: A Study of Negro Life in a Northern City* [1945]. Harcourt, Brace & World, 1962.

Epstein, Dena J. *Sinful Tunes and Spirituals*. Urbana: University of Illinois Press, 1977.

Erenberg, Lewis A. *Steppin' Out: New York Night Life and the Transformation of American Culture, 1890–1930*. Chicago: University of Chicago Press, 1981.

Fabre, Genevieve, and Robert O'Meally, eds. *History and Memory in African-American Culture*. New York: Oxford University Press, 1994.

Feelings, Tom. *The Middle Passage. White Ships/Black Cargo*. New York: Dial Books, 1995.

"Folklore and Ethnology." *Southern Workman* 25 (April 1896): 82.

Foreman, Ronald C. *Jazz and Race Record, 1920–1932. Their Origins and their Significance for the Record Industry*. Ph.D. dissertation, University of Illinois, 1972.

Frazier, Thomas R., ed. *Afro-American History: Primary Sources*. New York: Harcourt, Brace & World, 1970.

Frith, Simon, and Andrew Goodwin, eds. *On Record: Rock, Pop and the Written Word*. New York: Pantheon, 1990.

Fry, Gladys-Marie. "Harriet Powers: Portrait of a Black Quilter." In *Missing Pieces: Georgia Folk Art, 1770–1976,* edited by Anna Wadsworth, pp. 16–23. Atlanta: Georgia Council for the Arts and Humanities, 1976.

Fuller, Edmund L. *Visions in Stone: The Sculpture of William Edmondson*. Pittsburgh: University of Pittsburgh Press, 1973.

George, Zelma Watson. *A Guide to Negro Music: an Annotated Bibliography of Negro Folk Music, and Art Music by Negro Composers, or Based on Negro Thematic Material*. Ed.D dissertation. Ann Arbor: University Microfilms (8021), 1954. 302 pp.

Georgia Writer's Project, Work Projects Administration. *Drums and Shadows: Survival Studies Among Georgia Coastal Negroes*. Athens: University of Georgia, 1940.

Graveley, William B. "The Dialectic of Double-Consciousness in Black American Freedom Celebrations, 1808–1863." *Journal of Negro History* 67 (1982): 302–317.

Grundin, Eva Ungar. *Stitching Memories: African-American Story Quilts*. Williamstown, Mass.: Williams College Museum of Art, 1990.

Hampton, Henry, and Steve Fayer with Sarah Flynn. *Voices of Freedom. An Oral History of the Civil Rights Movement from the 1950s Through the 1980s*. New York: Bantam Books, 1990.

Harper, Michael S., and Robert B. Stepto, eds. *Chant of Saints. A Gathering of Afro-American Literature, Art, and Scholarship*. Urbana: University of Illinois Press, 1979.

Hasse, John Edward, ed. *Ragtime. Its History, Composers, and Music*. New York: Schirmer Books, 1985.

Hazzard-Gordon, Katrina. "Afro-American Core Culture Social Dance: An Examination of Four Aspects of Meaning." In *Perspectives of Black Culture,* edited by Harry B. Shaw, pp. 46–58. Bowling Green, Ohio: Bowling Green State University Popular Press, 1990.

Herskovits, Melville Jean. "Drums and Drummers in Afro-Brazilian Cult Life." *Musical Quarterly* 30 (4) (1944): 447–492.

Holway, John B. *Voices from the Great Black Baseball Leagues*. New York: Dodd, Mead, 1994.

Hurmence, Belinda, ed. *My Folks Don't Want Me to Talk About Slavery: Twenty-One Oral Histories of Former North Carolina Slaves*. Winston-Salem, N.C.: John F. Blair, 1984.

Hymn Book of the Colored M.E. Church in America. Jackson, Tenn.: CME Book Concern, 1891.

Hymns for the Use of the African Methodist Episcopal Zion Church. New York: AME Zion Book Concern, 1839.

Johnson, James Weldon, and J. Rosamund Johnson. *The Book of American Negro Spirituals* [1925]. Reprint, New York: Viking Press, 1937.

————. *The Second Book of Negro Spirituals.* New York: Viking Press, 1926.

Johnson, Thomas L., and Philip C. Dunn. *A True Likeness. The Black South of Richard Samuel Roberts [photographer] 1920–1936.* Columbia, S.C.: Bruccoli Clark, 1986.

Jones, Charles Price, compiler. *Jesus Only Nos. 1 and 2.* Jackson, Miss.: Truth Publishing Company, 1901 [Printed by the National Baptist Publishing Board].

Joyner, Charles W. "Soul Food and the Sambo Stereotype: Foodlore from the Slave Narrative Collection." *Keystone Folklore Quarterly* (Winter 1971): 171–177.

Keck, George R., and Sherrill V. Martin, eds. *Feel the Spirit: Studies in Nineteenth-Century Afro-American Music.* Westport, Conn.: Greenwood Press, 1988.

Lead Me, Guide Me: The African American Catholic Hymnal. Chicago: G.I.A. Publications, 1987.

Leon, Eli. "African Transformation in Afro-American Whole Quilt Patterns." In *Traditions in Cloth: Afro-American Quilts/West African Textiles* [Exhibition Catalog]. Los Angeles: California Afro-American Museum, 1986.

————. *Who'd a Thought It: Improvisation in African-American Quiltmaking.* San Francisco: San Francisco Craft and Folk Art Museum, 1987.

————. "'Wrapping Home Around Me': How the Patchwork Quilt Became a Medium for the Expression of African Values." In *Rambling on My Mind: Black Folk Art of the Southwest* [Exhibition Catalog], pp. 18–23. Dallas: Museum of African American Life and Culture, 1987.

————. "Cut It down the Middle and Send It to the Other Side: Improvisational Technique in African-American Quilts." *Threads* 19 (1988): 70–75, cover.

————. "Cross-Stripping Patterning in African Textiles and African-American Quilts." *Surface Design Journal* 15, (1) (1990): 6–8, 38.

————. *Arbie Williams Transforms the Britches Quilt.* Regents of the University of California and The Mary Porter Sesnon Art Gallery, UCSC, 1993.

Lewis, Earl. *At Work and at Home: Blacks in Norfolk, Virginia, 1910–1945.* Ph.D. dissertation, University of Minnesota, 1980.

Lift Every Voice and Sing: A Collection of Afro-American Spirituals and Other Songs. New York: Church Hymnal Corporation, 1981.

Longini, Muriel Davis. "Folk Songs of Chicago Negroes." *Journal of American Folk-Lore* 52 (203) (1939: 96–111.

Marks, Carole. *Farewell—We're Good and Gone: The Great Migration.* Bloomington: Indiana University Press, 1989.

Memory and Metaphor. The Art of Romare Bearden 1940–1987. Introduction by Kinshasha Holman Conwill. Essays by Mary Schmidt Campbell and Sharon F. Patton. New York: The Studio Museum in Harlem and Oxford University Press, 1991.

Moore, Stacy Gibbons. "'Established and Well Cultivated': Afro-American Foodways in Early Virginia." *Virginia Cavalcade* 39 (1989): 70–83.

Morgan, Kathryn L. "Caddy Buffers: Legends of a Middle Class Negro Family in Philadelphia." *Keystone Folklore Quarterly* (Summer 1966): 67–88.

Myers, Betty. "Gullah Basketry." *Craft Horizons* 36 (3) (1976): 30–31, 81.

Myrdal, Gunnar. *An American Dilemma: The Negro Problem and Modern Democracy* [1944]. Reprint, New York: Pantheon Books, 1962.

Natanson, Nicholas. "Robert McNeill and Black Government Photographers." *History of Photography* 19 (1) (1995): 26–30.

National Baptist Hymnal, The. Nashville, Tenn.: National Baptist Publishing Board, 1903 [National Baptist Convention, USA].

Nelson, Havelock, and Michael A. Gonzales. *Bring the Noise: A Guide to Rap Music and Hip Hop Culture*. New York: Crown, 1991.

New Hymn and Tune book: An Offering Praise for the Use of the African M.E. Zion Church of America. New York: AME Zion Book Concern, 1892.

Odum, Anna Kranz, collector and editor. "Some Negro Folk-Songs from Tennessee." *Journal of American Folk-Lore* 27(105) (1914): 255–265.

Osofsky, Gilbert. *The Making of a Ghetto. 1890–1930* (2nd ed.). New York: Harper Torchbooks, 1971.

Oszuscik, Philippe. "African-Americans in the American South." In *To Build in a New Land: Ethnic Landscapes in North America,* edited by Allen G. Noble, pp. 157–176. Baltimore: Johns Hopkins University, 1992.

Otto, John Solomon. "A New Look at Slave Life." *Natural History* 88 (1) (1979): 8+.

Pierson, William D. *Black Legacy. America's Hidden Heritage*. Amherst: University of Massachusetts Press, 1993.

Porter, Lewis. "An Historical Survey of Jazz Drumming Styles." *Minority Voices. An Interdisciplinary Journal of Literature and the Arts* 3 (1) (1979): 1–19.

Puckett, Newbell N. *Folk Beliefs of the Southern Negro* [1929]. Reprint, New York: Dover, 1969.

Ramsey, Bets. "The Land of Cotton: Quiltmaking by African-American Women in Three Southern States." *Uncoverings,* Vol. 9 of The Research of the American Quilt Study Group, edited by Laurel Horton, pp. 9–28.

Raniello, John, ed. *Prelude to the Blues: An Anthology of Black Slave Poetry*. Beverly Hills: Rainbow Press, 1969.

Reid, Ira De A. "The John Canoe Festival. A New World Africanism." *Phylon* 3 (4) (1942): 349–370.

Reidy, Joseph P. "Negro Election Day and Black Community Life in New England, 1750–1860." *Marxist Perspectives* (Fall 1978): 104–117.

Roach, Hildred. *Black American Music Past and Present* (2nd ed.). Malabar, Fla.: Krieger, 1992.

Romare Bearden: The Prevalence of Ritual. New York: The Museum of Modern Art, 1971.

Rose, Tricia. "Black Texts/Black Contexts." In *Black Popular Culture,* edited by Gina Dent. Seattle: Bay Press, 1992.

Sales, Grover. *Jazz: America's Classical Music*. Engelwood Cliffs, N.J.: Prentice-Hall, 1984.

Schuller, Gunther. *The History of Jazz. Vol 1: Early Jazz; Its Roots and Musical Development*. New York: Oxford University Press, 1968.

Shapiro, Nat, compiler. *Hear Me Talkin' to Ya; The Story of Jazz as told by the Men Who Made It*. New York: Dover Publications, 1966.

Shaw, Arnold J. *World of Soul: The Black Contributions to Pop Music*. New York: Cowles Education Corporation, 1969.

———. *Black Popular Music in America. From the Spirituals, Minstrels, and Ragtime to Soul, Disco, and Hip-Hop*. New York: Schirmer Books, 1986.

Showers, Susan. "'A Weddin' and a Buryin' in the Black Belt." *New England Magazine. An Illustrated Monthly*. New Series, Vol. 18. Old Series Vol. 24 (March 1898–August 1898): 478–483.

Sibley, David. "W. E. B. Du Bois: A Black Perspective on Social Space." In *Geographies of Exclusion: Society and Difference in The West,* edited by David Sibley, pp. 137–156. New York: Routledge, 1995.

Sobel, Mechel. *The World They Made Together. Black and White Values in Eighteenth-Century Virginia*. Princeton: Princeton University Press, 1987.

Sollers, Werner, and Maria Diedrich, eds. *The Black Columbiad. Defining Moments in African American Literature and Culture*. Harvard English in African American Literature and Culture. Harvard English Studies 19, pp. 42–51. Cambridge: Harvard University Press, 1994.

Southern, Eileen, ed. *Readings in Black American Music* (2nd ed.) [1971]. Reprint, New York: W.W. Norton, 1983.

Starks, George, Jr. *Black Music in the Sea Islands of South Carolina: Its Cultural Context, Continuity and Change*. Ph.D. dissertation, Wesleyan University, 1972.

Stavisky, Leonard Price. "Negro Craftsmanship in Early America." *American Historical Review* 54 (January 1949): 315–325.

Touchstone, Black. "Voodoo in New Orleans." *Louisiana History* 13 (Fall 1992): 371–386.

Twining, Mary A. "Echoes from the South: African-American Quiltmakers in Buffalo." *New York Folklore* 10 (3–4) (1984): 105–115.

Upton, Dell. "White and Black Landscapes in Eighteenth-Century Virginia." *Places* 2 (2) (1985): 59–72.

Vlach, John Michael. "Arrival and Survival: The Maintenance of an Afro-American Tradition in Folk Art and Craft." In *Perspectives on American Folk Art,* edited by Ian M. G. Quimby and Scott T. Swank, pp. 177–217. W.W. Norton, 1980.

Wahlman, Maude Southwell. "Aesthetic Principles in Afro-American Quilts." In *Afro-American Folk Art and Crafts,* edited by William Ferris, pp. 78–97. Jackson: University of Mississippi, 1983.

Wheat, Ellen Harkins, with contributions by Patricia Hills. *Jacob Lawrence: American Painter.* Seattle: University of Washington, 1986.

Wheat, Ellen Harkins. *Jacob Lawrence: The 'Frederick Douglass' and 'Harriet Tubman' Series of 1938–1940*. Hampton, Va.: Hampton University Museum, 1991.

White, Shane. "Digging Up the African-American Past: Historical Archaeology, Photography and Slavery" [Review article]. *Australasian Journal of American Studies* 11 (1) (1992): 37–47.

Wiggins, William H. "The Wooden Chains That Bind: A Look at a Shared Creation of Two Diaspora Woodcarvers." In *Black People and their Culture,* edited by Linn Shapiro, pp. 29–32. Washington, D.C.: Smithsonian Institution, 1976.

Wills, Garry. *Lincoln at Gettysburg: The Words That Remade America*. New York: Simon & Schuster, 1992.

Willis, Deborah, ed. *Picturing Us. African American Identity in Photography*. New York: The New Press, 1994.

Winfield, Arthur Anison F. *Slave Holidays and Festivities in the United States*. Ph.D. dissertation, Atlanta University, 1941.

Woodson, Carter G. *A Century of Negro Migration*. New York: Russell and Russell, 1918.

Woofter, T. J. *Black Yeomanry. Life on St. Helena Island* [1930]. Reprint, New York: Octagon Books, 1978.

Work, John, Jr. *American Negro Songs and Spirituals: A Comprehensive Collection of 230 Folksongs, Religious and Secular*. New York: Negro University Press, 1915.

Wright, Richard. *Twelve Million Black Voices*. New York: Arno Press, 1969.

Photo and Literary Credits

Photo

p. 02 © Nancy-Elizabeth Fitch; **p. 06** Library of Congress LC-USZ62-33994; **p. 10** Library of Congress LC-USZ62 8338; **p. 11** Library of Congress LC-USZ62 2574; **p. 12** Library of Congress LC-USZ62-10295; **p. 13** Library of Congress LC-USZ62-7356; **p. 16** National Museum of American Art, Washington DC/Art Resource, NY; **p. 17** From the Penn School Collection. Permission granted by Penn Center, Inc., St. Helena Island, SC; **p. 26** Hampton University's Archival and Museum Collection, Hampton University, Hampton, Virginia; **p. 35** Valentine Museum; **p. 37** © Chester Higgins, Jr.; **p. 179** Library of Congress LC-USZ62-25650; **p. 234** © John Michael Vlach; **p. 238** Library of Congress LCUS 262-15257; **p. 279** Courtesy of Kenrick Ian Grandison; **p. 286** Courtesy of Kenrick Ian Grandison; **p. 288** Courtesy of Kenrick Ian Grandison; **p. 290** Courtesy of Kenrick Ian Grandison; **p. 291** Courtesy of Kenrick Ian Grandison; **p. 292** Courtesy of Kenrick Ian Grandison; **p. 295** Courtesy of Kenrick Ian Grandison; **p. 297** (top) Courtesy of Kenrick Ian Grandison; **p. 297** (bottom) Courtesy of Kenrick Ian Grandison; **p. 298** Courtesy of Kenrick Ian Grandison; **p. 299** Courtesy of Kenrick Ian Grandison; **p. 300** (top) Courtesy of Kenrick Ian Grandison; **p. 300** (bottom) Courtesy of Kenrick Ian Grandison; **p. 308** © Grey Gundaker; **p. 309** © Grey Gundaker; **p. 315** © Grey Gundaker; **p. 346** © Maude S. Wahlman; **p. 348** © Maude S. Wahlman; **p. 349** © Maude S. Wahlman; **p. 374** National Museum of American Art, Washington DC/Art Resource, NY; **p. 377** National Museum of American Art, Washington DC/Art Resource, NY; **p. 378** National Museum of American Art, Washington DC/Art Resource, NY

Literary

Chapter 1 "From the Shores of Africa" in *There is a River: The Black Struggle for Freedom in Amer-* *ica,* © 1981 by Vincent Harding. Reprinted by permission of Harcourt Brace & Company.

"Slavery and the Circle of Culture," *Slave Culture. Nationalist Theory and the Foundations of Black America,* by Sterling Stuckey. NY: Oxford University Press, 1987: 10–43, 53–64. Reprinted by permission of Oxford University Press.

"Gullah Attitudes Toward Life and Death," by Margaret Washington Creel in *Africanisms in American Culture,* © 1990. Reprinted by permission of Indiana University Press.

From *Sapelo's People: A Long Walk into Freedom,* by William S. McFeely. © 1994 by William S. McFeely. Reprinted by permission of W.W. Norton & Company, Inc.

Chapter 2 From "History, Fable, and Myth in the Caribbean and Guianas," by Wilson Harris in *Caribbean Quarterly,* June 1970. Reprinted by permission of University of West Indies.

"The Association of Movement and Music as a Manifestation of a Black Conceptual Approach to Music Making," by Olly Wilson in *Report* of the 12th Congress, American Musicological Society, London, 1981: 98–105. Reprinted by permission of the American Musicological Society.

"An Aesthetic of the Cool: West African Dance," by Robert Farris Thompson. *African Forum,* Vol. 2, No. 2, 1966: 85–102. Reprinted by permission of the author.

"Primitive African Dance and Its Influence on the Churches of the South," by Pearl Primus in *The Dance Encyclopedia,* compiled and edited by Anatole Chujoy. NY: A.S. Barnes and Company, 1949: 387–89.

From "Easter Sunrise Sermon," by Reverend W.T. Goodwin in *Alcheringa,* © 1972.

Chapter 3 "Shotgun Houses," by John M. Vlach. *Natural History,* February 1997, © 1997 by American Museum of Natural History. Reprinted with permission.

"Poor People Done It Like That," by John M. Vlach in *Charleston Blacksmith. The Work of Philip Simmons,* © 1992. Reprinted by permission of University of South Carolina Press.

"Gracia Real de Santa Teresa de Mose: A Free Black Town in Spanish Colonial Florida," by Jane Landers in *American Historical Review*, February 1990. Reprinted by permission of American Historical Association.

Grandison, Kendrick Ian. "From Plantation to Campus: Progress, Community, and the Lay of the Land in Shaping the Early Tuskegee Campus." *Landscape Journal*, Vol. 15, No. 1 (Spring 1996), © 1996. Reprinted by permission of the University of Wisconsin Press.

"Tradition and Innovation in African-American Yards" by Grey Gundaker in *African Arts*, April 1993. Reprinted by permission of University of California at Los Angeles.

Chapter 4   "Another Face of the Diamond," by Judy McWillie. *Clarion*, Vol. 12, No. 4, 1987: 42–53. Reprinted by permission of the Museum of American Folk Art, New York.

"African Symbolism in Afro-American Quilts," by Maude Southwell Wahlman in *African Arts*, Vol. 20, No. 1, 1986. Reprinted by permission of University of California at Los Angeles.

"Vision in Afro-American Folk Art: The Sculpture of James Thomas," by William Ferris. Reproduced by permission of the American Folklore Society from *Journal of American Folklore* 88:348, April–June 1975. Not for further reproduction.

James Hampton: *The Throne of the Third Heaven of the Nations. Millennium General Assembly,* by Lynda Roscoe Hartigan. Courtesy of Museum of Fine Arts, Boston.

Chapter 5   "Negro Baptizings," by Ruby Terrill Lomax in *From Hell to Breakfast*, Number XIX, © 1944. Reprinted by permission of Publications of the Texas Folklore Society.

"Festivity and Celebration in a Black Methodist Tradition, 1813–1981," by Lewis V. Baldwin. *Methodist History*, Vol. 20, July 1982: 183–191. Reprinted by permission of *Methodist History*.

"Women and Ritual Authority in Afro-American Baptist Churches of Rural Florida," by Audrey L. Brown. Reproduced by permission of the American Anthropological Association from *Anthropology & Humanism Quarterly* 13:1, February 1988. Not for further reproduction.

"We Got Our Way of Cooking Things: Women, Food, and Preservation of Cultural Identity among the Gullah," by Josephine A. Beoku-Betts in *Gender & Society*, Vol. 9, Issue No. 5, pp. 535–555, © 1995 by Sage Publications. Reprinted by permission of Sage Publications, Inc.

"I Got the Blues," by Alan Lomax. *Common Ground*, Vol. 8, No. 4, 1948: 38–52. Courtesy of Alan Lomax.

Chapter 6   "Gullah: A Creole Language," by Charles Joyner. From *Down by the Riverside: A South Carolina Slave Community*. © 1984 by the Board of Trustees of the University of Illinois. Used with the permission of the University of Illinois Press.

"Ezekiel and the Vision of Dry Bones," by Reverend Carl J. Anderson. From *I Got the Word in Me and I Can Sing It, You Know. A Study of the Performed African-American Sermon,* by Gerald L. Davis. © 1985 University of Pennsylvania Press. Reprinted by permission of the publisher.

Chapter 7   "Oration in Memory of Abraham Lincoln," by Frederick Douglass in *The Life and Writings of Frederick Douglass. Reconstruction and After*, Vol. IV by Philip S. Foner, © 1975. Reprinted by permission of International Publishers Company, Inc.

Mary McLeod Bethune's "The Negro in Retrospect and Prospect." An Address delivered at the 1949 Annual Meeting of the Association for the Study of Negro Life and History (New York). *Journal of Negro History*, Vol. 35, 1950: 9–19. "For the Best and the Brightest," by Vincent Harding in *The Fifth Annual Memorial Lecture of the Society for Values in Higher Education*, © 1993. Reprinted by permission of the Society for Values in Higher Education.

Index

Aesthetics 15–18; 189–199; 200–212; 277; 290–300;
  305–329; 332–382
African American Spaces and Places 9–15; 231–331
African American Women 350–351; 384; 399–414;
  459; 500–501
Afro-Baptist Church 212–214; 386–391; 399–414
All-Black Towns 13
Anancy (African and African American folkloric
  spider god) 176–177
Anderson, Rev. Carl J. 460; 487–493
Atlantic Slave Trade 40–59

Baptism 384; 386–391
Bakongo Cross 36–37; 61–62; 80–82; 343
Baldwin, Lewis V. 384; 391–399
Beoku-Betts, Josephine A. 384; 414–432
Bethune, Mary McLeod 500–501; 511–514
Big August Quarterly 384; 391–399
Black Belt (Alabama) 236–237; 276–285
Black Methodism SEE BIG AUGUST QUARTERLY
Black Preaching 180–181; 212–214; 215–228
Blues (Blues-Jazz) 19–20; 385; 432–447
Brown, Audrey 384; 399–414. SEE AFRICAN
  AMERICAN WOMEN
Burials 34–35; 153–157

Circle
 Cosmology 25–28; 30–33; 38
 Dances and Ringshout or the Shout 32–33; 59–65;
  72–98; 113–137; 193–195
 Community 164–173
Clinton, President William Jefferson 497–498
Community 144–148; 164–173; 243–252; 276–304;
  383; 414–432; 459–460; 461–486; 501–502;
  518–531
Community-Building 164–173; 276–304
Cosmology 5–6; 25–40; 138–164
Creel, Margaret Washington 34–36; 138–164
Dance 6–9; 32–33; 65–104; 174–230
Davis, Gerald L. 460
Declaration of Independence 497
Dialectics 497

Discography 451–456
Double-Consciousness 10–11; 27
Double textuality 143–144; 459–486; 499; 503–511
Douglass, Frederick 498–499; 503–511
Du Bois, W.E.B. 8; 11; 14; 27; 90. SEE DOUBLE-
  CONSCIOUSNESS
Dunham, Katherine 7, 14

Easter Sunday Sermon 215–228
Election Day Festivals 104–113
Ethics 140–141; 200–212; 243–252

Ferris, William 18; 357–372
Filmographies 23–24; 229–230; 382; 456–458; 495;
  532
"For The Best and The Brightest" 518–531
Fort Mose (Gracia Real de Santa Teresa de Mose)
  232–233; 235–236; 252–276
Franklin, John Hope 498
Free Black settlements 252–276

Gilroy, Paul 1–2; 10
Goodwin, Rev. W.T. 181; 215–228
Grandison, Ian Kendrick 236–237; 276–304
Gullah (Culture and Language) 20–21; 34–40;
  113–120; 138–172; 243–252; 354; 384–385;
  414–432; 459–486
Gundaker, Gary 237; 305–329

Hampton, James 16; 334–335; 373–382
The Hampton Throne 334–335; 373–382
Harding, Vincent 28; 30–31; 40–58; 501–502;
  508–531
Harriet Jacobs Bible Quilts 120; 336; 343;
  350–351
Harris, Wilson 174–178; 181–188
Hartigan, Lyndia Roscoe 334–335; 373–382
Herskovits, Melville 14; 194; 454
Historically Black Colleges and Universities SEE
  TUSKEGEE INSTITUTE

History
   (Of) The Middle Passsage 40–58
   Spirit of African American History 1–25

Jefferson, Thomas 55; 497
John Kunering Ceremony 100–104
Joyner, Charles 459–486

King Jr., Dr. Martin Luther 497–498

Landers, Jane 235–236; 252–276
Limbo Dance 174–178; 181–188
Lomax
   Alan 385–386; 432–447
   John and Alan 194
   Ruby Terrill 384; 386–391

McFeely, William S. 30; 38–40
McWillie, Judy 332–333; 336–345
Marshall, Paule 33
Memory of Slavery SEE PAUL GILROY
Middle Passage SEE HISTORY
Murray, Albert 385
"The Negro in Retrospect and Prospect" 511–517.
   SEE SANKOFA

Nommo/Nummo 5; 20–22; 25–26; 232; 459–460;
   496
Non-Alphabetic Writing 15–16; 231–232; 333

"Oration in Memory of Abraham Lincoln" 503–511

Primus, Pearl 179–181; 212–214

Quilting 333–334; 345–347

Raboteau, Albert 193–195; 339
Rituals and Ceremonies 385–458

Sankofa 3; 500; 511–517
Sea Islands
   All Saintsd Parish 461–486
   Daniel Island 235; 243–252
   Sapelo (Hog Hammock) 164–172
Selected Readings 22–23; 172–173; 229; 379–382;
   447–451; 493–494; 531
Sermons 215; 228; 487–493
Shotgun House 233–234; 239–243
Simmons, Philip 234–235; 243–252
Spencer, Peter 384. SEE BIG AUGUST
   QUARTERLY
Spirit Yards 237–238; 305–325
Struggles for Freedom (Resistance) 41–42; 45–56;
   139; 252–275
Stuckey, Sterling 8; 32–33; 59–137

Text (Nature of) 1; 22
Textiles 17; 333–334; 345–357
Thomas, James 334; 358–372
Thompson, Robert Farris 180; 200–212
Tuskegee Institute 236–237; 276–304

Van Sertima, Ivan 176–177
Verbal Lanuage
   Dynamics 20–21
   Speechmaking 21–22; 409–412; 496–532
   SEE SERMONS
Vlach, John Michael 233; 239–252
Vodun (Voodoo) 186–187

Wahlman, Maude Southwell 333–334;
   345–357
Washington, Booker T. 13, 15. SEE TUSKEGEE
   INSTITUTE
Wilson, Olly 178; 189–199